THE YORKIST AGE

PAUL MURRAY KENDALL, Ph.D., L.H.D., formerly Regents Professor at Ohio University, is now Visiting Professor at the University of Kansas.

BOOKS BY PAUL MURRAY KENDALL

The Art of Biography
Louis XI
Richard the Third
Warwick the Kingmaker
The Yorkist Age
Richard the Third: The Great Debate (Ed.)

PAUL MURRAY KENDALL

THE
YORKIST
AGE

*Daily Life during
the Wars of the Roses*

The Norton Library
W · W · NORTON & COMPANY · INC ·
NEW YORK

First published in the Norton Library 1970

Books That Live
The Norton imprint on a book means that in the publisher's
estimation it is a book not for a single season but for the years.
W. W. Norton & Company, Inc.

SBN 393 00558 5

PRINTED IN THE UNITED STATES OF AMERICA

1 2 3 4 5 6 7 8 9 0

To John Calhoun Baker

PREFACE

THE object of this book is not to analyse but to recapture a part of the past. I have aimed at recreating the Yorkist Age as it was lived; and I have therefore avoided, when I could, dealing with pots and pans and concepts and constitution and government and economic change and religious attitudes, and have tried to show people using and acting out and responding to and being moved by these things and institutions and forces. My purpose has been to catch people in action, as wide a variety of people as the sources offered, exhibiting the diversity of human behaviour that makes up the texture of daily life.

Isolating a segment of time from the mesh of history is, admittedly, to deal in metaphor, not Truth. Yet, I believe that this figure of speech, The Yorkist Age, has more than a pale paper-existence, that it represents conditions of life in the fifteenth century differing from the medieval past as from the Tudor future—in sum, I have tried to demonstrate that the metaphor is apt and useful.

Like all historical writing, this is essentially an exercise of the imagination, for the imagination is a combining and associative faculty. As the novelist works imaginatively from the data of his experience, the historian works imaginatively from the more inert and 'outside' data of evidences preserved from the fangs of time. Documents cannot be strung together to make a history any more than personal anecdotes can be strung together to make a novel. The living tissue of Edward IV's day cannot be revived by a calendar of information. The goal of recapturing *the* fifteenth century is almost bound to result in a list of facts connected by 'craftily qualified' generalizations. The historian can only try to achieve *his* fifteenth century, hoping that it bears some resemblance to the vanished actuality.

7

Facts are brute, recalcitrant matter; they must be rubbed together in the mind before they will assume the shape of meaning. On the other hand, once 'touched up', they become artifacts. I have invented no scenes, no conversations, no details of action. Matters of conjecture have been so indicated. All dialogue in the book is quoted directly from primary sources; the surprising amount of it reveals the age's springing interest in social intercourse. If the reader detects that I have an enormous affection for these bygone people, I can but admit that, lacking such affection, I should not have been willing to spend so many months of my life in trying to live with them.

Since the society of the Yorkist Age can be recreated from such intimate documents as wills and household accounts and letters I have, whenever possible, let the men and women of the time speak in their own words; and that those words may flow as clearly now as once they did, I have presented them in modern spelling and punctuation.

Glancing at the table of contents, the reader may be surprised to notice that the Wars of the Roses are not dealt with until the end of the book. I have put this chapter last to indicate that the so-called wars had comparatively little effect upon the life of the time and that the reign of Edward IV represents a recovery from rather than an arena of civil strife. The Prologue offers a brief summary of events to orient the reader; he may, however, turn to the last chapter immediately, if he prefers, without seriously dislocating the coherence of the book.

The apparatus of scholarship applied to a social history in which a multiplicity of sources has been consulted and deployed would engender a forest of notes before which even the most intrepid reader might properly quail. In an appendix, therefore, I have listed the two dozen or so principal collections of letters and wills and the household accounts and chronicles and town records which offer the richest materials; and I have indicated the main additional sources that I have used for each chapter. This study is based on contemporary sources, including a few unpublished documents like Richard III's register of grants (Harleian MS. 433) and dispatches of Milanese ambassadors still remaining in manuscript. Tudor writers like Holinshed and Hall offer fuller accounts of events than fifteenth-century chroniclers but their works must be regarded as secondary.

As the result of a fellowship awarded by the John Simon Guggenheim Memorial Foundation I was able to pursue research for this book in England. I am indebted to the American Philosophical Society for a grant to microfilm Milanese dispatches in the Archivio di Stato, Milan; to the Research Committee of Ohio University for grants and other generous assistance; to the staffs of the London Library, the British Museum, the Institute of Historical Research of the University of London, the Ohio University Library. To this and other ventures Dr. Hollis Summers has contributed more than friendship could ask.

The dedication of the book to John Calhoun Baker, University president and statesman, is an inadequate way of saying thanks for his constant encouragement and for all kinds of assistance, tangible and intangible.

Finally, I salute two Carols and a Gillian for gracefully including the fifteenth century in their twentieth-century lives; and I am especially grateful to one Carol for an invaluable criticism of the manuscript. .

PAUL MURRAY KENDALL

Ohio University

CONTENTS

PRINCIPAL PERSONS

ROYALTY

KING HENRY VI (1421–71; reigned 1422–61 and 1470–71) of the House of Lancaster, murdered in the Tower

His wife, MARGARET OF ANJOU, daughter of 'Good King René', King of Naples, of Jerusalem, of Hungary, and ruler of none of them; Duke of Anjou, Lorraine, and Bar; Count of Provence

His son, EDWARD, PRINCE OF WALES, slain at Tewkesbury, 1471

KING EDWARD IV (1442–83; reigned 1461–70 and 1471–83) of the House of York

His father, RICHARD, DUKE OF YORK, killed at Wakefield, 1460

His mother, CICELY, DUCHESS OF YORK

His wife, ELIZABETH WOODVILLE, a widow with two sons when she became queen

His sons, EDWARD, PRINCE OF WALES, later Edward V (1470–83?; reigned April 9–June 26, 1483), reputedly put to death by order of Richard III;

RICHARD, DUKE OF YORK, who disappeared under the same circumstances as did his brother

His daughter, ELIZABETH, wife to HENRY VII

His brothers, GEORGE, DUKE OF CLARENCE, executed 1478; RICHARD, DUKE OF GLOUCESTER, later Richard III (see below)

His sisters, ELIZABETH, wife to John de la Pole, Duke of Suffolk; MARGARET, wife to Charles the Rash, Duke of Burgundy

His favourite mistress, JANE SHORE, wife to William Shore, mercer of London

KING RICHARD III (1452–85; reigned 1483–85), killed at Bosworth Field

His wife, ANNE, younger daughter of Richard Neville, Earl of Warwick, the Kingmaker

His son, EDWARD, PRINCE OF WALES, died 1484

KING HENRY VII (1455–1509; reigned 1485–1509), descendant of an illegitimate son (later legitimated but barred from the royal succession) of John of Gaunt, Duke of Lancaster; son of Edmund Tudor, Earl of Richmond, an illegitimate (?) son of Owen Tudor, a Welsh adventurer, and Katherine of France, widow of Henry V.

His wife, ELIZABETH, daughter of Edward IV

His mother, MARGARET BEAUFORT, COUNTESS OF RICHMOND, later Countess of Derby

KING CHARLES VII OF FRANCE (reigned 1422–61), Joan of Arc's 'gentle dauphin'

His son, KING LOUIS XI (reigned 1461–83), 'the universal spider'

PHILIP THE GOOD, DUKE OF BURGUNDY (died 1467), ruler of the Low Countries and the Burgundies

His son, CHARLES THE RASH, DUKE OF BURGUNDY, killed before Nancy, 1477

His natural son, ANTOINE, the great Bastard of Burgundy

LORDS

RICHARD NEVILLE, EARL OF WARWICK, called 'The Kingmaker', killed at Barnet, 1471

His daughters, ISABEL, wife to George, Duke of Clarence; ANNE, wife to Prince Edward, son of Henry VI, and then to Richard, Duke of Gloucester, later Richard III

His brothers, GEORGE, BISHOP OF EXETER, later Archbishop of York, Chancellor of England, 1460–67; JOHN, Lord Montagu, later Earl of Northumberland, and then Marquess Montagu, killed at Barnet, 1471; John's daughter, ANNE, third wife to Sir William Stonor

JOHN MOWBRAY, DUKE OF NORFOLK, besieged the Pastons' castle of Caister, 1469, died, last of his line, 1476

His wife, ELIZABETH TALBOT, a beautiful girl who dominated her husband and favoured young John Paston

JOHN HOWARD, KNIGHT; then Lord Howard; later Howard, First Duke of Norfolk, killed at Bosworth Field, 1485, fighting for King Richard III

WILLIAM DE LA POLE, DUKE OF SUFFOLK, favourite of Margaret of Anjou, murdered in the Channel, 1450

His wife, ALICE CHAUCER, grand-daughter of Geoffrey Chaucer

His son, JOHN DE LA POLE, Duke of Suffolk, a blustering lord who coveted Paston property

John's wife, ELIZABETH, sister of Edward IV

HENRY BEAUFORT, DUKE OF SOMERSET, favourite of Margaret of Anjou, killed at the battle of Hexham, 1464

THOMAS GREY, MARQUESS DORSET, elder son by her first marriage to Elizabeth Woodville, wife of Edward IV

JOHN DE VERE, EARL OF OXFORD, a Lancastrian whose father and elder brother were executed, 1462, by Edward IV; the 'good lord' of young John Paston

THOMAS COURTENAY, EARL OF DEVON, a turbulent Lancastrian lord executed after the battle of Towton, 1461

HENRY PERCY, EARL OF NORTHUMBERLAND, prisoner in the Fleet with John Paston; betrayer of Richard III at Bosworth Field; murdered 1489

His son HENRY ALGERNON PERCY, Earl of Northumberland, famous for his *Household Regulations*

JOHN TIPTOFT, EARL OF WORCESTER, Constable of England, humanist; executed by Warwick, 1470

ANTHONY WOODVILLE, LORD SCALES, later Earl Rivers, eldest brother of Edward IV's queen, jouster and humanist; executed by Richard, Duke of Gloucester, 1483

WILLIAM, LORD HASTINGS, Edward IV's Lord Chamberlain; one time 'good lord' to Sir John Paston; friend of Jane Shore; executed by Richard, Duke of Gloucester, 1483

GENTRY

THE PASTONS:

JOHN PASTON, ESQ., inheritor of the Fastolfe estates, died 1466

His grandfather, CLEMENT PASTON, yeoman, founder of the family fortunes

His father, Justice WILLIAM PASTON

His mother, AGNES PASTON (née Berry), daughter of a Hertfordshire knight

His wife, MARGARET PASTON of Mauteby

His sister, ELIZABETH PASTON, wife to Robert Poynings, sword-bearer to Jack Cade

His eldest sons, SIR JOHN, died 1479, a bachelor; YOUNG JOHN, later knighted and made Sheriff of Norfolk and Suffolk; Young John's wife, MARGERY BREWS

His daughter, MARGERY PASTON, wife to Richard Calle

His chaplain, SIR JAMES GLOYS

His bailiffs: RICHARD CALLE, steward and receiver, husband to Margery Paston despite the opposition of the family; JOHN PAMPYNG, beloved in vain by John Paston's daughter Anne; JOHN DAUBENEY, killed fighting for the Pastons in the siege of Caister Castle, 1469

SIR WILLIAM STONOR

His father, THOMAS STONOR, died 1475

His three wives: DAME ELIZABETH, widow and daughter of London merchants, friend of Thomas Betson, Merchant of the Staple; AGNES WYDESLADE, a West Country heiress; ANNE NEVILLE, daughter of John, Marquess Montagu, brother to Warwick the Kingmaker

His adviser, THOMAS MULL, a friend of the family

SIR WILLIAM PLUMPTON, of Yorkshire

His bastard son, ROBIN

SIR JOHN FASTOLFE, captain in the French wars, builder of Caister Castle

SIR JOHN FORTESCUE, Chief Justice, K.B., an ardent Lancastrian but later a member of Edward IV's council; famous for his works on English law

THOMAS DENYES, lawyer and Coroner of Norfolk, murdered in 1461, probably by the Parson of Snoring

PETER MARMION, owner of the manor of Nursling, Hampshire, who one day found himself chained up in his own hall with a dog collar

RICHARD PENONS, a Cornish gentleman, Justice of the Peace and notable pirate

MAYORS, MERCHANTS, AND
OTHER TOWNSPEOPLE

JOHN SHILLINGFORD, three times Mayor of Exeter and champion of the city against the Bishop of Exeter

WILLIAM CANYNGES, five times Mayor of Bristol, Merchant Adventurer

ROBERT STURMY, twice Mayor of Bristol, Merchant Adventurer

THOMAS WRANGWYSH, twice Mayor of York, Merchant Adventurer

SIR THOMAS COOK, Mayor of London, Mercer, despoiled by the Woodvilles

BARTHOLOMEW READ, Mayor of London, Goldsmith, who reportedly drank a jewel worth 1,000 marks

LAURENCE SAUNDERS, Dyer, rebel against the city government of Coventry

HARRY BUTLER, Recorder of Coventry, foe to Laurence Saunders

THOMAS BETSON, Merchant of the Staple, business partner of Sir William Stonor

RICHARD CELY, Merchant of the Staple, owner of the manor of Bretts Place, Essex

His sons: RICHARD, GEORGE and ROBERT

STEPHEN FORSTER, Fishmonger of London

His wife, AGNES, prison reformer

CLERGY

JOHN STAFFORD, Archbishop of Canterbury and Chancellor, friend of John Shillingford

GEORGE NEVILLE, Archbishop of York and Chancellor, brother of Warwick the Kingmaker

EDMUND LACY, Bishop of Exeter, foe of John Shillingford

MARGARET WAVERE, hysterical Prioress of Catesby

The wicked ABBOT OF WELBECK

JOHN SWYFT, the good Abbot of Beauchief

SIR JAMES GLOYS, chaplain to the Paston family

OTHERS

JOHN BOON, international adventurer, spy for Warwick the Kingmaker, later in the service of King Louis XI

JACK CADE, calling himself Mortimer, 'The Great Captain of Kent', killed shortly after the failure of his Rising of 1450

WILLIAM CARNSYOWE, 'The Great Errant Captain of Cornwall'

JOHN GOOS, heretic, burned

RICHARD HEYRON, lawyer, international promoter who embroiled the Duke of Burgundy, the King of France, the King of England, the Emperor and the Pope in his schemes

MARGERY KEMPE, the sobbing mystic of Lynn, dictated the first true autobiography written in English

WILLIAM WORCESTER, secretary to Sir John Fastolfe, book-lover and annalist

PROLOGUE

The Times

The Times

A BOHEMIAN lord and his retinue visited the England of Edward IV in the early spring of 1466. Crossing the Channel from Calais, they had such a stormy voyage that they 'lay in the ship as though they were dead'. They managed to revive sufficiently, however, to admire the White Cliffs and mighty Dover Castle, which, they were later told, had been built by evil spirits. Finally their vessel slipped into Sandwich harbour, and here the landbound Bohemians beheld another remarkable sight, a detachment of the English fleet riding at anchor. Like most visitors arriving at a Kentish port, they proceeded to London by way of Canterbury. They thought that the cathedral could hardly be rivalled in Christendom, an opinion 'on which all travellers agree'.

To the Bohemians and other visitors, England lay on the perimeter of the world, edged by the ocean that stretched westward no man knew whither—for Ireland was often hazily located by foreigners as somewhere between Land's End and Spain. A Milanese ambassador considered even Flanders so remote that he complained to his master at being 'planted here on the extreme shore of the earth's orb'.

Yet travellers coming to England during the Wars of the Roses were, almost all of them, surprised and charmed by what they found. When the Bohemians arrived—the first foreigners to leave a record of their impressions in this period—Edward IV had been wearing for five years the crown he had won after packed vicissitudes and victories. There was more fighting to come. Yet the Bohemians saw, or at least mentioned, no signs of a war-torn country; they heard, apparently, no laments for myriad lives lost in civil strife. What struck them most was the riches and fertility of the island: anticipating Shakespeare, they called it 'a little sea-girt garden'.

They saw, it is true, only the southern parts; and the countryside of England showed sharp regional contrasts. North of Trent and to the West, in the Marches of Wales, stretched hills, forests, heath, broken in the valleys by patches of farming unchanged for centuries. Village and manor house lay in the midst of two or three huge fields, one remaining fallow, which were subdivided by grass balks into the open strips of lord's demesne and peasant holdings. On hilly waste grazed thousands of sheep, many of them owned by Cistercian monasteries. The North and the Welsh Marches, poor in goods and rich in fighting men, continued to nurse feudal ideas and loyalties and feuds; they provided many of the armed bands that bellicose lords brought to the battlefields of the Roses. Bondmen laboured on the lord's land and paid servile dues in the lord's court. Yorkshire, Durham, Northumberland were dominated by massive castles and abbeys, planted upon moors that seemed to be rounded by the stamp of Roman legions and Celtic kings. On the borders, sewn with fortresses, Scots and English raiders were always burning villages and stealing cattle. A communication from King Henry VI to the Pope described the See of Hereford in the Welsh Marches—tamer than Northumberland—as 'situated on the confines of England and among a ferocious and uncivilized people'.

Down in Kent, on the other hand, the countryside was mostly enclosed into plots of arable and pasture by neat hedges and ditches. Riding up the Dover Road, travellers saw apple orchards, 'cherry gardens of the best', plum and pear and chestnut trees, fat cattle, and poultry. This intensive agriculture was carried on by small yeomen farmers, for the county enjoyed a special form of inheritance-by-equal-shares called gavelkind. There was no villeinage in Kent: birth in the county was sufficient proof that a man was of free condition. The harbours swarmed with traders, fishermen, and mariners. In the forest of the weald, now somewhat thinned, wood provided fuel for iron and glass works. Kent was famous for its heavy cloth—a single piece, some thirty yards long, weighed more than sixty pounds—and for its oysters and its ale. Beer supposedly came into England with the Reformation, but it was already being brewed in Kent, though the hops had to be imported. Situated on the route from London to the Continent, Kentishmen were an efficient and progressive race, proud of their independence of mind and quick to show it.

The manorial tradition of tilling open fields was to be found not only in the North and West but in the Midlands and, here and there, throughout the rest of England; but East Anglia and the southern counties, Cornwall, the Thames and Severn valleys, offered, like Kent, panoramas of enclosed holdings. The Bohemians, riding from London through Windsor and Reading to Salisbury, reported the land so tightly hedged and ditched—wood, arable, pasture—that travellers afoot or on horseback could not cut across fields but had to keep strictly to the highways. Everywhere the vistors saw vast flocks of sheep.

Yet in most parts of the country, towns and cultivated areas were still scattered among sweeps of forest and fen and waste. Though beginning to shrink, forests like Dean and Rockingham and Knaresborough covered hundreds of square miles. Rivers, drawn far larger than roads on mediaeval maps, offered serious barriers to communication, but were much used for the transport of freight and passengers. In the Fen district, towns like Croyland stood as islands above watery marshes. Once off a main highway, strangers to a region often had to hire guides in order to reach their destinations.

Ourselves travellers from the twentieth century, we can come a little closer to this England of the War of the Roses by seeing through the eyes of contemporary travellers. The Bohemians of 1466; Dominic Mancini, who described Richard of Gloucester's usurpation of the throne; Nicolas von Popplau, who met King Richard the following year (1484); a Venetian diplomat who set down his impressions (the well known *Italian Relation*) at the end of the century, and sundry Italian merchants looked through the aperture of their own customs and prejudices, but their dominant impressions show a surprising agreement.

They were struck by the lack of wolves in England, by the quantities of cattle, by the handsome parks, royal and noble, abounding in fallow deer and other game. Polydore Vergil, Henry VII's historian, singled out 'delectable valleys', the abundance of fish and fowl, and declared that 'the beef is peerless, especially being a few days powdered with salt'. The Venetian summed up the country as 'all diversified by pleasant, undulating hills and beautiful valleys; nothing to be seen but agreeable woods or extensive meadows or lands in cultivation; and the greatest plenty of water springing everywhere'. He was surprised at the paucity of growing grain, but 'this negligence is atoned for by an immense profusion of every edible animal . . . above all, an enormous number of sheep. . . . Common fowls, pea-fowls, partridges, pheasants, and other small birds abound here above measure, and it is truly a beautiful thing to behold one or two thousand tame swans upon the river Thames. . . .' Noting the fertility of the soil, the mining of tin, and above all the production of wool, he concluded that 'the riches of England are greater than those of any other country in Europe. . . . Every one who makes a tour in the island will soon become aware of this great wealth . . . for there is no small innkeeper, however poor and humble he may be, who does not serve his table with silver dishes and drinking cups. . . .' This observation was made only a dozen years after the last battle of the Roses (Stoke, 1487).

Like other travellers, the Venetian was also struck, however, by the emptiness of the countryside. 'The population of this island does not appear to me to bear any proportion to her fertility and riches.' He himself had ridden from London only as far as Oxford but upon inquiring of those who knew the North, 'was told that it was the same case there'. Travellers must have seen an occasional abandoned village and tracts of land once cultivated that had fallen back into waste; for the population of England had diminished. The land which supported some four or five million people in the thirteenth century now nurtured probably—only the merest estimate is possible—two and one-half or three millions. This radical shrinkage, due mainly to the ravages of the Black Death during the reigns of Edward III and Richard II, had been accompanied by enormous suffering and social turmoil; but it had produced, by the time of the Wars of the

Roses, a prosperous country of rising wages, steady or falling prices, low rents.

The inhabitants of the realm of England impressed foreigners as being so different from Europeans as to require considerable interpretation, sometimes laudatory but more often not. There was no doubt that the English were an entity, a nation; and the English themselves heartily agreed. They knew that no other land or folk could hold a candle to them. 'The English are great lovers of themselves,' our Venetian reported bluntly, 'and of everything belonging to them; they think that there are no other men than themselves and no other world but England; and whenever they see a handsome foreigner, they say that he "looks like an Englishman", and that "it is a great pity that he should not be an Englishman"; and when they partake of any delicacies with a foreigner, they ask him, "whether such a thing is made in *their* country?" ... It is not unamusing to hear the women and children of men forced to leave the kingdom lament ... that "they had better have died than go out of the world", as if'—the Italian adds scornfully— 'England were the whole world.' The German knight, Popplau, fifteen years before, used almost the same language: the English think they are the wisest people on earth and that 'the world does not exist apart from England'.

Perhaps this aggressive self-love sprang in part from a deep-grained conservatism, jarring to the more flexible Italians: 'If the king should propose to change any old established rule, it would seem to every Englishman as if his life were taken away from him. . . .' In fifteenth-century England the swan of enlightened patriotism had not yet spread its wings, but the cygnet of insularity and xenophobia was in lusty growth. The English had little use for foreigners, as the latter were only too well aware. Londoners could not believe that the long locks of the Bohemians grew from their skulls but insisted that they were glued on with bitumen, and whenever one of the party appeared, crowds stared rudely at him 'as if he had been some fabulous animal'. The Venetian declared emphatically that the English lumped all aliens together into a conniving lot who 'never came into their island but to make themselves masters of it and to usurp their goods'.

Most foreign visitors thought that the charms of the land far exceeded those of the people—though it must be remembered that tourists in all ages are apt to be critical of the treatment they receive. The Bohemians praised the English as a musical nation, 'for never in any place have we heard such sweet and pleasant musicians as here'; and they were grateful for English hospitality, declaring that 'in no land have we been shown greater honour. . . .' Popplau and the Venetian also found the English quick to offer dinners and entertainments. And no foreigner failed to wax enthusiastic about the loveliness—and most of them about the passionate natures—of English women, 'the greatest beauties in the world, and as fair as alabaster'. But summary verdicts on the men are crushing. 'I have nothing more to record of the English', wrote the journalist of the Bohemian party, 'except that they are, as it seems to me, so cunning and treacherous that a foreigner cannot be sure of his life among them. . . .' Popplau found Englishmen choleric by nature and pitiless when roused to anger, an opinion which echoes Froissart's of a century before. The German knight admired King Richard, but Richard's subjects 'surpassed the Poles in ostentation and pilfering, the Hungarians in brutality, and the Lombards in deceit. . . . The avarice of the people made everything in England dear'. Foreigners were a little afraid, it appears, of this tough, outspoken race that quarrelled fiercely among themselves, had conquered half of France and crowned their boy-king at Paris, and knew that, one and all, they were a remarkable people.

Native letters and documents, as well, testify to a darker side of English character during this period. Englishmen stood stiff upon what they regarded as their rights, reached for what was to be taken, and were often harsh and suspicious in their dealings. A middle class in town and country were clawing upward into the social and economic sun; they had not yet quite perceived, some of them, that life need not be so hard and that a man could prosper without ruthlessness.

Yet this grasping practicality was leavened by a rough-and-ready humour and the rudiments of a sporting instinct, qualities not easily recognized by foreigners. A puzzled Italian reported that the English 'have no idea of the point of honour. When they do fight it is from some caprice, and after exchanging two or three stabs with a knife, even when they wound each other, they will make peace instantly, and go away and drink together'. The Englishman of Edward IV's day also exhibited a sensibility and a capacity for simple delight as yet only haltingly articulate. He cultivated gardens and laid out parks. He enjoyed 'flowers white and red' and the green of fields, dogs and horses, the sea, the grace of swans, 'and the young rabbits that in a sunny morning sit washing their faces'. The loveliness of spring shines in his songs and carols; his ballads are bright with the brave poignance of star-crossed love. Though he thought himself an unmoved, no-nonsense sort of fellow, he had a child's love of colour—in his dress, his house, his church, the court of his king. His fondness for pageantry popped out at funerals as well as weddings. Give him any excuse and he would have braying trumpets, torches, cloth of gold, singing, actors posturing on stages, banners, minstrelsy, and whatever else he could devise of 'gorgeous ceremony'. He had not yet found his full voice or mined his genius or harnessed his energies by his imagination. But he was vigorously alive, a lusty and complex fellow not too easily penetrated by foreigners.

In the course of the fifteenth century this hardy race, harassed by a government at once feeble and oppressive, seized weapons to uncrown a king, Henry VI, and set a new dynasty, the Yorkist, upon the throne. A decade later, they again took arms to decide that the line of York should keep what it had won. On the death of Edward IV, his brother Richard, Duke of Gloucester, usurped the throne and doomed Edward's sons, only to be overthrown two years later by an almost unknown Welshman named Henry Tudor, of indirect and flawed Lancastrian descent. After assuming the crown (1485) Henry VII married Elizabeth, daughter of Edward IV, defeated a Yorkist invasion mastered all challenges to his rule, and thus brought the Wars of the Roses to an end.

Like the great Duke of Wellington, most of us began learning about the fifteenth century at Shakespeare's knee; the lesson was

flamboyant and administered at an impressionable age. Four
plays, the tripartite *Henry VI* and *Richard III*, dramatize a sweep
of history from the development of party strife and the breakdown
of government in the reign of Henry VI to the Tudor's victory
at Bosworth Field. These youthful dramas exuberantly chronicle
quarrels, riots, plottings, battles, murders, a never-flagging tale
of bloody action that projects the period 1422–1485 as full of sound
and fury signifying—except for a rousing evening in the theatre—
nothing. Part of this effect derives from Shakespeare's sources:
sixteenth-century historians painted highly coloured pictures of
fifteenth-century civil strife in order to emphasize the blessings
of strong Tudor rule. But much of the hurly-burly arises simply
from dramatic exigencies: the young Shakespeare, eager to
command his audience, zealously crammed the most violent
happenings of more than half a century into a dozen theatrical
hours. As a result, the chief men of the period rush jerkily about
like phantoms to be seen in early films; and the thirty years
1455–1485 show but tiny islands of peace amidst a sea of flailing
weapons.

England as a whole was undoubtedly more miserable during
the last decade before the outbreak of large-scale fighting (battle
of Northampton, 1460) than during the sporadic 'wars'. Your
average Englishman living through these times would probably
have been amazed to learn from a subject of Queen Elizabeth
the First that he had endured a generation of horrors.[1] The Wars
of the Roses were not, in our sense, wars at all, and there was only
one rose, the White Rose of York. The Red Rose was a Tudor,
not a Lancastrian, cognizance; the term 'Wars of the Roses' was
invented in the sixteenth century. Henry Tudor's triumph over
Richard III at Bosworth Field does not even signal the most
decisive date of the period: it did not begin a new form of
monarchy nor bring the Middle Ages to a close in a single
spasm.

The daily life described in these pages embraces a span of half
a century, roughly from 1445 to 1487. The arrival in England, in

[1] Even the fifteenth-century nobility, the class which suffered by far the
most heavily, was, on the whole, safer than the wives of Henry VIII.

1445, of Henry VI's beautiful and imperious French bride, Margaret of Anjou, crystallized the bitterness of factions, led to the loss of France, and provoked the formation of a party supporting Richard of York's demand for reform of the government. A cluster of battles fought in 1460–1461 gained the throne for York's eldest son Edward, crowned Edward IV. Except for Lancastrian outbreaks in the remote North and West, the realm quietly began pulling itself together under Edward's leadership. In the period 1469–1471 the king fought another series of battles to crush the alliance of his former mentor, Warwick the Kingmaker, and the Lancastrians. The so-called Wars of the Roses then ended; the remaining dozen years of Edward's rule told a tale of growing prosperity and stability. The battles of Bosworth (1485) and Stoke (1487) scarcely troubled the realm at all; they were waged by the immediate adherents of the king and his sworn enemies. A picture of England during the 'Wars of the Roses' is, essentially, an account of daily life during the reign of Edward IV, and during that reign of more than two decades, warfare, or widespread disorder shook the realm for a space of perhaps eighteen months scattered over several years.

The decisive date of this period, if we must have meaningful dates, is March 4, 1461. On that day Edward of York established a dynasty of politician-kings that lasted—with interruptions—until 1688. When the kings ceased to be politicians they ceased to be kings, as Charles I and James II were rudely taught.

English kings before Edward had been *politic*—canny in statecraft like Edward I, brilliant in administration like Henry II, or, like Edward III in his earlier years, adroit at keeping the barons contented. But a politic king is not a politician-king. Mediaeval kings were not politicians because, in the first place, they did not have to be so: their reign did not depend so much upon their rule as Edward IV's did. Secondly, the area of political manoeuvring was too narrow to represent the kind of activity which 'politician' connotes. There will be no politician-king until there is a critical popular will which must be courted and can be manipulated. King Edward IV possessed the talents of a politician, and the fifteenth century had developed in town and country a consequential 'middle class'.[1] London was the touchstone of Yorkist success. By and large, the capital and the adjacent parts of the realm that elevated Edward to the throne enthusiastically supported the Tudors, made the Reformation, and backed Parliament and Cromwell against Charles I.

The least-appreciated of English monarchs, Edward IV was Queen Elizabeth's great-grandfather in more than blood; it was he, not Henry VII, who revived the realm of England and set it moving towards the splendours of the sixteenth century. No king of that realm owned a more brilliant habit of victories coupled with a greater love of peace than Edward IV; no king of England since the Conquest was so familiar with his subjects and beloved by them as he; and no king of England up to that time, save William I and Henry II, performed so seminal a labour in reinvigorating the institution of the monarchy.

While Henry VII has been widely praised for squeezing his subjects by taxes and extortion (he ruled by his cashbox, Gairdner notes approvingly) and for being able to weather challenges to his throne that were sometimes merely the measure of his unpopularity—Edward IV has been generally ignored, despite the fact that he restored to peace a realm wracked by a generation of turbulence, broke the power of Warwick the Kingmaker, an overmightier subject than ever Henry VII had to face, and strengthened the realm and the monarchy by reforms and techniques usually labelled 'Tudor innovations'.

The scholars of one century produce the textbooks and popular histories of the next. Because Victorian writers felt obliged to endorse Henry VI's piety, to deplore the irregularity of Edward IV's home life, and to applaud Henry Tudor's 'rescuing' of England from Shakespeare's Wars of the Roses, King Edward and his subjects remain, in the popular imagination, but shadow-shapes in a jejune entertainment. Who would suppose, from the textbooks, that when Henry VII died, Sir Thomas More was moved to

[1] The term 'middle class' is of course anachronistic, particularly in its modern connotations. I use it for lack of a better, to identify in general the rising and expanding orders of yeomen, townsmen, professional men, squires and knights of recent vintage—social orders now interpenetrating each other and becoming increasingly mobile.

write a poem celebrating the end of a dark, oppressive reign; or that in commenting upon the life of Edward IV, Sir Thomas praised him as a great king?

These years of the fifteenth century adhere into more than an arbitrary slice cut from the flux of time; they own an identity not simply dependent upon the duration of the strife of the Roses or the regnal years of Edward IV. Taken together, the latter decades of Henry VI, the reigns of Edward IV and Richard III, and the first decade of Henry VII reveal a distinct style and tone of life, as distinct as any metaphorical halting of the march of time can be.

From that which was to follow, the period is clearly enough marked off in everybody's mind: though aware that mediaeval ideas and practices will linger, we readily sense the acceleration of change summed up in the great words Reformation and Renaissance, in the 'absolutism' of Henry VIII, the lustiness of capitalism, the discovery that England's destiny lies upon the oceans. But from that which preceded, the period is much less clearly distinguished: the fifteenth century is often lumped with the Middle Ages, dismissed briefly as more of same but running down and rather dreary. Yet the age has no less descernible a beginning than an ending: it is separated from the Middle Ages by a series of shocks and dislocations occurring in the fourteenth century.

Consider England in that typically mediaeval century, the thirteenth, the England of Henry III and Simon de Montfort and the building of Salisbury Cathedral. This realm knew itself to be part of something larger, Christendom, swayed by spiritual and profane ideas represented in Papacy and Empire (then locked in bitter struggle). Christendom was still engaged in a common enterprise, the Crusades; spoke and wrote a common language, Latin; and acknowledged the dominion of an ecclesiastical bureaucracy that monopolized the learning and abilities of the age. Papal legates, humbly welcomed by Henry III, helped him to govern; the Pope chose the bishops who filled English Sees; and numerous French and Italian clerics held English benefices.

Socially and politically England was tied to another entity, the realm of France. This second affinity was likewise expressed by language, the French, the mother-tongue of most of the English upper class. Knightly society spoke French, read French romances, aspired to the ideals of French chivalry. Henry III could think of no better way to resolve a quarrel with his barons than to request the arbitration of the French King, Louis IX, 'St. Louis'. Lords often owned lands in France and might have been born there. Simon de Montfort, the younger son of a French baron, found himself completely at home in the baronial society and at the royal court of England.

The towns, even London, counted for comparatively little in this rural England (though the London mob once pelted the queen with filth as she tried to shoot London Bridge). Feudalism, which took no account of and left no place for a middle class, still dominated in idea if it was decaying in practice; the countryside, much more heavily populated than it would be two centuries hence, was enjoying the ripe noon of the manorial system; though free peasants tilled plots here and there and servile dues were being commuted for money payments, villeinage was everywhere and the agricultural labour of villeins supported the picturesque international society of knight and cleric. Fighting exercised and entertained the lordly class: disorders usually sprang from quarrels of lord and lord, or lord and vassal, or nobles and king. Parliament was still, mainly, the king's high court of lords spiritual and temporal; the occasional addition of Commons after Montfort's time remained a novelty.

The great upheavals of the fourteenth century profoundly shook this society, loosened its structure, powered the dynamics of change. The life of England emerged from these shocks into the fifteenth century so altered that it can no longer be called mediaeval. A severe agricultural depression, the ravages of the Black Death and social dislocations consequent upon them, the Peasants' Revolt, a long, wasting war with France, the withering of Papal prestige following upon the Great Schism and Lollard attacks upon the Church Worldly—these forces and movements hastened the demise of feudalism, spurred an English sense of

nationalism at the expense of Christendom, severed the social
tie with France, loosened the bonds and jarred the certainties of
mediaeval socity.

Edward IV, not the Pope, filled vacancies in English bishoprics;
and if Edward had been insane enough to submit *his* quarrel, with
Warwick the Kingmaker, to the French King, Louis XI—hated
by all good Englishmen—popular indignation would probably
have toppled him from his throne. Serfdom still lingered,
especially in the remoter parts, but it was already becoming a
survival, an anachronism. A new social order had thrust itself
up into the world between knight and peasant, the townsmen and
yeomen-gentry on whom Edward IV and his successors grounded
their powerful rule. Parliament, still the King's high court, now
exhibited a Commons which had become the dominant element;
and even if its members were not yet quite ready to test their
power, they were indeed beginning to understand that they
represented all the commons of England. The blows of the
fourteenth century upset the crude but rigorous balances of
mediaeval society. Greater opportunities and differentiations of
estate and inequalities and variety of careers made life more
challenging, more complex, more uncertain. Enterprising men of
small means no longer needed to enter the Church—though many
continued to do so—in order to rise in the world.

Increasingly anti-clerical and bitterly anti-French, exuberantly
conscious of itself, Edward IV's England had become England.
Until the end of Richard II's reign the government, the courts,
the towns, kept their records in French or Latin; lords and knights
conducted their correspondence in French, when they corresponded at all. With amazing suddenness, in the reigns of Henry
IV and Henry V, 1399–1422, French well nigh disappeared and
Latin was fading. By the middle years of Henry VI, documents
of many kinds, the Rolls of Parliament, chronicles, letters were
cast in English, homely and sometimes laboured but often
wonderfully pungent, as when Margaret Paston hit off a man she
did not like as 'a flickering fellow and a busy'.

Though most people wrote letters only when they had to,
their pens vigorously threaded the ramifications of domestic

problems and the bitter-sweet web of human experience. Four great collections of family missives survive: the Paston Letters, written by members of a tough, intelligent Norfolk clan who in less than three generations rose from the yeomanry into the higher gentry; the Stonor Letters, reflecting the well-to-do squirearchy, long settled on their land but not above making business alliances and trading in wool; the Plumpton Letters, which reveal the turbulent lives of a hard-handed, litigious Yorkshire knight and his kin, and the Cely Letters, a three-cornered correspondence carried on by a family of Merchant Staplers from Calais and London and their Essex manor. Then there are the Shillingford Letters, that hit off the personality and portray the political struggles of a doughty West Country mayor in the most embattled moments of his life. Hundreds of other voices from this world have also been preserved—letters of kings and commoners, reports of frivolous goings-on in nunneries, chancery petitions and town records unfolding tales of suffering and knavery and valour and love and death. Nothing like these riches of self-relevation exist from the mediaeval past.

The tradition of Latin historical writing had well nigh ceased by the time Edward IV came to the throne, but municipal chronicles, artless though they be, and propaganda narratives were lighting the lamps of English prose: town clerks here and there were translating old documents, Latin or French, into the vernacular as well as creating fuller and more systematic records of their own day; morality plays and interludes satirized contemporary manners in the racy language of the market-place; and Sir Thomas More, who had grown to precocious boyhood before Edward IV's death, would soon produce in his exuberant history of Richard III the first of modern biographies. The century did not write the *Canterbury Tales*, but it printed them, and produced a reading public for them. The Englishness of England had arrived.

In looking at the past, we are easily bemused by the intricate interplay of likenesses and differences; aiming for the special tone and style of an age, we are more likely to overshoot the mark

than to fall short. To our time-charmed eyes, differences project
so picturesquely or repellently or seem so alien that they startle
us from feeling the deep ties of common experience that bind us
to those who have gone before. We tend, too, to forget our own
ills in viewing those of the past. Historians write of the 'disorders'
of the fifteenth century as if they themselves lived in a disorderless
society which is the norm of human behaviour; the term *disorder*,
dangerously relative, thus floats in space without a horizon of
reference to give it meaning. Fifteenth-century offences against
human dignity and life and property sometimes took forms
different from such present-day offences and so look dark in our
imaginations. This sense of difference inclines us to find the life
of former times more dangerous than our own—ironically
enough. In the bad moments of the Wars of the Roses, 'evil
fellowships' occasionally broke into men's houses, laid ambushes
on the highway for enemies, seized manors on fraudulent claims.
We exaggerate the amplitude and effect of this marauding because
in our own more tightly organized society criminal impulses
and lawless passions find another vent.

We think the roads of fifteenth-century England unsafe indeed,
ignoring the little hells of broken glass and blood and sheared
flesh that strew our own roads. Then, as now, most men completed their journeys without incident. John Shillingford, Mayor
of Exeter in the late 1440's, thought no more of making several
trips a year to London than do his present-day successors.

Though *modes* of thought, attitudes, styles of living, and what-
there-is-to-be-talked-about have changed, 'the olde daunce' of
marrying and rearing children and losing in death and hoping
for tomorrow and trying to get ahead and envying the neighbours and enjoying the evening air and laughing with friends,
the small pains and pleasures, the 'buzz and hum' of daily life,
went on during the Wars of the Roses much as it goes on today.

When Margaret Paston learned that her younger sons were
going to accompany her eldest, Sir John, on Edward IV's invasion
of France (1475), she wrote anxiously to him, 'For God's love,
and [if] your brothers go over the sea, advise them as ye think
best for their safeguard. For some of them be but young soldiers,

and wot full little what it meaneth to be a soldier, nor for to endure to do as a soldier should do. God save you all and send me good tidings of you all.' Sir John Paston, visiting Bruges some time after he and his second brother had enjoyed a sojourn there, reported to the younger John, 'Rabekyn recommends her to you; she hath been very sick, but it hath done her good, for she is fairer and slenderer than she was, and she could make me no cheer but always my sauce was "How fareth Master John, your brother?" wherewith I was wroth, and spake a jealous word or two, disdaining that she should care so much for you, when that I was present.'

Even in the midst of troubles that seem remote to us, the common chords of living sound across the ages. Some months after an armed fellowship of the Lord Molynes had forcibly taken possession of the Paston manor of Gresham, Margaret Paston began assembling weapons and men to counter-attack. She sent hasty word to her 'right worshipful husband' to bring cross-bows and quarrels, pole-axes, armour; then, after analysing the defences of the enemy, she went right on—with a request for '1 lb. of almonds and 1 lb. of sugar' and cloth 'to make your child's gowns . . . and a hood for me of 4s. a yard. . . .'

On the other hand, apparent likenesses sometimes turn out to be not so like, after all, for language is slippery and meanings shift from age to age. Words like 'Parliament', 'mercy', 'freedom', 'treason', 'good government', 'fair prices', meant rather different things, as we shall see, from what they mean today.

The values of life, in the fifteenth century, were still emblemized rather than analysed. The Church had saturated men's minds with concrete images of the extra-mundane world and taught men to project, in daily life, attitudes and claims by an elaborate symbolism. Indeed, the pompous ceremonies of the Church had come to be used in this age to symbolize the dignity of earthly institutions like gilds and municipal governments. Banquets were brought to an end by the serving of 'sotelties' (subtleties), sugar-and-pastry confections moulded into a tableau of St. George slaying the Dragon or the Trinity surrounded by saints or the Virgin and Child. That hungry fingers would soon leave these sotelties a sticky ruin did not call into question the appropriateness of the imagery. On certain subjects, men of the time shaped their thinking into parallel categories sealed off from one another.

The urge to emblemize produced the concept of the 'appropriate punishment'. Transported back to the London of November 12, 1478, we would see one William Campion taken from Bread Street prison and made to mount a horse. A 'vessel like unto a conduit full of water' was set upon his head; 'the same water (ran) by small pipes out of the same vessel' and gave Campion a continuous wetting as he was led through London streets, doubtless followed by a jeering crowd. 'And when the water is wasted, new water is . . . put in the said vessel again.' Thus was Campion punished for having unlawfully tapped conduit pipes in order to bring water secretly into his own house and the houses of some of his neighbours.

Though the middle classes in town and country were moulding their lives by manners and aspirations and a vigorous empiricism of which we are the heirs, there still survived at the fringes of life grotesque, sometimes savage, usages of an earlier day.

Down in Winchester a condemned thief who had prolonged his life by accusing many men falsely was at last 'appealed' by an honest tailor. The men were clad in white sheepskins from head to foot, given each an ash club with an iron point, and set to fighting in 'the most sorry and wretched green that might be found about the town', neither having had food or drink and 'if they need any drink, they must take their own piss'. At the first blow their weapons broke. They fell on each other with nails and teeth. Flinging the tailor to the ground, the thief leaped on him and bit his privy parts. In an agonized convulsion, the tailor got to his knees, seized the thief's nose in his jaws, and gouged an eye with his thumb. The thief then confessed his lies and was hanged; the innocent tailor was given a pardon, became a hermit, and died shortly thereafter.

In crushing a Lancastrian army at Mortimer's Cross (February, 1461), young Edward of York (soon to be Edward IV) captured and condemned to death Owen Tudor, the glib adventurous Welsh gentleman who had won his way to the bed of Henry V's widow, Katherine of France, and sired three sons by her (one of whom became the father of Henry VII). Even when the scaffold was erected in the marketplace at Hereford, the jaunty Owen hoped to circumvent death as he had circumvented so many other obstacles, 'weening and trusting always', Gregory reports, 'that he should not be headed [beheaded] till he saw the axe and the block; and when he was in his doublet, he trusted on pardon and grace till the collar of his red velvet doublet was ripped off. Then he said, "That head shall lie on the stock that was wont to lie in Queen Katherine's lap" and put his heart and mind wholly unto God and full meekly took his death.' His head was 'set upon the highest grice of the market cross, and a mad woman kemped his hair and washed away the blood of his face, and she got candles and set about him burning, more than a hundred'.

The world of the fifteenth century was both small and enormous.

It was small because the earth stood at the heart of the universe, and the hand of God lay close upon human life. The Cross was everywhere displayed, at the wayside shrine, in the marketplace, borne aloft in procession through the city streets. The Virgin, who had once been a woman, softened the terror of God; the saints, their tangible remains ever on view, were willing to work miracles in this world and put in a word for man at the Throne. Rituals, ceremonies, folk-tales, the blaze of images and wall-paintings and tableaux in stained glass helped to domesticate eternity. Heaven was hard to reach but not far away, and the reminders of heaven were everywhere.

So too did reminders of darker regions lie all about. As the Church in this century began to lose touch with men's sense of awe, the mysterious unknown curled tightly about human life; hungering for spiritual tidings, folk hearkened to the voices of darkness. The uncertainties, the violent reversals of fortune generated by the Wars of the Roses likewise pushed men towards superstition.

Pilgrims and chapmen and friars, vagabonds, royal messengers, wandering minstrels, sped the report of marvel and portent from town to town. Chroniclers recorded wonders as matter-of-factly

as they recorded political events. When conflict threatened or
conspiracy raised its head, bloody rains fell in various parts of the
country to warn of upheavals. During the late 1450's, as York and
Lancaster moved towards open warfare, a huge cock was seen in
the waters near Weymouth 'coming out of the sea, having a
great crest upon his head and a great red beard and legs half a
yard long. . . .' The learned John Warkworth, Master of St.
Peter's College, Cambridge, zestfully reported of the uneasy
year 1473, when Edward IV's brother George of Clarence was
stirring trouble, that several magical wells signalled disaster by the
abundance of their flow and 'also this same year, there was a
voice in the air, betwixt Leicester and Banbury . . . long time
crying, "Bows! Bows!", which was heard of forty men; and
some men say that he that cried so was a headless man'.

The Croyland chronicler records an even more gruesome
portent of the struggle between Edward IV and the Earl of
Warwick: 'A certain woman in the county of Huntingdon, who
was with child and near the time of her delivery, to her extreme
horror felt the embryo in her womb weeping as it were and
uttering a kind of sobbing noise. . . . We may suppose that even
the children unborn deplored our impending calamities.'

With superstition ran prophecy, mysteriously wise after the
event and often pungently ironic. The English, Philippe de
Commynes drily observes, are never unprovided with prophecies.
When the Duke of Suffolk was murdered by the crew of a vessel
called the *Nicholas of the Tower*, the tale immediately ran that the
Duke had 'asked the name of the ship, and when he knew it, he
remembered Stacy that said, if he might escape the danger of the
Tower, he should be safe; and then his heart failed him. . . .'
At the first battle of St. Albans (1455) the Duke of Somerset met
his end beneath an inn-sign bearing the picture of a castle; and a
report was soon current that the Duke had been told he should
die under a castle. A little later the same year, John Gresham sent
word to John Paston from London: 'Here be many marvelous
tales of things that shall fall this next month, as it is said, for . . .
one Doctor Grene, a priest, hath calculated . . . that before St.
Andrew's day next coming shall be the greatest battle that was

since the battle of Shrewsbury . . . and there shall die seven lords, whereof three shall be bishops. . . . I trust to God it shall not fall so.'

Prophecy was often manipulated for political ends. A Norfolk soothsayer named Hogan, in the nervous year of 1473, was sent under arrest to London 'for reporting of his old tales'. Sir John Paston wrote from the capital: 'Every man saith we shall have a do ere May pass. Hogan the Prophet is in the Tower; he would fain speak with the King but the King saith he shall not vaunt that ever he spoke with him.' Edward IV was well aware of the political dangers of prophecy. Some people believed that he condemned his brother George, Duke of Clarence, to death because of a prophecy which said that one whose name began with G would supersede Edward's heirs—though it seems likely that this prognostication was not invented until Richard of Gloucester had assumed the throne. Following that event, says Mancinci, the pat prophecy circulated that within a space of three months three kings would reign. In the uneasy times of Henry VII's accession to power, it was rumoured that 'all manner of prophecies is made felony'.

The Black Art, too spread its raven wings over the realm. Witches were solemnly burned; 'nigromansers' went to the scaffold. Witchcraft was used, like prophecy, as a political weapon. The arrogant Eleanor Cobham, wife of the 'Good Duke' Humphrey of Gloucester, was condemned for trafficking in magic to practice upon the life of Henry VI—Humphrey, his uncle, then being heir to the throne—and, after doing public penance, was consigned to prison for the rest of her days. The Duchess' accomplices did not get off so lightly. Margery Jordan, the Witch of Eye, was burned at the stake; and Roger Bolingbroke, a clerk, after being exhibited on a scaffold beside St. Paul's, dressed in his conjuring gown and his evil instruments 'hanging about his neck', was hanged, drawn, and quartered.

The formidable and heartily disliked Dowager Duchess of Bedford, mother of Edward IV's queen, was popularly believed to have procured the dazzling marriage of her daughter by putting a spell upon the king; and on one occasion she was formally accused of seeking the death of Warwick the Kingmaker, her family's enemy, by fashioning an image of 'a man-of-arms . . . broken in the midst and made fast with a wire'. The feckless Duke of Clarence loosed tales of witchcraft against the queen and her relatives, and similar charges played an undetermined but probably potent role in Clarence's own downfall. The Tudor story that Richard of Gloucester had violently accused the queen and Jane Shore of withering his arm (unwithered) helped to discredit the king whom Henry VII had defeated in battle.

Yet, if in many ways the world seemed small, it was also enormous. Groping along the axes of space and time, man peered into murky vistas. Westward from English shores stretched the Atlantic Ocean . . . whither? Even if not unknown, spaces were often undefined or difficult to traverse; the interplay of communications, even within the range of comparatively few miles, was frequently untrustworthy. Measured in time, the realm of England stretched across distances greater than the span of the United States. York was six or even seven days away from London: no two points on the globe connected by airline are that far apart today. Cornwall, still speaking Cornish, lay farther from the capital than York; and even the ride from Norwich to London required two-and-a-half or three days. Bad country roads, the necessity of finding fords across rivers or a way through marshes, travellers' lack of information about routes or distances, further prolonged journeys.

Time, too, often loomed uncharted and mysterious. Between Adam and Eve and the present, the span of years glimmered uncertainly. Brutus, the supposed Trojan founder of England, and Charlemagne and King Arthur mistily intermingled. The past was vaguely felt to have been a happier age than the present, but when or why it ceased to be nobody knew. People referred to a previous 'time whereof no man's mind runneth'—and let it go at that. Many men did not know exactly how old they were; they did not know the date of the year or the regnal year of the king. They dated by saints' days, even by Sunday collects, as when Agnes Paston concluded a letter, 'Written at Paston, in haste, the Wednesday next after *Deus qui errantibus*'.

Yet Englishmen of this age were beginning to demand more information about the world. Anxieties stirred by uncertain times, the growing hunger of literate and publicly active squires, merchants, lawyers for authentic or seemingly authentic news stimulated a more intense, more calculated political propaganda than had hitherto been seen in England. The Yorkists had much the better of it; the Lancastrian lords of the West and North, the passionate and feudal-minded Margaret of Anjou, ignored the changing temper of the realm; while their adversaries, appealing to Londoners and townsmen and gentry of the more progressive regions—in general, the South and East—enjoyed the support of ballad-mongers and pamphleteers.

In 1459–1460 a barrage of 'seditious bills' and jeering verses helped to bring down the crumbling Lancastrian government. Risings and invasions were heralded by proclamations: Jack Cade issued a manifesto of grievances as he led his Kentishmen to Blackheath; Warwick the Kingmaker used proclamations to justify his cause when he attacked the Lancastrians in 1460 and, ten years later, when he sought to dethrone Edward IV.

Victories were publicized in 'official' accounts: after Edward IV crushed the Warwick-inspired Lincolnshire rising of February–March, 1470, a narrative of the rebellion and the confession of the chief rebel, Sir Robert Welles, were disseminated through the realm; and the brilliant campaign of 1471 by which Edward regained his throne was memorialized in the *Historie of the Arrivall of Edward IV in England*, which was translated into French and sent to Edward's Burgundian ally. Richard III, at the outbreak of Buckingham's rebellion and when Henry Tudor threatened invasion, issued pronouncements attacking the character of his enemies and bidding for his subjects' support. Shorter bills and schedules listed leaders killed in battle or traitors attainted in Parliament.

Important news was also announced by word of mouth in market squares, sometimes in churches. On Easter Saturday, 1461, Edward IV's Chancellor proclaimed at Paul's Cross the decisive victory at Towton of the Sunday before; nine years later, Edward's flight from England was likewise published there.

'Tokens' and 'credences' were widely used in order to authenticate tidings. Information about the period which we dearly lack fails us because it was transmitted only by word of mouth; all that survives is the letter of credence bidding the recipient put trust in what the bearer will say. Tokens were employed by kings and commoners alike. Professor Armstrong has counted at least a dozen certain references to tokens in the Paston letters and about half a dozen each in the Stonor and Plumpton letters. Early on Easter Sunday morning, 1471, when Edward IV was settling accounts with his erstwhile mentor Warwick the Kingmaker at Barnet, men came pelting into London crying that Edward and his brothers had been butchered in a Yorkist rout. A little later, the citizens finally learned who had conquered when a messenger galloped through the streets holding aloft one of the king's battle-gauntlets in token of victory.

Queen Margaret, fleeing into Wales after the Yorkists had captured Henry VI at the battle of Northampton (July, 1460), 'durst not abide in no place that was open, but in private. The cause was that counterfeit tokens were sent unto her. . . . For at the King's departing . . . toward the Field of Northampton, he . . . commanded her that she should not come unto him till that he sent a special token unto her that no man knew but the king and she.'

Foreign traders, English and alien, provided one of the best sources of news, as they had done for centuries; they maintained an informal network of speedy messengers and sure tidings, since political changes could profoundly affect their ventures. Though the Prior of St. John's, Sir John Weston, sat on the King's council and tapped all official sources of information, he nonetheless was always pressing his friends the Cely family, Merchants of the Staple, to send him tidings; for the Staplers' town of Calais was one of the best listening-posts in Europe. London sent correspondents to both the Lancastrian and the Yorkist armies in 1471 in order to find out as speedily as possible which army was likely to arrive at its gates. Gentry coming up to London, besought by friends and kin in the country to keep them informed, spent much time gathering and sifting the reports current in the capital.

But there was never enough news, or sure enough news, to allay anxieties; tidings of high moment sometimes travelled very haphazardly; and successive tidings often differed wildly so that the truth could not be ascertained for days or weeks. Word of the capture of Henry VI in Lancashire (1465) was brought to Edward IV by a monk. Merest chance wafted the first news of the battle of Barnet across the Channel. A man who left London by boat the next day was taken at sea by the Easterlings, who landed him in Zealand. Somehow his knowledge of King Edward's triumph reached Edward's sister Margaret, Duchess of Burgundy, and she immediately sent to the Dowager Duchess the first written account of the battle to appear on the Continent. Early tidings were often false; bad news and good were likely to be exaggerated. A Milanese ambassador shrewdly discounted the over-optimistic reports, arriving after the battle of Towton, that Henry VI had been taken, observing, 'Vain flowers always grow in good news'. The farther tidings had to travel, the likelier they were to prove untrustworthy. At the time Edward landed, a fugitive, in the Duke of Burgundy's dominions (October, 1470), Duke Charles had received certain intelligence that he was dead; thirteen years later, a premature report of Edward's death which reached York was inscribed in the city records and never removed. The Milanese ambassador to the court of Louis XI of France wrote bitterly, at the time of Edward's campaign of 1471, 'We have such different reports that I cannot possibly find out the truth'. Edward had regained his kingdom before the end of the first week in May, but King Louis did not receive authentic word of this upset to his hopes until June 1.

At times of greatest crisis, emissaries from both sides criss-crossed the country bearing commands to raise men and spreading conflicting reports. 'Now go messengers by "twyne", contrary and contrary', wrote a chronicler of the wild days of March, 1461.[1] At the outbreak of Buckingham's rebellion against Richard III, in October 1483, a Northerner sent word that

---

[1] Queen Margaret's forces were retiring northward after just failing to take London, as the Yorkists, entering the capital, proclaimed Edward of York as King Edward IV.

'Messengers cometh daily both from the King's Grace and the Duke into this country'.

Because, in this uncertain world, men's hunger for news could not be satisfied, a crop of writhing rumours snaked through all the realm to plague peoples' minds. Reports of 'flying tales' and of dire predictions that there will be 'a work' or 'a do' appear again and again in the Paston letters. For lack of knowledge, even the merest hearsay was sought; on one occasion the town of Beverley paid a labourer to walk to the Earl of Northumberland's castle at Leconfeld 'to hear rumours'.

Like prophecy and witchcraft, rumour was employed for political ends. The Yorkists encouraged slanders on Margaret of Anjou's chastity and, in 1459-1460, stimulated reports of tyrannous exactions by the queen's government. Later, Warwick and then Clarence used rumour in trying to undermine King Edward's rule. During the reign of Richard III, Tudor agents spread a fog of slanderous tales; and Henry Tudor himself was plagued by rumour during the campaign that led to the battle of Stoke (1487), for Yorkist sympathizers so successfully sowed false word of the king's defeat that contingents marching to join him hastily turned homeward. The Lancastrians and Edward IV and Richard III and Henry VII all issued fierce commands against 'telling of tales and tidings whereby the people might be stirred to commotions'.

But beneath these jars and anxieties, currents of knowledge and perception flowed ever more strongly among a people who had not yet learned to bridle the range of human nature or distrust the mysteries of human existence. The men of the Yorkist Age conducted their lives, viewed human responsibility, and laid themselves open to experience more carelessly and generously than we do. They had a grander vision of man's destiny but expected much less of him. We draw a modest, perhaps cynical, circle, but demand that each individual fill it; the subjects of Edward IV drew an enormous circle, and took it for granted that man would cut a puny figure therein. Human frailties, consequent on the fall of man, were reprehensible but inevitable and

therefore could be condoned—witness the casual acceptance of
bastardy. Punishment had to be fierce and spectacular, for man,
hardened in sin, needed vivid deterrents; yet rulers exercised
mercies we find inexplicable because they are unrelated to the
question of guilt or innocence. To the people of this time human
mercy, like God's mercy, must be capricious, else how could it
be mercy. Traitors today are processed by the machinery of law
and condemned for faithlessness to a concept called the state.
In the fifteenth century, treason was personal, the desertion of an
oath made to a king. The traitor did not disappear into mech-
anized legal jaws, his fate on no man's hands. He confronted the
judgment of the man he had wronged and might therefore have
some hope of mercy. We shudder at the burnings and disem-
bowellings of the age; yet Edward IV, not once but repeatedly,
forgave treasons which would now be condignly punished. The
century knew how softly sin and how easily error slid into a
man's heart.

As people of the Yorkist Age were simpler and looser in judg-
ments of their fellows, so did they offer themselves more recklessly to the blasts of living. Exposing themselves raw to
experience, they were more like amoebae than we, if you will,
but then perhaps we are amoebae who—under the pressure of
neighbours, of the machine, of a depressed sense of possibility—
have put on overcoats and think we are overcoats. Fifteenth-
century men had not learned that it is better to fit in than to feel.
They were more irritable and excited and excitable than we; and
they consumed spectacles of blood and terror and images of
dissolution that we could hardly bear. Life was not only more
terrible, more tautly stretched between violent contrasts of piety
and cruelty, ostentation and nastiness, pleasure and pain, fairyland
and hell, but it was suffered with exposed nerves and a desperate
acquiescence in God's will. Today we confine ourselves to the
middle strings and discreet horns of the human orchestra; during
the Wars of the Roses men played the wild gamut of strains
from piccolo to doublebass. They liked life gamy—just as they
enjoyed heavily seasoned food, not only because spices covered
the taste of decaying meat but because they stung a man into a

heightened awareness of being alive. These people exhibit a more jagged range of emotions, quicker shifts of mood, a heartier and more immediate response to life than are to be observed today. By our standards, the subtlest are often obvious; the most foresighted, impulsive; the wariest, naïve. For many of them there was no middle distance, no tomorrow. Only today and eternity.

But among the pushing, literate, increasingly critical middle orders, tomorrow was appearing. That is how the century differs from what has gone before, in a greater prudence, precision, calculation, wariness; in a dimmer sense of custom, a keener sense of consequences; in a stronger and more confident desire to manipulate rather than to accept the way of things. Queen Elizabeth I might have found Edward IV attractively intelligent but somewhat barbarous; Edward I would probably have considered him valiant but supersubtle. Men were beginning to order their lives more pragmatically, more exactly, than their fathers had done. The measurement of work by the diurnal hours, the keeping of records and annals, the leap ahead in communications powered by the printing press, all showed an age of accelerating change. Invented in the fourteenth century, mechanical clocks now counted the division of the day in all towns and in the halls of the well to-do; and in the operation of businesses and municipal governments, a keener sense of the virtues of punctuality signalled heightened standards of efficiency. Englishmen were beginning to grip the world in both hands—rudely sometimes, as foreigners discovered, but zestfully.

The people of the Yorkist Age were aware too, as their forebears had not been, that life is various and plastic and mutable, that customs and values are susceptible to the transformations of time, and that their own lives in especial had broken from the scheme of the past:

Men's works have often interchange:
That now is nurture [good breeding] sometime had been
                                                    strange . . .

And after this shall things up rise
That men set now but at little price.

So conscious were they of changing perspectives and standards that they sought to slow the pace by creating appearances of stability—minutely specified household regulations that defied the uncertainty and flux of things, an elaborate system of courtesy, a devotion to tournaments and other archaic ceremonies, a clothing of old language for new ideas. Even as they strode vigorously to meet the future, the people of the age regarded, or considered it good form to regard, all 'newfangledness' with suspicion. Two of the Vices in the morality play, *Mankind*, probably composed during the last decade of Edward IV's reign, are called New-Gyse and Now-a-Days, and foul-mouthed, shiftless fellows they are. Yet though the Virtue, Mercy, warns mankind against them—

> Nice in their array, in language they be large . . .
> They heard not a Mass this twelfthmonth, I dare well say—

Mercy also takes care to qualify his condemnation:

> The good new guise now-a-days I will not disallow;
> I discommend the vicious guise.

Despite the upheavals of the Wars of the Roses, the latter decades of the fifteenth century, lit by both a setting and a rising sun, form a span of diffused prosperity and vigorous growth between the dislocations of the late fourteenth century and the grim days of Tudor land-enclosure and Tudor debasement of the coinage and widespread misery among the lower classes— 'these decaying times of charity', Stow called them. It may even be that we shall find in the reign of Edward IV the age that subsequent centuries looked back to as Merrie England.

I

The Mayor

The Mayor: At Home

AT six o'clock on a summer morning, church bells sounded the beginning of a town day. The doors of the Gildhall were thrown open. Preceded by the Serjeant-at-the-Mace bearing the gilded symbol of authority and by other officers, a ceremonious figure, respectfully saluted by early risers, made his way towards the church. Clad in scarlet and fur with a thick silver chain about his shoulders and a high furred hat on his head, he surveyed the awakening town with a ruler's eye. After he had lent his presence to the early Mass of market-day, his retinue reassembled about him, and he proceeded to the market-place to see that his constables were on the watch for 'fraudulent sellers of victuals'. Then, joined by other figures in scarlet cloaks, he returned to the Gildhall for a meeting of his council. In the person of the mayor, the town had once again asserted its dignity and recommenced its communal life.

This mercer or draper or grocer, serving his one-year turn as chief magistrate, better represents the spirit of the age, in many ways, than a lord or even an ambitious squire like John Paston. The reign of Edward IV has some claim to be called the golden age of the mayor.

Not until the fifteenth century did most of the chief towns, having won their struggles with local lords or ecclesiastics, secure from the king a charter of liberties including the right to organize themselves as counties. By the time of Edward IV they had won sufficient wealth and power to exert pressure upon the changing shape of English life; and, under the king, the mayor governed his municipality no less authoritatively and a great deal more tightly than the king governed the realm. Before the end of Henry VIII's reign, on the other hand, towns were beginning to blend into the national scene, mayors were becoming absorbed into the royal mesh of administration, some municipalities were losing their prosperity and population to the countryside, and the ever-growing capital, London, was shouldering its rivals into the subordinate role of sleepy provincial centres. The latter years of the fifteenth century struck, for towns, a moment of balance-within-change, when they had partially freed themselves from the forces of the past but had not yet begun to yield their individuality and pride to the new forces of the Tudor age.

London was far and away the largest city in the kingdom, three or four times as populous as any other, one of the great cities of Christendom. After London, the chief towns of England were widely scattered, each the focus of a broad tract of country. York, the second city with perhaps 15,000 inhabitants, was the Metropolis of the North. Her lovely white walls and battlemented gates enclosed a Minster completed in 1472, some three score churches and religious foundations, and an industrial and trading depot which supplied the needs of the largest and one of the wildest parts of England. Down the river Ouse sailed barges laden with wool and cloth bound for the Low Countries; up the river came barges freighting wine, stockfish, spices, tapestries, woad, pitch. These imports along with the products of the looms and metal-working shops of the city were packed by horse across moors and dales to abbeys and castles and bristling border towns like Carlisle.

Bristol, only a little smaller than York, could boast no Minster nor the historical tradition of the Eboracum of the Romans; but it was more famous as a trading centre and a port, home of enterprising merchants, shipbuilders, and mariners. Bristol vaunted its 'double walls' of water and stone, its stone-bound quays, its cloth industry, its merchant fleet, a harbour sheltered from storms and pirates, and its opening upon the Atlantic.

The Venetian diplomat of Henry VII's time observed that except for London, 'there are scarcely any towns of importance in the kingdom save these two, Bristol and York'; but Norwich, though declining, and Coventry were probably not far behind

York and Bristol in population. Norwich was then the greatest cloth town in England; the cloth woven in the villages of Norfolk had to meet the approval of the Norwich gilds. Coventry, magnificently walled and surrounded by a broad belt of common lands, was likewise a hive of weavers and dyers. Coventry blue thread was known abroad; her merchants freighted imports and exports on the Severn or to and from the Eastern ports; lords and gentry from all over England were happy to become members of the city's great religious gilds. Next in size after these towns came Winchester and Exeter and Canterbury and Colchester, Lincoln, Nottingham, Chester, Shrewsbury. Perhaps none of them had more than 5,000 people.

Of the four chief cities, only Bristol faced an expanding future, thanks to Columbus and the Atlantic. By the middle of Henry VIII's reign, the weavers of Coventry were crying for work, for the clothiers, seeking streams for fulling mills and freedom from municipal restrictions, had taken to the countryside. York was losing out to rising towns like Halifax, in industry, and to Hull, in foreign trade. With the decline in the popularity of worsteds, Norwich too declined, until grass was growing in the market-place.[1]

The smaller towns, like St. Albans, were rudely enclosed by a ditch-and-embankment and by wooden barriers that could be swung across the main entries to the market-place. All the chief cities armoured themselves in stout walls and gates and towers. During this age of sporadic warfare, most towns kept their fortifications up to the mark; repairs and additions were financed from murage dues collected from each citizen; occasionally a gild, sometimes a wealthy merchant, undertook to re-edify a section of wall. The town armoury contained artillery as well as small arms; in troubled times, guns were hastily mounted on towers and emplacements above the gates.

The girdle of their walls set cities off sharply from the rest of the realm, even though a ribbon of inns, hospitals and abbeys often lined the approaches. The men of the age were well aware of this

---

[1] With the coming of alien weavers, Norwich, however, recovered a measure of prosperity in the latter years of the sixteenth century.

bold separation. Manuscript illustrations show white towers and walls, with steeples and tiled roofs behind, rising dramatically from a pastoral foreground. Yet the walls enclosed stretches of field, greens, orchard closes of religious houses, garden plots; and most citizens owned a cow or two, some sheep, perhaps a pig, which were pastured on the common lands outside. Towns and townsmen of the Yorkist Age were more distinctly set apart from the land and yet also closer to it than their modern counterparts.

Near the gates of a town there frequently stood a hut with a bearded and verminous old fellow before it extending his alms bowl; this was the hermitage, a municipal institution: candidates applied to the mayor. The gate was guarded by sergeants, who sent sturdy beggars packing, examined the credentials of messengers on sweating horses, sometimes exacted toll from countrymen bringing provisions to market, directed a leper, rattling his clapper, to the lazar house down the road.

Once a traveller had passed the towered gates with their arrow-slits and portcullis and machicolated battlements, he was plunged into a reeking, noisy, crowded world. In its tortuous alleyways and swarming narrow streets, the English town of this period probably resembled nothing today so much as a Levantine or other Mediterranean city, where life is lived out-of-doors, unself-consciously, and at high pitch.

For his ideal city, Sir Thomas More provided streets only twenty feet wide; most town thoroughfares were probably narrower than this, with sudden widenings and turnings, the sky shut away by the upper storeys of gabled houses leaning ever nearer to each other. A 'channel' in the middle of the street or two smaller ones at the sides encouraged the rain to cleanse the public way, but the streets remained thick with every variety of filth, with rubbish swept from houses and with worse than rubbish sometimes dumped from upper windows. A dead animal might lie several days, before the constable of the ward got round to ordering somebody to remove it; even the dignitaries of London sometimes failed to set a good example: 'John Derby, Alderman, for so much as he refused to carry away a dead dog lying at his door, and for unfitting language which he gave unto the mayor, he was by a Court of Aldermen deemed to a fine of £1, which he paid, every penny'. The wares of shopkeepers, piled around doorways, and market stalls made the streets still narrower. A reckless horseman or carter drove citizens to the walls.

In the early morning, the 'Common Herd' escorted cattle out to pasture; boys collected swine and goats to feed in waste and wood; but there were always domestic animals 'going' in the streets. Ducks waddled in the water of the channels (forbidden); pigs rooted at garbage piles (forbidden); goats nuzzled at the food stalls (forbidden).

The life of the town clotted most thickly in the market-place, around the principal church, at the Gildhall—and these institutions were usually close together. Between the rows of market stalls, buyers fingered wares and bargained; hawkers offered fruit or chestnuts or pins and girdles, weavers' wives displayed on their arms a pile of 'dozens' (half-cloths twelve yards long). In the nave of the church a gild held a business meeting, while chantry chaplains sang for souls of the dead. Men bought and sold goods in the churchyard, dumped loads of rubbish there (forbidden), stored a load of hay or wood or iron (forbidden) until a purchaser could be found. Citizens trooped into the Gildhall to attend the court of the mayor or pay a fine or to have their wool weighed, while young people, if the main hall was large enough, played a game of tennis (forbidden).

The air hung heavy with smells and sounds. Beneath the 'boards' of butchers and fishmongers grew reeking piles of blood and bones and entrails. Horses, cattle added their steaming deposits to the muck of the streets. Down lanes hemmed by crowding tenements men scalded swine (forbidden within the city limits), adding to the stench produced by the tanners and whittawyers— workers in white leather—and dyers. Over ditches and streams running through the town, latrines were sure to be projecting (forbidden).

Sounds penetrated the town atmosphere as insistently as odours. Church bells were always going, saturating the ears. They sang and boomed above the arguments of the market, the shouts of small boys teasing a goose, laughter in the alehouses, the mutter of the Mass wafted from church doors, clatter of hoofs on rough paving, a hue and cry after thieves. Bells sounded the hours of the day and the perambulations of the night watch; they summoned substantial citizens to a meeting of the Common Council, announced the opening of city court, signalled the time of municipal elections. Bells rang for the feasts of the Church, for warnings of danger, for exercising the art of bell-ringing; and when discontents among the lower orders boiled up into riots, the wild tintinnabulations of the 'common bell' shouted their defiance of authority. But, most often, the bells rang in behalf of souls—for funerals and the 'month's mind' and the 'year's mind' or obit. Since the custom among prosperous citizens of leaving money for bells to be rung on their obits extended back tens of decades, this accumulation of piety kept the bells tossing all the hours of the day. Lesser notes blended into the din. The town crier rang his bell in the square to herald the latest proclamation from the mayor, or the king. Beadles from the craft gilds and religious fraternities walked through the wards ringing bells to inform the brethren and sisters of a funeral or a meeting. A lord rode through the high street with jingling harness. On All Hallows' Eve (October 31) and on All Souls' Eve (November 1) the bells tolled all night long; and every night, usually at nine P.M., the curfew bell sounded the closing of the city gates.

As poignantly as sounds and smells struck the senses, the whole existence of the city thrust itself upon the gaze of the inhabitants. Greatness and misery, business, sport, punishment were exposed to public view. Artisans in their shops had to work in full sight and must not pursue their labours after dark. Crime sat, pelted with filth, in the stocks on the green. Neither riches nor poverty shrank from the light of day. The dignity of power, the dark mystery of death, the humility of indigence, the splendour of wealth, the horror of a felon's end were acted out as if life were a perpetual morality play (as people once knew that it was). The mayor, taking the sun in scarlet surrounded by his officers, looked only like himself, master of the city. A lousy beggar showed his sores as he extended his alms bowl. Whoredom was shamed in a striped hood. Lords or abbots riding through town had their lordly way cleared by liveried servants. When a well-to-do citizen died, many-faced poverty congregated about the door: the fortunate ones would receive a gown, a meal, and perhaps 2d. The funeral procession blazed in the streets with banners of chanting clergy, poor men bearing torches, children in black gowns. Yet, if wealth looked even wealthier, poverty humbler and power more awesome, the great and the mean alike shared the spectacle; everybody acted in the drama and everybody knew his part.

The work day stretched long, but the panorama of street life offered plenty of entertainment. On a rude platform in the square, players of the town or of a parish, or a troupe from a neighbouring village, enacted the edifying drama of a saint's life, then pranced through a knockabout morality dominated by the bawdy-tongued Vice. Town minstrels, bright in livery and silver badges, played for civic processions, holidays, the arrival of a great lord, fairs and festivals. In the summer weather the minstrels of the King or of the Queen or of the Duke of Gloucester, making their seasonal tour, gave a concert on the green, complete with trained apes and marmosets to delight the vulgar; they could be sure of a fat tip from the city magistrates, perhaps a noble (6s 8d) or even as much as 10s. On occasion the 'Trumpets' of the Duke of Clarence or the Earl of Essex went blaring through the streets followed by streams of children. Threadbare mountebanks with only their tricks to recommend them danced and sang and juggled and beat their tabors while a girl balanced herself on two swords thrust into the earth.

On weekends and holidays wrestlers from neighbouring villages competed on the green for a ram's head. Cock-fighting and bull-baiting provided the crowd with bloodier amusement. Butchers were strictly forbidden to slaughter bulls until they had been baited. Numerous towns had an official called the 'Bull-ring Mayor' or the 'Warden of the Shambles' who made sure that all bulls ready for killing were first baited for the enjoyment of the citizenry. Archery continued to be a popular and patriotic sport, encouraged by Parliament and sometimes enforced by the mayor.

The municipality maintained butts and pricks where citizens practiced the yeoman art. 'Roving' was also very much in vogue. The Prior of Coventry complained bitterly that townsmen broke down his hedges and trampled his grain as they wandered on fine days, quivers on back, shooting at whatever targets took their eye. The Mayor replied stiffly that he was not responsible for damage done by individuals and that, furthermore, many towns including London, permitted roving. Over in France a young nobleman, issuing from a house just as an archer let fly at the door, was skewered like a chicken.

Men enjoyed a variety of other games as well, many of them frowned upon. Parliament, lamenting the decay of archery (it was being lamented before Agincourt), issued stern prohibitions against football and bowling games and other unmannerly pastimes, as well as against all forms of gambling. But in every town in England men kicked footballs in streets and bowled on greens and rattled dice in alehouses.

Punishments, too, were woven into the common experience of townsmen; for man was known to be sinful, the fabric of order was felt to be precarious, and only the strongest deterrents, the most emblematic examples could preserve society from falling apart into rapine and anarchy. A traitor or felon was lashed, face up, to a 'hurdle' and dragged at a horse's tail through town to the scaffold. Attended until the last moment by a priest or friar who held a cross before his eyes, the victim mounted the platform to behold a mass of faces, made a brief speech of repentance or perhaps a passionate declaration of innocence, forgave the hangman, and took the noose. Hanged and then quickly cut down while still alive, he was castrated and disembowelled and might still linger in agony while his entrails were burnt before his face. 'Jesus, yet more trouble', moaned one sufferer as the hangman's knife drove into him. This gruesome death was a ritual: every act had a symbolic significance going far back in time. A crazy old woman who shrieked a reproach to the Boy-King Henry VI and had not the wits to answer her accusers was pressed to death for her failure to plead. Men, women, and children crowded to watch these executions, sometimes jeering, sometimes in silence, sometimes with tears upon their faces. The gates of towns, the spikes on the towers of London Bridge sprouted a crop of heads, picked by kites and weathering.

Sometimes the great ones of the world imitated the capricious mercy of God in dramatizing their clemency. In July of 1447, five months after Humphrey, Duke of Gloucester, had died, or been murdered, while in the custody of his bitter enemy, the Duke of Suffolk, five of his followers, including Humphrey's bastard son Arthur, were condemned 'to be hanged, drawn, and their bowels burnt before them, and then their heads to be smitten off, and then to be quartered, and every part to be sent unto divers places by assignment of the judges'. They were dragged from their prison in Southwark, across London Bridge, through Cheapside, and out Newgate to Tyburn. 'And every man of them lay on hurdles in velvet doublets. And Arthur held a cross of gold between manacles. And all the time they prayed the people to pray for them as they were guiltless of any treason, which sight was full heavy to the commons.' Even the French ambassadors beholding the spectacle were moved. The men were hanged, but as they were strangling, the hangman suddenly cut them down. The Duke of Suffolk himself rode up to hand them pardons for their lives. 'And they came again through the city thanking God and the King of his grace.'

Lesser punishments were often grotesque and humiliating, and here and there customs from a more brutal age survived. In the Cinque Ports a thief was forced to be his own gaoler: his ear was nailed to a post or a cartwheel and he was given a knife to cut himself loose. When, surrounded by curious eyes, he had nerved himself to the deed, he had to pay a fine and foreswear the town. Those who bribed jurors were forced to display their guilt by a whetstone hung about their necks. Cuck stools stood ready to bring shrews and scolds to their senses. The one on Chelmsford Green, Coventry, frequently needed repair. In Nottingham, where the term 'scold' was defined to include men as well as women, the cuck stool was wheeled to the offender's door and then she (or he) was paraded to the four gates of the city. The standard punishment for fraud and other knavery was the stocks or the pillory, where a hail of vegetables and jeers sharpened the punishment.

City fathers tried to draw the line, however, at personal vengeance. The wife of Thomas Pynde, taverner of London, was defrauded by one Simon Ludbroke, who, committed to prison on October 27, was sentenced on December 13 to stand in the pillory for half an hour—at the suggestion of Thomas Pynde, though Thomas was warned to leave punishment to the law. Nevertheless, as soon as Ludbroke was clapped in the pillory, Pynde removed the ladder leading to the platform and then he and his friends plastered the hapless Simon with rotten eggs: the constable on duty there consumed a whole hour finding another ladder. But Pynde was haled before the mayor and aldermen and promptly committed to prison. Two days later, he humbly admitted his errors and was fined the enormous sum of £20, of which £10 was remitted.

Offences against morals were also vigorously aired. The Coventry Leet (court) condemned William Powet, capper, 'and his paramour' to be 'carried and led through the town in a cart in example of punishment of sin'. A few years later, John Got was let off more lightly, perhaps because he was the town gaoler. He was warned in court that he would lose his position if he 'commits fornication, especially with Elizabeth, wife of Thomas White'. At York, prostitutes were required to avoid the town and dwell in the suburbs. Elizabeth Judela, convicted in London of being 'a common bawd', was 'led from prison to the pillory in Cornhill with minstrelsey', wearing 'a ray [striped] hood on her head' and carrying a white rod in her hands. Dealers who tried to foist tainted victuals on the public had their stinking fish burnt before their noses or their fraudulent loaves loaded on their shoulders. In London a woman named Agnes Deyntee, who had sold 'corrupt and old butter, not wholesome for man's body', was condemned to stand beneath the pillory for half an hour with her dishes of rotten butter hanging about her neck and then to quit the city.

For minor offences, punishment fell more heavily upon the humbler citizens than upon the merchant aristocracy. The latter usually paid for their misdeeds by fines, whereas poor men cooled their heels for several days in gaol. Incarceration was likewise more painful for the man who had no money in his purse, for prisoners were expected to pay for their board and lodging. Though towns attempted to enforce a tariff of maximum prices a gaoler might charge for food, drink, and decent accommodation, ordinary citizens were sometimes miserably treated unless they had friends to help them. For a fee, a man was permitted to have his servant fetch his bed to the prison, and for another fee the gaoler—forbidden, for good reason, to brew or sell ale—would send out to the nearest tavern for drink.

Great prisoners of state like Henry Percy, whose Lancastrian father, slain at Towton, had forfeited the earldom of Northumberland, fared well in the King's prison of The Fleet. He was permitted four servants and an allowance of 26s 8d a week. When John Paston, who fell afoul of The Fleet for a few months, enjoyed a visit from his wife, Henry Percy and others made her such good cheer that the usually sober John was moved to write her a letter in verse. Humble men who languished in gaol were not forgotten, however. Wills of the time reveal that 'relief of poor prisoners' was one of the most exemplary forms of charity by which a man might demonstrate to Heaven his good intentions. Philip Malpas, the most unpopular London alderman of the century, left the princely sum of £125 for this purpose, and all over England men bequeathed money, food, gowns to the inmates of prisons. At the bottom of fifteenth-century thinking there was always the realization that while laws must be rigorously enforced, justice was a matter for Heaven.

But everything was a matter for Heaven. To twentieth-century eyes, town life in the reign of Edward IV appears supercharged with the ceremonies and reminders of religion. In York and London there was a church for every 500 inhabitants. Their steeples thrust above tiled roofs; their bells sounded the dominant tone of daily living; their altars and walls and windows offered a blaze of beauty unrivalled by secular buildings. Friars, priests, men in minor orders (like Chaucer's Somnour) were always to be seen in the streets. In the corporate life of the citizen, the activities of his gild and civic celebrations were all coloured with religious ceremonial; and the pattern of church observances determined his working hours. He downed tools at noon on Saturday for the Sunday holiday and at noon on the days preceding the half-dozen principal festivals of the Church. Counting days off for gild and municipal affairs and for Church holidays, a townsman probably enjoyed something like forty free days, exclusive of Sundays, during the year.

On the other hand, if the Church had impregnated the world, the world of the towns had come, by the fifteenth century, to use the pageantry and prestige of the Church as a means of expressing the dignities of secular life. The Church festival of Corpus Christi, falling on the first Thursday after Trinity Sunday—a likely season for fine weather—was now the day on which the gilds, *for the honour of the town*, demonstrated in processions and plays a vivid image of their importance.

A Corpus Christi Gild was specially dedicated, in most towns, to presenting the procession. At York, as in other cities, this gild included not only the principal townsmen but great lords and ladies like Richard, Duke of Gloucester and his wife and Richard's mother Cicely, Duchess of York. A parade of ecclesiastics, members of the Corpus Christi Fraternity, officers of the city, the craft gilds in their liveries, moved in a dazzle of torches and crosses and banners from Holy Trinity Priory to the Minster, where a renowned preacher delivered a sermon. In the midst of the procession was borne the shrine of silver gilt crusted with gems that housed a beryl vase containing the Sacred Elements. Along the route the fronts of houses were hung with tapestries and the doorways wreathed in rushes and flowers. This procession at York took place not on Corpus Christi Day itself, but on the day after; and in most of the other towns it was presented early in the morning; for the procession had ceased to be the heart of the festival. In the chief towns of the Midlands and the North, the Corpus Christi plays, staged by the craft gilds, were the thing.

None, it seems, enjoyed such fame as those at Coventry, or so allusions early in the next century suggest ('Oft in the play of Corpus Christi he had played the devil at Coventry': Heywood, the *Foure PP*). In Edward IV's time the merchants of Shrewbury, disloyally pretending that they were bound for business at Coventry Fair, so deserted their own celebration that they had to be restrained by municipal ordinance from leaving town. Coventry showed only ten plays on ten pageant-wagons, with one station in each of the ten wards of the city; but every play was a cluster of little plays and was produced by a cluster of gilds.

The small town of Beverley proudly offered thirty-six dramas, but then the stronghold of Corpus Christi playing lay in the North. York topped all other towns with a day-long festival of some fifty different pageants showing Biblical scenes enacted by about five hundred performers. Beginning at dawn, the wagons, marshalled on Toft Green, wound slowly through the streets, pausing to exhibit their sacred stories before the principal public places from Holy Trinity Priory to the Minster and before the homes of those who were rich, or pious, enough to pay a fee for the privilege. As in other places, the dramas were distributed among the gilds by a certain logic: the Shipwrights, Fishmongers, and Mariners drew on their experience to play the tale of Noah; the Goldsmiths made splendid the Three Kings coming from the East; while the Vintners portrayed the Miracle at Cana.

Banners bearing the arms of the city were planted at each station. A pageant-wagon, drawn by horses, rolled into position before the waiting crowd, the side-curtains were raised, and the actors launched into their parts. The spectacle was not all solemnity, for by this time many plays were enlivened by farcical moments. The Devil, a very popular character, leaped from a 'Hell-mouth' with firecrackers banging in his ears and tail; the ranting tyrant Herod, who flung himself into the street frothing at the mouth to beat his head on the cobbles, was such a favourite at Coventry that he rode, arrayed in his kingly dress, in the religious procession. The costumes for God, Abraham, High Priests, 'knights' were made of expensive stuffs; sometimes they were borrowed, or rented, from the gentry. Faces were painted, weapons gilded. What lacked in scenery was hidden by a lavish display of colours.

This was the city's day, when nobles and knights and squires as well as humbler countrymen came riding in to view the pageants and enjoy the Mayor's hospitality. In 1478 the mayor of York and his 'brethren' viewed the Corpus Christi plays from the house of Nicholas Bewyk; they paid 9s rental for Nicholas' front chamber and to the 'knights, ladies, gentlemen, and nobles then being in the city' they sent 40s worth of red and white wine (about forty-five gallons). It appears that, from Henry V to Henry VIII, all the Kings of England saw the Coventry plays at least once. Margaret of Anjou, Henry VI's ill-starred Queen, graced the celebration of 1457: 'on Corpus Christi Eve, at night, the Queen came privily to see the plays and on the morrow she saw all the pageants played save Doomsday, which might not be played for lack of day'. The wagons halted first at the dwelling of Richard Wood, grocer, where the Queen lodged. For refreshments, the Mayor sent her three hundred loaves of fine bread, a pipe of red wine, a dozen fat capons and a dozen fat pikes, panniers of peascods and pippins and oranges, two 'coffins' of comfits and a pot of green ginger. Among the lords and ladies attending the Queen was Lord Rivers, who twelve years later would be beheaded on Gosford Green, just outside the city walls.

Though the festival of Corpus Christi reached the height of its glory during the fifteenth century, the animating spirit among the gilds was already beginning to flicker. What had once been an act of faith, and then a zestful gesture of pride, had become a duty; gilds who were growing poorer, or so claimed, resented the money and time their members spent upon the pageants and tried, by one device or another, to wriggle out of their obligations. But the Mayor and aldermen were in firm control, and for the 'weal of the city' they held recalcitrant gilds and gild members rigidly to the mark.

Nothing better shows the really secular nature of the Corpus Christi celebration than the multiplication of town decrees designed to ensure the best possible production of plays. Gilds which had somehow escaped the duty of sponsoring a drama were forced to give financial aid to pageant-producing gilds. Dues called 'pageant-pence' or 'pageant-silver' were collected from each gild member; fines swelled the pile of coins in the 'pageant-box'; and everyone 'occupying' a craft who did not belong to a gild had to contribute towards the support of a play. All persons, churchmen as well as others, who made clasps, dog collars, and other 'gear belonging to the girdlers' at York paid twice as much in pageant-silver as members of the gild.

The city fathers had very much at heart the standard of acting and play production. Robert Eme, a man of such importance that he would one day become a sheriff, was informed that he 'and all other who play in the Corpus Christi pageant shall play well and sufficiently so that there be no slacking in any play, on pain of 20s to the wall fund'. Henry Cowper of Beverley was fined by the wardens 'because he did not know his part'. At Hock-time (second week after Easter), the magistrates of Worcester called the gilds together in order to determine which five of them would present their pageants in that year's festival. No city took greater precautions than York to ensure good acting: it was decreed 'unto perpetuity' that yearly at Lent 'there shall be called before the Mayor four of the most cunning, discreet, and able players within this city to search, hear and examine' all players and plays and pageant-wagons; 'all such as they shall find sufficient in person and cunning, to the honour of the city and worship of the said crafts', they will admit and all 'insufficient persons either in cunning, voice, or person they will discharge. . . .'

Producing the plays was an expensive business. Pageants had to be repaired and cleaned and strewn with rushes; rent must be found for the 'pageant-house', where wagon and gear were stored; clerks or schoolmasters were hired to revise the prompt book and copy out fresh parts and song sheets; the elaborate costumes frequently needed refurbishing or replacement; actors and minstrels and the prompter received a wage for their services; and rehearsals and moments of waiting before and after performances had to be eased with gallons of good ale. In 1490 the Smiths of Coventry expended a total of £3 7s 5½d on their pageant (something like £150 in modern money) and some gilds doubtless spent more.

A sampling of craft records shows a fraternity in the throes of play production: 'Paid at the second rehearse in Whitsun week in bread, ale and kitchen, 2s 4d. . . . Paid to the players for Corpus Christi day: imprimis to guard 2s, to Caiaphis 3s 4d, to Herod 3s 4d, to Pilate's wife 2s, to the minstrel 14d. . . . At Richard Wood's door for ale to the players, 5d. . . . For St. Mary's Hall to rehearse there, 2d. . . . Paid for a pint of wine for Pilate, 1d. . . . Paid for six skins of white leather to God's garment 18d, paid for making of the same garment 10d. . . . Reward to Mistress Grymesby for lending of her gear for Pilate's wife, 12d. . . . Four jackets of buckram for the Tormentors with nails and dice upon them. . . . Paid for the minstrels for the procession 2d and pageants 3s 6d. . . . Paid to Fawston for hanging Judas, 4d. . . . Paid to Fawston for cockcrowing, 4d. . . . For mending the white and black souls' coats, 8d. . . .'

Not many weeks after Corpus Christi came the celebration of the 'Common Watch', as it was called at Worcester, or the 'Marching Watch', as it was known in London and other towns. This was a double muster in arms, held on Midsummer's Eve (June 23) and on the Eve of Sts. Peter and Paul (June 28) to express the worldly pride of the city. At early morn, women and children trooped into the woods to cut fennel and hawthorn branches and other greenery for decking doorways. Men cracked street paving in order to plant small trees before their houses (forbidden). Servants heaped up piles of coal and wood; lanterns were hung out. As dark fell, bonfires blazed, citizens danced and sang and drank in the streets, and gildsmen gathered at their halls martially arrayed in jacks and sallets and bows and spears. Then, lighted by cressets and a multitude of torches, the craft gilds marched through the streets of the town. Sometimes the mayor and his officers sat before the Gildhall to review this display of municipal might. Sometimes the Mayor, clad in brigandines bright with scarlet velvet, led the procession on a war-horse. Half the city officers usually marched on the first night while the other half lined the streets; on the second night their roles were reversed.

Crowds packed the town to see the show. Drinking often led to words and words to broils. The Prior of Coventry, alarmed by the bloody fighting that erupted on these nights, begged the Mayor to appoint constables to patrol the wards. He also complained that his hedges were broken and his enclosures damaged by the masses of people gathering greenery. Down in Bristol that most famous mayor and merchant, William Canynges, decreed that at the conclusion of the parade on both nights the Mayor and Sheriffs should provide wine for the gildsmen. The Weavers and Tuckers (Fullers) were each assigned ten gallons, and, in all, twenty-six crafts received ninety-four gallons of wine, fetched by the gild servants in their own pots.

The city magistrates staged a year-long drama of ceremonies, quasi-religious and civic, all of them weaving a ritual pattern of municipal dignity. The election of the mayor, which usually took place in the autumn or shortly after the New Year, was followed by an oath-taking on the part of the successful candidate, after which the old mayor delivered to his successor his hat of office, the King's Sword, and the casket containing the city seals and keys. Down in Bristol, the whole company of 'substantial citizens' brought home 'the new mayor to his place, with trumpets and clariners, in as joyful, honourable, and solemn wise as can be devised'. After they had dined, some with the new mayor and the rest with the old, they assembled at the High Cross to walk in procession to St. Michael's and make offering. Then followed 'cakebread and wine' with the new mayor and Evensong.

After dinner on All Hallows' Day, the Mayor and Sheriff and council of Bristol, 'with many other gentles and worshipful commoners', walked, two by two, 'unto the Mayor's place, there to have their fires and their drinkings with spiced cakebread and sundry wines, the cups merrily serving about the house'. On St. Katherine's Eve (November 24), the Mayor and his 'brethren', after hearing Evensong, proceeded to the hall of the St. Katherine Gild, where they were treated to refreshments; then each of the city officers retired to his dwelling in order to be ready 'to receive the St. Katherine's players, making them to drink at their doors and rewarding them for their plays'.

St. Nicholas' Day (December 6) marked the opening of Christmas revelries. In the morning the Mayor and his fellows heard Mass and listened to a sermon by the Boy-Bishop; then, after dinner, they played solemnly at dice (a traditional part of the festival) until the Boy-Bishop arrived with a train of clerical attendants to give the town officers his blessing and be refreshed with bread and wine. The next day these magistrates were presented with their Christmas liveries, the Mayor receiving £8 worth of finest scarlet cloth as well as an allowance for furs, wine, minstrels (in all, more than £90). He was a busy man during this season dominated by the Lord of Misrule. The people of Bristol, like those of other towns, celebrated with mumming and gaming and dancing and brawls among visored rascals in dark streets. The Mayor heard sermons by friars famous for their preaching on the four Sundays of Advent; he inspected the wharves of Bristol to make sure that enough wood had been imported for the holidays, that sufficient 'small wood' was available for the poor, that extra supplies of food had been laid in since 'many strangers resorted to the town': and on Christmas Eve he issued the usual proclamation against wearing of masks, carrying weapons, and remaining in the streets without lights after curfew.

So, throughout the year, the pageant of municipal ceremonies continued, a co-mingling of customary rites and increasingly secular exuberance. When the officers of Canterbury led a 'riding of the bounds', small children accompanied the parade; and at every turning the Mayor gave them pennies so that the true boundaries of the city would be perpetuated in their minds.

The occasional arrival of mighty lords, the welcoming of king or queen, provided further occasion for pageantry. When the magistrates of York learned that their friend Richard of Gloucester (later Richard III) and the Scots Duke of Albany would reach York early on the morning of June 18 (1482) on their way to invade Scotland, it was ordered that 'all the Aldermen, in scarlet, and the Twenty-Four, in crimson, and every other man of craft in the city in their best array shall be ready the following morning —the Aldermen and Twenty-Four by four of the clock and every other of the city by three of the clock—at Miklyth Bar to attend of my lord of Gloucester's good grace. . . .'

On important occasions cities entertained royalty with a show that had long been a tradition of town life. After being greeted a mile or two beyond the walls by the Mayor and the 'most worshipful citizens', the King was welcomed at the gates by Biblical prophets or Dame Sapience or King Arthur in flattering rhymes. Before the principal church perhaps, the Four Cardinal Virtues continued the theme of praise. A conduit in the market-place ran wine, as angels, perfuming the visitor with smoking censers, piped a tune. Farther on, the Nine Worthies, a fight among wodewoses (wild men), a Jesse tree painted on canvas delighted the King's eye and ear. If he tarried overnight, there would be a parade to the church, and King, Lords, Mayor and Aldermen, and clerks marched with crosses and banners around the churchyard before hearing Mass—procession was the essence of display.

When Edward IV entered Bristol in early September of 1461, William the Conqueror welcomed him at the gate—a deft compliment to the victor of Towton—a giant delivered him the keys of the city, and at Temple Cross the King was treated to St. George on horseback 'upon a tent, fighting with a dragon, and the king and the queen on high in a castle, and his daughter beneath with a lamb. And at the slaying of the dragon there was a great melody of angels'.

Sometimes royalty preferred to dispense with ceremony, as when Margaret of Anjou, journeying 'suddenly from Kenilworth to Coventry unto her meat [dinner] . . . came riding behind a man then; and so rode the most part of her gentlewomen'. Her mode of transportation was not unusual. Edward IV's sister Margaret, departing from London to become the bride of Duke Charles of Burgundy, was borne through cheering streets upon the horse of the great Kingmaker, Warwick. Ladies of this age sometimes rode sidesaddle and sometimes astride; the custom of riding side-saddle had been introduced towards the end of the preceding century by Richard II's Queen, Anne of Bohemia.

Ordinarily, when Edward IV approached a town, the magistrates and wealthiest burghers—Mayor and Aldermen in scarlet and the citizens in violet or green or murrey—met him some distance beyond the walls, dismounted to kneel three times in the prescribed courtesy to royalty, made him a speech of welcome, then escorted him to his lodging and presented a gift of perhaps £50 or £100 in gold, fish, wine, and bread.

There was no difficulty in determining which were the chief citizens who should accompany the Mayor and make the largest contribution towards the expenses of the King's welcome. Distinctions in rank among townsmen, as among lords and gentry, were dramatized by dress and ceremony. The social stratum to which any citizen belonged could be penetrated at a glance.

Atop the heap stood the municipal oligarchy: 'The Clothing', 'The Scarlet', the 'probi homines', the 'superiores', the substantial men 'de bone condicioun'. They inhabited, in Bristol, towered mansions with vaulted cellars for the storage of wine; in London and other cities, gated dwellings built around a courtyard; or broad houses which fronted the street in carved beams and handsome windows. Their wives went abroad attended by servants. They themselves wore furs and velvet and expensive broadcloth and usually received every year, if they were members of the council, a gown of the city livery. They were masters of the chief religious and craft gilds. The wealthiest of them, the ones likeliest to become mayor, were mercers, drapers, grocers, goldsmiths. Towns like Bristol contained well-to-do weavers; dyers occasionally rose to prominence in Coventry; and here and there fishmongers and other victuallers were rich and powerful; but the chief offices fell usually to the merchant-traders of fifteenth-century towns.

Next came the 'middling' class, the comfortably-well-off 'shopholders': skinners and tailors and ironmongers and corvisors (shoemakers). Among their numbers were ambitious young men rising towards 'The Scarlet'. Shopholders wore russets and kerseys and might buy good black broadcloth for a Sunday suit. Beneath these were the humbler artisans, sellers of victuals, small shopkeepers, and journeymen who hoped someday to own a business of their own. Apprentices, too, formed a part of this class, which dressed in Welsh or Kendal friezes and cheap worsteds. Except for those who purchased the freedom of the city—immigrants from another town—apprenticeship represented the only path to citizenship and success.

These ranks made up the citizens, the enfranchised, who voted and 'bore scot and lot' (paid taxes) and belonged to gilds. At the bottom of the heap were the proletariat, unskilled labourers most of them, who lived in frail cots or crowded tenements and hired themselves out as best they could. At Worcester, such men wishing work were required to stand at the Market Cross by five in the morning in summer, six in winter, and wait patiently for someone to engage their services. Cities also numbered among their inhabitants members of the gentry who varied their country lives by spending a season in their town houses, as did the Pastons at Norwich; but not a few knights and esquires had wholeheartedly embraced the citizen's life of trade.

A tax assessment of a tenth on goods levied at Nottingham in 1472 reveals that one man paid 74s 7½d, while others paid as little as ¼d. Quarterly assessments at Coventry for street-cleaning and paying the town minstrels were divided thus: 'hall doors 1d, shop and cot doors ½d'. Constables making collections needed no official list of citizens ranked by income. When a subscription (not voluntary) went round for a present to the King or for money to pay soldiers going to the wars, each ward of the city usually contained a few men paying 20s or more, several contributing about 10s, while the great majority were taxed at 2s or less. The assessment represented an acknowledged status, not a precise percentage of income. In many towns the poor were spared, their neighbours making up the difference.

Yet, though cities displayed a strict hierarchy of prosperity and prestige, craft and religious gilds included all classes of the enfranchised. Towns were divided, spatially, into wards; socially, into strata determined by wealth; but the gilds were the organic cells of the town hive. Men knew themselves sons of Holy Church, subjects of the king, citizens of the town, but they were gildsmen to the bone. The two principal forms of association, the craft gild or 'mistery' and the religious fraternity, were in many ways much alike. Almost all craft gilds enjoyed a patron saint, charitable purposes, and religious ceremonies. Certain of the religious fraternities were based upon rank or upon associations of work or trade. In Bristol the trade gild of the Merchant Adventurers had its religious counterpart in the Gild of Kalendars; the Merchant Adventurers of York were also members of the Corpus

Christi Gild. Citizens usually belonged to a craft gild and at least
one religious fraternity.

Most splendid of the religious fraternities were the great town
gilds, remnants in some places of the Gild Merchant of an earlier
age, like the Gild of St. Mary at Lichfield, the Gild of Palmers at
Ludlow, the Trinity Gild of Lynn. Such gilds were often only
another name for the ruling oligarchy; sometimes they included
gentry, merchants, and nobles from all over England. The life of
Coventry was dominated by the Holy Trinity and Corpus Christi
Gilds; members of the ruling class belonged to both; and a man
marked for the mayoralty would become master of one gild
before taking office and master of the other upon ceasing to be
mayor.

The average citizen and his wife belonged to a religious
fraternity organized within their parish or including men of
similar occupation. They might pay an entrance fee of 5s or 6s and
2s a year in dues. The great fraternities asked much more. A
modest one like the Gild of the Resurrection, Lincoln, demanded
'4d to the light and 1d to the wax on entry' and 13d yearly in
four payments. Sick benefits might amount to 1s or more a week;
burials of members were as grand as the 'common box' would
allow, expenses being minutely specified. The religious fraternities
of the humbler classes could not afford to retain a chantry priest to
sing for souls but managed to sponsor a light at an altar in the
parish church; their members who were sick or temporarily
destitute received 1d or 2d a week. The Gild of St. Michael on the
Hill, Lincoln, firmly announced that 'whereas this gild was
founded by folks of common and middling rank', no one of the
status of mayor or bailiff could become a brother 'unless he is
found to be of humble, good and honest conversation', and no
one was to have any claim to office in the gild because of his rank.

Members of a religious gild celebrated their fraternal association
on 'the general day'. The brethren and sisters, after marching two
by two in their liveries or hoods to their parish church to hear a
Requiem Mass for deceased members, proceeded to an inn or
house, or their hall if they were prosperous, where they enjoyed
a banquet. After eating and much ale drinking and other pleasures

of good fellowship, they transacted gild business: moneys lent to members were accounted for; the old officers produced their reckonings; the company voted upon new regulations and elected officers for the coming year. Most gilds were headed by an Alderman; four 'skeveynes', or stewards, took charge of gild property; a Dean or Beadle summoned members to meetings; and a Clerk kept the minutes.

The general day fell usually upon the day of the patron saint or the Sunday thereafter. Some gilds held two feast days yearly, others as many as four. There were also 'morne speeches' and 'drinkings' and other get-togethers. A number of gilds staged a pageant on their 'day'. The fraternity of St. Elene, Beverley, chose the 'fairest youth' they could find, who was 'clad as a queen like to St. Elene [mother of Constantine] and an old man goes before carrying a cross and another old man carrying a shovel, in token of finding Holy Cross'. With the gild members following, two by two, 'they go in procession, with much music, to the church of the Friars Minors . . . and there at the altar of St. Elene solemn Mass is celebrated'. The Gild of St. Mary, Beverley, displayed 'one clad in comely fashion as a queen, like to the Glorious Virgin, having what may seem a son in her arms; and two others shall be clad like to Joseph and Simeon; and two shall go as angels, carrying a candle bearer on which shall be twenty-four thick wax lights'.

On the eve of the burial of a deceased brother or sister, the gild members assembled in church to hear Dirige and Placebo; next morning they bore the body to the church for Requiem Mass and then to the interment. The richer fraternities provided poor men clad as mourners carrying torches, a distribution of alms, and numerous Masses to be said for the soul of the deceased on the 'month's mind' and the 'year's mind'. Fines for misconduct were applied, in part, 'to the wax'—an equal or greater amount going to swell the fund 'of the ale'.

In the various parts of the realm, religious fraternities displayed special interests and attitudes. Those at Lincoln strongly supported pilgrimages: money was supplied to pilgrim-members, they were ceremoniously escorted from the city, and if they could give advance notice of their return, they were met at the town gates. In East Anglia, gild regulations evinced great concern about decorum on the general day, particularly unlicensed trips to the ale chamber. The fraternity of St. Martin, Stamford, sponsored the hunting of a bull by dogs, the animal then being sold. The fraternity of the Annunciation, Cambridge, would admit to membership no parson nor baker nor any wife unless she were the wife of a member. Numerous prosperous fraternities supported a schoolmaster and a school.

The craft gilds, or misteries, were as diversified as the religious fraternities. They included wealthy associations of mercers and drapers, gilds of artisans—cordwainers, smiths, girdlers—groups who rendered special services, like the 'Innholders', and unions of humble workers such as tilers and porters. The great London companies were divided into two gilds, one for the 'livery', the most prosperous members of the craft or trade, the other for the journeymen. Most misteries, however, included all classes of enfranchised workers or traders. Like the religious fraternities, their aims embraced churchly and charitable observances; but the principal object of such an association was to control the operation of a trade or industry.

Craft gilds enforced established prices, laid down rules governing hours and wages, set standards of quality and workmanship, and demanded the absolute obedience of all members to the warden and masters. 'Searchers' were appointed to inspect shops and workrooms in order to ensure the observance of gild regulations. The industry or trade over which a gild had the right of search established, in the eyes of the law, the kind of gild it was. Grocers, for example, dealt in a wide variety of wares, but they possessed the right of search only over spices.

When a craft-gild apprentice had served his time, usually seven years though in some misteries as much as ten or twelve, his master brought him before the wardens of the gild as a candidate for full membership, and the wardens in turn presented him to the Mayor as a young man who had qualified for town citizenship. The number of apprentices and journeymen a shopholder might employ was strictly limited, and the terms of apprenticeship were rigidly defined. Apprentices, drawn from yeoman families, gentry of the surrounding countryside, and children of the town, received board and lodging and some clothing and their training. A member of a rich manufacturing or trading gild, however, might demand as much as £5 as a premium for accepting an apprentice and a yearly payment as well. It was easier to become a smith than a goldsmith.

Every aspect of a man's business was controlled by his gild, and much of the rest of his life as well. In many towns members of a mistery were required to take a formal oath to their master and wardens so that if they afterwards defied the leadership of the gild they could be sued for breach of oath in ecclesiastical courts. The multiplicity of rules—prohibitions, requirements, reiterations of punishment and penalties—has a tyrannous ring; but the prime object of a craft gild was protection and defence, protection of its monopoly of goods or services, defence against those seeking to evade its jurisdiction or undermine its prices or compete with its members.

Gilds were all alike and all different. The Tailors of Exeter offer as good an example as any. Tailors worth £20 or more were required to be of the 'masters' fellowship of clothing', which meant paying an entrance fee of a silver spoon, buying a livery once a year, and giving 12d to the annual feast. Middling shop-holders were organized into the 'fellowship of the bachelors', who paid 8d to the feast. Journeymen and hired workers paid 6d. The Clothing and Bachelors met quarterly to regulate their affairs and then dined together, after which the journeymen were permitted to bear away the meat and drink that were left. The governors of the craft, the master and wardens, met every Thursday evening at nine o'clock to transact gild business. In the laying down of policy and enforcing of regulations they were assisted by a Council of Eight. No craftsman was permitted to employ more than three journeymen and one apprentice, unless he secured a special license. Every new apprentice had to pay a silver spoon to the gild; when he had completed his term, he was expected to furnish a breakfast for the master and wardens the day before he became enfranchised. Tailors moving to Exeter who were made 'free of the craft by redemption' (i.e., by purchase) offered an entry fee of 20s and also provided a breakfast.

Just as the craft gilds exercised a ubiquitous paternalism over their members, so did town governments assert an equally firm control of the gilds. The mayor was, in effect, the governor of every mistery. Since the ruling oligarchy was composed mainly of merchants, they had a vested interest in seeing that the victualling gilds provided cheap food of good quality, that the manufacturing misteries kept down the price of their wares, that the city's good name, and theirs, was not besmirched by shoddy cloth, that associations of middlemen-sellers did not drive up the cost of living.

In Bristol, as in other cities, the newly elected mayor summoned to him the masters of craft gilds, ordered them to proceed to their halls for the election of officers, and required those officers to take an oath upholding the right of the mayor to oversee and amend the administration of all gilds. Their regulations had to be submitted to the municipality for approval; the mayor could cancel or add what regulations he pleased.

On the other hand, the city government stood ready to uphold the authority of wardens and masters: recalcitrant gild members were not only fined by their mistery but were punished by the mayor with further fines and, in the case of continued defiance, by imprisonment. In Coventry, craftsmen were required to obey their warden on pain of 100s fine—many a craftsman made no more than 100s a year. Apprentices were enrolled before the Mayor, and their promotion to journeymen was registered in the city records. The municipal government settled all quarrels between gilds. When the Weavers and Corvisors of Coventry came to brawls over a conflicting business interest, the mayor promptly put a stern hand upon both parties, required the Weavers to contribute 20s and the Corvisors 100s to be used in 'drinkings' to re-establish good fellowship between the crafts, heavily fined certain gildsmen for trespass and assault, and forbade the Corvisors to use fancy trade names like 'queyres enamelling' for plain blackalyre cloth.

Rebellions flared against this iron control but were quickly put down. The Dyers of Coventry resented being under the thumb of the numerous drapers in the governing oligarchy. They set up secret regulations regarding methods of dyeing and prices, and attempted to hold their members to these regulations by oaths binding in ecclesiastical courts; but after a struggle the city brought the Dyers firmly to heel. The Bakers of Coventry on one occasion raised a riot, then marched out of the city, leaving the inhabitants breadless; but they were quickly constrained to make a humble submission and the ringleaders were fined and imprisoned.

The mayor likewise looked with a jaundiced eye upon any movement by journeymen or other workers to combine in order to assert their modest rights. Such associations were instantly crushed, sometimes to reappear in the innocent guise of religious fraternities and be again suppressed. Newfangled attempts at capitalism were also discouraged. When certain iron-makers of Coventry managed to coordinate the work of smiths and brakemen (who drew iron into rough wire) with the finishing operations of girdlers and cardmakers (makers of iron wool-combs), this combination was pronounced to be in restraint of trade—there were dark allegations of shoddy workmanship leading to the ruin of the crafts.

The mayor exercised the same hawklike supervision over the market-place. In the chief towns, he was King's Clerk of the Market, controlling the official weighing machine, 'The Beam', and Ulnager of Cloth. As one of his first acts, a new mayor dispatched his officers to bring in all weights and measures that they might be compared with the city's official standards. The Mayor, or his deputies, frequently sallied into the market-place to punish breaches of sanitation and to catch red-handed the ubiquitous regrator, male or female—that illegal middleman hated by the commons who bought up supplies of food to hold them for resale at a higher price. At the gates other officers were on the lookout for forestallers, almost as unpopular as regrators, who intercepted cart-loads of provisions even before they reached the market. The butchers of London sent forestallers as far away as Northampton.

Buying and selling in the market was hedged round by a thicket of regulations, beginning with the 'Assize' of bread and ale and wine established by Parliament; town decrees reiterated and amplified these Parliamentary enactments; and gilds of sellers added their own restrictions. The mediaeval notion of the 'just price' still prevailed, in theory. Townsmen liked to think that the object of industry and trade was not to make money but to provide goods and services to the community at the lowest prices consonant with allowing the fishmonger and the baker and the tavernkeeper a sufficient profit to continue in business. A profit of 1d in the shilling was considered sufficient for purveyors of food, of 2d in the bushel of grain for innkeepers, and of 2d on the gallon of good wine selling for perhaps 16d. The market existed for the town, not the town for the market: everybody subscribed to the idea but in the reign of Edward IV it had ceased to be a guide to business practice.

The massive array of market regulations had three main objects: to protect the commons against unscrupulous victuallers; to war on fraud in all buying and selling; and to favour townsmen over 'foreigns'.[1] Every ward had its 'ale-conners' who, when a tavernkeeper displayed a new bush, sampled the brew in order to rate it as first-class or as ordinary ale. Wine and fish and meat were inspected to ensure that they were 'wholesome for man's body'. Officers made the rounds of stalls and boards and shops to test weights and measures. In Coventry, searchers appointed by the Drapers examined cloth brought for sale to the 'Drapery', and the city ulnager scrutinized cloth manufactured in the city, before sealing it. The stalls of foreign fishmongers and foreign butchers were patrolled lest townsmen be offered tainted or overpriced victuals. In general, foreign sellers had to expose their wares in specified places and at specified times; foreign buyers were not permitted to appear in the market until citizens had had first choice.

These severe regulations, however, like other mediaeval legislation, sometimes represented an aspiration rather than an achievement. For one thing, they weighed more heavily on the little man than on the wealthy dealer. The enterprising and the

---

[1] 'Foreigns' were all people not inhabitants of the town; men from another country were usually referred to as aliens.

unscrupulous found plenty of opportunity for evasion. Rich victuallers grew richer, despite all attemps to maintain a just price. Regrators and forestallers were known to wax fat in the sun. The bigger the operation, the freer it was of control. One of the greatest benefits conferred by town franchise was the right to trade with other towns of the realm without paying toll, a right which was sometimes established by royal charter, sometimes by diplomatic treaties between towns. The great merchants maintained a vigorous circulation of goods.

With less success than they achieved in the control of gilds and markets, the city magistrates struggled to keep the municipality clean, orderly and decorous.

Educated men of this age knew very well that a deadly connection existed between filth and plague; and mayors and aldermen redoubled their injunctions against animals 'going' in the streets and against littering the town with garbage. But the careless commons were not yet sufficiently disciplined nor policed to obey. Yet plague, not the civil strife of the Roses, was the dominant fear of the age. Since the Black Death had appeared in England in 1349, it had struck again every few years, sometimes in one region, but often spreading over most of the realm. Clergy led the commons in penitential processions; the churches filled with fearful folk praying for salvation; and still this terrible death pounced on its victims—first a dizziness and then the fateful swelling beneath the armpit. The mournful bells of deathcarts sounded in the streets; the warning cross blossomed on doors; men staggered and were taken as they talked to friends in an ale-house. The disease attacked most viciously the young and the healthy and the well nourished. The upper classes suffered severely even though they could attempt flight.

1454, September: 'Here is great pestilence. I purpose to flee into the country' (from London).
1464, October 5: Venetian merchants arriving in Bruges from London reported that plague in the English capital was killing 200 people per day.

1465, August: 'They die right sore in Norwich'—Agnes Paston and her cousin Clere dared no longer stay there.

1467: People began dying of the plague in London in March; by July the deathrate had risen so alarmingly that Parliament adjourned in a panic; and in November the city was still so crowded with dead and dying that the opening of the law courts had to be postponed.

1471, September: ' . . . great death in Norwich . . . it is the most universal death that ever I wist in England.' Pilgrims told the Pastons that none of the places they had come through were any safer.

November: 'We know not whither to flee to be better than we be here.'

1479: One of the worst visitations of the age—'so universal a death I have never known'. The realm was so disorganized by terror that few records of this year survive. Edward IV secured a dispensation from the Pope permitting him and his chief courtiers to eat meat during fasting periods so that they might keep up their strength against the onset. Sir John Paston, his brother Walter, and probably his grandmother Agnes died this year of the disease. Young John Paston and his wife fled from their manor of Swainsthorpe to Norwich; when Norwich became a pit of death they could not move, for by this time the plague had reached Swainsthorpe.

1485, autumn: A new plague, the Sweating Sickness, perhaps imported by the French mercenaries of Henry Tudor, victorious at Bosworth, killed two mayors and six aldermen of London within a few days.

Our ancestors suffered plague and mysterious fevers and agues of the eye and aching teeth and festering ears and swelling of the joints and sudden paralysis and griping of the bowels, and yet, somehow, most of them managed to live hearty lives. Doctors and quacks bled patients and cast horoscopes and prescribed noisome concoctions . . . and often were less helpful probably than village 'wise women' with their simples.

Meanwhile, the city fathers of the English municipalities not only laid on prohibitions against unsanitary practices, but did the best they could to promote cleanliness. Most of the principal cities had sewers; pipes brought fresh water from springs and streams beyond the walls to conduits and 'bosses' in the streets; wells were dug at city expense. Women were not to do any washing at these conduits, and brewers and dyers and butchers were forbidden to send their apprentices with tubs to monopolize the public water supply. 'Skaldynge de hogges' and slaughtering of cattle had to be done outside the city walls; the butchers of London were required to cart entrails down to the Thames, where they were loaded on barges to be dumped into the river when the ebb was running strongly. Municipal carts periodically collected rubbish.

The mayors struggled also to repress rampant individualism, rudeness, and downright nastiness. Prohibitions had to be reiterated against digging clay or sand from public roads and greens and squares. At least one traveller during this period drowned as a result of riding into just such a hole in the highway, which had filled with water. Towns had to enact explicit decrees against 'scorning of strangers'; innkeepers were cautioned against bullying potential customers; shopkeepers were ordered to cease sallying into the street to grasp passers-by; victuallers were enjoined against cutting stockfish or saltfish on the same board on which they had cut flesh the week before. Not only did 'pissing in the churchyard' have to be forbidden by law but also pissing in the Drapery—except into the gutter running down the middle of the building.

After plague, fire was the great hazard of the towns; a blaze fanned by wind could quickly wipe out a block of wooden houses, for even the best fire-fighting equipment of the time, providently disposed, was cumbersome and slow. Fire-fighting regulations were probably better observed than the laws of sanitation. At Coventry, it was forbidden to curry leather within the city limits, for fear of fire. Thatched roofs and chimneys 'of tree' were prohibited in most cities. Certain men in each ward were required to store fire-hooks (for pulling down buildings), ropes, rings, and ladders. Each citizen was supposed to own a leather bucket. In Worcester, firehooks were available in three parts of the city, and citizens were appointed to haul water from the conduits by horse and cart, in case of fire.

Even fundamental orderliness was not easy to achieve in that age when men were quickly stirred to joy, tears, anger. Words in the streets soon led to blows and blows to bloodshed. With feeling the prologue to action and most men going armed with knife or dagger, towns sought to prevent weapon-carrying except by those of the rank of gentlemen or above—not that gentlemen were more pacific, merely more influential. Words were carefully hearkened to. A threat or 'unfitting language' was enough to bring a man before the mayor's court. In order to prevent feuding or the rise of factions, the magistrates of York rigorously investigated malicious gossip. Action had to be quick and penalties severe because there were never enough constables or sergeants to provide adequate policing of the city. Paid officers patrolled by day; the night watch was usually the duty of citizens, who evaded it whenever they could. Constables pursuing a malefactor were sometimes manhandled by that malefactor's friends or so vividly threatened that they rushed back to the mayor to report that they had been put in fear of life and limb.

In their pursuit of decorum, city magistrates kept as watchful an eye as they could upon sexual morals. 'Known' prostitutes were driven away or forced to wear a striped hood of shame and dwell in the suburbs. The mayor lectured adulterers in open court and exposed lecherous clerks to public ridicule in the stocks. Coventry required all single women up to the age of forty either to 'take chambers' in the home of honest folk or go into service, until they were married; and the mayor decreed that any person 'entreating for the favouring of any misliving woman' was to be fined 20s.

The menace of the 'sturdy beggar' was now beginning to fall upon the towns, though he would not become a widespread social evil until the hard times of the Tudors. In 1473 Edward IV's council issued a proclamation, to be read in all the cities of the realm, against vagabonds who feigned sickness or pretended to be pilgrims or passed for poor University clerks. They were a political danger, for they wandered from town to town 'sowing seditious languages'. After the accession of Henry VII, such proclamations were multiplied, and the King sent frequent orders to mayors to round up vagabonds and gamesters.

No wonder that the mayor had to be a wealthy man. Expressing the honour of the city in a year-long parade of ceremonies and governing a hardy race of townsmen with inadequate means that often had to be backed by sheer assertion of authority and personality, the merchant-turned-mayor had no time for his business or other private concern. During his year, he belonged to the city; and the city, saving the King's prerogative, belonged to him. On the record, most mayors of the time appear to have performed their duties with zeal, even with aplomb. The tough life of trade, the apprenticeship in rule offered by lower municipal offices provided a good school of government.

Surviving documents sketch two discernible types of mayors, with infinite variety between. One is the magistrate who governed in the glow of his fame as a merchant. It is not surprising that Bristol five times chose for mayor William Canynges, whose merchant's mark was known throughout Europe and who was the son of a renowned mayor. Canynges built and operated a fleet that included some of the largest merchant-vessels sailing under the English flag, kept almost a thousand men employed at times on his far-flung enterprises, entertained King Edward in his mansion, secured additional privileges for Bristol by presenting the King with a large sum of money, rebuilt one of the loveliest churches in the realm, St. Mary Redcliffe, and ended his days humbly within Holy Orders. Canynges was the very symbol of Bristol's proud sea-destiny.

The other pattern of mayors is represented by Thomas Wrangwysh, twice elected chief magistrate of the vigorous, and sometimes turbulent, city of York. Though he must have been a successful trader since he was Master of the Merchant Adventurers Gild, he achieved his chief fame in serving the Metropolis of the North. He won the friendship of Richard, Duke of Gloucester, the 'special good lord of York' and a man not easily impressed.

On several occasions when Edward IV or his brother Richard summoned soldiers from the city, Wrangwysh was chosen to be their captain; when York was negotiating a reduction of its 'fee-farm' (yearly tax), his fellow-townsmen elected him their chief Parliamentary representative. He appears to have been equally at home in the saddle and in the council chamber. Two characteristic moments of action suggest the force of his personality.

During his second term as mayor, in January of 1485, Thomas Wrangwysh ordered Sheriff Thomas Fynch to deliver one William Friston from gaol 'upon sufficient surety'. A servant of Fynch's named Raby not only disobeyed this order but treated the prisoner cruelly. Wrangwysh thereupon committed Raby to gaol and 'because Friston lay in the stocks without meat or drink, the Mayor commanded that Raby should have no meat or drink likewise'. Nevertheless, another servant of the Sheriff's secretly 'came by water' and provided Raby with 'sufficient meat and drink from Thomas Fynch's place'.

Wrangwysh, discovering the little game, summoned Fynch to appear in the Council Chamber. Though the Sheriff was able to show that he had no knowledge of the business, Mayor Wrangwysh commanded Fynch to prison. Fynch angrily declared that he would be his own gaoler and stalked off escorted by six Serjeants-at-the-Mace. But on the way a band of Fynch's adherents, heavily armed, 'took him with a strong hand from the said serjeants'. Tempers boiled as men in the streets instantly became partisans: 'There arose among the commons there present a great and jeapardous scrimmage and affray' in which divers men were hurt.

Hearing of the riot, Wrangwysh strode into the street at the head of his councillors, stilled the fight by his words and presence, and fetched Fynch back to the Council Chamber. 'The Sheriff then and there humbled himself unto the Mayor's commandment.' Men were still muttering in the streets, so Wrangwysh and his fellows themselves 'came forth with Thomas Fynch and put him in gaol'. That night, the Mayor permitted Fynch to go home, but not until William Friston had first been delivered from prison.

At the end of this same year, the city of York, still loyal to Richard III, who had been slain four months before at Bosworth, was daring to resist attempts by Henry VII, Richard's conqueror, and the Earl of Northumberland, Richard's betrayer, to force upon the city as Recorder a man named Grene, in the place of Miles Metcalfe, who had been an ardent supporter of Richard. Twice the King and the Earl peremptorily urged Grene's appointment and twice the city evaded these commands. On December 12 came yet a third letter from Henry VII, harshly ordering the city fathers to give Grene possession of the recordship. In Grene's presence the town clerk read this communication before the council, of which Thomas Wrangwysh, his term of mayor finished, was a member. Once again the council decided to continue their postponement of the issue. Grene flew into such a rage that he snatched the King's letter from the clerk and rushed from the chamber. The councillors had just the man to handle this situation. Three days later, Thomas Wrangwysh, King Richard's friend, returned the document to the clerk. With this quiet, resolute action he passes from history, in his way as symbolic of the age as William Canynges.

The Mayor: Abroad

DURING the reign of Edward IV the mayors of the chief towns of the realm not only administered local affairs but, like the princes of the earth, they devoted time and energy to foreign relations. England was still so loosely organized, politically, that mayors were required to deal with neighbouring gentry, magnates of the kingdom, the King himself, and Holy Church. Chief magistrates all pursued the same policy: to maintain the independence of the city, satisfy the King's demand for loyal and orderly rule, and diminish whatever temporal rights the clergy claimed to exercise within town walls.

Nothing so demeaned the dignity of the mayor and irked the sensibilities of the ruling oligarchy as outside interference with the affairs of the city. Towns of the Yorkist Age usually treated on terms of equality and mutual respect with nearby lords or the magnates of the realm. Gone were the days when a Mayor of Exeter was forced to acknowledge himself the Earl of Devon's man and humbly do the Earl's bidding or when an Earl of Northumberland or one of the Nevilles could overawe the city of York. Nobles were still able occasionally to bend a town to their will, though only during troubled times. Here and there townsmen accepted a lord's livery and became his adherent, but mayors emphatically joined their own prohibitions and penalties to proclamations of the King forbidding this practice. A citizen who wore a noble's colours was a potential source of disaffection, a traitor within the walls. For the most part, lords in this age cultivated the good will of towns.

The city of York enjoyed a profitable relationship with Richard

of Gloucester, who ruled the North from his castle of Middleham
in Wensleydale. When York wished to discharge an incompetent
clerk or remove from the River Ouse illegal 'fishgarths' protected by powerful interests or to secure a diminution of its fee-
farm, the city turned confidently to the Duke of Gloucester, who
never failed to plead its cause with his brother, Edward IV. When
the Duke learned that a servant of his named Redeheid had bullied
and insulted a citizen of York who was visiting Middleham Castle,
he sent Redeheid to the city under guard so that he might be
punished according to the judgement of the Mayor and Aldermen.
Shortly after this incident, a tailor, John Davyson, who was
bitterly at odds with Roger Brere, saddler, could think of no
better way to get his enemy in trouble than to spread the report
that Brere had made a jibe against the Duke of Gloucester. The
chief men of York were so much disturbed by this gossip that
William Melrig, who was falsely alleged to have heard Brere's
slanderous remark, was summoned before the Mayor, Sheriffs,
Chamberlains, and a concourse of citizens to make his emphatic
denial.

Henry Percy, Earl of Northumberland, went out of his way to
flatter the city, hoping to rival the Duke of Gloucester's popularity; but when the Earl brought pressure to have one of his
servants made Sword-bearer, the city fathers promptly decreed
that, since it was against the custom of York for a man to seek
office through outside influence, Percy's candidate was not to be
given the post, nor any other.

The city of Bristol was also allied with a neighbouring magnate.
In the fourteenth century the Lords of Berkeley had harassed
Bristol and used force to constrain its liberties. By the period of
the Wars of the Roses, however, the Berkeleys were trading in
wool and corn and wine with Bristol merchants and going into
partnership with Bristol shipowners to freight goods and rob
carracks of Genoa. In 1470 a feud which had lasted for a generation
between the Berkeleys and the Talbot Earls of Shrewsbury broke
into open warfare. Lord Lisle, son of the Countess of Shrewsbury,
rode forth at the head of hundreds of armed men. The Berkeleys
appealed to Bristol, and not in vain. A strong contingent of

troops sallied from the town and Bristol archers helped the little Berkeley army to crush the forces of Talbot on Nibley Green, where Lord Lisle was killed. Maurice Berkeley, son of Lord James, married the daughter of a mayor of Bristol. At her burial in 1517, the officers of the city escorted her coffin with 200 torches, followed by thousands of mourning citizens. After the interment there was a great 'drinking' in St. Mary's Hall, 'and I thank God', wrote the steward, 'no plate nor spoons was lost, yet there was twenty dozen spoons'.

On occasion, a great lord could still make his weight un-pleasantly felt, particularly if he was Richard Neville, Earl of Warwick (the Kingmaker), the greatest lord of all. When, in 1464, the Mayor of Coventry found it impossible to resolve a complicated quarrel between Will Huet and Will Bedon, he appealed to the King to decide the matter. Edward IV wisely requested the city to try local arbitration. Finally the Mayor himself gave a decision in Will Bedon's favour. Huet broke into such 'inordinate and seditious language' that the Mayor clapped him in gaol and reported his action to the King, who sent back his thanks for this prompt repression of Huet's unruliness. But Huet had friends who knew where to turn. They 'laboured unto my lord of Warwick', whose castle stood nearby. The Kingmaker, furious with Edward IV at this moment for his having secretly married Elizabeth Woodville, was only too glad to show that he could thwart Edward's authority. Unable to withstand the wishes of the mighty earl, the mayor reluctantly decreased the amount of money Huet was required to pay Bedon and freed him from prison. This interference, the town clerk noted angrily, was 'to our great rebuke'; and it appears that by this action Richard Neville lost the hearts of the governing class of Coventry.

Interference by the King was another matter, for the King was lord of most of the principal towns. Mayors displayed a somewhat ambiguous attitude toward royal intermeddling in their affairs. They bitterly resented any attempt by a citizen to appeal over their heads to royal authority. Too often such appeals forced city officers to make a journey to Westminster or brought a privy seal reprimanding the city for failure to keep proper order. When

Edward IV or Henry VII proposed a candidate for one of the town offices, the mayor and his fellows almost always accepted the royal nominee, but they clearly disliked this dictation.

On the other hand, mayors showed themselves quick to call for royal help if their rights were threatened or a local situation was getting out of hand, as Coventry had turned to the King to settle the Huet-Bedon affair. The city of Nottingham, troubled by citizens flaunting the livery of Lord Grey, took their problem to the royal council. In the Star Chamber, Edward IV himself straitly ordered Grey to give no more liveries in Nottingham and to cease stirring up broils in the city, and Grey meekly promised to obey the King's command. When rioting broke out in York over the enclosure of certain common lands, the city sent hasty word to Richard III to know how he wished the guilty parties to be punished. A quarrel between Coventry and Bristol over wharfage fees which Bristol exacted from Coventry merchants was, by mutual consent, submitted to the royal council. The Mayor did not like the King looking over his shoulder, but was glad to be able to turn to him, at need.

Edward IV and Richard III and Henry VII kept a close and jealous eye upon their cities. At the first sign of disorder, down from Westminster came a privy seal or a royal emissary rebuking the laxity of the mayor; but the royal government was also quick to acknowledge even small examples of authoritarian vigour by city magistrates. The King was much more sensitive to disorder in his cities than in his countryside; unruly towns advertised a weak central government.

Though most towns during the Yorkist Age kept on good terms with lords and with the king, they carried on a bitter warfare with another power. This great enemy lay within their very gates: the Church, robed in the might of tradition, wealth, the holy sacraments of the Faith Catholic. Priors, bishops, abbots clung to ancient privileges that, in the view of townsmen, grossly infringed municipal liberties, scorned communal pride, and thwarted the mayor's government.

The fight between Church and mayors had been going on for centuries; during the reign of Edward IV the rising power and prosperity of the towns increased the intensity of the struggle. One of the reasons Henry VIII so easily toppled the Church Temporal was that his townsmen had inherited from their fathers and grandfathers a fierce resentment against ecclesiastical claims to worldly domination.

Towns which had grown up on Church lands were the unlucky ones, helpless in the grip of precedent. However large and prosperous they had become, they were forced to remain within the small destinies that had been theirs when they were no more than straggles of cottages outside a priory gate or next a bishop's wharf. Towns like Reading and Bury St. Edmunds and Bishop's Lynn alternated riots and litigation in a desperate battle to shake themselves free—by the fifteenth century, parchment was more frequently the weapon than poleaxes—but the bishop's or the abbot's bailiff stood always ready to enforce his master's right if a mayor dared have a mace of office borne before him or the citizens tried to establish a market of their own. No matter how ingeniously, persistently, expensively the citizens pleaded their cause in the courts, the ecclesiastical lord but had to produce his musty charters and the fight went for naught.

In the fifteenth century, Winchester, ancient capital of Saxon kings, well nigh drowned in waves of ecclesiastical privilege. The Mayor ruled less than half his city; three of the town gates, the traffic of the river, the market were in the grip of the Church. Yearly, as the Bishop of Winchester's great fair of St. Giles was about to open, that prelate's officers closed all the shops and took over the rule of the city for the duration of the fair. When changes in the manufacture and distribution of cloth struck at the prosperity of Winchester, the citizens had neither the means nor the hope to fight misfortune.

The towns on royal domain, which included the chief cities, were able, however, to wage vigorous battle.

In the fifteenth century the city of Norwich, where dwelt a hardy civic spirit, struggled against a powerful combination of county magnates and local prelates. At one time or another the city was quarrelling with the Warden of St. Paul's Hospital, the Prioress of Carrow, the Abbots of Holme and Wendling, and the man who controlled the cathedral precincts, the Prior of Norwich. The Prior used fraud as well as force, buying the services of the city Recorder and other officers, calling on the armed retainers of his county friends to overawe the citizens. They fought back as best they could. Four times between 1433 and 1444 the King seized the franchises of Norwich into his own hands when disturbances reached the pitch of riot. Twice the aldermen and citizens, betrayed by the Prior's creatures, forcibly removed the city seal from the treasury to prevent the incumbent Mayor, fraudulently elected, from sealing away the rights of the community. To preserve their liberties, the citizens and their genuine mayors formed a mysterious association, 'Le Bachery', ostensibly a religious gild devoted to maintaining a light in the Chapel of the Blessed Virgin of the Fields, but actually a body formed to lay plans and concert action.

On Shrove Tuesday of 1443 'the King of Christmas' appeared in the streets of Norwich. A merchant named John Gladman headed a fantastic procession of one hundred and thirty people. He wore a paper crown and his horse was 'trapped with tinsel and other nice disguisy things'. Before him rode twelve men each representing a month of the year 'disguised after the season required, and Lent clad in white and red herring skins and his horse trapped with oyster shells after him'. But wild words were flying in the streets; men declared that the city was strong enough to slay the Bishop, the Abbot of Holme, and the Prior. Somewhere, somehow, violence flared. The bells began to ring. Suddenly three thousand citizens had swarmed to arms. They marched on the priory, ringed it with helmeted men, laid guns against the gates. The trembling monks were forced to deliver up a hated deed, which bound the city to pay the Prior four shillings a year, and to relinquish jurisdiction over certain lands. To prevent the Prior's county friends from helping him, the aroused citizens clapped shut their gates and manned the walls.

But they could not resist the King, and in this age the King's government favoured order and the *status quo* at any cost. Once again the municipal franchises were revoked. Down came a commission of lords and justices to investigate and indict. 'Many of the worthy men of the city fled into other countries over the sea for dread, with as much of their goods as they might have with them.' The franchises were restored three years later and King Henry VI himself visited Norwich in 1448; but the quarrel between the citizens and the Prior went on, sometimes riotously, sometimes litigiously, until Henry VIII put an end to all such quarrels.

In Canterbury, of all English cities, Town and Gown might be expected to enjoy peaceful relations. Before that marvel of Europe, the jewel-crusted shrine of Thomas à Becket—'gold was the meanest object to be seen there'—pilgrims poured a stream of offerings; and in the inns and cook-shops and taverns of the town they also left behind mounds of coins. The citizens of Canterbury held their muster-in-arms to commemorate the death of Becket. On a pageant wagon decked as an altar, boys enacted the slaying of the 'holy blisful martyr'. The four murderers plunged their swords into concealed bladders of blood to give realism to the scene, and a mechanical angel, suspended above, flapped its wings.

Yet not even their love of St. Thomas nor their takings from the pilgrims could reconcile the citizens to the Clerical pretensions that chafed their liberties. As doughtily as the men of Norwich, they carried on a running fight, and had for centuries, with the Abbot of St. Augustine's, with the Archbishop, and with the Prior of Christ Church.

The Mayor and the Abbot quarrelled about water rights; they disputed the privilege of arresting evildoers on a highway which belonged to the King but ran through abbey lands; they disagreed over the regulations of the fishmarket—Canterbury, stuffed with clerics, needed large supplies of sea food; all over England churchmen were constantly causing trouble by their efforts to provide convents, abbeys, chapters, friaries with sufficient fish.

The city quarrelled with the Archbishop over ecclesiastical immunities and restraints of trade. He held a city within the city, the walled borough of Staplegate, an affront to the citizens' pride and to their purses, which was exempt from all lay jurisdiction, the King's as well as the Mayor's. His Westgate and Wingham

tenants were likewise outside town authority. In 1467 the municipality complained bitterly—as it had done almost two hundred
years before—that the Westgate men, crowding their houses on to
the bank of the river, had caused the stream to drive against the
city walls and undermine them. Wingham men intercepted fish
bound for Canterbury, thus diminishing the city's provisions and
the city's tolls; but the citizens could do nothing about this hated
forestalling, for the Archbishop possessed a right to have a market
at Wingham. In 1480, however, the Mayor eased the city's
feelings with a harmless martial display. When the Archbishop's
officers seized a rent on certain land outside the city walls, the
Mayor collected a body of citizens, marched to the meadow in
warlike style, and on arrival served out wine to refresh his troops.

With the Prior of Christ Church, the city's most irksome and
formidable foe, there had been centuries of angry controversy.
Ugly incidents still occurred but in the fifteenth century the
warfare was waged mostly by protest or law suit. The Mayor
and the Prior were constantly at loggerheads over a variety of
issues—benefit of clergy which let criminous clerks off much too
lightly, right of arrest, abuse of sanctuary, payment of taxes,
control of the river, market jurisdiction.

Feeling boiled up in 1425 when a certain alien called Bernard
the Goldsmith escaped from the city prison and succeeded in
reaching the cathedral. He was hotly pursued by the bailiffs and
an angry crowd of townsmen. The fugitive tried to hide within
the rails of a monument to Archbishop Chicheley, but the furious
mob thrust arms and sticks between the bars, clawed at him and
beat him, finally tore him loose from his refuge, and began to
drag him down the nave. At that moment a band of cathedral
servants fell on the intruders. The prisoner was jerked from their
hands and they were driven out of the church.

The issue of taxation did not lead to violence but caused much
heartburning among the citizens. Right in their midst the Priory
of Christ Church possessed rents worth £200 a year and five
acres of land which contributed nothing to the city's support or
the city's tax burden. The citizens demanded that the prior should
at least help to maintain the town walls. This quarrel smouldered

until 1492, when the priory, having secured a portion of the wall, agreed to keep its stretch in repair.

In the streets of Canterbury bickerings and incidents were common. When a serjeant ventured on church ground with his mace, it was rudely taken away from him. Clerks fouled the city ditch with filth—deliberately, the Mayor declared. Much to the Prior's ire, the townsmen retaliated against clerical encroachment by breaking their Christmas customs. They no longer gathered as of old around the tomb of Archbishop Sudbury to say prayers for his soul, and when lords rode into Canterbury with the King's seasonal offering to St. Thomas, the citizens refused to accompany them in state to the cathedral.

The river and the market, however, were the great, the endless subjects of dispute. Mayor and Prior had amicably agreed upon straightening the course of the river, but the effects of this operation on the Prior's mill and on the city's mill led to bitter trouble. Each side claimed that the other's mill was injuring its own. In 1499 a water-war broke out. Summoning his forces, the Prior dug a trench which diverted water from the city mill, whereupon the Mayor assembled *his* forces, destroyed the offending trench, and constructed a dam to impound water for the city mill. Forth sallied the Prior's men to cut the dam. The Mayor led a little army to the river meadows, routed the enemy, seized their arms, and marched home in triumph. Next day he dealt the Prior a still shrewder blow: he dismantled the city market by the priory gate, on which priory tenants were always encroaching, and set up a market in open ground around St. Andrew's Church.

The Prior rallied his powers to oppose this indignity. Ecclesiastical tenants refused to sell in the new market; priory servants made themselves as unpleasant as possible when they came to buy fish. At the market stalls the citizens contributed their share of jostling and black looks and on one occasion seized a great halibut from the caterer of Christ Church as he was bearing it to the priory. When the Prior sought to by-pass the market by convoying fish from the seaside, the Mayor's men promptly confiscated the fish at the city gate, 'disappointing the brethren of their dinners'.

The outraged Prior finally brought suit at Westminster. The citizens took up the challenge zestfully, collected voluntary contributions to support the cause, and appointed the Mayor to conduct their defence. He and numerous aldermen made several trips to London, all of them expensive, the costs minutely recorded: hire of horses to Rochester, then hire of barges and cloaks for the journey to London; '3d paid at Sittingbourne in washing of my shirts'. In London the Mayor was constantly dispensing money to counsel: 10s one day, 19s another; 3s 4d daily to each of three lawyers for four days work at Westminster Hall; 37s 4d paid for the examination of sixteen persons, at 2s 4d a head, in the Star Chamber. There were other important 'incidentals' and money was not stinted: 16d paid by the Mayor for bread and drink and rent, when he assembled his witnesses in a house beside St. Paul's to rehearse them in their evidence 'against they came into the Star Chamber'. The Recorder of London received 20s for inspecting the city's bill of particulars and a treat in the buttery of the Palace of Westminster which meant a further payment 'in reward to the officers of the king's buttery for their good cheer 12d and to the cook of the king's kitchen 8d'. When the Mayor sent word home that gifts were needed to help make friends in proper places, several members of the Common Council hastened up to London with two great trout and ten capons.

Despite this drain of money and energy, the citizens of Canterbury must have been pleased with the generalship of their mayor, for the market never went back to the priory gate.

The most remarkable battle of the age between townsmen and the Church, however, took place in the West Country; it resists the erosion of time because the protagonist left a racy account both of the struggle and of himself.

Down at Exeter, in the early 1440's the hearts of the citizens daily waxed more bitter. Opposite their town hall rose the gates and walls of an alien power—the cathedral church of St. Peter, the Bishop's palace, and ecclesiastical precincts.

Indifferent to the city's good, the Bishop and his clergy and his tenants were planted in the very bowels of the city's life. 'Of time that no mind runneth' Exeter had been a city, the citizens asserted, long before there was such a thing as Bishop, Dean, and Chapter. The clergy retorted that the city government was a rank parvenu; when the bishopric was established by Edward the Confessor, no such upstarts as mayor and aldermen peopled the world.

Town claimed a right of way through the cloisters to the cathedral, which the Bishop, Dean, and Chapter maliciously kept locked. Gown retorted that the cloister doors were barred because ill-bred young people 'exercised unlawful games' there and defouled the walls and broke glass by playing tennis. Burghers who lived in the neighbourhood of a certain Bevys tavern, hard by the cathedral close, declared that the night was made hideous by the uproarious carousing and drunken quarrels of clerks. The clergy answered that they had no unruly folk within their precincts: such disturbances must have been raised by citizens and their precious mayor, who was himself 'cause and giver of example to all such misgovernance'.

The city chafed against flouting of its laws and injuries to its trade. Ecclesiastical tenants encroached on the High by erecting huge market stalls in front of their properties, refused to pay their taxes, evaded taking their turn at the watch. The canons were as bad or worse: they dumped their filth into a city lane; they appropriated postern gates in the city wall, and through these gates 'suspicious men and women have been let in and out' and 'divers men that should have been arrested conveyed away'. In the very palace of the Bishop, as well as in the houses of canons, the clergy sold wine which they had illegally imported without paying the city's custom duty of 4d a pipe or the city's retail tax of 12d a pipe. Furthermore, though this wine was often 'found corrupt', the Bishop had prevented the city officers from casting it into the gutter; indeed, the clerks had carried this foul wine to the port of Topsham, and shipped it back to Bordeaux to be mixed with good wine and reimported. The city's assize of bread, too, had been defied, and light loaves sold to the citizens; and the city's coroner had been driven off when he sought to hold his inquiry upon prisoners who had died in the Bishop's gaol.

The clergy, labelling these attacks slander, declared themselves 'oppressed and enthralled' by wolvish citizens. Old Bishop Lacy icily laid down the dictum that the church possessed a 'fee', a jurisdiction, entirely separate from that of the city, over which knavish city officers had no authority whatsoever. As tempers frayed, life in Exeter grew ugly with 'night-walking, evil language, visaging, shouldering, and all riotous rule'. To bolster his pretensions, Bishop Lacy applied to the King for a grant of authority. After all, the bishops on the royal council were his brothers, and pious Henry VI was only too happy to do what bishops requested. Edmund Lacy duly secured letters patent confirming his claim.

This move sounded the call to battle in the ears of the men of Exeter. Their right to rule themselves would become but a mockery unless they nullified the letters patent; and they could do this only by proving in court that the grant ran counter to the city's royal charter. They took their stand on a claim to possess a jurisdiction older than the Bishop's, for in the fifteenth century such a case was bound to be decided by the sheer weight of evidences, by what had been decreed in the past, however inequitable the decree was in the present. But in their hearts, they claimed the right to govern themselves because they were free men.

In this crisis they had a man to turn to, an alderman and merchant. Popular at home, he was known beyond the walls of Exeter, was an acquaintance of the Lord Chancellor himself. If any man understood the ways of the great world, where the suit would have to be fought, and could uphold the city's dignity while he was urging its cause, that man was John Shillingford. He came of an old county family, taking his name from the village of Shillingford, whence his forebears had moved into Exeter to embrace the life of trade. His father, famed for his learning in the law, was twice Mayor; doubtless John Shillingford had been sent to one of the Inns of Courts in London, where he learned worldly manners, polished his Latin, and acquired that knowledge of the law which was well nigh essential to men of property and position in fifteenth-century England.

At Michaelmas, 1444, the city elected him Mayor. Unaccountably, John Shillingford refused the office. Being a shrewd politician, as will appear, he perhaps determined to embark upon the struggle only if the city gave him a bold demonstration of its will to follow his banner. In any case, he got the bold demonstration. The principal citizens promptly applied to the King's council for a writ against their recalcitrant Mayor-elect. Early in the New Year (1445), a privy seal duly came down to Exeter ordering John Shillingford, on pain of £1000, to assume his duties.

He assumed them with a will. Soon the Bishop was blaming everything on 'the wilful labour of John Shillingford in whose time ever hath been great trouble'.

If he needed a spur, there occurred, not long after, an incident that stirred the citizens to fighting pitch. One Hugh Lucays, a tenant of the Bishop, 'the most or one of the most misgoverned men of all the city of Exeter or of all the shire', attacked a citizen in the King's High Street at the very door of the Gildhall. John Glasyer, a serjeant of the city, promptly arrested Lucays; but the prisoner broke away from his captor and hot-footed it for the Bishop's domain. Glasyer and another serjeant pursued him through the cemetery and into the cathedral and there laid hands on him. Immediately a swarm of clerks attacked the officers 'with swords, custellis, long knives, and Irish skenes'. Others clapped shut the cathedral doors in the faces of two city stewards who had 'followed freshly' only sixteen feet behind their fellows. By the time the stewards found an open door, the prisoner had been violently recovered; the serjeants appeared on the verge of losing their lives. When one of the stewards interposed his mace of authority, it was knocked aside with the blow of a custell that left a nick in it. The officers were glad to get out of the church unharmed.

The city angrily demanded the return of Lucays and the punishment of ecclesiastics who had interfered with the king's justice. The Bishop's men refused with equal heat: they knew nothing, they said, of Lucays' alleged misdeed; he was 'furiously driven into the said Cathedral Church by officers with swords, daggers and other invasive weapons against the peace drawn'; the godly ministers, habited for divine service, had laboured to save Hugh's life, 'as priests ought to do', without meaning any harm to the city officers; and if the mace was nicked, it was because the steward had smote John Pawton, a priest, on the head with it.

John Shillingford and his aldermen decided to provoke the Bishop to a suit, if they could. On Ascension Day, 1445, the Serjeant-at-the-Mace boldly arrested a servant of the cathedral chancellor; at the moment, this servant was in the very palace of the Bishop and was holding up from the ground his master's golden cope as the chancellor and his fellow ecclesiastics were going in solemn procession to the cathedral!

The bishop was not yet to be drawn. At the end of his term, Shillingford stepped down from office. But at Michaelmas, 1446, the city again elected him Mayor. Within a few weeks two more clerks were arrested on church ground. Then Bishop Lacy brought suit, claiming the enormous damages of £1000 for false arrest. But the Bishop and his counsel apparently recognized that the claim to a separate jurisdiction was weak. Therefore Edmund Lacy used his influence at court to secure a privy seal ordering the question to be decided by the Lord Chancellor and the two Chief Justices.

Shillingford at once opposed this move, for he knew well that he had a far better chance of winning at Common Law, where the evidences would count for more and vested interests for less. He fired off a protest to the Chancellor and another to the King, in which he boldly asserted that the privy seal ran counter to Magna Carta. These petitions were disregarded. Both sides began the process of submitting proofs, articles of complaint, replications to the adversaries' proofs and articles, rejoinders to the replications. As the legal battle reached its pitch, the city's comment on Shillingford's leadership was to elect him Mayor for the third time at Michaelmas, 1447.

In less than a year—summer of 1447 to late spring of 1448—the Mayor made seven journeys to London that we know about, and perhaps more. He was usually four days and nights on the road, stopping the second night at Shaftesbury and reaching the capital early on the morning of the fifth day. By hard riding, however, he managed on one occasion to cut a full day and night from this schedule. Over a span of eleven months these seven excursions—

three of them in late autumn or winter—cost him almost two full months of riding the roads.

Nor did he spare himself in London. He had to rise betimes; for business, even high affairs of state, began early. Men of 'worship' heard Mass in their private chapels by six or seven, depending on the season; humbler folk were stirring with the dawn. The city of Bristol, complaining to the King about the mischief one of his household men was committing, used the damning statement that 'he lieth in his bed till it be nine or ten at the bell daily, as well the holidays as the working days, not attending divine service'. On a typical day in London, John Shillingford first met with his lawyers, at Paul's cloister or at their chambers in the Temple; then he took boat to Lambeth to call upon the Chancellor at his episcopal palace (the Chancellor being John Stafford, Archbishop of Canterbury); if no formal session was to be held that morning and the Chancellor was too much pressed by affairs of state to spare a moment's talk, the Mayor took boat again to Westminster to keep his cause warm by chatting with Chief Justice Fortescue, KB, or Chief Justice Newton, CP. Perhaps he snatched a hasty dinner outside Westminster gate, where there were cook-shops galore and cooks crying 'hot pies'!

In the afternoon the Mayor of Exeter took boat again to Lambeth in the hope of another word with the Chancellor. Then once more he went down river to the Temple for a final totting up of the day's accomplishments with his counsel. Before he retired that night, or in the darkness of early morning, propping himself in his bed to write, he composed a report to his aldermen. He commented on the progress of the suit, the latest tricks of his adversaries, the disposition of the Chancellor; then he gave orders for what was to be done at home. These missives display a feeling for scene, an uninhibited self-revelation, a raciness of English, without parallel in any surviving documents produced before this time.

John Shillingford was careful to season the rightness of his cause with due attention to the Lord Chancellor's palate. He heralded his coming in the summer of 1447 by sending Archbishop Stafford seven great conger eels, four hundred 'buckhorn' (pilchards), and four crabs, which cost the city 40s (something like £60 today), plus 8s to the carrier for delivering the sea-food to London. When Shillingford came up to the capital in the autumn, he learned, the very morning of his arrival, that the Chancellor had asked Chief Justice Fortescue to dinner that day to discuss the suit, 'saying that he should have a dish of saltfish'. 'Hearing this, I did as me thought ought to be done, and by advice of the Justice and of our counsel, sent thither that day two stately pickerel and two stately tenches.' It was a happy thought, because two of the greatest lords of the land, the Duke of Buckingham and the Marquess (soon to be Duke) of Suffolk descended on Lambeth for dinner, and Shillingford earned for himself a hearty thanks.

Taking boat next morning to attend upon the Chancellor, the Mayor landed at Westminster Stairs as the bells of the palace clochard were ringing nine. Chance forced him to exercise his urbanity *extempore*. Just as he was mounting the steps, he 'met with my lord Chancellor at the broad door a little from the stair foot coming from the Star Chamber'. Bending his knee, Shillingford saluted 'him in the most goodly wise that I could and recommended unto his good and gracious lordship my fellowship and all the commonalty of the city of Exeter. He said to the mayor two times "Welcome" and the third time, "Right welcome, Mayor", and held the Mayor a great while fast by the hand, and so went forth to his barge and with him great press, lords and other, etc. and in especial the Treasurer of the King's Household, with whom he was at right great privy communication'. But the scene was too exciting for Shillingford to maintain his recital in the third person—'And therefore I, Mayor, drew me apart, and met with him at his going into his barge, and there took my leave of him, saying these words, "My Lord, I will wait upon your good lordship and your better leisure at another time". He said to me again, "Mayor, I pray you heartily that ye do so".'

The Mayor waited no longer than the following morning, Sunday. About eight o'clock he arrived at Lambeth Palace with one of his counsel and his town clerk. They were ushered through the outer chamber, where lesser folk cooled their heels, and came into the inner chamber. Beyond lay the privy chamber or closet, really a bedroom, but even the King himself used his bedroom for private consultations. 'We met and spoke with the Chancellor in the inner chamber, he at that time being right busy, going into his closet. And with right good language he excused himself that he might not speak with us at that time for great business, and commanded us to come again the morrow.' But John Shillingford did not mean to be put off so easily. 'I, Mayor, prayed him of one word at that time and no more, saying that I was informed that he was displeased of my late coming, and if he were so, I besought him to hear mine excuse. He said "Nay"; but that I was come in right good time and welcome, and at his departing into his closet he said, "Mayor, would God ye had made a good end at home". And I said, "Would God, my Lord, that we so had".' This sturdy answer made its impact; the Chancellor hesitated: 'he said, "Well, Mayor . . ." and bade me come again that same day afternoon'.

Savouring the bustle of high office and the presence of the great, Shillingford provides the only intimate picture of a fifteenth-century English statesman at work. When he was ushered into the Chancellor's inner chamber that afternoon, he found 'much people, lords and other, my lord treasurer, under treasurer, the privy seal, and divers abbots and priors, and many strangers aliens of other lands. And then came in the Duke of Buckingham and there was great business at that time'. Almost everybody but the lords was bidden to leave the chamber, but the Mayor of Exeter did not budge. 'I awaited my time and put me in press [i.e., made his way through the waiting line] and went right to my lord Chancellor and said, "My lord, I am come at your commandment, but I see your great business is such that ye may not attend". He said No, by his troth, and that I might right well see. I said, Yea, and that I was sorry and had pity of his great vexation.' John Shillingford might be only a provincial mayor, but he felt perfectly at ease rubbing shoulders with nobles and bishops and entirely confident of his *savoir faire* in the chamber of the Chancellor and Primate of England.

When finally the Mayor and his counsel and the Bishop of Exeter's counsel were summoned to appear before the Chancellor and two Justices one afternoon, Shillingford hit off the scene in a sentence: 'My lord took his chair and the justices sat with him, and both parties with their counsel kneeled before.' At another session—it was the day Shillingford's adversaries brought with them a new man named Orcharde, 'a great bear'—the Chancellor was 'right merry' and turning to the Mayor began recalling amusing experiences he himself had had in Exeter. Shillingford joined in, speaking 'to my lord in disport'. The Chancellor was reminded of some political high-jinks—'he could tell us how Germyn [former Mayor and at this time City Receiver] took the church the day of election, etc.' Shillingford had something good to add to that story: 'Germyn put his finger in his eye and wept'— but, alas, we shall never know the point of it all, for there is a hiatus in the manuscript.

When the Mayor came up to London in late January, 1448, he had to put off going to Lambeth until the Chancellor's buckhorn arrived from home. It finally came on February first, 'better late than never', as he reported grumpily, and so on going to Lambeth the next morning, he took part in the Archbishop's celebration of Candlemas Day. 'That day I was with my lord at Mass, and offered my candle to my lord's blessed hand, I kneeling down offering my candle. My lord with laughing cheer said heartily, "Graunt mercy, Mayor". Bidden to stay to dinner, Shillingford met "with my lord at the high table end [of the great hall] coming to meatward, and as soon as ever he saw me he took me fast by the hand and thanks enough too".' The Mayor modestly disclaimed the present of fish as 'too simple a thing considering his estate, but if I had been at home at this fair he should have had better stuff. I went forth with him to the midst of the hall, he standing in his estate [i.e., in formal style] against the fire a great while and two bishops, the two chief justices, and other lords, knights, and squires, and other common people great multitude, the hall full, all standing afar apart from him, I kneeling by him'.

Yet, though John Shillingford employed the graces and enjoyed the drama of high place, he never forgot that he was Mayor of 'a great commonalty' which was depending upon him to fight its battle. Urbane he might be, but when Chancellor or Justices started talking about concession, he turned hard as steel.

At one session, when the ecclesiastical party continued to evade an answer to the city's complaints by talking vaguely of evidences and proofs, Shillingford commented scornfully that though the suit was to be tried in London, they kept their 'agreements home in the chapter house', and he demanded that 'our articles should be answered before we proceed any further'. But the Chancellor and the Chief Justices, eager to avoid the onus of handing down a judgement, wanted to continue looking for a compromise. The old Archbishop gently twitted Exeter's champion on a rather vulnerable claim the city advanced, the exuberance of which leaves little doubt that it was drafted by the Mayor himself. To show that Exeter antedated by far the Cathedral of St. Peter, Shillingford had written that the 'city soon upon the Passion of Christ was by Vespasian besieged by time of eight days; the which obtained not the effect of his siege and so went forth to Bordeaux and from Bordeaux to Rome and from Rome to Jerusalem and there he with Titus besieged Jerusalem and obtained it and sold thirty Jews for a penny, as it appeareth by chronicles'.

Shillingford stoutly answered 'that that was no matter of our complaints, but put in to prove what the city was of old time'. The Chancellor changed his tune then, saying 'somewhat strangely and sharply that many of our articles were matter of noise [rumour] and slander, and to answer them would be cause of more grouching and ill-will. And I said, "If any such be, let them be laid apart, and those that be sum and cause of all this debate, let them be so answered".'

The two parties banged back and forth at each other, with the Chancellor and the Justices trying to interject a conciliatory note. 'I held my own.' When Archbishop Stafford commended the Mayor's good rule of the city while the suit was pending, Shillingford turned suddenly to one of his adversaries, Canon Kys: 'Kys, ye said to me at home that I did and said much thing more' than the Chancellor would approve of. 'Say ye here before my lord what it was. My lord sat still awhile, and Kys kneeling spake never a word, and thus passed over.'

When the session concluded and the parties withdrew down the hall, 'the Chancellor asked wine and sent me his own cup and to no more. I went right to my lord again before them all, and spoke with my lord privily a great while of divers matters'—which doubtless caused his opponents a deal of heartburning, for 'my lord at this time did me much worship'.

The Archbishop of Canterbury's treatment of the Mayor betokens the importance of townsmen in this age, as his marked favour to the man indicates the impact of John Shillingford's personality. The Chancellor's friendliness also hints—and Shillingford may have missed this—of his uneasy desire to placate the party which, though it had the better cause, he could not quite bring himself to declare for, against the pull of his loyalty to a brother bishop and his realization that many towns, likewise doing battle with the Church, would be heartened by Exeter's victory. At this very moment, the citizens of Canterbury were plaguing him with their rights.

Old John Stafford, Primate of England, was very much a man of his age. He had now been Chancellor through fifteen dismal years of King Henry's collapsing government. He had done his best to keep the wheels turning, to hold a balance between factions. More a politician than a prelate, he was no inspiring man of God, as doubtless the Archbishop of Canterbury should be, but a man of men, humane, mellow as old fruitcake, a peace-weaver in troublous times. When he resigned the chancellorship two years later, as the kingdom began to quake, he almost alone of the court party had incurred no popular odium. Perhaps he wore the purple without arrogance because he was not born to it, and looked kindly on sinners because he knew how sweet sin feels along a man's bones. A year before Shillingford first became Mayor, John Stafford had buried his mother under a handsome monument in North Bradley (Wilts.) church. History records her only as 'Emma of North Bradley', for John Stafford was the bastard son of a knight. He had climbed the long way upward by his abilities, and somewhere along the way—according to Gascoigne who disliked him—he had had a child by a nun.

Neither the prelate's greatness nor the Mayor's inflexibility kept the two men from getting on famously. On a Sunday morning when they were talking 'in my lord's inner chamber', Shillingford cheerfully remarked that as far as he knew, Bishop Lacy, 'a blessed good man in himself if he must be', had no more knowledge of 'the ground of this matter than the image in the cloth of Arras there!'

In talks with Chief Justice Sir John Fortescue, the Mayor yielded not an inch even to that famous lawyer. When Fortescue raised a point of ancient tenure in the Bishop's favour: 'I said nay, and proved it by Domesday.' Fortescue pressed 'great arguments by long time', alternating with amiable suggestions as to compromises. But 'all it was to tempt me with laughing cheer'. However reasonable some of Fortescue's proposals might be, John Shillingford would not abate a jot of his claims until he had consulted his constituents at home. 'It could seem if I did so that I had doubt of our right, where I have right none.' Fortescue replied, perhaps with a rueful smile, 'Ye did thereon as a wise man'.

At every stage of the proceedings in London, John Shillingford kept the chief citizens of Exeter fully informed and made sure of the city's support for every move. As soon as he and the lawyers had drawn up answers to the Bishop's bill of claims, he dispatched two copies of these answers to Exeter. One was to be pondered by Nicholas Radeford, the Recorder, who had a country seat near Exeter. The other copy he begged his aldermen to study diligently 'and if anything be therein too much or too little', they were to amend it with all the acumen they could muster. 'This done, I pray you to call before you at the hall the substance of the commonalty, praying every of them in my name and charging them in the most straitest wise to come before you in haste for the tidings that I have sent home to you; and that ye wisely declare before them these answers, so that they' give their voices manfully 'yea and nay' and promise to 'abide by the answers in all wise'. Shillingford, who unlike his ecclesiastical opponent had to woo and enlighten where he would command, added prudently that in advance of the meeting the aldermen should work on the citizens individually to secure their approval.

When the Bishop's party finally submitted a rejoinder to the city's articles, the Mayor dispatched a copy to Exeter, exhorting his fellows to bend their brains immediately to the problem of rebuttal, 'which is dark to my conceit as yet; but I trust to God it shall be right well with your good information and help thereto. I can no more at this time, but I pray you to be not weary to over-read all the writing that I have sent home to you; and if ye be, no marvel though I be weary, etc. and God be with you'.

He kept his 'brethren' up to the mark. Receiving from them a missive chockful of reminders he did not need, he commented with some sarcasm—'which letter in my simple conceit I in all things have well understood, and I am, and was before that letter, fully remembered of all things that is comprehended therein.' In fact, 'ye and I communed thereof the last whole day of my being at home at Exeter in my parlour. What is to do furthermore', he did not yet know, 'but I must do as I can, may, and dare do, eschewing variance [quarrel], breech, throwing off, and indignations especially'.

When the Mayor could not be in London himself, he kept up a steady pressure on the Chancellor by sending a deputy; and he armed that deputy with instructions as elaborate and precise, in their way, as any with which the King furnished his ambassadors. On one occasion his agent, Richard Druell, instead of using the instructions for private guidance, delivered the document to the Chancellor himself. Doubtless he received a hearty dressing down, for the next time Druell was sent to London, the Mayor, ashamed of the 'simpleness of writing' of the paper, ordered his agent to beg the Chancellor to return it 'for your better instruction'. But he did not want Archbishop Stafford to suspect him of insincerity: 'nevertheless, if my lord suppose any article comprehended therein be not true, it shall be proved true every point.'

When later Shillingford sent his Town Clerk to Westminster, he had clearly been turning over in his mind the usefulness of an indiscretion like Druell's. He dispatched a detailed memorandum to the clerk with orders: 'This matter written in haste I pray you to understand well, and have it in your hand when ye speak with my Lord Chancellor. And when ye may, take a time to deliver it to him, saying that this was sent after you in great haste for your instruction.' Just so, at this time, did royal ambassadors sometimes carry instructions ostensibly for their privy use but designed to be yielded with a show of reluctance, to the monarch they waited upon. By the next century most ambassadors went armed with two sets of instructions, only one of which was ever submitted for inspection.

The Mayor carefully noted the hours of his departure from Exeter, of his arrival in London; he came to Westminster 'at nine of the Bell'; he kept an appointment with the Chancellor promptly 'at ten of the clock'. He enjoined diligence and accuracy on his fellows; he worked out for his deputies detailed accounts of what they were to do and say as well as analyses of the city's legal strategy and estimates of the opponents' position. When his deputies reported to him, they were likewise expected to picture their activities in strict terms of hours. Though clocks were often located in churches and the hours were rung by church bell, God's time was giving way to man's time.

The letters of John Shillingford best preserve the daily life of the age, however, when the mayor happily indulges in displays of personality, the like of which are not to be found before this time. On one of his trips to London, he was unable to call upon the Chancellor immediately because the all-important present of buckhorn, which alderman Germyn was supposed to have shipped, had not yet arrived. 'And so,' he wrote home, in rueful irritation well seasoned with Shandyan humour, 'I have help enough backward and but little forward, as it at all times proveth. I pray you specially to thank much gentle Germyn *Quasi duceret euge euge* Germyn of his governance at this time, *id male gaude* Germyn [gentle Germyn who will doubtless pat himself on the back for the way he's handling matters, the bungler!]. I know right well he will excuse himself by blaming this false harlot his carrier, and the carrier likewise by the said Germyn; and so I may say *ait latro ad latronem* [thieves stick together] and *inter scabella duo anus labitur humo* [between two stools arse falleth to the ground]. Christ's curse have they both, and say ye amen *non sine merito*, and if ye dare not say so, think so, think so. Also I charge Germyn under rule and commandment of J. Coteler my lieutenant, that he do what he can, brawl, brag and brace, lie and swear well to, and in especial that the streets be right clean and specially the little lane in the back side beneath the flesh fold [cattle pen] gate,

for there lieth many oxen heads and bones
that they be removed away for the nones
against my coming as soon as I may by cokkis bonys!'[1]

An even more arresting piece of self-revelation was prompted by Shillingford's discovery that in answering the city's complaint of clerical carousing in Bevys tavern, the Bishop's men had accused him of all manner of vices.

'They have spat out the utmost and worst venom that they could say or think by me; blessed be God it is neither felony, nor treason, nor great trespass. But as for truth of the matter that toucheth me, many worthy men stand on the same case and have done much worse than ever I did, though that be to me none excuse. As touching the great venom that they mean of my living, I may and purpose to be at my purge, as I may right well upon my soul, of all women alive except one, and of her right a great while; therefore, I take right naught by [I am untouched by their slanders] and say sadly [earnestly] *si recte vivas* etc. and am right merry and fare right well, ever thanking God and my own purse. And I lying on my bed at the writing of this right early, merrily singing a merry song, and that is this, "Come no more at our house, come, come, come". I will not die nor for sorrow nor for anger, but be merry and fare right well, while I have money—but that is and like to be scarce with me, considering the business and cost that I have had: and like to have: and yet I had with me £20 and more by my troth. Wherefore, how that ever ye do, send me £20 in haste, as ye wish the speed of your matter and welfare of the city, I not shamed but pleased at this time; and see that ye fail in no wise, I marvelling much—for as much as I departed from you without any money of yours—that ye had not sent to me since some money by Germyn, Kyrton, or some other man.'

John Shillingford found himself interesting and took for granted that his fellows found him interesting too. This vivid projection of a little ego-drama, the calculated range of tone from earnestness

[1] The mayor wrote the lines as prose; they have been rearranged to show his obvious intention of rhyming. 'By cokkis bonys'—by God's bones—is a vulgar oath, characteristic of the Host in the *Canterbury Tales* and used by the Mayor for humour and the rhyme.

to comedy, and the whimsical anticlimax in the descent from
confession to cash—all smack of the post-mediaeval age of
psychological awareness. When Shillingford writes, however
exuberantly, of thirty Jews' heads sold for a penny, he is a child
of the Middle Ages; but when he revels in himself, he is a father
to the Elizabethans.

Towards the end of 1447 the Lord Chancellor, still reluctant to
hand down a formal judgement, persuaded both parties to have a
try at reaching an agreement at home. Accordingly, on December
14 John Shillingford wrote to one of the Bishop's counsel, beginning his letter by amiably proposing that they get busy with
negotiations. Then the true feelings of the man suddenly flashed
out: the city's desire to make an end did not arise from any doubt
of the justice of its cause, nor was 'I, John Shillingford' growing
timorous 'for any dread of great words of malice, slanders,
writings, to rebuke me and to make me dull to labour for the
right that I am sworn to uphold; for truly I will not be so rebuked
nor dulled, but the more boldlier will do my part as I am sworn
to'. Yet he was never 'the worse willed to all good communication
and reasonable mean to make a good end, for with the grace of
God I will be one man and the same man I have been'.

On second thought, John Shillingford decided that this passage
was hardly likely to promote sweet reasonableness at the treaty
table; therefore, holding to his prime duty as a negotiator, he
crossed it out and wrote simply, 'Ye may fully conceive that my
fellows and I would fain have peace, praying you to apply your
good will and favour to the same'.

Bishop Lacy's answer was to summon Shillingford to his manor
of Chudleigh, the message arriving only the evening before he
was bidden to appear. The Mayor was not to be commanded so
lightly. He sent a deputy armed with excuses, including the statement that 'I standing mayor and of power, and yet having no
power, may naught do, say, agree, nor assent without communication had with my fellowship, a commonalty which is hard to
deal with'.

As the great suit dragged on, feeling in Exeter grew bitterer.
The Mayor's refusal to be overawed by the Bishop was answered,

in the first months of 1448, by renewed scorn and defiance from ecclesiastical precincts. When the Assizes opened at Exeter, the Bishop's tenants, on pain of a forty shilling fine, were forbidden to take their turn at keeping watch and were told that, 'if any of the Mayor's officers entered into any tenement of the Bishop for to warn any man to come to the watch, they should break his head'. Whereupon the outraged Mayor 'made right great way-ward language to them'. Priests summoned before the city court refused to put in appearance. The clergy insisted on the release of one of the ecclesiastical tenants because he had work to do for the Bishop. The minstrel of another tenant 'made affray upon a woman and would have ravished her'. A priest stirred up a row, then took refuge in the church. Shillingford minced no words in letting the Chancellor know the source of all the trouble: 'now almost every man taketh colour by my lord Bishop.'

The Bishop's men retorted that clerical life and limb was no longer safe because 'there were many wild and unreasonable fellows of the city of Exeter'. When William Speer, the Town Clerk, demanded of a cathedral chaplain what cause he had to use such language, the chaplain answered 'with a high spirit' that some of the city serjeants had declared 'in William Gyfford's house in hearing of a priest that there should many a priest of the Close of Exeter lose his head on Midsummer Eve'.

Suddenly one morning Shillingford's old friend Canon Roger Kys appeared with the news that he had been sent as the Bishop's deputy to sound out the Mayor's intentions. But who should know better than Edmund Lacy that principals deal only with principals? Shillingford replied to this insult by telling Kys flatly that he would enter into no discussion with the Bishop by means of an intermediary. He knew right well, he reported to Arch-bishop Stafford, that the Bishop considered it *infra dig.*, because of the Mayor's 'simpleness and poverty', to negotiate directly. 'Nevertheless, simple as he was, he was Mayor of Exeter,' and had been commanded by the Lord Chancellor to deal with the Bishop himself. 'Wherefore he would boldly take it upon him.'

Bishop Lacy then tried a different tactic. At eight o'clock one morning, two of his officers rode into town to inform John

Shillingford that the Bishop himself would arrive that same day at one P.M. to treat with the Mayor. At this news Shillingford was 'foul astonished and encombered'. He declared emphatically that it was not the Bishop's place to come to him, but the duty of the Mayor and aldermen to attend upon the Bishop, as they would be happy to do. He scented the trap at once: 'this was hasty process', he bluntly told the Chancellor, 'and he conceived right well that it was done for to take him in a default'. Though showing contempt for the city by giving such off-hand notice, Lacy could pose as going to very humble lengths to reach an accommodation; and this is just what the Bishop did in a letter he afterwards wrote to the King.

The messengers demanded an instant answer: his lordship would be on the way at any moment. Shillingford refused to treat under these circumstances and demanded two hours in which to consult his fellows. This reluctantly granted, the Mayor was able to report in an hour that the city magistrates would give the Bishop a hearty welcome and wait upon him at his command.

So, when Edmund Lacy, Bishop of Exeter, arrived in his cathedral city at evensong, he received a fitting reception from his 'ghostly children'. The Mayor and aldermen escorted him to St. Peter's church. 'When my lord had said his prayers at the high altar, he went apart to the side altar by himself and called to him the Mayor and no more.' There in the rich twilight of stained glass, amidst the haunting forms of arch and pillar, the old Bishop in his vestments of state, a breath of incense wafting from their folds, condescended to inform the Mayor of Exeter that, at the Chancellor's commandment, he had come to listen to what he had to say. Therefore, let the Mayor be about it and speak up.

John Shillingford replied that his lordship need not have put himself out to ride to Exeter, 'for if he had sent for the Mayor' and his fellows, 'they would have come to him, as their part was, with right good will'. Shillingford then asked the Bishop to assign an hour the next morning for a formal meeting.

His lordship replied shortly that 'he might not tarry, but be gone anon'.

'The Mayor said that he could not commune with him suddenly and with so short warning and by himself.'

The Bishop 'said I should take whom that I would, there stood right enough about'. The haughty tone of Edmund Lacy drawls right down the centuries; the words sketch the lordly movement of the episcopal hand as it indicates Shillingford's fellows skulking in the distance.

The Mayor stood his ground: he needed time to consult and he reiterated his request for a meeting the next morning; 'and so with much hardness, prayer, and instance it was granted at ten o'clock'.

Promptly 'at ten at the bell' the Mayor, aldermen, and their counsel presented themselves in the cathedral. Nothing came of the meeting. Edmund Lacy rode off haughtily on Monday morning.

By the time the summer of 1448 was wearing away, John Shillingford realized that matters had reached an impasse dangerous for the city. Despite the pressure of his appeals by letter and in person, the Chancellor could not be brought to hand down a judgement. The Bishop was now pushing his damage suit and, in these circumstances, might well win it. And the city had spent a great deal of money, which apparently the citizens did not grudge in their hearts but must have felt in their purses. They had had to pay for 'many great ensearches, first in our treasury at home among full many great old records; afterwards at Westminster, first in the Chancery, in the Exchequer, in the Receipt, and in the Tower'. In addition to meeting the fees of their expensive London counsel and heavy travel expenses, the city had lined influential pockets—20s to the Sheriff of Devon, 6s 8d to one of his officers, 40s to that powerful courtier John Trevilian whom his many enemies called the 'Cornish Chough', tips to the Chief Justices' clerks, silver to cross numerous palms in the West Country and at London. Many more pounds dribbled away in fish and wine and game dispatched to the City Recorder, Nicholas Radeford; wine was required to refresh the aldermen at numerous discussions; dinners and suppers in Exeter warmed the stomachs of influential Devonians; buckhorn for the Chancellor and sturgeon for the Justices cost a pretty penny. In our money the sum of it all must have amounted to some thousands of pounds.

As John Shillingford's third term as mayor was running out, he and Bishop Lacy agreed to accept the arbitration of the two greatest lords of the region, Sir William Bonvile and Thomas Courtenay, Earl of Devon, themselves bitter enemies but temporarily reconciled. They awarded to the Bishop a jurisdiction separate from that of the city, and town officers were forbidden to make arrests on Church territory. On the other hand, Bishop Lacy was required to relinquish any damages he won in his suit; his men could arrest no citizens within the fee; the Bishop's tenants were required to take their turn on the city watch and pay city taxes; the special charter Bishop Lacy had secured from the King was annulled; and the Mayor and his officers kept the right to bear their maces of office on cathedral ground.

Not long after this award was given, John Shillingford died. He had not spared himself. During one of his talks with the Chancellor, 'my lord conjured me to make an end of this matter and if I did so I should be chronicled'. The Mayor did better: *he* chronicled his age, his town, himself.

3

Rebel Against the Mayor

TOWN government in England had never been democratic or fraternal or mild. But on occasion in the past the commons had joined with 'The Clothing', when towns were smaller and weaker, to fight the encroachments of lords or ecclesiastics. By the time of the Wars of the Roses, however, the great towns governed themselves under charter from the King and they were controlled by an oligarchy of money. Theoretically, every man enfranchised had an undefined right to participate in the election of the mayor and of the burgesses sent to Parliament. But the enterprising and ambitious had gathered the reins of power firmly into their hands.

Yet some cities had at least an air of greater freedom than others: the average citizen was more vocal and made himself more strongly felt, it appears, in York and Norwich and in some of the Cinque Ports than at Nottingham or Coventry.

On a January day in York (1483) as a number of men were 'sitting at the ale at Eden Berrys, in Gothyngate', somebody raised a lively question: 'Sirs, whom shall we have to our mayor this year?'

One Steven Hoghson answered, 'Sirs, one thing and it please the commons, I would we had Master Wrangwysh, for he is the man that my lord of Gloucester will do for'.

Robert Rede, a 'gyrdeler', was quick to retort, 'That may not be, for the mayor must be chosen by the commonalty, and not by no lord'. It appears that he added, 'My Lord of Gloucester will not be displeased whomsoever it pleases the commons to choose for their mayor'.

Methods of election were often complicated and differed from town to town. In some places, a handful of citizens appointed by the mayor chose a larger body who in their turn nominated two men for the office of mayor, from whom the mayor and aldermen then made their selection. In other towns, the mayor and his brethren nominated two men for the choice of the citizens, the 'substantial citizens', that is. Worcester was governed by two bailiffs, one 'high' chosen by 'Twenty-four of the great clothing', and one 'low' appointed by the Forty-eight, or Common Council, who were supposed to represent the commonalty. Both bailiffs, in fact, were members of the 'great clothing'. However the machinery might be rigged, the oligarchy of wealth kept government firmly in their hands.

These men undoubtedly enjoyed power and, in many cases, probably arranged commercial favours and illegal concessions for themselves and their friends. On the other hand, they worked hard and their lot was sometimes dangerous as well as thankless. Despite the perquisites of livery gowns and other allowances, mayors and aldermen not infrequently disbursed considerable sums of their money in upholding the dignity of their positions. Men who refused office were heavily fined or worse. In the Cinque ports, their houses were sometimes pulled down. When Stephen Fabyn, draper, elected Alderman of Bridge ward in London, refused to take the oath, protesting that he lacked 'the estate to maintain the dignity', he was promptly committed to Newgate prison until his assertion was proved, Men who sought, in advance, to be relieved of the duty of office-holding, whether for sickness or any other reason, were required to pay a composition of £5 or more, depending on their wealth.

Nothing was permitted to shadow the dignity of the mayor, visible emblem of the greatness of the city. Harry Butler, Recorder of Coventry, announced one day in a burst of self-inflation that he could commit the Mayor to prison if he wanted to. He was immediately put in his place with a heavy rebuke and maimed in his prestige by being required to walk in procession not directly after the Mayor but third in line. When an innkeeper was elected Mayor of Coventry, he was forced to remove his sign of business. A man who used 'unfitting language' against the mayor or his brethren was committed to prison until he was prepared to make a public submission, which meant going down on his knees before the mayor and abjectly begging for pardon, and then he had to pay a stiff fine and sometimes provide surety for good behaviour before he was released. Certain Bristol citizens of Irish extraction, led by Harry May, 'vaunt parloure and chief labourer', dared to bring suit before the Chancellor of England against the Mayor and council. For this contempt of the city's dignity, Harry and all his fellows were deprived of their franchise 'till they bought it again with the blood of their purses; and with weeping eyes, kneeling on their knees, besought the Mayor and brethren of their grace'. The magistrates of York ordained that any enfranchised man who was 'rebel henceforth to his mayor', or made slighting remarks about city officers, or disclosed anything said by the mayor and his councillors in council, would pay a fine of £10.

In February of 1484, Thomas Wrangwysh, elected Mayor of York for the second time while he was at London representing the city in Parliament, found when he reached Tadcaster on his journey homeward that the old Mayor and the aldermen and all the officers of York had ridden forth to bid him welcome. Other citizens came out to meet him as the parade moved toward the city and 'brought him worshipfully home to his own place'. But Thomas set an example of scrupulous respect for his office by firmly refusing to allow the sword or the mace to be borne before him: he had not yet taken his oath.

The dignity hedging a mayor served the practical purpose of helping him to clamp a tight control over his little realm. Awe eked out inadequate policing; a severe tone and multiplicity of regulations propped the *status quo*. 'The Clothing' were not indifferent to justice but held that their first duty was to enforce obedience. Everybody knew that men needed masters; order had to be imposed from above. The *superiores*, the oligarchy of enterprise and success, found their right to rule in the law of nature. The hearts of men being wild and sinful, governors must rule hardily. Besides, the King was always looking.

The town oligarchy solidly closed ranks in support of this system. The middling shopholder usually accepted it as in his best interests. But the swarming commonalty were by no means always content. In the world of the countryside, a yeoman might offend against the custom of the manor but he never questioned it, for that custom went back 'to a time whereof no man remembereth'; and the Yorkist Age, though stirred by new currents, was still powerfully gripped by the force of the past. But though submissiveness on the part of the town commons had long been a fact, it had never hardened into tradition. The humbler citizens nursed a day-dream that once all townsmen had been, if not equals at least brothers, and that the town corporation was a benefit held in trust for all. Therefore the authoritarian demeanour of fifteenth-century mayors did not pass without challenge. More money circulated from purse to purse; men went more richly and more warmly clad than in previous centuries; and the gulf between rich and poor did not yawn so bleakly as it would under the Tudors. But during the Wars of the Roses, nevertheless, towns exhibited plenty of discontent.

Grumbling led to stirrings of rebellion: black looks, angry verses nailed on the church door, the cry of 'false harlot', rashly flung at mayor or alderman. Political dissatisfaction was usually exacerbated by economic discontents. Flattened under a pyramid of gild rules and market regulations and town ordinances, the humbler citizens were likely to feel that they were kept down that others might rise. Rioting flared in Norwich and York and Coventry and Gloucester and other towns; the Gild of Tailors at Exeter waged a fierce battle throughout the reign of Edward IV against the domination of the town aristocracy.

All causes of discontent, all feelings of bitterness found their expression in the issue of the common lands which girdled cities in an expanse of open fields and enclosures and waste and woods. The right of each citizen to pasture animals on the town common was the most jealously watched of all municipal 'rights'. Resentment against the oligarchy's abuse of the privilege generated more violence than all other causes of discontent put together. A cow, a few sheep, often spelled for humble folk the difference between penury and decent subsistence. Perhaps even more poignant, pasture lands shared by all symbolized the dream of municipal fraternity. Each citizen of Coventry and York had, in theory at least, an equal 'stint' of common. At Launceston, richly endowed with common lands, the Mayor was permitted to pasture twelve animals; aldermen, ten; substantial citizens eight or six; ordinary citizens, four; and the rest of the enfranchised, two. Nottingham had a curious system of dividing its common lands yearly among its burgesses, an arrangement that easily led to trouble. In 1480, the commonalty angrily refused to accept the partition proposed by the Mayor.

No oligarchy held a tighter grip on its city than 'The Scarlet' of Coventry. A body of twenty-four *potentiores*, mostly former magistrates, chose the officers for the coming year; the mayor and the Twenty-four then selected another twenty-four to make up the council of Forty-eight, but the mayor was not obliged to consult the full council and usually made his decisions with the assistance of a small group of advisers. The town Leet, a legislative and judicial body which met twice a year, was composed of a jury of twenty-four, virtually identical with the twenty-four who elected the mayor and served on his council. The town government was beautifully self-perpetuating. Unlike the London oligarchy, constantly invigorated by new blood from the shires, certain families in Coventry held power decade after decade.

For many years the commonalty had stirred restlessly under this rule. In the late fourteenth century citizens rose in their wrath against malpractices of powerful victuallers. During the reign of Henry VI, popular discontents became focused upon the corrupt management of the common lands. 'The Clothing' and their friends nibbled away at these lands, enclosing a piece here and a piece there; and they 'surcharged' the municipal pastures (i.e., exceeded their stint) with sheep by the hundred.

During the latter half of the fifteenth century, ill feeling flashed into angry protests and acts of violence. These tumults cast up into the light of history the only rebel against a Mayor whose cause and career still survive. Like many rebels in all ages, Laurence Saunders belonged to the class against which he fought. He was a prosperous dyer, son of William Saunders, Mayor of Coventry in 1469, and therefore a member of 'The Clothing' who might look forward to an honourable career in the governing of the city. We know him only through the records of his enemies, the town authorities against whom he did battle for the commonalty. They called him a headstrong, proud man who 'would not otherwise be ruled than after his own will'. Fortunately, the Town Clerk recorded some of the petitions in which Laurence Saunders set forth the grievances of the commons and even noted satirical verses in which Saunders' adherents attacked the ruling oligarchy.

In 1469 a man named Briscow overreached himself in his encroachments on Coventry Common, and the pent-up feelings of the townsmen exploded into violence. William Briscow, gentleman, owned lands adjoining the London road about a mile south of the city and just across the river Sherbourne from common pastures. Briscow's father had been Mayor of Coventry in 1428, but with the money John Briscow had won in trade, William, like many another member of his class, had chosen to withdraw from the city and live the life of the gentry. Briscow's friends among 'The Clothing' had allowed him to enclose pieces of land on the edge of common fields and to pasture flocks of sheep in the fields themselves. In 1469, however, he carried his presumption too far by building a wall which obstructed the river. Angry citizens sallied from the gates and pulled the wall down. Briscow made the mistake of suing for trespass in the county courts.

This piece of ingratitude united, for once, the oligarchy and the commonalty. The Mayor and his brethren immediately 'remembered' Briscow's illegal enclosures and use of Coventry Common. On Monday, November 30, with the Mayor himself riding at their head, some five hundred citizens issued from the town, arrayed in jacks and sallets and brandishing a variety of weapons including mattocks, spades, axes—according to Briscow's petition to the King. They smashed Briscow's gates and hedges, cut down several great oaks, carried away wood, clay and gravel and 'riotously destroyed two swans nests'. At the command of the Mayor, an alderman summoned the 'Waits' of the city to play triumphal airs and bawl impromptu ballads 'in rehearsing of their said riots, and like as they had done a great conquest or victory'. The Mayor 'made them pipe and sing before the said rioters all the way to the city, a space of a large mile or more'. Soon after, the taverns were full of men 'avaunting and rehearsing of their great riot, saying that if your said beseecher sued any person that they would slay him'.

Encouraged by this success, citizens poured from the city a week later, on St. Nicholas' day (December 6), which opened the season of merriment and licence. This time they threw down hedges and trampled enclosures which the Priory of Coventry had erected on the edge of the Prior's Waste, land the city claimed as its own. Prior Deram was a much more powerful man than William Briscow, and when he let the city fathers know in vigorous language that he meant to bring suit for this outrage, 'The Clothing' quickly decided that the commonalty had been allowed to go too far. The Prior was bought off with certain pieces of disputed property. In order to give this concession an appearance of popular consent, the city fathers secured the express approval of 216 substantial citizens.

Laurence Saunders, whose father was then Mayor, signed among the 'approvers', his first appearance in the city records. Perhaps he was too young to protest. By the time a decade had passed, he had either changed his mind or considered himself strong enough to show his true sympathies.

He chose to strike for the commons in 1480, when he had just started up the ladder of preferment by being elected one of the two chamberlains of the city for that year. The chamberlains had charge of the city walls and therefore collected murage dues, and they supervised the common lands. They were required to 'pin in pinfolds' all sheep and other animals pastured in excess of the permitted stint, taking 4d for each score of sheep pinned.

One Saturday in the spring, Laurence Saunders and William Hede, chamberlains, refused to disburse the wages of workmen who had been hired to quarry stone for the repair of the city walls. Laurence declared 'presumptuously' that 'they that set them a-work should pay for them'. The Mayor clapped the chamberlains into prison. Hede soon made humble submission to the authorities, declaring that he had been led into his iniquitous ways only at Saunders' urging. At first sight, Laurence's refusal to pay the workmen seems to bear little relation to the grievances of the commonalty; but murage dues weighed heavily upon the humbler citizens, and the tax was the bitterer because the wealthy Prior of Coventry, though many a yard of his land marched along the walls, had refused for years to pay a penny.

Besides, this is the official version of Laurence Saunders' first rebellion. Laurence himself declared that he had been imprisoned by the Mayor because he fulfilled his sworn duty: he had been impounding all cattle which 'The Clothing' were pasturing in excess of their stint. When, on April 8, he pinned 200 sheep belonging to William Deister and refused to unpin them at the Mayor's command, he was clapped into jail and Will Deister got his animals back without having to pay a penny. What was worse, Laurence had no chance to defend himself in public or to pry open the whole question of privileged abuse of common pasture. The Easter Leet met on April 10. Laurence had powerful friends, even among the oligarchy, and they tried hard to free him; but the Recorder of Coventry, Harry Butler, had no intention of permitting Laurence to raise a rumpus in court, and he was not released until the afternoon of the 11th. A week later the Recorder bound the Chamberlains by recognizances of £10 apiece to 'obey the mayor's commandments in right or wrong'. On May 24, the Mayor fined Saunders and Hede £10, of which £6 was forgiven. But when Laurence demanded to be quit of his recognizance, the Recorder snarled that he 'should not be released thereof for the best piece of scarlet in England'.

Laurence had not learnt his lesson. All summer he went on impounding animals: 400 sheep belonging to the Prior; 400 belonging to Will Briscow; 300 more of the Prior's on still another day; 180 belonging to Robert Beveys. But the Mayor and Recorder released all the sheep, took not a single fine, and ordered Laurence to desist from his unwelcome officiousness. The indignant chamberlain declared that up to 1,000 sheep were illegally grazing on the common because their owners were 'maintained' by the Mayor and Recorder; he added that several fields now enclosed were, in fact, common lands. The Recorder furiously rejoined 'that he would make the said chamberlain to curse the time that ever he saw him and would make him to weep water with his eyes. And for to be revenged upon him, he said he would ride to complain about him unto our sovereign lord the King'.

But Laurence, ever the man of action, rode first, Securing permission from the Mayor to go to Southampton on private business, he took horse on September 20 and galloped off to Ludlow Castle to lay his charges against the oligarchy of Coventry before the Council of little Prince Edward, son and heir to Edward IV.[1]

On September 30 the Prince's Council ordered the city authorities to send a 'discreet person' to Ludlow to present their side of the story. The Mayor replied angrily on October 3 that no trouble existed which could not easily be settled 'amongst ourself'. He lashed out against 'the hasty, sinister and seducious suggestion and labour made by Laurence Saunders against the will of the governors of this your city'. Saunders was a subversive fellow who had 'openly disobeyed me and the rule of this city and by his power would induce commotion amongst the people'. William Shaw underlined this telling point: 'he would subdue us all if he might get assistance, to the worst example that ever was here.' The Mayor then sent off an imposing embassy of eighteen persons headed by Harry Butler, the Recorder, and John Thrumpton, Master of Holy Trinity Gild. They travelled in style, with a harbinger to ride ahead and provide lodgings, a cook to oversee the preparation of their meals, and twenty-eight servants. William Hede was included in the party to show how a good man could go wrong under Laurence's sinister influence.

After hearing the evidence of both sides, the Prince's Council made its decision on October 27. Laurence's proof of false dealing in the common lands could not be ignored: the Council ordered a full investigation and required the city government to pay such fines as were owing to the chamberlains. But however just may have been his complaint, 'the said Laurence' had acknowledged before the Council his 'obstinacy and disobedience to you Mayor,

---

[1] Laurence directed himself to Ludlow because the Borough of Coventry had once been an appendage of the Earldom of Chester. As Earl of Chester, Prince Edward might be regarded as the suzerain of the town; and he was, furthermore, the nominal head of the Council of Wales.

Recorder, and others having the rule of the said city', and therefore he was to be 'corrected and punished after his desert'. The
commons of Coventry were commanded to eschew 'all unlawful
assemblies' and use of violence.

The Prince's Council sent along a gentleman to see that the
rebellious chamberlain showed himself properly penitent. In St.
Mary's Hall, before the scarlet-gowned *superiores* and a silent array
of commons, Laurence Saunders pushed his knees to the floor and
humbly offered himself for correction. He was committed to
prison. To regain his freedom, he had to bind himself in the
enormous sum of £500 to appear at the next general sessions of
the court and in the meantime to 'be of good bearing against
the said Mayor'. This recognizance, the breaking of which would
mean ruin, was to be continued from session to session till the
rulers of the city were convinced that Laurence had had a genuine
change of heart. As a last artful flick of the whip, he was required
to pay the £15 11s 11½d that the Coventry delegation had spent
on their jaunt to Ludlow.

For the moment Laurence himself had to lie low, but the blow
he struck had shaken the city. The commonalty sorely grudged
the treatment which had been meted out to their champion; the
fraudulent dealings in common lands which he had brought to
light sparked a blaze of anger. On Lammas Day the following
year (August 1, 1481),[1] a mob smashed into Briscow's illegal
enclosures. Old Harry Butler, sick though he was, rode out to
quell the riot. One John Tyler, who gave the Recorder a piece of
his tongue, was forthwith committed to prison. On the Trinity
Gild feast day, Decollation of St. John the Baptist (August 29), a
swarm of citizens ruined the ceremony of their betters by ringing
the common bell and making a vain attempt to rescue Tyler. The
riot succeeded in embarrassing the authorities; for the King, quickly
apprised of the outbreak, fired off an angry privy seal to rebuke
the Mayor for failing to keep order and to command the incarceration of ring-leaders at Ludlow until the following Easter. But the
city buzzed with 'conventicles' and 'conspiracies', which all the

[1] Many of the Coventry pastures were 'common' only from Lammas Day, August 1,
until Candlemas, February 2; on August 1 the citizens made a ceremony of 'throwing
down the fences' of 'Lammas lands'.

diligence of the *potentiores* could not suppress. Matters grew so bad that in April of 1482 Edward IV dispatched another privy seal to reprimand the authorities for their slackness. Apparently Laurence Saunders and his friends had won so much backing, even among the oligarchy, that the Mayor dared not act vigorously.[1]

So far, no mention of Laurence Saunders himself; he had been biding his time. Hobbled by his recognizance and attempting politic means, he now laid before the Mayor and council a list of meadows illegally enclosed. The rulers of Coventry condescended to explain to their adversary why these enclosures had been permitted; and they even 'made him privy to the evidence of the city on this behalf'. Laurence, not to be fobbed off so easily, asked for a copy of this evidence 'to show to certain people as he should please'—probably old men among his following who would know if these evidences were valid. When he was harshly refused, he burst out against his enemies, demanded to be discharged of the recognizance which made him a slave to the Mayor's will and threatened that, if they would not discharge him, 'he would find the means to be discharged'.

The Mayor and his brethren held their fire until certain lords of the Prince's Council appeared in Coventry the Saturday before All Hallows' Day (October 26). With their full approval, the Mayor clapped Laurence Saunders into prison, where he remained until the Sunday after All Hallows. Then, 'by great instance made by his friends', he agreed before the Ludlow lords to seal a 'statute merchant' of £200 to obey the Mayor; and four of his adherents were bound in the crippling sum of £100 as surety for his good behaviour. When Laurence was finally released, the lords of the Prince's Council gave him a stiff warning: this was the second time he had been gaoled for disobeying his superiors and raising commotions among the people; 'they therefore bade him beware, for if he came a third time in ward for such matters, it should cost him his head etc.'

For twelve long years Laurence Saunders managed to remain silent. As he grew old in bitterness, his worldly affairs decayed.

---

[1] The privy seal declared that the rebellious elements were 'supported and favoured by divers persons having rule in the city'.

Fines and sureties had taken their toll; the wealthy cloth dealers
of the city undoubtedly sent their dyeing business elsewhere;
and probably Laurence, brooding over his injuries and the un-
redressed grievances of the commons, had little heart for making
money. He remained the hero of the commonalty; for in these
years the oligarchy tightened its grip on the life of the city and
discontents simmered. Humble cloth-sellers could no longer
vend their wares in the porch of St. Michael's Church; they were
required to sell in the Drapery, a building owned by the all-
powerful Holy Trinity Gild, where they had to pay stallage and
where searchers appointed by the Drapers closely scrutinized their
wares. Wool must be sold at the Wool Hall, and the city charged
a fee for weighing which drove up the price weavers had to pay for
their raw material. An ordinance requiring all apprentices to be
enrolled in the city registers and pay 13d was likewise deeply
resented; for if a small shopholder wanted a likely lad who was
penniless he had to find the money out of his own pocket, and
besides such a regulation demeaned the dignity of his gild. There
was so much grumbling against this measure that all those caught
in evasion were required to give surety of good behaviour. The
makers of pewter ware and the Tanners, perhaps because they
showed signs of defiance, were hauled into the Leet court on
charges of fraudulent dealing.

By Lammas Day of 1494—the day that symbolized all his
defeats—Laurence Saunders could keep quiet no longer. Some
forty men were in the street when William Butler, perhaps a son
of Laurence's old enemy the Recorder, now deceased, drove by
with a cartload of oats.

Laurence suddenly cried out, 'Sirs, hear me! We shall never
have our right till we have stricken off the heads of three or four
of these churls that rule us!' He appealed to the crowd to band
together against the oppressors—'If thereafter it be asked who did
that deed, it shall be said, "Me and they and they and me!" '

Having fired his hearers, he forced Butler to drive the cart into
the Crosscheping—the market-place—and there made him dump
the oats in the street. 'Come, sirs!' he shouted to the crowd.
'Take this corn, who so will, as your own!' Then he committed

William Butler to prison. The oats had probably been grown on land wrongfully enclosed, or Butler had illegally forestalled them at the gates.

The rulers of the city did not act for six weeks, perhaps alarmed by the spectre of rioting and daunted by Laurence Saunders' popularity. Then, on September 17, they once again thrust him into gaol and there he remained until he found sureties for the fine of £40 that was levied against him. In the Easter Leet of 1495, 'The Clothing' expelled the rebel from their midst: Laurence Saunders was henceforth forbidden ever to ride with the chamberlains on Lammas Day, on pain of losing his £40, and he was 'discharged from the mayor's common council, and all other councils hereafter to be taken and kept within this city for the welfare of the same'.

The commonalty seethed: the one man who dared to speak out for them, even though he wore the livery of both the Holy Trinity Gild and the Corpus Christi Gild, had been disgraced and put to ransom as if he were an enemy Scot. Eight days after Lammas of 1495, buzzing crowds gathered before the north door of St. Michael's Church. 'Some evil disposed persons unknown' —in the Town Clerk's view—had nailed up verses that spoke for them all:

> Be it known and understand
> This City should be free and now is bond.
>
> Dame Godiva made it free;
> And now the custom for wool and the Drapery.
>
> Also it is made that no 'prentices shall be
> But xiii pennies pay should he.
>
> And now another rule ye do make
> That none shall ride at Lammas but they that ye take.
>
> When our ale is tunned
> Ye shall have drink to your cake.
> Ye have put one man like a Scot to ransom.
> That will be remembered when ye have all forgotten.
>
> Caviat'.

Feeling the ground shake beneath their feet, 'The Clothing' decided to move cautiously. John Dove, elected Mayor in 1496, appears to have been a timid man. The city decided to forgive Laurence Saunders £20 of his £40 fine; his sureties paid half of the remainder. But the wrongs he had suffered and the grievances of the commonalty clamoured in his ears, and age had not withered him into prudence. He and his friends found a way to the Bishop of Rochester, a member of the King's Council. Forgetting what he had learned years ago about the trust that could be put in princes, Laurence appealed to King Henry VII. Early in 1496 the Mayor was requested, by privy seal, to forgo the remaining £10 of Laurence Saunders' fine and was ordered to do justice 'in the variance as touching the common [lands] which the said Laurence had informed the King's Grace to be in this city'. While Mayor Dove squirmed and wondered what to do, Laurence Saunders boldly came to his house one day in early summer.

'Master Mayor', said the old rebel, 'I advise you to look wisely on yourself, for ere Lammas Day ye shall hear other tidings. And many of these caitiffs that look so high now shall be brought lower. And ye know well, amongst you ye have of mine £10 of money which I doubt not I shall have again ere Lammas Day, or else three or four of the best of you shall smart.' Laurence then gave the Mayor a nasty parting shot: 'Therefore I advise you, bear upright the sword, at your peril; for ye shall know more shortly.' The sting in the reference to the sword was that Richard II had once ordered a mayor of Coventry to have his sword borne behind him because he had failed to do justice.

Despite this ghastly blow to his dignity, Mayor Dove did not dare commit Saunders to prison. Instead he addressed a frantic appeal to the city Recorder, none other than the infamous Richard Empson, the King's extortioner who enriched the treasury and his own purse by all manner of quasi-legal frauds. While Laurence's party and the oligarchy waited for word from Westminster, the incorrigible rebel struck again. On July 20 he strode into the 'gaol-hall' where the Mayor and his brethren were sitting in their pomp as judges. 'And then and there the said Laurence before a great audience said, "Master Mayor, I have brought you

a bill here. I pray you it may be read openly in this court".'
Finally the Mayor found his tongue and replied that the matter
required no such haste; Saunders would be given 'a reasonable
answer' the next day at nine of the clock—in private, of course.
The Mayor and his brethren knew very well that the 'bill' listed
fields and pastures wrongfully withheld from the common lands.

As he departed, Laurence could not resist taunting the Mayor
in public. 'Master Mayor,' he called derisively, 'hold upright your
sword.' To show that he had no fear of Richard Empson's
influence at court, he added, 'As for Master Recorder, I have
reckoned with him, before the King, and he shall be easy enough'.

But Laurence, as usual, was too sanguine. The anxiously
awaited privy seal from Henry VII announced that the city might
dispose of the case as it saw fit. At once an exorbitant surety
for good behaviour was demanded of Laurence Saunders. He
passionately refused, for he would be caught in no more golden
traps nor jeopardize his adherents, and besides, he had little money
left. Once again, he was clapped in gaol. Once again, he and his
friends made an appeal to the Bishop of Rochester.

The Bishop requested the Mayor to put Saunders under surety
so that he might appear before the King's Council at Woodstock
and air his charges. Laurence offered a sum which the Mayor
refused. The prisoner declared furiously that 'he would find no
other, whatsoever fell. Wherefore he remained still in prison'.
A few days later, two poems blossommed on the cathedral door:

You have hunted the hare, You hold him in a snare;	It had been as good nay [not].
Ye that be of might, See that ye do right,	Think on your oath.
For where that ye do wrong, Ye shall mend it among,	Though ye be never so loath.
Little small been [bees], That all about fleen,	They wag their wing.

Where they light,	And also sting,
The been will bite,	
Look that ye do right.	Beware of wappys [wasps].
Both day and night,	
Both early and late,	For after-clappys [dire conse-
Keep well your pate.	quences].

The second set of verses struck the chord sounded by the satiric poem of the year before:

The city is bond that should be free.
The right is held from the commonalty.

Our Commons that at Lammas open should be cast
They be closed in and hedged full fast.

And he that speaketh for our right is in the hall [gaol],
And that is shame for you and for us all.

You cannot deny it but he is your brother;
And to both Gilds he hath paid as much as another.

For any favour or friendship the commons with you find,
[Ye] pick away our thrift and make us all blind.

And [if] ever ye have need to the Commonalty,
Such favour as ye show us, such shall ye see.

We may speak fair and bid you good morrow,
But love with our hearts shall ye have none.

Cherish the Commonalty and see they have their right
For dread of a worse chance by day or by night.

The best of you all little worth should be
And ye had not help of the Commonalty.

Through the rest of the summer and into autumn, Laurence Saunders, lying in gaol, continued to send appeals to the King's

Council. Finally on November 10, two privy seals arrived. One directed the Mayor to take surety of Laurence Saunders in £100 and release him from prison so that he might confront, before the Royal Council, a delegation sent by the city; the second order permitted six of Laurence's friends to appear as his witnesses. Doubtless the old rebel was jubilant as he rode to London. What he received was a full hearing.

From Friday, November 18, until the following Tuesday, the Royal Council, including the Archbishop of Canterbury, the Archbishops of London and Rochester, the Chief Justice, and many other lords, listened to the complaint of Laurence Saunders, the answer made by the representatives of the city, 'the replication of the said Laurence and the rejoinder thereupon'. Order, as usual, was preferred before justice. At the conclusion of the hearing, Laurence was committed to Fleet Prison, 'there to abide until the King's pleasure was known what further punishment he should have'. As the gates of the prison closed upon him, the one great rebel against town oligarchy of the fifteenth century disappears from history. He had not acted wisely but he had played out his game dauntlessly to the end. And even in his old age he kept a green heart.

4

The Lord Mayor of London

LONDON had long called itself the King's Chamber, but for the Yorkist monarchs London was the touchstone of fortune as well as the first jewel of their crown. Edward IV wooed the city like a lover (and the city wives), shaped his policy with a delicate ear to its interests, honoured its officers, and traded by the side of its merchants.

During the Wars of the Roses, London was fast becoming the magnet of ambitious young men from all the counties of the realm. It was girdled by some of the most fertile lands in the kingdom. Highways converging on the capital channelled a swelling stream of goods to and from the city marts. The broad estuary of the Thames enticed the traffic of the seas. To foreigners, London blazed on the far western perimeter of civilization, the metropolis of the oceans. If Rome was the grandest and Venice the most romantic and Paris the largest of cities, travellers declared that London was the most enterprising and busiest, and marvelled to find it so lovely. A Milanese ambassador reported that the English capital was the 'wealthiest city in Christendom'. The Duke of Milan was further informed, in March of 1461 when the Yorkists had just entered the city, that Edward IV and Warwick would probably triumph over the House of Lancaster because they were backed by the Londoners, whose support meant everything.

These Londoners were 'by birth for the most part a mixture of all countries of [England]; by blood, gentlemen, yeomen and of the basest sort; and by profession, busy bees in the hive of this commonwealth'. It was a filthy, crowded, clamorous, opulent hive. Narrow streets ran all hugger-mugger, darkened by the leaning upper storeys of gilt and gabled houses. Towered gates and fine facades of stone and tenements leaning askew and shops overflowing with goods took the visitor's eye. Erasmus, a few years after this time, permitted himself to be appalled by the stench and dirt; but his nose, it must be remembered, had been thrown somewhat out of joint by his failure to find preferment and by an unfortunate argument with the royal customs which left him £20 the poorer. Yet, dirty the city certainly was, despite systematic efforts to combat the airy attitude of the inhabitants toward household rubbish and casual filth.

Italian visitors, accustomed to their sharply defined cities of stone, found the place an architectural hodge-podge. They thought the houses quaint and crazy, comfortable and often splendid on the inside with amazing depositories for wares, but built every-which-way as fancy and convenience dictated—houses with ground floor of stone supporting carved beams and 'pentices'; houses of half timber and whitewashed plaster, here and there a building of brick, the tented roof of a great hall, or an imposing municipal edifice with massive 'quadrant' like the Leadenhall. Lords and their liveried retinues inhabited spacious dwellings with courtyards and gardens. A hundred churches thrust their steeples into the London sky. Yet the dominant tone of London was sounded by business enterprise. 'Whatever there is in the city,' reported Dominic Mancini, 'it all belongs to craftsmen and merchants.'

The town embraced the river and—crown of the river—the Bridge. Land-bound Italians marvelled at the tides which coasted ships up to the heart of London and swiftly dropped them down again to the sea. The river and the town lived together like Venice and the Adriatic. A courtier in the reign of Queen Mary one day haughtily informed an alderman that the Queen 'in her displeasure against London had appointed to remove with the Parliament and Term [law courts] to Oxford. This plain man demanded, whether she meant also to divert the river of Thames from London, or no? and when the Gentleman had answered no, then, quoth the alderman, by God's grace we shall do well enough at London, whatsoever become of the Term and Parliament'.

Strangers bound for the English capital sailed up the Thames or rode through the thrifty enclosures of Kent. Coming from Calais, they crossed the Channel in a few hours—if the wind was fair and no Breton pirates showed sail. Landing at Dover or Sandwich, they rode to Canterbury to spend the first night and visit the tomb of St. Thomas à Becket, called by many the richest shrine in Christendom. The glitter of gold and precious stones was dominated by a great ruby, the Regal of France, which one day Henry VIII would wear upon his thumb. The second night was usually spent at Rochester. By midmorning of the third day, travellers were crossing Blackheath, where the remains of Jack Cade's great camp could still be seen. From the top of Shooter's Hill they caught their first sight of London lying along the river on a green breast of land that merged into the blue hills of Hampstead and Highgate.

If the visitors sailed up the Thames, they could see at Tilbury carracks of Genoa or other large ships, their cargo being unloaded into lighters. Occasionally, porpoises or even whales might appear, for two whales are recorded as disporting themselves only a little below Woolwich. The first view of London was sometimes gruesome. Between St. Catherine's and Wapping, pirates were hanged on short gallows at the low-water mark and left to remain until three tides had overflowed their bodies. To the right rose the chalky pinnacles of the Tower, while dead ahead could be seen the Bridge, one of the wonders of the world. Nineteen arches of shining white stone, broken by a drawbridge, supported a London street of shops and houses.

Hundreds of small boats plied up and down and across the river like restless water bugs. The fare was a penny; but in wet weather one could take a 'tilt boat' (a tented or covered boat) for 2d. Men impatient to cross the river stood on the many public stairs crying, 'Wagge! wagge! go we hence!' The richer the gown and the lordlier the manner, the better the service. Thomas Hoccleve confesses in one of his poems that in his misspent youth he thoroughly enjoyed being 'tugged to and fro' by watermen eager for his patronage because they knew he was good for a big tip. These boatmen were a tough lot. When the Lancastrian Lord Scales tried to slip away from the Tower under cover of darkness

—in July, 1460—they swiftly overtook his craft, murdered the unpopular lord who had been shooting guns against the city, and cast him on the steps of St. Mary Overy 'naked as a worm'. Not even the Mayor was safe from their irreverent tongues. In 1453 John Norman felt himself too old for the traditional ride to Westminster, where mayors took their oath of office before barons of the exchequer, and so he began the custom of going by water. The boatmen at once made a song for him—'Row, Norman, row to thy leman [lover].'

Among the small boats, the barges of the great glided westward to Westminster or down to Greenwich, floating caravans of carved wood and gilding, gay with banners and liveries of the oarsmen and velvet gowns. All over the river lay the traffic of the seas. A forest of masts and tackle bristled along the bank. Great cranes—amazing to the Italians—swung bales from ship to wharf. From the Tower to Blackfriars stretched quays and warehouses, broken by the battlements of Baynard's castle and the great stone bulk of the Steelyard, home of the Easterling traders.

But the visitor's gaze always came back to the Bridge. It was grander and longer than the Rialto, the Ponte Vecchio, the Pont Neuf. At the north and south ends stood stone towers with portcullises, often topped by a row of traitors' heads shredding in the rains. The drawbridge was worked from a third towered gate in the middle. Ship-traffic had become so heavy that after 1481 the drawbridge was raised no more; and the market carts from Kent, banging over the paving with iron-tyred wheels, did such damage that all 'shod carts' had to be forbidden. The Bridge was looked after by two wardens, who had at their disposal rents and gifts totalling several hundred pounds yearly. Still, the roadway was so pitted, in 1460, that when a mass of citizens were escorting the army of the Earl of Warwick into the city, several men-at-arms stumbled and fell, and, prisoned in heavy armour were trampled to death.

At ebb tide, the current swirled so dangerously through the nineteen arches that 'shooting the bridge' was only for the experienced waterman. On November 8, 1429, the Duke of Norfolk and his retinue took barge at St. Mary Overy between four and five in the afternoon and swung out into a swift ebb. A few minutes later, the little ship smashed on the pilings of the bridge. Most of the company drowned, but the Duke and two or three others managed to leap on to stone parapets and cling there until men lowered ropes to them. These piers were often thick with 'Petermen', so called because of the fishing nets they used, Peternets. The clear-flowing river, dotted white with swans, swarmed with fish; Petermen caught smelts and salmon and barbel and flounder and pike and tench.

At Galley Quay, nearest the Tower, an oar-banked Venetian galley disgorged bales of damask and velvet, spices and other luxury goods. Wool quay, farther west, was piled with 'sarplers' of wool destined for Calais. A grain ship from Prussia or a Flemish carvel laden with Holland cloth or a Spanish merchantman with a cargo of wood and madder and iron and oil might be lying at Brown's Wharf; for Stephen Brown, ex-mayor and grocer, dealt in a wide variety of goods. The basin at Billingsgate harboured coastal fishing vessels and larger ships, weatherbeaten from the Iceland voyage and full of cod that had been salted on the return trip. The wharves above the Bridge were used mostly by smaller vessels, by barges plying the Thames from as far away as Henley, and by lighters from ships anchored in the river to the east of the Bridge. The greatest wharf here belonged to the Steelyard, which received bulk cargoes of timber and cables and corn and pitch, and dispatched bales of broadcloths to all the markets of Eastern Europe. West of the Steelyard, ships freighting tuns of wine from Bordeaux tied up at 'The Three Cranes', the famous wharf of the vintners.

Vessels bringing provisions to be sold by retail at the dockside were required to distribute themselves evenly east and west of the Bridge. Eel ships, anchoring by night, were towed at early morning to Marlowe's Quay. Before the waiting housewives could board, a water bailiff searched for red eels and undersized eels, which were thrown into the Thames. He then supervised the weighers, who saw to it that Londoners got a fair measure of eels for their money. Other eel ships stayed in the river and sent lighters to the shore for their customers. At Billingsgate and at Queenhithe,

Norman vessels offered garlic and onions and salt for sale. Fish too could be bought on board but only after the Mayor or one of his representatives had examined the cargo and set a price. Rush-boats drove a thriving trade at the smaller wharves; servants bore away the fresh-smelling bundles on their backs to be strewed in halls and chambers.

The population of London in the reign of Edward IV numbered some forty or fifty thousand people, of whom about a quarter represented prosperous merchants and shopholders and artisans with their families. London had something like three or four times the population of York and of Bristol, about five times the population of Coventry and six times that of Norwich, and in the opinion of Italian observers it boasted no fewer inhabitants than Florence or Rome. Paris, the giant of the west, was at least four times as large.

The city extended little more than a mile along its river from the Tower to Blackfriars and less than that from the river to its northern walls. The perimeter of those walls is recalled today in the names of streets and underground stations. From the Tower, the wall marched northward to Aldgate, then westward past Moorgate and Aldersgate, and south by Newgate and Ludgate to Blackfriars bordered by Fleet Ditch.

The one surviving description of London as it looked at the end of Edward IV's reign was recorded by Dominic Mancini, who, leaving England just as Richard III was about to be crowned in early July of 1483, composed on his return to France an account of Richard's usurpation. To Mancini's eye, the great sinews of the city were the three principal streets running from east to west: 'London might justly complain of us for ignoring her', he writes toward the close of his narrative, 'as she is so famous throughout the world, and has deserved well of us. . . . On the banks of the Thames are enormous warehouses for imported goods: also numerous cranes of remarkable size to unload merchandise from ships. From the district on the east, adjacent to the Tower, three paved streets lead towards the walls on the west; these are the busiest in the whole city and almost straight. The one closest to the river and lower than the rest is occupied by liquid and weighty commodities: here are to be found all manner of minerals, wines, honey, pitch, wax, flax, ropes, thread, grain, fish, and'—adds the Italian, dead to the romance of commerce—'other distasteful goods'.

This was Thames Street, skirting wharves and warehouses and mansions of wealthy traders. The street swarmed with drays and sumpter-horses, sailors in exotic dress speaking exotic tongues, mercers-men and grocers-men and drapers-men hastening to the wharves, porters of the fishmongers bearing huge panniers of stock-fish and ling, Italian mariners and merchants from Galley Quay earning scornful glances for their gesticulations, tough Germans from the Steelyard shouldering their way. Petty Wales, that part of Thames Street from the Tower to Billingsgate, was so blocked by carts and cursing carters that even royal retinues issuing from the Tower were forced to wait fuming until the traffic jam untangled itself—so complained the inhabitants whose ears were daily assailed with a barrage of foul language. At the Bridge, Fish Street running northward was lined with fair houses and fine inns, 'The Bull', 'The King's Head', 'Paul's Head' in Crooked Lane—all so handsomely furnished and provisioned that visiting lords were happy to dine there. Westward stretched an array of large buildings: Fishmongers Hall and the Steelyard and Vintners Hall surrounded by the stone-crofted mansions of the wine dealers with their huge vaulted cellars.

The Steelyard, headquarters of the Easterlings, the merchants of the Hanse, looked like a fortress with its mass of stone buildings and wall and three arched gates fronting the street. The Hanse merchants lived under the strict rule of a head man and twelve councillors; they took their meals together; they were not allowed to marry and no woman was permitted on the property; they kept a suit of armour in every bedroom. A London alderman represented them in the city government, and they were given charge of one of the gates, Bishopsgate.

Thames Street had its cook-shops too, where folk might come to buy meals at a moment's notice. Fruiterers and cooks' boys shouted their wares—'hot peascods!'—'strawberry ripe!'—'cherry on the ryse [branch]!' These street cries and other pungent details of

London Life are described in the contemporary poem *London Lickpenny*, perhaps by John Lydgate, which pictures an innocent Kentish yokel, come to Westminster Hall to seek justice, wandering through the city, always discomfited because 'for lack of money I might not speed [prosper]'.

In the second street, part way up the slope from the river 'you will find', Mancini reports, 'hardly anything for sale but cloths'. He was remembering, however, only one section, Candlewick Street. Actually far from straight, this thoroughfare ran westward from the Tower as Tower Street, became the bustle of East Cheap, broadened into lines of mercers' and drapers' shops on Candlewick Street, and then twisted its way by Budge Row and Watling Street into St. Paul's Churchyard. Up Mincing Lane, to the north of Tower Street, dwelt Genoese merchants and 'galleymen'. Mark or Mart Lane, likewise running north, displayed houses and offices of Merchants of the Staple. East Cheap offered butcher shops and cook-shops and famous taverns like the 'Boar's Head'. Here occurred the memorable 'hurling' on Midsummer's Eve, 1410, when Henry IV's younger sons John and Thomas supped so rousingly that their retinues fell into a great brawl, which was only quelled after the Mayor and sheriffs had rallied an armed band of citizens. Though East Cheap was crammed and noisy and redolent of smells, the inns offered fine food; Sir John Howard found 'The Greyhound' a fitting hostelry in which to offer breakfast to Lord Audley. The Kentishman of *London Lickpenny* was deafened by street cries. 'Ribs of beef!'—'Pies!'—'Hot sheep's feet!'—'Rushes fair and green!' Pots 'clattered on a heap' as pewterers hawked their wares. Fishmongers behind their stalls urged passers-by to purchase 'melwell [cod] and mackerel'. Bands of ragged minstrels played for coppers on 'harp, pipe, and sawtry'. Others sang of *Jenkin and Julian*. Oaths split the air—'yea by cokke [God]!' and 'nay by cokke!' Here the best cook-shops in the city displayed steaming pasties and other hearty fare. Prosperous cooks often boarded the servants and retainers of lords visiting London. Such men would not sally into the street, as did their humbler competitors, who plucked at folk, even fine gentlemen, with greasy hands, trying to pull them into the shop. There were so many complaints that the Cooks Gild attempted to prohibit this un-dignified practice. But cooks were not the only offenders: smaller retailers of all kinds were always seizing people by the 'sleeve gown or otherwise'. Finally the city required the great companies to restrain their members, and even the lordly Mercers registered the edict in their minutes.

Running out of East Cheap to the west, Candlewick Street was the stronghold of the drapers. 'Great cheap of cloth!' the Kentish-man heard the smaller shopholders calling. Roomy establishments contained shelves piled with cloths of all colours and grades, tapestries, pillows, 'bankers and dorsers' to soften hard wooden benches. A room to the rear and a vaulted cellar held more bolts and bales; for drapers were importers and exporters as well as retailers.

Candlewick Street catered to gentry and lords from all over the country, who often bought cloth for their households when they came to London to attend Parliament or the court of the King or to nurse their lawsuits at Westminster. From William Bulstrode, Sir John Howard purchased counterfeit tapestries (painted cloth), and cushions covered with crimson and green velvet, as well as crimson cloth 'ingrained' (of the best dye) at 8s 6d yard; and he kept a running account that amounted to many pounds a year. On occasion, after Howard and Bulstrode had done business, the knight sent out for wine and wafers; once Sir John presented Bulstrode with a handsome pike that cost 16d.

By St. Swithin's Church on the south side of Candlewick stood the London Stone, wrapped with iron bars, a menace to unwary carters and an historic monument of which the exact meaning had been lost.

Budge Row (i.e., Fur Row) was the domain of the skinners; shops of leather-sellers and hosiers lined Soper Lane leading off to the north. There were more drapers in Watling Street. The parish church of St. Anthony held handsome tombs of mercers and grocers. The cross streets here were bright with carved timber work and painted gates leading into courtyards; for this was one of the wealthiest quarters of the city, and here too stood 'fair inns for receipt of carriers and travellers'.

Mancini recounts that 'in the third street which touches the centre of the town and runs on a level, there is traffic in more precious wares, such as gold and silver cups, dyed stuffs, various silks, carpets, tapestries, and much other exotic merchandise'. He found the shops here far more commodious than those in Continental cities: 'they are not encumbered with merchandise only at the entrance; but in the inmost quarters there are spacious depositories, where the goods are heaped up, stowed and packed away as honey may be seen in cells'. Mancini's third street was the most famous thoroughfare in the city. From Aldgate to St. Paul's, it ran as Aldgate Street and Cornhill to the Stocks Market; then came The Poultry and finally West Cheap or Cheapside or simply 'The Street', so renowned was it. Travellers from East Anglia riding into London through Aldgate often put up at the Saracen's Head Inn just inside the wall on the south side. To the north stood Holy Trinity Priory, the grandest monastery in the city, whose Prior was Alderman of Portsoken ward, a poor district of crowded tenements outside the walls to the east. Farther along Aldgate towered the magnificent parish church of St. Andrew Undershaft, so called because the maypole erected there rose higher than the steeple. Cornhill had been a grain market time out of mind. On the north side 'foreign butchers' set up their blocks and stalls on Wednesday and Saturday. Here too, daily except Sundays and feastdays, long bread carts from Stratford-atte-Bowe sold penny wheat loaves two ounces heavier than the standard London loaves. Half-way up the street, 'The Tun upon Cornhill' flowed with water brought from Tyburn in pipes. On the top was perched a cage where 'nightwalkers'—riotous folk 'flown with insolence and wine'—and bawds and priests caught tasting the flesh pots were incarcerated by the night watch. Stocks and pillory, on a wooden platform nearby, exposed to ridicule knaves who preyed upon the public by all manner of fraudulent schemes. In 1468 'divers common jurors' who had committed perjury were displayed in this pillory with paper mitres on their heads.

At the corner of Cornhill and Lime Street stood the Green Gate, the mansion of the unpopular alderman Philip Malpas, which was plundered by Jack Cade and his followers. Like other great houses,

the Green Gate was separated from the street by a row of tenements, here a frontage of nine shops broken by a gate leading into
the courtyard. At Bishopsgate Street rose the massive 'quadrant'
of the Leadenhall, which had been enlarged and rebuilt by the
famous Simon Eyre, draper and mayor of London. The Leadenhall housed a 'common granary', storage space for wool, a chapel
where divine service was held early every morning for market
people, and large enclosures in which aliens and 'foreigns' set up
stalls on Monday, Tuesday, and Wednesday to sell canvas, linen,
cloth of all kinds, ironmongery, and lead, and where country
people hawking provisions might find shelter for themselves in
wet weather. Cornhill clattered with the hoofs of sumpter-horses
packing wool from the Hampshire and Wiltshire Downs and the
Cotswolds to be weighed at the Leadenhall on the 'King's beam'
and sealed by the customs men. The bulky sarplers were then
carted down to the wool wharves. On a fine summer morning the
markets would be astir by four o'clock.

Farther along, still on the south side, stood two notable parish
churches, St. Peter-upon-Cornhill, with its library and grammar
school, and St. Michael's, whose six bells were 'accounted the best
peal of bells in England for harmony, sweetness of sound and
tune'. The largest, Rus Bell, named for the alderman who gave it,
rang nightly at 8 P.M. In the westward reaches of Cornhill 'up-
holders' sold secondhand clothes and cheap household stuff. The
hero of *London Lickpenny* saw hanging outside one of these shops
his hood which had been stolen only a short time before at
Westminster.

The open expanse of the Stocks Market was crowded with
stalls of fishmongers, butchers, and poulterers. To the north rose
the roofs of Grocers Hall, in which Edward IV feasted the Bastard
of Burgundy (June, 1467) to display for him the opulence of
London merchants. At the Great Conduit, where Bucklersbury
Lane curved up from the south, The Poultry became West Cheap.
This conduit, the oldest in the city, provided spring water brought
from Paddington, and like most of the other conduits in the city
was rebuilt and enlarged during Edward's reign. If the wind were
from the south, the passer-by pausing for a drink would smell the

odour of good English herbs mingled with a galaxy of exotic scents coming from the grocers' shops which lined Bucklersbury Lane. Grocers were apothecaries too and they sold treacle of Genoa and honey and sugar loaves and copperas and cubebs and liquorice, as well as spices and all manner of coarse goods in bulk. Housewives came to Bucklersbury Lane to purchase imported white Castile soap in a hard cake at 2½d the pound or a speckled grey soap from Bristol, 'very sweet and good', at a penny a pound or the ordinary cheap liquid black soap at ½d a pound.

First in the handsome reach of Cheapside stood the Standard and its cistern, originally of wood, but now being rebuilt in stone through a generous bequest of William Wells, former mayor. Here Lord Say was executed by the jeering followers of Jack Cade in 1450; and here at the beginning of Edward IV's reign, John Davy, a favourite of the King, had his hand cut off for striking a man before the Judges at Westminster Hall. Farther along the street rose the great cross erected by Edward I, now being rebuilt at a cost of well over £1,000 through the generosity of London citizens. At the top of Cheap another 'fair conduit', erected about 1430, refreshed passers-by. Near the Standard, on the south side, stood the church of St. Mary le Bow, so called because it was built on arches of stone. The famous Bow Bell rang curfew at 9 P.M. and, along with the bells of All Hallows Barking, St. Giles without Cripplegate, and St. Bride's in Fleet Street, sounded the hours at night. In 1472 John Donne, mercer, gave two tenements in Hosiers Lane for the maintenance of Bow Bell.

West Cheap, the pride of London, was the domain of the mercers and goldsmiths, the mercers living mostly in lower Cheapside in 'large fair houses' with commodious shops on the ground floor. Mercers Hall was situated on the north side, and around the corner, up St. Laurence Lane, was Blossom's Inn—so called because its sign showed St. Laurence the Deacon in a border of blossoms—which was the terminus for carriers from all over eastern England.

'Then into Cheap I gan me draw', reports the Kentish lad of *London Lickpenny*, 'where I saw stand much people'. Up Cheapside towards St. Paul's, the shops of the goldsmiths displayed an array of gold and silver plate, jewels and rings and ewers and mazers and standing saltcellars with covers. Foreign visitors were amazed at the precious wares the London goldsmiths had to offer. Their shops and houses extended up Guthran Lane, too, where stood their Hall, and they lay splendidly buried in the nearby churches of St. Vedast and St. Peter in Cheap and St. Matthew in Friday Street and St. John Zachary. In the year before Columbus discovered America, some of the goldsmiths were newly housed in a block of buildings which caused even a cool-eyed Venetian diplomatic agent to write: 'The most remarkable thing in London is the wonderful quantity of wrought silver. In one single thoroughfare, named The Street, leading to St. Paul's there are fifty-two goldsmiths shops so rich and full of silver vessels, great and small, that in all the shops in Milan, Rome and Venice and Florence put together, I do not think there would be found so magnificent an array. And these vessels are all either saltcellars or drinking cups or basins to hold water for the hands; for they eat off that fine tin, which is little inferior to silver [pewter].' He adds, 'The citizens of London are thought quite as highly of there, as the Venetian gentlemen are at Venice'. He was remembering the buildings on the south side of Cheap between Bread Street and Friday Street which Stow calls 'the most beautiful frame of fair houses and shops that be within the walls of London, or elsewhere in England . . . builded by Thomas Woode, goldsmith, one of the sheriffs of London, in the year 1491. It contains ten fair dwelling houses and fourteen shops, uniformly builded four storeys high, beautified towards the street with the goldsmiths arms and the likeness of woodmen, in memory of his name, riding on monstrous beasts, all which is cast in lead, richly painted over and gilt'. Woode intended these shops to be occupied by enterprising young goldsmiths, and he provided stocks of money that they might borrow to set themselves up in business.

Atop of Ludgate Hill towered St. Paul's, a massive pile 720 feet long, 130 feet broad, and 150 feet high, with a steeple that thrust almost 500 feet into the air, crowned by a copper gilt weathercock. Famous preachers of the day exhibited their skill at Paul's Cross, in the northeast corner of the churchyard; during the Wars of the

Roses, godly exhortations were sometimes replaced by political harangues. Paul's cloister, on the north side of the cathedral, contained a fine library in the East quadrant. The cloister buzzed with worldly voices, for lawyers were always to be found here walking up and down talking to their clients; as they discussed means of circumventing wills or upsetting land titles, they saw writhing on the walls about them the Dance of Death, copied in the reign of Henry VI from the famous murals in Paris and provided with sentiments by John Lydgate. Not far from Paul's Cross squatted a fat stone tower housing the four bells of St. Paul's, 'Jesus bells'—'the greatest I have ever heard', declares Stow.

Nearby, the Collegiate Church of St. Martin-le-Grand, chief sanctuary within the walls of London, was crowded with criminals and debtors and, sometimes, political refugees. North of Paul's on Newgate Street, the massive establishment of the Grey Friars contained a church 100 yards long, spacious cloisters, and a beautiful library, toward the building of which Richard Whittington had contributed £400. The library was 129 feet long and 31 feet broad, all panelled with wainscot; it offered readers twenty-eight desks and eight 'double setters' and was well stocked with books. Blackfriars, to the southwest of Paul's, had a hall so commodious that Parliaments and other assemblies were held there.

Mancini neglects to mention some of the greatest houses in the city, like Pountney's Inn and The Erber and Cold-Harbour, erected by merchants but now the London seats of lords. On Bishopsgate Street, Sir John Crosby, alderman, built Crosby's Place, whose roofs towered higher than those of any other dwelling in London; Richard, Duke of Gloucester, later occupied this handsome house and garden; and the great hall now stands in Chelsea to show the splendour of timber and stone in which 'The Clothing' of London housed themselves. Though the region east of St. Paul's might be called the aristocratic quarter, notable houses were scattered all over the city. In the same way, Candlewick Street belonged particularly to the drapers as western Cheapside to the goldsmiths, but Mancini notes that 'there are in the town many other populous quarters with numerous trades'.

An influential member of the gentry like Sir John Howard needed so much cloth for his household and himself that though he bought largely from Bulstrode of Candlewick Street, he dealt with drapers and mercers in several parts of London. He ran up large bills with John Porter, and to put his people in mourning for the death of his mother he purchased from Thomas Bernwey, also of Candlewick Street, ninety-six yards of black broadcloth and sixty yards of white frieze in one order. But Howard also bought fine crimson ingrain and green cloth from Gay of Fleet Street, paying £6 13s 4d in cash, in June, and giving an obligation to deliver the remaining £15 8s 6d at Michaelmas next coming. He patronized William Boylet, draper, in Thames Street and Robert Hardwick, draper, in Lombard Street. He sometimes ordered fine cloth from 'Leonard the tailor' in Southwark, who made it up into gowns for as little as 15d or 16d the gown, though the labour of lining a doublet might come to 2s or more. From Thomas Rowson, mercer, in Cheap, he purchased sarcenet; 'Lumpner the mercer' and Laurence Troyce sold him crimson velvet; but when he wanted to array himself for the Queen's coronation in 1465 and for the famous jousts at Smithfield in 1467 between the Bastard of Burgundy and Lord Scales, the Queen's brother, Howard went to Humfrey Gentile, an Italian draper who probably dwelt in Lombard Street. Here he bought black and red and crimson and green damask, black and crimson velvet, red and black satin, and six gorgeous yards of 'velvet on velvet pearled with gold', which cost some £50 a yard in modern money.

Though London was girdled by green fields, as Mancini reports, the city already thrust beyond its walls. To the east, Portsoken ward was a huddle of tenements and open spaces where weavers stretched their cloth on 'tenters', Bishopgate ward to the northeast, extended to the Priory of St. Mary Spital, a distance of some 600 yards. Moor-fields, to the north, offered marshy ground where young men shot at butts or played football. Then came the portions of Cripplegate and Aldersgate wards beyond the walls, not very thickly populated; and finally, to the northwest and west and southwest stretched the great ward of Farringdon Without, which included Smithfield and the Priory of St. Bartholomew and the numerous Inns of Chancery and Inns of Court and the shops of Fleet Street and the lovely grounds of the Temple running down to the river. Smithfield, at ordinary times, was a dusty, noisy stinking cattlemarket; but royal jousts were held in the square; and the Mayor and aldermen in full regalia came out during St. Bartholomew's fair to watch the wrestling.

Past Temple Bar ran the country highway of the Strand, London residences of the bishops lining the south side. Northward and westward from Charing Cross lay open fields. But turning to the south with the curve of the river, that rare Londoner who did not go by boat would soon arrive at Westminster gate, famous for its cluster of cook-shops and their aggressive owners. After a miserable experience in Westminster Hall, Lydgate's Kentish boy headed for London:

> Then to Westminster gate I went
> When the sun was at high prime.
> Cooks to me, they took good intent,
> Called me nearer, for to dine,
> And proffered me good bread, ale and wine.
> A fair cloth they began to spread—
> Ribs of beef, both fat and fine,
> But for lack of money I might not speed.

That industrious scribbler of verses and Clerk of the Privy Seal, Thomas Hoccleve, confessed how in his youth he emptied his purse in order to swagger it out as a gentleman—

> Where was a greater master eke than I
> Or better acquainted at Westminster Gate
> Among the taverners namely
> And cooks when I came early or late.
> I pinched not at them in mine agate
> [I never deigned to question the bill]
> But paid them as that they ask would
> Wherefore I was the welcomer aldgate [indeed].

On the river side of the courtyard at Westminster Palace, an arched gate led to a landing. The 'clochard' a massive stone tower about sixty feet high with a lead spire, housed three giant bells rung only for coronations, royal funerals, and triumphal occasions. 'Men fabled that their ringing soured all the drink in the town'. Near the entry to Westminster Hall stood the Clock House containing 'a cloche, which striketh every hour on a great bell, to be heard into the hall in sitting time of the courts or otherwise: for the same clock, in calm, will be heard into the city of London'. With the clock sounding the hours, and cooks at the gate crying their wares, 'Wretches hang that jury men may dine'; for Westminster Hall, the great edifice of William Rufus rebuilt in splendid style by Richard II, was thronged with suitors and witnesses and plaintiffs and defendants. The King's serjeants (attorneys) thundered in silken hoods to be answered by lawyers in their long gowns of 'ray' (striped) cloth. The Court of Common Pleas and the Court of King's Bench—with its marble seat for royalty, on which, at the beginning of his reign, Edward IV sat three days together to show that he meant to dispense justice— and the Court of Chancery, growing into great importance in this age, were all housed in Westminster Hall, from which stairs ascended into the courts of Star Chamber and the Exchequer. At the doors, Flemings hawked pins and girdles and fine felt hats and that handy invention, spectacles.

Across the river and outside the jurisdiction of London stretched the borough of Southwark. Impressed with its size, Mancini described it as 'a suburb remarkable for its streets and buildings, which, if it were surrounded by walls, might be called a second city'. Southwark offered Londoners a variety of entertainment: bear-baiting pits and cock-fighting rings and stews and bagnios which paid rent to the bailiffs of the Bishop of Winchester— prostitutes were once called the Bishop of Winchester's geese. The district also contained several churches and some mansions, including Sir John Fastolfe's, which was large enough for him to stuff it with old soldiers of the French wars when Jack Cade's thousands were marching up from Kent. There were notable inns too, 'The Tabard' made famous by Master, Geoffrey Chaucer, whose works were being enthusiastically read in this period, and 'The White Hart', which Jack Cade found grand enough to make his headquarters.

Mancini ends his description of the English capital with a flourish of praise: 'Did I intend to enlarge on the refinements of the inhabitants, the magnificence of the banquets, the ecclesiastical ceremonial, the adornment and opulence of the churches, I should embark on a larger work than I intended.'

In the Yorkist Age the decaying mediaeval city was re-edified into the final image of mediaeval splendour, but this civic pride, expressed in conspicuous consumption of wealth, pointed toward the worldly concerns of the future. Though a man of the four-teenth century would have found much in the London of Edward IV that was familiar, this was not the city of Edward III or Richard II. That city had been racked by the quarrels of factional politics; its liberties had from time to time been seized into the King's hands; much of its wealth and the greater part of its trade were still controlled by foreigners; and the parish churches and great religious foundations showed signs of wear. Under the Tudors, on the other hand, London would grow dirtier and more crowded and a deeper gulf would open between rich and poor. Stow lamented closely huddled tenements which obscured the lines of public buildings, the ugly hovels overrunning green fields with-out the walls. The burst of fanaticism and greed which ushered in the Reformation swept away glass, images, monuments of the parish churches. Miles Partridge, who broke up St. Paul's Jesus Bells and pulled down the Clochard, reportedly won these spoils playing dice with Henry VIII. The Priory of St. John of Jerusalem was demolished to provide stone for the Protector Somerset's house in the Strand.

In the earlier years of the fifteenth century Richard Whittington, thrice Mayor of London and the 'Sun of Marchandy' blazoned the theme of civic devotion which city magnates coming after him strove with splendid emulation to follow. He bequeathed money for Whittington College. He rebuilt churches and established conduits and 'bosses' of fresh water. That symbol of municipal power, Gildhall, begun in 1411, owed much to him: his money paved the hall with Purbeck marble, glazed windows in the hall and the mayor's court, edified the chapel and college and the fine library. After him, John Rainwell and William Wells and William Eastfield and Simon Eyre and Geoffrey Bullen, great-grandfather of the ill-fated Anne, and Edmund Shaa and Thomas Hill and many others left their coat of arms or merchant's mark or device punning upon their names on stone and glass and lead all over London as memorials of their civic generosity. They piped in fresh water for London's growing population and established schools and libraries and re-edified city gates and founded alms-houses and hospitals and rebuilt churches and gave away thousands of pounds to the poor and the sick, relieved prisoners and pro-vided dowries 'to poor maids' marriages'. In 1439, when the city was afflicted by a dearth of grain and prices shot beyond the reach of ordinary citizens, Stephen Browne, Mayor of London and grocer, sent into Prussia to buy grain on his own, and soon ships came sailing up the Thames to drive down prices and end the threat of famine.

London did not offer a show on Corpus Christi Day. The capital of the realm and King's Chamber had its own pageantry. With flapping banners and tapestries hung from windows and streets strewn with flowers and minstrels and trumpeters playing, London staged 'royal entries' and marked the coronation of kings and queens and provided a brilliant background for special occasions, as when, in 1467, the opening of Parliament coincided with a great joust between the Bastard of Burgundy and Lord Scales. Thousands thronged into the city for the excitements of Bartholo-mew Fair, where the Mayor, sheltered by a pavilion, presided over wrestling and shooting matches. Best of all the citizens loved the double festival of the Marching Watch, held on the Eves of St. John Baptist (June 23) and of St. Peter and Paul (June 28).

The three or four thousand citizens who formed the Marching Watch of St. John's Eve became the Standing Watch on the Eve of St. Peter and Paul. A store of provisions was laid in against the day; armour was burnished until it shone like glass. Early in the morning, women and children streamed out of London to plunder the surrounding countryside for flowers and green garlands. As evening approached, bonfires began to blaze. Tables, set up before the houses of 'the wealthier sort', were covered with meat and vessels of wine and many a pottle of ale which neighbours and passers-by were bidden to 'sit and be merry with'. Every man's door was shadowed with green birch, long fennel, St. John's wort, orpen, white lilies. Oil-burning glass lamps were set out on long standards. The Standing Watch lined the route of the march, aldermen wearing polished brigandines covered with velvet, ordinary citizens in jack and sallet.

Assembling in St. Paul's churchyard and down Ludgate Hill, the Marching Watch moved into Cheapside in ranks of armed men marshalled by gilds and led by the twelve great Livery Companies. The procession was lit by 700 cressets, iron baskets holding fires of coal and wood on long poles. Each cresset was borne by a poor man decked in a straw hat and painted badge, having beside him another poor man in like array with a bag of coals for a refuelling. Accompanied by trumpets and pipes and drums, the martial array swept between files of armed men, gild after gild gleaming in the flame of bonfires and cressets. Here came the 'Mayor's Watch', with the Mayor 'well mounted on horseback, the sword-bearer before him in fair armour well mounted also, (his) footmen and torch bearers about him, and two pages on great stirring horses following him'. Then appeared the Watches of the two sheriffs, only a little less grand.

As in the other municipalities of England, the richly harnessed citizens who dominated this parade constituted the mercantile oligarchy which governed the city. Of eighty-eight mayors during the century, the Mercers and Grocers and Drapers accounted for sixty-one; almost all the rest were Fishmongers, Goldsmiths or Skinners. Six other gilds contributed a few aldermen— the Tailors, Vintners, Ironmongers, Haberdashers, Salters, and Dyers. Such were the twelve great Livery Companies, established by royal charter, which dominated the other fifty gilds—more or less: there were always recombinations—and ruled the life of

London. The heart of the city government consisted of the Mayor, aldermen—one for each of the twenty-five wards—and the Common Council. The latter sounds a representative note but was in fact of small importance in the fifteenth century. Aldermen, who served for life, were nominated by the wards, four names being put forward, but the Mayor and his brethren could reject all four if they wished. Common Councillors were likewise nominated by the wards.

On October 13, the Common Council and the Masters and Wardens of the chief gilds assembled to choose two candidates for the mayoralty. The Mayor and aldermen then selected one of these men to be the new Mayor. In effect, the whole machinery of municipal elections was in the hands of 'The Clothing'.

During the reign of Edward IV the Mayor became Lord Mayor and aldermen began to be knighted in considerable numbers, 'to the great worship of the city'. The mayors of all towns jealously guarded their 'estate', but there was no eminence in municipal England like the dignity of the Lord Mayor of London. At Coronation banquets in Westminster Hall, the Mayor had the privilege of offering the King wine in a gold cup, presenting him at the same time with a gold ewer of water to temper the wine if His Highness pleased; after the King had drunk, the Mayor kept the cup and ewer 'for his fee'. The aldermen and certain substantial citizens attended upon the Butler of England at the banquet and were usually given places of honour. At court or in the great hall of a magnate of the realm, the Mayor of London sat with a Chief Justice of England and was outranked only by peers. How the city writhed in 1468 when the frivolous young Duke of Clarence, sitting on a commission of Oyer and Determiner to enquire into treasons, was given the opportunity of demeaning the Mayor. One day that worthy—Thomas Owlgrave, 'a lumpish man'—dozed off, and Clarence 'said openly in his derision "Speak softly, sirs, for the Mayor is asleep" '.

A story retailed in Tudor times about Sir Bartholomew Read, mayor in 1502, illustrates the high style in which the Mayor of London was expected to conduct himself. When Read, a goldsmith, held his mayoralty feast in Goldsmiths Hall—Gildhall had not yet been equipped with a kitchen—he invited the ambassador of France and several 'great estates of court', so that about one hundred persons sat down at three long tables to a feast of three courses. The first, of fifteen dishes, was served on vessels 'of new white silver'; the second, of twelve dishes, appeared on silver 'parcel gilt'; and the third, of ten dishes, came forth on silver 'all gilt'. As the guests ate their way through these courses, dishes were not removed to the kitchen but were placed 'within a park finely paled and cunningly dressed and garnished with all manner of sweet and goodly flowers in the midst of the hall. And after dinner the same meat was carried out at the gate, and immediately given to the poor, that were orderly placed in the street ready to receive of the same'.

At the conclusion of the banquet, an Italian jeweller produced 'a stone of great value, and said that he had offered the same to the Emperor, the French King and the King of England, but none of them would give the value thereof. The Mayor heard him and said: "Have ye offered it to our sovereign lord the King's Grace?" The stranger answered: "Yea". Then sayeth the mayor: "Think you the King's Grace refused it for want of treasure? Let me see it", said he and asked him what he valued it at. The stranger said a thousand marks [£666]. "And will that buy it?" sayeth the Mayor. "Yea", sayeth the stranger. Then the Mayor took the jewel and commanded one to bring him a spice mortar and a pestle and willed his officer to beat [the stone] to powder. And so he did. Then the Mayor called for a cup of wine, and put [the powder] in the cup and drank it off clean, and said to the stranger: "Speak honourably of the King of England, for thou hast now seen one of his poor subjects drink a thousand marks at a draft". And then commanded his money to be paid him'.

If this story seems pitched to a higher flight than truth could achieve, another example of the Mayor's pride is fully vouched for. In 1464, the King's serjeants-at-law held a dinner at Ely House, within the boundaries of the city, and invited the Mayor and aldermen of London and some lords of court, including the powerful and arrogant and learned John Tiptoft, Earl of Worcester. As the banquet was about to begin, the Earl was ceremoniously ushered to the seat of honour. Mayor Mathew Philip looked at his aldermen. Without a word, he abruptly left the hall, his brethren following him. They rode to the Mayor's house, where Philip nonchalantly spread before them a worthy feast. The serjeants, horrified at the awful lapse of which they had been guilty, hastily sent messengers to the mayor bearing 'divers sotelteys'—in an attempt to sweeten his temper—but when the messengers saw how lavishly the Mayor was entertaining at his own table, they retired in shame. Mathew Philip had vividly reminded everybody that, as a London chronicler notes, 'Within the jurisdiction of the city, the Mayor is supreme after the King'.

In 1481 Edward IV invited the Mayor and aldermen and certain of the most substantial citizens to a hunting party in Waltham Forest. Mayor Hariot enjoyed the King's favour because he 'was a merchant of wondrous adventures into many sundry lands by reason whereof the King had yearly of him notable sums of money for his customs, besides other pleasure that he had shown to the King before times'. When the Londoners reached the forest, they found a Robin Hood scene awaiting them: beneath great trees 'a pleasant lodge of green boughs had been erected for their dining place. And the King would not go to dinner till they were served. And they were well served and worshipful'; their meat was as beautifully cooked 'as if it had been dressed in a standing place'. Then red and white wine went round. After dinner the Londoners mounted their horses to hunt with the King and killed many deer. Nor did Edward neglect their wives: he sent the 'Mayoress' and the wives of the aldermen two harts and six butts and a tun of wine 'to make them merry with', and on this kingly fare the ladies feasted in Drapers Hall.

Despite passing perils and crises caused by the Wars of the Roses, the capital of England had never been so prosperous, so enterprising, so lovely.[1] 'London,' sang the Scot William Dunbar, enchanted by what he saw, 'thou art of Towns A *per se*!'

---

[1] That is, at the end of Edward IV's reign. London in the fourteenth century offered more spectacular examples, perhaps, of individual wealth but could not match the general prosperity of 1483.

Strong be thy wallis that about thee standis;
　Wise be the people that within thee dwellis;
Fresh be thy ryver with his lusty strandis;
　Blithe be thy churches, wele sownyge be thy bellis;
Riche be thy merchauntis in substaunce that excellis;
　Fair be their wives, right lovesom, white and small;
Clere be thy virgyns, lusty under kellis:
　London, thou art the flour of Cities all.

II

Other Important People

5

The King and the Royal Household

IN an age when the London ménage of the Earl of Warwick sometimes consumed six oxen for breakfast and when the King-maker spread before visiting Bohemian lords a feast of sixty courses, it behooved the King of England to surround himself with a household that expressed the uniqueness of his prerogative. Magnificence exemplified power. The Act of Resumption of Henry VII's first Parliament announced, 'Your honourable household must be kept and borne worshipfully and honourably, as it accordeth to the honour of your estate and your said realm, by the which your adversaries and enemies shall fall into the dread wherein heretofore they have been'.

Splendour not only bolstered royal authority but was an essential attribute of kingship itself, as Sir John Fortescue makes clear: 'It shall need that the King have such treasure as he may make new buildings when he will for his pleasure and magnificence; and as he may buy him rich clothes, rich stones, and other jewels and ornaments convenient to his estate royal. And often times he will buy rich hangings and other apparel for his houses and do other such noble and great costs as besitteth his royal majesty. For if a king did not so, nor might do, he lived then not like his estate, but rather in misery, and in more subjection than doth a private person.'

Feeble Henry VI and his rapacious courtiers fell far short of this kingly standard. As his government crumbled in the 1440's and 1450's, Henry's lords, battening on the royal lands and revenues, grew richer while Henry sank more hopelessly into debt. The King was carefully insulated from the public discontent stirred by

this state of affairs. Even clerks who preached before him had first
to submit their sermons to censorship.

It was a gloomy tatterdemalion court. Endowed with the
instincts of a monk, and with a clouding mind, Henry cared little
for show—at the sight of a low-necked gown he fled, crying
'Fy, fy, for shame!'—and he had no understanding of finances.
The establishment swarmed with impecunious hangers-on; at the
half dozen great religious festivals of the year, hundred of squires
and gentlemen hungrily thronged the court to live for several
days on the King's bounty. Meanwhile, serjeants and yeomen and
clerks of the royal household desperately petitioned Parliament
for wages long unpaid.

By 1449, the year before Jack Cade's rebellion, the King owed
£372,000; the expenses of his household amounted to the
enormous sum of £24,000—Edward IV spent about half that
much—whereas his basic revenues totalled only £5,000. A
correspondent of the Pastons reported from London on January 2,
1451, 'The King borroweth his expenses for Christmas'. During
the later 1450's, with Henry slipping in and out of madness and
his Queen, Margaret of Anjou, moving about the realm as she
began her duel to the death with the Duke of York, the royal
household as an institution of kingship virtually ceased to exist:
'The realm of England was out of all good governance,' a
chronicler summed up, 'for the king was simple and led by
covetous council and owed more than he was worth. His debts
increased daily but payment was there none; all the possessions and
lordships that pertained to the crown the King had given away.
And such impositions as were put to the people was spended in
vain, for he held no household nor maintained no wars.'

When Henry, in 1459, kept Easter at the Abbey of St. Albans, he
presented his best gown to the prior. His embarrassed treasurer had
to buy it back for fifty marks, much against the King's will,
because it was the only robe Henry owned that was presentable
for state occasions.

Thus the mediaeval tradition of the royal household withered.
Edward IV, ascending the throne in March, 1461, developed an
economical but splendid court, grounded on the precedents of

past households yet reaching towards a more sophisticated expression of kingship. He originated, in a sense, the mode of kingly living which, transmitted with embellishments by Henry VII, became the Renaissance taste and ostentation displayed by Henry VIII and Queen Elizabeth I.

When the handsome and merry and victorious young Edward of March rode into London with the mighty Warwick at the end of February, 1461, and the plundering hordes of Queen Margaret were forced to withdraw into the North, the happy Londoners sang, 'Let us walk in a new wineyard, and let us make us a gay garden in the month of March with this fair white rose and herb, the Earl of March' After assuming the Crown and then defeating the Lancastrians at Towton, this fair white rose and herb proceeded to make a gay garden which expressed his own enjoyment of the bright surfaces of life and also showed the realm that the House of York understood the proper style of kingship.

From the royal palaces the wintry gloom of Henry VI was banished, to be replaced by youthful laughter, love songs, the aroma of summer flowers. Chambers flashed with velvet and jewels and the new honorific badge of York, a collar of suns and roses which all members of the royal household of the rank of gentlemen and above were required to wear daily. When Edward and his court went hunting, tables heavy with roasted meats and sugared dainties were stretched in the shade of the trees, and silken tents grew like gargantuan flowers on the lawns. The King and his courtiers glided on the Thames in gilded barges, down to Greenwich or up to Shene (Richmond), jousted at Eltham, feasted at Westminster, made love by moonlight and torchlight, rose at dawn to hear Mass, broke their fast with a mess of meat and ale, and quickly took horse to be beforehand of the sun in their pursuit of royal disports.

The Duke of Milan's envoy, Count Dallugo, whirled from banquet to hunting party, was soon laid up with gout. Impressed and a little bewildered, he reported that the new King was chiefly inclined to pleasure. He soon inclined to it also and concentrated his diplomacy on securing some of the famous English dogs and horses for his master. Lord Hastings wrote complacently to the

court of France in 1463 that the Earl of Warwick had so
thoroughly trounced the Lancastrians and the Scots that the King
had no need to interrupt his pleasures of the chase. The citizens
of London threw open their gates to Edward in April of 1471,
Commynes suggests, because he owed money to goldsmiths,
drapers, vintners, victuallers, and was ardently championed by the
ladies of the capital—some of whom had probably received from
him favours never engrossed upon the patent rolls.

When Edward came to the throne at the age of nineteen, he
stood six feet four inches tall and was no less comely than gallant.
The Speaker of the Commons in his first Parliament was moved
to touch upon 'the beauty of personage that it hath pleased
almighty God to send you'. Commynes calls him 'a most handsome prince and very valiant . . . I don't remember ever having
seen a handsomer man than he was when Warwick drove him
from England'. Edward's manner was as winning as his appearance. Dominic Mancini, who knew the English court well,
reported that the King 'was of a gentle nature and cheerful
aspect: nevertheless should he assume an angry countenance
he could appear very terrible to beholders. He was easy of access
to his friends, and to others, even the least noticeable. Frequently
he called to his side complete strangers, when he thought that they
had come with the intention of addressing or beholding him more
closely. He was so genial in his greeting, that if he saw a new-
comer bewildered at his appearance and royal magnificence, he
would give him courage to speak by laying a kindly hand upon
his shoulder. To plaintiffs and to those who complained of injustice he lent a willing ear; charges against himself he contented
with an excuse if he did not remove the cause. He was more
favourable than other princes to foreigners who visited his realm
for trade or any other reason. He very seldom showed munificence
and then only in moderation.'

Like his predecessors, Edward was often called 'Your Grace',
a title he shared with dukes and archbishops; not until the Tudor
monarchs emphasized their power by ascending into a cloud of
awe did the King become, always, 'Your Majesty'.

This witty and amiable young King, exuberantly sensual,

fierce in battle as any of the fierce and valiant Plantagenet line and the first warrior of Europe (he fought some half a dozen major engagements and lost none), possessed a first-rate intelligence and the will to apply himself to building a strong monarchy. His optimism and his love of ease would sometimes lead him into serious trouble, but once roused, he donned the lion's skin—or the fox's—with invincible élan. Though, at the beginning of his reign, he seemed content to let his great mentor, Warwick the Kingmaker, guide the realm while he himself enjoyed the gay perquisites of kingship, he quietly set about creating a council of able men devoted to the royal interest; and within a few years he was blunting Warwick's authority and taking into his own hands —a little too sanguinely, a little too carelessly—the direction of affairs.

From the moment he ascended the throne he showed himself eager to dispense justice and to heal the wounds of civil discord. When his treasurer, the Earl of Essex, 'felt and moved' the King to favour John Paston in one of the Paston land disputes, Edward replied that 'he would be your good lord therein as he would be to the poorest man in England. He would hold with you in your right; and as for favour, he will not show favour more to one man than to another, not to any in England'.

Though Yorkist partisans grumbled, the King treated old enemies with kindness and worked to win their allegiance. After Henry Beaufort, Duke of Somerset, leader of the Lancastrians still stirring up trouble in the North, had surrendered Bamburgh Castle in December 1462, King Edward tried ardently to make the brave and unfortunate Duke his friend. He granted him a full pardon, gave him a command in Warwick's army, and then showed him high favour at court:

'The King made full much of him, in so much that he lodged with the King in his own bed many nights, and sometimes rode a-hunting behind the King, the King having about him not passing six horses at the most, and yet three were of the Duke's men of Somerset. Edward made a great joust at Westminster, that he [Somerset] should see some manner sport of chivalry after his great labour and heaviness. And with great instance the King made him to take harness upon him and he rode in the place, but he would never cope with no man and no man might not cope with him, till the King prayed him to be merry and sent him a token and then he ran full justly and merrily, and his helm was a sorry hat of straw.'

But such melancholy gestures[1] and all of King Edward's kindnesses, were not enough to reconcile the young Duke to the House of York. The King saw to it that Parliament restored Beaufort to his forfeited titles and estates, and made him several gifts of ready money. He even appointed the Duke and a band of the Duke's men as his special bodyguard. When Edward moved northward in the summer of 1463 and the men of Northampton beheld, with horror, their King guarded by Somerset and 200 of his followers— like 'a lamb among wolves'—they rose in wrath and fear, stormed the royal lodgings and would have slain Somerset before Edward's eyes, 'but the King with fair speech and grave difficulty saved his life for that time, and that was pity'. After Edward got Somerset safely away to Wales, he dispatched Somerset's men to garrison Newcastle, punctually paying their wages. The King also appreciated the loyal hearts, if not the violent tempers, of the citizens of Northampton: he 'full lovingly gave the commons a tun of wine that they should drink and make merry. Some fetched wine in basins, and some in cauldrons and some in bowls and some in pans and some in dishes'.

But the Duke could not endure his new Yorkist friends. In early December of 1463 he rode desperately for the North, having secretly written to his men in Newcastle to betray the town to him. He was almost caught in Durham, escaping 'in his shirt and

---

[1] Henry Beaufort's *tristesse* was doubtless genuine enough—Edward IV's father had slain his father, after all—but his display of it perhaps shows touches of the aristocratic melancholy now becoming fashionable on the Continent, for Beaufort had been an intimate friend of the Duke of Burgundy's son Charles. Olivier de la Marche the Burgundian chronicler and master of ceremonies, took for his motto, 'Tant a souffert la Marche'. Charles d'Orléans anticipated Hamlet in his plaint, 'Je suis celluy au cueur vestu de noir'. Even the much earthier Villon recorded, 'Je m'esjouys et n'ay plaisir aucun'. Lorenzo the Magnificent—well advanced in his teens before Charles d'Orléans died—shows the development of this attitude into zestful Renaissance gloom:

> Quant e bella giovinezza
> Che si fugge tuttavia!
> Chi vuol esser lieto, sia:
> Di doman non c'e certezza.

barefoot', and his Newcastle followers were forced to flee for their lives. He managed to join King Henry at Bamburgh Castle, which had again fallen to the Lancastrians. But in May of 1464 Warwick's brother John, Lord Montagu, defeated his forces at Hexham Field, and the axe of the headsman put an end to Henry Beaufort's violent story.

By this time Edward IV had married—with no ceremony but in a style of high romance. On May Day of 1464 he had ridden out from Stony Stratford with a handful of attendants as if to go hunting. Instead, he galloped to Grafton Regis, the manor of Richard Woodville, Lord Rivers, and there with only the formidable Lady Rivers and two gentlewomen as witnesses he wedded the eldest daughter of the house, Elizabeth, a beautiful widow with two small boys. A few hours later Edward returned jauntily to Stony Stratford, the first King since the conquest to marry one of his subjects. In after years lurid stories of the wooing circulated; Dominic Mancini heard that even when the impassioned Edward held a dagger at her throat, Elizabeth would not yield her honour, and in admiration of her virtue he had made her his consort.

For four months he nursed his secret, while Warwick the King-maker confidently drove forward his design of marrying his sovereign to the sister-in-law of Louis XI, Bona of Savoy. When finally the King disclosed the news at a meeting of the Great Council, he discovered that while his subjects enjoyed reading romances, they had no patience with a royal love-match. From the mighty Warwick to the merest London shopkeeper, the people of England outspokenly disdained a Queen who was only the daughter of a lord, and old Yorkists were angry that the King had chosen a woman whose father, eldest brother, and first husband had all done battle for the House of Lancaster.

Young Edward had undoubtedly married his Elizabeth 'pour sa beauté et par amourette', as a Burgundian chronicler reported, but he was also moved by shrewder considerations. Lord Rivers was a tough, handsome adventurer who had made his fortune by marrying the dowager Duchess of Bedford, Jacquetta of Luxembourg, and had sired almost a dozen sons and daughters. This ambitious Woodville clan, owing everything to the King, would be useful as a make-weight against the high-flying Nevilles; and if Lord Rivers and Anthony Woodville, Lord Scales—'men of very great valour', an Italian envoy found them—had once fought and suffered for Lancaster,[1] the marriage would demonstrate that Edward meant to bury old hates.

Yet, in the end, it turned out to be a fearful mistake, not only because it helped drive Warwick towards rebellion and saddled Edward with a swarm of hungry in-laws who did him little good, but also because Elizabeth Woodville was as ambitious, cold, and shallow as she was beautiful. In the King's later years she devoted herself to building a Woodville party, for Edward allowed her a large license in bestowing offices, perhaps as the price of her quietly accepting his liaison with Jane Shore;[2] and the court became a hothouse of intrigue and covert feuds. Jealous, greedy, fearful of the rancours she had stirred in the breast of the Duke of Clarence, she urged Edward on to execute his foolish brother George (1478); and thus she incurred the enmity of his loyal and able youngest brother Richard, Duke of Gloucester, who was, reports Mancini, 'so overcome with grief for his brother, that he could not dissimulate so well but that he was overheard to say that he would one day avenge his brother's death'. Considering that her son Edward might ascend the throne as a minor, she entirely surrounded him with Woodvilles and Woodville sup-

[1] That Lord Rivers became the King's father-in-law had its ironies, for Richard Woodville and his eldest son had years before felt the rough edge of the King's tongue, when Edward was only the seventeen-year-old Earl of March and lay at Calais in the winter of 1459-1460 with the Earl of Warwick and Warwick's father, the Earl of Salisbury, the three earls preparing to invade Lancastrian England (see *Epilogue*). In the early morning of January 7 a small detachment of Warwick's men swooped down on Sandwich, captured Henry VI's fleet, surprised in their beds Lord Rivers and his wife, laid hands on Sir Anthony Woodville as he came riding into town, and carried ships and captives triumphantly back to Calais. 'As for tidings,' one of the Pastons wrote soon afterwards, 'my Lord Rivers was brought to Calais and before the Lords with eight score torches, and there my Lord of Salisbury rated him, calling him knave's son, that he should be so rude to call him and these other lords traitors, for they shall be found the King's true liegemen when he should be found a traitor, etc. And my Lord of Warwick rated him and said his father was but a squire and brought up with King Henry V, and since then himself made by marriage, and also made Lord, and that it was not his part to have such language of lords, being of the King's blood. And my Lord of March rated him in like wise.'

[2] Mancini, a good witness, declares that the Queen 'attracted to her party many strangers and introduced them to court, so that they alone should manage the public and private business of the Crown . . . give or sell offices, and finally rule the very King himself'.

porters.[1] The moment Edward IV died, April 9, 1483, she launched a conspiracy to deprive Richard of Gloucester of the office of Protector of England during Edward V's minority and thus herself set in motion the train of events that led to Richard's usurpation of the throne.

Even before she had been five years a Queen, Elizabeth was credited—in a popular report that is backed, in its essentials, by substantial evidence[2]—with having procured the death of an earl because he had pricked her vanity. About the time of her coronation, in May of 1465, the Earl of Desmond, Deputy Lieutenant of Ireland, had come to England in order to clear himself of some charges brought against him and to pay homage to the King. Desmond was a man after Edward's own heart: cultivated, brave, convivial. One day when they were out hunting, Edward, in his direct and merry way, inquired of Desmond what he thought of the royal marriage. Desmond replied frankly: he esteemed the Queen's beauty and virtues but he thought the King would have done better to marry a Princess who would have secured him a foreign alliance. Edward accepted this answer in the spirit in which he had asked the question and sent Desmond back to Ireland loaded with presents. A little later, in casual jest, he reported the Earl's words to Elizabeth—being not yet well schooled in his Queen's character. Coldly furious, she dissembled her feelings and grimly awaited an opportunity to settle accounts with Desmond.

When, in 1467, the Earl of Worcester became Deputy Lieutenant of Ireland, he agreed to give the Queen her revenge. Desmond was indicted on a flimsy charge, and when he bravely came in to face his accusers, he was cast into prison and condemned to be beheaded. Shortly after he suffered on the block, two small sons of his were cruelly murdered. It is said that the Queen stole the King's signet to seal the death warrant; there is evidence that the King was not pleased with the news of Desmond's execution. By this time, probably, Edward was finding more amiable companions for his bed.

---

[1] Sir Thomas More: 'Everyone as he was nearest of kin unto the Queen, so was planted next about the Prince . . . whereby her blood might of youth [i.e. from his childhood] be rooted in the Prince's favour.'

[2] See Kendall, *Richard the Third*, p. 444, note 8 of Chap. VIII.

However mean her nature, Queen Elizabeth undoubtedly contributed to the developing sophistication of King Edward's household. Since so many people grudged her marriage because she was a mere lord's daughter, the Woodvilles were eager to remind the realm that, on her mother's side, she was the niece of the Count of St. Pol, one of the powers of Europe and an ornament of the court of Burgundy. That court was then the most magnificent in the western world, and the Queen and her kin set about creating in the royal household a tone of Burgundian elegance, a task made easier by the fact that close economic and political ties already existed between England and the dominions of Duke Philip the Good.

King Edward invited to his Queen's coronation her younger uncle, Jacques de Luxembourg, Seigneur de Richebourg; and 'Lord Jakes', as the Londoners dubbed him with cheerful irreverence (Jakes — privy), and his train of Burgundian knights lent their glittering presences to the jousts that inevitably concluded the coronation ceremonies.

In the spring of 1466 a group of visiting Bohemians headed by the Lord of Rozmital were deeply impressed by the decorum of the English Court. The King lodged them handsomely, put a herald and a royal councillor at their service, and showed the amplitude of his power with a banquet offering a choice of fifty courses—'as is their custom', recorded one of the party.

The ceremony which most struck the visitors, however, was the 'churching' of Queen Elizabeth, who had given birth to her first child, Elizabeth, in February. A procession of ecclesiastics, peers and peeresses, minstrels, heralds, conveyed the Queen to the service in the Abbey and from the Abbey to a banquet at Westminster Palace. The Lord of Rozmital dined alone at the King's table with 'the King's mightiest Earl'—undoubtedly Warwick— for etiquette forbade the King himself to be present. In the course of the dinner, royal gifts were distributed to the musicians and heralds and 'all who had been rewarded ran around the table shouting out what the King had given them'.

The guests filled four large chambers, through which Warwick conducted the Lord of Rozmital in order that he might behold the haughty and beautiful Queen of England. In a room bedecked with tapestries Elizabeth sat alone at table on a golden chair, attended by her mother and Edward's sister Margaret, who were required to kneel when the Queen addressed them. Not until the first course had been served were they permitted to sit, but the ladies in waiting remained kneeling for the full three hours that the banquet lasted, the Queen not deigning to utter a word to anyone. When the tables had been removed for merrymaking, the Queen's mother resumed her kneeling posture, and the Princess Margaret, even while dancing, was careful to make many curtsies to Her Highness.

Queen Elizabeth's cultivated brother Anthony, Lord Scales (later Earl Rivers), imitating the flamboyant chivalry of Duke Philip of Burgundy, had already become the premier knight of English tournaments. On an April morning in 1465 Lord Scales was holding converse with the Queen, kneeling before her with his bonnet sitting on the floor beside him. Suddenly the ladies of the court surrounded him; one of them tied round his shapely thigh a collar of gold and pearls with 'a noble flower of souvenance enamelled and in manner of an emprise' and dropped into his bonnet a little roll of parchment bound with gold thread. Thus Anthony Woodville learned that he was to perform a two-day joust with some nobleman 'of four lineages and without reproach'. Nucelles Pursuivant carried this challenge to Philip the Good's son Anthony, Bastard of Burgundy, one of the great jousters of the age, who, in the presence of his father and an array of courtiers, duly touched the flower of souvenance by way of accepting the emprise. Nucelles did well for himself, for the Bastard gave him 'the rich gown furred with sable' that he wore during the ceremony of touching the emprise and also a 'doublet of black velvet garnished with arming points, and the slits of the doublet sleeves clasped with clasps of gold'.

Two years after, in the late spring of 1467, the Bastard of Burgundy fulfilled his mission. The moment the news arrived that he was coming, the sheriffs of London were ordered to prepare lists in West Smithfield, ninety yards long and eighty yards wide; under their supervision workmen set about smoothing the ground with loads of gravel and building two grandstands, one for the

King and court, a smaller one for the Mayor and chief citizens. On May 29 the Bastard of Burgundy and his party sailed up the Thames in 'four carvels of forestage' fluttering with pennants and banners and tapestries. Next morning John Tiptoft, Earl of Worcester, Constable of England and therefore arbiter of chivalry, escorted the Bastard to the palace of the Bishop of Salisbury in Fleet Street, which was 'richly apparelled with arras and hanged with beds of cloth of gold'; the Bishop also put his country house in Chelsea at the Bastard's disposal so that he might 'essay his harness secretly'.

On Thursday, June 11, began what was to be the most famous English joust of the century. Peers and Knights of the Shire, in London to attend Parliament, swelled the crowd of citizens making their way to Smithfield. Olivier de La Marche, who had accompanied the Bastard of Burgundy, stored up all the details of the scene. He approved of the royal stage, 'very spacious and made in such a manner that there was an ascent by steps to the upper part where the King sat. He was clothed in purple, having the Garter on his thigh, and a thick staff in his hand; and truly he seemed a person well worthy to be King, for he was a tall, handsome Prince, kingly in manner. An earl held the sword of state before him, a little on one side; and around his throne were grouped twenty or twenty-five councillors, all with white hair; and they resembled senators set there together to counsel their master'. Below the King in massed ranks sat knights, esquires, and archers of the Crown.

Soon after Edward had assumed his state, the Mayor of London appeared at the head of a procession of aldermen and justices. The Mayor had his sword borne before him, but when he and his fellows kneeled before the King, the Mayor's sword-bearer held the point downwards in token of submission. Lord Scales now rode into the field, preceded by the Duke of Clarence and the Earl of Arundel bearing two helmets and followed by other lords carrying spears and swords. After doing reverence to the King, Scales entered his pavilion to arm himself. The Bastard of Burgundy then made his appearance; he preferred to don his armour in the open.

Finally the trumpets sounded, the two knights on their destriers thundered down the lists, lances couched. Neither scored a hit. Discarding much of their armour, they then charged at each other brandishing swords, but the Bastard's horse, somehow ramming its head into Scales' saddle, fell to the ground atop its rider. After the Bastard had been extricated and Scales had proved that he used no illegal armour on his saddle, King Edward asked the shaken Burgundian if he wished another mount. The Bastard replied that 'it was no season', and went to his chambers. Grimly he told Olivier de La Marche, 'Doubt not: he has fought a beast today, and tomorrow he shall fight a man'.

Next day they were to joust on foot with spears, then axes, but 'the King beholding the casting spears right jeopardous and right perilous, said, in as much as it was but an act of pleasaunce he would not have none such mischievous weapons used before him'. So Scales and the Bastard laid on with their axes, Scales striking with the head and his adversary with the small end of the blade. Fiercely they hacked at each other, axes clanging on armour, until the combat became so violent that 'the King cast his staff, and with a high voice, cried "Whoo!" Notwithstanding, in the departing there were given two or three great strokes', but at the King's command the heated warriors took each other by the hand and promised 'to love together as brothers in arms'. Scales won the admiration of the spectators by daring to fight with his visor up, and English versions of the combat suggest that the King intervened when his brother-in-law was getting the better of the Bastard; La Marche, on the other hand, asserted that he inspected Scale's armour and found great gashes in it from the under point of the Bastard's axe.

By the time Scales and the Bastard met in the lists (1467), King Edward, though still spending goodly sums, had already begun his conquest of debt. Determined to avoid the discontents which Henry VI's wasteful government had excited, he made a promise to Parliament in his frank, engaging manner: 'John Say [Speaker of the Commons], and ye, sirs, come to this my Court of Parliament for the commons of this my land, the cause why I have called and summoned this my present Parliament is that I proposes to live upon my own and not to charge my subjects but in great need and urgent causes concerning more the weal of themself, and also the defence of them and of this my realm, rather than my own pleasure.' But Edward's struggle with Warwick interrupted his design of establishing a solvent monarchy.

The short-lived regime of the Kingmaker (October, 1470— March, 1471) provided a public illustration of the importance of regal magnificence. As soon as Warwick entered London in October of 1470, King Henry was led from the Tower, robed in a long gown of blue velvet, and installed in the Palace of the Bishop of London. Six months later, as King Edward, having suddenly landed in Yorkshire, was driving south towards the capital, the Kingmaker's brother George, Archbishop of York, attempted to hearten the Londoners by parading Henry VI about the streets. But he was escorted by only a thin shell of armed men, he slumped on his horse lack-lustre of eye, and worst of all, he was clad in the same gown he had been wearing when he was removed from the Tower. His progress was 'more liker a play than a showing of a prince to win men's hearts, for by this mean he lost many and won none or right few, and ever he was showed in a long blue gown of velvet as though he had no more to change with'.

During the fugitive Edward's enforced sojourn in the Low Countries, he had plenty of time to observe the style of the Burgundian court. He spent several days with Duke Charles himself, and for a month he lived at Bruges in the palace of the Seigneur de la Gruthuyse, Governor of Holland. Charles of Burgundy, as cultured as he was violent of temper, continued the multi-faceted ceremonial that had made his father's household the most famous in Europe. The greatness of 'The Grand Duke of the West' was expressed in a rhetoric of furs and velvets and tapestries and jewels, in fantastic tournaments where knights wore golden chains to symbolize their bondage to love, in the creation of Flemish illuminators and bookbinders and weavers and tailors, in the music of the most brilliant composers then in Europe, in paintings of Memling and Van Der Goes and Van Eyck, in noble libraries and in bizarre palaces where unwary visitors had dust blown in their eyes or were dumped by a collapsing bridge into a pond, and in a severe, minutely regulated decorum that, passing to the court of Spain in the sixteenth century, reached its final efflorescence at the Versailles of Louis XIV.

When a relative of the Duke of Brittany visited the wife of the Count of Charolais (Charles, then Philip's heir), it required a council of state to decide that the visitor must make two obeisances, upon which the Countess might advance three steps. A dinner which Charolais gave for Margaret of Anjou at Bruges provoked an intricate display of the dialectic of etiquette. Before the meal, the refugee Queen invited the Count to wash with her. 'Knowing his duty and following in the footsteps of his father [as a pattern of courtesy],' he politely refused despite reiterated invitations. When water was brought for Margaret's young Prince, the contest in manners started afresh. The Count would have no part of washing with the son of a king, though driven from his kingdom, while Margaret and Prince Edward averred that such miserable persons as they did not deserve the honour which Charles insisted on paying them. Protestations became heated while the dinner cooled, but Charolais' inverted pride was inflexible. That evening the court at Bruges hummed with intense discussions of the issue. Messengers sped to Duke Philip at Hesdin with news of this weighty affair of protocol. A great debate ensued between Philippe Pot and Philippe de Croy. Asked for his opinion by the Duke himself, the chronicler Chastellain judiciously agreed with Pot that, far from being 'over nice', as Croy maintained, the Count of Charolais had properly upheld the decorum of the Court of Burgundy.

After King Edward regained his throne in the spring of 1471, and became the unchallenged master of his realm, he set about in good earnest to clear off his debts, enlarge his revenue, and reorganize his household.

From the first years of his reign, the King had enthusiastically embarked on a career in trade, exporting thousands of broadcloths and sacks of wool. He conducted his operations through 'alien factors', probably to avoid playing favourites among his native merchants; and his ventures soon became so extensive that his chief factors had to employ sub-factors to help handle the King's flourishing business. By 1470, though now engaged in his struggle with Warwick, Edward had become an importer as well. In February of that year, at the port of London alone, twenty-five ships arrived or departed with royal cargoes; the imports included figs, raisins, oil, sugar, oranges, hops, copper, wainscots, fans, soap, spectacles, and one popinjay. The following June an Italian carrack, docking at Sandwich, unloaded 390 bales of woad and 27 butts of sweet wine consigned by 'John de Nigro, factor of Alan Mounton, factor of the king', and 613 bales of woad, 32 barrels of alum, 7 bales of wax, 23 bales of 'paper scribable', 14 sets of harness, white wine, wormseed, and other products shipped by Thomas de Pounte, 'factor of Alan Mounton, factor of the King'.

In the last half of his reign Edward expanded his operations: he began to export quantities of tin and lead; he purchased a number of ships—to strengthen the royal navy as well as to turn a profit—and he encouraged native ship-building by allowing a new vessel to make its first voyage free of customs duties and subsidies. The Croyland chronicler, who knew him well,[1] observes that he filled his treasury 'out of his own substance and by the exercise of his own energies . . . like a private individual living by trade'.

King Edward likewise overhauled the leaky Customs service, appointing 'men of remarkable shrewdness'; he developed a system of auditors and surveyors to increase the yield of the royal domain; he scrutinized land titles in order to exact fines from those who had illegally seized property; and he reorganized the royal administration in more ways 'that can possibly be conceived by a man who is inexperienced in such matters'. The Truce of Picquigny (1475) brought him an annual subsidy[2] of £10,000 from Louis XI.

Edward possessed a remarkable talent for managing people as

---

[1] The material for this portion of the *Chronicle* was probably furnished by John Russell, Bishop of Lincoln, one of Edward's best diplomats.
[2] 'Tribute,' said the English; Louis called it a pension.

well as finances. Forced loans had long been unpopular; besides, they had to be repaid. Gifts offered a richer source of revenue, and who could better charm purses than the genial King of England? The projected expedition to France (of 1475) gave him a patriotic theme. He began by calling before him individually his lords spiritual and temporal and gently inquiring what they might be willing to grant him toward the war. They readily promised goodly sums, perhaps not quite aware what they were doing. Edward then summoned the Mayor and aldermen of London and applied the same treatment. It worked so well that the King sent for all the wealthier citizens of the capital, women as well as men, and again reaped a good harvest. According to reports, one widowed lady, 'much abounding in substance and no less grown in years', offered £20 but upon receiving a kiss from the handsomest man in Europe promptly doubled the gift.

Edward then took to the road. The kingdom was small, the King had a marvellous memory for names and faces and the power they represented.[1] He knew all his lords spiritual and temporal, fewer than one hundred men; he knew the principal citizens of London and of the larger provincial towns; he knew most of the gentry in each county. The close watch he kept upon affairs and his wide acquaintance with his subjects are revealed in a mishap that befell the Cely family. One autumn afternoon in 1481, when old Richard Cely and his son Richard were hunting with their greyhounds, a hart from a royal forest in Essex was driven across the Thames and killed at Dartford. Young Richard wrote anxiously to his brother George that on the information of a man named Brandon they were indicted for the slaying of the hart 'the which we never saw nor knew of'—which, indeed, had been killed, Richard declared, by Brandon or his men. Young Richard betook himself to Sir Thomas Mongomery, Steward of the Forest of Essex. After protesting his innocence, he presented Sir Thomas with 100s, 'the value of a pipe of wine', and deposited

[1] 'Men of every rank wondered that [King Edward] a man so fond of boon companionship . . . and sensual enjoyments, should have had a memory so retentive that the names and estates used to recur to him, just as though he had been in the habit of seeing them daily, of nearly all the persons dispersed throughout the counties of this kingdom; and this, even if in the districts in which they lived they held the rank only of a private gentleman.'—*Croyland Chronicle*, p. 484.

3s 4d in the palm of one of Sir Thomas's gentlemen; and thus Mongomery became their 'special good master in this matter'. Now the Celys, though Merchants of the Staple and gentlemen landowners in Essex, held-no offices in London and were not among the wealthiest merchants of the capital. Yet Richard Cely had hurried to Sir Thomas Mongomery, not because he was so much troubled by the indictment itself but in order 'to have us out of the book ever it be showed the King'.

An Italian visitor to England in the spring of 1475 has left an account of the way in which Edward 'plucked out the feathers of his magpies without making them cry out'. Journeying from place to place, the King called before him all those worth £40 or more and explained that in order to invade France he must have money. 'Everyone seemed to give willingly. I have frequently seen our neighbours here who were summoned before the king, and when they went they looked as if they were going to the gallows; when they returned they were joyful, saying that they had spoken to the King and that he had spoken to them so benignly that they did not regret the money they had paid. From what I have heard, the King adopted this method: when anyone went before him, he gave him a welcome as if he had known him always. After some time he asked him what he could pay of his free will toward this expedition. If the man offered something proper, he [the King] had his notary ready, who took down the name and the amount. If the King thought otherwise, he told him, "Such a one, who is poorer than you, has paid so much; you, who are richer, can easily pay more"; and thus by fair words he brought him up to the mark. And in this way it is argued that he has extracted a very large amount of money.'

But King Edward meant to cut down wasteful expenditure as well as to increase his income. After he had reconquered his kingdom, in the spring of 1471, he turned his mind to creating a royal household which if it did not rival the extravagant court of Burgundy, might none the less express, economically, the princely tastes of the House of York. When Louis de la Gruthuyse, with whom the fugitive Edward had dwelt at Bruges, arrived in September, 1472, to be suitably rewarded for his hospitality by his erstwhile guest, the entertainment devised for the Burgundian lord, minutely described by Bluemantle Pursuivant, reveals the heightened manners of the English court.

As soon as Gruthuyse arrived at Windsor, the Lord Chamberlain, Hastings, conducted him to greet the King and Queen and then escorted him to the three chambers 'richly hanged with cloths of arras and beds of estate' which had been prepared for his sojourn. After Gruthuyse had supped with Lord Hastings, they repaired again to the king, who led them to the queen's principal chamber. A tableau of royal domesticity was unfolded for the visitor's benefit. Queen Elizabeth sat with her ladies playing various bowling games with pins of ivory. The minstrels struck up and there was dancing, the King treading a measure with little Elizabeth, his eldest daughter. Bluemantle does not bother to say so, but at the end of the evening the King and Gruthuyse undoubtedly shared a 'void', a parting cup of ypocras and wafers and spices. The next morning Gruthuyse heard the Mass of Our Lady sung by the choristers and children of the royal chapel. The King presented his guest with a covered cup of gold garnished with precious stones including a piece of unicorn's horn some seven inches long. Edward and Gruthuyse then spent the day hunting, and Gruthuyse accumulated more treasures: the half dozen bucks they had coursed with greyhounds and buckhounds, the King's own horse—'a fair hobby'—and a cross bow encased in velvet of the King's colours stamped with the royal arms and badges. Though it was almost night by the time they gave over the chase, Edward insisted on showing his visitor the royal gardens and 'vineyard of pleasure'.

In the evening Queen Elizabeth entertained with a banquet in her chambers. The Lord Gruthuyse and his son dined at the royal board; a lower table exhibited 'a great view of ladies, all on one side', and at a table in the outer chamber the Queen's gentlewomen sat in a row facing Gruthuyse's principal servants. After supper the boards were removed, the minstrels sounded a tune, and there was dancing again.

About nine o'clock the King and Queen and a train of courtiers accompanied Gruthuyse to three 'chambers of pleasaunce all hanged with white silk and linen cloth and all the floors covered with carpets'. The first chamber displayed a bed 'of as good down as could be got', draped with cloth of gold furred with ermine and canopied in cloth of gold, the side curtains being of white sarcenet. The second chamber, decorated all in white, contained a feather-bedded couch 'hanged with a tent knit like a net' and a cupboard. In the third chamber baths stood ready 'covered with tents of white cloth'. The King and Queen left their guest to the ministrations of the Lord Chamberlain. Hastings presided over the disrobing of Gruthuyse, disrobed himself, and both men entered the baths. When they had soaked in the warm water, they partook of green ginger, diverse syrups, comfits and ypocras.

A few days later, King Edward led Gruthuyse before an assembly of the three estates of Parliament and created him Earl of Winchester. Then followed a banquet, during which poor Garter King of Arms was deprived of the pleasure of crying 'Largesse!' when Gruthuyse distributed generous tips, because he had 'an impediment in his tongue'. There had been of course a procession, to the Abbey: for in this age the Crown in person as well as the Crown jewels must be exhibited. Few kings could grace a procession like the towering Edward of York clad in a gown of cloth of gold lined with red satin. When he left Bruges early in 1471 to sail for the reconquest of his realm, he planned to go by barge to the nearby town of Damme; but on learning that the good people of the city had been hoping for a sight of his imposing presence, he cheerfully walked to Damme to give his hosts pleasure.

About the time that Gruthuyse came to England, King Edward was setting in motion the reorganization of his household. Ordinances of previous kings were searched for precedents; Edward's officers proposed ways of increasing the efficiency of their administration; and finally a council of lords spiritual and temporal that included the Dukes of Clarence and Gloucester as well as 'the wise and discreet judges and other sad, advised, and well learned men of England' contributed their experience to the undertaking. As a result of these deliberations—keyed to the theme, 'The King will have his goods dispended but not wasted'—an elaborate set of regulations was drawn up, the famous *Black Book of the House-hold of Edward IV*. This ordinance established the numbers and grades of attendants, their duties, their allowances of food and fuel and light. Chief emphasis fell upon the 'below-stairs' machinery to enforce allowances and control expenditure in 'this honourable household and lantern of England'.

The refreshments for the King at All-Night—one loaf of bread, half a gallon of wine—when Squires for the Body undressed him as he talked with his familiars, and truckle-beds were pulled out for these Squires to sleep on; the duties of the Serjeant of Con-fectionery; the number of candles nightly allowed the Serjeant-usher of the Countinghouse; where the Yeoman of the Laundrey ate; how the Serjeant of the Ewery and Nappery was to stable his horses; the servants that a duke 'in this court sitting in the King's Chamber shall have eating in the hall'—every cost and motion of the household was regulated. The minuteness of specification is like an heroic spell to banish waste and inefficiency and forever freeze the court of Edward IV into a magnificent, but economical, decorum compounded of a thousand measured attitudes.

At the heart of the royal court stood the King's Chamber, swathed in the service, honorific and menial, of more than 400 persons. Physically the chamber consisted of three apartments: the outer or audience chamber, where King Edward received ambassadors and dined in state; the inner or privy chamber, where he took counsel with advisers or enjoyed a game of cards, and the bed chamber to which he might retire for still more privacy. The Lord Chamberlain, Edward's favourite, William Lord Hastings, presided over this establishment, 'Chief Head of rulers in the King's chamber'. The hierarchy of stately attendance numbered Knights for the Body, alternating eight week tours of duty, and the more numerous King's Knights; Squires for the Body, usually four; Squires for the Household, twenty of whom were always waiting 'upon the King's person in riding and going at all times and to help serve his table from the surveying board'. These Squires were 'accustomed winter and summer in afternoons and in evenings, to draw to lords' chambers within court, there to keep honest company after their cunning, in talking of chronicles of kings and of other policies, or in piping or harping, singing, to help occupy the court and accompany strangers'.

Next in importance after the Knights and Squires came four Gentlemen Ushers, learned in 'all the customs and ceremonies used about the king', who enforced the protocol of the royal chamber and supervised the Yeoman of the Crown—'most seemly persons, cleanly and strongest archers, bold men'—and the slightly less honourable Yeomen of the Chamber, whose duty it was 'to set boards, hold torches, watch the King, go messages'. At the bottom of the heap ten Grooms of the Chamber and four pages tended the fires and made the beds and did the cleaning, the pages being directed to see that dogs did not dirty the rooms.

At his board in the Chamber, Edward was served by a 'Sewer for the King', who was expected to be 'full cunning' in the elaborate ceremonial of presenting dishes and who was required to talk 'with the master cook of the King's diets and appetites'; but before the sewer bore dishes to the table, they had to be inspected by the 'Surveyor for the King'. At Edward's side when he ate stood a Doctor of Physic 'counselling or answering to the King's grace which diet is best'.

A master surgeon was on hand too, but he was usually relegated to the hall. To him were delivered the old cloths and towels of the nappery, out of which he made 'plasters for the sick officers of the court'. The King's barber was to be treated 'after that he standeth in degree, gentlemen, yeoman, or groom'. When he shaved the King, a Knight or Squire for the Body was required to be present, whether to add dignity to the occasion or to keep a careful eye upon the razor, the *Black Book* does not say. 'This barber shall have every Saturday at night, if it please the King to cleanse his head, legs, or feet, and for his shaving, two loaves, one pitcher of wine.' Thirteen minstrels were ordained to make music for court ceremonies and to announce entries and departures of the King by 'blowings and pipings'; they played trumpets, shawms, and small pipes, 'and some are string men coming to this court at five feasts of the year'. The royal chapel, famous all over Europe for the beauty of its singing, was staffed with a Dean, twenty-six clerks and chaplains—'clean voiced, eloquent in reading, sufficient in organ-playing'—and eight Children of the Chapel, who probably enjoyed the services, along with the henchmen and royal wards, of the 'Master of Grammar'.

The Black Book also lays down the conditions under which lords were to be entertained at court, the number of attendants they might bring with them and the allowance of food and light and fuel they were permitted. These attendants, together with the servants of the chief functionaries below the rank of Squire of the Body, ate in the hall, a swarm of men which included 'strangers' whom the marshal considered important enough to receive the King's hospitality.

To supply and maintain and keep the accounts of this 'Household of Regal Magnificence' a 'Domus Providencie' or Providing Household worked busily behind the scenes. The Steward, with his white wand of office, the Treasurer of the Household, 'the second estate next the Steward', and the Comptroller, sitting 'at the board of doom [judgement] within the household, that is, at the green cloth in the countinghouse', ruled the invisible world that propped the royal show. The principal duties of the countinghouse fell upon the Cofferer, the two Clerks of the Green Cloth, and the Clerk of Comptrolment, who had in their charge the Check-roll, the master list of those entitled to wages and allowances of food and fuel in the household. John Paston learned, from his brother Clement, that his son John, trying to make his way 'in the King's house' in the summer of 1461, was unfortunately 'not taken as none of that house; for the cooks be not charged to serve him, nor the sewer to give him no dish, for the sewers will not take no men no dishes till they be commanded by the comptroller'.

The clerks of the Countinghouse received a daily 'brevement' or accounting from the multiplicity of offices which fed or provisioned the household—the bakehouse, the pantry, the buttery of ale, pitcher-house and cup-house, Great Spicery, acatry or meat purchasing, and a dozen others.

The Black Book estimated the cost of maintaining the royal household at £13,000 a year, a sum a little greater than that which the King actually expended towards the end of his life. Though contemporaries regarded his household as becomingly splendid, Edward spent less money on it than either Henry VI or Henry VII.

The court of Edward IV was graced by taste and learning as well as more obvious grandeurs. In the earliest letter of King Edward that has survived, written when he was twelve, he and his elder brother Edmund (killed at Wakefield, 1460) reported to their father that, 'and where ye command us by your said letters to attend specially to our learning in our young age that should cause us to grow to honour and worship in our old age, please it your highness to wit that we have attended our learning since we came hither, and shall hereafter'. Edward was literate in Latin. Letters he wrote in French are extant, and in the famous interview with Louis XI on the bridge at Picquiny in 1475, Edward and his 'adversary of France' conversed alone for some time. Warwick the Kingmaker too spoke and wrote French easily as did Edward's closest friend, the Lord Chamberlain Hastings, and other nobles. After Edward returned from his enforced residence in the Low Countries, where he had seen the library of the Seigneur de la Gruthuyse, second only to the ducal library which was one of the wonders of Europe, he began to enlarge his collection of books; scribes and illuminators of Bruges were set to work to produce beautiful manuscripts, more than a score of which are preserved in the British Museum.

The wardrobe accounts of 1480 include payments for the binding of six of these folios in velvet and blue and black silk, with laces and tassels of silk, buttons of blue silk and gold and copper, and gilt clasps decorated with roses and the royal arms. When the King went down to Eltham to hunt, a number of these tomes, packed in 'coffins of fir' were sent along. Edward's library contained histories—Froissart's works and the writing of Josephus and Titus Livius as well as Waurin's and Hardyng's and Capgrave's chronicles which were dedicated to him—French translations of Boccaccio's *Decameron* and *De Casibus* and St. Augustine's *De Civitate Dei* and conventional religious tracts like *La Forteresse de Foi*. A Yeoman of the Crown acted as keeper of the King's books, and when Edward took to the road, a place was set aside in one of the carts carrying household stuff for the transport of such volumes as it pleased the King to take with him.

The education of the King's elder son and heir, Edward, elaborately prescribed in a set of ordinances issued for the instruction of his tutors, foreshadows the emphasis which the Tudor Age was to place upon the learning of its princes. Edward began his formal schooling at the age of three when he was sent to dwell at Ludlow Castle as nominal head of the Council in the Marches of Wales. He was given an impressive household, his chief officers being John Alcock, Bishop of Rochester, president of the council and principal teacher of the Prince; the accomplished Anthony Woodville, Earl Rivers, his governor; and Lord Richard Grey (the Queen's younger son by her first marriage), his councillor.

'The Prince was to arise every morning "at a convenient hour, according to his age", hear matins in his chamber, go, as soon as he was dressed, to his chapel or closet to attend mass, after mass eat his breakfast, between breakfast and dinner give his time to "such virtuous learning as his age shall suffer to receive", during dinner listen to the reading of "such noble stories as behooveth to a prince to understand and know", and after dinner return again to his learning. Later in the day he was to be given instruction in "such convenient disports and exercises as behooveth his estate to have experience in", then he was to go to evensong, and after evensong he was to eat his supper. Only when supper was over was the poor little fellow to be allowed to relax and enjoy "all such honest disports as may be conveniently devised for his recreation". But happily eight o'clock was to find him in bed with the curtains drawn, and those who attended at the last ceremonies of the ceremonious day were bidden to "enforce themselves to make him merry and joyous towards his bed". Around that bed careful watch was to be kept every night and all night, and that disease might not steal in and rob the King of God's "precious sonne and gift and our most desired treasure", a physician and a surgeon were to be ever at hand. Nor was the moral welfare of the child forgotten; for no swearing or ribald words were to be tolerated in his household, least of all in his presence, and no "customable swearer, brawler, backbiter, common hazarder, [or] adulterer" was to be retained in his service.'[1]

Shortly before King Edward died, these household regulations were revised to fit the advancing years of the Prince, now twelve; he was, for example, permitted to stay up until nine P.M. By this time an Italian humanist, seeking his fortune in England, had dedicated a poem to him and praised his learned accomplishments.

In other ways, too, King Edward and his family signalled their forward-looking concern for education: the craft of printing was introduced into England under the auspices of the House of York. Toward the end of the 1460's, William Caxton, merchant adventurer, gave up his governorship of the English merchants in the Low Countries to take service with King Edward's sister Margaret, now Duchess of Burgundy. She encouraged him to finish his translation of *Le Recueil des Histoires de Troyes* and probably prompted the dedication of one of the first books he printed in Bruges, *The Game and Playe of the Chesse*, to the Duke of Clarence, Margaret's favourite brother. When Caxton returned to his native London in 1476 to set up a printing press at the Sign of the Red Pale in Westminster, he undoubtedly came armed with letters of introduction from Duchess Margaret to the English court.

He immediately found patrons in the royal family and among the lords of Yorkist England. He dedicated volumes to Edward, to Edward's son the Prince of Wales, and to Edward's brother Richard (Richard III). Caxton left the printing of the classics to the presses of France and Italy; the works he produced reflect the interests of the newly developed reading public. He translated the *Mirror of the World* for that 'worshipful man, Hugh Bryce, alderman and citizen of London', printed chronicles and devotional exercises and books of manners and the poetry of Chaucer and Gower and Lydgate.

Edward and his brother Richard too were princely builders. The Croyland chronicler asserts that when it came to adorning palaces and churches, and 'building castles, colleges and other

---

[1] Scofield, *Edward the Fourth*, II, pp. 55-56; for the entire ordinance, see J. C. Halliwell, *Letters of the King of England*, London, 1846, I, pp. 136-44.

distinguished places, not one of his predecessors was at all able to equal [Edward's] remarkable achievements'. Of the three greatest monuments to perpendicular architecture which came into being during this age, Edward made gifts to Eton College Chapel; he and Richard contributed hundreds of pounds to that poem in glass and stone, King's College Chapel, and he himself began the rebuilding of the Chapel of St. George, Windsor. Even when he was departing on his military expedition into France, in 1475, he found money to keep his skilled artisans at work; and shortly after he had returned to London, he rode down to Windsor eager to see what had been accomplished during his absence. He urged on the enterprise so ardently that by the spring of 1478 there was a dearth of stone cutters in England: the best of them were all working at Windsor. William Wayneflete, Bishop of Winchester, who was then engaged in building Magdalen College, had to secure from the King a special dispensation in order to find enough stone-cutters to proceed. When Edward was interred (April 1483) in his chapel, at least part of the building was already roofed in lead.

The King stuffed this edifice with costly ornaments—£50 'for the making the head of an image of St. George and for gold to perform the same'; £160 for 'an image of Our Lady of gold with Our Lord in his arms'—and purchased copes of white silk damask 'embroidered with angels with diverse minstrelsies', and yards of 'white velvet with black spots, white damask with flowers of divers colours, blue velvet tissue cloth of gold', and other expensive materials. He apparently began gathering a library for the chapel, perhaps containing editions of the classics printed in Italy, for the King arranged to pay £210 (£8/9,000 today) to a 'merchant stranger' named Philip Maisertuell 'for certain books by the said Philip to be provided to the King's use in the parties beyond the sea'.

The intellectual ferment that glorifies the Tudor age was already stirring in the reign of Edward IV. Men were beginning to journey into Italy to drink of the heady fountains of humanism at Padua and Bologna and Florence. The most accomplished of these men, King Edward and his brother Richard drew into the service of the state as councillors and ambassadors. Edward IV probably made more use of the learning of his age, relatively, than Henry VIII did of his.

The Kingmaker's slippery brother George, Archbishop of York, exemplifies the quickening aspirations of the time, the reaching for fresh intellectual experience. He was made Chancellor of the University of Oxford when he was scarcely in his twenties. Before he was thirty he became Chancellor of England. A thorough worldling, clever and cultured, if not erudite, he corresponded with famous scholars; he collected manuscripts; he employed a Greek scribe to copy out classical masterpieces for his library. The Burgundian chronicler Chastellain, not easily pleased, found him 'very stately and eloquent'. Of another stamp was John Shirwood, Bishop of Durham and Richard III's representative at the Vatican. King Edward's brother was so moved by his erudition that he besought the Pope to make Shirwood a cardinal because he was such an ornament of learning in England.

Edward's court was intellectually enlivened by laymen as well as clerics. The fifteenth century, flushed with the germinating forces of the Renaissance, produced a blaze of princes. Few were more flamboyant than John Tiptoft, Earl of Worcester, and the Queen's brother, Lord Scales, later Earl Rivers John Tiptoft resembles the lord of an Italian city state, whereas Anthony Woodville appears as a forerunner of the accomplished, melancholic and curiously ineffectual Earl of Essex.

Educated at Balliol College, the brilliant Earl of Worcester became Treasurer of England when he was still in his twenties. Toward the end of Henry VI's reign he departed for Italy, accompanied by a lordly retinue. After spending a little time in Venice, he made a pilgrimage to Jerusalem and on returning to Italy, studied Latin and law at Padua, met the leading humanists of the Peninsula, heard John Argyropoulos lecturing on Greek in Florence, and began ardently collecting manuscripts, many of which he later left to Oxford University. An Italian humanist declared that the Earl, in avidly assembling a library, had robbed Italy to adorn England.

He returned to his native land not many weeks after Edward ascended the throne, and the young King seized immediately upon his talents. Within a few more months he was made a member of the King's council, Constable of the Tower and finally Constable of England, an office which in his ruthlessly capable hands spearheaded the drive to crush Lancastrian resistance. He commanded forces in the North; he led fleets against the Scots and French; and he was indefatigable in council. Some time during these crowded years, if not when he was in Italy, he translated Cicero's *Essay on Friendship* and the *Orations of Cornelius Scipio and Gaius Flamineus*, later printed by William Caxton, who declared that the Earl 'flowered in virtue and cunning to whom I knew none like among the lords of the temporality in science and moral virtue'. The commons, however, did not share Caxton's enthusiasm. They hated Worcester's severity, grumbling that he 'judged by law of Padua', but they trembled before his bold features and protruding eyes. When, in 1470, he ordered the execution of some seamen of Warwick's, captured as the Kingmaker fled to France, he added a spectacle never before seen in the realm; their trunks and heads were impaled on stakes. After this he was known as the Butcher of England.[1] He pursued the service of the new monarchy as zealously as he pursued his studies. Cold, enigmatic, tinged with cruelty and responsive to the new statecraft of Italy, he was more likely to weep at a torn manuscript than a severed head.

When King Edward was forced to flee the realm in September of 1470, the Earl of Worcester was caught hiding at the top of a tree in a forest in Huntingdonshire. Warwick, ruling in London, assigned to the Earl of Oxford, whose father and brother Worcester had condemned to death, the pleasure of presiding over his arraignment. On Monday, October 15, 1470, he was speedily found guilty of treason, condemned to be led on foot from Westminster to Tower Hill, and there beheaded. He began his last journey on Wednesday, but the streets were so packed with men and women yelling execration at this Italianate villain and struggling to tear him to pieces that the officers were forced to take shelter for the night in Fleet Prison. The next afternoon, the impassive earl, as brave as rigorous, was conveyed to Tower Hill

[1] There seems to be little difference between heads and trunks thrust on stakes and heads spiked on city gates, but your ordinary Englishman disliked 'newfangledness', especially with a foreign flavour.

by a powerful armed guard. Ignoring the jeers and curses of the blood-thirsty crowd, Worcester declared on the scaffold—when an Italian friar reproached him for his cruelty—that he had governed his actions by the good of the state. *Raison d'état*! There speaks the voice of Machiavelli and the coming age. Worcester's last earthly utterance, however, was completely mediaeval. He requested the headsman to perform his office in three strokes in honour of the Trinity.

Anthony Woodville, the Queen's brother, was a courtier, in an age not quite ready for the courtier, rather than a man of state; and in his contrarieties he seems almost Elizabethan. Pilgrim and knight, worldly and ascetic, he was moved both by the vision of the Grail and of the Good Life. He was the most famous jouster of the age and a patron of Caxton. He translated three devotional works which Caxton printed; yet he was also given to penning mediaeval ballads against the Seven Deadly Sins. Though he counted himself a staunch son of Holy Church, he seems to have developed an intimate piety, half mystical. The blows that fell upon his family and the perils that he himself suffered in the course of Warwick's struggle with King Edward[1] produced in him a profound religious experience. Henceforth, he told Caxton, he had resolved to dedicate himself to the cause of God. He perused the philosophers; he went on pilgrimage to the shrine of St. James of Compostella and talked of fighting the Infidel. He was appointed by Pope Sixtus IV Defender and Director of Papal causes in England, and beneath the rich robes of an earl he often wore a hair shirt.

In the lists he dazzled beholders as much by the opulence and originality of his costumes and his gracious deportment as by his skill in arms. Others won the prizes in jousts held at Westminster, January of 1478, to celebrate the marriage of King Edward's second son, but the cynosure of all eyes was Anthony Woodville, who appeared in the field 'horsed and armed in the habit of a white hermit' accompanied by his hermitage 'walled and covered with black velvet'.

---

[1] His father and brother John were executed by Warwick in the summer of 1469; he himself shared King Edward's flight to the Low Countries and the Yorkist reconquest of the realm.

In the work-a-day world, he commanded military expeditions and went on diplomatic missions, at the same time that he was governor of Edward's heir and thus headed the Council of the Welsh Marches. He could not claim the erudition of John Tiptoft, Earl of Worcester, but he was none the less a patron of learning. When he journeyed beyond the Alps, he seems to have sought inspiration equally from the holiness of famous shrines and from the golden reawakening of the cities of Italy. None could say whether he was more moved by the culture or the sacred authority of the Papal court. Among the people, he was famed for his ceremonious feats of arms; among the élite, for his accomplishments of mind. Imprisoned by Richard of Gloucester in the uncertain days that followed the death of Edward IV, he was condemned to be executed as Richard moved to usurp the throne. On the eve of his death, as a final reckoning with the world, he composed a pathetic plaint upon the mutability of life, entirely mediaeval in feeling:

> Somewhat musing
> And mourning
> In remembering
> Th'unsteadfastness;
> This world being
> Of such wheeling,
> Me contrarying,
> What may I guess? . . .
>
> Methinks truly
> Bounden am I,
> And that greatly,
> To be content;
> Seeing plainly
> Fortune doth wry
> All contrary
> From mine intent.

The chroniclers offer a glimpse of King Edward keeping at Westminster the last Christmas (1482) that he would ever see.

Chambers resounded to the music of minstrels; dancing and elaborate 'disguisings' beguiled the hours. 'The King ordered many performances of actors'; he frequently kept his state in the great hall or walked in ceremonial processions 'clad in a great variety of most costly garments, of quite a different cut to those which had been seen hitherto in our kingdom. . . . They gave that prince a new and distinguished air to beholders, he being a man . . . remarkable beyond all others for the attractions of his person. You might have seen the royal court presenting no other appearance than such as fully befits a most mighty kingdom, filled with riches and with people of almost all nations, and boasting of those most sweet and beautiful children, the issue of his marriage with Queen Elizabeth'. By this time Edward had solved his financial problems. For three years he had carried on a war with Scotland, without asking Parliament for money, and he died worth a fortune, 'the first English King to do so since the twelfth century'.

King Edward's health had been failing for the past two years.[1] He had revelled long o' nights, but he had worked long days, too. At the beginning of April he caught a chill, and though his illness did not appear serious, he grew ever weaker and died on April 9. He fell three weeks short of being forty-one years old.

The fierce struggle to establish a powerful central authority had taken its toll. The past was crowded with lost illusions and friends turned enemies. The sanguine young monarch hoping to dispense justice had become a ruler grimly and wearily enforcing order. Despite the amplitude of his might, the wit of Mistress Shore and the love of his subjects, the conqueror of Warwick, once an illness laid him a-bed, let death take him, apparently without a struggle. When he lost his ebullience, he lost everything.

Though Henry V when he died was held in greater awe, no King of England since the conquest was so deeply mourned by so many of his subjects as Edward IV. More than a decade after Henry VII came to the throne, a Spanish ambassador, noting that

[1] The city of Canterbury, on seeing the King in 1482, noted that he was not well. Edward was severely shaken at Christmas time (1482) by bad news from overseas which even his brother Richard's successful campaign in Scotland could not soften. Louis XI forced England's ally, Maximilian of Austria, now ruling in the Low Countries, to sign a humiliating treaty, in which the French King repudiated his promise to marry the Dauphin of France to Edward's daughter Elizabeth.

that King was heartily disliked by his people, added that 'they love the Prince [Henry's heir, Arthur] as much as themselves because he is the grandchild of his grandfather [Edward IV]'.[1]

Sir Thomas More, no mean judge of character, and somewhat closer to King Edward than modern historians, has this to say about him: 'he was a goodly personage, of heart courageous, politic in council, in adversity nothing abashed, in prosperity rather joyful than proud, in peace just and merciful, in war sharp and fierce. . . . At all the time of his reign he was with his people so benign, courteous, and so familiar that no part of his virtue was more esteemed.' When Queen Elizabeth I called herself 'mere English', she was speaking in the vein of her great-grandfather.[2]

[1] Elizabeth (Edward's eldest daughter) was married to Henry VII ; she too was much beloved for her father's sake.

[2] Literally, too: Edward IV had more native blood in his veins than any king since the Conquest.

6

Lords and Gentry

THE life of the land changed least. Probably nine of every ten
subjects of King Edward IV dwelt in the country; and their lives
were framed, like the lives of their forefathers and of their sons, by
the round of the seasons, the boundaries of the manor, and the
custom of the manor court. Though the realm was officially
divided into shires, sokes, 'honours' and 'liberties' (where the lord's
writ ran supreme), hundreds, and boroughs—rural England was,
organically, a web of manors. The great house, or abbey, dominated the social skyline; the master of the manor ruled a little
enclave of officers, servants, tenants, and sub-tenants.

A man of the fourteenth century riding through the countryside of the Yorkist Age would find much that was familiar.

Many a manor house was still surrounded by two or three great
open fields, the lord's demesne and peasant holdings, separated
into strips by balks of sod. Peasants, bond or free, lived in a huddle
of cottages and ploughed the land with scrawny oxen. On the
common meadows they pastured a cow and a few sheep; and in
the woods and waste beyond, they kept a pig or two 'going' and
took branches 'by hook or crood' for firewood and repairs.

In the late autumn the peasant ploughed the demesne, on his
days of labour service, and his own strips for the planting of
wheat. Not long after Candlemas (February 2) he was ploughing
again, since oats and peas were sown around Easter. Then it was
time to put in the barley. Oxen rather than horses dragged the
plough: they were more manageable and cheaper and when they
were past service they provided meat. In the harvest season the
peasant cut the lord's grain, closely watched by bailiff and reeve

to prevent him stealing extra time for his own crop. Around Martinmas (November 11) a great slaughtering of animals gave him and his family more meat than at any other season of the year. Otherwise they subsisted mainly on boiled bacon, an occasional chicken, worts and beans grown in the cottage garden, cereals. Hares from the lord's warren, fish from his stew pond, pigeons from his dovecot found their illicit way on to the table. The sale of a little wool put ale instead of water in the family drinking mugs.

Tenants appeared before the lord's steward at the manor court and paid the same feudal dues as their fathers: merchet, a fine levied when a villein's son or daughter married; chevage, a fee which permitted the villein to dwell off the manor; heriot, a death-duty, usually the best beast; and other fines depending upon the custom of the manor. This custom meant more in the lives of the peasantry than what King and council decreed or what happened in Parliament. Manor customs showed a common pattern, but there were regional variations. In Cornwall, for example, when a stranger died within the boundaries of a manor, the lord received his best beast or his best garment or best jewel. Even within regions each manor had its special laws which wove the texture of daily life.

But a man of Chaucer's time, pausing to look more closely at the Yorkist countryside, would find many changes from his day. Begun long before the fourteenth century, these changes had been accelerated by the shocks of the Black Death, the Hundred Years War, the Peasants Revolt (1381); and in the six decades between the death of Chaucer and the accession of Edward IV they had produced conditions of life and of land tenure that added up to a manorial system quite different from that which prevailed when Chaucer was born in 1340.

Almost everywhere fields had fallen back into waste or wood. Whereas the realm in the early fourteenth century had supported something like four-and-a-half million people, it now had a population of perhaps fewer than three million. There was a glut of land and a scarcity of men. While tenants and labourers therefore prospered, most lords had ceased to farm their demesnes because labour costs were too high, feudal claims too hard to enforce, and the price of crops too low. Now lords leased out their land to live as a rentier class, and they readily commuted for money the labour services no longer valuable to them. In the accounts of the time there frequently occurs a subtraction for 'decayed rents', either lands bringing a lower income than in the past or lying idle.

With the agricultural situation so favourable to tenants, land-lords often found it difficult to collect rents. Margaret Paston's 'Cosyn Calthorp' sent her 'a letter, complaining in his writing that forasmuch as he cannot be paid of his tenants as he hath been before this time, he purposeth to lessen his household and to live the straitlier'. Reports of bailiffs and stewards groan with lists of tenants who have failed to live up to their indentures. 'As to Skilly, farmer of Cowhaw, we entered there and said we would have payment for the half year past and surety for the half year coming, or else we would distrain and put him out of possession and put in a new farmer. Item, as to the farmer of the manor of Langston, we . . . took no distress but entered the lands . . . and as for Kyrley Hawe, I was with the farmer yesterday, but he will pay no penny nor be bound neither. . . .' Distraining was often a nasty business, breeding ill will between tenant and landlord. Even Sir James Gloys, the tough Paston chaplain who spent much of his time as a land agent, once admitted that though he had tried on several occasions to distrain upon a certain tenant, 'I could never do it but if I would have distrained him in his mother's house, and there I durst not for her cursing'.

For tenants of all kinds the Yorkist Age appears like a sunlit plateau between the gloomy valleys of mediaeval villeinage on the one side and of the hard Tudor days of leaping prices and ruthless estate management on the other. At the beginning of Edward IV's reign villeinage was fast dwindling; when King Edward died, eviction of tenants to permit land enclosures was causing complaints but had not yet become menacing. Sir John Fortescue complacently contrasted the miserable, half-naked spiritless peasant of France with the warmly clad, meat-eating, ale-drinking, independent English yeoman; and alien visitors journeying through the countryside were equally impressed by the handsome parks of nobles and gentry and the air of prosperity among the lower orders. Changes in manorial tenures, in manorial occupations, in manorial industry were creating diversity of fortune and rank among the yeomanry. The monolithic order of peasants had now split into a variety of destinies.

Though villeinage still existed, particularly in the North and parts of the West, it was already a survival, one that would linger as late as the days of Queen Elizabeth I, and the distinction between bond and free was rapidly blurring. Chaucer saw the men of 1381 take pitchforks and mattocks and assault their betters in a desperate attempt to sweep away serfdom and beat down the statutes that held men in thrall. But in Jack Cade's rising of 1450 no such motives were at work, for villeinage was no longer a social and economic issue.

Villeins were now being called 'customary tenants' or 'copyholders'—because they held their acres by a copy of the court roll of the manor—and they were winning for themselves a security recognized by law. Before Edward IV came to the throne, they were successfully appealing to the Chancellor against eviction; and in 1467 the Common Law, eager not to be left behind, came to their support. Chief Justice Danby declared that if a lord ousted his customary tenant 'he does him a wrong, for his tenant is as well inheritor to have the land to him and his heirs according to the custom of the manor as any man is to have his lands at common law'. When a villein's copyhold was upheld in the courts and he paid rent to his lord in lieu of labour-service, he was already merging into the ranks of free men. People were coming to think of servile tenures rather than servile tenants.

The status of yeomen, enormously broadened, now ranged from the humblest free man to men like the bailiff Richard Calle, who read French and cast up accounts in Latin, and Clement Paston, who probably signed himself gentleman before the end of his life and whose son rose to be a Justice. Even if all his land were leasehold, a yeoman could lay a solid foundation for his family and go to war as a gentleman. Bishop Latimer's father 'was a yeoman and had no lands of his own, only he had a farm of 3 or 4 pound by year at the uttermost [i.e., that was the rent he paid]; and hereupon he tilled so much as kept half a dozen men. He had walk for an hundred sheep, and my mother milked 30 kine. He was able, and did find the King a harness, with himself and his horse, while [until] he came to the place that he should receive the King's wages. I can remember that I buckled his harness when he went into Blackheath field [the rising against Henry VII in 1497]. He kept me to school. . . . He married my sisters with five pound or 20 nobles apiece. . . . He kept hospitality for his poor neighbours. And some alms he gave to the poor, and all this did he of the said farm. Where [as] he that now hath it payeth 16 pound by year or more and is not able to do anything for his prince, for himself, or for his children or give a cup of drink to the poor'.

A yeoman might, like Clement Paston, have part of his farm in 'bond land', another part at leasehold, and some in freehold. The enterprising copyholder, with a large family to help him, was taking on additional acres at copyhold and also leasing property. The yeoman-lawyer, the yeoman-bailiff, the mercenary archer invested their winnings in land.

The account books of Sir John Howard point the signs of the times. His steward noted that on the manor of Stansted Hall seven men who owed in harvest time from one-and-a-half to six days' work had failed to perform these 'journeys' for the past five years. Sir John leased this manor to two yeomen, Thomas Davy and his son John, for a period of seven years at £10 a year; with good luck and hard work, the Davys were probably able to realize as much income as a squire owning a manor worth £70 or more. With so much land available, yeomen could bargain for low rents and long leases and could often shift the onus of repairs to the landlord. 'Please you to remember the bill I sent you at Hallowmass,' Richard Calle wrote John Paston, 'for the place and lands at Boyton which Cheseman had in his ferme [i.e., rented] for 5 mark [66s 8d]. There will no man have it above 46s 8d . . . and yet we cannot let it so for this year without they have it for 5 or 6 year.'

Manorial occupations had broadened too. In his spare time a

small yeoman-farmer might carry on the trade of smith or carpenter, while his wife set up as a brewer. Yearly Sir John Howard
hired carpenters and other skilled labourers; he paid John Mendam,
a smith, 30s a year and a livery gown. A yeoman's son might lease
land for himself or take service in a household or try his fortune
in town by becoming an apprentice or, if he showed himself adept
at book-learning, he might win his way to one of the Inns of
Court. If he could draw a stout bow and his heart was stirred by
the *Agincourt Carol* he could enroll himself as one of the 'tall
fellows' in a lord's retinue or adventure oversea as a mercenary in
the pay of Charles, Duke of Burgundy, and share the violent ups
and downs of that spectacular career. When Sir John Paston was
about to depart for Calais in the retinue of its governor, Lord
Hastings, he asked his brother young John to try to recruit four
archers for him, 'likely men and fair conditioned and good
archers and they shall have 4 marks by year and my livery'. These
were not élite archers. An archer 'de maison' or élite archer,
Warwick the Kingmaker once assured Louis XI, was worth two
ordinary soldiers, even English ones. In 1467 Sir John Howard
contracted for the services of such an archer, a man named Daniel,
offering him £10 a year, two gowns, and 'a house for his wife to
dwell in at Stoke'. As an extra inducement he gave Daniel 12d,
two doublets worth 5s each, and a new gown, and sent him off
to a shooting match with 20d more jingling in his purse. When
Howard next journeyed to London, he went to Fyshlock the
bowyer and bought himself a bow for 2s, but for his élite archer
he paid 10s 6d for two bows, gave him a new case, a shooting
glove, bowstrings, and, a short time later, two more bows costing
13s 4d and a sheaf of arrows—probably the best target arrows
obtainable, for they came to 5s.

The appearance and the organization of numerous later-fif-
teenth-century manors likewise betokened changing times.
Enclosures in Kent and a few other shires were not new, but now
many parts of England were covered with a network of fields,
arable and meadow, separated by hedging and ditches. Peasants
as well as landlords pushed along the movement, exchanging their
strips of open field so that each might fence and thus more

efficiently work a property of his own. This drive to enclose land began the transformation of mediaeval agriculture, usually credited to the next century.

The industrial manor, now rapidly growing more common, represented the greatest change from the past. Sir John Fastolfe's manor of Castle Combe down in Wiltshire, Chaucer would have found quite unfamiliar and a man of the thirteenth century, incomprehensible. Flocks of sheep pastured on the meadows; but Castle Combe, as a result of Sir John's shrewd management and the growth of the cloth trade, was transformed in one generation into a hive of industry. Fastolfe had stimulated this movement by buying red and white cloth by the hundreds of yards from his tenants to make liveries for his soldiers, purchasing yearly 'to the value of more than £100'. As clothiers, escaping from the gild restrictions and the limited supply of power in the towns, settled in increasing numbers on the manor, sheep-herders crowded the village of Overcombe, while weavers and fullers and dyers built cottages at Nethercombe. The hillsides above the combe were covered with cloths drying on tenters; new fulling-mills and a gig-mill were built. The rattle of dice resounded in taverns, Sir John's fishponds were heavily poached, and some lusty artisans even dared to keep greyhounds, a privilege supposedly reserved to their betters, and coursed hares in the woods and fields of the manor. Finally taverns were ordered closed at nine o'clock in summer and eight o'clock in winter; and playing at dice and backgammon was prohibited, except at home until 9 P.M.

As early as 1435 a villein, William Haynes, who spent £30 rebuilding his house and contributed £20 to erecting a church tower, died possessed of goods and chattels worth something in the neighbourhood of four or five hundred pounds, say £20,000 in modern money. His widow Margery gave him a fine £27 funeral, probably, like Enoch Arden's, one of the costliest the region had ever known, paid almost £150 in fines for permission to possess her husband's goods and to marry again, lived like a lady with two French servants in her household, and died owning a grain-mill, a fulling-mill, two houses she herself had erected, and lands and tenements.

The nerve centre of the manor was the manor court, where once a month or several times a year tenants bond and free met, as required by 'suit of court', to regulate their affairs according to the custom of the manor. As the little drama of the court unfolded, the lord's steward sat at a table with a big book before him and noted down facts of tenure, accusations and excuses, as 'presented' by 'tithing-men', elected yearly, and by a jury of tenants. The steward also dispensed justice if the lord possessed view-of-frank-pledge, franchisal police powers.

Glancing through a few of the rolls that have been preserved, one can see the 'homage' of the little manor of Michell choosing a reeve for the coming year and two officers to taste ale and weigh bread. All brewers were automatically charged with having violated the assize of ale; any who were then able to prove them-selves innocent were excused. A free tenant was 'presented', paid his relief and did fealty for his lands. The steward read out a record of stray cattle pinned in the lord's pound, heard pleas of debt and trespass, and collected fines and fees accruing from the annual fair held on St. Francis's Day.

At the court of Standon manor, held on Wednesday after Michaelmas in 1455, twelve jurors 'presented' a number of tenants owing fines, who ranged from the 'Lord of Rugge' and the 'Lord of Weston' and a prior to a group designated simply 'free men'; all were further 'amerced' [fined] 2d. John Voxe, presented for unjustly felling two ash trees in his close, was ordered to pay to the lord the estimated value of the trees, 4d. A second tenant, who was one of the jurors, had fished in the lord's pool and taken fish. Still another juror was accused of breaking the lord's hedge on demesne land and there pasturing 'six oxen and three steers unjustly'; but the man asserted that he had a perfect right to do this and 'put himself upon his charter granted of ancient time by the lord. . . .' A miller 'took of the lord the water-mill there' for a term of twenty years at an annual rent of 56s 6d, payable in two instalments.

On a Wednesday after Hock Day (second Monday after Easter Sunday) towards the end of Edward IV's reign, four tithing-men of Carshalton manor presented, and a jury of twelve sworn free men confirmed, that two millers had taken excessive tolls, and that three men had shown themselves to be 'common breakers of hedges to the common harm'. Three tenants paid fines to the steward for the privilege of brewing ale till Michaelmas next. A man and his wife surrendered seven acres of land so that it might be bestowed upon a squire and his two sons, who were duly admitted as tenants and paid a fine of two capons. The tithing-men further presented that Henry Lee, ordered at the last view-of-frankpledge to repair the King's road to the fulling-mills pond, had not yet done so; he was warned that if he did not complete the work by the next 'view', he would be amerced 6s 8d. John Foxe, chaplain, was accused of assaulting John Merkely with a 'chip' of no value and of attacking William Pounchon with a knife, price one penny, Pounchon having drawn blood from Foxe with a bill.

At a court-leet of the Abbot of Peterborough, tithing-men and constables and surveyors of roads presented offences. All ale-sellers were, as usual, written down as guilty. Butchers were reminded that the churchyard must be cleansed every Saturday of the bones and filth their dogs brought there. Henry Roby was accused of being a petty briber and 'untrue to his neighbours'. Complaints were heard that the common sewer had not been repaired and that the Abbot was exacting unjust tolls of carts and carriages.

During troubled years and even on occasion when the realm was comparatively peaceful, manor courts could become the scenes of angry quarrels, sometimes boiling up into violence, as rival claimants of a manor appeared at the same instant to hold court. A landlord with a shaky title or a powerful enemy not only was forced to fight expensive law-suits but he had to provide a retinue of stout fellows to back up the authority of his steward. The worst sufferers, however, were the tenants. The Wars of the Roses disturbed the lives of manor dwellers far less than did tenurial disputes.

John Paston sent his agent Thomas Howes and a party of men to interrupt a court being held on the manor of Cowhaw, which he claimed by virtue of a wardship he owned. 'At the first Oyez,'

Howes reported, he and the Paston steward, Bartholomew Ellis, promptly strode into the assembly and 'there was long Bernard sitting to keep a court'. Ellis announced that he had come to hold the session and ordered long Bernard ' "to cease . . . for ye have none authority". Quoth Bernard, "I will keep both court and leet, and ye shall none keep here; for there is no man hath so great authority." Then quoth Bartholomew, "I shall sit by you and take a recognisance as ye do". "Nay," quoth Bernard, "I will suffer you to sit but not to write." "Well," quoth Bartholomew, "then forcibly ye put us from our possession, which I doubt not but shall be remembered you another day," etc.' Bartholomew then turned to the unlucky tenants: ' "Sirs," quoth he, "ye that be tenants to this manor, we charge you that ye do neither suit nor service, nor pay any rents but to the use of John Paston and T.H.; for, and ye do, ye shall pay it again. . . ." And thus we departed, and Bernard kept court and leet'—the tenants no doubt gloomily meditating on their predicament.

Some years later, young John Paston showed himself even more vigorous than Bartholomew in such a situation, though he had less protection. Suddenly learning that a man named Gornay to whom Sir John had leased the manor of Saxthorpe but not the right to keep a manor court, was none the less holding court there, young John, 'ere the court was all done, came thither with a man with me and no more, and there, before him and all his fellow-ship . . . I charged the tenants that they should proceed no further in their court upon pain that might follow of it, and they letted [ceased] for a season. But they saw that I was not able to make my part good, and so they proceeded further; and I saw that and set me down by the steward and blotted his book with my finger as he wrote, so that all tenants affirmed that the court was interrupted by me as in your right, and I required them to record that there was no peaceable court kept, and so they said they would'.

A few months later, on Holy Rood Day (May 3), young John again interrupted a manor court that Gornay was trying to hold. He spoke politely, however, and Gornay promised to discuss his differences with Sir John, for which young John had cause to be thankful. Urging his brother to come to terms with Gornay, he reported that 'it lieth not in my power to keep war with him; for and I had not dealt right courteously upon Holy Rood Day I had "drunk to mine oysters", for young Heydon had raised as many men as he could make in harness to have helped Gornay; but when Heydon saw that we dealt so courteously as we did, he withdrew his men and made them to go home again, notwithstanding they were ready, and need had been. And also my Lord of Norfolk's men will be with him against me I wot well, till better peace be'.

The hardships of tenants on a disputed manor were intensified when one of the claimants insisted that they give surety for payment of rent; for the other claimant usually countered by assuring them that he would 'save them harmless' if they broke the surety. The Paston bailiff John Pampyng describes these manoeuvres in a report to John Paston, who was struggling with Justice Yelverton for possession of the manor of Cotton: 'I have been at Cotton and spoke with Edward Dale, and he told me that Yelverton and Jenney were there on Friday and took a distress of 26 or more bullocks of the said Edward's in the Park and drove them to a town thereby. . . . And when the said Edward understood the taking of the said beasts he went to Yelverton and Jenney and bound him in an obligation of £10 to pay them his ferme at Michaelmas; which I told him was not well done, for I told him ye had been able to save him harmless. Nevertheless as for money, they get none of him readily nor of the tenants neither, as he can think yet. The said Yelverton dined on Friday at Cotton and there charged the tenants they should pay no money but to him. . . .'

No franchise was more jealously guarded than the right of holding a manor court. Not only did the fines, amercements, and other dues put ready money into the lord's coffers; but the holding of the court constituted the fundamental exercise of possession and expressed the fact of lordship itself. Violent disputes over land that turned the manor court into an arena and caused landowners to ride with a band of armed men at their backs, open assaults on manors and forcible entries sprang from deeper causes than troubled times and greedy hearts. The whole complicated system of feudal tenures, interpreted by centuries of accumulating law, had broken down, and no other system had quite been developed to take its place. The Common Law had not kept pace with accelerating change; the Court of Chancery was just emerging from infancy. Feudal terms and provisions were distorted to express concepts no longer feudal. Land held as tenure had given way to land understood as property, but the courts lagged behind. Abuses rushed in to fill the gap. Men secretly transferred property and then sold it, so that the new owners found their rights contested by titles they had never heard of. Land was sometimes conveyed by 'fines', registered in the court of Common Pleas, but the court had not developed a machinery of public notification.[1] The system of trusts and uses—holding land in trust for the use of somebody else—caused further confusion. Long ago the friars had managed to get round the prohibition against owning property by vesting it in laymen who held it for their use. Lords and gentry, finding many advantages in this system, had adopted it for themselves, and in the Yorkist Age it was one of the commonest forms of land holding. But faithless trustees and executors claimed property as their own or disputed among themselves the right of sole administration. In this age of clouded titles, marriageable girls qualified their willingness to accept a husband with the proviso, 'if it so be that his land stand clear'; and courts and Chancery were clogged with suits.

Furthermore, an economic situation now unfavourable to landlords caused nobles and gentry to seek every means to enlarge their holdings. At the same time that great families like the Nevilles brought together vast tracts of property by fortunate marriages and Yorkist partisans benefited by the confiscation of Lancastrian estates,[2] other men bought up doubtful claims and corrupted trustees in order to get their hands on property.

Sir John Fastolfe and John Paston had as many as a dozen legal actions going on at once. Of Sir William Stonor's three legal counsellors, one appears to have been specially retained to watch

---

[1] The first important step to correct these abuses was taken in the Parliament of Richard III by means of two statutes, one against 'privy and unknown feoffements', the other requiring property transfer by fines to be officially publicised.

[2] Sir John Howard, granted an estate of 1,000 marks confiscated on Sir Nicolas Latimer, sold the property back to Latimer for that price and gracefully offered the money to King Edward.

out for any suits being heard at Westminster that might affect Stonor interests. There were so many lawyers in Norwich that the city tried to limit their numbers by municipal decree. Prudent squires sent their sons to the Inns of Court in order to arm them with the legal training that had become almost a necessity in the management of property. Agnes Paston advised her son Edmund 'to think once of the day of your father's counsel to learn the law, for he said many times that whosoever should dwell at Paston should have need to [know how to] defend himself', a prophecy that proved to be only too accurate.

Law-suits were so expensive and time-consuming, the chances of securing a favourable verdict were so uncertain, and even successful suits so frequently brought no relief, that men turned, when they could, to arbitration, as Mayor Shillingford had finally consented to seek arbitrators for Exeter's quarrel with Bishop Lacy. A letter from Lord Scales to John Paston illustrates the procedure: 'For as much as I and others stand feoffed in the lands of Thomas Canon [an example of trusts and uses], which is in variance between you and him, if ye will do so much as for your part choose 2 learned men and the said Canon shall choose other 2, they to judge this matter as they shall seem of right and reason. And if so be that the said Canon will not do so, I will not let you to sue him after the form of the King's law.'

The Paston letters unfold a far more crowded tale of violence in land dealings than any other contemporary source. In 1450 a war-band of the Lord Molynes assaulted the Paston manor of Gresham and forcibly removed Margaret Paston from the premises, which were then looted. Fifteen years later, on Tuesday, October 15, 1465, the Duke of Suffolk rode into Norwich at the head of 500 men, ordered his confederate, the Mayor, to lay hands on all men of the Paston affinity, and then sent his forces to smash the lodge and mansion on the manor of Hellesdon and occupy also the adjoining manor of Drayton, both lying across a stream from Suffolk's place at Costessey. Twelve days later, Margaret Paston wrote mournfully to her husband that she had ridden to Hellesdon 'and in good faith there will no creature think how foul and horribly it is arrayed but if they see it. There cometh much people daily to wonder thereupon, both of Norwich [less than five miles distant] and of other places, and they speak shamefully thereof'. Four years later, the Duke of Norfolk besieged and captured Caister Castle from the Pastons.

That such spectacular resorts to violence were uncommon, the sight-seers thronging from Norwich indicate, and the indication is supported by the records of the time. But forcible entries were not confined to Paston properties. Henry Makney had for years waged a feud in the law-courts with John Colyngrygge over the Makney place, 'a pretty manor of brick' in Berkshire. When his rival achieved momentary possession, Makney wrote to Sir William Stonor, 'Colyngrygge and I be at open war: I purpose to enter in the manor of Makney with God's grace on Monday or Wednesday, and if I have need, I pray you send me a good lad or 2 that I be not beat out again'. Stonor himself ran the gamut of suits, attempts at arbitration, and violent altercations with the Fortescue family over his Devon manor of Ermington; only after a generation of trouble was the quarrel happily settled by the marriage of Sir William's son and daughter to a son and daughter of the Fortescues.

The Paston place near Norwich was not the only Drayton that John de la Pole, Duke of Suffolk, assaulted in his time. The manor of Drayton, Oxfordshire, was owned by Peter Idley, a well-to-do squire who was for a time Comptroller of the King's Works. He wrote a book of *Instructions to His Son*, in the course of which, like Agnes Paston, he advised his boy to seek legal training:

> I conceive thy wit both good and able;
> To the law, therefore, now have I meant
> To set thee, if thou wilt be stable
> And spend thy wit that God hath sent
> In virtue with good intent;
> Then shall I help thee as I can
> With my goods till thou be a man.

But this eldest son Thomas predeceased his father; and when Peter Idley himself died at the end of 1473, a bitter battle developed between Thomas's widow Alice and Peter's second son William over the manor of Drayton. In the first weeks of 1474 Alice hurried up to London to complain to the royal Council that William was attempting forcibly to evict her. William promptly countered by bringing charges of debt and trespass against her; and in consequence she found herself 'divers times arrested' and frustrated in her efforts to get justice from the King's Council, as she set forth in a petition to the Chancellor.

In the autumn of the following year, William Idley presented a counter-petition and won a decree that Alice should make reasonable provision for him from the estate. But the quarrel smouldered. Some five years later the case was submitted to the arbitration of four learned men, who reversed the Chancery decision and awarded the manor of Drayton to Alice.

But William had friends with stout fellows at their beck and call. Sir William Stonor and his father, Thomas, had been appointed among the executors of Peter Idley's will. It seems likely that Sir William backed William Idley's cause, for the Stonors possessed a connection with the Duke of Suffolk, Sir William's mother being apparently a natural sister of the Duke; and William Idley, assembling men in July of 1481 to attack Drayton, was able to enlist Suffolk's full aid. On the 16th Idley's band swarmed on to the manor 'with the maintenance of the Duke of Suffolk being there in person'. They 'brake the houses and walls of the same in divers places, took and led away the beasts and goods, and beat and chased out all the servants and other persons being within the same'. Suffolk was not content merely to direct operations. 'In his own person [he] pulled the said Alice out of her chamber and put her out of the said manor. . . .' After Alice appealed to the Royal Council, a privy seal directed Sir William Stonor and Humphrey Forster, Justices of the Peace, to restore her and her son Richard to possession of the manor; the record stops there.

As a result of economic pressures, uncertainties over title to land, the weakness of the Lancastrian government, and the system of livery and maintenance which gave each magnate a band of retainers to make good his local domination, the gentry of the realm in the last two decades of Henry VI's reign scrambled to secure 'good lordship' as they had never scrambled before. Not that they liked taking sides among the proud, touchy nobles of England: when an agent of Sir William Plumpton, whose 'lord' was the Earl of Northumberland, approached Lord Hastings to seek Hastings' good offices in making Plumpton a Justice of the Peace, King Edward's favourite—one of the most genial peers in England—fixed the man with a haughty eye and 'answered thus, that it seemed by your labour and mine, we would make a jealousy betwixt my Lord of Northumberland and him; Sir, I took that for a watchword for meddling betwixt lords'. But what was a man to do when, in the 1440's and 1450's, 'misrule doth rise and maketh neighbours war'?

There was nothing new in the act of seeking good lordship; it was common before the Conquest and it would continue, under changing forms, virtually until the First World War. By the reign of Henry VI the old feudal connection based on land tenure was extinct. It had been replaced by 'bastard feudalism', as it is now named, which was already firmly established in the latter years of Edward III. This system depended upon a cash-and-influence nexus called 'livery and maintenance'. In return for his services—usually armed services—a 'retainer', often bringing with him numerous adherents, received from his 'good lord' money or other compensation and wore the lord's colours ('livery'); and, in addition, if the retainer was harassed by the law or by enemies, the lord promised to give him protection ('maintenance'). This system of allegiance-by-indenture, permitting men of means to build up powerful followings, flourished in the climate of growing disorder afflicting the last decades of Henry VI's reign, its ranks often swelled by its victims and its violence condoned at court.

The captain of Lord Molynes' band who seized the Paston manor of Gresham had himself been dispossessed of lands by the Duke of Suffolk and so was forced to wear Molynes' livery in order to earn a living. When John Paston brought suit against Molynes, he was informed that the sheriff 'hath writing from the King that he shall make such a panel to acquit the Lord Molynes'.

Caught between the rivalries of ambitious lords, the gentry looked to the nearest man of power; and the nearest man of power, competing for influence with his peers, eagerly welcomed the connection. Sir William Stonor put himself within the orbit of the Marquess Dorset; Sir William Plumpton sought the good lordship of the Earl of Northumberland; John Damme of Sustead looked for protection to John Paston. The men who fared best were those who avoided dependence upon a party chieftain or those who managed to pick the winning side, like young John Paston.

The bitter land-feud between the lords of Berkeley and the famous warrior-Earl of Shrewsbury and his scarcely less martial Countess illustrates 'the world right wild' of the 1450's. An early historian of the Berkeleys found in the court records, from 1445 to the end of Henry VI's reign, 'matter of riot, force, violence, and fraud enough to blot more paper than I intend in the whole life of this lord [James, Lord Berkeley]'. In these broils the town of Berkeley was so devastated that its fee-farm fell from £22 to £11 and less.

The Shrewsbury clan held the immense advantage of being among the chief supporters of Henry VI's court party; and in 1451-52 they were able with impunity to harry Lord James with armed bands and law-suits, 'which storms to avoid he was enforced to keep home and to man his castle with some strength for his defence and preservation, and his sons being also embroiled in many troubles kept close with their father'.

In September of 1452 the Shrewsbury heir, Lord Lisle, urged on by his mother and having corrupted a Berkeley servant to deliver up keys, stormed into Berkeley Castle early one morning 'with great numbers of people warlike arrayed and there took the said Lord James and his said four sons in their beds and there kept them in prison in great duress by the space of eleven weeks, by the commandment of the said Countess . . . ever awaiting the hour of their cruel death'. Not content with forcing them to sign certain prejudicial indentures, the Countess, on November 4, had the Berkeleys conveyed by force to Bristol. In the presence of the mayor they were bound by statute-merchant in the terrifying sum of £12,280, which they signed 'for dread to be murdered'. Then the Berkeleys were haled by the 'riotous fellowship' back to Berkeley Castle, only to be forced in a few weeks to appear at Cirencester before a commission of inquiry, rigged by the Countess of Shrewsbury, and there to make such pleas as the Countess dictated. In the end, Lord Berkeley lost all the disputed lands and was kept out of his castle for two years.

After Edward IV came to the throne the Berkeleys petitioned, in the foregoing terms, against these violent proceedings. The now widowed Countess answered stoutly that Berkeley fellow-ships had despoiled the countryside, even torturing a blind man to make him reveal his gold. At the request of the oppressed populace Lord Lisle had entered Berkeley Castle merely to round up evil-doers; and the Berkeleys, far from being under duress, had freely resigned their ill-gotten gains to the House of Shrewsbury. The feud smouldered until the turbulent early months of 1470, when the battle of Nibley Green brought victory to the Berkeleys and death to Lord Lisle.

The worst excesses of bastard feudalism in the last years of Henry VI are dramatized in the sad story of Nicholas Radeford. Recorder of the city of Exeter, he lived comfortably on a country estate and was much courted by the mayor and aldermen with presents of fish, wine, and game. Not long after John Shillingford died (about 1449), Radeford exchanged his pleasant life for the dangers of his time by becoming a counsellor of Sir William Bonvile. For years Sir William and the hot-headed Thomas Courtenay, Earl of Devon, had bitterly disputed the leadership of the county. In the middle 1450's these two proud magnates called up their retainers, broke out banners, and fought a fierce battle outside the walls of Exeter; after which the victorious earl stormed into the city and carried off some of Bishop Lacy's canons to hold for ransom. Shortly before this affray, a band of armed men burst the gates of Nicholas Radeford's manor house and pounded at his doors. When trembling servants let them in, Radeford discovered that their leader was the son of the Earl of Devon. The old man was brusquely informed that he must present himself at once before the Earl. He called for a horse, but by this time Courtenay's men were pillaging the manor and had led off all the animals. Radeford was brutally ordered to walk. In the darkness he started down the road, hustled by jeering ruffians. When he had gone but a bow-shot from the manor gates, his tormentors drew swords, smashed his skull, and left him dead on the road like a dog.

Edward IV laboured throughout his reign to break the system of livery and maintenance and with it the dominion of the over-mighty subject. The evil had taken deep root; but after Edward had crushed the greatest network of baronial strength, the Nevilles and their adherents, he made notable headway in the last decade of his reign. As Henry VII would do after him, Edward excluded lords from his government and undercut their power in the shires by enlarging the judicial functions and winning the loyalty of the country gentry. By the end of his reign the relationship between Sir John Weston, Prior of the Order of St. John, and the Cely family, Merchants of the Staple, expressed the tie of lordship which was replacing bastard feudalism. The Celys did not hold their Essex manor of Sir John, nor did they become his armed retainers; but they called him their good lord, they wore his livery when they accompanied him on a journey of state, they received intimate reports of his diplomatic missions, and they in turn supplied him with the latest news from Calais.

The comparatively tranquil existence of Sir William Stoner, in Edward IV's days, probably represents the normal life of the upper gentry. He had occasional trouble with tenants; he fought numerous legal battles; his quarrel with the Fortescue family over the manor of Ermington produced one flare-up of violence. On occasion Sir William experienced the pressures of 'lordship'. In 1478 Lord Strange of Knockin wrote to him in an idiom which by this time was beginning to grow old-fashioned:

'Between this [6 October] and Easter I will and desire that ye nor Cottesmore [Sir William's brother-in-law] distrain not nor trouble my tenants no more: and between this and the next half year I will that ye both see me, and if ye deal as ye ought I will be your good lord, and eke I dare better displease you than ye me: and as for the ferme [a disputed rent] I will do nothing without my lord of Gloucester, and I trust in all things he will defend me and my tenants, and I am friended so to help myself. . . .'

When even so great a magnate as Richard Neville, Earl of Warwick, purchased two manors in the county of Norfolk, he caused his uncle and party chief, The Duke of York, to write to the gentry of the neighbourhood, requesting them 'as far as right, law, and good conscience will, to have in favourable recommendation' the Earl's officers; and Warwick himself heartily prayed John Paston that 'ye will show to me your good will and favour . . . and be my faithful friend, wherein ye shall do to me a singular pleasure and cause me to be to you right good lord. . . .'

Nowhere among the records of the time is the hunt for 'good lordship' illustrated in such detail as in the Paston letters; on the other hand, to take the Paston quest as representative is a little like describing the activity in the Place de la Concorde during the Terror as a typical eighteenth-century street scene. East Anglia, especially Norfolk and Suffolk, and the Paston family were special cases.

East Anglia was a special case because it was crammed with potentates and exhibited an intenser political rivalry, national and local, than most other regions. Like eighteenth-century Europe, it had its congeries of ambitious powers, alliances and counter-alliances, shifting balance of forces, and cherished claims and pretensions which generated diplomatic skullduggery or open war. Until he was murdered in the Channel in 1450, Queen Margaret's favourite, William de la Pole, Duke of Suffolk, dominated the eastern counties with the help of powerful creatures like Sir Thomas Tuddenham and John Heydon, Recorder of Norwich. Even after the Duke's death, his widow Alice and Tuddenham and Heydon managed for a decade to keep the Suffolk interest paramount and to maintain a grip upon the city of Norwich. The Lancastrian Lord Scales and the hated court favourite Thomas Daniel controlled northern Norfolk; the Lancastrian Earl of Oxford, with his chief seats in Essex and Norfolk, exerted great influence; the Lancastrian Sir Miles Stapleton—'that knavish knight', John Paston called him—made use of a turbulent menie. The Pastons and Sir John Fastolfe and John Damme of Sustead and other gentlemen, who suffered from the oppressions of Suffolk retainers, looked to the old Duke of Norfolk, brother-in-law and adherent of Richard, Duke of York, and to York himself.

In 1459–60 there occurred almost simultaneously a violent shift in the fortunes of John Paston and in the balance of powers in Norfolk. Six months before the Yorkists gained control of England, Sir John Fastolfe died (November, 1459), leaving in a nuncupative will made on his death-bed all his properties in Norfolk and Suffolk to John Paston. Paston wore out his heart and inflicted a miserably harried existence upon his wife Margaret in a desperate struggle to hold this magnificent inheritance. He never succeeded in achieving the good lordship necessary to protect his holdings, perhaps because he knew that gaining such lordship would cost him some of his manors.

By the time John Paston had got the Fastolfe properties in his hands, the political situation in Norfolk looked to be far more favourable to him than it had ever been before. Edward IV had ascended the throne; Sir Thomas Tuddenham would shortly be executed and John Heydon had ceased to be a menace; the Lancastrians Thomas Daniel and Lord Scales were dead; and the Earl of Oxford and his eldest son, early in 1462, were executed on a charge of plotting to restore Henry VI. It appeared to be a world for good Yorkists to bustle in. John Paston, perhaps by virtue of his new position, was elected Knight of the Shire for Warwick's Parliament of 1460; he appears to have spent a brief period in Edward IV's household; and he was again chosen to represent the shire in Edward's first Parliament of 1461. The murdered Duke of Suffolk's son John held no such sway as his father had done; the new Lord Scales, Anthony Woodville, would in a few years become King Edward's brother-in-law; seventeen-year-old John Mowbray had succeeded his father as Duke of Norfolk and represented the chief Yorkist strength in the county; and another good Yorkist, Sir John Howard, had been appointed Sheriff of Norfolk and Suffolk.

But the appearance of good fortune turned deceptive. The parliamentary election of 1461 was marred by charges of fraud; Sheriff Howard and John Paston quarrelled; from court, Paston's

son Sir John sent word to his father that 'It is talked here how that
ye and Howard should have striven together on the Shire Day
[election day], and one of Howard's men should have struck you
twice with a dagger, and so ye should have been hurt but for a
good doublet that ye had on at that time.'[1] Though further
troubles caused the King to order a new election, John Paston
kept his parliamentary seat; but Edward IV commanded both
Howard and Paston to appear before him to explain the violence
that each blamed upon the other. John Paston, already engaged
in a struggle to protect his properties, failed to heed the summons.
Young King Edward meant to dispense justice and he meant to be
obeyed. John's brother Clement reported that on October 11
[1461] the King had angrily declared, 'We have sent two privy
seals to Paston by two yeomen of our chamber, and he dis-
obeyeth them; but we will send him another tomorrow, and by
God's mercy, and if he come not then he shall die for it. We shall
make all other men beware by him how they shall disobey our
writing.'

When John Paston at last hurried up to Westminster, he was
sent to Fleet Prison. Still, though Sir John Howard was the King's
'servant', Edward scrupulously investigated the quarrel and,
deciding that John Paston was guiltless, ordered him released. By
this time hungry men on all sides were trying to bite chunks out
of the Fastolfe inheritance. To secure the good lordship he desperately needed, Paston had got his eldest son, Sir John, introduced at court, but the young man lacked money or friends or
address, for he was soon forced to come home again. Paston had
better luck with his second son, young John, who, almost of an
age with the Duke of Norfolk, became a member of the Duke's
household.

But the Norfolk interest was already aiming at Caister Castle,
which the old Duke had coveted; and from his manor of Costessey
the Duke of Suffolk greedily eyed the manors of Hellesdon and

---

[1] Sir John Howard himself possessed such a 'doublet of [de]fence', which, in his own
hand, he describes in his account book as being reinforced in front by 18 folds of white
fustian, four folds of linen, and one fold of black fustian; and in the back by 16 folds
of white fustian, four folds of linen and a fold of black fustian; the sleeves were likewise
lined with layers of fustian and linen.

Drayton. The Duke of Norfolk appears to have been a low-tem-
peratured young man, given to sullenness and irresolution and
easily led. He was in the hands of his council, whom at a later date
Edward IV sharply rated for their irresponsibility, and of his
beautiful wife Elizabeth Talbot. John de la Pole, Duke of Suffolk,
was even less able and more dangerous than the Duke of Norfolk.

His great-grandfather on his mother's side was Geoffrey
Chaucer and on his father's side, Michael de la Pole, the most
brilliant merchant of his day; but these likely strains had done
little for the Duke. Lethargic and irascible, he had a taste for
violence but none for either war or statesmanship. He played no
part in the struggle between Lancaster and York. Though his
eldest son John, Earl of Lincoln, was named heir to the throne by
Richard III, he did not support Richard in the campaign of Bosworth Field, and he did not lift a finger in the reign of Henry VII
while Lincoln and his other sons conspired and failed and perished.
Perhaps the gruesome fate of his ambitious father had stamped
upon him a determination to stay out of trouble; but other forces
moulded his life too. His mother, Alice Chaucer, was a domineer-
ing figure, rather like Agnes Paston but with more power. His
wife Elizabeth, sister of Edward IV, had been given to him so that
the only remaining Lancastrian Duke might be kept firmly within
the Yorkist orbit. It appears that John de la Pole suffered from
frustration as well as indecision and found occasional relief in
blustering about the countryside with a band of armed men at his
back.

What opened the flood-gate of John Paston's woes, however,
was that his chief co-executors, Justices William Yelverton and
William Jenney, turned against him, asserted that they had equal
powers in the Fastolfe estate, and charged that the nuncupative
will was a forgery. They put their own men in certain Fastolfe
manors, sold their supposed rights in others to powerful figures
like Gilbert Debenham, steward of the Duke of Norfolk, and
supported the Duke's claim to Caister to gain his good will. With
fertile ingenuity Justice Yelverton fought Paston in manor courts,
sued him for trespass in the local courts of the shire, brought actions
against him at Westminster, haled him into the ecclesiastical courts

on a charge of trumping up the Fastolfe will, and at one time tried to curry favour with the King by suggesting to Edward's brother-in-law, Anthony Woodville, Lord Scales, that he might well secure Caister since the Pastons were of servile origin and had no right to hold such land at all.

When John Paston stayed at home to protect his properties and to counter law-suits, the legal battle in London went against him; when he hurried up to London to fight his enemies there, they brought on their suits in the county courts and had him proclaimed an outlaw for non-appearance. In 1464 and again in 1465 he suffered further incarcerations in Fleet Prison because he could not be everywhere at once. Meanwhile, the Duke of Suffolk, buying up trumpery titles, began to harry the manors of Drayton and Hellesdon, and his mother Alice, announcing that Cotton belonged to her, held a manor court there.

No wonder Richard Calle, beaten from manors and roughly handled in Norwich, despairingly informed his master that 'ye must seek some other remedy than ye do, or else in my conceit it shall go to the Devil. . . .' Paston's family and friends begged him at any cost to find a protector. 'Spend somewhat of your good now and get you lordship and friendship,' he had been advised much earlier, '*quia ibi pendet tota lex et prophetae* [for thereby hangs all the law and the prophets]'. Margaret Paston and others urged him to turn to the de la Poles: 'Sundry folk have said to me that they think verily, but if ye have my lord of Suffolk's good lordship, while the world is as it is ye can never live in peace. . . .' Richard Calle thought that if his master could win the Duke of Norfolk's favour, 'he should make all well, for they fear him above all things'. But John Paston struggled on alone until he died in London in 1466, wrecked by his ambitions.

His two adult sons, on whom the fight devolved, appear almost like figures in a morality play: Sir John, the unsteady man fashioned for failure; and young John, the man of sense likely to succeed. Humiliated by his father who had thought him a drone and dilettante and forced him to moulder penniless at home, Sir John now rode jauntily up to London to take his place in the world of Court and to dally with grandiose schemes for winning the good lordship that had eluded John Paston; while young John, with but a small portion of his own, loyally laboured to hold together his brother's precarious estate. After tourneying at Eltham by the side of the king himself and that master-jouster, Lord Scales, Sir John wrote excitedly to his brother in April of 1467, 'I would that you had been there and seen it, for it was the goodliest sight that was seen in England this forty years, [considering that there were] so few men.' To which young John replied dryly, 'By troth I had rather see you once in Caister Hall than to see as many king's tourneys as might be betwixt Eltham and London.' There lies the story of their lives until Sir John's death in 1479.

Buoyantly, Sir John tried to advance in two diametrically opposite directions at once. In 1468 he became engaged to Mistress Anne Haute, a relative of the Woodvilles, and thereby thought that he had secured himself with the Queen's family, especially when Anthony Woodville, Lord Scales, announced openly that he meant to protect the Paston interests. In the same year Sir John somehow fell under the spell of the smooth-tongued George Neville, Archbishop of York (brother of Warwick the King-maker), at the moment when the Nevilles, arch-enemies of the Queen and her kin, were moving to win every possible adherent in order to bring low the King who had flouted Warwick's scheme of a French alliance and had driven George himself from the chancellorship. Sir John lent a goodly sum of money to the Archbishop and persuaded his mother to raise an additional sum; for the Duke of Norfolk and his council were now asserting that they intended to seize Caister.

In exchange for his money, Sir John enjoyed a heartening performance by the Nevilles in October of 1468. A correspondent reported to him, 'Ye may tell my Lord of York [the Archbishop] that it is open in every man's mouth in this country the language that my Lord of York and my Lord of Warwick had to my Lord of Norfolk in the King's chamber, and that my Lord of York said, rather than the land should go so, he would come dwell there himself.' Norfolk gallantly explained that it was his wife who was urging him to seize Caister and said that he would 'entreat her'.

The following spring, Sir John tried to activate, with young

John doing the work, the Woodville flank of his campaign for lordship. On the way north to quell what seemed to be a minor rising, the King, accompanied by a number of Woodvilles, came through East Anglia to visit Our Lady of Walsingham and raise men. Though the Duke of Norfolk was bringing 200 adherents in blue and tawny livery to swell the royal forces, Edward IV bluntly informed William Brandon, a councillor of the Duke who tried to put in a word against the Pastons, 'Brandon, though thou can beguile the Duke of Norfolk and bring him about the thumb as thou list, I let thee weet thou shalt not do me so; for I understand thy false dealing well enough.' He added that if Norfolk continued threatening Caister and 'did anything that were contrary to his laws. . . . Brandon should repent it, every vein in his heart. . . .'

Meanwhile, arriving in Norwich with the King, the Queen's kin made honeyed promises to young John Paston that both the Dukes of Norfolk and Suffolk would be brought to heel through Woodville influence. As soon as the royal party moved out of Norwich they would show Edward the smashed manor-house at Hellesdon and tell him all about Suffolk's wrong-doing. But when the damage was pointed out, the King merely remarked that 'as well it might fall down by itself as be plucked down'; if it had been plucked down, the Pastons should have sought legal redress. Though everybody, including the King, disliked the Duke of Suffolk,[1] Edward made clear that he intended to show special favour in no quarter by telling the Pastons 'to let the law proceed'. Young John concluded this recital to Sir John by a disillusioned estimate of Woodville 'good lordship': 'for all their words of pleasure, I cannot understand what their labour in this country hath done good; wherefore be not over-swift till ye be sure of your land, but labour sore the law.'

But labouring sore was not Sir John's *forte*, and he swung back immediately to the Neville connection, which now put him in close touch with young John de Vere, Earl of Oxford, whose father and brother had been beheaded in 1462 and who had just

[1] The fact that Alice Idley in her petition to the Royal Council (see above, p. 208) dared to emphasize the part played by Suffolk in the attack on the manor of Drayton shows the Duke's lack of influence at court.

sealed his alliance with the Nevilles by marrying one of the King-maker's sisters. For a moment in early August [1469] Sir John's hopes must have soared, for Warwick and his cohorts defeated a royal army and took King Edward captive—hunting down and executing in the process Sir John's erstwhile friends Earl Rivers and his youngest son Sir John Woodville. But by the time the Duke of Norfolk laid siege to Caister Castle a few weeks later, the realm had grown so 'queasy' and it was becoming so difficult to keep Edward caged, that Sir John's Neville friends could do no more for him than send down a servant of the Duke of Clarence on a vain mission to try to secure a truce.

After young John had been forced to surrender Caister, Sir John continued to lead his attractive bachelor life in London, though the Duke of Norfolk's 'gallants' threatened young John and all Paston supporters with death and though the county was scan-dalized that Sir John did nothing for the family of John Daubeney, faithful Paston agent slain in the attack on Caister. People were 'saying that he might do no more for us but lose his life in your service and mine', John reminded his brother, 'and now he is half forgotten among us'. Before summer, the Earl of Warwick and the King's brother George, Duke of Clarence, had fled to France, the Pastons' new friend John, Earl of Oxford, managed to follow them across the Channel, and slippery George Neville, Arch-bishop of York, was under guard at his great manor of The Moor in Hertfordshire.

But Paston hopes almost immediately flared up again. By October, King Edward was in flight for the Low Countries, the Kingmaker ruled at Westminster, and his adherent, the Earl of Oxford, now held sway in East Anglia. John Paston wrote jubilantly to his mother on the 12th, 'I trust we shall do right well in all our matters hastily; for my Lady of Norfolk [Duchess Elizabeth, who clearly counted for more than her husband] hath promised to be ruled by my Lord of Oxford in all such matters as belong to my brother and to me; and as for my Lord of Oxford, he is better lord to me, by my troth, than I can wish him. . . . The Duke and the Duchess [of Norfolk] sue to him as humbly as ever I did to them. . . . As for the offices that ye wrote to my

brother for and to me, they be for no poor men; but I trust we
shall speed of other offices meetly for us, for my Master the Earl of
Oxford bideth me ask and have. I trow my brother Sir John shall
have the constableship of Norwich Castle, with £20 of fee. . . .'

So could fortune smile on men who dared to link their destinies
to the ambitions of great magnates. But hardly six months passed
before the Yorkists landed in Yorkshire, and Sir John and young
John donned harness and took horse under the banner of the Earl
of Oxford, to hunt down 'yonder man Edward'. Two weeks later
they fought in Oxford's wing of the Neville-Lancastrian army on
the fog-shrouded Field of Barnet. Warwick and his brother John,
Marquess Montagu, were slain; the Earl of Oxford fled for Scotland; young John Paston, wounded in the hand by an arrow,
and his elder brother came into London as prisoners.

The quest for good lordship had failed once again. For the next
few months the Paston brothers had to concentrate their energies
on securing royal pardons. But King Edward and his age were
more tolerant than later times of rebels and broken oaths of
allegiance. After the Pastons made a half-hearted attempt to
resume the Woodville connection, young John was accepted once
again as a 'servant' of the Duke of Norfolk: he was much liked by
the Duchess, who had made her husband accord him and his little
garrison the honours of war in the surrender of Caister. Sir John,
returning to his London ways, knitted up his tie with the Archbishop of York.

The night before Edward had entered London, with Warwick
and the Lancastrians in pursuit, George Neville bought his pardon
from the King by sending secret word that he would deliver up
Henry VI, whom Warwick had appointed him to guard. There is
no record that, after the battle of Barnet, he visited St. Paul's to
gaze upon the bodies of his two brothers, which for three days
were exposed, naked save for loin-cloths, on the stone floor to
prove to the world that the House of Neville was finished. Now
the Archbishop of York was intriguing once more against Edward
IV, probably with Edward's incorrigible brother George, Duke of
Clarence.

Sir John wrote happily to his mother early in January, 1472, that he had secured his pardon, 'for comfort whereof I have been the merrier this Christmas . . . and before Twelfth [Night] I came to my Lord Archbishop, where I have had as great cheer and been as welcome as I could devise'. But within three months, King Edward, grown tired of George Neville's scheming, had him arrested and sent as a prisoner to Calais.

The resilient Sir John soon found a new tie of lordship. From time to time he had been courting—in an off-hand way that irritated young John—the Duke and Duchess of Norfolk; now, however, he pinned his hopes to an even more influential magnate, the amiable William, Lord Hastings, the King's greatest friend. Again he had chosen a bitter enemy of the Woodvilles. Anthony Woodville, now Earl Rivers, hated Hastings because he had lost the governorship of Calais to the Lord Chamberlain. The Queen's eldest son, the Marquess of Dorset, hated Hastings because they were strenuous rivals for the boon companionship of their sovereign. The Queen herself hated Hastings because he was 'secretly familiar with the King in wanton company'.

The Lord Chamberlain warmly welcomed Sir John's service, and for the rest of his life the elder Paston spent much time at Calais as a member of Hastings' retinue. This listening-post on the Continent, this trading and naval enclave steeped in the business dealings of the Merchants of the Staple, gave Sir John a bachelor life that he enjoyed. The winds of Europe blew the latest news by land and sea into the town. Distinguished visitors spiced the social activities of garrison and merchants. On one occasion the young Lord Zouch was reported to be coming and Sir Thomas Hungerford's daughter and young Lady Harrington—'these be three great jewels', Sir John reported happily to his brother.

The girls of Bruges in their high caps were only a short ride away, the stews of St. Omer an even shorter. Doubtless Sir John visited the Duke of Burgundy's funfair castle of Hesdin, close by, where blasts of wind blew up the ladies' skirts and where in the famous chamber hung with Jason tapestries,[1] described by William Caxton, the ducal engineers somehow simulated thunder and

[1] Depending on whether his mood was pious or pagan, Duke Philip of Burgundy ascribed the origin of his chivalric Order of the Golden Fleece to Jason or to Gideon.

lightning, rain and snow. It was exciting to be able to send home the latest tidings of the Duke, that firebrand of the age. In 1474 Charles the Rash gathered all his horses and all his men and laid siege to the little German town of Neuss on the Rhine; and while Europe watched and wondered as the siege went on month after month, Louis XI, 'the universal spider', with infinite patience and infinite cunning wove the Duke a world to destroy himself in. But the surfaces of life held Sir John's eyes: Burgundian banners waving over black-and-violet pavilions, the famed chivalry of Burgundy wheeling before the city walls, lances flashing in the sun—'I think that I should be sick but if I see it', he confessed to his brother.[1]

His duties were apparently light and he had plenty of leisure for reading his books. In an energetic moment, in order 'to avoid idleness at Calais', he sent word to young John, 'I must have mine instruments [i.e., deeds and estate-papers] which are in the chest in my chamber at Norwich. Pray send them me hither in haste. . . .' All in all, he summed up for his brother, 'Calais is a merry town'.

Meanwhile young John stuck doggedly to managing his brother's properties and trying, through the good graces of the Duchess of Norfolk, to get Caister back. On his side, Sir John had better luck with Lord Hastings than with any other 'good lord' he had essayed. As King Edward was returning to England, after his French invasion of 1475, he asked the Duke of Norfolk some pointed questions about the ownership of Caister. But death played the trump card. The Duke died in 1476 at the early age of thirty-two, and the Pastons quickly and quietly reoccupied Caister Castle. When Sir John himself perished of the plague in the dreadful year of 1479, however, his affairs were still so precarious that his last letter shows him struggling to scrape together £10 in order to come home.

[1] Sir John's former friend, Anthony Woodville, Earl Rivers, showed himself more prudent in his estimate of Charles, Duke of Burgundy. After a tour of Italian towns and shrines, during which the eternal banditti lurking outside the Eternal City plundered him of his baggage, Rivers had ridden into the Burgundian camp before Morat, in June of 1476. Premonition or a respect for those 'froward carls', the Swiss, or the sight of the Duke's unruly army, English archers exchanging insults and knife-thrusts with Italian mercenaries, led Rivers to take a hasty departure the day before the battle. Duke Charles sneered at the Earl, but the next evening his army had been smashed to bloody ruin and he himself was a galloping fugitive, eyes glazed with mad dreams.

Young John, now master of the Paston fortunes, found himself saddled with debts, mortgages, law-suits, the long-continued quarrel with the Duke of Suffolk, and an even more serious dispute with his Uncle William who was now trying to win a share of John's inheritance. Within half a dozen years, however, by shrewd management and hard work he succeeded in holding what remained to be held and in establishing himself as one of the leading squires of Norfolk. Much depended, however, on where he elected to seek good lordship, and had he not made the choice he did, the Pastons would probably not have produced Henry VIII's greatest admiral and become, in the century that followed, Earls of Yarmouth.

When Richard III ascended the throne, June 26, 1483, he created John Howard, now Lord Howard, Duke of Norfolk; and Howard became at a stride not only the dominant figure in East Anglia but, after the soon-to-be extinguished Duke of Buckingham, probably the greatest subject in the realm. Twenty-five years before, John Howard and John Paston had had a serious political quarrel; Howard and John Paston's sons had fought on opposite sides at Barnet; and on an occasion in 1474 young John Paston had some sort of brush with Howard, apparently while he was hunting. On the other hand, years before this Sir John and Gilbert Debenham had had 'words at London and Debenham should have struck him, had not Howard been [there]'; and in 1469 young John had entertained Howard at dinner along with others of the King's retinue. This sparse record offers little insight into Paston's attitude towards John Howard in 1483; there is no knowing whether his subsequent conduct sprang from dislike long cherished or from subtler calculations.

The new Duke of Norfolk, for his part, did all he could to gain young John Paston's adherence. He confirmed the Pastons in possession of Caister Castle; and when, on the outbreak of Buckingham's rebellion, he hastily requested John to 'come hither, and bring with you six tall fellows in harness', he signed himself 'your friend, J. Norfolk'. There is no indication that John responded to this summons; but he probably at least showed himself friendly to the duke, for Howard's last surviving letter, written on the eve of Bosworth, in which he reported that 'the King's enemies be a-land' and asked John Paston to join him at Bury, concludes 'Your lover, J. Norfolk'.

But John Paston sat on his estates and let others decide the fate of England by arbitrament of battle. The invading army of Henry Tudor was led by John, Earl of Oxford; and in the 1470's after the Earl had been captured and imprisoned in Hammes Castle near Calais—from which he had escaped to join Henry Tudor in France—John Paston had shown kindnesses to the poverty-stricken Countess of Oxford. Perhaps all these years he had remained loyal in his heart to the chief he had followed on the mist-wrapped plateau of Barnet.

In any case, Henry Tudor's triumph at Bosworth made the Earl of Oxford one of the two or three mightiest subjects in England, and the Earl of Oxford made John Paston a trusted councillor and Sheriff of Norfolk and Suffolk. In 1487 John fought with Oxford at the battle of Stoke and was knighted by Henry VII on the field. By the time he disappeared from history he had become so great a man in East Anglia that the erudite Bishop of Durham, one of the ornaments of the New Learning, wrote to him to propose that 'for as much as I have coals and other things in these parts and also ye have in those parts corn, wine, and wax' they might strike up a trade 'whereby our familiarity and friendship may be increased in time to come'. In the end, the stay-at-home younger brother won the girl he loved[1] and achieved the position in the great world which had slipped through the fingers of the high-flying elder brother. All Sir John left behind him was a bastard daughter, Constance, to whom Margaret Paston bequeathed 10 marks in her will.

As the manor organized the working of the land, the household of the manor framed the life lived on the land. The great English households dominated society from the days of Penda of Mercia to those of Edward VII, their functions and significance shifting in each successive age to fit the social idiom of the times. Just as, in the fourteenth century, feudal hospitality gave way to seignorial

[1] See Chapter 10: The Marriage Hunt.

ostentation and the sprawling menies of 'bastard feudalism'; so in the Yorkist Age the great household swarming with the retainers of 'bastard feudalism' was beginning to be transformed into the aristocratic ménage of the Tudor period. Between them, Edward IV and Henry VII put an end to the petty kingship of the over-mighty subject; but a great hall stuffed with officers and servants and followers continued to signify status long after it had ceased to represent political power. In the first years of Henry VIII's reign the Earl of Northumberland maintained a household of 166 people; the year before the descent of the Spanish Armada, the Earl of Derby had 118 servants at his beck and call.

Until his death in 1471 Warwick the Kingmaker maintained one of the greatest households of Yorkist times at Middleham in Wensleydale, Yorkshire. Here the King's youngest brother Richard, Duke of Gloucester, served along with several noble-men's sons as a henchman in the 'schools of urbanity'; and here in the darker days when King Edward had begun to challenge the power of the Nevilles, barons and knights and yeomen wearing the badge of the Ragged Staff crowded the great hall. Assiduously courting popularity—an agent of Louis XI reported that wherever Warwick appeared 'it seems to the people that God has descended from the skies'—the Earl kept up a lavish London establishment, and anyone acquainted with a member of the household was permitted to carry away as much meat from the kitchens as he could thrust upon a long dagger.

Edward's spoiled and shallow brother George, Duke of Clarence, surrounded himself with a household of 299 people, and when he journeyed from manor to manor he took 188 of them with him. After Warwick's death Richard of Gloucester became Lord of the North and held court at Middleham, a house-hold more serviceable than ostentatious—for he was Warden of the West Marches and Constable and Admiral of England—to which the whole country north of Trent, townsmen as well as gentry, turned in time of need. The Duke of Norfolk at Framling-ham Castle and the Earl of Northumberland at Wressel and Leconfeld in eastern Yorkshire continued the traditions of Mow-bray and Percy greatness.

The household regulations of Edward IV sketch the establishments proper to the upper ranks, from duke to esquire of the
household. A duke might be expected to spend, as George of
Clarence did, £4,000 a year on his household (equivalent to
perhaps £120,000 or more today), about three-quarters of which
would go for food and wages; and when a duke came to court,
his chief household officers, steward and treasurer, received the
same service meted out to barons. A marquess fittingly spent
£3,000 a year; an earl, £2,000; a viscount, £1,000; a baron,
£500; and so on down to an esquire of the body, £50. During
Edward IV's reign there were probably some 600 lords, gentry,
and townsmen with incomes of £100 a year or better; these were
the men who maintained the web of great households within
which English society had its being.

Since 'attendance' projected the strongest signal of status, everybody from duke to gentleman kept as many officers and servants
as his purse would support. A retired London tailor left his business
to his son on condition that 'when that I or my wife walketh out
my said son shall let me have an honest man child to wait upon me
and an honest maid child to wait upon my wife, at his own proper
cost if we desire it'. To be—or claim to be—of gentle blood
and hold no household was the heart of misery. A Yorkshire lady
wrote sadly to her brother, 'My sister Dame Isabel liveth as heavy
a life as any gentlewoman born, [on account of which] I fared
never well since I saw her last month. House such, hath neither
woman nor maid with her, but herself alone. And her husband
cometh all day to my husband and saith the fairest language that
ever ye heard. But all is wrong, he is ever in trouble. . . .' She added
in a flash of outraged pride: 'And brother, I yede [went] to the
Lord Scrope to have seen my lady [Scrope's daughter], and by my
troth I stood there a large hour, and yet I might neither see lord
nor lady . . . and yet I had 5 men in a suit [livery]: there is no such
5 men in his house, I dare say.'

The scramble to keep a great household quickly led to extravagance and debt. A friend of the Pastons rounded on one of John
Paston's swaggering enemies with: 'That is the guise of your countrymen, to spend all the good they have on men and livery gowns

and horse and harness and so bear it out for a while, and at the last they are but beggars; and so will ye do. . . . As for Paston, he is a squire of worship, and of great livelode, and I wot he will not spend all his good at once, but he spareth [saves] yearly 100 mark or £100; he may do his enemy a shrewd turn and never fare the worse in his household, nor the less men about him. Ye may not do so, but if it be for one season. I counsel you not to continue long as ye do. I will counsel you to seek rest with Paston.'

From the manor at Ewelme, Oxfordshire, an officer of the Duke of Suffolk wrote on January 17, probably of 1471, to Thomas Stonor begging him to explain to the Chancellor why the Duke could not yet come to Parliament: 'The more part of my lord's servants were sent into Suffolk to the household there against Christmas, and the remnant of his servants that were here awaiting . . . be forth with my lord's wife into Suffolk to bring her thither. . . . I dare say he hath here at this day awaiting upon his lordship not a dozen persons. And so my lord might not come at London himself at this time to his worship, and his servants from him.'

Thomas Stonor's son Sir William soon fell into extravagant ways, zestfully abetted by his first wife, Dame Elizabeth. An uncle-by-marriage wrote to him anxiously, 'For God's sake beware now . . . and stablish your household sadly and wisely with a convenient fellowship so as ye may keep you within your livelode. . . . I pray you that ye will not over-wish you nor over-purchase you nor over-build you, for these three things will pluck a young man right low. Nor meddle not with no great matters in the law. . . . And, sir, as it is told me, ye do make a fair new garden; in the which I pray you for my sake to set two herbs, the which be Patience, Thyme.' Dame Elizabeth, daughter and widow of merchants, so much enjoyed playing the great lady with her 'menie of boys' that her friend Thomas Betson, Merchant of the Staple, several times gently warned her 'to remember large expenses and beware of them'.

In the most flamboyant—and cynical—gesture of the day, Henry Stafford, Duke of Buckingham, after he had helped the Duke of Gloucester to arrange the execution of Lord Hastings

(June 13, 1483), showed the amplitude of his means by immediately taking into his service all of Hastings' 'feedmen'.

Since wages, one of the chief items of expense, fell due faster than rents came in, even the greatest lords were often pinched for ready money; the grandfather of the foregoing Duke of Buckingham put off a creditor by confessing, 'I have but easy stuff of money within [sic] me, for so much as the season of the year is not yet grown'—he was helpless until harvest time arrived and the Michaelmas rents came in. The Duke of York, leaving some jewellery in pledge, borrowed £437 from Sir John Fastolfe in 1452; ten years later the debt had not yet been completely repaid. The Stonors, the Plumptons, the Pastons were almost constantly plagued by debts and embarrassed by a shortage of cash. To provide a tomb for his father, Sir John Paston had to sell the cloth-of-gold pall, which his mother had already borrowed money on. But then in all ages, it seems, the rich tend to be poor in purse, a perpetual mystery to the threadbare creditor.

The rise of John Howard, one of the key figures of the Yorkist Age, was owing in part to the fact that among his ranging talents he possessed the capacity to manage money; his household kept pace with his position and his interests but also with his means. Even when he was but a knight, he put some 130 people in mourning gowns at the death of his first wife. Substituting for the Duke of Norfolk as Earl Marshal at the joust between Lord Scales and the Bastard of Burgundy, Howard spent at least £200 to accomplish his honorific duties, trapped himself and his horse in silks and polished steel, and was served by a retinue of seventy men in livery jackets. Yet he seemed always able to lend large sums of money: to the king, to his needy cousin the Duke of Norfolk, to neighbouring clothiers and chapmen, to yeomen archers serving with him on campaign. He built ships, for himself and for Edward IV, and commanded fleets. When the Bastard of Burgundy got word in London of the death of his father, Howard was chosen to speed him homeward across the Channel. In the spring of 1470 he attacked Warwick's flotilla in the Narrow Seas and wrested several prizes from it. A dozen years later he led a great raid into the Firth of Forth which left a trail of burnt shipping in Scots

harbours. Meanwhile Edward IV had entrusted him with important diplomatic missions, and after the Treaty of Picquigny (1475)
he had become the chief English envoy to the court of Louis XI.

Lover of Colchester oysters and of the sea from which they
were ripped, this hardy Essexman (he seems to belong more to
Essex than to Suffolk) enlivened his chambers with music and
plays. On October 18, 1482, 'my lord made covenant with
William Wastell of London, harper, that he shall have the son of
John Colet of Colchester, harper, for a year, to teach him to harp
and sing, for the which teaching my lord shall give him 13s 4d
and a gown'. Howard maintained in his household 'Thomas the
Harper', at least one adult singer, and four child singers for his
chapel. His account books show him enjoying music of all kinds—
the humble drone of a village bagpiper, my lord of Gloucester's
trumpeters, the 'Wayts' of London who carolled for him when he
visited the capital. Actors found a warm welcome in his hall.
Richard of Gloucester's players and the Earl of Essex's players
doubtless performed more sophisticated morality dramas than the
troupes from neighbouring towns who also trod his boards. He
enabled likely village lads to study at Cambridge, collected books,
and was free with alms. But he did not waste his money on idle
servants; and even after he became Duke of Norfolk he sat down
every Saturday night with his steward and annotated the accounts
in his own hand.

A generation later, Henry Algernon Percy, Earl of Northumberland, left such menial tasks to his battery of officers. Percy's
household regulations, imitating royal ordinances as the Earl
imitated royal state, probably offer a tolerable likeness of the
households of George, Duke of Clarence, and other magnates of
the Yorkist Age. Supporting an establishment of 166 people,
133 fewer than that of Clarence, the Earl was attended at meal-
times by five henchmen, three of them at his 'finding' and two
'at their friends' finding', and was served by gentlemen sewers,
butlers, cupbearers and carvers. Twenty attendants waited upon
him in the great chamber in the morning, eighteen in the afternoon, and thirty in the evening. Seven gentlemen singers and five
chapel children sang Mass for him. My lord's six chaplains, headed

by a Dean of the Chapel, included 'the almoner, and if he be a maker of interludes then he to have a servant to the intent for writing of the parts', and a 'master of grammar'. At dinner and other festive occasions three minstrels played on taboret (drum), lute and rebec (primitive violin).

Like the royal household, the Earl's establishment was managed in the countinghouse, where his four chief officers watched over the activities of yeomen, clerks, and grooms, including 'a groom for the mouth and a groom for the larder'. Northumberland had a secretary and a clerk of the signet to compose letters at his dictation; a herald and a pursuivant, clad in his arms, bore these messages with fitting dignity. When he removed from Wressel, he was accompanied by a riding household of fifty-seven persons, preceded by harbingers and kitchen officers to arrange for suitable lodgings; and behind this princely cavalcade jolted seventeen carts, bearing my lord's minutely specified baggage. In the autumn, when his officers were taking inventory and Wressel was being cleaned and fumigated, the Earl retired to one of his smaller manors, where he managed to get along with a retinue of forty-two people, called his 'secret household'. Tens of estate officers, parkers and keepers and bailiffs and surveyors and huntsmen, did quarterly tours of duty to swell the 'attendance' in the household. Nothing was left to chance or even to the impulse of generosity or piety. The Earl's gifts and the Earl's good works were as carefully embalmed in his ordinances as the modest breakfast of fish that he ate on 'scamlyng days', Mondays and Saturdays in Lent. At Requiem Mass sung for the souls of the Knights of the Garter, my lord offered 4d; he gave his barber 12d for every shaving and bestowed 6s 8d on the children of the chapel when they sang a 'Respond' called *Exaudivi*. The messenger who 'bringeth his lordship his New Year's gift from the king upon the New Year's Day, if he be a special friend of my lord's' received '£6 13s 4d, and if he be a servant of the King's and but a particular person, 100s'. Yearly the Earl's household consumed £25 19s 7¼d worth of spices. His total annual expenditure came to £933 6s 8d (viz. £2,000 suggested for an Earl in the *Black Book* of Edward IV). The House of Percy was now in decline and this stay-at-home lord did nothing to restore its fortunes. He died with cash assets of £13 6s 8d and debts amounting to £17,000.

Just as nobles and gentry of the Yorkist Age imitated the King's household, so too did they imitate the King in maintaining a council. The council of a magnate like the Duke of Norfolk, consisting of his chief household and estate officers, lawyers retained in his service, two or three neighbouring lords and knights, frequently served as a local court of arbitration. Richard of Gloucester's council at Middleham became such an effective instrument of justice in the 1470's that after Richard became king he created the Council of the North, which the Tudors continued. John Paston won his way to the rich Fastolfe inheritance as Fastolfe's most trusted councillor; Paston in turn had a council which included his receiver Richard Calle, and the faithful John Daubeney, who was killed in the siege of Caister, and John Damme, master of Sustead Manor.

The great households brightened the lives of country-dwellers by their round of seasonal entertainments. Easter Week ushered in the spring with a mixture of secular and religious pageantry. The Earl of Northumberland, clad in a robe of violet broadcloth furred with seventy-five skins of black lamb, 'to as many poor men as my lord is years of age . . . and one for the year of my lord's age to come' gave gowns with hoods attached, linen shirts, wooden platters full of bread and meat, ashen cups brimming with wine, leather purses each containing as many pennies as the Earl's years; and then he gave his own gorgeous gown to the poorest man that could be found among those crowding his doors.

As summer approached, the household began to be cheered by all manner of itinerant shows as the King's minstrels and trumpeters, his bearward and bear took to the roads along with similar entertainers from the halls of dukes, barons, and wealthy gentry. Village bagpipers and city minstrels and players, troupes of 'rude mechanicals' from surrounding hamlets, jugglers and quacks and friars with wondrous relics performed in the hall or in the courtyard. At all times board games formed a staple diversion for the lord and his household; and games of cards, introduced in this age, became immediately popular. Sir John Howard and the

Duke of Norfolk whiled away winter evenings while they were on the King's service in Wales by playing cards with the Duke's steward. This officer had at least one very lucky evening, for Sir John had to borrow from him 13s 4d so that the Duke could pay his score and Sir John then borrowed four marks to pay his own score. Chess beguiled many an hour. Howard paid a 'limner' of Bury 20d for painting two chess boards. Another old game, 'tables' (backgammon) still held its own, and, like cards, provided a genteel form of gambling. On one occasion Howard managed to lose 27s 4d during an evening's play.

Seasonal entertainments reached their climax in the celebration of Christmas. On the Eve of St. Nicholas (Dec. 5) one of the children of the chapel or a child from the village appeared at the service dressed as St. Nicholas, and the household trouped from the chapel into the hall for singing and games. On the day itself a 'boy-bishop', arrayed in state, preached a sermon and was then feasted. Depending on whether he kept Christmas at Wressel or Leconfeld, the Earl of Northumberland yearly received the Boy-Bishop of Beverley or the Boy-Bishop of York. This lad often received costly gifts and if he was clever of tongue or well coached, his sermon might be written down and preserved.

Now the master of the revels began rehearsing entertainments, and the Lord or Abbot of Misrule led his boisterous crew in mummings and 'disguisings', forerunners of the Tudor masque, and persuaded the lord to gamble at dice with them, a tradition of the season. Sir John Howard sent to London or Colchester for wildfire and cloth and other 'stuff for disguising'. Even quite modest households burst into a bloom of entertainments on the twelve days from Christmas to Twelfth Night. After the death of Margaret Paston, her daughter-in-law Margery (Brews) sent her eldest little boy to my Lady Morley 'to have knowledge what sports were used in her house in Christmas next following after the decease of my lord, her husband; and she said that there were none disguisings nor harping nor luting nor singing nor none loud disports, but playing at the tables and chess and cards. Such disports she gave her folks leave to play and none other.'

On Christmas Day the boar's head was borne to the high table to the accompaniment of songs and carols. At the lawyers' inns in London a cat and a fox were sometimes hunted round the festal boards, and the Lord of Misrule, riding into the hall on a mule, held a fantastic court. On New Year's morning children of the chapel and minstrels sang at the chamber doors of the lord and his lady. Horsemen arrived with gifts from the king and queen and from friends, kinsmen, well-wishers; while the lord's messengers rode abroad on the same errand. When Sir John and Lady Howard kept Christmas with the newly married Edward IV at Eltham (1464), Sir John gave the royal heralds 10s, the minstrels 10s, the trumpeters 10s, the officer of the cellar 20s, the pantry 20s and the buttery 20s. He presented the King with a 'courser' named Lyard Duras which had cost him £40 and the Queen with a courser called Lyard Lewes which cost £8. Servants and officers of the household often gave gloves to their master and mistress and might receive in return gifts of money which equalled a quarter of their wages. The Earl of Northumberland bestowed a noble each (6s 8d) on his three henchmen, 20s on the Abbot of Misrule, and 20s on the master of the revels 'for the overseeing and ordering of his lordship's plays, interludes, and dressing what is played before his lordship. . . .'

Outdoors, too, the changing seasons brought numerous diversions and folk ceremonies. Hunting and poaching were the chief sports in the greenwood. Merchants as well as gentry were securing licences in ever increasing numbers to enclose parks and build warrens. Even when the Celys were riding into the Cotswolds on business, they flew their hawks at game along the road. Hunting was expensive; a good hawk was hard to come by and cost as much as a horse. English dogs—greyhounds and mastiffs— and English and Irish horses were highly regarded on the Continent. Louis XI, probably the master hunter of the age, many times sent across the Channel for dogs and horses. The Duke of Milan once armed an agent of his with 1,000 gold ducats to buy hunting animals in England because they were 'of rare excellence'.

The quieter pleasures of walking were also appreciated. Sir William Sandes, who owned a manor adjoining one of the Stonor manors, sent word to Sir William Stonor that Stonor's farmer 'is

a troublesome fellow. . . . Sometime as I walk in my recreation I
may see that in your woods he hath made great waste. . .'. The
sport of tennis was enjoyed in town and country. In London one
day Sir John Howard lost 3s 4d in a game with Sir Robert
Chamberley. The execution of Richard Skeres, London skinner,
was much lamented by one of the chroniclers because Skeres had
been 'one of the cunningest players at the tennis in England, for
he was so deliver [agile] that he would stand in a tub that should
be near breast-high and leap out of the same . . . and win of a good
player'.

Encouraged by Parliament and authority everywhere, archery
continued to be a popular sport with all classes, though, as Sir John
Fortescue pointed out, it 'may not be done without right great
expenses, as every man expert therein knoweth right well'. The
Grocers of London had archery butts in their garden; a salter bequeathed a new bow to each of twenty neighbours in his parish
'that useth the sport of shooting'. When Sir John Howard rode
abroad he enjoyed watching champion village bowmen display
their art and he himself often took a hand in the sport. One day
at York he lost at the pricks (slender wands) 8d and at the butts
another 8d and spent 4d treating to ale and bread. On country
greens village and manor teams competed at wrestling; and all
over England men bowled and kicked footballs, though these
pastimes were frowned on as effeminate.

The election of Knights of the Shire sometimes furnished the
gentry a hearty gastronomic diversion. In the verdant April
weather of 1467, Sir John Howard and Sir Thomas Brews conducted a successful campaign at Ipswich, in the course of which
they refreshed the voters with a feast that included 8 oxen, 24
calves, 24 sheep, 20 lambs, 30 pigs, 12 pheasants, 108 capons, 240
chickens, 120 rabbits, 800 eggs, 140 pairs of pigeons, 32 gallons of
milk, £3 9s worth of bread (at a penny for a big loaf), wine by the
hogshead costing £3 13s 4d, as well as 13s 2d for 'wine at gentlemen's lodgings besides', 20 barrels of double beer (best beer), 16
barrels of single beer, 8 bushels of flour for doucettes (pastries),
24s worth of drinkings at taverns. The meal was prepared by four
cooks, receiving 13s 4d, aided by twelve labourers who got 4s

and by six lads paid 18d. Howard and Brews must have ridden
into Ipswich with a long train of supporters, for the cost of
stabling horses at inns during the day came to 44s 6d. The two
Knights of the Shire had to settle a bill of £40 17s 6d (something
like £1,500 today.)

Folk games and ceremonies responded to the changing seasons
as inevitably as burgeoning hawthorn or the browning hillsides of
autumn. In the North the beginning of field work after the
Christmas festivities was marked by Plough Monday. Men and
boys dragged a plough about the village, did a dance in fantastic
costumes, and took up a collection; anyone who failed to contribute was likely to have the path before his door ploughed up. At
Easter-time the 'wythe', a garland of branches, was ceremoniously
borne into the manor house, and all true hearts were expected to
'pay to the wythe'. Then came 'hocking' on the second Monday
and Tuesday after Easter Sunday. On the Monday women caught
and bound men with ropes and would not release them till they
had paid a forfeit; the next day men 'hocked' women; sometimes
chains were stretched across a road so that a toll might be exacted
of all who passed. Sir John Howard, riding home in April of 1464,
paid 16d 'in hocking at Sudbury', and when he arrived in his own
village of Stoke Neyland he gave 12d 'to the hock-pot', which was
probably donated to the parish church. The church likewise benefited from church-ales, at which parishioners on a fine spring day
gathered in the churchyard to drink the brew which the church-
wardens had produced for the occasion. 'Rush-bearings' saw
young people decking altars and nave with greenery while a
village fiddler played for dancing in the churchyard and cemetery.
In the North the church precincts became the scene of the 'Sum-
mer-game': an unmarried girl and an unmarried young man were
crowned King and Queen of Summer and kept their state upon
thrones surrounded by 'knights' and other functionaries.

During the Yorkist Age, May Day ushered in the gayest season
of the year with vernal ceremonies that would wither a little not long
after; for the Reformation, not without cause, smelled paganism
in the rites of the day. Before dawn young people were trouping
into field and wood to 'bring in the May', crowns and garlands of

spring flowers; and many a 'green gown' was given, with or without vows, in forest glades. Ale flowed on the green as boys performed Morris dances and sword dances taught them by their fathers. Robin Hood and Maid Marian presided over the village pageant; for the reign of Edward IV signals the ripest age of the Robin Hood legend. Sir John Paston one day complained to his brother John that he had been deserted by a servant whose idleness he had long condoned: 'I have kept him these three years to play St. George and Robin Hood and the Sheriff of Nottingham'.[1] As late as the brief reign of Edward VI (1547-53), Bishop Latimer found himself unable to preach on May Day in a certain country town because there was no one to listen to him: 'It is Robin Hood's day,' he was told. 'The parish are gone abroad to gather for Robin Hood.'

Mentions of Robin Hood first began to occur in the latter half of the fourteenth century. By 1439 a petition in Parliament called for the arrest of Piers Venables of Derbyshire, who 'in manner of insurrection went into the woods in that country, like as it had been Robin Hood and his menie'. A 'Robin of Holderness' stirred up riots in the East Riding of Yorkshire in the spring of 1469 a few days before Sir John Conyers, calling himself Robin of Redesdale, fomented a rising on behalf of the Earl of Warwick. Robin Hood ballads blossomed in the propitious air of Edward IV's reign—one of the earliest extant refers to 'Edward, our comely King'—for Robin Hood and the English yeomen rose into prominence together. He represented their sturdy independence, their romantic dreams of the good life, their private image of themselves: he is lord of the forest, prince of wits, a nonpareil of archers, a master poacher, a true-hearted subject, an untrusser of fat rich rascally prelates; and if he must meet a tragic end it will be the Church, in the shape of a nun, who will do him in. Minstrels singing ballads of Robin Hood knew where their audience lay:

> God have mercy on Robin Hood's soul
> And save all good yeomanry!

[1] The passage is usually interpreted as meaning that Sir John hired the man for his acting abilities, but the context makes clear that Sir John regarded him as good for nothing else.

Scattered among Robin Hood's forests and expanses of waste, the manors and villages of the realm were connected with each other and with the cities by a network of roads that earned no encomiums in the records of the day. Old Roman highways, their surfaces sometimes much broken but their foundations still solid, fanned out from London to form the principal roads of England: the much-travelled route to Canterbury and Dover; the road through Winchester and Salisbury and Shaftesbury to Exeter; Watling Street running northwest to Chester and beyond; the Ermine Street striking northward through eastern England; the Icknield Way in East Anglia. A network of subsidiary routes had sprung up during the Middle Ages, often no more than tracks across a heath or a rough detour from the highway to take in a town that had appeared since Roman days. The average road was a country lane running through deep woods and across sweeps of moor and marsh, un-signposted, generating forks and branching tracks to puzzle the traveller, sometimes ending abruptly at a ford that had disappeared under high water.

The records of manor courts and towns, wills and other documents complain of 'foul ways' and decayed bridges and flooded causeways and stretches of highway described as 'broken, hollow, and ruinous . . . and dangerous in winter'. Repair of bridges, fords, roads was the responsibility of the manor or borough through which they ran; but abbots and lords and corporations not infrequently failed their obligations, or their tenants, as the fines recorded on manor court-rolls show, neglected to replace broken pavements and clean out ditches.

During the turbulent decade of the 1450's and at other times when the realm was shaken by discord, hedges and forests served on occasion as places of ambush for the accomplishment of private revenge. 'Ten rioters lay in await in the highway under Thorpe Wood upon Philip Berney, esquire [Margaret Paston's uncle] and his man, and shot at them and smote their horses with arrows, and then over-rode them and broke a bow on the said Philip's head and took him prisoner, calling him traitor.' Berney never regained his health after this beating and fifteen months later 'passed to God with the greatest pain that ever I saw'. As William Tresham,

Speaker of the Commons of Parliament, rode to meet the Duke of York in the late summer of 1450, he was waylaid at dawn one morning near Thorpeland Close, Northamptonshire, by a band of armed men hiding behind a long hedge, who 'feloniously issued out and smote him through the body a foot and more and gave him many and great deadly wounds and cut his throat'.

But every age has its spectacular crimes of violence. Robbery was a much more common fate than ambush. Sir John Fortescue pointed with some pride to the robberies committed in the realm as proof that the English had much more spirit than the French: 'It hath often been seen in England that three or four thieves, for poverty, hath set upon seven or eight true men and robbed them all. There be more men hanged in England in a year for robbery and manslaughter than there be hanged in France for such cause of crime in seven years.' The Venetian diplomat, who perhaps had been told some tall tales, thought that there was 'no country in the world where there are so many thieves and robbers as in England; in so much that few venture to go alone into the country excepting in the middle of the day, and fewer still in the towns at night, and least of all in London'. Without question, there was a deal of highway robbery, as there would be until the nineteenth century.

Yet, though roads were often bad, and sometimes unsafe, at all seasons of the year travellers imperturbably made their way up and down the realm. After all, much of the information about foul ways comes from wills in which men left money for road repair, and from municipal and manor documents which indicate that steps were being taken to improve conditions. Gilds and towns and private individuals contributed funds for upkeep of bridges, streets, causeways, fords. The roads were probably better than they would become in succeeding centuries; for most traffic, passenger and freight, was borne on horseback, and heavy carts and carriages had not yet scored deep ruts. The Pastons and the Stonors and the Celys and the Plumptons make nothing of the badness of the roads. John Shillingford gives no sign of considering it a hardship to ride from Exeter to London several times in mid-winter. Probably as many people in the reign of Edward IV as in the twentieth century reached their destinations without incident.

Travellers on horseback often averaged between thirty and forty miles a day, and special messengers, hiring relays of horses, made even better time. John Shillingford informed his aldermen in the autumn of 1447, 'I rode from Exeter on Friday and came to London on Tuesday betimes [early] at seven at clock.' The following year on a Wednesday in May he left Exeter at seven in the morning and 'the next Saturday thereafter at seven o'clock in the morning I came to London'. Depending upon the season, the weather, the moon, and the traveller's urgency, the journey from Exeter to London, about 170 miles, could be accomplished in four or five days. The Pastons sometimes rode from Norwich to London in less than three days, but the trip usually took a full three days and occasionally a traveller entered London on the morning of the fourth day.

Bishop Redman, a Visitor of the Praemonstratensians, covered the distance of about 170 miles from Torre Abbey to the capital in four days. A delegation of citizens left Shrewsbury on a Wednesday and arrived in London in time for dinner (usually about 11 A.M.) on Saturday, covering 153 miles in three and a half days. They slept at Wolverhampton on Wednesday night, at Daventry on Thursday, spent Friday night at St. Albans, and rode into London the next morning. People leaving the capital bound for the Continent usually passed the first night on the Dover road at Rochester, the second night at Canterbury, and reached Dover by noon of the third day. With luck, they might be in Calais by nightfall for when wind and tide were right and no Breton corsairs showed sail, communications between Dover or Sandwich and Calais were rapid. A Cely letter written in London on November 9 was answered at Calais on the 12th. Young Richard Cely on September 2, 1480, sent a letter from Dover to his brother George at Calais asking him to be at Boulogne the following day, and George fulfilled the rendezvous.

The chief waterways of England carried a heavy traffic. After Edward IV visited Croyland Abbey in the fens in the early summer of 1469, he took ship and sailed up the Nene to Fotheringhay Castle. Barges plied the Ouse, the Trent, the Severn, the Thames, the Avon, the Medway, and even smaller streams. The Stonors, like other gentry, dispatched many a bale and barrel of stuff purchased in London to Henley, the river journey taking about four days. Dame Elizabeth Stonor received a rude shock when bargemen refused her packages because they had not yet received their money for previous shipments: 'Truly,' she wrote in virtuous amazement, 'I never had a thing carried by them but that I paid them truly before.'

The first royal postal system in England—Louis XI had invented the device a few years before—was instituted by Edward IV in 1482 in order to receive speedy tidings of his brother Richard's expedition into Scotland. Ten men were stationed along the road from London to Berwick, a distance of some 335 miles, so that each man rode a relay of about thirty miles. Richard himself, when he became King, revived the system in 1484; it appears that he increased the rapidity of transmission by adding extra riders so that each had but twenty miles to cover.

Though well-horsed messengers galloping main roads could achieve more than fifty miles a day, when travellers struck off into the countryside to reach a small town or manor, they often had to fee a native in order to find their way. Setting out for Yorkshire, Sir John Howard hired a guide for the dangerous crossing of The Wash; on leaving Pontefract he needed another guide to show him the way to Cawthorne; and when he rode into Lancashire he and his party lost the road and were rescued by 'a maid that taught the way over Didsbury Forth'—at which point the Howard account book almost bursts into a ballad. Even when quite close to home, men sometimes had to open their purses in order to reach their destinations. Sir John Howard's Norwich draper, Portland, had to be guided to Long Stretham in his own Norfolk county; and apparently the journey proved difficult, for he paid 8d for the service.

Geoffrey Chaucer would have found himself at home on the roads of the England of Edward IV. He would meet parties of pilgrims journeying to Our Lady of Walsingham or to Canterbury, country knights riding to a 'Shire Day' with a cavalcade of friends and tenants, a lord and his lady in crimson velvet heading a retinue of servants and a train of carts as they moved from one manor to another, a gay clerk with a hawk on his fist, friars and pardoners tramping their rounds from village to village, chapmen with shoulder-bag or sumpter-horse stuffed with merchandise, a Yeoman of the Crown riding hard with privy seals in his pouch. . . .

But at times Dan Geoffrey would be bound to realize that the world had changed a little since the days of the ill-fated Richard II. There was a greater diversity of travellers and of traffic. Men dressed as yeomen were riding surprisingly good horses and perhaps had a servant or two at their shoulders. Many more trains of pack-animals laden with bales of cloth were plodding the roads now; and clothiers in amazing numbers were riding with their employees from village to village to bring thread to the weavers or cloth to the dyers. Most surprising of all, perhaps, common carriers were plying regular routes from town to town and from all the chief towns to London.

The common carrier and his cart, or more likely his sumpter-horses, had begun to make his appearance in England about the time of Chaucer's death in 1400. By the beginning of the reign of Edward IV, in 1461, he had become an institution. From as far away as Exeter and Bristol and Shrewsbury and York and Lincoln and Norwich carriers made their way to London on more or less scheduled journeys. The inns in the capital where they ended their trips were as well-known as twentieth-century railway stations. When Sir John Paston was looking for a parcel from home, he sent a servant to Blossom's Inn in St. Margaret's Lane off Cheapside. Carriers seem to have adhered quite well to their timetables. Writing on a Sunday in London, Sir John asked for stuff to be sent him so that he could have it by the coming weekend. Margaret Paston requested her men in London to send her food and cloth 'by the next carrier'.

When people shipped money or jewellery by carrier, they sometimes resorted to stratagems. Thomas Makyn, requesting his master in London to send him 40s by the Oxford carrier, added, 'Buy a pound of powdered pepper to carry the money privily, or else two pounds of rice, for that makes great bulk.' John Paston once suggested, 'Peradventure with some trusty carrier might some money come trussed in some fardel, not knowing [unknown] to the carrier that it is no money but some other cloth or vestment of silk. . . .' Directions like these do not necessarily betray doubt of a carrier's honesty. Since carriers were responsible in law for the goods they transported, they undoubtedly charged a much higher rate for money and jewellery, and Makyn and John Paston were perhaps thinking of cheating the carrier rather than of being cheated by him.

Historians have generally neglected the role of the common carrier in transforming manor life during the Yorkist Age. Before he appeared on the scene only lords and the wealthiest gentry could afford to keep men in their service to fetch and carry goods and missives. Manor-dwellers were largely dependent on the products of their fields and of the shops in a neighbouring town; and family news and tidings of affairs in the realm came to them haphazardly and often at long intervals.

With the advent of the common carrier, the London market stood at the yeoman's gate; he could communicate readily with friends in London; and he might receive frequent news of the great world. The quantities of letters written in this age attest more than the spread of education: there had now arrived a sure and steady means of dispatching them. The growing sense of nationalism, the rise of an informed yeomanry, the greater sophistication and enlarged comfort of manor life, and the increasing domination of London in the Yorkist Age all owed something to the common carrier.

Churchmen and The Church

THE Church lay upon the realm, ubiquitous as the damp English air. It had so embedded itself in lay society that, like two plants that have worked their way into each other's vitals, these institutions had achieved an apparently inseparable accommodation, giving and taking. The English Church was now so old, so massive, so complex, and it had so saturated the daily life of the people that one could hardly say where religion ended and secular existence began. It was believed that the Church owned one-third—and, in fact, it probably did own almost one-quarter—of all the land of England.

Men were baptized into the community of Christendom, they were married at church door, they were laid to rest in church ground, their souls were fortified by church prayers. King, lords, wealthy townsmen and gentry all began the day by hearing Mass in their chapels; for daily Mass expressed status as much as furs and a retinue of servants. Ordinary folk attended services on Sundays and on the principal feasts of the Church. This observance was enforced by law as well as piety; back-sliders and other offenders against Holy Church were forced to do penance on town greens and in churchyards for all to see.

For attacking a priest with a spade, Richard Tylly of Taunton was excommunicated; when he submitted himself some months later for correction, he was required 'with bare head and feet and clothed only in a shirt and breeches and holding in his hand the spade [to] walk in procession around St. Mary Magdalen on two Sundays and on one Sunday similarly [to] walk round the chapel of St. James, and also [to] walk once round the market-place of

Taunton, and when he comes to the middle of it stand still for a time at the discretion of the chaplain with a whip in his hand who follows him. . . .'

From King to peasant, everyone bore candles round the church at Candlemas, crept to the Cross on Good Friday, watched miracle plays on Corpus Christi, listened to the all-night ringing of the bells on All Hallows Eve, had friends and kin among the clergy, enjoyed the preaching of an eloquent friar and the pillorying of a rascally clerk, and, when spring had unbound winter's icy chains with sweet showers, took to the road to go on pilgrimage. Pilgrimages were undertaken to fulfill vows; they were also holiday excursions offering folk the opportunity of seeing the 'countries' of the realm and exchanging stories with strangers and hearing the latest news and enjoying a respite from the daily routine. In one of Margaret Paston's first extant letters to her husband, she informed him what she and Agnes had done to try to cure him of an illness he had suffered in London: 'My mother [in-law] behested another image of wax of the weight of you to Our Lady of Walsingham and she sent four nobles to the four Orders of Friars at Norwich to pray for you, and I have behested to go on pilgrimages to Walsingham and to St. Leonard's [Norwich] for you.' On a June day in 1470 young John Paston casually mentioned to his brother Sir John, 'I propose to go to Canterbury on foot this next week, with God's grace'; perhaps he was honouring a vow he had made when Caister Castle was besieged the previous summer. Even the Duke and Duchess of Norfolk walked barefoot to Our Lady of Walsingham.

From every shire's end cavalcades of pilgrims jogged through the May weather to shrines all over England. An astonishing number, from all ranks, managed the long, hard journey to the Holy Land. The most popular pilgrimage beyond the shores of England was to the shrine of St. James of Compostella in Spain. In early spring shipowners of Bristol and the southern ports busied themselves to secure licences from the King to transport pilgrims by the hundreds. On these profitable voyages the ship's hold was rudely partitioned off into 'cells' or turned into one gigantic dormitory, where pilgrims, who supplied their own

bedding, lay in closely packed rows, their feet extended towards
a central aisle. Those with dainty stomachs brought fresh food
with them; cackling of geese and squawking of chickens mingled
with the groans of the seasick. In stormy weather grinning sailors
brought round bowls so that their troublesome cargo would not
foul the ship. The miseries of the voyage and the heartlessness of
the mariners were celebrated in many a song:

> Men may leave all games
> That sail to Saint James!
> For many a man it gramys [grieves]
>   When they begin to sail.
> For when they have taken the sea
> At Sandwich or at Winchelsea,
> At Bristol or where that it be,
>   Their hearts begin to fail. . . .
>
> A boy or twain anon climb high
> And overthwart the sail-yard lie—
> 'Y how! taylia!' the remnant cry
>   And pull with all their might.
> 'Bestow the boat, Boatswain, anon,
> That our pilgrims may play thereon;
> For some are like to cough and groan
>   Ere it be full midnight. . . .'
>
> . . . This meanwhile the pilgrims lie
> And have their bowls fast them by
> And cry after hot malmsey,
>   'Thou help for to restore'.
>
> And some would have a salted toast,
> For they might eat neither boiled nor roast;
> A man might soon pay for *their* cost,
>   As for one day or twain!
> Some laid their books on their knee
> And read so long they might not see—
> 'Alas, mine head will cleave in three!'
>   Thus saith another certain.

Then cometh our owner like a lord
And speaketh many a royal word
And dresseth him to the high board
    To see all thing be well.
Anon he calleth a carpenter
He biddeth him bring with him his gear,
To make the cabins here and there,
    With many a feeble cell.

A sack of straw were there right good,
For some must lie them in their hood;
I had as lief be in the wood
    Without meat or drink;
For when that we shall go to bed,
The pump was nigh our bed's head—
A man were as good to be dead
    As smell thereof the stink!

Sanctuaries continued to offer a haven for criminals and debtors and victims of injustice and political refugees. As Warwick the Kingmaker approached London in October of 1470, King Edward having fled to the Low Countries, die-hard Lancastrians and Neville supporters emerged from sanctuaries as numerous Yorkists, including some bishops of the royal Council, hurriedly entered them. Edward's Queen abandoned the rooms in the Tower which she had had specially decorated for her confinement and betook herself to Westminster Abbey, giving birth there the following month to her first son, later Edward V. Though the privilege of sanctuary was common to Christendom, it was apparently nowhere so widely practiced and so formalized as in England; for almost all foreign visitors commented upon the system. Every church was, in a measure, a sanctuary; by long custom certain ones were regarded as particularly privileged; but the only really secure havens were those possessing a papal bull and a royal charter.

A criminal, hotly pursued, headed for the nearest sanctuary, pounded up the nave and threw himself upon the altar. If he had more time, he rang the bell at the 'sanctuary door', claimed his privilege and was admitted to the precincts. In theory, he was then safe for forty days, though men sometimes spent much longer than that in sanctuary. If, on the other hand, officers of the law or his enemies closely besieged the place so that the felon could not escape, he had the option of sending for the chief magistrate of the town and confessing his crime, after which he took an oath to leave the realm. He then emerged from sanctuary clad in shirt and breeches only and holding a candle. Escorted by a constable to see that he kept to his route, he made his way to a designated port. If no ship was about to sail, he was required every day to walk into the water up to his knees, or sometimes to his neck, crying, 'Passage, for the love of God and King Edward's sake!' until a vessel took him over the sea. To the Venetian diplomat this custom seemed as picturesque as it does to later ages, and he wrote a lengthy account of it for his government. Though there were strict injunctions against molesting a 'king's felon', all such criminals did not succeed in finishing their journey. A widow dwelling outside Aldgate 'had long time cherished and brought up (out of charity) a certain Breton born, which most unkindly and cruelly in a night murdered the said widow sleeping in her bed, and after fled with such jewels and other stuff of hers as he might carry: but he was so freshly pursued that for fear he took the church of St. George in Southwark and challenged privilege of sanctuary there, and so abjured the king's land. Then the constables brought him into London, intending to have conveyed him eastward; but so soon as he was come into the parish where before he had committed the murder, the wives cast upon him so much filth and ordure of the street that they slew him out of hand. . . .'

Sir Roger Clifford was condemned, as an abettor of Buckingham's abortive revolt of 1483, to be drawn from Westminster to Tower Hill and there beheaded. As he was dragged, bound to a 'hurdle', past London's most famous sanctuary, the church of St. Martin le Grand near the top of Cheapside, his confessor managed to cut his cords; and in a trice Sir Roger was running desperately for the gate which meant life. As he almost reached it, he was tripped up, seized by royal officers, and rebound to his hurdle, in what agony of mind can be imagined. The Church clung as tightly to its right of sanctuary as to its other privileges. After Sir William Oldhall, outlawed in 1452 for supporting the Duke of York, took refuge in St. Martin le Grand, a band of Lancastrian lords came one night and removed him 'with great violence'. But the Dean of St. Martin's, bundling up his charters, hastened to complain to the King; and in the teeth of the royal favourites he was able to procure the return of Sir William to the sanctuary.

The visible embodiments no less than the powers of the English Church struck the minds of visitors. Though they came fresh from viewing the grandest religious monuments of the Continent, they expressed amazement at the number and beauty of the churches, the repertory of relics, the opulence of England's renowned shrines. The Bohemian lords thought the churches of London surpassed any they had ever seen, and these churches possessed so rich an array of relics that it would take two scribes at least a fortnight to describe them. 'Never in any country,' declared one of the travellers, 'have I seen more beautiful churches and monasteries than in England. For they are all covered on top with lead and tin and within they are adorned in a truly wonderful fashion.' Spending Easter in Salisbury, the Bohemians noted that on Maundy Thursday and Good Friday the congregation dined in the cathedral 'in memory of the Last Supper, and mirrors are set up on the altar'. But nothing of course could equal the glories of the shrine of St. Thomas in Canterbury Cathedral, which 'is so rarely embellished with pearls and precious stones that no more splendid tomb can be found in Christendom, nor one where greater miracles occur'. The relics, too, were exciting: a tooth of John the Baptist, a finger of St. Urban, a lip of one of the Murdered Innocents, and three thorns from the crown of Christ. When Erasmus 'did' St. Thomas's shrine, he was shown jewels 'larger than the egg of a goose', the prior touching every gem with a white wand as he told its name, value, and donor. Touring the ecclesiastical sights of London with a fellow Silesian, the German knight Popplau saw among other wonders 'some jars out of Cana in Galilee'.

Surviving churches only hint at the stained-glass windows bright with saints, the Last Judgement flaming on the walls, altars shining with silken banners and service of silver and gold. But even the ruins of the great monastic establishments of the North and West eloquently suggest their former grandeur. Poor betrayed Robert Aske[1] said wistfully in the hard days of their dissolution that the abbeys 'was one of the beauties of this realm to all men passing through the same'. The Venetian diplomat, after reporting that 'there is not a parish church in the kingdom so mean as not to possess crucifixes, candlesticks, censers, patens, and cups of silver', continued, 'Your Magnificence may therefore imagine what the decorations of those enormously rich Benedictine, Carthusian, and Cistercian monasteries must be. These are, indeed, more like baronial palaces than religious houses. . . . And I have been informed that amongst other things many of these monasteries possess unicorns' horns of an extraordinary size'. The Venetian quoted the English proverb about the abbeys of Glastonbury and Shaftesbury, 'that the finest match that could be made in all England would be between that abbot and abbess'—though, in fact, the Abbot of Westminster and the Abbess of Sion would have outdone them.

It appeared to the Venetian, and to others, that the clergy of England represented the most powerful and wealthiest force in the realm, 'nor is the saying that is so common in this country without cause—"that the priests are one of the three happy generations of the world" '. A papal agent named Aliprando, who was unceremoniously arrested at Calais and made an undignified escape clinging to the back of a horse, blamed his experience on 'these old prelates, abbots or other fat priests who rule [the king's] council'. But the Venetian and Aliprando were wrong. It was the world which had won the Church. From the bishops and abbots who sat in the King's council or occupied a place among the Lords of Parliament, to the parish clergy and the family chaplain, churchmen served secular interests at the command of their lay patrons; and the whole complex institution of the Church had become so impregnated with worldly preoccupations that if these

[1] Leader of the Pilgrimage of Grace, a northern rising against Henry VIII's Reformation.

should be brought under sharp attack, the edifice had no other prop to keep it from tumbling to the ground.

Mitred abbots lived in a style befitting their rank as peers of the realm. The kitchen of the Abbot of Glastonbury still hints at the lordly splendour of the appointments when he entertained distinguished visitors at dinner. On occasions of state the Abbot of St. Albans dined on a platform raised fifteen steps above the rest of the hall, and the monks who served him performed a hymn at every fifth step. Operators of great estates and massive establishments, abbots defended their temporalities with worldly zeal. The Abbot of Glastonbury wrote to Lord Wenlock's widow, 'Madame, I am informed that ye propose to trouble me in the law. . . . Madame, if ye will trouble with me, I promise you I shall open such things that shall turn you to as much trouble as I shall have by you, I doubt me thereof right naught. And I trust to God the best man of law in England will be on my side and right stiff against you. Madame, in such doing is none avail, neither to you nor to me. Wherefore, if it please you to be in peace, I will thank you thereof. If ye will needs go to plea, I trust to God. Answer you.'

Sometimes the worldliness of abbots took an even more pronounced form. In 1480 Dan William Brekenok, Inspector General of the Cluniac monasteries in England, upon paying a visit to the Abbey of Bermondsey discovered 'great ruin and decay, as well of the said monastery as of religion within the same'. When Abbot John Marlowe contumaciously refused to answer to the charges against him, the Inspector clad himself in a retinue of learned dignitaries and 'descended again to the said monastery of Bermondsey'. Abbot Marlowe was waiting for him, backed by a doctor of laws and a multitude of lay people, who laid hands on the Inspector and 'pulled him from his doctors, notaries, and other his learned counsel and had him to secret prison'—from where he somehow managed to appeal to the secular law, declaring that his gaolers meant to murder him, 'or otherwise mischief him contrary to the law and all good conscience'.

The prelates who went on diplomatic missions for Edward IV

and sat in his Council and held great offices did not represent an ecclesiastical domination of the realm. They did not occupy high place because they were bishops and deans; they had become bishops and deans because they served the King well and he had thus cheaply and effectively rewarded them. For numerous lesser officers, like the clerks of the Wardrobe, special livings were set aside as their preserve. Ambitious boys found their way to the universities and entered the Church to make a career for themselves; and Edward IV chose these learned, able, vigorous men—like Thomas Rotherham and John Russell and John Morton, all of whom rose to be Chancellor—to advise him and to carry out his policies. Such prelates often held several benefices and, busy at Westminster, saw little of their bishoprics.

An English Church with a royal Supreme Head did not come into being in the reign of Henry VIII. During the Yorkist Age there was an English Church, as there had been for centuries, and the Supreme Head of it, though not so officially titled, was King Edward IV. He refused to admit papal bulls and papal agents into his realm when he pleased; he nominated bishops and deans and presented to benefices, and through his civil servants, who were also the chief officers of the Church, he kept Convocation completely under his thumb and squeezed great sums of money from it. The Pope continued to collect First Fruits and other perquisites, to provide to a limited number of benefices, to confirm the selection of bishops and abbots, and to be acknowledged in England as the Head of Christendom; but the Holy Father himself had no doubts about who was master of the ecclesiastical establishment: Martin V declared acidly, 'It is not the Pope but the King of England that governs the Church in his dominions.'

Like bishops and deans, the parish priests—the clergy closest to the average man—were often engrossed in the world. They were likely to be poor, in a society growing more prosperous, and ignorant or rudely lettered before parishioners whose standards of education were rising. Benefices held by royal officers and pluralistic prelates were farmed out to vicars for a miserable wage. To make ends meet, monasteries and nunneries had been permitted to 'appropriate' churches, that is, to pocket the proceeds of the living and hire curates for a small stipend to carry out the duties. Furthermore, priests were increasingly drawn from the humbler ranks. During the Yorkist Age far fewer of them had independent means than in preceding centuries. The average living now paid about £8 to £9 a year. Consequently peasant-priests and starveling curates spent a great deal of time farming their glebe land, usually forty to sixty acres, and trying to market their produce. Many country parsons with a flair for agriculture leased additional lands to improve their incomes. Barely maintaining the services of the Church, some of them hardly able to do more than gabble through a Paternoster, they differed little from the mass of their parishioners.

The church edifice itself, invaded by the world, had become the centre of town and village life. Men talked law-suits or crop prices and women had neighbourly chats while Mass was being said; sometimes the nave became quiet only at the Elevation of the Host. The church served as a handy meeting-place, where enemies might confer on neutral ground, arbitrators decide a land quarrel, a young man with marriage in his mind arrange to meet a young girl and her family. At Sandwich, elections were held in one parish church and the council met in another; at Rye the municipal accounts were audited yearly in the church. Public announcements of all kinds were made during the service. Men were 'warned' about the meeting of a manor court or a village gathering. At the outbreak of the Lincolnshire Rebellion in 1470, Sir Robert Welles instructed the clergy to declare in all the churches of the shire that 'every man must be at Ranby Hawe on Tuesday in readiness to resist the King'.

As Edward IV used bishoprics to reward his councillors, lords and gentry with benefices to bestow expected the recipients to do them worldly services. When William Worcester complained to Sir John Fastolfe that he was unpaid, that hard-fisted old knight merely remarked that he was sorry Worcester was not a clerk so that he could present him with a benefice. Parsons and chaplains acted as land agents, stewards, counsellors. The Paston family, with more than twenty livings to bestow, worked their clergy hard. The Vicar of Paston, a member of the family council, kept an eye out for dissatisfaction among the tenantry and reported on men he thought disloyal. The Rector of Titchwell, writing 'in all goodly haste for the matter is of substance', warned that 'this day in the grey morning three men of my Lord of Norfolk with long spears carried off three good horses'. The Rector was eager to take action, 'for such an open wrong unremedied knew I never'. The Parson of Melton collected rents; the Vicar of Stalham took inventory of sheep and lands at Sparham.

The family chaplain served as secretary, schoolmaster, and often as land agent too. Sir John Fastolfe's chaplain, Thomas Howes, was kept so busy serving writs and letting land that he could have had little time for saying Mass. James Gloys, the Paston chaplain from about 1448 until he died in 1473, completely identified himself with the worldly interests of his patrons. He owned a goodly collection of books; he understood all the Paston business; and when trouble broke he could be counted on to act boldly.

Not long after he joined the Pastons he had made himself so unpopular in their service that in the village of Oxnead, a Paston manor, he was attacked in the street by two men and 'driven into my mother's place for refuge'. That afternoon he was assaulted again and so many threats were uttered against him that Margaret Paston sent him up to London to her husband to get him out of harm's way. His letters to his master show him leasing lands, distraining for rent, threatening recalcitrant tenants, defying Paston enemies. To arrest a man named Bettes, he trailed him to a manor court being held by a certain Gonnor. But Gonnor spoke so fiercely, Gloys reported to John Paston, that the bailiff of the Hundred 'durst not arrest the said Bettes. Then I took it upon me and arrested him myself as he sat by Gonnor'. Gonnor 'set all the tenants upon me and made a great noise'. Though his prisoner was taken from him and he was threatened with being bound like a criminal, Gloys coolly rode away, telling Gonnor 'if that he abode in Norfolk he should be made to seek the skirts of his saddle ere Easter.

'And if he had kept his way that night, I should have kept him true covenant; for I lay await upon him on the heath as he should have come homeward, and if I might have met with him I should have had Bettes from him. But he had laid such watch that he had aspied us ere he came fully at us; and he remembered . . . that four swift feet were better than two hands, and he took his horse with the spurs and rode to Felbrygge Hall as fast as he might ride.' Lying there in ambush, his eyeballs shining in the twilight, James Gloys was clearly a formidable man, if not a formidable man of God. When the Duke of Suffolk threatened the manor of Drayton, Margaret Paston informed her husband that she could send only 'Thomas Bonde and Sir James Gloys to hold the court in your name and to claim your title; for I could get none other body to keep the court . . . because I suppose they were afraid of the people that should be there of the Duke of Suffolk's party'. When Bonde and Gloys arrived, they found some sixty of Suffolk's men there, 'some of them having rusty pole-axes'. Though James Gloys 'had the words', it was Thomas Bonde the enemy preferred to lay hands on, trussing him up like a felon.

Shortly after the death of John Paston, in 1466, the family gathered in London to concert measures for protecting the estate; but they soon realized that they must 'send a letter to Richard Calle and to Sir James Gloys to come up to London in any wise. For there is no man can do in divers matters that they can do. . . .'

But now there came a change. Margaret Paston, bitterly resenting her eldest son's spendthrift ways, came to depend more and more upon James Gloys, much to the disgust of Sir John and young John. Very early Gloys had aroused jealousy by his capacity to insinuate himself into the good graces of the ladies of the family, even winning the favour of John Paston's fearsome mother, Agnes. 'But and we among us give not him a lift,' one of the Paston men wrote angrily, 'I pray God that we never thrive.'

Four years after the death of John Paston, young John was informing his brother that there was no money to be got out of their mother, for 'she and her curate [Gloys] allege more poverty than ever was'. Two years later (1472) he was referring to Sir James as 'the proud, peevish, and ill-disposed priest to us all. . . . Many quarrels are picked to get my brother E[dmund] and me out of her house; we go not to bed unchidden lightly, all that we do is ill done, and all that Sir James and Pekok [a steward] doth is

well done. Sir James and I be twain [at odds]. We fell out before
my mother with 'Thou proud priest and thou proud squire, my
mother taking his part. . . .' A few months later, young John
continued the tale: 'Sir James is ever chopping at me when my
mother is present, with such words as he thinks "wrath" me and
also cause my mother to be displeased with me . . . and when he
hath most unfitting words to me, I smile a little and tell him it is
good hearing of these old tales. Sir James is parson of Stokesby
by J. Berney's gift. I trow he beareth him the higher.' When Sir
John learned of Gloys' death the following year, he had only this
to say: 'I am right glad that [my mother] will now do somewhat
by your advice; wherefore beware from henceforth that no such
fellow creep in between her and you. . . .' Gloys had been many
things to the Pastons; chaplain seems to have been the least of
them.

In espousing the interests of their patrons, parsons and chaplains incurred the ill will of parishioners and manor tenants who
looked upon such clerks as hard-fisted bailiffs rather than ministers
of the faith. As a result of obeying the orders of Agnes Paston, the
Vicar of Paston, as he began to say Mass one morning, was
suddenly set upon by officers of the sheriff, heartily abetted by
some of his flock. In terror he 'sold away 20s worth of stuff; and
the residue of my stuff, I have put it in sure hands'. Taking refuge
in Bromhom Priory, he wrote hastily to his mistress, 'The great
fray that they made in the time of mass, it ravished my wits and
made me full heavily disposed. . . . It is told me that if I be taken,
I may no other remedy have but straight to prison.'

Letters, proceedings in Chancery, and the testimony of ecclesiastics themselves reveal numerous cases of parish clergy unpleasantly
at odds with their parishioners. Parsons complained of being
cheated by their flock or threatened or assaulted. According to
William Russell, Vicar of Mere, a member of his parish loosed a
dog on him which bore him to the ground and bit his arm in
three places. He only saved himself from death, he declared,
because 'he smote the said dog with the church door-key under
his ear and with that the said dog departed'. Enraged parishioners
dragged a parson from his church, 'set him openly and shamefully

in the stocks', and then cast him into prison. Quarrels frequently arose over the exaction of excessive 'mortuaries'. When certain members of the parish of Roseland, near Falmouth, refused to pay these death fees, the priest procured their excommunication. In retaliation, a band of men made such an uproar in the church the Sunday before Christmas that 'the parishioners went home without Mass'. On Christmas day the men reappeared, armed, threatened to kill the priest, and 'would have chased [him] out of his chancel by the windows . . . wherefore the said parson was very glad to escape secretly while others of the parish treated with them'.

On the other hand, priests were sued for forgery, theft, breach of trust, and accused of a rogue's gallery of crimes ranging from adultery to murder. The Parson of Snoring incited an armed band to drag a man from his house and slay him. Sir John Fastolfe testily inveighed against a parson who 'fished my stanks at Dedham and helped to break my dam and destroyed my new mill'. An outraged father complained to the Chancellor that William Roddok, priest, 'a limb of the Devil', had seduced his daughter. John Mallery, Vicar of Lewesham, 'spoke with a loud voice' in the pulpit, urging his flock to band together and capture and kill the sheriff or any other officer who tried to serve a royal writ. On the following Tuesday when a king's bailiff rode into town, Mallery 'rang the great bell' and something like a hundred persons 'with swords, clubs, bows and arrows' swarmed upon the bailiff.

Thomas Stonor received a petition from 'your poor beadmen and tenants of your lordship of Didcot, which be greatly wronged and ungoodly treated by the parson of Didcot'. The parish had kindly given him permission 'to go to school to Oxenford' on his promising that he would find a substitute to perform his offices. But once the parson rode off to Oxford, 'the divine service and other sacraments were not kept as they ought to be, to great unease to the parish'. In the buying and selling of their grain, the parson cheated them or maliciously interfered with their dealings; he was always quarrelling with them and harrying them, 'to great heaviness of the parish, the parson to be so unkind'. The parson's man, Robert Dobson, 'called divers men, knaves and harlots and churls . . . and the said parson maintained him therein. They were so bold that twain of the parson's men lay await upon John Pepwite in Bagley; and there they beat him, and, except [for] people of Abingdon, likely to have killed him. This man recovered and came home. And upon a Sunday after Evensong the mother of this same man and the man also made an outcry upon the parson among all the parish . . . which were heavy to hear of, if it should be written.'

An oration prepared for a Convocation of the clergy[1] paints more vigorously than any lay source the widespread hostility which encompassed churchmen. Pleading that his fellows should 'make ourselves good shepherds, not mercenary ones', lamenting that 'the clerical body should be divided by discords within itself', the author warns that clergy and laity 'are two armies unequal in worldly power, and one will destroy the other' unless harmony is restored. The vices and the quarrels of churchmen 'provoke the laity of our time to attempt . . . unbridled enormities against the Church. Fearing no censure, they even indict clergymen for fictitious crimes; drag them to examinations; throw them into squalid prisons to make them empty their barns, while some are even fixed in pillories or fastened to the gibbet. . . .

'There are scarcely ten in any diocese who do not yearly suffer either in their person or their purse. Hence parsons do not reside on their benefices; yet . . . they are publicly inveighed against for their absence. All the regard and devotion of the faithful to the priests have become chilled; and tithes, oblations, and other benefits to the churches fall to nothing.' The orator is more concerned to hide abuses from the laity than to reform them: 'I wish that all preachers who would suggest anything . . . to prelates or ecclesiastical persons for their emendation would choose a place apart to announce the crimes of their pastors, where the horned cattle will not be present with us; where they who erect their horns to strike the pastors of their churches and to disperse their flocks may not learn from us what is objectionable in us.'

---

[1] This Convocation, which was to have met in mid-April, 1483, was cancelled because of the death of Edward IV on April 9.

The greatest embarrassment to the Church was the floating population of clerks in Minor Orders and unbeneficed priests. This underworld of the establishment, often ragged and quick-fingered and lewd, swelled the proletariat of the towns and trouped about the countryside only too ready for mischief. Such 'criminous clerks' might be seen sitting in the stocks pelted by a jeering crowd or being booted out of town 'with minstrelsey'. Their amorous exploits formed the stock-in-trade of much popular poetry; they spread rumours and haunted taverns and gulled the credulous.

The world had also invaded religious establishments set apart from the world, the monasteries. Monks and nuns had long ago resigned spiritual leadership to the friars; but by the fifteenth century the friars too had lost much of their good fame and their zeal. They still maintained a reputation for learning and for delivering catchy sermons spiced with fables; but the Four Orders had grown increasingly wealthy and lethargic, and they were more celebrated for their magnificent halls like those at Black-friars and at the Grey Friars in London than for lives dedicated to St. Francis's ideal of poverty. The educated laity were beginning to scorn their jigging sermons and easy penances and begging tricks. When the Yorkists became alarmed early in 1454 by reports that the Duke of Somerset was sowing spies in their households, it was believed, typically, that many of these agents were disguised as friars. By the reign of Edward IV, their diminishing numbers were having to be bolstered by recruits from the Continent.

The regular clergy, monks and nuns, showed an even sadder decline from the ages when their establishments had stood as fortresses of Christian devotion, even of civilization, in a brutalized world. Now life outside monastic walls had grown rich in opportunities for living, while the life within had shrunk into a meagre routine of existence. During the Yorkist Age there were something like 600 religious houses, three-quarters of them being monasteries. Most of them were quite small, averaging about fifteen inmates; many had even fewer and numbers were everywhere declining. Travellers who extolled the magnificence of the monastic life in England were remembering only the few great abbeys, and they did not closely examine what went on within. By the end of Edward IV's reign religious houses probably counted no more than 2,000 nuns and about 7,000 monks.

These houses were frequently not only small but miserably poor. The Premonstratensian monastery of Begham, Kent, contained only eight canons in 1478; the number had dropped to six by 1497. Buildings were sagging into ruin; the monastery owed hundreds of pounds; one run-away canon had been wandering in the world for at least three years. The Premonstratensians at Malden, Essex, had a community of only six in 1482; there were eight at Blanchland, Northumberland, and the place was so broken down as to be hardly habitable. Nunneries, particularly those in the North, exhibited the same conditions. In some places it was almost impossible to carry on divine services; bishops were constantly urging abbots and prioresses to recruit novices.

Debt and dilapidation were not entirely the fault of the monks and nuns. Their revenues were heavily taxed both by Church and State; over-generous hospitality depleted funds; feudal incidents and the perquisites of patrons took their toll; income from land was falling; and though there were ever fewer monks and nuns, expenses mounted because more comforts had to be supplied. Still, there was a good deal of bad management and sometimes worse than bad management. Abbots and prioresses, lazy or fond of power, often failed to make the required yearly accounting to their brethren and sisters and badly muddled their finances. They failed to keep buildings in repair, disposed of lands and woods at a low figure in order to lay hands on ready money or to please a powerful neighbour, and recklessly sold 'corrodies'— life annuities of board and lodging—which if folk lived too long or ate too much cost the establishment dear.

On occasion mismanagement turned out to be criminal negligence and fraud and embezzlement, usually coupled with even more picturesque vices. Lurid immoralities were never widespread, but there certainly existed unscrupulous abbots and wicked prioresses[1] who plundered the funds of the community, sold lands and cut down woods and pawned sacred vessels for their own gain. Perhaps no more than twenty-five or fifty of the some 600 religious houses exhibited shocking evils during the Yorkist Age; but these became the scandal of their neighbourhoods, and the 'shiten shepherd', as Chaucer's parson knew, often soiled his monastic sheep.

Conditions at Littlemore Priory, near Oxford, reveal how hard it was for nuns to resist the blandishments of gay University clerks. In the course of an episcopal visitation, nuns and prioress hurled violent accusations against each other. The nuns asserted that the Prioress had had a daughter by Richard Hewes, priest, of Kent, who still visited her. She disposed of the 'pans, pots, candlesticks, basins, sheets, pillows, featherbeds, etc.' of the Priory to accumulate a dowry for this daughter. She commanded the nuns to say that all was well when a visitation occurred. Those who rebuked her evil life she thrust into the stocks. She had pawned almost all the jewels belonging to the house and provided neither sufficient food nor clothing nor pocket-money for the convent. One of the nuns, it was charged, had had a child within the past year; and a girl about to become a novice was so appalled by the evil life of the prioress that she went elsewhere.

When the erring Prioress was quizzed by the Bishop, she ended by admitting most of the charges. Though removed from office, she was permitted to carry on its duties for the time being—a concession which reveals how few nuns in this age were capable of managing a convent, even badly. It is not surprising that when the Bishop visited the Priory a few months later, he uncovered fresh scandals. The Prioress now complained that one of the nuns 'played and romped' with boys in the cloister and refused to be corrected. When she was put in the stocks, three nuns broke the door and rescued her and burnt the stocks; and when the Prioress summoned aid from the neighbourhood, the four recalcitrants smashed a window and escaped to friends, 'where they remained two or three weeks'. Other nuns played and

[1] The most wicked of all was fortunately a creature of legend, the nun of Kirklees who betrayed Robin Hood to his death. But that a nun should be chosen for the role is significant.

laughed during Mass, even at the Elevation. The Prioress, in turn, was charged with punishing the nuns because they had told the truth at the last visitation. The nun she had put in the stocks was blameless; another nun had been struck on the head; and Richard Hewes had paid a recent visit to the Priory.

Prioress Margaret Wavere of Catesby provided endless gossip for the neighbourhood and kept her nunnery in a constant uproar. She let buildings fall into ruin, put the nuns on short rations, gave out no money for clothes. For her own benefit she sold woods, pawned part of the silver service, made away with spoons and table cloths 'fit for a king'; and forced her charges to perform manual labour unworthy of their delicate upbringing. She had a priestly lover, William Taylour, a frequent visitor at the nunnery, with whom she strolled boldly in the gardens of the village of Catesby. Often moved to violent anger, even during divine service, she tore the veils from nuns, dragged them about the choir by their hair, screamed epithets like 'beggar!' and 'harlot!' at them. The visiting Bishop required her to see no more of William Taylour, but she, like the Prioress of Littlemore, was permitted to continue as head of the nunnery.

The worst offenders among abbots usually coupled violence to immorality. When Bishop Redman visited the Abbey of Welbeck in 1482, the canons reported 'great enormities and disgraceful things, the scandal of which is spread abroad'. The Abbot was letting the place fall to pieces; he had disposed of lands, woods, tithes of the monastery to 'great men'; he had pledged or pilfered all jewels and plate so that 'he did not have a single silver cup to set before us in our present visitation, nor one dish, napkin, silver salt cellar or any other vessel, to his great confusion'. Divine service often had to be diminished or omitted through an 'entire lack of oil, wax, and wine'. The fields around the Abbey presented a miserable spectacle—woods reduced to an expanse of stumps, enclosures unditched and unhedged, barns empty of stock.

As a result of his relations with a number of women, the Abbot had gathered to himself several children, 'who had hitherto been supported out of monastery goods'. He spent his time playing 'at tables and other games the whole day and night with buffoons and other such persons'. This conduct had infected two of the brothers, who were found guilty of incontinence, apostasy, and rebellion. Bishop Redman did what he could: the Abbot was relieved of his post and with the two sinning canons was sent in disgrace to the monastery of Barlings to do penance until the next visitation; meanwhile, the house remained in abject poverty, 'and the brethren bewail their lot'.

Conditions became so intolerable, early in 1461, in the Abbey of Beauchief, Derbyshire, that Canon John Swyft appealed for an investigation by means of a vividly allegorical letter in which the monastery was pictured as 'cast down and inexterminably lying in the dungeon of inordinate sin, enormous misrule and wretchedness; and in the prison of unrecoverable subversion, ruin, destruction, importable poverty and indigence; and under unpiteous presumption, and full ungentle and cruel gaolers', who were guilty of 'all manner of extortions, usurpations, collusions, riots, and devastations'. Alarmed by this awesome intelligence, Bishop Redman hastened to make an investigation, and the substance of the Canon's charges were borne out. The Abbot was convicted of a variety of 'notorious crimes', including incontinence and perjury; but he and seven of his accomplices fled before Bishop Redman arrived, and had to be excommunicated. Canon Swyft himself was elected Abbot, and a few years later the Abbey was found to be in a satisfactory state except that cloister silence was not always observed and the canons sometimes did a little tippling after Compline.

Outwardly, the daily round of the monastic life was unchanged. Monks and nuns broke their sleep about two A.M. and trooped from the dorter into the choir to say Matins and Lauds. The service of Prime began at six in the morning in winter, an hour later in summer as with the rest of the services. Three hours later came Tierce-Sext, and then None at midday in winter. The religious were left free in the afternoon for individual devotions or labour. Vespers were said towards the end of the day, and the routine of services concluded with Compline, usually at seven P.M. in winter. Monks and nuns were then supposed to retire immediately to the dorter and go to bed. In moving from service to service it was ordered by the *Syon Rule* that 'none shall jut upon other wilfully, nor spit upon the stairs going up or down, nor in none other place reprovably but if they tread it out forthwith'. During the services 'none shall use to spit over the stalls nor in any other place where any sister is wont to pray . . . for defouling of their clothes'.

Except among the Carthusians—with their proud motto of 'Nothing reformed because nothing to reform'—and the Bridgetine Nuns and the Observant Friars, the disciplines of the religious life had, by the reign of Edward IV, become much relaxed. St. Benedict's well-balanced trinity of duties—divine service, labour, and cultivation of mind and spirit—which had once kept monastic existence fresh and vigorous, no longer satisfied the average man and woman who entered into enclosure.

Monks now constituted probably less than half of the population housed by a well-to-do abbey; and the proportion among nuns, except in the poorer convents, was not much greater. In the reign of Henry VIII the thirty monks of St. Peter's, Gloucester, were attended by eighty-six servants. Much earlier, Bicester Priory employed more than twenty-five people to look after the prior, eleven canons, a few clerks of the chapel and novices. Not only were religious houses staffed by cooks, butlers, bakers, brewers, and farm hands, but they frequently called upon the services of barbers, laundresses, tailors, carpenters. At Athelney in 1455 the visiting bishop ordered the monks to cease employing a tailor to fit their habits and a barber to cut their hair and shave them. The austerity of monastic diet had also vanished; the religious ate meat and enjoyed numerous 'pittances', special dainties.

Monks and nuns had likewise ceased to follow the precious tradition of intellectual accomplishments. With the exception of the *Croyland Chronicle*, monastic chronicles almost entirely died out during the Yorkist Age; the regular clergy had lost interest in copying manuscripts or creating works of art or fostering learning. Even the primary function of monasticism, the praise of God, was neglected or scanted or became a desultory observance. Episcopal visitations reveal that monks and nuns not infrequently found it too difficult to rise in the middle of the night and raise their voices in an icy choir. At Peterborough, in 1487, only about a dozen of the forty-five monks ordinarily obeyed the schedule of divine services. At another monastery there were 'but four who attend choir in time of divine service, while the others . . . spend their time in idleness'. Sometimes the Abbot of Ramsey found only eight monks out of thirty present for Matins; and on occasion, but two or three appeared for High Mass. Even those who managed to attend were not blameless: they dozed or gossiped or slipped away when they thought nobody was looking. At St. Neots, the monks relieved the tedium of their existence by chatting 'with secular folk as though they were at market'. The commonest fault was gabbling through the service to get it over with, leaving out syllables and skipping pauses and thus making nonsense of plain chant. Satan found this lapse so widespread and so fruitful that he detailed a special devil, Tutivillus, to collect in a long bag hung about his neck all the omitted words and tortured phrasings dropped by the negligent, and his master expected him to fill no less than a thousand bags a day.

Monastic life had fallen into the doldrums simply because the flame had gone out of it[1]—except for the few monks and nuns with a genuine religious vocation.

Into monasteries drifted the lethargic, the miserable, the confused, happy to exchange the vigorous give-and-take of secular life for a routine existence padded by comforts and not very demanding. Nunneries were even more worldly than monasteries, because by the Yorkist Age they had become aristocratic boarding houses. Girls of the peasant and artisan class did not enter convents as a rule; they could not furnish the requisite dowry. To demand such a fee of a prospective novice was of course forbidden, but the practice was firmly and universally observed. The daughter of a lord or a knight or a wealthy merchant either married or

---

[1] 'In 1514 . . . when Bishop Foxe of Winchester founded Corpus Christi College, Oxford, he at first intended a house for monks; but his friend Bishop Oldham of Exeter expostulated "What, my lord, shall we build houses and provide livelihood for a company of bussing monks, whose end and fall we may live to see? No. No, it is more meet a great deal that we should have care to provide for the increase of learning, and for such as who by their learning shall do good in the Church and commonwealth".' A. R. Myers, *England in the Late Middle Ages*, p. 223.

entered a nunnery; there was no other career open to her. London merchants paid as high as £100 to place a daughter in a suitable religious establishment. Girls of small means could enter these genteel portals only if they were fortunate enough to live in a community where a philanthropist or a religious fraternity, like the Gild of Palmers at Ludlow, made money available for the purpose. Fathers in the upper ranks of society frequently left sums to daughters with the designation that the bequest was to be used as a religious or a marriage dowry. A man with an expensive son and half a dozen girls soon began turning convents over in his mind; for though, in addition to a goodly amount in cash, a novice was expected to bring with her a bed and other furnishings, the cost of placing a daughter in a convent was somewhat less than that of finding her a suitable husband. Nunneries likewise offered a quilted existence to well-to-do widows who had no desire to marry again and were weary of worldly cares; and they also served, unfortunately, as a dumping-ground for retarded or feeble-minded or deformed girls of aristocratic families.

Since the great civilizing and spiritual mission of monasticism had withered away and since religious houses now sheltered many men and women without true vocation, it is not surprising that monks and nuns led humdrum lives and that they slipped into worldly ways in order to lighten the tedium of their hours. Such is the picture drawn by the record of episcopal visitations.

Arriving with his retinue of doctors and secretaries and servants, the Bishop sometimes preached a sermon to begin the visitation. Then he gathered the religious community into the chapter house in order to explain the purpose and nature of his inspection, of which the establishment had been informed in advance. These preliminaries accomplished, he called before him one by one the whole community, beginning with the abbot or prioress and descending in order of rank and seniority. Sometimes everybody said that all was well and the Bishop, if he agreed, ordered an *omnia bene* to be inscribed on the record; but on many occasions the Bishop's secretary was kept busy writing down the accusations brought by the head against the members and the complaints of the community against the head. At the end of the inquiry, the Bishop investigated all serious charges and summed up his findings in an address to the monastery. On returning to his episcopal palace, he entered a record of the visitation in his register and sent a copy of it to the respective house.

The Bishop's ears were often assailed by the usual symptoms of petty living—back-biting and malicious gossip, personal jealousies, an enormous concern for comforts and privileges, and all the minor infringements of religious discipline that boredom could devise. A sacristan, reported to be a violent fellow, had made a 'doublet of [de]fence' out of church vestments. A monk of Ulverscroft Priory found his metier in rambling 'about in the woods and copses . . . looking for the nests of wood-birds and catching other creatures of the wood'. An abbot's chaplain, 'having cast off his regular habit, dressed in a tunic with a cap on his head' and went fowling at night. The records buzz with complaints against tippling and overhearty eating. At Peterborough, 'after Compline the young monks come down from the dorter and so do set to drinking, sometimes with the abbot . . . and are rendered altogether unfit for being present at Matins'. Some monks at Ramsey 'say that they are ailing and cannot attend choir; and yet they are good eaters and drinkers'. Gay dress was likewise a fruitful subject of complaint: at Kirkby Bellars the 'canons do wear clasps in their boots . . . and now of late the young canons do carry purses adorned with orphreys and silk, that hang down from their belts to their knees. . . .'

The passages of the *Croyland Chronicle* dealing with abbey history sketch the placid but stagnant back-water of religious enclosure in this age. The writer is much concerned with the material comforts and splendours of his house: 'We deem Stephen Swynshed worthy of remembrance, who presented to the vestiary a choice cope with a similar alb . . . equal in value to a sum of twenty pounds and more. . . .' Brother Thomas Leverton, we learn, bequeathed an annual income of 4s so that 'there might be faithfully supplied, in the lower hall only, a cheese in summer for the supper of the convent, and another in winter. . . .' At the same time the writer froths with indignation at the men of surrounding villages, 'our powerful neighbours, not to call them enemies' who encroach on lands claimed by the abbey; and he cries upon the Lord to protect his house against 'the ever hostile, ever malicious comnalty' who 'just like so many ravening dogs . . . perpetrated many enormities, in fishing, fowling, and plundering the nets. . . .'

Nuns were apparently worse than monks in drumming their tattle into the Bishop's weary ear. They accused the prioress of treating them harshly and not giving them enough to eat and cutting off the clothing allowance so that they went about in threadbare garments. They disclosed that she 'dresses more like a secular person than a nun', that she 'wears golden rings exceedingly costly and carries her veil too high above her forehead'; that she has cut down woods and sold corrodies and pawned jewels without telling them. Sometimes they whispered that she entertained men in her private chambers and gambled with them 'at tables'. The prioress, in turn, had already informed the Bishop that the nuns squabbled among themselves and told malicious tales and contumaciously refused to be corrected. They insisted on keeping monkeys and squirrels and birds and dogs which dirtied the house and sometimes made a mockery of divine worship. They were forever breaking the rule of silence. Instead of going to bed after Compline, they sometimes wandered in the garden and gossiped and played games and occasionally even danced to a harp. They were so difficult to deal with that the prioress certainly should be excused for failing to tell them all about the finances, which they were too addlepated to understand anyway.

Worse still, monks and nuns would not stay where they belonged, in the cloister. Enclosure was the essence of the religious life, but in the Yorkist Age it was impossible to enforce. Monks *would* go hunting and poaching and stroll into the village for a drink at the tavern or to watch a wrestling match on the green. Chaucer and Langland spoke for the fifteenth century as well as their own times in their comments upon monastic worldliness. Chaucer's monk, it will be remembered, 'gave not of that text a pulled hen. That saith that hunters be not holy men' and that condemned 'a monk out of his cloister. . .'

Full many a dainty horse had he in stable:
And when he rode, men might his bridle hear
Gingling in a whistling wind as clear
And eke as loud as doth the chapel-bell
Where this lord was keeper of the cell. . . .

and where he should have been upon his knees in prayer instead of enjoying the spring breezes in a furred gown. Langland knew the monk as 'a roamer by streets' and the monk's prior as 'a pricker [rider] on a palfrey from manor to manor. An heap of hounds at his arse as [if] he a lord were'.

Records of visitations in the fifteenth century bear out Chaucer's and Langland's picture. The Abbot of Humberstone, it was said, would not take the trouble to visit sick monks in the infirmary but 'he visits the girls of whom he is fond in the town'. At Newnham Priory the inmates kept so many hunting hounds that in order to feed them 'the alms of the house are very greatly wasted' and the dogs 'also snatch food from the canons' tables'. Two monks at Dunstable devoted themselves to their thirty-nine hives of bees, 'the profits of which they have retained entirely for their own use'. On occasion monks and nuns sallied forth to visit each other's houses, though the practice was strictly prohibited.

Nuns, it appears, enjoyed breaking the rule of enclosure as much as monks. Chaucer's Prioress, the charming and well-bred Madame Eglentyne, should not have been on pilgrimage at all. Considering the gamey company among whom she rode, it is not hard to see why the Church wanted no pilgrim-nuns. Not many fifteenth-century convent inmates, however, were so giddy as the erring sister 'who on Monday night did pass the night with the Austin Friars at Northampton and did dance and play the lute with them in the same place until midnight, and on the night following she passed the night with the Friars Preachers at Northampton, luting and dancing in like manner'. But though nuns listened demurely as the Bishop lectured them on the evils of breaking enclosure, they had no intention of immuring themselves in the convent; and they were able to think up a galaxy of excuses for going out—their parents were ill or one of the family was getting married or they had to go to market or they must make confession at a neighbouring monastery. . . . The nuns at East-bourne complained that their extravagant and worldly prioress had put the convent in debt some £40 because she 'frequently rides abroad—and pretends that she does so on the common business of the house, although it is not so—with a train of attendants much too large and tarries long abroad; and she feasts sumptuously both when abroad and at home, and she is very choice in her dress so that the fur trimmings of her mantle are worth 100s. . . .'

The worst breach of enclosure, and the sin which the Church abhorred most of all, was 'apostacy', the breaking of vows in order to wander in the world. Girls and men, lacking in religious vocation and susceptible to love-longing, sometimes dared mortal shame and the pains of Hell by taking to their heels with a lover. Nuns were usually seduced by a neighbouring chaplain or vicar or a monk from a nearby house; but occasionally they went off with men they had met on their excursions into town. Agnes Butler, of St. Michael's, Stamford, disappeared for a day and a night with an Austin Friar; shortly after, she could not resist a wandering harp-player and lived with him for a year and a half at Newcastle. But she returned. Apostates almost always returned, sooner or later, temporarily or for good.

The moment their flight was discovered they were excom-municated. Their sin was published abroad, and, on pain of excommunication, all folk were forbidden to help them in any way. Who would risk cursing for a run-away monk or a draggle-tailed nun? If the Church could not find them or frighten them into returning, it called upon the State; and, in the end, between Church and State, the guilty ones were usually apprehended. Often they returned of their own accord, shamed and hungry and disillusioned. A pregnant nun, cast off by her lover, knelt in the dust before the convent gate and implored mercy. Though some prioresses tried to refuse admission to their fallen charges, the Bishop always insisted that they be taken in so that they might cleanse their souls with harsh penances. This was the Church

Merciful; but a soiled wanderer in the world, driven back to enclosure by force or because she had nowhere else to go, hardly bolstered the morale of her sisters.

Even when they remained within their houses, monks and nuns were invaded by the world. The system of granting corrodies not only lightened the purse of a religious house but also lamed the spirit of enclosure and distracted the praise of God. To begin with, numerous communities had corrodians thrust upon them: the King and the family of the founder and perhaps the Bishop might possess by charter the privilege of appointing a certain number of corrodians to a house; such corrodies were used as means of rewarding faithful servants with a pension. In addition, people eager to turn their life-savings into such a 'livery' in order to guarantee themselves a tranquil and secure old age were usually able to find needy priors and prioresses willing to grant corrodies cheaply in order to get their hands on a little ready money. Thus, husbands and wives and children and servants and pets, corrodians all, plumped themselves down within monastic walls and troubled the quiet air of enclosure with the full-blooded, bustling, noisy ways of ordinary living.

Bishop Alnwick discovered that the Prioress of Langley had sold a corrody to John Fraunceys and his wife for a mere 20 marks (£13 4s) and that the couple had been consuming the substance of the convent now for six years. At Nuncoton two corrodians, each of whom paid 20 marks, had been enjoying board and lodging for twelve and twenty years respectively. It appears that a gentleman named Thomas Foster bought one corrody from the Prioress of Thetford, but then moved himself, his wife, three children, and a maid into the convent where they lived for many a long day. After Bishop Grey had visited the nunnery of Godstow, he gave order that 'Felmersham's wife with her whole household and other women of mature age be utterly removed from the monastery within one year next to come seeing that they are a cause of disturbance to the nuns and an occasion of bad example by reason of their attire and those that come to visit them'. At St. Michael's, Stamford, 'Richard Grey, lately boarding in the priory together with his legitimate wife, had got one of the nuns with child', and he continued to live in the convent for some time after the Bishop had ordered his removal. The pets were often worse than the people. The Prioress of Langley complained that Lady Audley 'has a great abundance of dogs, in so much that whenever she comes to church there follow her twelve dogs, who make a great uproar . . . hindering them in their psalmody, and the nuns hereby are made terrified'. And at Legbourne 'Margaret Goodesby, a secular woman, lies of a night in the dorter among the nuns, bringing with her birds, by whose jargoning silence is broken and the rest of the nuns is disturbed'.

Bishops who faithfully carried out their duties of visitation could not help on occasion being depressed by the failure of spiritual force within monastic walls. Of Huntingdon Priory, Bishop Grey sadly recorded, 'We found no good thing in the same which might be likened to religion save only the outward sign. . . . Alas for sorrow! religion is no more; love is driven out.' The figures best symbolizing the flagging fires and the habitual worldliness of monasticism in this age are not spectacular characters like the wicked Abbot of Welbeck and the hysterical Prioress of Catesby; but rather the 'jargoning' birds in the dorter and the Prioress of Gracedieu and her chaplain. The chaplain, a good hearty countryman, shocked the nuns sometimes because after cleaning out the stables he conducted divine service without washing his hands; and at harvest season the prioress went out into the fields to watch him gathering in the grain and 'at evening she comes riding behind him on the same horse'.

Throughout the fifteenth century the gap between the *image* of the Church and the *fact* of the Church widened; and it widened before the eyes of a generation of men increasingly dominated by fact rather than custom, increasingly critical of appearances, increasingly concerned with determinable values and their money's worth.

Yet what perhaps might have surprised Geoffrey Chaucer and William Langland most about the reign of Edward IV was that the Church still reared its massive walls of power and privilege to the sky, and that few voices were raised to demand that it be parted from its wealth. Henry VIII's spoliation of the Church in the 1530's, far from abruptly striking out a new historical direction, more nearly represents the lagging fulfilment of a course charted a century and more earlier. When Chaucer died in 1400 the Church had been under severe attack for more than two decades. The followers of John Wycliffe, the Lollards, found increasing support among gentry and townsmen; and many men not infected by the Lollard heresy were crying out against the corruption and unmerited wealth of the ecclesiastical establishment and clamouring for its lands, goods, revenues to be put to secular use. Langland boldly predicted the day when the State would lay hands upon the Church:

> Then shall the Abbot of Abingdon and all his issue forever
> Have a knock of a king and incurable the wound.

The Lollards and the anti-clerical party were strong enough in the reign of Henry IV (1399-1413) to prepare a petition for Parliament demanding the seizure of the temporalities of the Church and proposing that the proceeds should be used to create fifteen earldoms, provide lands for 1500 knights and 6200 squires, support 100 almshouses, and pour £20,000 a year into the royal treasury. One measure of the changes fermenting during the Yorkist Age is the difference between this curiously naïve scheme, flavoured with feudal thinking, and Henry VIII's policy of binding gentry and townsmen to his cause by sharing his spoils with them.

Henry V, fanatically orthodox, halted the advance of anti-clericalism and set out to destroy Lollardry with iron and fire. A desperate uprising led by Sir John Oldcastle and other conspiracies were ruthlessly crushed. In thus showing themselves to be rebels as well as heretics, the followers of Wycliffe forfeited the support of the influential classes and were forced to go underground. By the 1430's of Henry VI's reign violent anti-Church feeling was apparently dying away. A lull in organized assaults upon the establishment lasted for a century (1430-1530). Then the massive ivy encrusting the oak was severed by a royal axe.

A multiplicity of causes engendered this surprising lull. For one thing, in the reign of Henry VI the realm grew increasingly distracted by the hopeless French war and mounting anarchy at home. For another, in the reigns of Edward IV and Richard III and Henry VII the realm of England, recovered from the manifold shocks of the previous century, was becoming increasingly prosperous; there was plenty of land for the enterprising, and townsmen and gentry could find a way to worldly advancement without bothering to untruss the Church. But by the time Henry VIII had sat twenty years upon his throne, land was growing scarce and the middle classes more pushing; and King Henry himself was spurred by needs that Edward IV and Henry VII had not felt, and owned an authority that his grandfather and his father spent their reigns in patiently building.

During the fifteenth-century lull, the attack upon the Church shifted from the national to the local level, shifted inwardly to the minds of men, shifted from abuses to inadequacies. Cities and boroughs battled bitterly against what they had come to consider an alien authority in their midst. Mayors like John Shillingford and towns like Exeter regarded themselves as true sons of the Faith Catholic, but they were no longer willing to identify that faith with the worldly institution that thwarted their civil government.

While townsmen openly battered at the walls of Church privilege, Lollardry gnawed away in the dark at the foundations of doctrine. The movement had lost its intellectual headquarters, for Oxford had been severely purged of heretics and the books of Wycliffe and of Bishop Pecock—condemned for basing his assault on Lollardry upon reason rather than upon ecclesiastical authority—were ceremoniously burnt. By the generality of the upper classes Lollards were regarded as fanatical subversives; and north of Trent Lollardry was almost universally despised—in one of the York plays a devil, Tutivillus, is described as 'a master Lollard'. Though no heresy-hunter like Henry V, Edward IV dutifully handed over heretics to the Church when he found them, as he had willingly confirmed the ancient privileges of the Church; for the Yorkists, though they in fact transformed the government of England and kept the ecclesiastical establishment in tight subjection, had won their way to the throne as champions of legitimacy in the state and traditionalism in religion.

Lollards and their books continued to be burned; mayors and sheriffs were warned to be on the look-out for subversive elements. Edward IV felt impelled in December of 1475 to create an imposing commission, headed by his brothers the Dukes of Clarence and Gloucester, to inquire into treason and Lollardries and heretical errors in Dorset and Wiltshire. Lollardry, though no longer intellectually or socially presentable, exerted a significant pressure upon the Church during the Yorkist Age.

The heresy was kept alive and spread mainly by poor priests and town artisans. Weavers were particularly prone to Lollardry—was this precise, prudent craft congenial to proto-Puritans or did sitting at the loom encourage sturdy contemplation? Scratch an itinerant weaver of the reign of Edward IV and you would often find a Lollard. When captured by officers of the Church and put to a severe interrogation, many heretics flinched before the sudden reality of a fiery death and abjured their errors. These might be seen of a Sunday in Yorkist England parading about a churchyard clad only in shirt and breeches and shouldering a bundle of faggots, pausing at the command of a parish priest to recant aloud their miserable errors.

But not a few held courageously to their opinions, or, having once recanted, when caught a second time—which automatically meant death regardless of further repentances –bravely faced the flames. In the London mayoralty year of 1466-67, Gregory's *Chronicle* relates, 'there was an heretic burned at Tower Hill, for he despised the sacrament of the altar; his name was William Balowe and he dwelled at Walden. And he and his wife were abjured long time before. And my Lord of London [the bishop] kept him in prison long time, and he would not make no confession unto no priest but only unto God, and said that no priest had no more power to hear confession than Jack Hare. . . .

'At the time of his burning . . . [the] parson of St. Peter's in the Cornhill laboured him to believe in the holy sacrament of the altar. And this was the heretic's saying: "Bawe! Bawe! Bawe! What meaneth this priest? This I wot well, that on Good Friday ye make many gods to be put in the sepulchre, but at Easter Day they cannot arise themself but that ye must lift them up and bear them forth, or else they will lie still in their graves." '

Whoever wrote this portion of the *Chronicle* sounds more impressed than hostile; and martyrdoms must often have made a deep impact, even upon pillars of society who were good Catholics. When a popular parish priest, Richard Wyche, and his servant were burned at Tower Hill, 'there was [so] much trouble among the people that all the [officers of the] wards in London were assigned to watch there day and night'. What in fact happened was that a mob of weeping men and women scrabbled to bear away Wyche's ashes as if he were a saint; some erected a cross to mark the holy spot; others sold commemorative images of wax; until by command of Henry VI the mayor and sheriffs drove away the people and degraded the place with dung 'so that no more idolatry could be done there'. It was reported that the Vicar of Barlings, in order to enrich himself with offerings, had doctored the phenomena of martyrdom by surreptitiously mixing incense with the ashes.

Few who witnessed the last hours of John Goos could have remained unmoved; the very style of Fabyan's recital betrays *his* feeling: 'And in this year [1473-74] was one John Goos, a Lollard, burned at Tower Hill for heresy; the which before dinner was delivered unto Robert Byllysdon, one of the sheriffs, to put in execution the same afternoon; where he [the sheriff] like a charitable man had him home to his house and there exhorted him that he should die a Christian man and renounce his false errors. But that other, after long exhortation heard, required the sheriff that he might have meat, for he said that he was sore hungered. Then the sheriff commanded him meat, whereof he [par]took as [if] he had ailed nothing and said to such as stood about him, "I eat now a good and competent dinner, for I shall pass a little sharp shower ere I go to supper." And when he had dined, he required that he might shortly be led to his execution.'

Itinerant weavers trudged from market-place to market-place, ostensibly seeking work but in reality looking for kindred spirits or likely converts among the town artisans. In a candle-lit gathering of humble folk, most of them probably illiterate, these propagators of the new faith read aloud portions of the Bible translated by Wycliffe and such Lollard works as *The Wycket* and *The Lantern of Life*. The opinions of these heretics often differed now in details, for their intellectual fountainhead had been forcibly dried up; but their main beliefs are revealed in the interrogation of James Wyllys before the Bishop of London in August of 1462.

Typically, he was of Bristol and he was a weaver; he had secured portions of the Bible in English and learned heretical doctrine from 'a certain William Smyth of Britol', who had been condemned for his opinions by the Bishop of Worcester and burned. Wyllys 'obstinately says and holds' that when he communicated on Easter Day 'he received nothing at that time except material bread . . . and that it is not the true Body of Christ. . . . Also that a sinful priest has not the power of absolving anyone in confession from the stains of his sins, nor does it profit a man to confess to a priest. . . . Also that images are not to be adored . . . because these images are stocks and stones. . . . Also that there is no place of Purgatory. Also that the Mass is of no value. . . . That the saints being in Heaven do not need the goods of men on earth. . . .' Wyllys ended by abjuring his errors, but since he had recanted once before to the Bishop of London, he was handed over to the secular arm as a relapsed heretic and committed to the fires.

Lollards were to be found mainly in the southern half of England, in regions that draw a circle about London: East Anglia and Lincolnshire and Coventry and Bristol and the Channel counties and the capital itself. It was the men of these districts who propped Tudor authoritarianism and welcomed the Tudor Reformation, as their grandsires had supported the New Monarchy of Edward IV and their descendants would back Parliament and Cromwell against a King who, like the Lancastrians and the fifteenth-century Church, had lost touch with the facts.

The Venetian diplomat—thinking at first of the upper classes—
reported that the English 'all attend Mass every day and say many
paternosters in public . . . nor do they omit any form incumbent
upon good Christians. *There are, however, many who have various
opinions concerning religion*'. A comment he makes on politics
illuminates this statement: 'If the King should propose to change
any old established rule, it would seem to every Englishman as if
his life were taken from him. . . .' The English clung to customary
practices but tended to think as they pleased. And one day
thinking would irradiate practice.

In a way difficult to apprehend today—unless the subject is
shifted from religion to politics—Englishmen of the fifteenth
century were able to keep separate the unpleasant manifestations
and unwarranted privileges of the establishment from the faith
which it enclosed, though even faith had become infected by the
forms which bounded it. The clergy themselves were so
numerous, in all the ranks of Major and Minor Orders, that they
were well understood to represent a cross-section of the fallible
world. Almost everyone had kinsmen and friends in the
Church. Though Margaret Paston preferred her son Walter to
become a 'good secular man than to be a lewd priest' and though
in her lifetime she had known clerks who were worse than lewd,
she did not object to Walter's becoming a good priest and she
thought nothing of making this observation itself to a priest, her
chaplain James Gloys. Furthermore, the age was tolerant of
frailties, even clerical frailties, to a degree hard for more efficient
times to appreciate.

The Englishman of Edward IV's day had little use, however,
for the apical figure of Christendom, the Pope. 'Pope's curse,'
men thought, 'would not kill a fly.' Representatives of the Holy
See were sometimes roughly handled by royal officers at ports of
entry; the agent Aliprando, who fled in rage from Calais, believed
that anti-papalism was fostered even by the bishops of the royal
Council, 'who have represented to the King that he must have all
who come from Rome arrested. . . .' The Pope was a foreigner,
a needy Italian potentate, who tried to squeeze money from
England to carry on his petty Italian wars and to support a hungry,

corrupt bureaucracy.[1] Sir John Paston, in reporting to his brother that he had applied to the Curia for an annulment of his troth to Anne Haute, remarked cynically, 'I have answer again from Rome that there is the well of grace and salve sufficient for such a sore, and that I may be dispensed with; nevertheless my proctor there asketh 1,000 ducats. . . .' Sir John was informed that the Pope every day put a multitude of such cases through the mill.

People were also looking with a jaundiced eye on the papal privilege of sanctuary. However it might be propped by Popes' charters, it was a messy, unjust, unseemly business. Behind the sanctuary gate irresponsible debtors laughed at their creditors, and criminals waited till night to sally forth and rob honest citizens. In the turbulent 'fifties Londoners became so exasperated by the plunderings of a criminal gang who made St. Martin le Grand their headquarters that a mob attacked the sanctuary and waged an all-night battle with the robbers, in which two of the citizens and one of the criminals were killed. The town of Rye quietly solved the problem by decreeing, privilege or no privilege, that "as Holiness becomes the Lord's House", the church and its precincts henceforth would offer no more protection than "the houses of the free men, especially as to arrests and other matters" '.[2]

While resentment against the Church Worldly continued to gather force from many directions, the Church Spiritual too was no longer satisfying the religious hungers of men. The every-day and the eternal had become confused in a way that did not uplift

---

[1] A passage from the morality play *Mankind* (circa 1475) suggests that the Pope was sometimes treated very casually indeed in ribald conversation. Two of the Vices, Nought and Now-a-Days, are chaffing each other:

> Now-a-Days: Also I have a wife; her name is Rachell.
> Betwixt her and me was a great battle;
> And fain of you I would here tell
> Who was the most master.
> Nought: Thy wife Rachell, I dare lay 20 lies.
> Now-a-Days: Who spake to thee, fool? Thou art not wise!
> Go and do that longeth [belongs] to thine office—
> Osculare fundamentum!
> Nought (addressing the Virtue, Mercy):
> Lo, master! lo! here is a pardon by limit;
> It is granted of Pope Pockett.
> If ye will put your nose in his wife's socket,
> Ye shall have 40 days of pardon.

[2] The nuisance of sanctuary lingered long after the Reformation, however.

the former and degraded the latter. Saints, through their remains, were addressed like good fellows who would do a favour if properly rewarded. In gestures of faith, like pilgrimage, the action often usurped what supposedly gave it meaning. The banquet which celebrated the installation of John Shillingford's friend John Stafford as Archbishop of Canterbury was brought to a climax by the serving of a 'soteltie' sculptured to form 'a god-head and the Son of God glorified above; in the Son, the Holy Ghost "voluptable"; St. Thomas kneeling afore him with the point of a sword in his head. . . .' Idea could hardly escape contamination from such form. Even John Tiptoft, the erudite and very religious Earl of Worcester, concluded, on the scaffold, a thoroughly Machiavellian defence of his severities as Constable by requesting the executioner to lop off his head in three strokes, in honour of the Trinity.

As the awesome and the commonplace blurred, simple folk looked for the marvellous in witchcraft and superstition. Among the ever-growing middle ranks of gentry and townsmen, there was developing a movement towards private religion, not unorthodox but essentially outside the church. People were pondering the writings of the Yorkshire mystic, Richard Rolle, and the *Scale of Perfection* of Walter Hilton and Thomas à Kempis's *Imitation of Christ* and the anonymous *Cloud of Unknowing*. These devotional works and others enabled men to pursue the religious quest in their homes or in their minds while the priest at the altar said Mass.

The Church of the Yorkist Age was permeated by the world and therefore susceptible to worldly measurement, and that measurement was growing ever more informed, critical, and detached.

Merchants, Pirates, Aliens and Lawyers

SETTING aside the capital of the realm, Bristol was the town for trade. And even London, though it had almost everything else, could not claim the Atlantic Ocean. The emblem of Bristol was a ship—embroidered on the banners of the city troop that fought for Edward IV at Towton, engraved in the city seal, stamped upon the bells from its foundries. Bristol was cradled between wharves that stretched along the Avon and the Frome. On the other side of the Avon the suburb of Redcliffe was a hive of weavers. The lowland between the rivers swarmed with sailors. In Marsh Street a fraternity for mariners, maintained by a levy of 4d a ton on cargo arriving in the port, supported a priest and twelve poor sailors who prayed for merchants and seamen 'labouring' on the seas. Shanties echoed through the streets. One day the bemused town clerk found himself scribbling in his records:

Hail and howe! Rumbylowe!
Steer well the good ship and let the wind blow!
Here cometh the Prior of Prikkingham and his Convent.
But ye keep the order well, ye shall be shent [ruined],
With hail and howe! etc.

Wharves and warehouses and vaulted cellars were piled with cloth to be exported and hogsheads of wine come from the South; and many a ship sailed up the Avon, deck heaped with fish, for Bristol was the Yarmouth of the West. Trade flowed in and out of the town by land and sea: men of Bristol collected and distributed goods in Wales, up the Severn to Coventry and

Chester, and across the southern counties; and won for themselves the trade routes of the Atlantic.

Files of packhorses carried cloth woven or warehoused in Bristol to the port of Southampton to be loaded on the Italian galleys, and the same horses came back freighted with silks and velvets to be worn by the merchant aristocracy. Bristol also drove a flourishing trade with London, less than three days away for carriers going by Chippenham and Newbury. Bristol dealers preferred to sell their cloth at the Steelyard, the entrepôt of the Hanse, rather than to native traders, for the Easterlings paid hard cash while Londoners wanted credit and tried to settle part of the debt in 'cards, tennis balls, bristles, tassels, and such other simple wares'.

While the merchants of eastern England dealt mainly with the Baltic and Holland and Flanders and northern France, the men of Bristol had pushed westward and southward. Their vessels, equipped now with several sails and improved compasses that enabled them to navigate more effectively than their fathers, drove across great cold seas to faraway Iceland. Ships by the tens headed into the Atlantic laden with cloth and on their return were coasted up the Avon gorge by the mighty tide of the Severn, bringing from Ireland hides and linen and fish, from Gascony wine, from Spain wine and iron and leather and oil and soap and dye-stuffs.

In this age one of the boldest Bristol merchants, Robert Sturmy or Sturmyn, Mayor in 1453-54, dared to challenge the Italians for the trade of the Mediterranenan. Sturmy's stout ship, the *Cog Anne*, set forth in the grey November weather of 1446 with 160 pilgrims bound for the Holy Land and a cargo of wool and tin. Down the Atlantic and between the 'Straits of Marrok' the *Cog Anne* made its way and on to Pisa, where the wool and tin were sold to friendly Florentines; and early in December the vessel deposited its pilgrims safely at Joppa. On the journey home, however, the *Cog Anne* ran afoul of a wintry tempest and was dashed to pieces on the rocks of the Peloponnesus.

Far from losing heart, Robert Sturmy himself sailed for the Levant in the summer of 1457, probably in the great merchantman the *Katherine Sturmy*, which he himself had built, 'specially for war'. The *Katherine Sturmy* and its accompanying caravel carried lead, thousands of pieces of tin, 600 sarplers of wool, and 6,000 pieces of cloth—a cargo worth upwards of £20,000 (more than half a million in modern money). Before he left Bristol, Sturmy made his will: 'And for as much as I am passing over the sea under the mercy of God, I bequeath my body to be buried where it is most pleasing to God.' And so it turned out. Sturmy reached the Levant in safety, successfully disposed of his merchandise, and began the long return journey, probably with a cargo of spices. But the Genoese had got word of his venture and were determined that no Englishman should break their trading monopoly. As Sturmy neared Malta, he came upon a fleet of Genoa lying in wait for him. Apparently no quarter was given. Neither Robert Sturmy nor his two ships ever came back to England. Philip Meade, then Mayor of Bristol, angrily sued all the Genoese in the realm before Henry VI's Council; and after a long legal battle the Italians were condemned to pay £6,000. Not until Tudor days would Englishmen begin to penetrate the Mediterranean, where brave Robert Sturmy had shown the way.

The developing trade with Iceland formed the toughest and most venturesome part of Bristol maritime enterprise. Early in the century, the men of that strange, distant island seldom saw a ship, not even the six vessels a year promised them by the Norwegian government. Then the fishermen of Hull and Boston and Lynn rebelled against the irksome restriction that forced them to haul all catches made in Norwegian waters into the Staple port of Bergen, and they began to make the long voyage to Iceland fishing grounds, soon joined by the men of Bristol. The King of Denmark, alarmed by the invasion, forbade Englishmen to visit Iceland, though he sometimes issued special permits, as did the King of England. But English fishermen and merchants sailed through fearsome seas, licences or no licences. They set forth in the spring, summered off the Iceland coast, and returned in the late summer or early autumn. Great merchantmen of Bristol, cocky doggers of Hull and Lynn clustered round the coasts. Their crews went ashore as they pleased to 'build houses, erect tents, dig up the ground, and carry on fishery as if it were their own property'. Occasionally the English landed on the island in full martial array with trumpets blaring and banners whipping the air. Danish officials accused them of murder and pillage and rapine, even charged them with kidnapping or buying children—and it appears that they did carry off a few. But the officers of the King of Denmark were not popular with the natives, and when a party of Englishmen captured and bore away the Danish governor, a chronicle representing the views of the Icelanders recorded tersely, 'Few were sorry at that'.

When a Danish governor, Björn Thorleifsson, arrived with a a strong escort at Ríf in 1467, he found English merchantmen and fishers carrying on a lively business. Before he could make any attempt to enforce his king's prohibitions, the English fell upon him and his men like a thunder-clap, and 'Björn the Mighty was smitten to death', his house sacked, and his son held for ransom. But when Björn's wife heard what had happened, she announced, 'There shall be no weeping but rather gather men!' Donning a shirt of mail—and thrusting a woman's dress over it for seemliness —she and her warriors 'came with craft upon the English and slew a great company of them, except the cook, who got his life very narrowly for that he had before helped their son'. This bold lady then sailed for Norway to report to the king; he is said to have found her 'a woman pleasant to behold'.

Bristol merchants like William Canynges exported wheat and wine and quantities of cloth, especially brightly coloured cloth, to Iceland, and they also introduced such products of civilization as glasses, combs, caps and shoes, hardware, and small beer. From Iceland they brought home fish, fresh fish salted on the voyage or the iron-hard dried codfish, 'pisces durus, vocatus Stockfysh'. A merchant whose vessel freighted £600 worth of fish might sell the cargo for £1,000.

The most famous citizens of Bristol, like Robert Sturmy and William Canynges, were shipbuilders and shipowners as well as merchants. Canynges possessed a princely fleet of ten vessels, totalling some 3,000 tons (burden) and employing 800 men. The largest, the *Mary and John*, was of 900 tons and cost 4,000 marks

(£2,600) to build—a marvel of the time, for most English vessels were smaller than those of Italy and Spain. Freight rates were so profitable to shipowners that if all ten of Canynges' ships were normally employed, he might in a single year enjoy a gross return of £10,000. But the risks, too, were enormous: ships that bravely outlasted tempests might fall to pirates, or ship and cargo could be tied up for months if the vessel was sequestered by the King to defend his coasts or do duty with his fleet.

Edward IV was the first King of England who systematically encouraged the building of a merchant marine, as he initiated so many other 'Tudor innovations'. To stimulate ship-building, he offered a first voyage free of customs and subsidies, he forbade merchants to freight cargoes in foreign bottoms if English ships were available, and he himself became the greatest trader in the realm.

Before the end of his reign, the daring merchants of Bristol were already probing the future. In the summer of 1480, John Jay sent two ships sailing westward into the Atlantic, navigated by a Welshman named Lloyd, 'the most scientific mariner of all England', to search for a land called 'The Ile of Brasile'. After being tossed on stormy seas for two months, the vessels were forced to put back into an Irish port. But the following year another expedition set forth. And one day soon a man named John Cabot would come to Bristol.

Still, Bristol and York and Southampton together could not equal London as a trading centre. By the end of the Yorkist Age the capital dominated the commerce of all England, and the marks of its merchants were known throughout Europe. The marts of London, operating twelve months in the year and sending forth streams of chapmen and offering their goods to the remotest manor by means of the common carrier, were beginning to drive into decline the great mediaeval fairs. Stourbridge Fair, St. Giles at Winchester, the fairs of Cambridge and Salisbury and Coventry, survived the fifteenth century, but the Yorkist Age broke their grip on the trade of the realm. The Grocers of London refused to allow their members to offer goods for sale at any fair, and the Mercers followed suit. When the Haberdashers began to cut into the Mercers' business by vigorous trading at the fairs, the Mercers worked to persuade all Companies to ban attendance there; and they might have succeeded except that Parliament, under pressure from fair-towns all over England, forbade such a boycott.

No Company better demonstrates how the merchants of London dealt in imports and exports than the Grocers, second in importance only to the Mercers. The Grocers traded *en gros*, in bulk; all of them, or almost all, were retailers as well as wholesalers; and no merchants bought and sold so wide a range of goods as they. Their company grew out of an amalgamation in the fourteenth century of the Pepperers or Spicers and the Canvas dealers or Corders and the Apothecaries. In the fifteenth century they provided many a Lord Mayor for London (though fewer than the Mercers), their wharves and warehouses stretched along the Thames, and the names of their wealthiest members, like Stephen Browne, were known all over the Continent.

Their company was governed by a master, usually a London alderman, and two wardens, who were assisted by a committee. The wardens were expected to trade with the company funds, at their own risk, and to show a profit. In 1450 the Grocers had a capital of about £500, which by 1488 had grown to over £1,000. In a single year the wardens turned a profit of £41 through deals in pepper alone. The Grocers lent their money out to members of the company or to other merchants, sometimes for as low as 8½ per cent interest but more often at the going rate of 12 per cent—for usury, like adultery, was prohibited by the Church but firmly entrenched in society.

The building and decoration of Grocers Hall, one of the handsomest company edifices in the city, cost about £600. Behind, stretched a lovely garden for the 'consolation and pleasure' of the members. Hedged with whitethorn, the garden offered a fig tree and a melon bed and wortleberries and grapes ripening in the sun against a parlour wall; while lavender, roses, and other blooms sweetened the air. The tired grocer might refresh himself by practicing archery at the butts or relax in a 'fair arbor'. There were 'six pots of tin for birds to drink of';

several gardeners were required to tend to 'divers delicate seeds' and potted plants, and to prune vines and trees.

Like the other great companies, the Grocers were divided into Livery and non-Livery members, the latter being required to ascend into the former when their incomes reached a certain figure. In 1470, seventy-five members were in the Livery, and one hundred and two were out of it. These 'Bachelors of the Grocery' had their own officers and a separate social life. An ambitious young journeyman who wished to set up in business for himself needed considerable capital, though if he had friends he might be able to launch himself on credit. In 1480 the company established £40 as the minimum that such a young man must have, but it did not enforce this figure very long.

Grocers were able to demand premiums of their apprentices, paying 20s to the company for each apprentice they took; for in good times a journeyman grocer could easily command £5 or £6 a year, and board, and if he were especially apt, up to £20. Furthermore, the Grocers did not mind if such a young man did a little trading on his own in order to accumulate capital. The Mercers, on the other hand, who regarded themselves with some reason as the aristocrats of international trade, were much more strict: by 1503 they were requiring £100 as the minimum capital with which to set up shop, and they did not allow their young men to trade for themselves—though the young men did it anyway, hiding merchandise in taverns and 'other secret trading places'.

In theory, the Grocers devoted themselves to importing, or buying from importers, spices and canvas and all manner of ropery and drugs and unguents and soap and confections. But they traded far more widely than their amalgam of gilds implied; and many of them were exporters as well as importers. When a bargain in fish came their way, they dealt in fish. They won for themselves most of the trade in French and Flemish garlic, cabbages, onions, and apples. Nearly all the fruits of the Mediter-ranean—oranges and almonds and figs and dates and raisins—that Italian carracks and Spanish merchantmen brought to Southamp-ton found their way into the hands of grocers, who often dis-tributed them from that port instead of trans-shipping them to

London. They imported quantities of wine, too, but then almost everybody traded in wine, mercers and drapers and ironmongers and fishmongers and goldsmiths and tailors, as well as nobles and gentry. Wine was so liquid an asset that it was used as a medium of exchange, even for the payment of debts. Grocers also imported iron and steel from the Baltic or from Spain and carried on a brisk business in dye-stuffs, woad and madder, scarlet grains, saffron.

Still, spices and drugs—'subtle ware', as they were called—accounted for the major portion of their trade. They could claim no monopoly—Stephen Forster, fishmonger, once purchased 22 bales of pepper for £529—but they dominated the market in these exotic goods. Even the wealthiest grocers, who might import up to £4,000 worth of stuff a year, kept retail shops, usually in Bucklersbury Lane, and those shops were stuffed with honey, licorice, dyes, alum, soap, brimstone, paper, varnish, salt, vinegar, garden seeds, canvas, rope, musk, incense, rice, sugar loaves, treacle of Genoa, mercury, and all manner of syrups and spices. When Sir John Howard was in London in September of 1466, he bought from his apothecary 'a little barrel of water for the sickness . . . a little box of preservative . . . a pot of treacle'.

London trade, then, was not departmentalized by the merchant gilds. A man did not have to be a vintner to import wine, nor a fishmonger to deal in fish, nor a grocer to sell canvas; and goldsmiths, tailors, skinners might be found handling all these commodities. The advantages of being a grocer if one dealt in grocery were two-fold: trade secrets and 'know-how' were shared; and the officers of the company enjoyed, by royal charter, exclusive supervision of spices and heavy commodities. What determined the major trading area of a company was the 'right of search' which it exercised. The Grocers had charge of the king's beam for weighing exports and imports in bulk and possessed the office of 'garbling' (inspecting and grading) spices and drugs. Their garblers examined all bales of pepper to see if pepper dust had been fraudulently added, and their searchers could enter at will any shop which sold grocery ware.

But the trade of England which made her most famous throughout Europe and prosperous at home rested upon the backs of her sheep, as it would until the Industrial Revolution. Not until the sixteenth century would the Lord Chancellor seat himself upon a woolsack; but it was in the Yorkist Age that the prosperity won from wool and woollen cloth first wrought itself into a loveliness of stone and brick and gilded wood. Up and down the country Merchants of the Staple and 'broggers'—middlemen in wool— and Merchant Adventurers and clothiers vied with each other in building handsome houses, their merchants' mark proudly gilded above the front door, and in rebuilding parish churches in the Perpendicular style, whose eloquent spaces and entrancing geometry of straight lines and expanses of glass and fan vaulting gave a man the most dazzle for his money. These merchants bequeathed themselves and their wives to the centuries in church brasses, where the woolpack or the sheep or sometimes the clothier's shears reveal what made it all possible. Thomas Paycocke's timbered mansion in Coggeshall, inns and houses in Suffolk villages, the reaches of golden stone in Chipping Camden and Northleach and Broadway and elsewhere in the Cotswolds, the towered churches of Somerset, the church of St. Mary Redcliffe, Bristol, re-edified by William Canynges—these offer a more telling picture of life during the Wars of the Roses than chronicles of battle.

England held a European monopoly of the best grade of wool, 'chief treasure in this land growing'. Its nearest rival, Spanish wool, had to be liberally mingled with English wool for the making of fine cloth:

> All nations affirm up to the full—
> In all the world there is no better wool.

Exported by the thousands of sacks on Italian galleys sailing through the 'Straits of Marrock' and dispatched in even greater quantities across the Channel to Calais and thence into the Low Countries, English wool fed the looms of the clever artisans in Florence and Venice and Milan and was turned by the weavers of Bruges and Mechlin and the cities of Holland into luxurious woollens prized by all Europe. In 1437 a shrewd economist[1] expressed in a poem called *The Libelle of Englysche Polycye* the convictions of the London merchants about English trade. Two points in particular were hammered home: England must have a strong navy in order to 'keep the Narrow Seas', whereby English shipping will be protected and foreign merchants can be constrained to divert their trade, now enriching the Low Countries, to the ports of England. In the second place, English diplomacy must take into account the monopoly of wool and thus bring the Flemings to see what side their bread is buttered on:

> The little land of Flanders is
> But a staple [market] to other lands, iwys [truly]. . . .
> By draping of our wool in substance
> Live their commons, this is their governance;
> Without which they may not live at ease.
> Thus must them starve or with us must have peace.

The export of wool, it is true, was declining as the cloth business expanded; and even after the revival of trade under Edward IV no more than about 9,000 sacks were exported annually, whereas in the heyday of wool in the fourteenth century more than 30,000 sacks had left English shores in a year. During Edward IV's reign, however, the men who dealt in wool, the worshipful Company of the Merchants of the Staple, still considered themselves 'the flower of English merchaundy'.

Records reveal the name of more than 300 Staplers doing business in this period. Most of these were London merchants, but there were a number of provincial Staplers too, like John Barton of Holme, beside Newark, who jauntily inscribed in a window of his house:

> I thank God and ever shall—
> It is the sheep hath paid for all.

---

[1] Probably Adam Moleyns, later Bishop of Chichester and a royal Councillor; murdered in 1450 (see Epilogue: *Wars of the Roses*).

The Staple itself, the official channel through which the wool trade was required to pass, had been fixed since 1426 at Calais, within easy sailing distance of London and the Channel ports and but a short ride from Bruges and Ypres and the great Flanders fairs. Four-fifths of the wool that left England went through Calais.

The *Cely Papers* and the *Stonor Letters* reveal that the structure of the wool trade required a network of trusty agents. It was a good business for a partnership like that of Sir William Stonor and Thomas Betson, or for a family group like the Celys with their office in Mark Lane and their country manor of Bretts Place, Essex. Old Richard Cely depended most upon his eldest and steadiest son, Richard. The sporting George usually had his mind on his horse Py and his hawk Meg even when he was bargaining with Flemish buyers, whose names his pen struggled to reproduce. Robert the Black Sheep could not keep his thoughts on business at all for running after girls in London or gambling with dice at Calais. William, a cousin, was making his way as an apprentice or journeyman.

In the spring of 1480 Robert was lingering at Bruges, afraid to come back to Calais because he had been charged with desertion in the bishop's court. He had somehow got himself betrothed to one Joan Hart, and Joan's relatives were trying to wring money out of Robert's father. Old Richard Cely countered by demanding the return of the gifts which the prodigal Robert had showered on the girl. Finally Joan's people gave back a girdle of gold with silver buckle and pendants, a gold ring with a little diamond in it, a damask carpet.

Whenever he got in a scrape, Robert piteously applied to brother George, for old Richard Cely but too well understood his son's 'childish dealings', and young Richard too turned a deaf ear, pointing out to George that one loan would inevitably lead to an application for another. Perhaps George was the more inclined to sympathize with Robert because he himself was not a pillar of rectitude. On one occasion his servant wrote to him from Calais, 'Also I let you know, where ye go and eat puddings the woman is with child'. Some nine months later George was informed that 'Margery' needed new clothes for her churching . . .'

'as she had the other time'. A few weeks later, he learned that Margery's infant daughter had died.

While old Richard Cely managed affairs in Mark Lane, young Richard rode off through late spring sunshine and rain, hawk on fist to let fly at a heron by the way, in order to purchase wool in the Cotswolds. William Cely was stationed at Calais to receive and house the sarplers. George went to the Sinxon Mart at Antwerp, the great summer fair, to collect money due from Flemish buyers and to stir up new business. The Betson-Stonor partnership worked in the same way. Down in the country Sir William Stonor supervised the clipping and packing of wool from his own manors and his neighbours'. Thomas Betson in London, assisted by two apprentices, saw to the weighing of the wool at the Leadenhall and the warehousing of the sarplers till the wool fleet sailed. Meantime a third apprentice had departed for Calais in order to take charge of the shipment there; and then Thomas Betson crossed the Channel and went on to the Flanders Fairs, where he collected debts in a bewilderering variety of coin and arranged for the transfer of funds to London by bills of exchange. A half century later, John Johnson, Merchant of the Staple, was carrying on his business in almost exactly the same way. Young Richard Cely spelled somewhat more phonetically than Johnson —St. Olave's church becomes 'Sent Tolowys scryssche'—but on the other hand, Richard Cely never had to worry about a wayward aunt who at St. Omer made such indiscreet Protestant remarks concerning heathen images and whores of Babylon that she almost ended her days in one of the Emperor's dungeons.

There were some half a hundred different grades of English wool, ranked according to the localities in which the sheep pastured; and they were also labelled according to age, for Flemish merchants were required to take one sack of 'old wool', of the previous season's clip, for every three sacks of new wool they purchased. Though 'March wool' from a small area in Shropshire and Herefordshire fetched the top price of 14 marks a sack (£9 6s 8d), the clip from the great flocks grazing in the Cotswolds, worth 12 or 13 marks the sack, was so sought after that 'Cotswold' meant wool of best quality. Then came the wool of Hampshire and Wiltshire, priced at 7 marks the sack; the clip in Kent and Yorkshire brought only 4½ marks; and Surrey and Suffolk wool went for about 50s a sack.

Spring was the season for the Stapler to ride into the country in order to purchase wool from sheep-owner or brogger. He shipped his sacks in the 'wool fleets' that periodically sailed for Calais during the summer. In the autumn he again took to the road to 'cast a sort' (examine samples) for next spring's purchases and bought wool-fells (hides) produced by the November slaughtering.[1]

On a May morning, the streets of Northleach and Chipping Camden and Burford and Stow clattered with the horses and hummed with the talk of Staplers and hawk-eyed Italian buyers and a few London mercers and drapers out to turn an extra penny in wool and farmers and broggers and members of the fellowship of wool-packers. Like Thomas Betson, whom they knew, the Celys swore by Cotswold wool; they dealt mainly with William Midwinter and John Busshe of Northleach, both flourishing broggers, the former of whom left £600 and broad lands when he died in 1501.

After a Stapler purchased wool, it was baled by a wool-packer and his men, who were appointed by the Staple to grade wool impartially as 'indifferent persons'. Stringent regulations forbade mixing earth, hair, sand, or rubbish with the wool, or mislabelling it, or not packing it in the county of origin. In the country, the fellowship of wool-packers served to protect the Stapler against fraud on the part of the middleman; but these same packers also examined the sacks when they reached Calais, and then they protected the good name of the Staple from sharp

---

[1] Old Richard Cely 'to George Cely at Calais, writ at London the xxij day of May', 1840: '[By] a letter from you written at Calais the xiij of May . . . I have well understood of your being at the marts [Flanders fair] and of the sale of my middle wool desired by John Destermer and John Underhay, wherefore by the Grace of God I am a-busied for to ship this aforesaid sarplers, the which I bought of, William Midwinter of Northleach, xxvj sarplers the which is fair wool, as the wool-packer Will Breton saith to me, and also the iij sarplers of the rector's is fair wool, much finer wool nor was the year before, the which I shipped afore Easter last past. The shipping is begun at London but I have none shipped as yet but I will after these Holy Days, for the which I will ye order for the freight and other costs. This same day your brother Richard Cely is ridden to Northleach for to see and cast a sort of fell for me and another sort of fell for you. . . .'

practice on the part of merchants, or so they were supposed to do.
Will Breton, the Celys' favourite packer, was a much-travelled
man, moving about from Southampton to the Cotswolds to
London to Calais.

After the bulky sarplers, each holding two or three sacks, had
been brought to London—or another of the Staple ports—and
been weighed and registered at the Leadenhall by royal 'customers',
they were warehoused until there was a sailing for Calais. For
the Narrow Seas were coursed by Scots and Breton privateers,
and in the early summer the wool ships sailed in fleets with
convoys. 'Conduct money' was a standard part of the freight-
rate. Wool ships set forth not only from London and Boston and
Lynn and Ipswich but also from such tiny ports as Walberswick
on the Suffolk shore and Rainham and Bradwell in Essex and
even from towns along the Medway like Maidstone, though
such vessels could have been little more than barges of about
30 tons.

As a hedge against disaster, merchants shipping in the wool
fleets scattered their cargoes among half a dozen or more vessels.
Communications from London specify in detail the locations and
markings of the wool or wool-fells. A list of such descriptions
prepared by young Richard Cely for his brother George at
Calais includes 'in the *Thomas* of Newhithe [on the Medway],
Robert Hewan master, a pack lxiiij fells Cotswold; they lie
behind the mast and Betson's fells lie above them'. The Cely and
Stonor letters echo with sighs of relief that a fleet has come safe
to port. 'Blessed be Jhesu', wrote Betson's apprentice, Thomas
Henham, 'I have received your wools in safety!' Enemy cruisers
as well as storms were always to be feared: 'Robert Eryke was
chased with Scots between Calais and Dover. They scaped
narrow.'

From the buying of the wool in the Cotswolds to its sale in
Calais, the trade was supported on a structure of credit. The
Celys usually paid their brogger, William Midwinter, half the
price on delivery and the remainder in two instalments at intervals of three months or even longer. From the Dutch and Flemish
buyers riding into Calais, the Staplers customarily received as

'earnest money' or 'God's penny' a third of the selling price in coin and the rest 'at six months and six months'. When the wool market became sluggish, even more lenient credit was extended; and rebates were given to buyers with a good reputation for paying. The Flemings and Dutch were charged interest, but this, like fluctuations in price, was concealed by manipulating the rate of exchange. An ambitious apprentice not only needed to know French and Flemish and Latin, but he had to master the shifting values of the many kinds of coin that poured into Calais: Andrew gilders and the Arnoldus gulden (much debased) and Carolus groats and old crowns and new crowns of France and Davids of Utrecht (much debased) had to be calculated against Scots riders and Burgundy riders and Rhenish florins and Nimwegen groats and a dozen other coins. English money was solider than most of the coinages: on May 10, 1484, 30s Flemish were required to buy 20s English.

In order to collect the money due them, George Cely and Thomas Betson had to ride into Flanders at all seasons to attend the fairs, the Cold Mart in winter and the Easter Pasche Mart and the Sinxon Mart in summer and the October Balms Mart. Staplers like the Celys who did not have a great store of capital were under the constant strain of meeting their obligations to English middlemen by means of remittances from Flanders. These took the form of bills of exchange drawn on Lombard banks or on Merchant Adventurers with offices in London and Antwerp. In June of 1480 young Richard Cely wrote hastily to his brother George that he had bought £91 13s 4d worth of fells from Midwinter and had to pay £40 down within five days and the remainder in two payments at Bartholomewtide and Hallowstide; 'Sir, I pray you have these days in remembrance, my poor honesty lies thereupon.'

The poor honesty of the Celys did not always stretch as far as it might have done. Despite stringent regulations of the Staplers and inspections and re-inspections, there were a number of ways of beating the game and the Celys were old Calais hands. It appears that on one occasion at least they concluded a sale with Flemish buyers who had come to England, which was prohibited. On another, when the Lieutenant of the Staple, inspecting a shipment of Cely wool newly arrived at Calais, designated sarpler No. 24 to be opened for examination, William Cely, knowing it to be of middle wool and 'very gruff', persuaded the 'indifferent packer' to cast out sarpler No. 8 instead, which was of 'fair wool'; and once the numbers of the two sarplers had been exchanged William was able to write home contentedly, 'Your wool is awarded by the sarpler that I cast out last'. It is not surprising that Flemish buyers constantly complained to the Staple that the wool sacks they opened in Bruges did not contain the 'fair wool' they had purchased at Calais.

The fellowship of wool packers owned a rich repertory of 'deceitful sleights' which they practiced for their own benefit or that of a generous customer; and the Celys' friend William Breton was master of them all. 'Bearding and clacking' was a favourite device; by thus 'forcing' the wool, that is, removing all impurities such as tarry marks, one sack paying only the ordinary custom and subsidy sold for three times as much as the normal sack. The trick of 'inwinding' produced a sack of outwardly fair and inwardly inferior wool. Records reveal that one of William Breton's most cherished frauds was to cut the feet off fells and then stuff them into a sack labelled 'Cotswold wool'.

In one year the Celys, not among the wealthiest Merchants of the Staple, did more than £2,000 worth of business, which brought them a gross profit of perhaps £300. A sack of good Cotswold cost at Northleach something like £8; by the time the expense of transportation to London had been added and the custom and subsidy of 40s per sack and freightage to Calais (about 6s 6d a sack), the wool offered to a Flemish dealer had cost the Celys £11 and they received for it perhaps 19 marks (£12 13s). Thus they made a gross profit of about £2 on a sack; but favourable rates of exchange and other advantages might drive the profit up to £3.

At high-roofed Calais, garrisoned by English troops and occupied by English landlords and ruled by the Staple, the merchants lived like a community of initiates vowed to serve the god of the wool-trade. They talked of bargains and of the doings of the sinister French King (Louis XI) and enjoyed tidings come hot from the court of the Emperor or from the camp of the Duke of Burgundy. They were required to live in licenced lodgings, which were provided with a high table for merchants (board perhaps 3s 6d a week) and side tables for apprentices and lesser fry (board at 2s 6d). Though the town was surrounded by dreary marshes, a Stapler might ride out, hawk on fist, to take a glass of wine with other good fellows at Guisnes or Hammes; and on occasion the married men challenged the bachelors to a bout of archery. Since Calais was reputed for its bargains in all manner of wares, Staplers and visitors always had shopping to do for their friends. The Celys bought goshawks, onion seed, Gascon wine, pickled Meuse salmon, lambskins, mink, tapestries, armour, sugar loaves, fine Louvain gloves. When Sir John Howard came to Calais in 1466, he purchased Holland cloth by the hundreds of yards, draperies and bedding, ribbons, laces, not forgetting five yards of white damask costing 5s 6d as a gratuity for his hostess.

Although the worshipful Merchants of the Staple continued to be a great and famous company throughout the Yorkist Age, they had been surpassed before the end of Edward IV's reign by their younger and freer rivals, the Merchant Adventurers. Under the leadership of the Mercers of London the Adventurers had secured their final charter of incorporation earlier in the century; and though, after a bitter battle, they failed to make much headway against the Hanse traders in the Baltic and the Germanies, they had won a virtual monopoly of the export of English cloth to the marts of the Low Countries. Domiciled at Bruges and then at Antwerp in the 'English House'—of which William Caxton, mercer, had been governor before a newfangled craft caught his eye—the agents of London mercers and other merchants from all over England sold white, unfinished broadcloths by the thousands and bought for the home market a variety of 'mercery' ranging from tennis balls to spectacles.

Lords and abbots and knights and yeomen-farmers who owned large sheep-runs were not troubled by the shrinking wool trade; for they now sold much of their clip to the new race of men who supplied the cloths for the Merchant Adventurers to export, the clothiers. Though in Norwich and Coventry and Salisbury and Bristol quantities of cloth were still being manufactured under the stiflingly regulated, cumbersome gild system—the weavers working for the dyers or the dyers for the fullers, the cloth passing from independent artisan to artisan—those infant capitalists, the clothiers, had created an industry in the freedom of the countryside and were busy building fulling-mills and gig-mills (the gig was a machine to raise nap) along swift-flowing streams. They financed and managed all the processes of cloth-making. Through borough and manorial villages passed files of pack-horses as the servants of the clothiers transported thread from carders and spinners to weavers and took bales of cloth from the weavers to the fulling-mills.

Artisans, their independence lost, sometimes complained angrily that clothiers pared their pay or made them take half their wages in cheap mercery wares. Often the goodman no longer worked in his cottage but trudged early in the morning to the clothier's mansion and there on the top floor occupied one of a row of looms. A number of clothiers, however, felt a paternal obligation to their workers. Thomas Paycocke of Coggeshall, whose house with its carved beams still fronts the village street, bequeathed 6s 8d to a former apprentice, Humphrey Stonor; 20s 'to Thomas Goodday, shearman, and each of his children 3s 4d apiece'; and a variety of sums to other Gooddays of Sampford and Stisted and Coggeshall. To 'John Beycham, my weaver' he left £5 and 'a gown and a doublet'; Robert Taylor was forgiven whatever money he owed and received 3s 4d in addition. 'I bequeath to all my weavers, fullers, and shearmen that be not afore rehearsed by name 12d apiece, and will they that have wrought me very much work have 3s 4d apiece. Item, I bequeath to be distributed among my combers, carders, and spinners summa £4.'

Not many years after the close of Edward IV's reign, the names of the great clothiers rang up and down England as if they were legendary characters of romance: Thomas Dolman of Newbury; the Tames of Fairford; the Springs of Lavenham in Suffolk; and

John Wynchcombe, immortalized by Thomas Deloney as Jack of Newbury. When Thomas Dolman retired from clothmaking, the Newbury weavers lamented. . . .

> Lord have mercy upon us, miserable sinners,
> Thomas Dolman has built a new house, and turned away
> all his spinners.

The Tames would entertain Henry VIII in the mansion that cloth built. Thomas Spring married a daughter to a son of the Earl of Oxford, gave £200 to rebuilding Lavenham church, and left money for 1,000 masses to be said for his soul. James Terumber, or Tucker (the alias suggests that he began life as a fuller), so handsomely rebuilt the village of Trowbridge that clothiers in all the region round were moved to emulate his good works.

Cloths were manufactured in a wide variety of sizes and colours —kerseys and straits and statutes and dozens and medleys and blod and many others. Three kerseys or four straits were roughly equivalent to one broadcloth; dozens, the cloth that the country weaver brought into Coventry and was permitted to sell 'hanging on his arm' were half-broadcloths. Blod, a red cloth, very popular, brought from £1 to £2 the cloth; medleys ranged in price from 24s to almost £4 a cloth. But the cloth which the Merchant Adventurers usually exported was the 'broadcloth of assize', twenty-four yards long and two yards wide, as established by Parliamentary statute. Most of these cloths were exported unfinished, for the artisans of the Low Countries, hard pressed by the competition of English looms, had been forced to concentrate their industry on dyeing and shearing and napping.

Nothing could obstruct the rising tide of trade generated by the Merchant Adventurers. When Philip the Good, Duke of Burgundy, besieged by his merchants crying that English cloth was ruining them, forbade the Adventurers to import into Flanders, they simply moved their 'House' from Bruges to the Imperial city of Utrecht and continued a thriving business. Merchants of the Staple fought bitterly to break the Adventurers' monopoly, but just as mercers who dealt in wool were required to put themselves under Staple regulation, so too the Staplers who exported cloth were forced to pay the fees exacted by the Merchant Adventurers and abide their rules. Early in his reign Edward IV, himself a great Adventurer, issued a new charter to the company which gave them all they wanted. They were permitted to draw up ordinances in order to govern all trade with the Low Countries, except that in wool and tin; and every English merchant exporting or importing in the dominions of the Duke of Burgundy was required to pay them a fee and submit his business deals for their approval.

The Mercers of London formed the mainspring of the organization: the 'Court of Adventurers' was held in Mercers Hall, the Governor in the Low Countries was almost always a mercer, and the Mercers spent large sums—which they assessed upon the Adventurers—in securing privileges and conducting trade diplomacy. But grocers, drapers, haberdashers, skinners, and some tailors and fishmongers also belonged to the association and had a voice in its decisions.

Like the Staplers, the Merchant Adventurers shipped their wares in fleets, which were convoyed by heavily armed vessels; and the sailings of these cloth-armadas usually coincided with the times when the four great seasonal fairs of Flanders were about to begin. In 1475 the Wardens of the Mercers informed the Governor of the English House at Antwerp, 'There be divers ships here appointed, as well by drapers, grocers, haberdashers, and the assent of the fishmongers as by our fellowship, which now by God's grace shall come to the Balms Mart'. The articles of 'mercery' which the English merchants purchased at the fairs to import into England were likewise shipped in convoyed fleets. The Governor apportioned freight rates and 'conduct money' and saw to it that the vessels were properly victualled, 'tackled and [furnished] with habiliments of war'. Traders who shipped on their own when space in the fleet was available were required to pay their share of the charges.

The term 'Merchant Adventurers' had once referred to all foreign traders, except Staplers, 'adventuring' anywhere; but the increasing power and prosperity of those exporting cloth to the

Low Countries attached to their association the generic label, 'Merchant Adventurers of England'. Just as the London Mercers dominated this body, so this body in turn dominated all the other Adventurers of the realm. The Merchant Adventurers of Bristol, however, exported cloth—each 'at his adventure'—mainly to France and Spain and Iceland, the small number who traded with the Low Countries forming a separate body controlled by the overseas Governor. The Merchant Adventurers of York were nearly all in the Netherlands trade; along with the Adventurers of Newcastle and Hull they sent forth their own fleets to the Flanders Fairs and elected a Governor and claimed to be independent. But they were required none the less to obey the regulations and pay the 'outrageous contributions' enforced by the London company. The Adventurers were all a proud lot, their spirit exemplified by the Adventurers of Hull who accepted into their fellowship only those who lived 'by the way and means of buying and selling and by great adventure'.

Their merchant-king, Edward IV, carefully guided his foreign policy in the interests of the Adventurers and made them partners in his diplomacy. Many times, through the Mayor of London, he summoned them to Westminster so that he might hear their wishes, explain his negotiations with Burgundy, and appoint some of their members to take part in or to instruct his embassies to the Duke. Not yet accustomed to a king who understood the importance of trade, the Adventurers in 1464 shrank from Edward's request that they negotiate a renewal of mercantile intercourse and asked the Mayor of London to persuade the King 'in the most pleasant wise' to use his own diplomats. But in 1467 and 1468 William Caxton, at King Edward's request, was heading delegations of Adventurers who treated with the Duke of Burgundy's representatives regarding the sale of English cloth and the fixing of a standard rate of exchange.

In the 1470's Caxton and other Adventurers again took part with royal diplomats in trade negotiations with the Burgundians, as King Edward continued to press his ally, Duke Charles, to accord advantageous terms to English merchants. A set of instructions he and his council drew up in 1474 ordered his ambassadors to 'insist with all diligence' that (1) the Duke permit a free market for English cloth in his dominions; (2) the sale of Spanish and Scottish wool be curtailed and better provision be made for Newcastle wool; (3) the negotiatiors establish standard values for the various coinages circulating in the Low Countries; (4) 'searches made upon Englishmen hereafter be not made in fields and highways without the towns, but in good towns and more honestly than hath been used aforne and in late days'; (5) tolls and customs be 'set in certain' and not altered upwards; (6) English merchants receive permission to export from the Low Countries 'horses, harnesses, all manner artillery and habiliments of war'; and (7) 'rovers, men of war, or enemies unto England' should be excluded from the Duke's ports and territories. Throughout his reign the King worked to further the prosperity of his foreign traders. Henry VII's treaties of mercantile intercourse with the Netherlands represent no more than a continuation of Edward IV's solidly established policy.

The Merchant Adventurers rode the forces of the future. Whereas the export of cloth in 1354 had amounted to only 4,774 pieces, at the close of Richard III's reign England was shipping abroad almost 70,000 broadcloths a year, worth something more than £100,000; and whereas in the fourteenth century the lion's share of foreign trade had fallen to alien merchants, by the end of Edward IV's reign the volume of trade carried on by aliens was less than two-thirds that of the Merchant Adventurers alone. In the sixteenth century the Merchants of the Staple would close their books forever, when the demands of native looms forced an embargo on the export of English wool; and the once-thriving cities of Flanders would sink into decay.

Merchants of all kinds who entrusted cargoes to the sea were splendid gamblers: profits were great and so were the perils. Many a ship never reached its destination or arrived with blood spattered on the deck and an empty hold. But that was the merchant's way, to venture; it was not only his livelihood but his life. John Johnson, Stapler of Tudor times, speaks also for the merchants of the Yorkist and all other ages: 'God having appointed me to be a merchant . . . I am compelled to enter into much business, and to take money and much things in hand. . . . If it please God, I may live to see the end. If not, his Will be done, for I make no other reckoning, supposing not to displease God to be occupied while I am here in that which is my calling. . . .'

From 1449 until 1475, except for brief intervals of truce, England was at war with France. An enemy even more to be feared at sea was the Hanseatic League; a long history of quarrels ended in the rupture of relations in 1468, following which the Easterlings carried on an intense and all too successful naval war with the English until 1474. After King Edward made peace with the Hanse in that year and signed the Treaty of Picquigny with Louis XI the following summer, English foreign trade began to soar.

The merchant's greatest enemy remained the pirate, though there is nothing very distinctive about piracy during the Yorkist Age. It had flourished in the fourteenth century and it would go on flourishing under the Tudors. During the fifteenth century piracy reached its apogee of success during the last bad years of Henry VI; the failure of Henry's government to keep the seas and the ill-concealed partnership between some of Henry's lords and pirate chieftains drove the merchants of the realm into the arms of the Yorkists. The coasts of England and the Low Countries and France and Spain all harboured pirates; but the Celts had raised the occupation to a fine art. The indefatigable Breton sea-thieves of St. Malo zealously vied for leadership with their Cornish brothers of Polruan and St. Ives and, above all, Fowey. A Cornish gentleman might be a Justice of the Peace and a considerable land owner in his region, but he could hardly regard himself as respectable unless he possessed shares in a piratical balinger or two. The system which enabled pirates to thrive despite commissions of enquiry, commands to arrest goods and persons, and orders for restitution, is writ large in the records of Henry VI's collapsing government.

On December 7, 1451, a Gascon squire, associated with four merchants of Bristol, freighted *The Kateryn* of Bayonne with wine, iron, saffron, ivory, and other merchandise. Covered by letters of safe-conduct from Henry VI, *The Kateryn* made a good voyage despite wintry seas and on Christmas Eve lay off St. Ives. A piratical pinnace, also called *The Kateryn*, promptly put out from town, captured *The Kateryn* of Bayonne as she lay peacefully at anchor, took her into the harbour and despoiled her of the cargo. One of the Bristol merchants, William Joyce, who was on board and witnessed the piracy, hurried off to Lostwithiel, showed the ship's safe-conduct to the sheriff in the shire hall and demanded that it be publicly read. An influential man in West Cornwall, Richard Penpons, Justice of the Peace, then came forward and observed quietly that the letters of safe-conduct had not been properly drawn up and that the ship had been lawfully seized. Penpons, of course, was the principal owner of *The Kateryn* of St. Ives.

It took Joyce five years to secure a hearing in Chancery, and even then he did not dare to mention Richard Penpons, who appears to have been a stalwart Lancastrian, and the case came to nothing. The accession of Edward IV to the throne in 1461 seemingly gave Joyce his opportunity; by December of that year he had procured an inquiry into the case, and in August of 1462 Henry Bodrugan and other officers, accompanied by Joyce, moved on St. Ives to arrest the pirates. But these worthies, incited by Penpons, suddenly issued forth in such warlike array that Joyce and Bodrugan fled for their lives, pursued for ten miles. The Bristol merchant was so angered by this treatment that, in a third bill, he finally ventured to accuse Penpons directly. Now become a good Yorkist and again Justice of the Peace, Richard Penpons answered stoutly, as he had a decade before, that the safe-conduct did not protect the ship; and it appears that Joyce, for all his years of labour, received neither justice nor his goods. One of the commissioners who had been appointed to inquire into the case of *The Kateryn* of Bayonne, Thomas Bodulgate, was a great landholder, a friend of Penpons, and an enterprising pirate.

Both Edward IV and Richard III took measures to check the evil, and sea traffic became safer than it had been in Henry VI's last years; but Cornish piracy still had a long history before it.

As far as English merchants, and Englishmen generally, were

concerned, aliens who came into the realm to make their homes or to trade or even to visit, were hardly less objectionable than pirates. The nascent nationalism of the fifteenth century generated a dislike of foreigners in all European countries; but by common consent xenophobia flourished in England as it did nowhere else, for the English were regarded as more set in their prejudices and more arrogant in their national pride than any other people on earth.

The Scots of course did not count as aliens; they were simply the enemy—a more inimical and personal enemy perhaps even than the French, because they looked rather like Englishmen and dared to use a language that parodied the noble English tongue. All over the north parts of the realm and even as far south as Norwich, the bitterest slander that could be hurled against a man was to call him a Scot. The records of the city of York buzz with indignant complaints against 'children of iniquity' who have defamed a true-born Englishman by noising it abroad that he came from over the border. John Harrington, the town clerk, was so exercised by this outrageous accusation, brought against him by Thomas Wharfe, that he hastened to solicit testimonials from Sir John Ashe, Lady Fitzhugh, Sir John Conyers, and Sir Robert Harrington that he was no 'false Scot'. 'If this slanderous report,' Ashe wrote fiercely, 'come to the ears of some young men of the blood that he [Harrington] is of, it will grieve them, I doubt not, which I pray you desire the said Thomas Wharfe to remember.'

Aliens domiciled in England were no less disliked than transients. Beginning with the reign of Edward III, many Flemings had settled in the realm to ply their clever fingers at the loom. Villages and towns of East Anglia had their 'alien quarters', where men said *brod* instead of *bread* and *case* instead of *cheese* and sometimes received hard looks from their fellow-townsmen. Journeymen were always grumbling against the competition of domiciled aliens, and the masters of the journeymen complained just as bitterly, for somewhat different reasons. A petition of 1514 strikes the customary note: the realm 'is so inhabited with a great multitude of needy people, strangers of divers nations, that your liege people . . . cannot imagine nor tell . . . what occupation they

shall use to put their children'. The Cordwainers of London, their
hearts wrung because their countrymen wore shoddy shoes not
manufactured by themselves, expressed 'ruth and pity . . . to see
great loss and decaying of all the king's subjects of this realm that
have the use and wearing of such false stuff'.

Sometimes these men and women trying to make a new life
for themselves and their children in the green, prosperous land
of England received worse than harsh glances and verbal drub-
bings. When agents of Warwick the Kingmaker, in 1468, were
rousing the anger of London artisans against Edward IV's ally,
Charles, Duke of Burgundy, a group of citizen-conspirators
planned to cross the Thames in boats under cover of darkness in
order to visit their wrath upon the Flemings; and only the last-
minute discovery of the plot prevented an orgy of thumb-cutting
(head-chopping, some said) in Southwark. In the autumn of 1470
and again in May of 1471, Kentish supporters of the Earl of
Warwick stormed into Southwark, maltreated Flemish and
Dutch weavers and burned their 'beer-houses'.

Foreign ambassadors sometimes discovered that diplomatic
courtesies did not extend beyond the royal court. Though
England and France were supposed to be the best of friends in
1478, Louis XI's envoy, the Bishop of Elne, had such a harrowing
experience that at moments, he afterwards declared, he almost
despaired of his life. Some of his troubles, it may be, stemmed from
the rough English humour of the day rather than from malice.

Whenever the Bishop or one of his retinue ventured from their
lodgings, a crowd collected to yell 'French dogs!' and jeer him on
his way. More irascible Londoners shouted that the ambassador
was no better than a French spy who ought to be drowned in the
river, and they raised such a clamour that King Edward had to put
the most obstreperous of them under arrest. But even when the
Bishop of Elne followed the royal Court to Windsor, he did not
find peace. One day the villagers, raising the old cry of 'French
dogs!', made a rush at some of his servants. In the riot that followed a royal archer seized a club and brained a Frenchman with
a blow that stretched him senseless on the ground for more than
an hour. Edward offered to have the archer's offending hand cut

off, but the Bishop vetoed the punishment—doubtless wisely—on the grounds that the King of France would not like it. By the ambassador's own confession, every time thereafter that he saw an Englishman touch a bow, he thought his last moment had arrived.

Even the King was not above enjoying himself at the expense of the somewhat timorous Bishop. On one occasion he drew my Lord of Elne aside and inquired innocently if it were true, as a herald of his had just reported on returning from France, that King Louis was looking forward to the Bishop's arrival in order to cut off his head. The ambassador summoned enough dignity to reply that people who told tales like that were 'mauvais gens'. Edward pushed the joke still further by urging the Bishop to run no risks and promising to take good care of him if he sought asylum in the realm. When the envoy answered tartly that if he wanted to fly from France he would choose some other land than England, King Edward was so delighted with the retort that he sent the Comptroller of the Household to offer Louis' ambassador a present of 2,000 crowns for his expenses—which the Bishop had to refuse for fear of what his suspicious master might think about it. Even a diplomatic envoy enjoyed no immunity from the prejudices of the populace. But then, the Bishop of Elne was a Frenchman.

Alien merchants were regarded with suspicion, disdain, and righteous indignation. The English, reported the Venetian diplomat, 'have an antipathy to foreigners, and imagine that they never come into their island but to make themselves masters of it and to usurp their goods'. Six decades before, *The Libelle of Englysche Polycye* had thundered:

> And thus they would, if ye will so believe,
> Wipe our nose with our own sleeve!

Native complaints—parliamentary and municipal and individual—against aliens and their practices ran the gamut of commercial perfidy.

The most welcome, or better, the least unpopular, were probably the Easterlings. The citizens of York disliked them because they rode about smelling out bargains and trying to unload their Teutonic wares upon the northern markets; but then the men of York were a conservative lot. The Merchant Adventurers of London bore the Hanse traders a bitter grudge and had long quarrelled with them because the Hanseatic League refused to accord to the Adventurers in German towns the same privileges that the Easterlings enjoyed at their Steelyards in London and Boston; but London merchants were the only really steadfast supporters of the sea-war with the Hanse, 1468-74. Otherwise, the Easterlings were quite cheerfully tolerated. The goods they brought into the realm like timber and pitch and potash and cables were all useful materials and they were cheap. Secondly, the Germans bought cloth for export from all parts of the realm; and whereas the Merchant Adventurers had to send mostly unfinished cloth to the Low Countries, the Easterlings provided work for English dyers and shearmen by purchasing quantities of finished cloths to be disseminated over Europe as far as Novgorod. When the royal Council broke with the Hanse in 1468, artisans of Gloucester and other towns petitioned in the Easterlings' behalf.

The greatest volume of animus was called forth by the trader of Italy. As far as the English were concerned, the only good Italian was the Italian who remained at home; and even he would probably rob you when you made a pilgrimage to Rome. The Staplers and the Merchant Adventurers heartily disliked those dark-eyed, saturnine strangers, mounted on sleek horses, who rode through the Cotswolds buying up the best wool or halted in Wiltshire and Hampshire villages to purchase the best white broadcloths. Old Richard Cely gloomily wrote to his son George, in October of 1480, 'I have not bought this year a lock of wool, for the wool of Cotswold is bought by Lombards. . . .' Londoners also grumbled against the Italian brokers of Lombard Street.

In the 1450's English merchants had bitterly resented the Italian factors of Henry VI's favourites, who had secured for themselves all sorts of fat pickings. Feelings grew so hot that in 1456 an incident between a mercer's boy and an Italian led to a violent riot; the following year the city's wrath boiled up again, and mobs plundered numerous Lombard dwellings. Not long after, the Earl of Warwick, Captain of Calais, made himself very popular in the capital by dispatching a small fleet to sail up the Thames and capture at Tilbury three vessels which Italians, with special royal licences, were loading with wool and cloth.

The merchants of Italy stirred English ire in general because they brought into the realm expensive luxury goods which tended to corrupt the native character and in exchange for these fripperies they bore away honest wool and cloth and gold. *The Libelle* protested against

> Apes, japes, and marmosets tailed,
> Nifles, trifles that little have availed,
> And other things with which they blear our eye. . . .

The Italian merchants, it was devoutly believed, practiced all kinds of frauds to do the native competitor in the eye. They bribed wool-packers to beard and clack wool, and thus further undermined English character. They paid in ready money for the best cloths and wools, quickly sold them for cash at a five per cent loss, and then lent that cash to English merchants at exorbitant rates of interest. They foregathered in each other's lodgings, driving secret bargains to the destruction of native traders; they dawdled in the country selling goods, which they were forbidden to do; and whereas they were supposed to export wool only through the 'Straits of Marrock', they fraudulently secured licences to ship to the Low Countries and there competed with the Staplers.

The Commons of Parliament inveighed against all these nefarious transactions and tried, in vain, to erect a wall of prohibitions. Transient aliens were given a limited number of days in which to complete their business in England, and they were forbidden to sell at retail. Prohibited from taking gold out of the realm, they were required instead to buy English goods with the moneys they received for their wares. In order that their transactions with each other might be scrutinized, they were ordered to 'go to host', that is, to live in the houses of English merchants, who were empowered to oversee all their dealings.

When the Commons[1] of Richard III's Parliament of 1484 drew up a very strong petition against 'The Merchants of Italy', however, the king and his advisers attached an important condition— 'Provided alway that this act . . . in no wise extend . . . any let, hurt, or impediment to any artificer or merchant stranger of what nation or country he be . . . for bringing into this realm, or selling by retail or otherwise, of any manner books written or imprinted, or for the inhabiting within the said realm for the same intent, or to any writer, limner, binder, or imprinter of such books, as he hath or shall have to sell by way of merchandise. . . .' To King Richard and his counsellors goes the honour of having devised the first piece of legislation to foster the art of printing and the dissemination of books.

The Parliamentary Commons of Edward IV and Richard III and Henry VII busied themselves with all manner of economic legislation. When the Duke of Burgundy forbade the importation of English cloth into his dominions, the Commons retaliated with an embargo on manufactured articles from the Low Countries; at the request of the 'gentlewomen of London' who held a virtual monopoly in England of the manufacture of silk goods, they repeatedly forbade the importation of competing articles from abroad; and when they feared for the noble sport of archery, they required aliens to import a certain number of bow-staves with all other merchandise. They passed a multiplicity of regulations in an endeavour to regulate domestic prices and set standards of quality for the staples of living like bread and ale, and they enacted numerous statutes designed to prevent fraudulent practices in the production of cloth. But this legislative tinkering with the economy could not be closely enforced and was probably not always helpful. The merchant class had to petition Richard III to annul an act against deceitful dyeing and stretching of cloth because the bill had done more harm than good.

In these Parliaments there sat a group of men who strongly stamped the period with their attitudes and activities and who,

[1] The terms 'House of Commons' and 'House of Lords' did not come into use until the next century.

with townsmen and gentry, were coming to dominate England in the Yorkist Age. These members of Parliament belonged to the professional classes, drawn in their increasing numbers from the town oligarchies and from yeomen and country gentlemen. They had common aspirations and a common bond of education and outlook, for most of them were lawyers or had been trained in the law at one of the Inns of Court or Chancery.

As a result of the decline of the Church, the spread of education, and the rise of the middle classes, the lay lawyer and civil servant and estate-supervisor of the fifteenth century replaced the mediaeval clerk as the managing force of the realm. One reason why the Yorkists triumphed and Edward IV could begin building a nation-state was that a strong central authority suited the interests and the talents of these men.[1]

The professional classes (an awkward but inevitable term) had, in the reign of Henry VI, begun sitting in Parliament for towns and boroughs which, out of indifference or poverty or a desire for a strong voice at Westminster, were willing to choose them as representatives instead of their own citizens. Cities like London and York and Bristol and Nottingham still elected fellow-townsmen, whom they honoured and paid well and who were the chief spokesmen for the trading interests; but places like Ipswich—one of its representatives in 1469 had agreed to sit for nothing if given

---

[1] It has been remarked that the Commons of Edward IV's Parliaments were much more docile than those of the preceding Lancastrian era. This so-called docility, however, seems to have at least partly represented a genuine satisfaction with the executive. Lancastrian Parliaments had clamoured for reform of the government, resumption of royal lands alienated by Henry VI's feckless generosity, reduction of debt and better management of finances. The government of Edward IV applied itself with marked success to all these problems.

Historians more interested in the past as a seed-time of the future rather than as a living entity have accused King Edward of neglecting Parliamentary institutions; in fact, though he summoned but six Parliaments, their sessions extended over more than half the years of his reign. Between 1475 and the last assemblage in 1843, Edward held only the brief Parliament of 1478 ; but to suppose that he was therefore oppressing the realm is to put seventeenth-century ideas into fifteenth-century heads. The king was never more popular than during these years; and far from yearning to be summoned to Westminster, his people were undoubtedly surprised and grateful that he succeeded in waging war with Scotland for three years without asking for a grant of taxes. 'Money,' remarked Sir Thomas More, 'is the only thing that withdraweth the hearts of Englishmen from the Prince.' Young John Paston spoke for his age when, in March of 1473, he wrote to his brother Sir John, representing Yarmouth in Parliament, 'I pray God send you the Holy Ghost among you in the Parliament House, and rather the Devil, we say, than ye should grant any more taxes.'

the freedom of the town—and smaller boroughs were glad to be canvassed by ambitious 'outsiders'—country gentlemen or London lawyers or estate-managers of great lords or civil servants or members of the royal household. In 1463 John Sackville, Esquire, agreed to sit for Weymouth in return for a barrel of mackerel delivered at Christmas; a member for Dunwich accepted his salary in herrings; other representatives received no fee at all.

Professional men had discovered that a seat in Parliament offered them the opportunity to make worthwhile contacts, to render good service to the King or to a patron, to exert influence, and perhaps, since increasing numbers of Parliamentary petitions, drawn up in the form of bills, were being presented for the approval of Commons, to earn a little money or good will in putting such petitions in proper form. While the more important royal officials usually sought election as Knight of the Shire, the smaller fry found places for themselves in borough representation. In the latter years of Henry VI and during the reign of Edward IV fewer than a third of the boroughs sent two of their own citizens to Parliament. In 1478, 17 per cent of the Commons consisted of careerists in the royal service, and more than two-thirds of the boroughs returned one or two outsiders. This revolution in the composition of the Commons marched side by side with a managerial revolution; the essential tone of Tudor government was already sounding in the Yorkist Age.

The official world of clerkdom was no longer the domain of the Church. Clerks of the Privy Seal, clerks to the Signet, clerks of the Exchequer and in the Chancery were drawn increasingly from the ambitious middle ranks of laymen. Early in the century Thomas Hoccleve, continually scribbling complaints about his salary and achieving no more than a corrody at the end of his service, did not fare very well; but many who followed him won annuities from the King or the hand of a royal ward (a minor heiress) and ended their careers as landed squires. Conversely, landed squires, seeing the rewards to be won in the service of a king or a great lord, became clerks and estate-managers. William Marchall, a clerk in the Chancery, owned property at Standlake and Woodstock,

Oxfordshire, and doubtless signed himself 'gentleman'. Peter Idley, a squire of the same county, moved upward through the royal service from Bailiff of the Honour of Wallingford to Gentleman Falconer to the King and Under-Keeper of the Royal Mews and Falcons, and from that sporting post advanced to become Comptroller of the King's Works throughout the realm. The chief clerkship of the Treasury was now held by a knight, frequently a man of legal training, who during the reign of Edward IV usually sat at the royal Council board.

This development of a lay professional class is symbolized by the changing status of the King's secretary. A comparatively minor official under the Lancastrians, he became an officer of great importance in Edward IV's reign, for Edward made extensive use of the Signet Seal which was operated by the secretary. Richard III's secretary and councillor John Kendall,[1] once a Yeoman of the Chamber, achieved a prominence in the government fore-shadowing the elevation of Henry VIII's secretary, Thomas Cromwell, to the position of First Minister, formerly held by the Chancellor.

The management of finances through the King's Chamber, more flexible and efficient than the Exchequer, and the payment of receipts from the royal domain into the Chamber—adminis-trative techniques often ascribed to the Tudors—were solidly established by the Yorkist kings. The old royal domain, the Duchy of Lancaster, and the great confiscated properties like the Clarence lands were put in the charge of professional receivers, auditors and surveyors. These experts in land management rode all over England on regular circuits, probably a book of Chaucer or Lydgate or *The Dictes and Sayings of the Philosophers* or *Tully of Old Age* in their saddle bags and the hope of retiring as a gentle-man upon land in their hearts. Lords and gentry, eager to increase their rent-rolls and improve their household accounting, likewise offered posts to the professional classes. For the office of Clerk of the kitchen in the Household of Lord Hastings, Governor of Calais, young John Paston recommended his friend Richard Stratton as 'well witted, well mannered, a goodly young man on

[1] For an account of the role he played, see P. M. Kendall, *Richard the Third*.

horse and foot; he is well spoken in English, meetly well in
French, and very perfect in Flemish; he can write and read
[i.e., Latin]'.

The Paston letters offer the fullest picture of members of the
professional class in the service of the gentry. Richard Calle, John
Daubeney, and John Pampyng worked loyally and, it appears,
effiiciently for the Pastons as estate-managers, advisers, and, on
occasion, as warriors; and, it must be admitted, not one of them
received the full measure of his deserts from the Paston family.
Richard Calle, chief steward and receiver, held manor courts in
defiance of threats and violence, was more than once roughly
handled in the streets of Norwich because of his devotion to
Paston interests, and yet found himself bitterly estranged from the
Pastons because he dared to seek a wife in the family. The affairs of
John Daubeney, killed at the siege of Caister, were so ill looked
after by Sir John Paston that young John wrote in shame to
remind his brother of their obligation. Brave and faithful John
Pampyng disappeared from Sir John Paston's service without
receiving the smallest annuity or even a word of commendation.

Battling to protect the Paston estates, John Pampyng risked
assault and endured imprisonment. He reveals his life in a letter he
wrote to John Paston, senior, in which he describes his attempt
to come to terms with Justice Yelverton and Justice Jenney, who
were forcibly encroaching on manors claimed by the Pastons:
'To speak with them as ye commanded me, I tarried not but rode
to Ipswich to my bed; and there at The Sun was the said Yelverton
and Jenney and Thomas Fastolfe; and mine host told me that the
same afternoon they had been at Nakton, but what they did there
I cannot tell; and when I was understood (to be) your man, Hogon,
Jenney's man, asked surety of peace of me; and Jenney sent for an
officer to have had me to prison; and so mine host undertook for
me that night. And this day in the morning I went to St. Laurence's
Church; and there I spake to them and told them ye marvelled
that they would take any distress or warn any of your tenants
that they should pay you no money. And Yelverton said ye had
taken a distress falsely and untruly of him. . . . And he said he was
enfeoffed as well as ye; and as for that, I told him he wost other

[knew otherwise] . . . and so I told him that he should be served the same within few days. And he said . . . if ye took upon you to make any trouble in his land ye shall repent it. . . . And so I am with the gaoler, with a clog upon mine heel for surety of the peace; wherefore please your mastership to send me your advice' —a very modest request!

Even after they had valiantly defended Caister against the besieging force of the Duke of Norfolk, the Paston stalwarts had no assurance of continued employment. Young John Paston, trying to discover his older brother's intentions, wrote fervently, 'By my troth, they are as good men's bodies as any alive, and specially Sir John Stille [a chaplain] and John Pampyng. And [if] I were of power to keep them . . . by troth they should never depart from me while I lived.' But Sir John Paston had a gift for choosing rascally servants who deserted him on a minute's notice and for failing to cherish the men who had propped the Paston fortunes. Two years after the siege of Caister, Margaret Paston was urging young John 'to move [Sir John] to take John Pampyng to him, or else to get him a service in the chancery, or in some other place where he might be preferred, for it is pity that he loseth his time so here. . . .' She added, 'For divers other things which ye shall know hereafter I would that he were hence in haste.' This veiled remark, when coupled with what Sir John wrote two years after (1473), suggests that Margaret Paston was thinking of more than Pampyng's welfare. Her younger daughter, Anne, had ventured, like her elder, Margery, to fall in love with a man who had shown himself leal and intrepid in the family service. But she was not to be permitted to follow her ungrateful sister's path. To heal the quarrel between Yelverton and Paston, Anne was betrothed to Justice Yelverton's grandson. John Pampyng had become an embarrassment if not a danger. 'Item,' Sir John wrote to his mother from London, 'I pray you take good heed to my sister Anne, lest the old love atween her and Pampyng renew.' John Pampyng thereupon disappears from the lives of the Pastons, in these words of Sir John's: 'Among all other things, I pray you beware that the old love of Pampyng renew not. He is now from me; I wot not what he will do. No more.'

As for lawyers, they thrived in this litigious age. Clement Paston laid the foundations of his family's fortune when he borrowed money to send his son William to one of the Inns of Court; and young John Paston, educated probably at Cambridge and at one of the Inns, re-edified that fortune when he became chief councillor of the Earl of Oxford. It is notable, too, that when the Mayor of Canterbury was pressing his suit in London against the Prior of Christ Church he was always having to send messengers into the country in order to consult with his counsel; the London lawyers retained by Canterbury apparently all owned manors to which they retired as often as possible.

Instead of seeking a royal office or taking the livery of a lord or knight or rising in the legal profession itself to become a Serjeant-at-law and perhaps a Justice, a lawyer might make a distinguished career for himself as the Recorder of a town or even as town clerk. Harry Butler and John Dudley, successive Recorders of Coventry, were figures of national prominence. Miles Metcalfe, Recorder of York, was rich enough to contribute £100 when the city was collecting money to give a present to Richard III and was so beloved by the corporation that they defied Henry VII rather than remove this devoted adherent of King Richard. Thomas Urswyck, Recorder of London, played a decisive part in opening the gates of the capital to King Edward in April of 1471, and was 'knighted in the field' by Edward in consequence of his good services.

In the Yorkist Age even the more modest post of Town Clerk offered attractive rewards and prestige. John Harrington, Clerk of the Court of Requests—that branch of the royal Council which dealt with poor men's causes—served also as Town Clerk of York. Cities were everywhere having their records re-copied, brought up to date, and maintained in greater detail than formerly—a process so extensive that paper was beginning to replace the more expensive parchment—and able lawyers therefore found a ready market for their services. Thomas Caxton, perhaps a brother of William Caxton, successively sold his services to Tenterden, Lydd, Romney, and Sandwich. Even after he had resigned his office at Lydd, the town frequently retained him to conduct its business with London or negotiate with the King; and when in 1470 the municipality fearfully entangled itself in the Wars of the Roses by first sending a troop of men to fight for Warwick and then rushing a contingent to the aid of King Edward, Thomas Caxton was made treasurer of the town, then bailiff, and was given a town clerk of his own training.

The well-educated layman did not always find the path of the professions a smooth climb. Though William Worcester subsequently achieved fame as an annalist, his letters to the Pastons portray a disillusioned man, ill-rewarded by a hard master, Sir John Fastolfe, whom he served long and faithfully as secretary. 'And whereas ye of your pleasure write me or call me Master Worcester,' he told John Paston, 'I pray and require you forget that name of mastership, for I am not amended by my master of a farthing in certainty [I receive no annuity], but of wages of household in common *autant comme nous plaira* [being subject to dismissal at his pleasure] . . . I have 5s yearly, all costs borne, to help pay for bonnets that I lose. I told so my master this week, and he said [to] me yesterday he wished me to have been a priest . . . to have given me a living. . . . And so I endure *inter egenos ut servus ad aratrum* [among the downtrodden as a slave yoked to the plough]. Forgive me, I write to make you laugh. . . .'

Scriveners, whose position was rather low among professional ranks, often conducted schools, and a few in London apparently published and sold manuscripts on a considerable scale; but, like William Worcester, some of them found the rewards of education meagre. William Ebesham, who copied out books and treatises for Sir John Paston, addressed him on one occasion, 'beseeching you most tenderly to see me somewhat rewarded for my labour in the Great Book which I wrote [for] your good mastership'. Sir John, always out of funds, had apparently fobbed Ebesham off previously by asking him to present his bills through John Pampyng: 'I have often times written to Pampyng, according to your desire, to inform you how I have laboured in writings for you. . . . And God knoweth I lie in sanctuary at great costs, and amongst right unreasonable askers. . . . And in especial I beseech you to send me for alms one of your old gowns. . . . I have great myst [need] of it,

God knows, whom I beseech preserve you from all adversity. I am somewhat acquainted with it.'

Members of the gentry seeking careers and career men rising into the gentry had in common not only their ambitions and their legal training but also a strong sense of profession. A friend of John Paston's, in the course of castigating a Paston enemy, remarked, 'I would ye should do well, because ye are a fellow of Gray's Inn, where I was a fellow'. A fierce pride in the English Common Law and in English parliamentary and judicial institutions rings through the works of Sir John Fortescue. In England, a king dispenses justice through judges; he is provided with expert advice by a royal council; and only Parliament can make laws. Hence Fortescue urged that justices and councillors and royal officers and members of Parliament be well-educated in order to preserve the unity and liberties of the realm. The Inns of Court provided a humane as well as a legal education. Students there not only attended sessions at Westminster, disputed points of law, and were treated to lectures by the great lawyers of the day; but they also read history and literature, became proficient in English and French and Latin, and learned 'singing and all kinds of music, dancing, and such other accomplishments as [were] suitable to their quality and such as [were] usually practised at court'.

These professional men, gentry and rising gentry, were a bookish lot, the backbone of the readers of the nation. Richard Calle lost a French book when Lord Molynes' men plundered the manor of Gresham. John Pampyng, who dealt with Ebesham the scrivener and was regarded by Margaret Paston as fit for a chancery post, must have had some interest in books. Sir John Paston and young John Paston and Sir John Howard, all of whom acted in one capacity or another as professional men, were book collectors. Indeed, in the counties of Norfolk and Suffolk alone a network of literary patrons can be traced, which included Sir John Fastolfe; the de Veres; Sir Miles Stapleton; John Denston, coroner of Suffolk and J.P.; Sir John Howard's first wife, Katherine; the Lady Isabel Bourchier, sister of the Duke of York; Agatha Flegge, wife of John Flegge, esquire, of Suffolk; and others. Unfortunately, the works they commissioned or encouraged were, none of them, written by men of much talent.

It was not an age of great literature, but pens were busy upon paper none the less; and a very considerable number of the poems, prose works, and translations which appeared were produced by members of the gentry, by professional men, and by officers in royal government:

> William de la Pole, Duke of Suffolk: author of poems in English and French
>
> John Tiptoft, Earl of Worcester: scholarly translator
>
> Anthony Woodville, Earl Rivers: poet and translator
>
> Sir Thomas Malory: author of *Morte Darthur*
>
> Peter Idley, Esq.: author of *Instructions to His Son*
>
> Stephen Scrope, gentleman: scholar and translator
>
> Gilbert Banester, poet and musician, Master of the Children of the Chapel Royal, owner of lands and tenements, 'of East Greenwich, in the County of Kent, gentleman': translator of the Tale of *Guiscardo and Ghismonda* and composer
>
> John Metham, 'a simple scholar of philosophy' and a Cambridge man, probably professionally employed by Sir Miles Stapleton: author of various prose works and of a poem in rime royal, *Amoryus and Cleopes*
>
> John Hardyng, Constable of the Castle of Kyme, employed as a diplomatic secret agent: author of Hardyng's *Chronicle*
>
> Thomas Hoccleve, Clerk to the Privy Seal: poet
>
> George Ashby, Clerk to the Signet: poet
>
> William Gregory, Mayor of London: chronicler
>
> William Caxton, Merchant Adventurer: writer, translator, and printer
>
> William Worcester, secretary to Sir John Fastolfe: annalist and historian
>
> Henry Lovelich, skinner: translator of a poem on *The Holy Grail*.

Even when Richard Langport, clerk of the royal Council, girded on his harness and rode with Edward IV to fight at Towton, he brought at least one book with him, an expensive one, and after he lost it on that bloody battlefield, King Edward granted him 5 marks in recompense.

No collection of letters written by a member of the professional classes has survived; and therefore we cannot pry intimately into the life, opinions, and operations of a lawyer or estate-manager in the same way that we look through the window of the Cely letters at a family of merchants or live with the Stonors and Pastons the lives of the gentry. Fortunately or unfortunately, the professional man whose career has left the most vivid impact in contemporary documents is a magnificent rascal named Richard Heyron. And his complex, bizarre story persistently illustrates the co-mingling of likenesses and differences that haunts all comparisons of the fifteenth century with our own age.

The chronicler Fabyan provides a garbled, fragmentary version of Heyron's history; modern scholars, like Scofield in her biography of Edward IV and Power and Postan in Studies in *English Trade in the Fifteenth Century*, have corrected Fabyan's errors; but the climax of the tale, buried in dispatches of Milanese ambassadors, remains to be told.

Richard Heyron is instantly recognizable as the type of brilliant and unscrupulous promoter. The intricate mesh of dealings, his capacity to inspire trust and find money, his knowledge of expedients, his use of bribery and propaganda and legal smoke-screens, his success in keying enterprises to great international issues strike at once a familiar note. On the other hand, the strings he pulled and the particular methods his time offered him will be of no use to his twentieth-century descendants. Sometimes in prison, apparently for long periods holed up in sanctuary, as a wandering exile, he was able for twenty-five years—and for another five after his death—to involve in his schemes the Duke of Milan, the Duke of Burgundy, the Kings of England and France, Maximilian King of the Romans, and Emperor Frederick III, and the Pope.

Richard Heyron called himself a London Merchant of the Staple, but it would be surprising to discover that he had not studied law at one of the Inns of Court, for by his legal manipulations he made his mark in the world. Fabyan characterizes him as a 'merchant of pregnant wit and of good manner of speech', a description that hardly does justice to his ingenuity and plausibility. He makes his first appearance in the records at a time well suited to his talents, the confused and violent days at the end of the year 1459.

Driven from England, the Earl of Warwick and the Duke of York's son Edward, Earl of March (later Edward IV), took refuge early in November at Calais, Warwick's stronghold, where they remained until they triumphantly made good their return to the realm in June of 1460. During this interval Richard Heyron appeared at Calais, acting as merchant-factor and probably legal adviser as well to the Earl of Wiltshire. This wealthy lord, one of the handsomest and most hated men in England, prime favourite of Margaret of Anjou, had good reason to fear the return of the Yorkists; and in the winter of 1459-60 he gathered all the coin, jewels, and costly goods he could lay hands on, stuffed them into five hired carracks, and sailed to Holland. Heyron's mission at Calais was to dispose of an enormous quantity of wool that the Earl had somehow come by, a cargo variously estimated to be worth £18,000 to £24,000 (something like three-quarters of a million in modern money). Since nobody hated the Earl of Wiltshire more than Warwick did, Heyron apparently passed the wool off as his own, and when the Yorkists turned to the Staplers for money, he discreetly offered a loan of 2,000 marks and 300 sarplers of wool.

Warwick, however, quickly discovered the truth, probably through the Staplers themselves, promptly seized all the wool and consigned Heyron to prison. But prisons are not made to hold such men as Heyron. He managed to smuggle messages out of Calais by means of one of his servants, Richard Copin; and when he learned that Copin had been arrested with incriminating letters on him, Heyron succeeded in escaping from Calais and joined the Earl of Wiltshire in Holland. Soon after, he proceeded to Bruges and offered the Council of the Duke of Burgundy 10,000 crowns (£2,000) for letters of marque, but Philip the Good, favouring the Yorkists and fearing the Lancastrians, wanted no part of such a risky proceeding.

Undaunted, Heyron not only made his way back to England but apparently avoided the consequences of his association with Wiltshire and his escape from Calais; for in the Christmas season of 1460—by which time the Yorkists were ruling England in Henry VI's name—he boldly demanded that the royal Council force the Staplers to reimburse him for the 'restraints' they had put upon his wool (he could scarcely accuse Warwick of having seized it!). The suit was dismissed. Within a few months Edward IV was proclaimed King, the Lancastrians were crushed at Towton, and the Earl of Wiltshire, captured after the battle, had his head cut off and all his goods confiscated. Heyron promptly brought suit against his fellow-merchants before the Council of the new King, claiming that the Staplers were responsible for the loss of his wool. Again the suit was dismissed, on the grounds that the wool had been the property of the Earl of Wiltshire and now belonged, like the rest of Wiltshire's possessions, to the King. Heyron, his schemes apparently exploded, was sent to prison, but he soon escaped to sanctuary and comfortably resumed plotting.

By some means, known only to men like Heyron, he managed to worm himself into the favour of the King's secretary. The secretary, doubtless for a good price, procured a document authorizing Heyron under the King's seal to prosecute his case against the Staplers in foreign courts. At the same time Heyron and his agents were befogging the whole issue by spreading in court circles the story that the Staplers were accusing the King of favouring Heyron's cause so that the Yorkists would not have to pay back what Warwick had wrongfully taken from Heyron, and by sowing rumours in the city that the King, angry with the Staplers because they had slandered him, meant to support Heyron's case.

Leaving behind him this miasma of confusion, Heyron with his usual facility made his way to the Continent to put his precious document to use. In Flanders he procured the arrest of three English merchants and sued them and other Staplers in the courts of the Duke of Burgundy for the recovery of goods that he now valued at £24,000. The Staplers vigorously fought the case, however; and after winning a judgement against Heyron, they secured a royal edict that Heyron was to pursue no further legal action outside the kingdom.

But Richard Heyron, far from beaten, now transferred his activities to France. He always had plenty of money to scatter in the right places, for his backers stood to win a fortune if Heyron could make good his claim; and he understood the politics of Europe as well as he understood the art of managing men. One of the increasing tensions between the Duke of Burgundy and his overlord, the King of France, had grown out of a dispute over the right of the citizens of Flanders to appeal from the ducal courts to the Parlement of Paris. Still relying on his fraudulent authority to sue in foreign lands, Heyron now took his case to the French Parlement, hoping that Louis XI might support him as a means of emphasizing his dominion over the Duke. But Louis, ardently seeking the friendship of England through the good offices of Warwick, allowed the matter to hang fire. Heyron then tried to put pressure on the French King by turning to the exiled Lancastrians, headed by Margaret of Anjou and her shadow-chancellor, Sir John Fortescue. In a memorandum drawn up between 1468 and 1470, Fortescue pointed out to Louis' advisers—somewhat cynically—that money spent in backing a Lancastrian invasion could be recovered 'by means of a suit that Richard Heyron, English, is pursuing in the court of Parlement, provided that the King is willing to show him favour'.

Nothing seems to have come of this interesting suggestion, but after Warwick had driven Edward IV from England and restored Henry VI to the throne in the autumn of 1470, Richard Heyron was probably among the Lancastrian exiles who returned to the realm. Before he was able to profit by the Yorkist overthrow, however, Edward had fought the battles of Barnet and Tewkesbury (spring of 1471) and regained his throne. Heyron once more beat a retreat into sanctuary, and this time he remained there, at Westminster or in the church of St. Martin le Grand, for at least two years, because, as will appear later, he negotiated an interesting deal in London in 1473 and he could hardly have been a free man. Through his agents, in the meanwhile, he continued to press his suit before the Parlement of Paris; but after King Edward and

King Louis signed the Treaty of Picquigny in 1475, Parlement dismissed the action.

Still able to find resources, Richard Heyron now turned to the Pope, for like Sir John Paston he knew that the Roman Curia sold ointments for many sores. King Edward's proctor at the Vatican was able to block Heyron's appeal, however, and he was informed that he must reopen his case in England. Meanwhile Parliament, in 1478, ordered proclamation to be made in London that Heyron must 'surcease' his suits against the Staplers in foreign courts on pain of outlawry and confiscation of goods.

Heyron's answer to this apparently crushing reverse was to betake himself to Rome with a full purse. And despite the original Papal refusal to act and the operations of King Edward's proctor and the decree of the English Parliament, Heyron succeeded in obtaining from Pope Sixtus IV, in November of 1480, a Bull which upheld his claims against the Staplers and threatened them with excommunication if they did not do him justice. When the Celys' friend Sir John Weston, Prior of the Order of St. John, was sent by King Edward the following year as ambassador to the Vatican, one of his missions was to persuade the Apostolic See to abandon Richard Heyron. Weston exposed Heyron's train of chicaneries; but, as he wrote to George Cely, he found the indomitable Heyron strongly entrenched in papal favour: 'I promise you, he is greatly favoured and he would have made a foul work and [if] remedy had not soon been found.'

Finally in February of 1482 King Edward and his Council, heartily weary of the matter, drew up a long statement of Heyron's fraudulent procedures and ordained his case closed unless he sought a hearing in England. This pronouncement and Weston's mission put paid to Heyron's hopes of winning the Wiltshire gold at the end of the rainbow. Fabyan completes the story by declaring that the Staplers 'purchased an absolution' from the Pope and that Richard Heyron 'after long being in Westminster as a sanctuary man, without recovery of his costs or duty, died there, being greatly indebted unto many persons'.

The first part of the statement may well be true, and there is no reason to doubt that Heyron was greatly indebted to the speculators who backed him; but he did not die a sanctuary man in Westminster.

Dispatches of Milanese ambassadors reveal that even while Richard Heyron was driving on his suits against the Staplers, he had managed to lay hands on another obligation of grandiose proportions. In 1473, while he was sheltering in a London sanctuary, he secured from a man named John Wodye a deed that empowered him to collect an international debt which had been outstanding for half a century and which, though it certainly looked fishy, had stirred up a good deal of trouble. Back in 1406 Edmund Holland, Earl of Kent, in marrying Lucia Visconti, a daughter of the Duke of Milan, had been promised a dowry of 70,000 florins, guaranteed by the merchant community of the city. According to the story Wodye furnished Heyron, the dowry was never paid; when Lucia died a widow in 1424 she appointed William Anderby and Thomas Huyvet her executors; and when William Anderby, outliving Huyvet, died in 1461, he appointed John Wodye *his* executor. By virtue of this appointment, Wodye, claiming that the Duke of Milan owed him 70,000 florins, was able to purchase letters of marque against the merchants of Milan and of Genoa (ruled by Milan). By this time all the Viscontis had sunk into the grave. The great Francesco Sforza, now ruling Milan, complained to Edward IV in 1464 that as a result of Wodye's trouble-making Milanese and Genoese traders had almost ceased doing business in England. When Warwick restored Henry VI in 1470, the merchants of Milan petitioned Sforza's son to ask King Henry to annul the letters of marque, on account of which they had 'suffered great losses in England'. The Duke therefore requested Louis XI, Warwick's ally, to use his influence in the matter, but Edward IV had regained his throne before anything could be done.

As soon as the Wiltshire case was finally quashed in 1482, Richard Heyron turned with undiminished zest and ingenuity, and apparently undiminished funds, to prosecuting the Wodye claim upon the Visconti dowry. By this time he must have been a man well up in years. In England he was outlawed; he had been expelled from the dominions of the Duke of Burgundy for debt;

he no longer dared set foot in France; he had been unmasked at the Papal court. He therefore transferred his operations to the Holy Roman Empire, settling at Speyer. By this time his two chief agents were his nephew, John Skiby, 'well versed in his manners', and one John Raynold, who claimed to be 'citizen and merchant of England' but who was probably an inhabitant of Metz. According to one of the diplomats of the Duke of Milan, Raynold was as slippery a customer as Heyron: he 'could not venture himself in England or Flanders owing to his malpractices'. Among other exploits, he had gulled credulous folk who believed the rumours that Duke Charles of Burgundy, killed at Nancy in 1477, was still alive and would one day reappear, 'and by such practices he lived for ten years'.

Richard Heyron could hardly have invented an Emperor more suitable to his purpose than Frederic III. Throughout his long and inglorious reign he had showed himself mean, shifty, avaricious, and perennially impecunious. As Commynes put it, 'He endured everything in order to spend nothing.' There was little in the way of parchment sealed that could not be secured, for a fee, from the Imperial court, and Richard Heyron was still able to find money and reach the right pockets to put it into. On September 9, 1484, the Emperor dispatched letters to the Kings of France, Spain, England, Portugal, Bohemia, and Denmark, requesting them to aid Richard Heyron, the legitimate heir of Lucia Visconti, who had petitioned the Emperor for justice in his struggle to secure payment of the Visconti dowry. Though such letters had far less force, and were much less expensive, than letters of marque, they may have enabled Heyron to exact some reprisals against Milanese merchants; for six years later, the Duke of Milan was complaining to the King of England that traders of Milan continued to be molested. But before Richard Heyron could develop grander plans or enjoy much benefit from the Imperial letters, he died at Speyer—'miserably at the hospital', according to a Milanese ambassador—on August 14, 1485, as Richard III and Henry Tudor were marching towards Bosworth Field.

Even Heyron's ghost, however, was powerful enough to trouble international politics. He bequeathed the claim upon the Visconti dowry to his associates, John Raynold and John Skiby, who for the next five years made themselves as thorough nuisances as ever Heyron had done. Twice rebuffed by the Duke of Milan, Raynold and Skiby had raised enough money by September of 1490 to secure letters patent from the Emperor authenticating the claims of the heirs of Richard Heyron and authorizing reprisals against the subjects of the Duke of Milan. Not many weeks later, the Count Palatine and the Margrave of Baden seized Milanese cargoes being freighted down the Rhine and cast their owners into prison. It was a fleeting moment of triumph. After a flurry of international diplomatic correspondence, King Henry VII took the merchants of Milan under his protection and requested the Emperor and his German princelings to give no aid to Heyron's heirs, who, if they had a case, must bring it into English courts. There the tale of highly resourceful means applied to even more highly doubtful ends comes to a conclusion. Richard Heyron was undoubtedly a most charming and persuasive man who made love to the occupation he chose for himself. He would have gone far, though he might not have achieved such fame, if he had taken service with King Louis XI of France.

III

The Household

9

The Fabric of Life

SUBSTANTIAL townsmen and the gentry were interpenetrating each other's lives in increasing numbers, even as within their own ranks they were showing an increasing variety of degree and status. 'Substantial townsmen' include a Mayor of London knighted by the King, an alderman and draper of Coventry whose income equalled that of a squire of the royal household, a tailor of Winchester worth no more than £20 who had managed to secure a post as 'customer' in the port of Southampton and thus wrote himself 'gentleman'. The elastic term gentry now covered a social span from peasant-yeomen to cadets and female lines of the nobility and embraced sons of merchants settled on land, lawyers or auditors of mean stock who had purchased country property, knights and squires tracing (somewhat vaguely) from the Conquest, and a man like Sir John Howard, related to the Mowbray Dukes of Norfolk, who was wealthier and more influential than many barons.

Merchants were buying land to found a family based on the gentility of an estate. Gentry established business connections with merchants, sought wives among the well-provided daughters and widows of The Clothing, and—less eagerly but not infrequently—married their daughters to the sons of merchants. About one-third of the aldermen of London during the Yorkist Age married into the gentry.

The great merchants lived in dwellings much like the manor houses of prosperous knights and squires. The mansion of Stephen Browne, grocer and twice Mayor of London, occupied a whole block between Thames Street and the river. Built behind his wharf, this residence had an oak-panelled hall, 40 by 24 feet, running north and south and was entered from the court by a flight of stone steps. As in most houses of this kind in town or country, the buttery and pantry and kitchen, lying to the north, were screened off from the hall, an arrangement still to be seen in Oxford and Cambridge colleges, while an entry from the south end led into a series of family chambers, including a chapel. Between these a passage opened into the 'great parlour', not much smaller than the hall, with bay-windows looking out on the panorama of Thames shipping. This timbered edifice stood on a vaulted undercroft of stone, storage cellars extending beneath much of the building. The entrance court, measuring about 60 by 40 feet, was reached through a gateway in the north wing which contained a row of shops fronting on the street. Browne's chapel was as much a mark of status as a clue to his piety: the Pastons put forward as one of the proofs of their gentility the fact that for many years the family had been licenced by the Bishop to attend divine service in their own chapel.

Other dwellings, not so grand but still spacious, faced the street in the more usual town style and reached upward for their space: hall and kitchen offices occupied the floor above the shop; parlour, chapel, a principal bedchamber were on the second floor, with more chambers on the third. Smaller residences were built in 'frames' of two or three or even more. A 'triplex' erected in Friday Street contained large shops over cellars, halls nine feet high with kitchens on the first storey, and on the storey above, three rooms for each household, eight feet high and probably wainscoted.

Down in Bristol, Merchant Adventurers built themselves city estates that embraced a groined stone cellar and warehouse and hall and parlour and chambers and a tower; perhaps the men of Bristol fancied towers because they were used to standing on the high 'forestage' of a ship to see the coast of Spain come up out of Biscay. The Paston place in Norwich would appear, from the address of a letter, to have been built around a court: 'To John Paston, Esquire, or to Roose dwelling afore Mistress Paston's gate.' Wills and the surviving houses themselves reveal that even villages, particularly those enriched by the cloth trade, boasted gracious dwellings with carved and gilded fronts brightening the street, like Thomas Paycocke's place at Coggeshall and James Terumber's celebrated mansion in Trowbridge.

People quite well off, however, occupied houses much less spacious than these. A London mercer possessed only one bed-chamber for his wife and seven children; and a haberdasher's house had apparently only two bedrooms in use, one with two beds, the other with five. Servants and apprentices and older children must often have slept on pallets in the hall, which was more and more becoming the domain of the household 'below-stairs'.

The Londoner of middling means lived in a house like that of a draper in St. Christopher's parish: a shop hung with painted buck-ram, a storeroom, and a wainscoted hall screened from kitchen and buttery occupied the ground storey; and on the floor above were three bedchambers. Artisans and shopholders of still more modest means lived in rows of dwellings, each of which consisted of a shop and small storage room behind, with 'solar' upstairs that served as parlour and bedchamber. Humble citizens crowded shop and family into one room. These mean tenements, wedged against great houses or squeezed together along narrow alleys, often measured no more than 6 by 10 feet. Shops with solar might have frontage of about 10 feet and a length twice that with a small garden at back. Four properties in Cheapside occupied a total frontage of 49 feet and ranged from 32 to 43 feet long. The mean-est houses rented for a few shillings a year; a tenement Sir John Howard let to a hosier in Crooked Lane fetched about 40s a year; whereas Stephen Browne paid a quitrent of £19. A grocer's shop in Cheapside with 'a place above it', presumably an establishment with a hall, rented for £4 6s 8d a year.

During the Yorkist Age magnates and even royalty sometimes preferred to put up at a merchant's house rather than to sojourn in the local abbey or castle. Doubtless Edward IV found the mansion of William Canynges more comfortable, when he was entertained there in 1461, than most of his own palaces. Canynges' house had a tower with four bay-windowed parlours, expanses of glass, and tiled floors. Even the haughty Margaret of Anjou chose, in 1456, to accommodate herself and her waiting women in the home of Richard Woode, merchant of Coventry, rather than to stay at the priory.

Gardens of even the larger houses were often quite small but, from the evidence of wills and letters, highly prized. A London garden might offer a pear and an apple tree, a bed of herbs and simples, flower borders, a well, and a privy. John Baret of Bury made provision in his will so that his niece Janet Whitwelle, who was bequeathed the use of certain chambers in his house, might have 'easement of the well in the yard, and easement of the privy in the same yard. And she to have a key of the great garden gate, to go in when she will and her servants and what friend she will call to her, and a place of the garden assigned to her for herbs and for wood to lie in'.

For 'consolation' a man found it good to stroll among his flowers and meditate on God. So death took Sir John Heveningham, who 'went to his church and heard three Masses, and came home again never merrier and said to his wife that he would go say a little devotion in his garden and then he would dine; and forthwith he felt a fainting in his leg and sat down. This was at nine of the clock, and he was dead ere noon'.

Houses in small towns rented for much less than those in London, but incomes in the provinces were correspondingly lower. A serjeant-tailor in the Great Wardrobe was allowed £5 a year for a house, whereas down in Canterbury a mason who supervised all building in the Priory of Christ Church received a rent allowance of only £1. The dwelling of a lawyer in Warrington, Lancashire, contained 'one fair hall', two chambers, and a kitchen; stable, barns, appleyard, almost an acre of land, 'and a fountain of springing water' completed the premises, for which the lawyer paid but 3s 3d yearly. Edmund Filpot, of Twickenham, though only a bricklayer, possessed a 'dwelling house and place with thirteen small tenements to the same annexed', as is revealed in the register of Richard III's chancery; for poor Edmund had had to secure 'a protection for requiring of alms' because his property and 'all his goods therein' had been 'suddenly burned, to his utter undoing;

who before, kept after his degree a great household, by which many poor creatures were refreshed'.

The manor houses of the gentry varied as much in size and pretentiousness as the residences of substantial townsmen. Sir John Fastolfe, grown rich on the French wars and by shrewd management of lands, built himself a great castle at Caister, which, along with the lovely brick pile of Tattershall Castle, Lincolnshire, was one of the last fortifications in England erected as a private dwelling. 'A rich jewel,' Sir John's secretary William Worcester called it. The walls enclosed an elaborate chapel and great hall and 'winter hall,' chambers for the master and chambers for guests and for servants, a 'great chamber' leading out of the 'Summer Hall', a white chamber next to it, and a 'white-hanged chamber'—almost thirty rooms in all.

Older manor houses still had the look of castles, being moated and walled; others, built around a quadrangle, presented heavy walls and narrow apertures to the outside with more gracious windows facing on the courtyard; while still others were sprawling farmhouses. The Pastons' manor of Gresham had towers at each corner but the drawbridge had been replaced by a causeway and sprays of hedge lined the entry to the house. Leland, in the next century, described Sir William Stonor's chief seat at Stonor, Oxfordshire, as 'a fair park, and a warren of conies, and fair woods. The mansion standeth climbing on an hill and hath two courts builded with timber, brick, and flint'. The brick portions of the manor house probably sprang from the building zeal of the first Thomas Stonor, who in the reign of Henry V bought 200,000 bricks at Crockernend for £40, paid £15 to have them carted to Stonor, and hired Flemish workmen to lay them. The Stonor letters mention the usual array of rooms—hall and parlour chamber and several other chambers; and one of Sir William Stonor's correspondents refers to his 'study'.

From the records of a chantry established in Bridport, a country house of modest size can be reconstructed. The founder of the chantry bequeathed his dwelling, probably on the outskirts of the town, for his two chantry priests to live in. The house contained a hall with kitchen and buttery adjoining, chambers for each of the priests, and apparently a guest chamber and a servant's room. House and garden were enclosed by a stone wall, hedge, and palings. Another ecclesiastical dwelling, the parsonage on the Paston manor of Oxnead, is pictured in a memorandum apparently drawn up for a prospective incumbent:

'The church is but little, and is reasonable pleasant, and repaired. And the dwelling place of the parsonage is well housed and repaired, hall, chambers, barn, dove-house, and all houses of office.

'And it hath a dove-house worth a year 14s 4d.

'And it hath two large gardens . . . whereof the fruit is worth yearly 26s 8d.

'And there longeth to the said parsonage in free land adjoining to the said parsonage 22 acres or more, whereof every acre is worth 2s; to let, £3 4d. . . .

'And it is but an easy cure to keep, for there are not past 20 persons to be yearly houseled.

'The parsonage stands by a fresh river-side.

'And there is a good market-town called Aylesham within two mile of the parsonage.

'And the city of Norwich is within six mile of the parsonage.

'And the sea is within ten mile of the parsonage.'

In town or country mean dwellings probably showed little change from those of a hundred years before. Village cots, made of wattle and daub or rude planks, had but one room with a beaten earth floor and a smoky hearth in the centre of it. Peasants with a few coins in coffer dwelt in cottages that contained a kitchen and a chamber under the eaves.

An esquire of the times of Edward III transported to the London or the countryside of Edward IV would have found most dwellings familiar in appearance; but home life during the Yorkist Age had become markedly more comfortable, and a larger proportion of the population was able to enjoy these comforts. All over England, except in the North, cheerless castles were being allowed to fall into decay. Other castles and old-fashioned manor-houses now showed large windows, fire-places built into the walls (replacing the central hearth with smoke-louvre cut in the ceiling), and additional airy parlours and solars. Increasing numbers of houses were being constructed of brick in London, the eastern counties, and the Thames valley. On his manor of Hunsdon in Hertfordshire, Sir William Oldhall, one of the Duke of York's chief adherents, erected a brick tower 80 feet square and 100 feet high, propped on each side with seven buttresses 'of great width' and crowned by an 'over-storey' or oriel with gilt vanes, and that enterprising squire John Paston is to be found modernizing manors by adding several wall-chimneys.

Social and architectural change reveal a growing demand for privacy, a privacy lighted by as many windows and as vividly upholstered as a man's purse would allow.

Like the lords of the time, knights and merchants were no longer content to share the hurly-burly of the hall with servants and retainers and apprentices and casual strangers. If a London mercer still ate dinner in his hall with his journeymen and apprentices and if a country gentleman shared his meat with his bailiff and reeve and farmhands, both men were afterwards likely to retire with their wives to the intimate comforts of the parlour, which in smaller places might also be the chief bedchamber.

The parlour, or 'chamber', though not new in the fifteenth century, had become the distinctive emblem of Yorkist houses. Within his river-front mansion Mayor Stephen Browne undoubtedly entertained in the 'great parlour', dined there with his wife, and played at tables, watching the sails on the river, white against green Surrey fields. Mayor Shillingford of Exeter had a parlour large enough to receive all his aldermen; a century before, they would have gathered in the hall. Joan Buckland, of Edgcott, Northamptonshire, dined in state in her parlour, for it contained a 'high dais' with a trestle table and a 'long green table'. Baldwin Coksedge, gentleman, of Felsham in Suffolk, left to his wife Denyse a 'new house called a parlour' on his manor of Upwode Hall; and John Baret of Bury built a residence around a parlour rather than a hall.

William Marchall, clerk in the Chancery and a property owner in Oxfordshire, likewise followed the fashion by adding a parlour to his place. He got word one winter day from his agent that 'two carpenters had been working continually for seven weeks since Michaelmas, and for three weeks past had wrought by candle-light evening and morning in one of the wool-houses; they had framed half the chamber floor and all the chief work of the jetty with goodly windows in two bays; the principal timbers were true heart of oak, and the rafters of elm; "doubt you not your chamber floor shall be strong enough and ye shall couch pipes of wine thereon, and then ye shall not bend it with dancing lightly . . .".'

Sleeping quarters were also becoming less indiscriminately crowded. Men were erecting houses with numerous bedrooms so that the master and mistress might have a chamber of their own with other rooms provided for children, guests, and servants. Sir Thomas Urswyk, Recorder of London knighted 'in the field' by Edward IV, had nine bedchambers in his country house at Dagenham, including rooms for his chaplain and his clerk and a nursery for the children. Sir John Rudston's house in Cornhill not only contained a number of bedrooms but a 'maiden's chamber' and a 'brushing chamber' and a special larder for preparing fish. John Olney's place in Milk Street had as many as eight chambers which might be either bedrooms or parlours. Even after that 'witty and eloquent' Mayor and Mercer of London, Sir Thomas Cook, had lost most of his fortune as a result of running afoul of the greedy Woodvilles, he could not bear to relinquish the pleasures of privacy and built himself 'a little mansion fore-against the east end of the Friars Augustins' which dispensed with a hall but contained five rooms for himself, including a study and a countinghouse, chambers for his wife, and a chapel.

Amenities and conveniences did not keep pace with the move-ment toward privacy but they were growing more elaborate and more numerous. Bedrooms of any pretensions contained chamber-pots. The merchant or knight who demanded the latest in comfort equipped his chamber with a portable night-stool provided with a stock of cheap cloths 'for wiping the nether end', a covering of coloured cloth, and a cushion to conceal the hole in the daytime. A servant was expected to tend to this convenience first thing in the morning and to be on hand, when his master used the stool, with a basin of water and a towel. London mansions had a privy in the garden and one upstairs, with leaden urinals in the court-yard and cess-pits having exit pipes for proper disposal of sewage. A modest 'frame' of dwellings offered a privy for each pair of houses; the poor, crowded into one room, used street conven-iences. A woman living in Queenhithe connected the latrine in her solar with the street gutter by a wooden pipe; but such enter-prise was no longer tolerated in London and she had to make other arrangements. Kitchen slops, all manner of liquid and casual refuse continued to be thrown into the street.

Manor houses and town mansions were usually supplied with wells. Some Londoners possessed rainwater cisterns from which gutters might run into the kitchen. Those fortunate enough to dwell by the Thames used river water. Others depended upon municipal conduits and 'bosses' and wells. Even modest households owned numerous basins, ewers, lavers, of silver or pewter or latten (a cheap metal alloy much used). Some large houses had 'lavatoria', systems of hanging basins with drain pipes down to gutters. William Honyboorn of Bury, a dyer, bequeathed to his daughter 'my best hanging laver standing in my parlour'. Bed-rooms were often equipped with 'chaffers' for heating water.

Complete immersion depended, it appears, on status and indi-vidual taste. Many town labourers and peasants were doubtless satisfied with the rite of baptism. Men of moderate means some-times numbered bath-tubs among their possessions. Lords and lordly merchants owned a bathing-tent, which consisted of a tub cushioned with sponges and shrouded in sheets or richer textiles that hung from a framework. A servant used smaller sponges for soaping his master and for rinsing him with hot herbs and aromatics. Public bath-houses in towns still continued the Roman tradition. When Sir John Howard was sojourning in London, his steward sometimes recorded a payment of 6d 'for the bagnio'. Many of these 'stews', particularly those in Southwark, were little more than fancy houses of prostitution. On one occasion that old roué, Duke Philip of Burgundy, wishing to honour an English embassy that met him at Valenciennes, hired the bath-house of the town for the envoys, complete with *filles de joie*. During the reign of Edward IV, however, London offered at least three respectable bath-houses for women and two for men. For Mak and Tib there was the country brook or the river Thames or the consolation of knowing that many physicians regarded bathing as an open invitation to the plague. Surviving information about bathing habits tends to be haphazard. The widow of a merchant willed to a friend 'a bowl basin to wash his feet in'. William Stonor, on a visit to one Master Marmion, disbursed 15d to a barber for cleaning his head.

The washing of clothes, on the other hand, was attacked much more systematically. Men and women of any consequence were expected to appear in clean garments. Handbooks of manners emphasize to city apprentice or yeoman's son that he must at all times present himself in 'fresh and clean array'. A London tailor was sent to prison for forcing an apprentice to go to bed 'foul-shirted and full of vermin'. For the servants of a manor house a stream nearby provided laundry facilities; the clothes of Londoners were washed on the banks of the Thames. Most towns forbade women to monopolize the public conduits in doing their laundry. Professional laundresses were common. On journeys about the country or when he was in the capital, Sir John Howard had his shirts washed for a penny. London records reveal the activities of 'Beatrice le Wimplewasher' and 'Massiota la Lavendere'. The heavy wool gowns and hangings, elaborately sleeved doublets and delicate linens must have challenged all their ingenuity and courage.

Many halls, as well as humble cottages, were still heated by a smoky central hearth, an ancient arrangement that would persist here and there for another century—conservatives declared the smoke to be medicinal—but the new fashion of wall-chimneys was fast spreading in town and country. Shops in London and other cities offered wide stone fireplaces at which customers might warm themselves; in the houses of the well-to-do, such fireplaces, equipped with decorative andirons and tongs and bellows, were to be found in hall and parlour and principal bedroom. Braziers, conveniently wheeled, provided heat at need for other chambers.

In the dwellings of all but the poorer classes, candles furnished the chief means of artificial lighting. The wills of the period abound in bequests of candle-holders made in a variety of metals, shapes, and sizes. Parlours and halls of wealthy men were lighted by chandeliers suspended from the ceiling and by wax torches thrust into sockets on the walls. Candles were not cheap, especially the ceremonial tapers weighing five pounds or more, for wax was an imported article; and even tallow cost four times the same weight of lean meat. The two chantry priests of Bridport used about 18 pounds of candles a year. The household of the Duke of Clarence consumed an average of three dozen a night from All Hallows to Easter, and the chandler's bill for a year ran to £64 (more than £2,000 in modern money). Torches and oil-burning lanterns provided portable illumination. Cottages flickered in the smoky flame of home-made rushlights.

If such artificial illumination marks little change from a former time, the light of day itself flooded halls and parlours and chambers. Only householders of rather slender means or old-fashioned tastes now stopped openings in the walls with thin horn, oiled linen and the like. The delight in sweeps of glass expressed in the perpendicular architecture of churches also showed itself in the domiciles of the day. A merchant in Southwark planning an addition to his house wanted eighteen windows in each of the two upper storeys of the new wing. Sir John Howard was able to buy glass from an Ipswich glazier at 5d a foot. Though by no means a luxury, then, glass was still sufficiently costly and new so that people bequeathed windows like gowns in their wills and some-times carried off glass panes when they moved from one dwelling to another. The Parson of Oxnead, on leaving the rectory, carted away all doors and windows. Gerhard von Wesel, forced to leave the Hanse Steelyard in London, was in mortal fear that he would not be allowed to remove the new glass he had installed. He had heard that the rent-gatherer was 'loath that John my child should take away such reparations as I have made in my chamber, as glass windows and other things'. Though distressed at losing £20 worth of glass, Gerhard was mainly concerned lest 'others should mock me to scorn with my father's arms and marks in glass windows and other places'. The practice of treating windows like furniture continued to cause quarrels and law-suits until the time of Henry VIII, when it was enacted that windows were part of a house rather than movables.

Movables themselves showed little change from Chaucer's day and would show little for some decades after the Yorkist Age. Even in palaces, furniture was quite scanty and, though often richly carved, simple in design. A book illustration shows Henry VIII, grown old, sitting on a chest and playing his lute; the chest constitutes the only furniture of the chamber. Several drawings in Flemish manuscripts picture Philip of Burgundy or his son Charles, rulers of the most splendid court in Europe, standing beneath a 'cloth of estate' and consulting with their councillors, likewise standing. People of the fifteenth century, it appears, stood a great deal more than we do; and when they did sit, gentlemen were content with a bench or a joint-stool or a chest, while ladies often bestowed themselves upon cushions placed about the floor.

Hall and parlour usually contained one or two trestle tables, folded against the wall when not being used for meals; benches and 'forms'; and perhaps one chair. Permanent tables, especially small three-legged affairs, were becoming increasingly popular as the age drew to a close. Bedchambers, except for the elaborate bed itself, often contained no more than a chest and a 'truckle bed' for an attendant to sleep on, which was pushed underneath the large bed during the day. In the wills of the period tables receive no more than casual mention, cushions and joint-stools are bequeathed by the dozen; but chairs are described with evident pride. Joan Buckland owned a 'carven chair' and another chair 'of beyond sea making'. Sir William Stonor was informed on one occasion that the new 'chair for the mistress is made after your device'. The spaces of Sir John Fastolfe's great hall contained two chairs, one red and one green, and there were two others in his winter hall.

Floors of stone or planks were strewn with rushes. The chantry priests in Bridport changed their rushes quarterly, but wealthier households in spring and summer probably freshened chambers with flowers and aromatic herbs at more frequent intervals. Erasmus, however, mentions rooms in which only the upper layer of rushes was regularly removed, leaving at the bottom indescribable abominations. Tile flooring was beginning to come in, probably under the influence of the close political and mercantile tie between England and the Low Countries. The Drapers of London had a tiled hall and parquet flooring in the kitchen. The hall at Crosby's Place, like that of Gildhall, was paved with unpolished Purbeck marble.

But flooring, furniture, architectural ornament created only the framework of an interior. Wall hangings and canopied beds and cupboards displaying plate sounded the tone of a house, expressing the owner's wealth and taste and status. Like costume and etiquette, rich stuffs helped to force life up into an allegory of consoling significance. Here again Burgundian influence was probably strong. In accents of wonder young John Paston described to his mother the wedding of Edward IV's sister Margaret to Charles of Burgundy, at Bruges. 'I have no wit nor remembrance to write to you half the worship that is here; as for the Duke's court . . . I heard never of none like to it, save King Arthur's court.'

Fifteenth-century wills from all parts of England reveal men and women, even in the contemplation of death, affectionately telling over their cloths of Arras, their curtained beds—puffy clouds of colour—and their jewels and gowns and plate, ivory 'tables' (backgammon), chess sets, silver spectacles. Wills turn up other things too: fondness for servants, appreciation of friendships, kindness to employees, a benevolent interest in the poor of the parish or of surrounding villages, and, for the present-day reader, occasional curious touches. In 1463 John Baret of Bury left to Lady Walgrave a 'musk-ball of gold with pearls and lace'.[1] A decade later, Sir John Paston, courting for his brother a widowed Lady Walgrave, playfully carried away her musk-ball. The same John Baret bequeathed to Thomas Brews, who would one day become young John Paston's father-in-law, a cramp-ring of silver

---

[1] A musk-ball was an ornamental perfume dispenser, worn on clothing or carried in the hand.

gilt and black enamel. Cramp-rings, frequently mentioned in wills, were supposed to have achieved their efficacy against cramp through being blessed in a special ceremony on Good Friday by the King or, more often, the Queen. Sir Thomas Cumberworth of Somerby, Lincolnshire, whose will reveals a household and estate abounding in beautiful stuffs, gowns, money, cattle, jewellery, armour, began his bequest to his niece Anneys with a 'pair of beads of coral gauded with gold'. Perhaps they reminded him of Madame Eglentyne—

> Of smal coral about her arm she bore
> A pair of beads, gauded all with green,
> And thereon hung a broach of gold full shene—

for Sir Thomas coupled this gift of beads with 'My boke of the talys of Cantyrbury'.

Halls, parlours, bedchambers were swathed in tapestries or woollens of solid colours or painted cloths, in 'bankers and dorsers' flung over benches, and in cushions by the dozen. Lords and gentry, moving from manor to manor, often took a number of their hangings with them. An inventory of 'the stuff that is left within the manor of Stonor . . . from year unto year' enumerates, among a host of articles ranging from '1 wood axe' and '1 flesh axe' to '1 Grail', hangings of black say (fine serge) for the hall along with two cushions covered with grey skin, two of red worsted, and two of tapestry work with 'knots'. The parlour, warmed by a fireplace, contained a feather-bed with 'a red coverlet with green chaplets' and also a 'green coverlet with pots and ostrich feathers'. The 'little chamber annexed unto the parlour', was hung with cloth striped purple and green. Three other chambers displayed hangings of red and green stripes and in one of them was a bed curtained in red and green. The Stonor chapel not only shone with coloured glass and painted images but was provided with vestments of purple velvet lined with green sarcenet, albs of Breton linen, 'carpets for the sacrament' with a canopy of silk, copes of purple velvet lined with tawny sarcenet, the Trinity cut in alabaster, and, among other rich objects, a case for the Sacred Elements of white and blue velvet barred with red velvet and embroidered with a 'trail of ivy'.

Alicia Langham, of Snaylwell, Suffolk, who appears to have been only moderately well off, was able to leave one daughter a tapestry depicting the history of Robert of Sicily, perhaps her grandest possession, and a second daughter, a nun, a 'hanged' bed and a carved wooden coffer made in Prussia. Some people liked rooms decorated all in one colour, as did Joan Buckland who slept in a 'chamber of red'. Many retired naked, but they sank into feather beds smothered in pillows and blankets and sheets, and were protected against draughts, even against air, by closely drawn curtains.

Tapestries 'of Arras' were the most expensive hangings; next came good woven stuff in solid colours with figures or a border; and for men of narrower means, mercers and drapers stocked 'counterfeit Arras', cheap painted cloths. The people of this age delighted in bold designs and bright hues, though gentler colours like 'applebloom' and mulberry and grey were coming in. One set of parlour hangings displayed 'ten countries bordered with histories of the bible' while other 'hallings' and bed curtains abounded in elephants, unicorns, dragons, pelicans. The Iron-mongers of London owned two hangings 'with peacocks, vines, and wells with the seven planets counterset'. The finest Arras were enormously dear: Sir Thomas Cook first got into trouble with the Woodvilles when he refused to sell at a loss a tapestry depicting the Siege of Jerusalem that had cost him £800 (about twice the yearly income of most barons).

An inventory of the goods Sir John Fastolfe stuffed into Caister Castle offers a repertory of the sort of hangings with which the rich surrounded themselves: the 'nether hall' was enlivened by a cloth of Arras 'with a giant in the middle, bearing a leg of a bear in his hand'; the hanging behind the dais offered 'one wodewose [wildman, a favourite figure] and one child in his arms'; while the west side of this hall was covered with a 'cloth of the Siege of Falaise'. Other tapestries depicted the Adoration of the Shepherds; three archers shooting at a duck in the water; a gentlewoman harping by a castle; the Nine Worthies; 'a man drawing water in the middle of the cloth out of a well'. A less costly 'halling of deep green' covered a wall space eleven yards long and four yards wide. 'Bankers' relieved the simplicity of benches with cloths showing a bear holding a spear, a man shooting at a bloodhound, and other studies from life or fancy. One of the many tapestried bed-hangings pictured 'a gentlewoman being there in the corner with a whelp in her hand and an Agnus Dei about her neck'. Coverlets were no less vivid. Even Sir John's cook was lulled to slumber by a 'red coverlet of roses and bloodhounds' heads'.

Next after hangings, the men and women of this time prized the workmanship and the massiveness of their plate. People of means liked to emphasize their status by covering dinner tables with a profusion of silver, at the same time displaying on a cupboard in hall or parlour a collection of plate as large as that which was being used. The Venetian diplomat reported that the amount of plate for sale in the shops of London could not be matched in Milan, Rome, Venice and Florence put together, and that 'no one who has not in his house silver plate worth at least £100 is considered by the English to be a person of any consequence'. Most of this plate consisted of huge 'salts' or salt cellars with elaborate covers, cups and goblets and ewers and basins and chargers, 'for they eat off that fine tin [pewter] that is little inferior to silver'. Mazers, drinking bowls of wood bound in silver with a medallion or figure at the bottom, were often given pet names. Sir John Fastolfe's inventory lists more than 500 pieces of plate, ranging from 'a cup of gold with a ewer' and '6 Paris cups of silver of the months' to 'great chargers' and numerous salt cellars, one 'well gilt with many windows' and another 'like a bastille all gilt with roses'. A widow, no more than well-to-do, could refer casually to 'all my silver vessel (26 platters) and 32 saucers that I am served withal daily'. Forks had made their appearance: John Baret willed to a friend his 'silver fork for green ginger'.

Kitchen utensils ran to rather massive instruments like axes and mortar-and-pestles and iron frying pans and ladles and brass pots. Sir John Howard's papers reveal him setting up in housekeeping his daughter and her husband with the following gifts: a frying pan, a gridiron, two ladles and two skimmers; 6 spoons, 2 salts 'parcel gilt', 3 basins and 2 ewers, 2 long pots of tin; 16 yards of banker, many yards of green and blue worsted, a hanging bed of red worsted, a carpet, and, to his son-in-law, a gown of chamlet, furred. Shortly after Howard married for the second time he delivered to his lady, for the furnishing of one of his manors, 80 yards of Holland cloth, 7½ yards of green velvet and almost the same amount of crimson velvet, a bed curtained in crimson damask and one hung with tapestry, 32 yards of Arras, and '4 pieces of new Arras come late from Calais'.

In the same extravagance of materials and design the people of the period quilted their bodies. The Venetian diplomat summed up native dress in a sentence: 'They all from time immemorial wear very fine clothes.' Despite sumptuary legislation by Parliament, regulations by gilds, cautions of the Church and barbs of satirists, Englishmen dressed to the height of their bent; and their bent was for luxurious cloth, exciting colours, and a cascade of flashing ornaments. Men dressed gaily, not only to spice their lives and to express, or counterfeit, their 'estate' but also to exploit a means of conspicuous consumption in an age when such means were limited but were becoming less so. The costume of the upper ranks demonstrated an excess of materials that flagrantly disregarded the contours of the body and the requirements of efficiency or that, in the case of indecently short doublets, flouted propriety in order to emphasize the supreme rights of fashion. In almost Elizabethan style Thomas Hoccleve railed against the outrageousness of dress; perhaps he was a little soured by the pinched means his salary as a clerk to the Privy Seal confined him to:

> But this methinketh an abusion,
> To see one walk in a robe of scarlet
> Twelve yards wide, with pendant sleeves down
> On the ground, and the fur therein set
> Amounting unto £20 or better.
> And if he for it paid, hath he no good
> Left him wherewith to buy himself an hood.
> So poor a wight his lord to counterfeit
> In his array! In my conceit it stinketh!

So many wasteful yards of cloth and windings of fur are used in gowns, Hoccleve goes on, that tailors and skinners will soon have to abandon their shops and take to the fields in order to have room enough to carry on their crafts.

Playing cards preserve in stylized form the dress of the day, for playing cards came into England during this period and were illustrated in the contemporary fashion. Indeed, the present-day conception of mediaeval costume in general and of the dress proper to fairy princes and princesses represents actually the styles of the Yorkist Age.

Women's robes showed little change from the past except that they had grown longer. The Bohemian visitors of 1465 were struck by the length of trains at court. Ladies wore necklines low and square-cut, with sleeves puffed or flowing. They expressed themselves most characteristically in their headdresses, elaborate construction's trailing clouds of fine linen. In the earlier decades of the century, horned headdresses were popular, satirized by John Lydgate in *A Little Short Ditty Against Horns*, in which he assured ladies that 'Beauty will show though horns were away'. Women also fancied headdresses in the shape of hearts or butterflies or crescents or wound them into towered turbans. During the reign of Edward IV, the emblem of the fairy princess made its appearance, the steeple headdress, a long cone tilted at an angle of some 45 degrees and trailing lawn to the ground. Too painfully heavy to wear for long, the steeple was replaced before the end of the century by much simpler gear. The portrait of Edward IV's Queen, Elizabeth Woodville, shows how a great lady arranged her face to suit her headdress. Eyebrows and even forehead-hair were severely plucked in order to simulate a very high brow, continued by the lines of the headdress, and to create a smooth, masklike appearance which dramatized the difference between a woman and a woman of rank.

Gowns were gathered with cinctures of silk and velvet tipped with an enamel-and-silver pendant or a jewel-studded leather tag dusting the ground. Kerchiefs, brooches, rings, collars, and other ornamental 'devices' lovingly enumerated in wills, highlighted the comparative sobriety of gowns. Ladies were fond of expensive rosaries of coral and often wore them wrapped round their wrists. In January of 1467 Sir John Howard presented his second wife with five gowns, including a green velvet and a crimson velvet and a black velvet all furred with miniver and ermine; but he also gave her no less than nine rings set with precious stones, six plain gold rings, four chains and collars, among them a 'device of gold in fourteen links' set with four rubies, three diamonds, seven pearls.

Men dressed in a more extreme style than women, dictated more rapid changes of fashion, wore a greater variety of garments, and, if surviving records tell a true story, spent more on their clothes. A few months after Margery Brews and young John Paston were married, Margery informed her husband that she had only two gowns for winter wear, 'my black and my green-Alyre'; whereas John could afford to leave behind in his brother's London chambers 'my tawny gown furred with black and the doublet of purple satin and the doublet of black satin'. Hoods and variations on the hood like chaperones had now mostly gone out except for use in wet weather or on a journey; though in the earlier part of Henry VI's reign lirapipes were still being worn, a sort of loose turban of cloth with a long streamer hanging down the side or thrown over the shoulder. During the Wars of the Roses hats made of velvet or fur or leather or a variety of cloths assumed peaked or bulbous or pot-shaped forms; but before the end of Edward IV's reign there had appeared the trim velvet cap, often jewelled or bearing insignias and badges.[1] Men no longer wore their hair short as in Henry V's day; now it hung to the shoulders and fops occasionally let it grow so long they could scarcely see. The faces of the upper ranks were clean-shaven.

The doublet provided the chief masculine opportunity for extravagant finery, though short gowns could also be very 'fetis' (fashionable). Courtiers wore doublets with fiercely padded shoulders and suave, tight waists. The sleeves had become wild concoctions of velvet and damask and satin, dripping to the floor or wrapped around the arms in so many folds and layers as to look like barrels, or slashed to show the lining and sometimes laced. Devotees of fashion wore doublets and demi-gowns so indecently

[1] See the portrait of Richard III, p. 191.

short (only the hose cloth covered the privy parts) that they were prohibited in the sumptuary law of 1463. Hose cloths came in a rainbow of shades, the two legs often showing different colours. Shirts worn beneath the doublet were of fine Holland cloth.

Shoes completed the extravagance of shoulders and sleeves. Their points or 'pikes' were often so long that in order for their wearer to move at all, they had to be ornamentally chained at the knee.[1] Certain London cordwainers, for reasons unknown, secured a papal Bull limiting the length of pikes to two inches, on pain of cursing; but the Bull was derided, the Cordwainers Gild secured privy seals from the King permitting them to make pikes as long as they pleased; and those members of the craft who had sought to discourage high fashion were made to see the error of their ways. For riding or hunting or tramping about their estates, men wore boots coming to the calf or full-length 'boteux'.

While young courtiers and those aping courtiers indulged themselves in doublets of crimson velvet or green damask, 'The Clothing' of the towns and the conservative ranks of lords and gentry probably spent more of their money on long gowns, expensively furred, weightily sleeved, and lined with bright silks or satins. The repertory of furs extended from lordly ermine and marten and sable through beaver, budge (lamb), fox, otter, to squirrel and rabbit, and even cat. On shopping expeditions in London Sir John Howard, before he became a baron or a duke, purchased crimson jackets and purple jackets and black velvet doublets and doublets of damask, a tawny cloak lined with velvet, other cloaks black and white, long gowns of crimson velvet lined with silk and of green velvet and of chamlet furred, a short gown of russet velvet furred with marten, and—for ceremonies at court —a doublet of cloth of gold. He bought leather boots for 3s a pair, while three pairs of ordinary shoes cost only 2s; a fine hosecloth was worth 4s; and to make livery gowns for his household officers and servants he purchased good warm cloth of russet or murrey

---

[1] So famous on the Continent were the pointed toes of English shoes and the martial prowess of Edward IV that a Netherlands chronicler ends his badly muddled account of the battle of Towton by declaring that after the Earl of Warwick had fled, King Edward and a small band of followers won an almost miraculous victory by dismounting to fight on foot after prudently tearing off the 'beaks' of their shoes.

(mulberry, one of the colours of the House of York) and black broad-cloth and friezes of various colours, costing from 2s to 4s or 5s a yard.

'The Clothing' achieved an array of gowns by virtue of their positions in municipal life: the great scarlet gown, furred, of an alderman, striped gowns representing the livery presented yearly by the mayor to his brethren, winter and summer gowns in the colours of gild or company or religious fraternity. It is not surprising that the wills of townsmen rustle richly with the itemizing of gowns bequeathed to kin and friends. When the Mayor of London rode out to Blackheath at the head of a train of citizens to welcome the boy-king Henry VI home from France in 1432, he appeared in 'red crimson velvet, and a great velvet hat furred royally, and a girdle of gold about his middle, and a baldric of gold about his neck trilling down behind him'. When Londoners welcomed Edward IV to the city, the Mayor and aldermen in their scarlet headed a procession of several hundred substantial citizens clad alike in violet or green or white gowns.

Sumptuary legislation in the reign of Henry IV prohibited all those beneath the rank of knight, except for mayors and ex-mayors of London, York, Bristol, and their wives, from wearing fine fur and gold ornaments; whereas by the second year of Edward IV's reign (1463), aldermen and sheriffs everywhere might display the same luxury of dress as esquires and gentlemen worth £40 a year. But sumptuary legislation was only a gesture, a vain attempt to preserve the security of the good old days by maintaining on parchment distinctions of rank that had already disappeared, or were fast disappearing, from the street.

Men enjoyed the glitter of ornaments as much as women, studded their fingers with rings, wore belts of jewelled leather and silver, slung heavy chains of precious metals around their necks, and, if they were men of court, displayed in Lancastrian days the honorific collar of SS and in the households of Edward IV and Richard III the Yorkist collar of suns and roses.[1] Fashionable cos-

---

[1] The white rose of York; a ballad celebrates Edward IV as The Rose of Rouen (his birthplace). The device of suns derives from an experience Edward had just before his victory at Mortimer's Cross (Feb. 3, 1461), when 'over him, men say, [were] three suns shining'; and he was quick-witted enough to persuade his men that this peculiar atmospheric effect was an omen of success.

tume was designed to set man off from the animals, to dissociate
him from labour, to suggest the weight of his purse, to indicate
his status or profession, and to dramatize his breeding, perhaps his
comforting uniqueness.

The same urges and attitudes demonstrated by the furnishings
and the costumes of the age likewise find their expression in the
cooking and serving of meals. The English took their food
seriously, sometimes ritually, and usually in large quantities.
Travellers during the Wars of the Roses rarely failed to make some
comment upon the subject. The Bohemian lords were amazed at
the dinner of fifty courses given them by King Edward, only to
become still more amazed when that overmightiest of subjects,
Warwick the Kingmaker, set before them sixty courses. The
German Popplau discovered that the English spent largely on
feasting and good living; but in his opinion the cooking was
hardly adequate and the natives were satisfied with dishes that
were coarse to his palate. A papal agent handled roughly at Calais
wrote bitterly to the Duke of Milan that the English were all
gluttons and devils. Polydore Vergil, only a few years after the end
of our period, smacked his lips over the beef, which he thought
'peerless, especially being a few days powdered with salt'.

The Venetian diplomat has more to say about English food and
cooking than any other visitor of the time. He emphasized the
great variety of seafood, singling out particularly salmon, 'a most
delicious fish'; and he was also struck by the 'immense profusion'
of edible animals, wild and domestic. He noted that the English
drank great quantities of beer and ale, liquors which the Venetian
himself came to enjoy after a little experimentation, finding them
especially refreshing when he was overheated. Much wine was
drunk too, but from his observation people preferred—even
ladies of distinction—to go to a tavern to enjoy their wine rather
than to serve it at home. He was above all impressed by the
importance attached to food by all degrees of men. 'They have a
very high reputation in arms . . . but I have it on the best authority
that when war is raging most furiously, they will still seek for good
eating and all their other comforts. . . . They take great pleasure in
having a quantity of excellent victuals and also in remaining a long

time at table, being very sparing of wine when they drink it at their own expense', nor do they consider 'it any inconvenience for three or four persons to drink out of the same cup', a custom on which Erasmus likewise commented.

'They think that no greater honour can be conferred or received than to invite others to eat with them or to be invited themselves; and they would sooner give five or six ducats to provide an entertainment for a person than a groat to assist him in any distress.' The Venetian enjoyed the 'magnificent banquet' lasting 'four hours or more' given by the Lord Mayor of London on the day he assumed office and estimated that 'there must have been 1,000 or more persons at table'. But at a dinner given by the Sheriffs—'to which I went, being anxious to see all I could'—he was even more impressed by 'how punctiliously [the guests] sat in their order, and the extraordinary silence of everyone, insomuch that I could have imagined it one of those public repasts of the Lacedemonians that I have read of'.

Professional cooking was done by men, aided by kitchen boys who were often apprentice-cooks. Cooking was a man's profession because it was man's work: it took muscle to wield the 'flesh-axe' and sever a boar's head and to hack and beat the dried fish and to brandish a vigorous pestle in pounding salted meat to pulp in a big marble mortar. As in all ages, cooks held a high position among household servants. When Master Stamford, the Duke of Norfolk's cook, fell ill, Sir John Howard lent the Duke 6s 8d to cheer the man's spirits, and a few days later Master Stamford received another 6s 8d (equal to a week's wages or more of a skilled artisan). When Sir John himself dined out, he seems to have left tips only for the cook: at the Abbey of St. Ossith's, 20d to the Abbot's cook; and after dining with King Edward's favourite, Lord Hastings, 'to the cooks of my Lord Chamberlain, 5s'. In great establishments the kitchen was often a separate building, circular with a cone-shaped roof topped by a louvre for ventilation, as may be seen at Glastonbury.

Three principal meals divided the day, hours varying according to the season of the year: breakfast at six or seven; dinner, the main meal, from nine till noon but usually about ten or eleven; and supper in the neighbourhood of four P.M. Lordly households also made provision for 'All-night', a snack eaten in the bedchamber before going to bed. All ranks faced much the same kind of breakfast. After Edward IV or Sir John Paston had heard Mass, they broke their fast with ale and bread and boiled beef or mutton or herring, while the yeoman or small shopholder fortified himself for the day's work with ale and bread and a bit of bacon or a piece of cheap fish. When Sir John Howard, on a hunting expedition, paused at a country tavern for breakfast, he satisfied himself with bacon, oatmeal liberally sprinkled with saffron, and the usual ale and bread. Supper was often not much more than a somewhat enlarged breakfast. Dinner was the serious meal of the day; and when guests arrived or a holiday season came round, it was expected to express the status of the family.

The diet of the Yorkist Age immediately presents three striking characteristics to men of a later and less gastronomic time: the variety of meats and fish and the dishes made out of them; the abundance of stews and thick soups and pies and 'fritters'; and the gargantuan consumption of spices. Choice of food was then bounded by the season of the year and the decrees of the Church. Since, in most parts of England, cattle could not be pastured over the winter, there took place a great slaughtering of animals at Martinmas (November 11). This meat, salted by the butcher or at home, became, along with salt fish, the staple of winter meals. At Lent, even salt meat disappeared from the menu, but people enlivened the diet of fish by purchasing quantities of figs and raisins and almonds and dates and nuts. One late spring a Bristol merchant refused a shipload of these dainties brought from Spain because it had missed the season; that is, Easter was already past. The coming of spring, so sensitively recorded in the lyrics of the period, not only meant the loveliness of new green in hedge and wood but it also signalled the approach of fresh meat. Not very good meat, at least on the table of the average man. Cattle tended to be lean and stringy. Meat was often consumed either within three days of slaughter or much later and thus it tended to be green and tough or very high. Winter and summer, game offered a relief to palates weary of dried or salted flesh.

Still, there was no lack of variety. In the autumn wives laid up quantities of stockfish, salt eels, salmon, red herring, white herring, cod, ling. Rivers and stewponds and the ocean supplied fresh fish in season. On one visit to Colchester, Sir John Howard enjoyed messes of marlin, shrimp, flounder, haddock. People also ate porpoise, swordfish, sturgeon, whale, dogfish, and other creatures.

There was likewise an extensive repertory of game. Merchants and gentry secured warrants from well-placed friends to shoot, or have killed for them, deer in the royal forests or a nobleman's preserve. The more prosperous men of the middle ranks now enclosed their own parks and warrens. For many years the citizens of London had held, by charter, common hunting rights in Middlesex, Surrey, and the Chilterns. London employed a Common Hunt at a salary of £10 a year, a gentleman learned in the art of venery who looked after horses and hounds. Supposedly hunting was 'the sport of the gentle'—as it had once been supposedly only the sport of kings. By law, no man was to own greyhounds or other hunting dogs unless he had lands worth 40s a year or was a clerk with a salary of at least £10; but, like sumptuary laws, such restrictions only emphasized the break-down of mediaeval rank. And among the lower orders the fine art of poaching flourished. In addition to venison and, on special occasions, boar, the subjects of King Edward IV loaded their tables with swans, cranes, heronsews, pheasants, curlews, peacocks, widgeons, bustards, plover, mallards, woodcocks, seagulls, quail, snipe, partridges, larks, and a variety of small birds including blackbirds.

The diet of an ordinary family, such as that of a small shopholder or yeoman farmer, can be seen in the household expenses of the two chantry priests at Bridport, who had an income between them of about £11 or £12 a year. They ate beef, mutton, pork and the usual variety of fish, both salted and fresh; they sometimes treated themselves to oysters, mussels, whelks, cockles. They freshened their Lenten diet with fruits and nuts of Spain. They bought dried peas and oatmeal in quantity. Sugar, a luxury, they could do without, using honey. From their garden they gathered

grapes and apples and pears and doubtless fresh vegetables as well.
Like everybody else in England, except the poor, they seasoned
their dishes with cloves, pepper, ginger, saffron, mustard, and
other spices.

For spice was the *sine qua non* of fifteenth-century cooking. The
popular notion that a mediaeval meal consisted mainly of a mighty
joint from which diners dug great gobbets of dripping meat is
wide of the mark. Roast meat and roast game appeared on the
table but it was usually cooked in or served with a heavy sauce of
spices, and for every such comparatively simple preparation in
the cook books of the day, there are a dozen recipes for soft, mixed
concoctions, stews and soups and morteux and pies and leches.
Spice was undoubtedly used to conceal the taste of near-rotten
meat; but this is hardly the whole story. Spice, after all, was to
cooking what colour was to clothing; one of the chief spices of
life was spice..

Venison might be roasted or boiled, but it was more likely to
appear in a stew called venison frumenty. The meat was leched—
cut into strips—and put into a soup made of wheat boiled in milk
to which the yolks of eggs, sugar, and salt were added. Another
favourite soup, called blandissory, began with a mixture of
ground almonds, beef broth—or fish broth—and sweet wine
boiled. After this stock had been strained and boiled again, capon
or fish, first pounded to pulp in a mortar and then 'tempered'
with milk of almonds and sugar, was put into the pot. Blanched
almonds were added and the soup served piping hot. 'Fylettys en
Galentyne' offered chopped roast-pork, fried onions, and beef
broth which had been boiled with pepper, cinnamon, cloves and
mace, to which was added a garnish of salt and bread steeped in
vinegar. 'Maumenye Ryalle' was still more challenging: a mixture
of strong wine, 'the best that a man may find', and 'a good quantity of powdered cinnamon' was fortified with soft pine-cones
washed in wine, white sugar, and cloves, this concoction being set
to boil; almonds, steeped in wine and then boiled in ale, were
added; after which pulped brawn—for lack of partridge or capon
—and ginger and salt and saffron and a sweet wine and a further
quantity of sugar completed the dish.

Cook-books divide solider fare into leched meats, baked meats, and meats roasted or boiled. A popular leche, 'Brawn in Comfyte', was prepared by grinding fresh brawn in a mortar, tempering it with almond meat and straining into a pot, to be then boiled with sugar and cloves. The resultant mixture was thickened with cinnamon and ginger, put into a linen cloth and pressed into any shape desired. After being leched, this concoction was garnished with bare boar-ribs and served. Baked meats were usually enclosed in pastries cheerfully called 'coffyns'. Fresh pork, for example, was pulped in a mortar, mixed with eggs, and strained into a pot, to which were added pine-cones and raisins; after being fried in fresh grease and spiced with pepper, ginger, cinnamon, sugar, saffron, and salt, this mixture was poured into a coffyn, and the cook must then 'plant the coffin about with dates and raisins and small birds or hard-boiled eggs, and endore [add a golden glaze] with yolks of eggs and saffron', after which the coffin went into the oven to be baked. Fish tarts were organized in much the same way, except that wine, fat eels, and cubebs were included. When certain birds such as pheasant and certain fish, like lampreys, were to be roasted, they should be brought into the kitchen alive, bled, 'and allowed to die in their blood'.

On festal occasions 'Cokyntryce' appeared upon the boards. In order to create this exotic, 'take a capon and scald him and draw him clean and smite him in two in the waist; take a pig and scald him and draw him in the same manner and smite him also in the waist; take a needle and a thread and sew the fore-part of the capon to the after-part of the pig and the fore-part of the pig to the hinder part of the capon; and then stuff them as thou stuffest a pig [Pig stuffing: eggs and breadcrumbs, salt, saffron, pepper, and mutton suet; boiled]; put him on a spit and roast him, and when he is enough, endore him with yolks of eggs and powdered ginger and saffron, then with the juice of parsley without; and then serve it forth for a royal meat'.

Sweets sometimes took the form of cheesecakes, pancakes, fritters, often rather like their modern descendants; but other sweets offered mixtures of almond milk and rice flour and sugar and spices and fruits. People enjoyed a 'cold ioncate' (junket) of cream, rose-water, and sugar. Pastries like doucettes consisted of a mélange of cream, egg yolks, sugar or honey, and saffron, poured into a hot coffin and 'served forth'. After discussing 'frumenty with porpoise', a man might be ready for something more delicate like 'flowers of violet', which had been boiled and pressed and pounded into pulp, then tempered with almond milk and rice flour and sugar.

When the remains of the meal had been cleared from the board, fruits and nuts and cheese were served. In his *Book of Nurture*, John Russell particularly recommends hard cheese to ward off the constipation likely to ensue from the eating of sweets.

On ordinary days the King or a great lord was content with two courses offering a choice of perhaps three or four dishes each; gentry like the Pastons probably had a somewhat narrower menu. Formal dinners given by the Mayor of Bristol or York or by a baron or the upper gentry usually offered three courses at the high table, two courses for the hall at large. A typical menu for such a dinner ran like this:

First course	*Second course*
Frumenty with venison	Cokyntryce
Maumenye Ryalle	Blandissory
Heads of boars	Pigs roasted
Fylettys en galentyne	Herons roasted
Roast swan	Mutton tart

Third course
Plover
Curlew
Snipe or small birds
Doucettes
Junket

Fruit, wafers, sweet wine.

At the end of each course a 'soteltie' was borne to the table—a magnificent confection of sugar and eggs and pastry shaped to represent such diverse and intricate subjects as St. George Slaying the Dragon, Hounds Pulling Down A Stag, or the Trinity watching over the Virgin Mary.

In the great households, hall and parlour were in the charge of a marshal. Master of protocol and overseer of feasts, he had to make sure that the hall was aired in the early morning, rushes freshened, tables and forms cleaned, and, if necessary, the hangings beaten. As people began coming into the hall for dinner, the marshal indicated their proper places at table, according to rank, and decided what strangers should be honourably entertained. He kept an eye on the butler, who laid the cloth on the high table, set the mighty salt cellar just a little below the middle of the board, and dealt out trenchers and napkins for the master and his guests. With great ceremony—making appropriate flourishes with his hands and arraying towels and napkins in intricate designs—the butler then arranged bread and drink upon the table. Only the master was served with new bread; the others at his table had bread one day old; those in the lower hall, bread four days old; and trenchers were made from bread four days old. If the host were of blood royal, the butler and sewer went through the rites of assay—now honorific—the butler using 'cornets' of bread to dip delicately into the viands and pouring the wine into the cover of the cup in order to taste it. The end of the dinner brought an elaborate ritual of basin-proffering for the washing of hands, removal of dishes, and placement of the surnap, which must be 'trailed' along the board in a manner minutely prescribed. 'Broken meats', that is, food left upon the trenchers, were deposited in the alms dish.

The most famous banquet of the age was the feast given by the Kingmaker's brother George to celebrate his enthronization as Archbishop of York and to remind the realm that, although King Edward had dared marry Elizabeth Woodville against Warwick's wishes, the House of Neville could outsoar if it chose the splendour of the House of York.

The Earl of Warwick himself acted as Steward for the occasion; brother John, then Earl of Northumberland, was Treasurer; while Edward's favourite, Lord Hastings, served as Comptroller. Sixty-two cooks laboured to prepare 104 oxen, 6 wild bulls, some 4,000

sheep, calves, and pigs, 500 stags, 400 swans, and a galaxy of
other meats, which guests by the thousands—some 6,000 according to report—washed down with 300 tuns of ale, 100 tuns of
wine, and a pipe of ypocras. Then came 13,000 sweet dishes
followed by an array of 'sotelties', one of which depicted Samson
pulling down the pillars. Dukes and duchesses, earls, countesses,
abbots and deans and lords and ladies, mayors, judges were seated,
table by table, in chamber, gallery or hall, according to the lore
of rank; and in addition to lesser officers who brought the dishes,
the Archbishop was served by a gentleman usher, marshal, butler,
sewer, carver, cupbearer, and chaplain.

The arts of feasting were conspicuously displayed at funeral
obsequies; and these ceremonies themselves, like furnishings and
costume and hospitality, tended in the fifteenth century to flaunt
the worldly status of a sublunary being rather than to express the
laying in earth of a tired son of Holy Church, the return to his
Maker of a worm of God.

The ceremony began with a Placebo, or vespers service, on the
eve of the burial, followed then or early next morning by the
Dirige, funeral Matins. On the day of the funeral a procession of
kinfolk, friends, fellow-gildsmen, clerks, hired mourners—as
grand as purse could afford—bore the bier to the church for
Requiem Mass and interment, after which came a dinner for all
the participants except one. Poor men and children, furnished
with mourning gowns, held tapers or torches about the hearse
during the ceremonies. At the Dirige for John Paston the blaze
of torches made such a smoke that windows had to be removed
from the church in order to let in air. Attendance of the clergy
was not left to piety or friendship. Fees were frequently offered
to all friars, monks, nuns, priests who would ornament the service
and lift their voices in chant.

Quite often the pomp of funeral services was not only appreciated by the family but vicariously enjoyed by the subject himself
before his death, as in making his will he precisely marshalled his
last rites. John Baret of Bury lovingly stage-managed every
moment of his burial: 'I will have at my Dirige and Mass 5 men
clad in black in worship of Jesus's 5 wounds and 5 women clad in

white in worship of Our Lady's 5 joys, each of them holding a torch of clean wax', they each to 'have 2d and their meat. I will that on the day of my interment be sung a Mass of prick-song at Saint Mary's altar in worship of Our Lady at 7 of the clock by the morning or soon after [and] that the Mass of Requiem may begin forthwith when that is done, to speed the time for the sermon. . . . The which Mass of Our Lady I will the Saint Mary priest keep in a white vestment which is ready made against the time, bought and paid for, with a remembrance of my arms and my "reason" [motto] thereto, *Grace me govern*. . . . Item, I will that each man that sings prick-song on the day of my interment at Our Lady's Mass have 2d and the players at the organs 2d and each child 1d and that they [be] prayed to dinner the same day. Item I will the Alderman [Mayor of Bury], burgesses, gentlemen and gentlewomen have a dinner the same day that I am interred, with other folks of worship, priests, and good friends, and also my tenants, to which I am much beholden to do for them all, for they have been to me right gentle and good at all times, and therefore I will each of them 4d to drink when they pay their farm [rent]. . . . Item I will the prisoners in the gaol have one day's bread, meat, and drink, and each person 1d, and the keeper to have 2d'.

The funeral expenses of Thomas Stonor amounted to £74. John Paston's must have been still higher, for he died at an inn in London. A priest and a woman took charge of the bier, and twelve poor men bearing torches walked about the cart as it jolted for six days over the roads from London to Norwich. The little cortege was met outside the city gates by a procession of friars from the Four Orders. Dirige was sung at St. Peter's Hungate in the presence of the same friars, 38 priests, 39 boys in surplices, 23 sisters from Norman's Hospital, and 26 clerks, as well as the Prioress of Carrow and her maid and an anchoress. Another procession then bore the body to Bromholm Priory, near Paston, where final rites were held. The funeral dinner must have accommodated many of John Paston's friends and well-wishers, for two men spent three days flaying the animals to be consumed, and the guests were offered tens of geese and chickens and capons,

41 pigs, 49 calves, 34 lambs, 22 sheep, 10 oxen, milk and cream by the gallon, and ale and beer by the barrel.

The voice of the century sounds most strongly, however, in the increasing elaboration of memorial services that followed interment and in the emphasis on Masses to be said for the soul of the deceased. The ceremony of the 'Thirty-Day' or 'Month's Mind' was becoming almost as grand as the burial itself. Some people made provision for bells to be tolled day and night during the interval and for tens or even hundreds of Masses to be said by relays of priests. The 'Year-Mind' or obit was celebrated with almost as much pomp as the Thirty-Day. Gentry and merchants arranged in their wills for chantries.[1] Sir John Fastolfe hoped to establish in Caister Castle a College where seven priests and seven poor men would sing for his soul perpetually; but most wealthy folk, lords or mayors, were content with a chantry of one or two priests. These might perform their services at an altar erected as part of the tomb, and thus came into being those delicate creations in stone which are to be found in many of the cathedral and parish churches of England. People of middling means endowed a priest to sing Masses at an altar in the parish church for a term of years, often five or seven.

Numerous wills specify that when a chantry priest said Mass for the soul of the deceased, he must without fail identify the subject of the service—'and after the Gospel to stand at the altar's end and rehearse John Baret's name openly'. Men hoped for heaven but they also envisaged with satisfaction their names forever ringing on the dear damp air of England.

Other attitudes can be discerned, however. In the towns particularly, at least a few men were beginning to react against the worldly pomp in which death was swathed. Thomas Betson, gentlest of merchants, requested 'the costs of my burying to be done not outrageously, but soberly and discreetly and in a mean [moderate] manner, that it may be unto the worship and laud of Almighty God'. Though the funeral of many an alderman filled the streets with banners and tapers and trains of poor men and

[1] The term *chantry* originally referred simply to the provision for the service but has since become associated with the place where the service was held.

ranks of singing clergy and though a merchant like Sir William
Taylor ordered that 'only £100' be spent on his obsequies, Sir
Thomas Hill directed that his 'body be brought over earth in
honest wise according to my degree without any pomp or
blandise of the world. . . . I utterly forbid any Month's Mind to
be kept solemnly for me after the guise of the world. . .'. A mercer
wrote emphatically, 'I warn you, I will none Month's Mind have.'
Decades before the Reformation, Puritan London was already
beginning to take shape.

The Marriage Hunt

IN the Yorkist Age almost everybody married. A spinster was a woman who spun yarn; a bachelor was an unliveried member of a London gild. Except for nuns, and widows who took the order of chastity, women married early and married again as often as they lost husbands. By the time Grace de Saleby, a great heiress, had reached the age of eleven, she was joined to her third husband who had paid 300 marks for her.

Town labourers and peasants of the vill loved where they looked and married where they loved. Mak and Tib were freer as well as poorer than their betters. Tib watched him play football on the village green; he noticed when he walked with her to church on Whitsun how well daisies suited her dark hair. Perhaps on a summer morning he gave her a green gown and then the banns were cried and they were married.

Occasionally love also had its way at the apex of society. The Scots king, James I, while a prisoner for long years in England, fell in love with Lady Jane Beaufort, married her, and wrote *The Kingis Quair* to celebrate his passion. Young Edward IV, entranced by the beauty of the widowed Elizabeth Woodville, wedded her secretly at her family's country seat on May Day of 1464; but, as we have seen, his subjects grumbled and grouched that he had chosen beneath his dignity and failed to strengthen the realm by a foreign alliance.

In the fifteenth century all the upper ranks of English society held to the conviction that marriage represented an instrument of worldly advancement. Townsmen and gentry formed one vast web of wife-and-husband hunters; parents, brothers and sisters, relatives, friends joined in the chase. A wealthy knight or merchant was scarcely interred before estimates of the widow's financial position went flying by word of mouth and letter through many a family network.

The business of marriage often began early, for a boy was considered to be of age at fourteen, a girl at twelve. Child marriages were not uncommon. St. Stephen's Chapel, Westminster, was the scene of a brilliant royal wedding in January, 1478, when King Edward IV gave away the bride, Anne Mowbray, aged six, to his younger son, Richard, Duke of York, aged four. John Rigmardin, three years of age, made his way to the church in the arms of a priest, who coaxed him to utter the words of the marriage ceremony; in the midst of the service the boy announced that he would learn no more that day, whereupon the priest answered, 'You must speak a little more, and then go play you'. A sadder experience befell James Ballard, eleven, who was married to his wife, Anne, at 'ten of the clock in the night without the consent of any of his friends, by one Sir Roger Blakey, then curate of Colne. . . . And the morrow after, the same James declared unto his uncle that the said Anne, being a big damsel and marriageable, had enticed him with two apples to go with her to Colne and to marry her'. Mistress Elizabeth Bridge, thirteen, complained that her bridegroom, John Bridge, about thirteen, never used her 'lovingly in so much that the first night they were married the said John would eat no meat at supper, and when it was bedtime, the said John did weep to go home with his father. Yet nevertheless by his father's entreating and by the persuasion of the priest, the said John did come to bed to Elizabeth'—who made this deposition— 'far in the night; and there lay still till in the morning in such sort as the deponent might take unkindness with him; for he lay with his back toward her all night. . . .'

Wardships were bought and sold like any other investments; a guardian had the use of his ward's fortune until the child came of age and not infrequently purchased the wardship in order to marry an heiress to his son or provide a husband with broad lands for his daughter. Some of these transactions showed the darker side of covetousness and left wounds upon the child's mind that never healed. Young people hardly entered upon puberty were married off not only by guardians but by parents as well with no apparent consideration for the child's happiness. A correspondent of the Pastons, John Wyndham of Felbridge, who had fallen in love with the widow of Sir John Heveningham, announced that if she would have him he would pay off her husband's debts of 300 marks, and he proposed to get the money by selling his son in the marriage market for 600 marks. Stephen Scrope declared bitterly that his father, Sir John Fastolfe, had sold his wardship for 500 marks to Chief Justice Gascoigne, in whose household he was treated so negligently that 'I took sickness that kept me a thirteen or fourteen years ensuing, whereby I am disfigured in my person and shall be whilst I live'. Scrope added, 'He bought me and sold me as a beast, against all right and law, to mine hurt more than 1,000 marks'. The Church, which tolerated marriage only as an inferior form of Christian living, paid small heed to the dangers of child marriage except to require that the principals of such a marriage have the right to repudiate it when they came of age, which, considering the years at which boys and girls were held to have come of age, was but a frail safeguard. The law did little better for wards: upon reaching their majority, they might sue their guardian on grounds of 'disparagement' if they had been matched below their degree.

On the other hand, one of the tenderest courtships of this or any period took place between Thomas Betson, when he was already a Merchant of the Staple, and Lady Stonor's daughter by her first husband, Kathryn Riche, who was probably no more than twelve or thirteen when she was affianced. Betson expressed his exquisite feeling for the little girl he was one day to marry in a letter he wrote her when he was on one of his business trips to Calais: 'Mine own heartily beloved Cousin Kathryn, I recommend me unto you with all the inwardness of mine heart. And now lately ye shall understand that I received a token from you, the which was and is to me right heartily welcome. I understand right well that ye be in good health of body and merry at heart. And I pray God heartily to his pleasure to continue the same: for it is to me very great comfort that ye so be, so help me Jhesu. And if ye would be

a good eater of your meat always, that ye might wax and grow
fast to be a woman, ye should make me the gladdest man of the
world, by my troth: for when I remember your favour and your
sad [earnest] loving dealing to mewards, forsooth ye make me
even very glad and joyous in my heart: and on the other side
again, when I remember your young youth, and see well that ye
be no eater of your meat, the which should help you greatly in
waxing, forsooth then ye make me very heavy again. And therefore, I pray you, my own sweet cousin, even as you love me, to
be merry and to eat your meat like a woman. And if ye so will do
for my love, look what ye will desire of me, whatsoever it be, and
by my troth I promise you by the help of our Lord to perform it
to my power.

'I can no more say now, but at my coming home, I will tell you
much more between you and me and God before. And whereas
ye full womanly and like a lover remember me with manifold
recommendation in divers manners, ye shall understand that with
good heart and good will I receive and take to myself the one half
of them; and the other half with hearty love and favour I send
them to you again; and over that I send you the blessing that our
Lady gave her dear son, and ever well to fare.

'I pray you greet well my horse, and pray him to give you four
of his years to help you withal, and I will at my coming home
give him four of my years and four horseloaves till [as] amends.
Tell him that I prayed him so. . . . I pray you, gentle cousin,
commend me to the Clock and pray him to amend his unthrifty
manners, for he strikes ever in undue time, and he will be ever
afore and that is a shrewd condition. I trust to you that he shall
amend against mine coming, the which shall be shortly with all
hands and all feet, with God's grace. . . . And Almighty Jhesu make
you a good woman, and send you many good years and long to
live in health and virtue to his pleasure. At great Calais on this side
of the sea, the first day of June, when every man was gone to his
dinner, and the clock smote nine, and all our household cried after
me and bade me come down, come down to dinner at once! And
what answer I gave them, ye know it of old. I send you this ring
for a token.'

As Kathryn grew towards womanhood, Thomas's affection seems to have blossomed into love. At times he showed himself properly jealous. 'I am wroth with Kathryn,' he complained to her mother, 'because she sendeth me no writing. I have [written] to her divers times and for lack of answer I wax weary; she might get a secretary if she would and if she will not, it shall put me to less labour to answer her letters again.' On Trinity Sunday of 1478, two years after he had written the letter from Calais, he confessed to Kathryn's mother: 'I remember her full oft, God know it. I dreamed once she was 30 winter of age, and when I woke I wished she had been but 20; and so by likelihood I am sooner like to have my wish than my dream. . . .'

Within a few weeks the marriage had been arranged for the late summer. But now suddenly Thomas Betson became a harried male. Because he was in London and the Stonors in the country, Kathryn's mother thrust upon him the terrifying responsibility of seeing to her trousseau. 'Madam, I can little skill to do anything that longeth to the matter ye wot of [i.e., the marriage]; therefore I must beseech your ladyship to send me your advice how I shall be demeaned in such things as shall belong unto my cousin Kathryn, and how I shall provide for them: she must have girdles, 3 at least, and how they shall be made I know not. And many other things she must have; ye know well what they be, in faith I know not: by my troth, I would it were done, [rather] than more than it shall cost.'

By the end of the summer Thomas had married his Kathryn at last, and it appears that they settled down to a happy life together. When he died eight years later (1486) Kathryn had borne him two sons and three daughters. She married again, and by her second husband, William Welbeck, a haberdasher, she had another son. But on her death in 1510 she asked to be buried by the side of her first love, Thomas Betson, in All Hallows Barking.

Thomas Betson had a gentler heart than most, then and now, and his wooing and marriage are hardly typical though certainly not unique. Love-liking could blossom within the social framework of the arranged marriage. Young men and young women, schooled to the system, enjoyed the marriage hunt; no less than their parents and friends, they seemed able to couple financial considerations with romantic interest. Those who made advantageous matches considered themselves fortunate. Falling in love happened after the wedding ceremony.

Parents of a girl often refused to contract a marriage for her that did not meet with her approval and sometimes listened to her desires. After the arrangements for dowry and jointure had been agreed upon, or looked to be so, the young people were given a limited opportunity to become acquainted with each other and discover if their feelings marched with their finances. When Sir John Paston approached Lady Boleyn, wife of the Lord Mayor, about one of her daughters for his brother John, she was not impressed by the position of the Pastons; but 'what if he and she can agree', she wrote, 'I will not let [hinder] it, but I will never advise her thereto in no wise'.

Yet, despite these gentler considerations, worldly prospects dominated the marriage hunt. When a young London mercer of no standing proclaimed his engagement to the widow of a wealthy vintner he was felt by the Mercers Company to have brought off a magnificent coup—'which is a worship to the fellowship, a young man out of the livery to be preferred to such a rich marriage'—and he was promptly promoted to the livery.

Some of the great fortunes of the city of London came about when matrimony produced a merger of business interests. Young George Irlond, a grocer, put his hands on nearly £3,000 by means of a marriage; another grocer, the famous Mayor John Wells, took for his second wife a widow who brought him a dowry of £764 and an equal amount in trust funds for her children with which she was permitted to trade. Wealthy city widows were besieged with suitors, and it appears that some of them were not above playing a female version of Volpone.

A draper, thinking he had safely completed a marriage contract with a widow, though the marriage itself she postponed, lavished his time and his money for three years in conducting her business affairs, 'intending it should have been for his own weal and profit in time coming'. He generously spent more than £20, with this and that, on her and her friends, and to keep her heart warm he loaded her with gifts, of which, however, he kept a careful record.[1]

After this draper—who turns out to be George Bulstrode, perhaps the son of draper William who did so much business with Sir John Howard—sailed off gallantly to Spain to buy £400 of merchandise for his widow, she began to smile upon a rival; and when he came home she refused to have anything more to do with him, 'not fearing the damnation of her soul'. This sad story came out after she had died, worth £2,000, and Bulstrode sued to collect what he felt was owing to him.

Marriage was such a nice business of mating destinies and finances that a good deal of bargaining enlivened the 'courtship'. The friends of the young man wanted the largest possible dowry; the parents of the girl were concerned about her jointure and sought to pin down the amount of land or money which the young man's family were prepared to give the couple. William Nightingale, a draper, secured with his bride £100, a gold ring, a grey fur, a horse, and a 34-year lease of a quay. A London goldsmith marrying a St. Albans girl with a dowry of £40 settled on her property worth 10 marks.

Gazing upon the animated scene of this marriage market and not realizing perhaps that the English were more reserved than his own countrymen, the Venetian diplomat concluded that the

---

	£	s	d
[1] 'a pair of great beads gauded with gold	2	2	
a great ring of fine gold with a great pointed diamond	10		
a small chain of gold with a little Agnus Dei of gold	3	6	
a signet of gold with her arms graven in stone and a ruby and emerald stone set in same	3	2	6
a great ring of fine gold set with a "Turkesshe" which I had made for her in Seville	3	5	2
a popinjay which I might have sold to my Lady Hungerford for 5 marks	2	6	8
for seven plight and a quarter of fine lawn	3	12	6
for six ells of fine Holland cloth for kerchiefs	1	16	
for a fur of fine budge	2	2	
for 18 "pampilions" at 20d, and 60 "tavilleons" at 2d	2		
for a Venice corse of gold and a Seville corse and ribbons and laces	1	5	8
for divers dainties as figs and raisins, dates, almonds, prunes, capers, sugar and other spices, lampreys, "conervais", pomegranates and oranges	6		
for ypocras which she caused me to make for her and for her friends at divers times, 8 gallons; for a hogshead of white wine; in all	2	11	8
for year's gifts [New Year's gifts] at divers years to her servants and to her friends and kinsfolk	1	18	8'

people of England lacked hearts. 'Although they are very much inclined to carnal passion, I never have noticed anyone, at court or amongst the lower orders, to be in love; whence one must necessarily conclude either that the English are the most discreet lovers in the world or that they are incapable of love. I say this of the men, for I understand it is quite the contrary with the women, who are very violent in their passions. Howbeit the English keep a very jealous guard over their wives, though anything may be compensated in the end by the power of money. . . .

'I saw one day that I was at court a handsome man of about 18 years of age, the brother of the Duke of Suffolk, who, as I understood, had been left very poor. . . . This youth was boarded out to a widow of 50 with a fortune, as I was informed, of 50,000 crowns [£10,000]; and this old woman knew how to play her cards so well that he was content to become her husband and patiently to waste the flower of his beauty with her, hoping soon to enjoy her great wealth with some handsome young lady. . . .'

Was the Italian right about the lack of romantic courtship in England? There was certainly no lack of love literature. English men and women doted on chivalric romances; the lyrical poems of the age sing plangently of love; and in the ballads star-crossed lovers drive violently towards passionate ends. By hearsay, at least, the age knew the madness and nobility of love. Perhaps most young men and women were content to sigh over the former and to seek the latter in the sensible marriage their parents arranged for them.

Yet Mayor William Gregory commented in his chronicle upon the slaughter at Towton Field (March, 1461), 'Many a lady lost her best beloved in that battle'. If this sentiment seems to sound a merely conventional note, the same can hardly be said of the moral which Gregory draws from the romantic marriage of Edward IV and Elizabeth Woodville: 'Now take heed what love may do, for love will not nor may not cast [forecast] no fault nor peril in nothing.' Of the half a dozen or so marriages of which there is more than passing mention in the Paston letters, three turn out to be fervent love matches, and not one of them developed within the accepted framework of parental arrangements.

Crimes of passion were by no means rare. Writing of the Yorkist victory at Northampton in July of 1460, Gregory considered the fate of a single man worth as much space as the whole battle. 'And that good knight Sir William Lucy that dwelt beside Northampton heard the gunshot, and came unto the field to have helped the King, but the field was done, ere that he came; and one of the Staffords was aware of his coming, and loved that knight's wife and hated him, and anon caused his death.'

A Yeoman of the King's Chamber, a man named Fazakerley, was sent to Ludlow to arrest certain of the Duke of York's retinue, including one Sharpe. Fazakerley and Sharpe's wife had been lovers. When the officer of the Crown tried to carry out his mission, he was slain by the enraged husband, and the commons of Ludlow rose in support of the deed. A tailor's apprentice became so miserably lovelorn that his master haled him into the gild court, where he was sternly reproved because he had wasted his time falling in love and 'used the company of a woman which was to his great loss and hindering for as much as he was so affectionate and resorted daily unto her'. In the reign of Henry VII another apprentice, 'having an inward love to a young woman and the young woman having the same unto him', was rash enough to reveal his marriage plans and on his wedding day found himself clapped into prison by his master. He petitioned the Chancellor for his freedom on the grounds that he had served seven years of his apprenticeship and that this cruel prohibition of his marriage was 'contrary to the laws of God and causeth much fornication and adultery to be within the said city'. A draper's apprentice was imprisoned after he had made a runaway marriage with a silk-woman. In general, however, young people in the business world of London married much later than the sons and daughters of the gentry; for in the great companies apprenticeship lasted ten years and a young man was unable to seek a wife until he was twenty-four or twenty-five. Furthermore, wards, who were under the protection of the municipal court of orphans, seem to have been much more carefully and suitably placed in marriage than children whose wardships were purchased by lords and gentry.

Despite, then, the cynical observations of the Venetian diplomat and the ubiquitous pursuit of the marriage hunt, love was a force to be reckoned with. Most parents of the time undoubtedly believed that once their children were settled as befitted their station, they would find love within the bounds of marriage. It appears that young men and women did so. The wills of the period reveal expressions of affection and trust on the part of the husband for the wife, who frequently is appointed as her husband's executor with full power to act as she thinks best. Letters tell the same story. Defeated in battle and about to be executed by Warwick the Kingmaker, the gallant William Herbert, Earl of Pembroke, addressed his last worldly thoughts to his wife: 'Pray for me and take the said order [of widowhood] that ye promised me, as ye had in my life my heart and love.' Though re-marriage was the general rule for widows, a number of them did take a solemn oath before a bishop to live henceforth in chastity.

The marriage hunt among the gentry is zealously pursued through the Cely letters and the Stonor letters and the Paston letters.

While young Richard Cely was buying wool in the Cotswolds in April of 1482, his favourite dealer, William Midwinter, after discovering that he was not 'in any way of marriage' told him about a young gentlewoman 'whose father's name is Lemeryke and her mother is dead and she shall dispend by her mother £40 a year as they say and her father is the greatest ruler as richest man in that country and there have been great gentlemen to see her and would have her'. Richard said that he was interested indeed. When next he came to Northleach, Midwinter informed him that if he would 'tarry Mayday' he 'should have a sight of the young gentlewoman and I said I would tarry with a goodwill'.

The rendezvous was naturally set for Northleach Church. Master Lemeryke, a Justice of the Peace, was to have sat that day at Northleach but sent one of his clerks instead and tactfully took himself out of the way to Winchcombe. Perhaps Richard was feeling a little nervous, for when he went to the church he had his friend William Breton, the wool packer, by his side and kept Breton with him throughout the day. 'I and William Breton were saying Matins when they came into church,' the young lady and her stepmother, 'and when Matins was done they went to a kinswoman of the young gentlewoman and I sent to them a pottle [half gallon] of white romney and they took it thankfully for they had come a mile on foot that morning. And when Mass was done, I came and welcomed them and kissed them, and they thanked me for the wine and prayed me to come to dinner with them and I excused me and' they made me promise to drink with them after dinner and I sent them to dinner a gallon of wine and they sent me a heronsew roast and after dinner I came and drank with them and took William Breton with me and we had right good communication'—which is not surprising since the way had been so well smoothed with wine. 'The person pleaseth me well, as by the first communication. She is young, little, and very well favoured and witty, and the country speaks much good of her. All this matter abideth the coming of her father to London that we may understand what sum he will depart with and how he likes me. He will be here within three weeks.' Richard concluded by praying his brother George to 'send me a letter how ye think by this matter'.

Wine and May Day and the comely face of Mistress Lemeryke would appear to have got the courtship off to a propitious start. But perhaps the father did not find Richard a good match or offered too small a dowry, for nothing further is heard of the matter. Only ten days later, the young man reported to his brother that new prospects were opening up: 'Sir Harry Bryan, the bringer of this, labours me sore to go and see Rawson's daughter; I am beholden to him for his labour.' Perhaps the pretty face he had seen in Northleach was still before his eye, for he added 'I have many things in my mind but I have no leisure to write, ye may understand part by my letter that I sent you before this'.

The hunt to provide Thomas Stonor's son and heir William with a fitting bride unfolds a cast of characters reminiscent of Ben Jonson's comedies of humour: the stern father, too much a figure of awe to his son; William himself, diffident, and rather easily discouraged; and the mainspring of action, the bustling family friend, ripe with stratagems to aid love's cause. The Stonor correspondence reveals even more clearly than the Paston letters the mixture of financial bargaining and amorous language, the birth of love from the womb of worldly goods. The delicate balance of the two forces was adjusted by an inner logic, known to everyone then but since well nigh lost.

The game began with a jubilant communication from the family friend and kinsman, Thomas Mull, to Thomas Stonor: young William 'hath been with a full goodly gentlewoman and commoned [talked] with her after love's lore: and for certain I know that each of them is verily well content of other'. After an analysis of the lady's financial position, Mull urged Thomas Stonor to be 'good father to my cousin in counselling, helping, and preferring after your heart's pleasure: for and [if] I should marry, I would he should choose for me'. He concludes, 'As it is said, there is of late fallen to my mistress's father 300 marks more after the death of my Lady Kyriell'. Not long after, young William reported to his father, 'I have comfortable demeanour of my mistress, but [except] as to the very purpose, yet I hope well'.

The lady began to indicate somewhat more emphatically, however, the amount of jointure she expected, and young William drew off, abashed. Thomas Mull, alarmed at William's timidity, dispatched a letter to him rich in the biaxial lore of fifteenth-century love—the lore that governed life, not literature: 'Whereas I feel by your writing that my mistress hath not that goodwill of you as sometime ye owed her, sir, ye may owe her right good will, howbeit that it be not in so hearty wise as ye did before.' Mull continues in this vein of nice distinctions: Had she 'said to you these words, "Sir, I would not have you, but if so be that I may have a £100 or 200 marks with you in jointure", then ye might conceive that she had loved your land better than yourself. But I understand that the words were these: "Sir, I may have 300 marks in jointure, and I to take the less when I may have the more, my friends would think me not wise etc: howbeit your father will not give me so much, yet let him do well to you." In which words I understand no utter nay. But and ye in your mind conceive that she has given you an utter nay, then never speak more of the matter. . . .

'But [if] the case were so that she would be agreeable to have you with £40 or 80 marks jointure, would your heart then love as ye have done before? This question would I know of you, for and I know your disposition on this behalf, I trow to God all this love and matter of love would be revived again in short season. Since your departure she hath been vexed and troubled with the throes of love more fervently in her mind than ye have been since vexed with her sayings. . . . She may revolve at her liberty but without controlling everything that longeth to love's dance; for though the flame of the fire of love may not break out so that it may be seen, yet the heat of love is never the less but rather hotter. I dare depose for her that the sharp and unwary changes from thought to thought and oft remembrance of the troubly waves of love have so pushed her to and fro in her own mind, that she desireth as sore after relief, as far as she may for shame, as the man in the water desireth to be relieved from drowning in the peril of the sea. But danger [pride] and shame will not suffer her to speak it without it be so that there be some new motion made to her etc.' Thomas Mull concludes happily, 'The means whereof I have encompassed in my mind, which by the mercy of God I will attempt, if it so be ye can be pleased that way, and that in short time.'

He soon developed a complete plan of campaign, as he explained to William's father. The instrument, a priest who had entrée to the lady's household, agreed to forward the cause of love by raising the subject of William Stonor and noting the lady's reaction. When the priest had been with her four days, Mull planned to send her a letter; the priest would call the bearer 'cousin' so that he would be bidden to stay under the lady's roof. After she had read the letter, 'if the priest feel her verily pliable, the messenger shall speak with her himself'. To make sure the secret agent played his part well, Mull fortified him with a memorandum detailing just what he was to say to the lady. All that was now necessary, thought Mull, was for Thomas Stonor to buck up his son: 'for God's sake, let him walk with you, and give words of good comfort, and be good father unto him. For, sir, he is disposed to be a muser and a studier'—a disposition which the father should do his best to eradicate.

But it all went up in smoke, how or why there is no knowing. The next recorded episode in the hunt occurs two years later. This time William's younger brother Thomas was urging him on, though humbly admitting that on the last occasion he had tried to help his brother in the lists of love he had made a mess of it. The lady in question was probably Elizabeth Ryche, who became William's first wife. 'Brother Stonor, I never longed so sore to speak with you as I do now, marvelling greatly that ye be long hence, remembering how greatly in conceit [high in favour] ye stand in London with a gentlewoman and the great labour that is made for her against you: and greatly it is noised that but ye beware she shall be taken from you. . . . I would not for my horse and harness and all my other goods that in this matter ye took a rebuke.'

Having wedded his wealthy London widow, William now encumbered with exhortations his brother Thomas who, taking part in Edward IV's bloodless invasion of France in 1475, got himself in some sort of scrape at Calais. Thomas was grateful for his brother's solicitude but not for the advice: 'Sir, I thank you for your good counsel, and certainly I think to do thereafter: but ye may thank my sister, your wife, that ye be of so good disposition to advise me to leave all folly, for that comes of the holy sacrament of wedlock, which I pray Jhesu send me soon to after I come home: for I fear me that till that time that that yoke of wedlock lie in my neck as it does now in yours, youth shall run in me as it has done in you aforetime. . . .'

After his shy beginning, William Stonor became an adept at the marriage hunt. On the death of Elizabeth, he married a West Country woman with broad lands; and when she died a year later, he won for his third bride Anne Neville, an heiress who had seen much trouble in her life. She was the daughter of the Kingmaker's brother John, Marquess Montagu, who, like Warwick, was slain at Barnet. Shortly after their marriage, William Stonor packed her off to Taunton so that she might impress his new friend the Marquess of Dorset, son to Queen Elizabeth. Anne wrote to her husband a lonely letter which, one can only hope, moved his heart: 'Sir, I recommend me unto you in my most hearty wise, right joyful to hear of your health: liketh you to know, at the writing of this bill I was in good health, thinking long since I saw you, and if I had known that I should have been this long time from you I would have been much loather than I was to have come into this far country. But I trust it shall not be long ere I shall see you here, and else I would be sorry, in good faith. . . .' She signed herself wistfully, 'Your new wife Anne Stonor'.

In the Paston letters the marriage hunt is pursued through three generations. Early in the fifteenth century William Paston, the yeoman's son who rose to be a Justice, secured the hand of Agnes Berry, daughter of a well-to-do knight. It is impossible to imagine Agnes as a gay or affectionate girl. She is always the fearsome matriarch—or more tactfully, a woman of pronounced character—tough and acquisitive as the times themselves. About 1440 she and Justice William matched their eldest son John with the heiress of a nearby squire, Margaret Mauteby, who joined the manor of Mauteby to the growing Paston lands.

The marriage hunt opens nine years later when old Agnes and her son John were seeking a marriage for his sister Elizabeth, a pursuit which, for a reason never made clear, went on for a decade. The family were considering Stephen Scrope, a widower, son of Sir John Fastolfe's wife by a former marriage. Scrope has earned a small place in histories of fifteenth-century literature by his translations of Cicero and Christine de Pisan; he was then some fifty years of age and disfigured, as we have seen from his own words. Agnes sought to overcome any scruples or doubts John might have: 'My cousin Clere thinketh that it were a folly to forsake him unless ye knew of another as good or better; and I have essayed your sister, and I found her never so willing to none as she is to him, if it be so that his land stand clear.' She gave John an additional prod, 'Sir Harry Inglose is right busy about Scrope for one of his daughters'.

But a secret letter Elizabeth Clere then wrote to John Paston explains why young Elizabeth might be ready to give herself to an ugly widower almost three times her age. 'She was never in so great sorrow as she is nowadays, for she may not speak with no man, whosoever come, nor with servants of her mother's', without Agnes making nasty insinuations. 'And she hath since Easter been beaten once in the week or twice, and sometimes twice on one day and her head broken in two or three places.' The poor girl managed to enlist the sympathy of a friar, who bore a message to Elizabeth Clere: she 'prayeth me that I would send to you a letter of her heaviness, and pray you to be her good brother, as her trust is in you; and she saith, if ye may see by his evidences that his children and hers may inherit and she to have reasonable jointure, she hath heard so much of his birth and his conditions that, and ye will, she will have him whether her mother will or will not, notwithstanding it is told her his person is simple [i.e., unattractive], for she saith men shall have the more duty of her [respect for her] if she rule her to him as she ought to do'. Cousin Clere warned John Paston that his sister was so unhappy she might take a desperate step: 'Think on this matter, for sorrow oftentime causeth women to beset themselves otherwise than they should do, and if she were in that case, I wot well ye would be sorry.' She concluded, in a sudden pang of fear at her daring to cross the indomitable Agnes, 'I pray you burn this letter, that your men nor no other man see it, for and my cousin your mother knew that I had sent you this letter, she should never love me'.

Fortunately for young Elizabeth, the marriage negotiations with Scrope fell through, but Agnes continued to make her daughter miserable. 'It seemeth by my mother [-in-law's] language,' Margaret Paston wrote to her husband four years later, 'that she would never so fain to have been delivered of her as she will now.'

In the spring of the following year Sir William Oldhall appeared briefly as a prospective bridegroom; a few weeks later, the Pastons had gone so far with William Clopton for his son John that an indenture was drawn up in which Elizabeth's dowry was set at 400 marks, she to have a jointure of lands worth £30 a year. John Clopton hoped that Agnes would provide Elizabeth with a worthy trousseau, pointing out that 'my mistress, your mother, shall not be charged with her board after the day of the marriage'. He wanted to confer with Paston without delay, 'for the sooner, the liefer me; for, as to my conceit, the days be waxen wonderly long in a short time'. But the Cloptons are heard of no more.

In July of 1454 Lord Grey de Ruthyn, one of the magnates of the realm, hastily informed John Paston 'that and your sister be not yet married, I trust to God I know where she may be married to a gentleman of 300 marks of livelode [property], the which is a great gentleman born, and of good blood'. Paston replied cautiously that his sister was not yet insured to any man though several offers were pending, but before he could say more to his lordship he must know the gentleman's name and place of residence and other pertinent facts. As he had probably suspected, it turned out that the gentleman was a ward of Lord Grey, who cared only for the dowry which would go into his own pocket.

Four years later, Elizabeth was unhappily settled in the house-hold of Lady Pole; but by January of 1459 she had at last found a husband. Her life with Robert Poynings was short but it must have been exciting, for he was an adventurous man who thrust himself into the turbulence of his age. Though he was Jack Cade's sword-bearer and carver, he managed to escape the vengeance which pursued Cade's followers—'Many a good man's heart he hath', William Worcester declared. In February of 1461, he was killed fighting for Warwick the Kingmaker and the Yorkists at the second battle of St. Albans. The first letter that Elizabeth, married, wrote to her mother begins with a charming shyness: 'and as for my master, my best beloved that ye call, and I must needs call him so now, for I find none other cause, and as I trust to Jhesu none shall, for he is full kind unto me, and is as busy as he can to make me sure of my jointure . . .' and from there on Elizabeth is entirely concerned with the finances of her marriage.

The hunters warm to their work after the death of John Paston in 1466. The letters exchanged by his eldest son, Sir John, who loved to play the courtier in London, and the next son, young John, who stayed at home to protect the family estate, open a window on to the world of the young knights and squires of the time: they talk of girls and clothes and books, exchange ribald observations, toss in a Latin or a French phrase occasionally, console each other in their ills and misfortunes, and give and receive news about the doings of the great. One of Sir John's friends thought him a nonpareil of matchmakers, even though he could still profit from Ovid's advice: 'And as to *De Arte Amandi* I shall send it you this week, for I have it not now ready; but me-thinketh Ovid's *De Remedio* were more meet for you, but if [unless] ye purposed to fall hastily in my Lady Anne P.'s lap, as white as whale's bone, etc. Ye be the best chooser of a gentle-woman that I know'—for everyone but himself.

In the early summer of 1468 he met at Calais a lady named Anne Haute. Not long after, they became engaged. But Sir John remained single, perhaps because her Woodville kin never did much for him, perhaps because he lost interest in Mistress Anne or could not bear to relinquish his bachelor's existence. He spent the last years of his life seeking an annulment of their betrothal, and died some months after he had finally managed to free him-self.

Within a year of his father's death, this best chooser of a gentlewoman was busily seeking a bride for his brother and on occasion tutoring him in the art of courtship. 'By privy means' he had been sounding Lady Boleyn about one of her daughters, but she was showing so little enthusiasm that Sir John, who had his dignity to think of, 'disdained in mine own person to common with her therein'. In Sir John's opinion, the only hope was for John to speak to her himself, 'for without that, in my conceit it will not be'. He was ready with a fund of advice on how to approach both mother and maid: 'Ye be personable, and peraven-ture, your being once in the sight of the maid, and a little dis-covering of your good will to her, binding her to keep it secret,' matters may go well. 'Bear yourself as lowly to the mother as ye list [please] but to the maid not too lowly nor that ye be too glad to speed nor too sorry to fail.' Despite this knowing counsel, 'the maid' apparently withstood John's arts, perhaps because he had little land of his own and few prospects of acquiring more.

Two and a half years later, in March of 1470, Sir John was still spurring on the hunt for brother John, even though the world had taken arms and Edward IV was about to march into Lincolnshire to put down a rising fomented by the Kingmaker. The Paston quarry, unfortunately, had no intention of immediately dwindling into a wife: 'Item as for Mistress Kathryn Dudley, I have many times recommended you to her, and she is nothing displeased with it. She recketh not how many gentlemen love her; she is full of love. I have beaten the matter for you—your unknowledge [without your knowing it], as I told her. She answereth me that she will no one this two year, and I believe her; for I think she hath the life that she can hold her content with; I trow she will be a sore labouring woman this two year for need of her soul.' Sir John was also forced to write of another prospect: 'Mistress Gryseacresse is sure to St. Leger, with my Lady of Exeter, a foul loss.'

For the next year and a half the Paston brothers were too much embroiled in the violent politics of Warwick the Kingmaker's restoration of the House of Lancaster to find time for marriage hunting; but a few months after they had fought on the losing side at Barnet, young John was trailing a girl of Yorkist family, Lady Elizabeth Bourchier. After Sir John had an interview with the lady, he sent out feelers to discover the effect and reported that his brother had apparently not yet learned the lessons Sir John was trying to teach him: 'ye have a little chafed it, but I cannot tell how; send me word whether ye be in better hope or worse.'

Three years later young John, now about thirty, showed himself weary of the single state. 'I pray, get us a wife somewhere,' he had written earlier, 'for *melius est nubere in Domino quam urere* [a somewhat mangled version of St. Paul's concession that it is better to marry than burn]'. Now he himself, at Norwich, was taking the lead in the marriage hunt and suggesting stratagems to Sir John. One of his warmest prospects was the daughter of a London draper, Harry Eberton. 'Ere ye depart out of London, speak with Harry Eberton's wife and inform her that I am proffered a marriage in London which is worth 600 mark and better'; Sir John was then to say that his brother, 'for such fantasy as I have in the said Mistress Eberton' would still prefer to deal with the Ebertons even though Eberton would not give so much 'as I might have had with the other'. Sir John was to hint that his brother might even better his last offer and that if the mother was willing, John would come posting up to London, within a fortnight 'for that cause only'. The 600 mark marriage sounds like a conventional move in the bargaining, but young John did have two other lines out: 'also, sir, I pray you that ye will common with John Lee or his wife, or both, to understand how the matter at the Blackfriars doth, and that ye will see and speak with the thing yourself and with her father and mother, ere ye depart.' John likewise had his eye upon a widow in the same quarter. 'Also, that it like you to speak with your apothecary, which was sometime the Earl of Warwick's apothecary, and to weet of him what the widow of the Blackfriars is worth and what her husband's name was. He can tell all, for he is executor to the widow's husband.'

By the time summer weather had yielded to the grey skies of November, Elizabeth Eberton and the Blackfriars widow had gone the way of all the former prospects. The 'thing' at Blackfriars was about to 'be wedded in haste' to one Skeerne—'as she told herself to my silkmaid [dressmaker], which maketh part of such as she shall wear, to whom she broke her heart [revealed her inmost feelings] and told her that she should have had Master Paston; and my maid weened it had been I that she spoke of; and with more, that the same Master Paston came where she was with twenty men and would have taken her away.' This romantic flight of fancy had not appealed to Sir John: 'I told my maid that she lied of me, and that I never speak with her in my life, nor that I would not wed her to have with her 3,000 marks.'

But fresh game was afoot. Young John had a friend named Dawnson and the two men were hunting hard for each other. Dawnson, up in London, had been in touch with Lady Walgrave, the widow of a knight. Sir John, with rather patronizing amusement, was seconding Dawnson's efforts: 'I have commoned with your friend Dawnson and have received your ring of him: and he hath by mine advice spoken with her [Lady Walgrave] two times: he telleth me of her dealing and answers, which if they were according to his saying, a fainter lover than ye would and well ought to take therein great comfort, so that he might haply sleep the worse three nights after. . . . Within three days, I hope to set

you in certainty how that ye shall find her forever hereafter. It is
so, as I understand, that ye be as busy on your side for your
friend Dawnson; I pray God send you good speed in these works;
yet were it pity that such crafty wooers as ye be both should
speed well, but if ye love truly.'

Three weeks later (December 11, 1474) Sir John sent word to
his brother that he had given himself without stint to the pursuit
and 'done my devoir to know my Lady Walgrave's stomach',
but he had little comfort to offer. She had refused to keep John's
ring even though Sir John in a burst of eloquence that he could not
forbear repeating told her 'that she should not be anything bound
thereby but that I knew well ye would be glad to forbear the
lievest [dearest] thing that ye had in the world, which might be
daily in her presence [and] that should cause her once a day to
remember you—but it would not be'.

Worse still, Sir John learned the next morning from his go-
between—an indispensable agent in the marriage hunt—that
Lady Walgrave wanted back her musk-ball, which he had taken
in a playful moment, protesting that he must send it to his brother.
Sir John called again upon the lady and redoubled his blandishments. He had not dispatched his brother the musk-ball, he told
her, 'because I wist well ye should have slept the worse; but now,
as God help me, I would send it you and give you my advise not
to hope overmuch on her which is an overhard-hearted lady for
a young man to trust unto'—though he assured Lady Walgrave
that brother John was in fact incapable of not trusting her. At
these words she ceased to demand the return of the musk-ball;
'wherefore do ye with it as ye like. I would it had done well; by
God, I spake for you so, that in faith I trow I could not say so well
again. I send you herewith your ring and the unhappy musk-ball'.
The effort had exhausted Sir John: 'make ye matter of it hereafter
as ye can; I am not happy to woo neither for myself nor none
other.'

Two years passed and young John, in May of 1476, was still
alerting his brother to the chase: 'I understand that Mistress
Fitzwalter hath a sister, a maid, to marry. I trow . . . she might
come into Christian men's hands.' But the marriage hunt was

almost over for John Paston: he was about to find not only a
bride but something he had apparently never bargained for, love.
The girl was Margery Brews, daughter of Sir Thomas Brews,[1]
a well-known figure in Norfolk with whom John Paston must
have been acquainted all his life. But somehow Sir Thomas's
eldest daughter had grown to womanhood without his being
aware. John's friend Richard Stratton had first spoken of her,
and spoken so enthusiastically that John, some time in the latter
part of 1476, plumed up his courage and his pen and wrote her a
letter that Richard engaged to deliver:

'Mistress, though so be that I, unacquainted with you as yet,
take upon me to be thus bold to write unto you without your
knowledge and leave, yet, mistress . . . I beseech you to pardon
my boldness, and not to disdain, but to accept this simple bill to
recommend me to you. . . . I have heard oft times Richard
Stratton say that ye can and will take everything well that is well
meant. . . . Mistress, I beseech you to think none otherwise in
me . . . but that I am and will be yours and at your commandment
in every wise during my life. Here I send you this bill written
with my lewd [ignorant] hand and sealed with my signet to
remain with you for a witness against me and to my shame and
dishonour if I contrary it. . . .'

John and Margery met and spoke and fell in love. Sir Thomas
Brews looked askance at John Paston's meagre portion; but
delays and bargaining added romantic poignancy to the courtship instead of dominating it. The Brews were much more openly
affectionate with their children than the Pastons, and Margery was
her father's and mother's favourite. Though Sir Thomas meant
to see that his daughter received her due in worldly state, he
treated young John very kindly and clearly approved of him as a
son-in-law.

Dame Elizabeth Brews was love's advocate itself. Early in the
courtship she wrote secretly to John to report the disposition of
her husband, to suggest what help John might ask of his mother,
and to encourage his ardour. 'And, cousin, that day that she

---

[1] On one occasion he was elected to Parliament along with Sir John Howard; see
Chapter 6 for an account of their campaign tactics.

[Margery] is married, my father will give her 50 mark. But and we accord, I shall give you a greater treasure, that is, a witty gentlewoman, and if I say it, both good and virtuous; for if I should take money for her, I would not give her for £1,000; but, cousin, I trust you so much that I should think her well beset on you and ye were worth much more.' Early in February of 1477, Dame Elizabeth, mindful of the season, invited John to pass a weekend at the Brews country seat at Topcroft. She made no attempt to conceal Margery's feelings: 'Ye have made her such advocate for you, that I may never have rest night nor day, for calling and crying upon to bring the said matter to effect, etc. And, cousin, upon Friday is St. Valentine's Day, and every bird chooseth him a mate; and if it like you to come on Thursday at night and abide till Monday, I trust to God that ye shall so speak to my husband that we shall bring the matter to a conclusion; for, cousin,

> It is but a simple oak
> That is cut down at the first stroke.'

Soon a letter arrived from Margery herself, and once we hear her voice, we understand why John fell in love with her. She felt too deeply and she was too honest to make use of even a shred of feminine wiles: 'Right reverend and worshipful and my right wellbeloved Valentine . . . if it please you to hear of my welfare, I am not in good health of body, nor of heart, nor shall be till I hear from you:

> For there wots no creature what pain that I endure
> And for to be dead I dare it not 'dyscure' [discover].

And my lady my mother hath laboured the matter to my father full diligently, but she can no more get than ye know of, for the which God knoweth I am full sorry. But if that ye love me, as I trust verily that ye do, ye will not leave me therefore; for if that ye had not half the livelode that ye have, for to do [though I might have to do] the greatest labour that any woman alive might, I would not forsake you.'

Though John had promised Dame Elizabeth not to add fuel to
the fire by writing to Margery until a financial settlement was
agreed upon, this letter elicited from him an enthusiastic acceptance
of the Valentine invitation, to which Margery replied at once to
express her joy 'that ye be purposed to come to Topcroft in short
time, without any errand or matter but only to have a conclusion
betwixt my father and you. And as for myself, I have done in the
matter that I can or may, as God knoweth; and I let you plainly
understand that my father will no more money part withal on
that behalf [i.e., for the dowry] but £100 and 50 marks, which is
right far from the accomplishment of your desire.

'Wherefore, if that ye could be content with that good, and my
poor person, I would be the merriest maiden on ground; and if ye
think not yourself so satisfied, or that ye might have much more
good, as I understand by you afore; good, true, and loving
valentine, take no such labour upon you as to come more for
that matter but let it pass and never more to be spoken of, as I
may be your true lover and bedewoman during my life.'

Perhaps at Dame Elizabeth's or Margery's urging, a friend of
the Brew's family, one Thomas Kela, now took a hand by
writing an encouraging letter to young John Paston: 'Right
worshipful sir, I recommend me unto you, letting you know, as
for the young gentlewoman she oweth you her good heart and
love, as I know by the communication that I have had with her
for the same.

'And, sir, ye know what my master and my lady hath proffered
with her, 200 marks. And I daresay that her chamber and raiment
[trousseau] shall be worth 100 marks. And I heard my lady say,
that, and the case required, both ye and she should have your
board with my lady three years after. And I heard my lady say,

> That it was a feeble oak
> That was cut down at the first stroke.'

Apparently the Valentine's weekend was a happy one, except
for concluding the marriage settlement. In early March, John was
back at Topcroft, writing excitedly to arrange a meeting between

Margaret Paston and Dame Elizabeth at Norwich. 'Mother, the matter is in a reasonable good way . . . for I trow there is not a kinder woman living than I shall have to my mother-in-law, if the matter take, nor yet a kinder father-in-law than I shall have, though he be hard to me as yet.' John was having the Paston place in Norwich stocked with ale and bread for her arrival on the Wednesday; he wanted Dame Elizabeth to be invited to 'dine in your house on Thursday, for there should ye have most secret talking'. He experienced an unusual flurry of anxiety about his mother's health: 'Beware that ye take no cold by the way towards Norwich, for it is the most perilous March that ever was seen by any that now liveth.' The next day John sent word to his brother Sir John at Calais that 'touching myself and mistress Margery Brews, I am yet at no certainty, her father is so hard; but I trow I have the good will of my lady her mother and her. . . .' He rapidly touched on a number of other matters, concluding, 'I pray you pardon me of my writing, howsoever it be, for carpenters of my craft that I use now, have not their wits their own'.

Shortly thereafter love's heaven clouded over. Sir Thomas was willing to offer 300 marks of dowry and board the couple for three years if necessary, provided that John could secure from his family the manor of Swainsthorpe; and he was even willing to use the dowry money he had saved for his other daughters to lend John the £120 that would purchase the manor. But he insisted that he must be repaid by John's family or friends and not by John himself out of his own goods or the marriage portion.

Margaret Paston was willing to squeeze some money from her manors. Sir John had responded to first news of the courtship with blithe approval: 'Bykerton telleth me that she loveth you well. If I died, I had rather ye had her than the Lady Walgrave; nevertheless she singeth well with an harp.' But after his mother had asked him to help the lovers and young John had twice applied to him and he had heard from other sources that he was rumoured to be playing the niggard to his brother, Sir John replied angrily to the man who had risked his life to hold Caister Castle for him, 'You need not to pray me oftener than once to do what might be to your profit and worship'. Item by item he demolished the notion that he had resources available to help satisfy Sir Thomas Brews' demands. He added, in a burst of irritation, 'I need not to make this excuse to you, but that your mind is troubled', and proceeded to work himself into a state of poorly concealed self-justification mingled with reproaches masquerading as a high moral attitude: 'I pray you rejoice not yourself too much in hope to obtain thing that all your friends may not ease you of; for if my mother were disposed to give me and any woman in England the best manor that she hath . . . I would not take it of her, by God.

'Stablish yourself upon a good ground and grace shall follow. Your matter is far spoken of and blown wide, and if it prove no better, I would that it had never been spoken of. Also that matter noiseth me [the affair has generated gossip] that I am so unkind that I let all together [I alone am preventing the match]. I think not a matter happy, nor well handled, nor politickly dealt with, when it can never be finished without an inconvenience. . . . If I were at the beginning of such a matter, I would have hoped to have made a better conclusion, if they mock you not. This matter is driven thus far forth without my counsel, I pray you make an end without my counsel. If it be well, I would be glad; if it be otherwise, it is a pity. I pray you trouble me no more in this matter. . . .'[1]

It was hard. Sir John was getting on for forty; he suffered bouts of illness and was always harried by debt; and now young John, his pupil in the marriage hunt, had ungratefully managed to find for himself the very mate, as everybody kept dinning into Sir John's ears. Besides, the elder brother probably realized that he would never marry and could not suppress a jealous pang that John and Margery were destined in the end to possess his all. He soon began to come round, however, and wrote to his mother that he had no objections to John's being given the manor of

---

[1] The rhetoric of this passage indicates that a scholarly reputation remains to be made in showing that Shakespeare had access to the Paston letters or, more probably, that the plays were written about one hundred years earlier than is generally supposed, perhaps by a secretary in Sir John Paston's employ. The latter thesis is all but proved by the fact that an Alicia Langham of Snaylwell, Suffolk—*the Pastons owned a manor of Snaylwell* (maladroitly located in Cambridgeshire)—left 12d in her will, dated 1451, to the pauper of Snaylwell, one William Shakespeare.

Swainsthorpe, though he refused to obligate himself to Sir Thomas. Feeling that he had put himself in an ungracious light, he promised John, 'I shall be to Sir Thomas Brews and my lady his wife a very son-in-law for your sake and take them as ye do, and do for them as if I were in case like with them as ye be'.

But spring wore away and the marriage was no nearer. Sir Thomas was apparently not yet satisfied by the attitude of Sir John, head of the Paston family. Then in June the two mothers came together again at Norwich. When Margery's father still proved obdurate, John in a fever of stratagems dictated a long letter for his mother to send to Dame Elizabeth and a second letter for her to send to himself which he might show to the Brews. In early August, Sir John had so softened that he was offering to be of some help; though he was still making clear that if his practised hand had manipulated the negotiations, difficulties would have melted away. By that time, however, love had somehow conquered; John was conspiratorially scribbling memoranda to himself like 'to keep secret from my mother that the bargain is full concluded'; and before autumn was very far advanced, he had won and wedded his Margery in a ceremony which passed unnoticed in the Paston letters.

Margery, married, loses not a jot of her charm. Her first surviving letter to her husband, of December 18, 1477, begins with the accustomed formality of the age, 'Right reverend and worshipful husband, I recommend me to you, desiring heartily to hear of your welfare'; then goes on to detail the gowns and the girdles that she needs for the winter. But she soon works into her own vein: she needs a girdle badly, 'for I am waxed so fetis [fashionable] that I may not be girt in no girdle that I have but one. . . . John of Damme was here, and my mother discovered me to him, and he said, by his troth that he was not gladder of no thing that he heard this twelvemonth than he was thereof.

'I may no longer live by my craft, I am discovered of all men that see me.

'I pray you that ye will wear the ring with the image of St. Margaret that I sent you for a remembrance, till ye come home; ye have left me such a remembrance, that maketh me to think upon you both day and night when I would sleep.' All men who read the Paston letters must fall a little in love with Margery, gay and witty and loving. So she continued to the end—she died in 1495—as irresistible as when she entertained John Paston for a Valentine's weekend. Her few remaining letters are called forth by John's sojourns in London, to which she never became reconciled.

In November of 1482 she wrote him a budget of news headed by the usual formal salutation, but towards the close she could not keep back her feeling: 'I marvel I hear no word from you, which grieveth me full evilly,' and she added a postscript, 'Sir, I pray you, if ye tarry long at London, that it will please you to send for me, for I think long since I lay in your arms.' John's family was growing; Margery reports the good health of 'all your babies'. Two days after, she was writing to him again, and this time formal salutation collapsed into 'Mine own sweetheart, in my most humble wise' etc. John was again in London two years later and Margery sent him on Christmas Eve her last surviving letter: 'I am sorry that ye shall not at home be for Christmas. I pray you that ye will come as soon as ye may. I shall think myself half a widow because ye shall not be at home.'

Meantime, the marriage hunt swept on. Less than six months after he was married, John was doing for his brother Edmund what Sir John had once done for him: 'I heard while I was in London,' he wrote to his mother, 'where was a goodly young woman to marry. . . .' Three years later, Edmund, who had married the widow of William Clippesby in the meanwhile, had begun to hunt for his younger brother William: 'Here is lately fallen a widow in Worsted,' he wrote hastily to William, 'which was wife to one Bolt, a Worsted merchant and worth £1,000. . . . I will for your sake see her' etc. etc. Our view of the marriage hunt is cut off in the early 1490's with Edmund Paston prospecting for John's eldest son. 'Merchants or new gentlemen I deem will proffer large,' wrote the great-grandson of Clement Paston, yeoman.

The Paston letters record a more turbulent love match than that of Margery and John, one that is almost the stuff of ballads. In the troubled spring of 1450, Thomas Denyes, a lawyer in the Earl of Oxford's household, fell headlong in love with a Norfolk widow named Agnes. She was worth better than 500 marks, but there seems no question that Thomas Denyes was moved by passion rather than calculation. From then on he was little use to the Earl of Oxford, whose seat at Wivenhoe, Essex, was much too far away from Norwich. The Earl proved sympathetic and wrote to John Paston requesting him to 'move' the gentlewoman in Denyes' behalf, for she had apparently not given Thomas much encouragement. Oxford promised to 'show our bounty to them both if it please her that this matter take effect', and he offered graciously to visit Agnes himself if it would forward Denyes's suit. The lady might have looked higher, but Oxford's 'good lordship', John Paston's labours, and Denyes's impassioned siege of her heart won the day.

A few years later a man named Ingham and his son Walter laid claim to some of Agnes' property. The mercurial Denyes plotted a revenge which even by the standards of that time was foolhardy in the extreme. He forged a letter from the Earl of Oxford to Walter Ingham, requesting Ingham to come to Wivenhoe. Then Denyes hired ruffians and set an ambush on the road which he knew Ingham would travel. The unfortunate man was set upon, beaten so viciously that he was apparently left for dead, and for the rest of his days went on crutches.

The Earl of Oxford was furiously angry at being so compromised and saw to it that the law moved promptly. Denyes was clapped into Fleet Prison, his servants and friends were harried, and his wife, who was with child, was thrown into Newgate. From the Fleet, Denyes wrote frantic letters to John Paston begging for help. To his credit, his anguish was all for the suffering of his Agnes: 'In augmenting of my sorrow I weened my wife should have died, for after she was arrested she laboured of her child, waiting either to die or be delivered, and she hath not gone eight weeks quick.' Fortunately, the warden of Fleet Prison managed to get the poor woman temporarily admitted to bail. John Paston had no sympathy with Denyes but he was moved by the wife's plight and risked writing to the incensed Earl to remind him that after all the match had been made by his good offices and that therefore he and Paston himself owed the lady their aid: 'If she be destroyed by this marriage, my conscience thinketh I am bound to recompense her after my poor and simple power. . . . For God's love, my Lord, remember how the gentlewoman is encumbered only for your sake and help her.' John Paston must have been of some assistance, for 'Woeful Denyes', as he signed himself, wrote an incoherent letter of mingled thanks and appeals: 'Ever I beseech your mastership . . . that ye like to do my wife help and comfort in her disease [trouble]; for if she were not, God knoweth I should soon shift [die]. And truly I have no thought nor sorrow but for her. I pray you, succour my wife, for she is widow yet for me and shall be till more is done. . . .'

Somehow Thomas Denyes managed to wriggle out of his difficulties. By 1461 he had become a good Yorkist; he apparently fought for Edward IV at Towton, for he was at York immediately after with the Yorkist army. He made complaints to King Edward about a Norfolk man named Twyer. Twyer was sufficiently powerful that he did not have to depend upon the law, like Walter Ingham. When Denyes returned to Norfolk, a band of armed men, led by the sinister Parson of Snoring, dragged him from his house, carried him off to a place near Walsingham, and murdered him. The Parson of Snoring and four of his accomplices were set in the stocks, but Denyes' murderers apparently never stood trial.

The most poignant love match recorded in this age blossomed secretly in the very bosom of the Paston family. A few years after the Pastons had finally married the unhappy Elizabeth to Robert Poynings they began to look for a husband for Margery, the eldest daughter of John and Margaret. In September of 1465 John Paston the younger asked his mother, then in London, to visit the Rood of the North door of St. Paul's and the Abbey of St. Saviour, Bermondsey, 'and let my sister Margery go with you to pray to them that she may have a good husband ere she come home again. . . .'

About the year 1467 J. Strange of Norwich began negotiating for Margery's hand for his nephew John who could offer her a

£40 jointure and an inheritance of 200 marks. But by this time Margery, unbeknownst to her parents, had fallen in love; and she had looked no farther than her father's household. She had been secretly wooed and won by Richard Calle, the able young bailiff of the family lands. Well educated, he owned an establishment of some sort at Framlingham, the principal seat of the Duke of Norfolk, whose father had originally recommended him to John Paston, and if the Pastons did not look upon him as gentry, he probably considered himself a gentleman—an ambiguity of rank typical of the fifteenth century. When Richard was away tending to the Pastons' complex affairs, he wrote letters to Margery to keep his love warm. Finally, when the two of them managed to steal a moment alone, the girl pledged her troth to him, an irrevocable step.

Honourably Richard informed Margaret Paston of his love for her daughter. She indignantly refused to listen to him. Margery was whisked out of his sight and so bullied by the family that she showed them some of Calle's letters. Richard Calle then informed the Pastons that he and Margery had plighted troth and that nothing could stand in the way of their marriage. Margaret Paston, already harried by a larger crisis in her affairs, badgered her daughter to declare that she had given no such engagement, and for a time the frightened girl could not bring herself to confirm her lover's word.

The revelation of the troth-plight could not have come at a worse time. During this spring of 1469 the Duke of Norfolk was openly preparing to lay siege to Caister, young John Paston was holding the castle with a handful of men, and in London Sir John anxiously sought to win the support of influential lords. In this taut moment of edgy nerves, Richard Calle persuaded a friend of his to sound young John Paston indirectly on the subject of his claim to Margery's hand; and the friend, it appears, misled Calle by a false optimism so that he ventured to write to Sir John, indicating that young John had given his approval to the match.

Sir John exploded in a letter to his brother; young John forcefully denied that Calle had had any comfort of him: 'I conceive . . . that ye have heard of R.C.'s labour which he maketh by our ungracious sister's assent; but whereas they write that they have my goodwill therein, saving your reverence, they falsely lie of it.' Young John had told Calle's friend that though 'my father, whom God assoil, were alive and had consented thereto, and my mother, and ye both, he should never have my good will for to make my sister to sell candle and mustard in Framlingham. . . .'

What must have especially exasperated the family was that Richard Calle was never more indispensable than at this moment. He was, in fact, making his headquarters at Caister with young John. Not long after the latter had penned his indignant letter to his brother, Calle also wrote to Sir John. He made no further mention of himself and Margery but he quietly underlined his service to the family by itemizing all that he was doing to gather money and keep the wheels of the household turning; and he did not scruple to add, 'and of all this twelvemonth I have not had one penny for my wages'. The situation had become intolerable for Richard. Only Margery could loose herself and him from the toils of frustration in which they writhed. Somehow he managed to smuggle a letter to her.

'Mine own lady and mistress, and before God very true wife, I with heart full sorrowful recommend me unto you, as he that cannot be merry, nor nought shall be till it be otherwise with us than it is yet, for this life that we lead now is neither pleasure to God nor to the world, considering the great bond of matrimony that is made betwixt us, and also the great love that hath been and as I trust yet is betwixt us, and as on my part never greater; wherefore I beseech almighty God comfort us as soon as it pleaseth him, for we that ought of very right to be most together are most asunder; me seemeth it is a thousand years ago since that I spake with you. I had liever than all the goods in the world I might be with you. Alas, alas! good lady, full little remember they what they do that keep us asunder; four times in the year are they accursed that let matrimony; it causeth many men to deem in them they have large conscience [i.e., easy morality] in other matters as well as herein. . . .

'I understand, Lady, ye have had as much sorrow for me as any gentlewoman hath in the world; would God all that sorrow that ye have had had rested upon me, so that ye had been discharged of it, for i-wis [truly], Lady, it is to me a death to hear that ye be treated otherwise than ye ought to be. This is a painful life that we lead. I cannot live thus without it be a great displeasure to God. . . .

'I had sent you a letter by my lad, and he told me he might not speak with you, there was made so great await [watch] upon him and upon you both. [Then] John Threscher came to him in your name and said that ye sent him to my lad for a letter or a token which I should have sent you [i.e., via the boy], but he trusted him [Threscher] not; he would not deliver him none. After that he [Threscher] brought him a ring, saying that ye sent it him, commanding him that he should deliver the letter or token to him [Threscher], which I conceive since by my lad it was not by your sending, it was by my mistress's and Sir James [Gloys's scheming].

'Alas, what mean they? I suppose they deem we be not insured together [betrothed], and if they so do I marvel, for then they are not well advised, remembering the plainness that I broke to my mistress at the beginning, and I suppose [by you broken also, if] ye did as ye ought to do of very right; and if ye have done the contrary, as I have been informed ye have done, ye did neither conscientiously nor to the pleasure of God, without ye did it for fear, and for the time [i.e., under pressure of circumstances] to please such as were at that time about you; and if ye so did it for this service it was a reasonable cause, considering the great and importable calling upon [harrying] that ye had, and many an untrue tale was made to you of me, which God knows I was never guilty of. . . .

'I suppose, and ye tell them sadly [earnestly] the truth, they would not damn their souls for us. Though I tell them the truth, they will not believe me as well as they will do you; and therefore, good lady, at the reverence of God be plain to them and tell the truth, and if they will in no wise agree thereto, betwixt God, the Devil, and them be it, and that peril that we should be in, I beseech God it may lie upon them and not upon us. . . .'

Richard strove to hearten Margery by reminding her that whatever the Pastons did, 'this matter is in such case as it cannot be remedied', and with simple dignity he asserted that, considering what he deserved of the family, 'there should be no obstacle against it'. If Sir John and his brother were so much concerned about status, let them look to their own marriages, for 'the worshipful that is in them is not in your marriage'.

Margery now plucked up her courage and announced plainly that she was betrothed to Richard Calle. The moment her lover found out that she had proved true, he complained to the Bishop of Norwich that whom God had joined together the Pastons were trying to keep apart. The Bishop, a friend of the family, sympathized with their point of view and ignored the appeal; but Richard Calle and Richard's friends gave him no peace. Reluctantly he sent word that Margery should be brought before him. Her mother enlisted the aid of the fearsome Agnes to delay matters until the girl was browbeaten into submission. Nobody knew better than Margaret Paston that in the eyes of the Church troth-plighting was as binding as matrimony itself. Ironically enough, only a few months before, when she heard that Sir John had engaged himself to Mistress Anne Haute, she had written to him that toward 'God ye are as greatly bound to her as [if] ye were married, and therefore I charge you upon my blessing that ye be as true to her as [if] she were married unto you in all degrees'.

August was now reaching its end. Richard and Margery's little drama of true love was being played against the background of a realm shaken by alarums of war. Warwick the Kingmaker had defeated the King's friends in battle and taken the King captive. The land quaked with rumours and uprisings. And now the young Duke of Norfolk, calling up his tenants and followers by the hundreds and sending for guns from Yarmouth, at last laid siege to Caister Castle.

At this critical moment in the Paston affairs, the Bishop of Norwich finally insisted that Margery be brought before him for examination. In vain did Margaret and Agnes seek to postpone matters until all of John Paston's executors could be called together 'for they had the rule of her as well'; and Sir John Paston, desperately seeking help for Caister, could only write darkly to Margaret that he would divorce the lovers by one means or the other. When the ladies called upon the Bishop, 'he said plainly that he had been required so often for to examine her that he might not now nor would no longer delay it, and charged me, on pain of cursing, that she should not be deferred but that she should appear before him the next day'. The angry mother answered flatly that she 'would neither bring her nor send her; and then he said that he would send for her himself, and charged that she should be at her liberty to come when he sent for her'. The Bishop made it clear, Margaret explained to Sir John, that he too was shocked by Margery's conduct and hoped that she would deny the engagement, 'for he woost well that her demeaning had sticked sore at our hearts'.

Next day Margery was brought to the Episcopal Palace. Calle had been summoned also, but the two were not permitted to see each other. The Bishop felt no compunction about putting pressure on the girl to deny her vow; before he judged by the canons of the Church he permitted himself to speak in the language of the world. He 'said to her right plainly and put her in remembrance how she was born, what kin and friends that she had, and should have more if she were ruled and guided after them; and what rebuke and shame and loss it should be to her if she were not guided by them'. He ended by telling her that she ran the awful risk of being outcast from her family, friends, and position. Then he asked her to tell him precisely the words that she and Richard Calle had used to each other.

Margery had taken her life in her hands now and did not falter. After she repeated the oath she and Richard had sworn, she boldly added that 'if those words made it not sure', she would say whatever had to be said to make it sure 'ere she went thence, for she said she thought in her conscience she was bound, whatsoever the words were'. Margaret confessed to Sir John that 'these lewd words grieveth me and her grandma [Agnes] as much as all remnant'. The Bishop did not like it either; he told Margery, and so did his chancellor, 'that there was neither I nor no friend of her would receive her'. But Margery was not to be shaken. 'Then Calle was examined apart by himself' to see if 'her words and his accorded, and the time, and where it should have been done'.

The stories agreed. The words were binding. The Bishop did what little he could for the family: despite Calle's protests he declared that, in case other impediments might be found, he would postpone giving final judgement until after Michaelmas (September 29).

The moment the hearing was over, a messenger hastened to bring the news to Margaret Paston, waiting at Agnes' place in Norwich. 'When I heard say what her demeaning was, I charged my servants that she should not be received in my house. I had given her warning, she might have been aware therefore, if she had been gracious.' In her bitterness Margaret Paston went so far as to send to some of her friends in Norwich asking them not to receive the girl if she applied to them. When Margery was escorted to the Paston door, Sir James Gloys gave himself the pleasure of turning her away. The Bishop of Norwich then placed her at the home of Roger Best until his decision should be announced. Margaret Paston was sorry 'that they are encumbered with her' but she took a savage satisfaction in the fact that such upright people would not treat Margery leniently. 'I pray you', she ended her mournful recital to Sir John, 'that ye take it not pensively, for I wot well it goeth right near your heart, and so doth it to mine and to other; but remember you, and so do I, that we have lost of her but a brethele [a worthless one]. . . .' Even if 'he [Calle] were dead at this hour, she should never be at mine heart as she was'.

Though the Duke of Norfolk grudgingly took the Pastons under his protection after he had won Caister, the family and their friends and tenants were menaced daily by Norfolk's 'gallants'. Richard Calle, however, remained loyal. He refused to gather any more money from the Paston lands unless he was specifically requested to do so; he made known that he stood ready to deliver all the account books and leases and other important estate papers in his possession; but he sent word to Margaret Paston, she reported to Sir John, that 'he will not take no new master till ye refuse his service'. The Bishop pronounced his judgement that Margery and Richard were indissolubly engaged. Richard then retired with the girl to Blackborough nunnery, near Lynn, until the banns had been pronounced and they could be married.

The Pastons realized that they could not do without Richard Calle's services. From London, Sir John even wrote home mildly that he wished the marriage of Richard and Margery to be delayed until the Christmas season. Margery's name never again appears in the Paston correspondence, and Sir John and young John finally broke with their bailiff; but for many long years Richard Calle continued to be of service to Margaret Paston. Upon her death in 1484, she bequeathed £20 to the eldest of the three sons of 'Margery my daughter'. His name was John.

Wives

WHAT the Victorians and subsequent generations have called home
life existed in the fifteenth century only among the humbler
classes. The young couple whose destinies had been linked by
parental arrangement settled down to create not a home but a
household. The attitudes of the age did not encourage privacy,
intimacy, or demonstrations of affection; households were frequently on the move or scattered; and the business of living,
among the merchants and gentry, often required husbands and
wives to be apart.

The King and his lords moved from manor to manor, as they
had for centuries, to keep watch upon their lands and to consume
the produce thereof; it was easier to bring the household to the
estate than to transport the yield of the estate to the household;
besides, at periodic intervals sewage had to be removed from the
cellar pits which lay below the 'garderobes' and castles 'sweetened'
before they could be again comfortably lived in.

On a smaller scale, the upper classes in town and country
emulated the nobles. Families like the Celys shuttled back and
forth between their manors and their London dwellings and
offices. The Stonors and the Plumptons and the Pastons shifted
households from estate to estate, paused in a nearby town to spend
a season, came up to London for shopping and legal business. Sir
John Howard owned places in Colchester, Harwich, and the
capital; the Pastons possessed two dwellings in Norwich and
property in London. In the last years of his life John Paston appears
to have spent more time on the banks of the Thames than at home
in the country. When powerful men were trying to tear pieces

from the Paston holdings, a Paston son held down one manor, John's wife Margaret maintained possession of another, while John himself fought the legal battle in London.

When Sir William Stonor was looking after his sheep in Oxfordshire or riding into the West Country to survey his property there, his wife Elizabeth spent weeks at a time in London keeping an eye on his business interests. She had London in her blood, for she was the daughter of an alderman, grand-daughter of a famous mayor and chronicler, William Gregory, widow of a wealthy mercer, and sister-in-law of Sir William Stocker, knighted by Edward IV for the part he played in the defence of London in the spring of 1471. Elizabeth had probably brought about the partnership between the Stonors and Thomas Betson, Merchant of the Staple, which Sir William found very profitable. Enjoying her new role of landed lady, she proudly described to her husband how she had waited upon the King's sister Elizabeth, Duchess of Suffolk, when the Duchess called upon her 'lady mother' (Cicely of York), and she maintained a 'menie of boys' and indulged in other extravagances for which Thomas Betson gently chided her; but she seems to have been most herself when she sojourned in the city to further the operations of the partnership. Coming from the manor of Stonor, she was sometimes met at Windsor by Thomas; they had a merry journey to London—so Betson reported to her husband—and Sir William sent up venison and boar to grace their table.

Husbands and wives, or either of them when the other was absent, 'broke up household' on occasion and became 'sojournants'. Sometimes they 'went to board' in London or a provincial town; sometimes they found quarters in an abbey; sometimes they took up residence in the manor house of a friend or kinsman or anyone who would have them. John Paston's brother William wrote to his nephew Sir John, in April of 1467, that Margaret Paston and a friend, James Arblaster, and 'I have appointed that we shall keep no household this term [in London], but go to board; wherefore we advise you to purvey for us a lodging near about my Lord Chancellor[1] that be honest, for Arblaster will none

---

[1] Warwick's brother George, Archbishop of York, who had a mansion near Charing Cross.

other. Item, as for you . . . get your chamber assigned within my Lord's place, and get chamber alone if ye may, that Arblaster and I may have a bed therein if it fortune us to be late with you there'.

While King Edward invaded France in the summer of 1475, his mother Cicely, Duchess of York, settled with all her household at the Abbey of St. Bennet, Holme, Norfolk, and announced that she would remain till the King 'came from beyond the sea, and longer if she liked the air there'. Barons and their wives did not think it beneath their dignity to 'go to board', and it was not unusual even for wealthy gentry like the Stonors to take such boarders. On one occasion, though, Jane Stonor wrote hastily to her husband that Lord Morley desired to lodge with them but she did not want him, declaring that she would rather 'break up household than take sojournants, for servants be not so diligent as they were wont to be'.

Fifteenth-century families, it seems, were restless and liked change, but sometimes their removes were dictated by economy. After Margaret Paston had strained her resources, in the autumn of 1469, to aid her son Sir John, she angrily sent word to him from Norwich that 'it is noised that I have departed [shared] so largely with you that I may neither help you, myself, nor none of my friends; which is no worship, and causeth men to set the less by us; and at this time it compelleth me to break up household and to sojourn; which I am right loath to have to do if I might otherwise have chosen, for it caused great clamour in this town that I shall do so'.

However intimate and affectionate the relations between husband and wife, the etiquette of the times demanded a formality that echoed their positions as master and mistress of a household. Following the requirements of 'common form', Margaret Paston began her letters to John, 'Right worshipful husband, I recommend me to you, desiring heartily to hear of your welfare'. The husband was the lord of the family as the King was the lord of the realm and God was the lord of life. Obedience to him was a law of nature; the Scriptures enjoined it and the Church preached it. The cardinal virtue and the prime duty of a wife was submissiveness. If a husband became angry or dissatisfied, it was to be assumed that the wife had failed in her function:

> That man that shall ye wed before God with a ring,
> Love thou him and honour most of earthly thing;
> Meekly give him answer, and not as an attirling [vicious one],
> And so mayest thou slake his mood, and be his dear darling.

Such is the burden of all the handbooks and verses of instruction. The wife must be tuned like an Aeolian harp to respond to the slightest breeze of her husband's will or whim.

At only one moment did she withdraw into a world of her own, when she was about to give birth to a child. Whether she was the Queen or a great lady like the Duchess of Norfolk or a squire's wife, she gathered midwives and her favourite waiting-women about her and took to her chamber with doors and windows shut and a hot fire burning. Men, even physicians, were excluded from this rite, which often began several days before the baby was born. When Queen Elizabeth was expecting her first child—the Princess Elizabeth—one of the royal physicians named Master Dominic assured Edward IV that 'the Queen was conceived with a prince'; and so positive was Master Dominic that 'by his counsel great provision was ordained for christening the said prince'. In order 'to have great thank and reward of the King', he stationed himself in the Queen's privy chamber so that he might be first with the joyful tidings. 'When he heard the child cry, he knocked or called secretly at the chamber door and asked what the Queen had. To whom it was answered by one of the ladies, whatsoever the queen's grace hath here within, sure it is that a fool standeth there without.'

If the manuals of manners insist that a wife must find her destiny within the character of Patient Griselda, the life of the age itself reveals that women, even as they were bringing child after child into the world—and mourning the early demise of several of them —were often the sturdy partners of their husbands' enterprises.

In the world of the towns, wives played an active part in business. When Margaret Paston wanted her menfolk to purchase cloth for her in the capital, she told them to go to 'Huy's wife', whose wares were cheapest and best. Wives of well-to-do London merchants had almost a monopoly of embroidering and garnishing cloth with jewellery and of the manufacture of silken girdles and other finery made of silk; their businesses were so flourishing that they were able to demand a premium of £5 of their girl-apprentices. Dame Elizabeth Stokton finished cloth for export to Italy. Widows not infrequently carried on their husbands' enterprises and prospered. One lady, managing a large import-export trade, earned the admiration of London by her shrewd, tough dealing. A fishmonger's heiress, four times married, went in for tailoring and brewing; the widow of a fishmonger owned a metal shop. Margery Kemp, married to one of the wealthiest merchants of Lynn, confessed that she could not bear any other wife to 'be arrayed so well as she'; and so she started a brewing business and then bought a horse-mill for the grinding of corn. Among the lower orders, wives often added to the family income by becoming brewers, bakers, and tavern-keepers; and it is sad to relate that they were every bit as celebrated for their short weights and false quarts as their masculine rivals. The unfortunate Bishop Pecock, condemned for heresy, declared that, if a husband so desired it, a wife should use her spare time in contributing to the support of the household.

For better or worse, towns generally recognized the independence of married women in business. At Worcester and elsewhere husbands were exempted from financial liability in case their wives were sued as a consequence of their dealings. The wife was 'sole merchant'. When a married man was to be made a citizen of York, he appeared with his wife and both of them were admitted as 'free burgesses'. As in all ages, some husbands found their spouses only too masterful: 'Ulveston is steward of the Middle Inn [of the Temple] and Isley of the Inner Inn, because they would have offices for excuse for dwelling this time from their wives.'

The wife of an ambitious yeoman, joining field to field, or of a landed squire like John Paston carried on a year-long campaign to keep her people fed and clothed. Gone were the mediaeval days when manors had to be almost entirely self-sufficient; but the household still brewed its ale and baked its bread, and the provident mistress had always to be planning for the future. In November enough meat to last over the winter must be salted and fish for the Lenten season laid in. 'Mistress, it were good to remember your stuff of herring this fishing time,' Richard Calle reminded Margaret Paston one autumn. 'You shall do more now with 40s than you shall at Christmas with five marks [66s 8d].' In the course of one month a manor household of modest size consumed 8 quarters [4 bushels] of wheat, 18 quarters of barley and malt brewed into ale, 3 beeves, 6 pigs, 22 sheep, 2 lambs, 1 capon, 333 pigeons, 1 heron, 460 white [pickled] herrings, 18 salt fish, 6 stockfish.

Many households no longer wove their own cloth, but wives and waiting-women had to make up cloth into clothing not only for the family but for servants as well; at least one gown or a livery jacket was usually included in yearly wages. Often the shops of a nearby town could not supply what was needed. 'As touching your liveries,' Margaret Paston reported to her husband from Norwich, 'there can none be got here of the colour that you would have, neither murrey, nor blue, nor good russets, below 3s a yard at the lowest price, and even so there is not enough of one cloth and colour to serve you.' As for buying in Suffolk, nothing was to be got there unless 'they had had warning at Michaelmas, as I am informed'.

Fortunately, the institution of the common carrier had opened up to manor-dwellers the world of goods that might be purchased in London, so that a pregnant wife, though buried deep in the country, could write her husband to send oranges and dates 'by the next carrier'. Wives of the gentry forwarded intricate shopping lists to their men in London. Jane Stonor would bid her husband remember 'the gentian, rhubarb, bays, silk, laces, treacle'. Barges taking four or fives days to make the trip brought Stonor purchases to Henley: rushes, spices, a basket of glass, gowns, a mustard quern, fish, wine.

Margaret Paston sent instructions 'to buy me three yards of purple schamlet, price the yard 4s; a bonnet of deep murrey, price

2s 4d; a hose-cloth of yellow kersey of an ell. I trow it will cost 2s; a girdle of plunket ribbon, price 6d; 4 laces of silk, 2 of one colour and 2 of another, price 8d; 3 dozen points with red and yellow, price 6d; 3 pair of pattens [work shoes]. . . . I was wont to pay but 2½d for a pair, but I pray you let them not be left behind though I pay more; they must be low pattens; let them be long enough and broad upon the heel'.

Sir John Paston was much concerned on one occasion about three pots of treacle he was dispatching to Norfolk: 'There is one pot that is marked under the bottom 2 times with these letters M.P., which pot I have best trust unto; and next him, to the "wryghe" pot; and I mistrust most the pot that hath a "krotte" above in the top, lest that he hath been undone. And also the other 2 pots be printed with that merchant's mark two times on the covering, and that other pot is but once marked but with one print; notwithstanding, I had like oath and promise for one as well as for all.'

Robin Plumpton, bastard son of Sir William, found himself floundering in mercantile meshes when shopping one April in London for his Yorkshire family. To begin with, Sir William wanted to pay as little as possible for a cope, probably for the chaplain of his chapel, and he expected an embroiderer to come all the way from London to work for him: 'As for your cope, I have cheaped diverse [bargained widely], and under a hundred shillings I can buy none that is either of damask or satin with flowers of gold. . . . And if ye will have it to be made here, it will stand ye to 6 marks [£4] or more, with the orfrey [gold-work] and making, and that is the least that I can drive it to. . . . And as for an embroiderer, I can find none that will come so far, but any work that ye would have, to send hither and they will do it. . . .'

Poor Robin had a much worse experience with 'the cloth of my ladies'. One Henry Cloughe 'put it to a shearman to dight, and he sold the cloth and ran away'. Henry had him arrested, sued him, and secured judgement to recover the cloth; but when the rascally shearman 'should deliver it, he delivered another piece'. Fortunately the indefatigable Henry discovered 'where he had sold it; and so it is had again and it is put to dyeing, and as soon as it is ready I shall send it by the carrier'.

Tradesmen of those days understood, as well as any of their successors, the high style to employ with the gentry. Thomas Bradbury, mercer, who would one day be Lord Mayor of London, wrote to Lady Stonor, 'Madame, the sarcenet is very fine. I think most profitable and most worshipful for you, and shall [last] you your life and your child's after you; whereas harlotry [cheap, flashy stuff] of 40d or 44d a yard would not endure two seasons with you: therefore for a little more cost, me thinketh most wisdom to take of the best'. On the other hand, when bills remained unpaid some merchants did not mince matters. 'Madame', one wrote to Sir William Plumpton's wife, 'ye know well I have no living but my buying and selling; and, Madame, I pray you send me my money. . . .'

In troubled times, when men sought to 'cut large thongs from other men's leather', wives of lords and gentry like Lady Berkeley and Margaret Paston did more than manage households. While John Paston was fighting in the courts at Westminster, Margaret carried on a harsher warfare at home. She undertook to distrain for arrears of rent, carried off cattle or ploughs from scowling tenants, and if somebody managed to secure a writ for their return, she defied the sheriff himself as long as she could. She gathered money, negotiated leases, barricaded herself in manor houses threatened by enemies, and sent up to her husband in London detailed budgets of news.

The bonds of marriage and the burden of affairs that wives sometimes had to shoulder find fullest expression in this age in these letters of Margaret Paston. Indeed, she is probably more intimately revealed than any other woman in the history of the world up to her time.[1] There have been preserved almost one hundred letters she wrote to her husband and her sons and almost fifty they wrote to her. In them lies the story of a marriage, loving but wracked by John Paston's ambitions.

---

[1] Similarly, we probably know more about Louis XI of France than about any man who lived before him. The fifteenth century is the first age in which biographical materials began to be preserved on a modern scale.

The Paston letters offer a glimpse of young Margaret, after her marriage had been arranged, meeting the man who was to be her husband, as reported by her future mother-in-law Agnes: 'And as for the first acquaintance between John Paston and the said gentlewoman, she made him gentle cheer in gentle wise and said he was verily your son. And so I hope there shall need no great treaty betwixt them.' They married and they fell in love, she with a touching surrender of herself, he with as much depth as his acquisitive nature permitted.

When she learned that he was recovering from a bout of illness in London, she hastened to let him know that 'by my troth I had never so heavy a season as I had from the time that I woste of your sickness till I woste of your amending, and yet mine heart is in no great ease, nor nought shall be till I wot that ye be very hale. . . . I would ye were at home . . . now rather than a gown though it were of scarlet'. After they had been married for more than a decade she concluded one of her missives to him, 'I pray you that ye be not strange of writing of letters to me betwixt this and that ye come home. If I might, I would have every day one from you.'

This shy, affectionate girl was soon transformed into the hard-worked partner of John Paston's ambitious enterprises and learned perforce to play a man's role in the world.

In 1448 Lord Molynes, an adherent of the Duke of Suffolk, seized John Paston's manor of Gresham. After repeated attempts to secure justice had failed, John re-entered the manor in October of 1449, when Suffolk's affairs were going badly and Molynes had other things to think about.[1] That winter John had to go up to London, as usual, to defend his interests. Therefore Margaret Paston, still a girl in her twenties, installed herself in the mansion at Gresham, a stout manor house, half-fortified and surrounded by a wall with a strong gate.

On January 28, 1450, the manor was attacked by a band of Lord Molynes's men, armoured in brigandines or jacks and sallets, some waving swords and glaives and battleaxes, others with bows and arrows, and still others bearing the new-fashioned hand guns.

[1] See Epilogue: 'Wars of the Roses.'

They were prepared to lay a siege *en règle* if necessary: they had with them large shields for sheltering archers or hand-gunners, ladders, pans with burning fire, pick-axes, long-handled hooks, and battering rams. John asserted that they were a thousand strong, which means there were undoubtedly several hundred and they must have looked more than a thousand to Margaret, who had only twelve men with her.

As they battered down the gate and swarmed towards the house, she resolutely took to her chamber, barred the door. Her men dared to put up a fight, several being wounded, but soon her room was surrounded by a yelling horde. They were not a disciplined war-band, she wrote to her husband, but 'a company of brothel [evil louts] that reck not what they do, and such are most for to be dreaded'. Unable to frighten her out, they dug her out—mined through the walls and carried her bodily off the grounds, while doorposts were smashed and the house was rifled to the bare walls and men shouted that if her husband or his friend John of Damme had been found within, it would have been the end of them.

Even now Margaret refused to beat a retreat to Paston or to take refuge within the walls of Norwich. She moved down the road but a short distance, to Sustead, John of Damme's place, and there she stubbornly remained. Molynes's men forced tenants to pay rents, sold and gave away Paston goods, scoured the neighbourhood for Paston supporters, uttered continued menaces against Paston and Damme. 'Here dare no man say a good word for you in this country, God amend it,' Margaret wrote. She was collecting information about the brutalities committed at Gresham, trying to protect her men and stir up public opinion, and sending reports to John, still in London.

After she had dispatched a message, at her husband's request, to demand that her tenants be left in peace, the leader of Molynes's band, a man named Barow, politely appeared with but two companions at the entrance to Sustead. Margaret came out but made no move to open the gates:

'I prayed them that they would hold me excused that I brought them not into the place. I said in as much as they were not well-willing to the good man of the place [John Damme], I would not take it upon me to bring them in to the gentlewoman. They said I did the best, and then we walked forth, and I desired an answer of them. They said to me . . . that there should no man be hurt of them that belongeth to you. Nevertheless I trust not to their promise, in as much as I found them untrue in other things.

'Barow and his fellows spoke to me in the most pleasant wise. They said they would do me service and "plesans", if it lay in their power to do aught for me, save only in that that belongeth to their lord's right. I said to them, as for such service as they had done to you and to me, I desire no more. . . .

'I conceived well by them [i.e., I could tell from the way they talked] that they were weary of what they had done. Barow swore to me by his troth that he had rather than 40s and £10 that his lord had not commanded him to come to Gresham.'

She reminded Barow that threats had been uttered against her because she dared to remain in the neighbourhood, and his disclaimers she had little confidence in. Still, she was not so worried about herself as about the loss of the manor; and that troubled her less than the dangers environing her husband: 'I hear said that ye and John of Damme are sorely threatened always, that though ye be at London ye shall be met with there as well as though ye were here; and therefore I pray you heartily, beware how ye walk there, and have a good fellowship with you when ye shall walk out.'

As Margaret brought numerous children into the world and reared them and managed the Paston household, she continued throughout the rest of her husband's life the struggle to carry out his exacting commands. To add to her burdens, her mother-in-law began quarrelling with John. After being assailed by Agnes's complaints and getting other reports of her trouble-making, Margaret wrote unhappily to her husband, 'In good faith I hear much language of the demeaning between you and her. I would right fain, and so would many more of your friends, that it were otherwise between you than it is. I pray God be your good speed in all your matters and give you grace to have a good conclusion of them in haste, for this is too weary a life to abide for you and all yours'. A letter from Chaplain Gloys to his master indicates that Margaret was not exaggerating her difficulties with Agnes: 'At the reverence of God, let some interposition go a-twixt you and my mistress your mother ere ye go to London, and all that ye do shall speed the better, for she is set on great malice, and every man that she speaketh with knoweth her heart, and it is like to be a foul noise [over] all the country without it be soon ceased.'

The task of trying to protect her husband's estates, attacked in every quarter, so told on Margaret Paston's spirit that in 1465 a Paston adherent wrote in alarm to John Paston, 'Sir, at the reverence of Jesu, labour the means to have peace; for by my troth the continuance [of this] trouble shall short the days of my mistress . . . for certain she is in great heaviness. . . .'

But the Paston affairs grew worse rather than better. Margaret and her eldest son, Sir John, had to mount guns at Drayton to defend the manor against an attack by some 300 of the Duke of Suffolk's men. The faithful steward, Richard Calle, was roughly handled in Norwich by the Duke's followers. His chief concern, however, was for his mistress. After forthrightly telling his master that something must be done immediately to halt the inroads of his enemies, he added, 'I beseech you to pardon me of my writing, for I have pity to see the tribulation that my mistress hath here, and all your friends. . . .' Margaret herself wrote despairingly a few days later, 'Affrays have been made on Richard Calle this week, so that he was in great jeopardy in Norwich . . . and great affrays have been made upon me and my fellowship. . . . If God fortune me life and health, I will do as ye advise me to do, for in good faith . . . what with sickness and trouble that I have had, I am brought right low and weak. . . .' But Margaret Paston, ailing or weary, continued to play a man's part till the day of her husband's death; and for years afterwards, she laboured anxiously to prevent her eldest son, Sir John, from letting the Paston lands slip through his fingers.

The Lady Isabel, wife to James, Lord Berkeley, proved herself even more indefatigable and strong-willed than Margaret Paston, and her bold and zealous defence of family interests cost her dear. While the forces of the Earl and Countess of Shrewsbury so harried Lord Berkeley and his sons that they had to immure themselves in Berkeley Castle, the Lady Isabel heartened and counselled her husband and doughtily carried on her legal battles at Westminster. A letter she wrote to him from London bespeaks her spirit and decisive personality: 'Right worshipful and reverend lord and husband, I commend me to you with all my whole heart, desiring always to hear of your good welfare, the which God maintain to increase ever to your worship.

'And it please you to hear how I fare; Sir, Squall and Squall; Thomas Roger and Jacket have asked surety of peace of me, for their intent was to bring me into the Tower. But I trust in God tomorrow that I shall go in bail unto the next term, and so to go home and then to come again. And, Sir, I trust to God and [if] you will not treat with them but keep your own in the most manliest wise, ye shall have the land for once and end.

'Be well ware of Venables of Alderley, of Thom Mull and your false council. Keep well your place. The Earl of Shrewsbury lieth right nigh you and shapeth all the wiles that he can to distrusse [untruss] you and yours. For he will not meddle with you openly no manner of wise, but it be with great falsedom that he can bring about to beguile you, or else that he caused that ye have so few people about you [and] then he will set on you. For he saith he will never come to the king again till he have done you an ill turn.

'Sir, your matter speedeth and doth right well, save my daughter costeth great good. At the reverence of God send money or else I must lay my horse to pledge and come home on my feet. Keep well all about you till I come home, and treat not without me, and then all things shall be well with the grace of Almighty God, who have you in his keeping. . . . Your wife, the Lady of Berkeley.'

Lord James, who knew how much he needed her, hurriedly pledged Mass-book, chalice and numerous vestments from his chapel and so was able to send her twenty-two marks. Not many months later—apparently after the Shrewsbury forces, with the 'great falsedom' Lady Berkeley prophesied, had taken her husband and sons captive—the Countess of Shrewsbury and her supporters arranged at Gloucester a commission of inquiry designed to bedevil the Berkeleys still further. Isabel, 'following her husband's business as solicitor', bravely faced the commission to fight for Lord James's rights. The vengeful Countess promptly imprisoned her in Gloucester Castle 'and kept her there so that she might not be delivered till she was dead'.

Other ladies of the age managed affairs almost as aggressively as the redoubtable Countess of Shrewsbury. When the castle of Bokenham fell to the Crown, in the turbulent last years of Henry VI, John and William Knyvet seized possession of it in defiance of royal authority. Armed with a writ, John Twyer, J.P., and two other officers came to the castle to oust the intruders. They were suffered to enter the outer ward but found that the inner draw-bridge across a deep moat had been raised. When Twyer shouted a demand to be admitted, there appeared 'at a certain little tower' of the drawbridge John Knyvet's wife Alice, backed by some fifty persons in warlike array. Alice explained the situation very clearly: 'Master Twyer, ye be a Justice of the Peace and I require you to keep the peace, for I will not leave the possession of this castle to die therefore; and if you begin to break the peace or make any war to get the place of me, I shall defend me. For rather had I in such wise to die than to be slain when my husband cometh home, for he charged me to keep it.'

Alice's manner must have been as emphatic as her words: 'for fear of death and mutilation' John Twyer and his companions hastily withdrew. Her terror of what her husband would do if she failed his orders sounds like a rhetorical flourish, or perhaps a touch of flattery to soothe Master Twyer's masculine pride.

At least one woman undertook to ply the dangerous trade of international agent. The Lady of Calais is nameless, she appears for but a moment, but she has earned a place in the story. Warwick the Kingmaker, fleeing to France in May, 1470, brought with him King Edward's discontented brother George, Duke of Clarence, who was married to Warwick's elder daughter Isabel. Under the benevolent auspices of Louis XI, Warwick treated with Margaret of Anjou, at Angers, for an alliance that would restore her husband Henry VI to the English throne at the price of her son's marriage to Warwick's younger daughter Anne. George of Clarence, now an embarrassing piece of excess baggage, remained in Normandy.

He was in a dangerous state of mind: fuming and sulky. When he had married Isabel, his father-in-law had held out to him the glorious prospect of supplanting his brother Edward on the throne. Now, after betraying his family and risking his neck, he had been cast aside with the sop that providing Henry VI's son and Anne Neville had no heirs, Clarence would succeed to the Crown.

At this explosive moment, there landed at Calais a lady who announced that she was on her way to serve and comfort the poor Duchess of Clarence, who had given birth to a stillborn son during the flight across the Channel. Calais, nominally faithful to King Edward, was governed by John, Lord Wenlock, Warwick's most trusted lieutenant. Wenlock had refused to let his chief land at Calais but had sent him a secret message promising that when Warwick had got help from France, Wenlock and the garrison would do their part.

So Wenlock was naturally suspicious of any lady coming from King Edward's England who asserted that she wished to go to the Duchess of Clarence. The lady then admitted that she had a secret mission: the King, eager to make peace with Warwick, was prepared to offer all sorts of attractive concessions. The lady displayed documents to prove her point. Wenlock, convinced and delighted, sent her on her way.

Though England and France were at war and the Normandy coast was being harried by the fleet of the Duke of Burgundy, she apparently had no difficulty in reaching the Duchess of Clarence. Her mission, however, was neither to comfort the Duchess nor to offer peace terms to Warwick. On behalf of King Edward she begged the Duke of Clarence to return to his family allegiance and produced assurances, which her stratagem at Calais had kept safe from Wenlock's eyes, promising that all would be forgiven if George would abandon his father-in-law. The lady was persuasive as well as resourceful; Clarence sent back word that as soon as opportunity offered he would do as his brother wished. Some nine months later, in early April of 1471, he led his army, ostensibly marching to Warwick's aid, into the Yorkist camp. The subsequent history of the lady is unknown;

but King Edward loved ladies, admired bravery, and had a generous heart: she was no doubt well rewarded.

Though foreigners had little good to say about the men of England, finding them choleric and fierce and avaricious, these visitors regarded English women as one of the wonders of the island: disconcertingly bold and free but the loveliest ladies alive.

The Bohemians who arrived in 1466 were impressed by the kissing they encountered: 'When guests arrive at a lodging they are expected to kiss the hostess and her whole household. But to take a kiss in England is the equivalent of shaking hands elsewhere, for the English do not shake hands.' A generation later, Erasmus revelled in the custom: 'Wherever you go,' he wrote a friend, 'you are received on all sides with kisses; when you take your leave, you are dismissed with kisses. If you go back, your salutes are returned to you. Whenever a meeting takes place there is kissing in abundance; in fact whatever way you turn, you are never without it.' This fashion, Erasmus pronounced happily, 'cannot be commended enough'.

Nicholas von Popplau was a good deal less gallant but even heartier in his appreciation of the bold beauties whom he met. 'One hears much of the Venusberg,' he noted, 'but as far as my experience goes—and I have wandered far and wide myself and heard many a tale from far-travelled men—there is no land which can be more justly compared with it than England.' Perhaps misled by all the kissing, he recorded complacently that English women 'are like devils once their desires are roused, and when they take a fancy to someone whom they can trust they grow quite blind and wild with love, more than the women of any other nation'. Even the Portuguese girls could not make him forget the hot-blooded women of England, who, in addition, were very beautiful, particularly those dwelling around Cambridge. Adultery was common and English inns were full of handsome creatures eager to flaunt their charms: 'Scarcely had he entered an inn before the womenfolk were after him, saying, "Dear master, whatever you desire, that we will gladly do". And if then out of politeness he made as if to shake hands with them, they, nothing daunted, would offer their lips for a kiss. Should he fail to comply, they would go away abashed, but return in half an hour and very respectfully offer him food and drink. He suspected that they did all this in the hope of robbing him both of his purse and his virginity.'

There must be something in what Popplau says about the girls to be met with in English taverns; half a century before the German's visit, that hard-worked clerk to the Signet and journey-man-poet, Thomas Hoccleve, sang of 'Venus' female lusty children dear', whom he encountered at the Paul's Head, 'That so goodly, so shapely were and fair. And so pleasant of port and of manner'. After a day's work of driving pen across parchment, Hoccleve loved 'To talk of mirth and to disport and play' with these delicious creatures, while they all drank sweet wine and ate 'wafers thick'. Naturally, he took care of the reckoning: 'To suffer them pay had been no courtesy.' Hoccleve, confessing himself a shy and modest chap, was well content with no more than an occasional kiss.

But upriver at Westminster, in the gay court of King Edward IV, men were readier to enjoy what the ladies of London were willing to offer. Two of Edward's greatest lords, the witty and genial Lord Chamberlain Hastings and the young Marquess of Dorset, the Queen's son by her first marriage, boasted of their amorous exploits in the city and stole each other's mistresses. The King outdid them, at least according to song and story. When his mother objected to his marrying a widow with two children, Edward replied cheerfully—so the tale runs—that though a bachelor, he had some children too.

The only woman of the age to become a legend was Edward's favourite mistress, Jane Shore, wife of a London mercer (not goldsmith, as the stories have it). She is celebrated in ballads, but best account of her comes from the pen of a man who saw her when she was old and poor.

'The King would say,' wrote Sir Thomas More in his *Historie of Kyng Rycharde the Thirde*, 'that he had three concubines, which in three divers properties diversely excelled. One the merriest, another the wiliest, the third the holiest harlot in his realm as one whom no man could get out of the church lightly to any place but it were to his bed. The merriest was this Shore's wife, in whom the King therefore took special pleasure. For many he had, but her he loved, whose favour to say the truth (for sin it were to belie the devil) she never abused to any man's hurt, but to many a man's comfort and relief: where the King took displeasure, she would mitigate and appease his mind: where men were out of favour, she would bring them in his grace. For many that had highly offended, she obtained pardon. And finally in many weighty suits, she stood many men in great stead, either for none, or very small rewards, and these rather gay than rich: either for that she was content with the deed's self well done, or for that she delighted to be sued unto, and to show what she was able to do with the King, or for that wanton women and wealthy be not always covetous.'

Bemused by her history, More tries to understand how it came about: 'This woman was born in London, worshipfully friended, honestly brought up, and very well married, saving somewhat too soon; her husband an honest citizen, young and goodly and of good substance. But forasmuch as they were coupled ere she were full ripe, she not very fervently loved for whom she never longed. Which was haply the thing that the more easily made her incline unto the King's appetite when he required her. The respect of his royalty, the hope of gay apparel, ease, pleasure and other wanton wealth, was able soon to pierce a soft tender heart. But when the King had abused her, anon her husband (not presuming to touch a king's concubine) left her to him altogether.'

To learn the secret of her charm, More sought out men who had known her in her glory. 'Proper she was and fair: nothing in her body that you would have changed, but if you would have wished her somewhat higher. Thus say they that knew her in her youth. Albeit some that now see her (for yet she liveth) deem her never to have been well visaged. Whose judgement seemeth me somewhat like, as though men should guess the beauty of one long departed, by her scalp taken out of the charnel house. Yet delighted not men so much in her beauty, as in her pleasant behaviour. For

a proper wit had she, and could both read well and write, merry
in company, ready and quick of answer, neither mute nor full of
babble, sometime taunting without displeasure and not without
disport.'

More preserves the scene in which Jane Shore passed from the
light of fame. 'When the King died, the Lord Chamberlain
[Hastings] took her. Which in the King's days, albeit he was sore
enamoured upon her, yet he forbore her, either for reverence, or
for a certain friendly faithfulness.' After Richard of Gloucester
had beheaded her protector, 'he caused the Bishop of London to
put her to open penance,' going before the cross in procession
upon a Sunday with a taper in her hand. In which she went in
countenance and pace demure so womanly, and albeit she were
out of all array save her kirtle only: yet went she so fair and lovely
that her great shame won her much praise, among those that were
more amorous of her body than curious of her soul.'

Despite this public exposure of her light living Jane Shore
could still charm a man, even such a man as the King's Solicitor,
Thomas Lynom, who had first looked into her eyes to accuse her.
Careless of all worldly considerations, he reportedly made a
contract of matrimony with her while she lay in Ludgate Prison—
so 'marvellously blinded and abused' was he 'with the late wife
of William Shore', as King Richard III, hearing the news, hastened
to write to his Chancellor, John Russell, Bishop of Lincoln. The
King begged Russell 'to send for him, in that ye goodly may
exhort and stir him to the contrary'. Yet, though Jane Shore had
carried secret messages for his enemies, the Woodvilles, and
though the match could hardly contribute to the dignity of his
very new regime, the King showed a sympathetic understanding
of Lynom's plight: 'If ye find him utter set for to marry her and
it may stand with the law of the church, we be content (the time
of marriage being deferred to our coming next to London) that,
upon sufficient surety being found of her good a-bearing', she be
discharged from Ludgate and 'committed to the rule and guiding
of her father, or any other by your discretion, in the mean season'.
She did not marry Thomas Lynom, but withdrew into obscure

_____
[1] A few weeks before he was crowned Richard III (July 6, 1483).

poverty to grow old and one day to show young Thomas More a face he could not forget.

Still, though Jane Shore shines as the ballad-heroine of the age and though foreigners, in paying tribute to English women, did not go beyond their free ways and lovely faces, records remain to show that the greatest ladies of the realm, as well as wives of gentry and merchants, could play masterful parts in a society apparently dominated by men.

Margaret of Anjou flashes across the English scene like an exotic tropical bird, magnificent but fierce, frantically beating its plumage in a wild, hopeless, ineluctable migration and finally dashing itself bloodily upon rock.

She shared the destiny of her family, the valiant and talented and curiously flawed House of Anjou. Her father, 'Good King René', laid claim to a brilliant array of titles—King of Naples, King of Hungary, King of Jerusalem—and could win, or hold, none of them; he cheerfully settled for a career of patronizing artists, devising fantastic tournaments, and writing poetry. Margaret's brother Duke John, regarded everywhere on the Continent as the very pattern of martial prowess and lordly charm, failed in all his enterprises.

At the age of sixteen Margaret, dowerless but beautiful and learned, became the bride of Henry VI. She brought with her, into a tough practical land where the knightly exploits of King Arthur were no more than reading matter, the haughty seignorial attitude and the archaic chivalry of her House. By the time she was twenty-one years old (1451) she was ruling England and beginning her passionate struggle to crush the House of York.

Henry was meekly content to follow her lead and she had enough spirit for two. A Milanese agent reported that the Queen, 'a most handsome woman though somewhat dark', kept a rigid state: when Duchesses and even her five-year-old son spoke to her, 'they always go on their knees'. The Mayor of Coventry discovered, when he headed a procession escorting her from the city, that he must himself bear his mace of office, as he was accustomed to doing only for the King. A Paston correspondent noted wryly, 'She is a great and strong-laboured woman'.

She soon became the stuff of legend. Among the tales that circulated on the Continent in the '50's and '60's, a Milanese ambassador reported the rumour, current in March of 1461, that 'the Queen of England after the King had abdicated in favour of his son, gave the King poison'. The envoy adds callously, 'At least he has known how to die, if he was incapable of doing anything else'.

Once the Yorkists had captured King Henry at Northampton in July of 1460, Margaret's history becomes a fairy-tale of disasters by land and sea, the saga of a forlorn but indomitable princess wandering the world to display the 'tragedie' of fallen greatness and the violence of her mistakes.

From Coventry, Margaret and her little son fled westward with only a handful of attendants. She was waylaid in Cheshire, robbed of all her possessions, threatened with death, but managed to escape and made her way to Harlech Castle. The following year, after the battle of Towton, she and King Henry and their little prince were galloping for Scotland with victorious Yorkists hot on their traces. Insensitive to English feelings, Margaret bought a refuge by delivering the frontier town of Berwick to her hosts.

She soon left her hapless husband with the Bishop of St. Andrews and journeyed to France to get aid from Louis XI, at the price of mortgaging Calais. With her gallant friend Piers de Brezé she then sailed to reconquer the North. But Margaret had only to take ship to raise a storm. A tempest smashed her fleet; as her own vessel foundered she and Brezé managed to escape in a small boat and reach Berwick. The expedition failed. A few months later, the Queen and her son, fleeing through a dense forest, fell into the hands of a robber band. Fortunately, one of the ruffians was so moved by her distress that as the bandits quarrelled over the spoils, he loaded Queen and Prince on his horse and bore them to safety.

In 1463 Margaret once again left Scotland, this time for the Low Countries to beg help from the chivalrous Philip the Good, Duke of Burgundy.

Like one of the goddesses who descended periodically from Olympus to disrupt the schemes of Greek and Trojan on the

ringing plains of Troy, the erstwhile Queen of England, reaching
Sluys at the beginning of August, was determined to blast a con-
ference of Burgundian-French-Yorkist diplomats at St. Omer
which boded ill for the House of Lancaster. For resources, she had
only her unquenchable spirit and her protector, Brezé: 'ne
credence, ne argent, ne meubles, ne joyaux pour engaiger'. She
and her son and her seven woman attendants depended even for
their food on Brezé's purse.

She left her prince and most of her followers at Bruges. Disguised—or costumed—in the garments of a peasant-woman, she
drove off in a humble cart accompanied by the ever-faithful Brezé.
A few hours after she reached St. Pol, Philip of Burgundy made
his entrance. She rushed into the street to greet him. He tried to
pay homage to her as a queen. She tried to throw herself upon
him as a helpless princess. It was an affecting scene, but the old
Duke could not be moved from his Yorkist alliance. Next day he
uncomfortably took his departure; only after he was well on the
road did he send back to Margaret a princely diamond and a
goodly sum of money. Then he dispatched his sister and her
daughters to console the afflicted Queen. With that devotee of
chivalry, the Burgundian chronicler Chastellain, taking it all
down, Margaret poured out one evening for the princesses of
Burgundy the high perils and misfortunes she had endured in
England—like Aeneas relating the fall of Troy to Dido.

For seven long years Margaret then dwelt in poverty, surrounded by a ragged court of dispossessed Lancastrians, on an
estate in her father's Duchy of Bar, dreaming of revenge and
awaiting the turn of Fortune's Wheel. The schooling in arrogance
and hate she gave her prince glows red in a comment by a Milanese
ambassador: 'This boy, though only thirteen years of age, already
talks of nothing else but of cutting off heads or making war, as if
he had everything in his hands or was the god of battle.'

When she got word that Warwick and Edward IV were
beginning to quarrel, she demanded aid from Louis XI in such
high terms that the sardonic King, showing her letter to a Milanese
ambassador, remarked, 'Look how proudly she writes'. But in
the summer of 1470 Louis had to use all of his magnificent battery

of persuasion to convince her that she must ally herself with her bitter foe, Warwick. When the Queen and the Kingmaker met at Angers, Margaret assuaged her feelings a little by keeping the Earl a good quarter of an hour on his knees while he humbly begged her pardon.

After Warwick had reconquered the realm for Lancaster she waited too long—she who so often had not waited long enough—to bring her prince to England. On the very day that the Earl lost all at Barnet she landed at Weymouth. Urged to action by over-confident West Country Lancastrians, she rode the panicky miles to Tewkesbury in an agony of fear for her son. A Yorkist band who discovered her hiding in a house of religion brutally broke the news of the defeat and death of the heir of Lancaster.

Margaret was brought to the Tower of London the same night that her feeble-witted husband met his death there. A few years later Edward IV ransomed her to Louis XI for 50,000 crowns. Heartbroken, all pride spent, she lingered in life on one of her father's estates until August of 1482. At her death, all she possessed that anybody wanted was her dogs. Louis XI wrote impatiently to demand them: 'She has made me her heir, and . . . this is all I shall get. I pray you not to keep any back, for you would cause me a terribly great displeasure.'

One of Margaret's greatest enemies likewise had a masterful temper, and a history crowded with triumphs and sorrows. Handsome and high spirited Cicely Neville[1] became the bride of Richard, Duke of York, and proved a bulwark of his career. Neither child-bearing—she bore a dozen children—nor the dangers of the time prevented her from accompanying her husband into France, into Ireland, up and down the shires of England. Her eldest son Edward was born at Rouen; George, at Dublin; Richard at Fotheringhay.

In October of 1459, when the Duke and his brother-in-law the Earl of Salisbury and Salisbury's son Warwick had assembled their forces at Ludlow to await an attack by King Henry's army, the

---

[1] The prolific Neville clan had disputed with the Percies for the control of the North and produced Warwick the Kingmaker and wives for half a dozen of the chief peers of the realm.

sudden defection of Warwick's troops forced the Yorkist leaders to flee in the night for their lives. Duchess Cicely with her daughter Margaret (later Duchess of Burgundy) and her two youngest boys, George (later Duke of Clarence) and Richard (later Duke of Gloucester and Richard III) had to be left behind in Ludlow Castle to the mercies of the Lancastrians.

Next morning the King's troops burst into Ludlow, hot for loot. Cicely did not await them behind the castle walls. When the rabble rushed into the market-place, they found the Duchess standing proudly at the market-cross with her three children: perhaps she had hoped in this way to save the town from pillage. But Ludlow and the castle were robbed to the bare walls, and Cicely was borne off to Coventry to witness the attainder of her lord and his followers in a Parliament packed with Lancastrians. King Henry, as kindly as ineffectual, allowed her 1,000 marks a year for her maintenance and put her in the custody of her sister, the Duchess of Buckingham, whose husband was one of the chiefs of the court party.

On one of Buckingham's manors she stayed, 'kept full strait and many a great rebuke', until the following summer, when Warwick and her son Edward Earl of March invaded England from Calais, captured the King at the battle of Northampton and set up a Yorkist government. Then Cicely and her children came to London to await the arrival of the Duke of York from Ireland. Within a few days of his landing at Chester, he sent word asking her to meet him at Hereford, and away she went at once, as fast as she could 'in a chair [carriage] covered with blue velvet' drawn by 'four pair coursers'. That the world was still 'right wild' made no difference to her.

Three months after she joined her husband, who came to London with clarions blowing before him and the full arms of England waving above him, for he meant now to claim the throne, the Duke was killed at Wakefield (December 30, 1460) and his head set to mouldering on Micklegate bar at York. A few weeks later, Queen Margaret's host of Northerners, smashing Warwick's army at St. Albans, were approaching the gates of London. Cicely, fearful for the lives of young George and Richard, got them on board a ship which took them safely across the Channel to the protection of the Duke of Burgundy; but she herself stuck to her post in the apparently doomed city. In less than a fortnight, her son Edward of March entered the capital, was proclaimed King Edward IV, and marched northward for a showdown with the Lancastrians.

Cicely remained in London as chief representative of the House of York to stiffen the trembling loyalties of the citizens. Rumours and fears swept the capital. Then, in the first days of April, a messenger galloped into the courtyard of Baynard's Castle, her great mansion on the Thames, and a few minutes later Duchess Cicely was reading out to the throng in her chambers her son's autograph letter announcing the destruction of the hopes of Lancaster at Towton Field. William Paston wrote hastily to his brother John to say that he had seen and handled the precious missive. Shortly after, it was reported that 'the Duchess of York . . . can rule the King as she pleases'.

But Cicely's struggles were not finished. In September of 1464 King Edward disclosed his secret marriage to Elizabeth Woodville, widow and daughter of men who had fought for Lancaster. Both commons and lords—especially that all-powerful lord, Warwick the Kingmaker—bitterly disapproved of this marriage to a woman, however beautiful, who was not a princess; but apparently nobody was so outraged as Cicely. She made a fearful scene, berated Edward as if he were no more than a naughty child at her knee, and denounced his marriage so violently that for years afterwards rumours were flying that she had publicly declared her son a bastard. An Italian visitor heard, almost two decades later, that in a towering passion she had offered to declare Edward's illegitimacy before a commission of inquiry.

A few years after, however (1470-71), she was secretly working on George of Clarence to renounce Warwick and return to his family allegiance; and in the winter of 1477-78 she doubtless pleaded, though in vain, with her son King Edward for the life of that same feckless son George.

She lived, a religious recluse in Berkhamsted Castle, to see her son Richard usurp the throne from her grandsons and die at

Bosworth Field, her grand-daughter Elizabeth become the wife of Henry Tudor, Richard's conqueror, and the children of her own daughter Elizabeth, Duchess of Suffolk, conspire and fail and perish as the Tudor (Henry VII) eradicated the remaining sprigs of the White Rose.

Henry Tudor's mother, Margaret Beaufort, was no less powerful a personality, and her son owed her even more than King Edward owed to Cicely. She was likewise a bluestocking of the age. Bluestockings leave few traces in times such as these, but there was apparently no lack of them. In East Anglia several ladies patronized writers, whose talents unfortunately were small; and doubtless the accidents of time have obscured the fame of women in other parts of the country who encouraged the arts and were ornaments of learning.

Margaret Beaufort's portrait tells much about her: the narrow expressive face reveals self-discipline, intelligence, with a glint of the wry humour she transmitted to her son lurking in the eyes. Richard of Gloucester's usurpation of the throne, in June of 1483, suddenly gave her the opportunity to unleash her remarkable talents. Her third husband Thomas, Lord Stanley, a shrewd and shifty lord, became King Richard's Steward of the Household; at Richard's coronation the Lady Margaret herself bore Queen Anne's train. Yet, across the Narrow Seas in Brittany, her son by her first marriage, Henry Tudor, *soi-disant* Earl of Richmond, watched and waited upon events; he represented, through his mother's descent, the remaining hope of the line of Lancaster.

After his coronation, King Richard with a train of nobles including Lord Stanley went a long progress into the West and North; but the Lady Margaret remained in London, the nerve-centre of the kingdom, her ear tuned for signals of disaffection. They were not long in coming. From the sanctuaries, full of Woodville adherents, issued a buzzing of conspiracy to rescue little Edward V and restore him to the throne. Woodville relatives and friends were secretly gathering followers in Kent and Surrey and the western counties. Henry Tudor's mother immediately began stirring Beaufort retainers and other old Lancastrians. Her messengers made their dangerous way to Brittany. She put herself in touch with the Woodvilles and was soon hearing from a precious pair in Wales. John Morton, Bishop of Ely, a consummate intriguer who was nominally the prisoner of the Duke of Buckingham, Richard's greatest supporter, had won over his vain, shallow captor to attempt King Richard's overthrow. In London the Lady Margaret sat at the centre of webs of intrigue, manipulating thread with delicate fingers.

The Woodvilles, however, were working to restore Edward V; Buckingham wanted the throne for himself; Lady Margaret had still other ideas. She now made herself the Athena of the conspiracy. Her clever man of affairs Reynold Bray, secretly riding to Buckingham's castle at Brecknock, helped John Morton to convince the Duke that he must throw his support to Henry Tudor. Then came the nicest stroke of all. Lady Margaret's agents, filtering through the southern counties, spread the word that Edward V and his brother were dead. While the Woodville followers were still confused by this news, Lady Margaret loosed the astonishing tidings that the mighty Duke of Buckingham, outraged at Richard's crimes, would take up arms with the conspirators to put Henry Tudor on the throne.

Under this artful management, what had been three competing plots became one. At just the right moment Lady Margaret wove the master strand of the web. A smooth-tongued physician of hers succeeded in making his way past King Richard's guards to talk with Edward IV's widow, Elizabeth Woodville, who had taken sanctuary at Westminster. The dowager Queen was assured that her sons were dead, but that she might secure her revenge and still become the mother of kings if she agreed to the marriage of her eldest daughter Elizabeth to Henry Tudor. Her ready acceptance was dispatched to Woodville adherents, and Lady Margaret now sent her able chaplain, Richard Fox, into Brittany in order to concert a landing on the south coast with the movements of Buckingham and the Woodvilles. An astute woman, Lady Margaret had chosen astute servants; when the moment struck, Bray and her physician and Fox and others were ready to accomplish her designs.

Through no fault of Henry Tudor's mother, the plot failed

miserably; King Richard, a first-rate commander, quickly crushed
the rebellion, executed Buckingham and restored order. Lady
Margaret got off lightly; she was put in the custody of her ostensibly loyal husband. Reynold Bray even received a pardon.
Henry Tudor sailed back to Brittany to wait for two more years.

Lady Margaret, assisted by Bray in England and Morton and
Fox on the Continent, prepared the way for her son's successful
invasion of August, 1485, by collecting money and promises of
aid, and doubtless by helping to create the fog of rumours that kept
King Richard uneasy and his kingdom jumpy.

After Henry VII won the throne, he showed himself a grateful
son, though, as Bacon remarked dryly, he was anything but a
uxorious husband. He did not mind owing much to his mother
but hated to owe anything to the Yorkist blood in the veins of
his beautiful wife Elizabeth. The Athena of the Tudor hopes
became, in effect, the Queen of the Tudor triumph. Screened by a
lattice, the Lady Margaret and her son cozily watched the coronation of Elizabeth. According to report, she held her daughter-in-
law in considerable subjection; it is certain that she was until her
death the dominant lady of the reign. Her new position gave her
scope to express her piety and taste; and her encouragement of the
arts, her religious bequests, her endowments in support of learning
showed her a fitting progenitor of the Tudors who came after.
She was in more ways than one a kingmaker.

A woman who, though only the widow of a London citizen,
even more remarkably foreshadows things to come, earned her
fame in the early years of Edward IV's reign. Agnes Forster and
her husband Stephen, a wealthy fishmonger and one-time mayor
of London, chose to express their charity, as many were doing in
this age, by working for the worldly, rather than the heavenly,
weal of their fellow-townsmen. They became interested in prison
conditions. Ludgate Prison had been specially built for citizens
held for debt or petty crimes, in order to spare them the miseries
of lying in Newgate with the worst sort of criminals. Moved by
the overcrowding of the prison, Agnes and her husband began
constructing an addition to Ludgate, a massive 'quadrant strongly

builded of stone', which contained a sizeable exercise ground and 'fair leads to walk upon, well embattled, all for fresh air and ease of prisoners'. They endowed the building as well,

> So that for lodging and water prisoners here nought pay,
> As their keepers shall answer at dreadful doom's day

—so end the verses, graven in copper, which were affixed to the 'quadrant'.

Stephen Forster died before the work was completed, but Dame Agnes pursued her humanitarian cause with increased zeal. She not only watched over the completion of the Forster addition, but spent her days in Newgate and Ludgate and the sheriffs' gaols studying the prison life of London. Many men and women were leaving sums in their wills to provide food and clothing for prisoners, but Agnes Forster was a proto-Elizabeth Fry, the first woman on record to concern herself with the penal system rather than with the plight of individuals.

In December of 1463, Dame Agnes turned over to the city the Ludgate Addition, and at the same time she laid before the Mayor and aldermen a set of proposals for the reform of all London prisons. They knew a good thing when they saw it: 'At the request and prayer of the well disposed, blessed and devout Dame Agnes Forster, for the ease and relief of all poor prisoners being in the gaol and "Counters" of the city', they promptly enacted her reforms. These articles fall under three main heads: preventing gaolers from mulcting prisoners by overcharging for bed and board, three shillings a week being the maximum allowed; checking the brutality of the keepers and regulating the practice of putting prisoners in irons; and, perhaps most important of all, making provision to see that no man languished in gaol without due cause. Every year at the feast of St. Matthew the Apostle (September 21) two curates and two 'commoners' of the city were given the power to enter any gaol at any time in order to investigate the complaints of the prisoners, to enforce the observance of the new articles, to survey the dispensing of alms and to inquire into the causes for which every inmate was imprisoned.

Two years later, Dame Agnes herself became a kind of gaoler; a French lord, the Sieur de Graville, who had been captured fighting for the Lancastrians in the North, was entrusted to her care until he was able to ransom himself. Since his hard-hearted son, a high officer of Louis XI's, made no move to help his father, Graville apparently remained under Dame Agnes' roof for twelve years. Doubtless the pangs of exile were lightened for the poor old man by the care Dame Agnes bestowed upon him. Edward may have chosen her to keep Graville for him because of her fame as a prison reformer, but it turns out that the man to whom Graville owed his ransom was named John Forster, probably the warrior son of a woman who was in her way also a warrior. Dame Agnes owned books, too, and knew how to take care of them. When she kindly lent out some law volumes, she had the borrower sign a deed that required their return 'when her ladyship will command them'.

In a very different key a Norfolk woman, Margery Kempe, sounds the same note of changing times. She began life like many another burgher's daughter of Bishop's Lynn. She married, had children, managed a household, and for a time set up in business for herself as a brewer. But she began to experience visions and hear voices. She put on a hair shirt and spent long hours praying in church. Finally, separating from her husband, she took to the road, convulsed, and spiritually arrogant and abysmally humble by turns. She made her way to the Holy Land. On her return, she spent months at Rome, dependent on charity for food and shelter; after that, she wandered penniless through Europe.

Later she sailed to the great shrine of St. James of Compostella in Spain; then, driven by divine compulsion, she plodded the roads of Germany. She was at times a dreadful trial to her fellow pilgrims and wayfarers, for she broke into clamorous fits of weeping which became the special mark of her holy possession. Once she had fourteen crying spells in one day. Still, though pilgrims avoided her company or deserted her on the road, she always met with someone to help her, feed her, guide her to where she wanted to go.

The upper clergy found her a nuisance. Often summoned

before bishops on suspicion of heresy, she remained unabashed. Here is her own report[1] on how she appeared in the palace of the Bishop of Worcester: 'When she came into the hall, she saw many of the Bishop's men in clothes freakishly cut in the fashion of the day. She, lifting up her hands, blessed herself. And then they said to her: "What devil aileth thee?" She said again: "Whose men be ye?" They answered back: "The Bishop's men." And then she said: "Nay, forsooth, ye are more like the Devil's men." Then they were angry and chid her, and spoke angrily to her.' The Bishop himself, though, gave her his blessing and put money in her purse.

But she had a stormier experience when she was brought before the Archbishop of York. He rounded on her at once, called her heretic and sent for fetters. When she burst into tears, the prelate asked harshly, 'Why weepest thou, woman?' She replied: 'Sir, ye shall wish some day that ye had wept as sore as I.' After quizzing her sharply on her faith and finding nothing wrong, the Archbishop told her: 'I am evil informed of thee. I hear it said that thou art a right wicked woman.' Though she 'trembled and shook', she retorted, 'I also hear it said that ye are a wicked man. And if ye be as wicked as men say, ye shall never come to Heaven, unless ye amend whilst ye be here.' In the end, the exasperated prelate ordered her to swear that she would leave his diocese instantly. When she refused, he called for a man to take her away. The man wanted a noble (6s 8d) for the unpleasant task, but the Archbishop would give no more than five shillings to 'lead her rapidly out of this country'.

In her last years she returned to Bishop's Lynn. She received a cold welcome home, for 'a reckless man, little caring for his own shame, with will and of set purpose, cast a bowlful of water on her head as she came along the street'. Some of her compatriots treated her badly, for her mysticism was dreadfully noisy; but others were moved by her holiness, and famous doctors came to Lynn to talk with her.

Before she died, she felt compelled to record her story; after difficulties she found a priest willing to take down her dictation (in the 1430's). Caxton's successor, Wynkyn de Worde, published

[1] In dictating her autobiography, she spoke of herself in the third person.

a small pamphlet of extracts from the work, but fortunately in 1934 the complete manuscript came to light.

Margery Kempe reports her life and her personality no less than the special ardours of her faith. She made no bones, for example, about how repellent to others her crying spells were: 'She never knew the time or the hour when they would come, and as soon as she found that she would cry, she would suppress it as much as possible so as not to annoy people. For some said it was a wicked spirit vexed her: some said it was a sickness: some said she had drunk too much wine: some would she had been at sea in a bottomless boat: and thus each man had his own thoughts.'

Her narrative gives homely details of her life on the roads of Europe as she begged from city to city, tagging along with a company of poor folk: 'When they were without the towns, her fellowship took off their clothes, and sitting naked, picked themselves. Need compelled her to await for them and to prolong her journey. She was afraid to put off her clothes as her fellows did, and therefore, through being with them, had part of their vermin, and was bitten and stung very evilly both day and night. She kept on with her fellowship with great anguish and discomfort and much delay, until they came to Aachen.'

While waiting at Bristol for a ship to take her to St. James, she was 'houseled every Sunday with plenteous tears and boisterous sobbings, with loud cryings and shrill shriekings, and therefore many men and women wondered upon her, scorned her and despised her. . . . On Corpus Christi Day . . . as the priests bore the sacrament about the town with solemn procession . . . she cried, "I die! I die!" and roared so wonderfully that the people wondered upon her. . . .' When finally she boarded ship with her fellow-pilgrims, 'it was told her if they had any tempest they would cast her in the sea, for they said . . . the ship was the worse for she was therein'.

Once when she reached Calais, footsore and 'overcome with labour', on her way back to England, 'there was a good woman had her home to her house, the which washed her full cleanly and did her on a new smock and comforted her right much. . . . While she was there abiding shipping three or four days, she met there

with divers persons which had known her before. . . .' She hoped
to cross the Channel with them but they refused to let her know
'what ship they purposed to sail in. She speried [queried] and spied
as diligently at she could' and thus learned their intentions; but
'when she had borne her things into the ship where they were . . .
they purveyed them another ship ready to sail'. Abandoning her
belongings, she hastily joined them, 'and so they sailed all together
to Dover. Perceiving through their cheer and countenance that
they had little affection to her person, [she] prayed to Our Lord
that he would grant her grace to hold her head up and preserve
her from voiding of unclean matter in their presence, so that she
should cause them none abomination. Her desire was fulfilled so
that, others in the ship voiding and casting full boisterously
and uncleanly, she . . . might help them and do what she would'.

But when they reached Dover, 'each one of that fellowship got
him fellowship to go with . . . save she only, for she might get no
fellow to her ease. Therefore she took her way toward Canterbury
by herself alone, sorry and heavy in manner that she had no fellowship and that she knew not the way'. But Providence was never
far from Margery. Early in the morning she 'came to a poor man's
house, knocking at the door. The good poor man, huddling on
his clothes, unfastened and unbuttoned, came to the door', and
shortly after, he was leading her to Canterbury on his horse.

Margery Kempe's story is the first true autobiography composed in England; and it is written in English. Thus it signals the
particular quality of fifteenth-century life. Margery knew that
she was a Child of God and with flamboyant humility she calls
herself throughout her narrative 'the creature'; but she also knew
that she was a remarkable person who had experienced more of
life than most folk.

Children

IN the tough, pushing world of the fifteenth century, children were not coddled nor did their upbringing occupy the centre of family life. Parental love, parental hopes were forced into harsh channels of expression which strained and often soured the feelings themselves. Children of the upper classes were sent while very young into strange households to make their way, and married early. Parents worked for the worldly advancement of their sons and daughters, but most of them apparently did not consider that enjoying children constituted a part of the pleasure of living.

Mothers like Margaret Paston sometimes tried to shield their sons from a father's rigour. Thomas and Elizabeth Brews, of Norfolk, were warm, affectionate parents. A letter from young Richard Cely to his brother George at Calais sounds an ageless maternal theme: 'Our mother longs sore for you. William Cely wrote that we be like to have war with France and that makes her afraid.'

But instances of such parental feeling do not often occur. Stephen Scrope, who complained so bitterly about his own upbringing, wrote casually, 'For very need I was fain to sell a little daughter I have'; he regretted only that he had to make the bargain 'for much less than I should have done by possibility'. Whatever lay in the hearts of parents, in their minds they assumed that children must become pawns in the family game of advancement, whose wishes and whose expressions of individuality were irrelevant, not to say intolerable. Consequently, the first and last duty of a child was humble obedience. Chaucer's squire serves as a model:

> Curteis he was, lowely and servysable
> And carf biforn his fader at the table.

The handbooks of the period multiply their injunctions on the subject:

> Reverence thy parents dear, so duty doth thee bind:
> Such children as virtue delight be gentle, meek, and kind.
>
> And, child, worship thy father and mother,
> And look that thou grieve neither one nor the other,
>
> But ever among thou shalt kneel down,
> And ask their blessing and their benison.

Disobedience was immoral, ungodly, inconvenient, and it met with swift punishment. Children were liberally beaten as part of their training; a child was a *tabula rasa* and it was the duty of parents to write emphatically thereupon the lessons of life:

> But as wax receiveth print or figure
> So children be disposed of nature.

Children learned very early and were expected to observe throughout their lives the formal terms in which obedience was expressed. William Stonor writes, 'My Right reverend and Worshipful Father, I recommend me unto your good fatherhood in the most humble wise that I can or may, meekly beseeching your good fatherhood of your daily blessing'. Young John Paston addresses his mother, 'Right Reverend and Worshipful mother, I recommend me to you as humbly as I can think, desiring most heartily to hear of your welfare and heart's ease, which I pray God send you as hastily as my heart can think'. When Sir John Paston, in his middle thirties, so far forgot himself as to begin a missive to his mother with an abrupt 'Please it you to weet that I have received your letter'; Margaret Paston tartly brought him to heel: 'I think ye set but little by my blessing, and if ye did, ye would have desired it in your writing to me. God make you a good man.'

Children were schooled according to the same principles by which they were reared. The wax was pliable but stubborn; learning and a little grace had to be beaten into the young:

> He hateth the child that spareth the rod;
> And the wise man saith in his book
> Of proverbs and wisdoms, who will look,
> 'As a sharp spur maketh an horse to run
> Under a man that should war win,
> Right so a yard may make a child
> To learn well his lesson and to be mild'.

Agnes Paston had no doubt about proper teaching methods: 'Pray Greenfield [a master in London] to send me faithfully word by writing how Clement Paston hath done his devoir in learning. And if he hath not done well, nor will not amend, pray him that he will truly belash him till he will amend. So did the last master, and the best that ever he had, at Cambridge.' This method of instruction was not new and it would last for a long time to come.

What was new was the spread of schooling itself. The mediaeval day was long past when only clerks could read and write and even a noble was content to make his mark. By 1489 reading and writing had become so common that a distinction had to be drawn in law between the literate layman and the clerk. The middle classes, urban and gentry, were making their energies felt throughout all the fabric of the realm.

Children were offered a diversity of educational opportunities: municipal schools, gild schools, schools established in hospitals by the bequests of wealthy men, schools started by scriveners or Bachelors of Arts, schools attached to chantries and to colleges of priests. Chaplains and parsons often tutored children of the neighbourhood as well as the households of their patrons. Abbeys and nunneries here and there still carried on their mediaeval tradition of educating the young. Robert Stillington, Bishop of Bath and Wells, and Thomas Rotherham, Archbishop of York, founded schools in their native towns. Aliens set up academies to teach languages. Men like Agnes Paston's Master Greenfield tutored boys looking to enter one of the Inns of Chancery or Inns of Court.

Though individual churchmen did much for education, the Church as a whole did not take kindly to the establishment of new schools. The city of Coventry had to ask the Prior to refrain from bullying parents into sending their children to his school instead of the municipal school. A prerogative, a source of profit was threatened. In London, the Church blocked for a time the founding of additional schools, but schools came into being anyway; by 1450 there were probably at least a dozen and may have been two or three times that number.

The majority of English men and women could not read and write; but the majority of English men and women were peasants on the land. The gentry and rising yeomen, all 'The Clothing' of the towns and most of the middling townsmen could read and write English, women as well as men. Most of the sons of merchants and gentry had some training in Latin because accounts were kept in that language and it was essential for the professions or the management of land. Of one hundred and sixteen Londoners who appeared as witnesses in a consistory court between 1457 and 1476, forty per cent were registered as literate, and 'literate' meant able to read Latin. A commercial education was offered in private schools and tutoring establishments. Bishop Stillington made provision in his school for three masters to teach grammar, music, and writing, 'and such things as belong to the scrivener's art'.

The surviving memorials of the period—letters, household accounts, wills, deeds, charters—all reveal a concern for education, an assumption that schooling is essential for success in life. A baker requests his son to be reared 'in all learning'; an alderman hopes his will be inclined 'to cunning learning and erudition'; a vintner dwells on the necessity of schooling until the age of sixteen. Even the wondrous pageants that ornamented the marriage of Margaret of York to Charles, Duke of Burgundy, did not make John Paston forget about a favourite page of his: 'And mother,' he wrote from Bruges, 'I beseech you that you will be good mistress to my little man and to see that he go to school. Pray Sir John Still [a Paston Chaplain] to be good master to little Jack and learn him well.'

Oxford and Cambridge still slumbered in their mediaeval curricula of Latin rhetoric and scholastic philosophy. The tradition of student unruliness continued: Sir William Stonor's servants were so badly beaten at Oxford that they refused to do their master's errands in the town; the German, Popplau, found the loveliest, and lightest, ladies near Cambridge, and visiting bishops found the giddiest nuns in convents around Oxford. Yet Oxford and Cambridge were changing, despite themselves. Poor boys, supported by enlightened members of the gentry like Sir John Howard and Sir William Stonor, now came to the universities with no intention of entering Holy Orders; they aimed at an ever-increasing choice of lay careers, many of them going on to the Inns of Court. Sons of wealthy merchants and gentry were also coming in considerable numbers, and even an occasional lord's son, to prepare themselves for public and private responsibilities. This new generation squeezed from the churchly learning of the past, secular careers and a love of books.

The spectacular rise of the Paston fortunes was owing to an investment in education by Clement Paston at the beginning of the century. Almost all we know of Clement comes from an account put about by Paston enemies, the effect of which on the twentieth-century reader is the reverse of what was originally intended: 'First, there was one Clement Paston dwelling in Paston, and he was a good plain husbandman, and lived upon his land that he had in Paston, and kept thereon a plough all times in the year. The said Clement yede [went] at one plough both winter and summer, and he rode to mill on the bare horse-back with his corn under him, and brought home meal again under him, and also drove his cart with divers corns to Wynterton to sell, as a good husbandman ought to do. Also, he had in Paston a five score or a six score acres of land at the most, and much thereof bond land [i.e., held by servile tenure] to Gemyngham Hall, with a little poor water-mill running by a little river there. Other livelode [property] nor manors had he none there, nor in none other place. . . .

'Also, the said Clement had a son William, which that he set to school, and he borrowed money to find him to school; and after that, he yede to [one of the Inns of] court and learned the law. . . .'

Young William was soon appointed Steward to the Bishop of Norwich; important men turned to him for advice, made him a trustee of their properties. He became Serjeant-at-law in 1421 and eight years later, a Justice of the Court of Common Pleas at a yearly salary of 110 marks. Thus the son of an industrious yeoman rose to be one of the hundred or so most influential men in England. He made a good marriage to Agnes Berry, heiress of a Hertfordshire knight, who brought him several properties, and he himself joined estate to estate until at his death his heir John was one of the important land owners of Norfolk. The other sons of Justice Paston, like John, were educated at Cambridge and probably, like him, at one of the Inns of Court.

John Paston's two eldest sons Sir John and John undoubtedly had a university education and probably were likewise trained in the law. A younger son Walter went to Oxford; he made the journey under the eye of the family chaplain, Sir James Gloys, who was given strict orders by Margaret Paston to make sure that Walter was put 'where he should be' and 'set in good and sad rule'. Margaret hoped that her son would 'do well, learn well, and be of good rule and disposition', but she did not want him to be 'too hasty of taking of Orders that should bind him, till that he be of twenty-four years of age or more, though he be counselled the contrary, for often haste rueth. . . . I will love him better to be a good secular man than to be a lewd priest'. He stayed five years at Oxford, spending about £12 or £13 a year. In the spring of 1479 he was hoping to take his degree at the same time as Lionel Woodville, brother to the Queen, for this young man could be expected to contribute liberally to a feast given by the Bachelors. Lionel did not take his degree at that time, but Walter became a Bachelor of Arts in June and reported that he was able to spread a very satisfactory dinner: 'and if ye will know what day I was made Bachelor, I was made on Friday the seventh, and I made my feast on the Monday after. I was promised venison against my feast of my Lady Harcourt, and of another man too, but I was deceived of both; but my guests held them pleased with such meat as they had, blessed be God.' Venison was apparently the traditional dish for such pleasant ceremonies; a correspondent of Sir William Plumpton wrote, 'Please your good mastership to wit, there is a clerk at York, the which purposes to say his first mass the Sunday next after the feast of the Nativity of Our Lady the Virgin; and if ye would vouchsafe that he might have a morsel of venison against the said Sunday', the writer would be grateful.

John Paston's youngest son William was sent to Henry VI's famous foundation, Our Lady of Eton, the only Paston of this time, so far as is known, who attended that school. He was lodged in a dame's house in town, under the tuition of a Fellow of the college. The impecunious Sir John, now head of the family, expected his mother to support William at Eton, an idea which was not to her liking; and William's fees and board bills were often months in arrears. On one occasion he informed his second brother John that he had met a young gentlewoman at a wedding; she appeared to be well endowed with worldly goods and he hoped that his brother would make some marital inquiries; his final comment does not suggest that he was deeply enamoured, however: 'and as for her beauty, judge you that when ye see her, if so be that ye take the labour, and specially behold her hands, for and if it be as it is told me, she is disposed to be thick.' He reported complacently of his educational progress, 'And as for my coming from Eton, I lack nothing but versifying, which I trust to have with a little continuance'. He then cites an example of his Latin, not very promising, and adds proudly, 'and these two verses aforesaid be of mine own making'. On another occasion he begged young John 'to send me a hosecloth, one for the holidays of some colour, and another for the working days, how coarse so ever it be, it maketh no matter; and a stomacher, and two shirts, and a pair of slippers. And if it like you that I may come by water and sport me with you at London a day or two this term time, then ye may let all this be till the time that I come. . . .'

Sir John Howard, too, owed much to education. He was probably, like John Paston, a Cambridge man who studied law at one of the Inns of Court. Though he had the advantage of high birth—his mother was a Mowbray—if he had not made himself a man of learning, it is doubtful that he could have risen to become one of King Edward's chief diplomats and a magnate whose household accounts could contain the casual item, 'For a grey nag to send to the French king, 36s 8d'. Periodically he journeyed to London to fetch his two young sons, Thomas and Nicholas, from school, probably at St. Bartholomew's Hospital.

Education was frankly equated with worldly success, but there is plenty of evidence to show that this utilitarian spirit by no means choked the love of learning and the enjoyment of books. Scriveners were kept busy copying manuscripts for the lay reading public. Sir John and his younger brother John strew their letters with Latin and French tags; their friends joke with them about Ovid's *Art of Love* and there is talk of other books too. Sir John fancied himself as a collector. The moment he heard that the family chaplain, Sir James Gloys, had died, he immediately asked his mother to buy Gloys's books if they were available and pack them up to London. Not that he had any money to spare— 'if it like you that I may have them, I am not able to buy them; but somewhat would I give, and [as for] the remnant, with a good devout heart, by my troth, I will pray for his soul. Wherefore if it like you by the next messenger or carrier to send them in a day, I shall have them dressed here, and if any of them be claimed hereafter, in faith I will restore it.' The books were still very much on his mind a few days later: 'I beseech you that I may have them hither by the next messenger, and if I be gone, yet that they be delivered to mine hostess at The George, at Paul's Wharf, which will keep them safe, and that it like you to write to me what my payment shall be for them.' On the same day he impatiently addressed his brother John: 'I pray you remember so that I may have the books . . . which my mother said she would send me by the next carrier.' A few weeks later Sir John was still fretting: 'I hear no word of my books; I marvel. No more.'

It finally turned out that the best book in Sir James's collection had been claimed, though Margaret Paston promised to try to get it for him; the rest were valued at 20s 6d. But by this time Sir John, at Calais, was plagued by debts and had his thoughts on preparations for the coming invasion of France (1475) so 'that as for the books that were Sir James's, I think best that they be still with you, till that I speak with you myself. My mind is now not most upon books'.

But clearly his mind often was upon books. The volumes owned by him and his brother John present a fair cross-section of the reading tastes of the gentry. He possessed several romances, poems by Chaucer and Lydgate and Hoccleve, a few religious and devotional books, a number of chronicles, works on war and heraldry, the *De Senectute* and the *De Amicitia* of Cicero and Ovid's *De Arte Amandi*. That tough old fighter, Sir John Fastolfe, had a collection almost as large. Sir John Howard was another ardent book collector. When in 1481 Sir John, now Lord Howard, commanded a naval expedition against the Scots which left a trail of burnt shipping in the Firth of Forth, he took with him not only steel harness and serpentines but French romances and French treatises on dice and chess and *Les Dits des Sages*.

William Worcester, annalist and humourist, who spent long years in the hard service of Sir John Fastolfe, once characterized himself to John Paston, in the third person: 'Item, Sir, I may say to you that William hath gone to school, to a Lombard called Karoll Giles to learn and to be read in poetry or else in French; for he hath been with the same Karoll every day two times or three, and hath bought divers books of him, for the which, as I suppose, he hath put himself in danger [i.e., debt] to the same Karoll. . . . He would be as glad of a good book of French or of poetry as my Master Fastolfe would be to purchase a fair manor.' When William Caxton set up in business at the sign of the Red Pole close by Westminster Abbey, in 1476, England was ready for him and his marvellous machine.

The lord's girl and the baker's boy and the squire's son and Margaret Paston's daughters and the girls of London mercers and tailors and fishmongers were not very long reared or schooled in the family household. They were all apprenticed, whether as apprentices proper or as pages or attendants in somebody else's household. It was the universal belief in England, except among the poor, that the best possible upbringing for a child was to thrust him out

of the family as soon as possible to learn the ways of the world and
continue his education under other auspices. A child who remained
at home too long became an eyesore, an affront to the fitness of
things.

This system amazed, even shocked, the Venetian diplomat.
'The want of affection in the English is strongly manifested toward their children; for after keeping them at home till they
arrive at the age of seven or nine years at the utmost, they put
them out, both males and females, to hard service in the houses of
other people, binding them generally for another seven or nine
years. All these are called apprentices, and during that time they
perform all the most menial offices. Few are born who are
exempted from this fate, for everyone, however rich he may be,
sends away his children into the houses of others, while he in
return receives those of strangers into his own.

'When I inquired their reason for this severity, they answered
that they did it in order that their children might learn better
manners. But I, for my part, believe that they do it because they
like to enjoy all their comforts themselves, and that they are
better served by strangers than they would be by their own
children. Besides which, the English, being great epicures and very
avaricious by nature, indulge in the most delicate fare themselves
and give their household the coarsest bread and beer and cold meat
baked on Sunday for the week, which, however, they allow them
in great abundance. Whereas if they had their own children at
home, they would be obliged to give them the same food they
made use of for themselves.

'If the English sent their children away from home to learn
virtue and good manners and took them back again when their
apprenticeship was over, they might, perhaps, be excused; but
they never return, for the girls are settled by their patrons, and the
boys make the best marriages they can, and, assisted by their
patrons, not by their fathers, they also open a house and strive
diligently by this means to make some fortune for themselves.'

Though the Venetian scrambles together the urban system of
apprenticeship and the general practice of sending children—
whether the sons and daughters of lords or prosperous yeomen—

into other people's households and though the motives he darkly
suspects are somewhat more amusing than convincing, the letters
of the time bear out in detail the picture that he paints. Since the
Venetian was domiciled in London and knew that society best,
he devotes the rest of his account to what he saw in the capital:
'The apprentices for the most part make good fortunes, some by
one means and some by another; but, above all, those who
happen to be in the good graces of the mistress of the house in
which they are living at the time of the death of the master,
because by the ancient custom of the country, every inheritance
is divided into three parts: for the church and funeral expenses,
for the wife, and for the children [this is, in fact, the 'Custom of
London']. But the lady takes care to secure a good portion for
herself in secret first, and then she, being in possession of what she
has robbed, of her own third, and that of her children besides,
usually bestows herself in marriage upon the one of those apprentices living in the house who is most pleasing to her, and who was
probably not displeasing to her in the lifetime of her husband;
and in his power she places all her own fortune, as well as that of
her children, who are sent away as apprentices into other houses.
. . . No Englishmen can complain of this corrupt practice, it being
universal throughout the kingdom.'

The Venetian was not far wrong in lumping lords' sons placed
in great households with yeomans' or shoemakers' sons bound in
indentures to a weaver. The motives, the play of human feelings
were much the same, however different the training and the
prospects of the children. An apprentice had the skills of the craft
and some manners beaten into him and competed with other
apprentices for the favour of his master, or his mistress. A squire's
daughter in the household of a knight was expected to learn the
intricacies of good behaviour and needlework, to have enough
of schooling to read and write and keep accounts so that she
would be useful to her husband, and to secure the patronage of her
mistress. In the household of the King or of a magnate of the
realm, lords' sons were instructed in polite learning, manly
exercises and the art of pleasing superiors. The social gamut was
wide but not the range of purpose behind the system.

Pages in great households were called 'henchmen'. Richard of Gloucester, brother of Edward IV, was one of several henchmen in the household of Warwick the Kingmaker. In the household of the Earl of Northumberland at a little later period, there were three henchmen living on the bounty of the Earl and two 'at their friends' finding'. Edward IV's Queen, the beautiful Elizabeth, had an establishment of her own at Smithfield, which included a schoolmaster to teach her henchmen and the royal wards in her charge. Edward's ordinances make careful provision for the training of the six or seven lads who were fortunate enough to win places as royal henchmen and who thus in ceremonial parades rode on either side of the 'haunch' of their sovereign.

The 'Master of Henxmen' was required 'to show the schools of urbanity and nurture of England, to learn them to ride cleanly and surely; to draw them also to jousts; to learn them [to] wear their harness [and] to have all courtesy in words, deeds, and degrees; diligently to keep them in rules of goings and sittings. Moreover, to teach them sundry languages and other learning virtuous, to [play the] harp, to pipe, sing, dance, with other honest temperate behaving; and to keep daily and weekly with these children due convenites [hours of meeting] with corrections in their chambers according to such gentlemen.[1] This master sitteth in the hall, next unto [but] beneath these henchmen, at the same board, to have his respects unto their demeanings, how mannerly they eat and drink, and to their communication and other forms curial [courtly], after the book of urbanity'.

Sir John Fortescue, the most famous political thinker of the age, urged that gentry and nobility should have their young reared in the household of a great lord that they might learn virtue and manners; princes and the sons of magnates should be educated at the King's Court: 'I cannot but highly commend the magnificence and state of the King's palace, and I look on it as an academy for the young nobility of the kingdom to inure and employ themselves in robust and manly exercises, probity and a generous humanity.' Fortescue's words recall the most famous page of this

---

[1] That is, being of high birth, henchmen were not to be beaten in public but in the privacy of their own rooms.

period, young Thomas More, son of a witty butler of Lincoln's Inn, who was born not long after William Caxton set up his printing press at Westminster under the curious eyes of Edward IV's court. Thomas was received into the household of Cardinal Morton, Henry VII's Chancellor, 'where, though he was young of years, yet would he at Christmastide suddenly sometimes step in among the players, and'—though never having studied the play—'make a part of his own there among them, which made the lookers-on more sport than all the players beside. In whose wit and towardness the Cardinal, much delighting, would say of him unto the nobles that divers times dined with him, *'This child here waiting at the table, whosoever shall live to see it, will prove a marvellous man'*. Whereupon for his better furtherance in learning, he placed him at Oxford. . . .'

During the Yorkist Age so many ambitious boys were striving in merchant's shop or squire's household or lord's hall to forge a career for themselves, that there now developed a literature of instruction for the aspiring young, which on the Continent had appeared long before.

These practical manuals of how-to-behave and how-to-get-ahead agree so closely that they seem to copy one another. They are usually pitched to appeal to the sons of 'middling' townsmen and yeomen rather than to scions of the upper classes; yet one of the simplest purports to be addressed to 'young babies, whom blood royal. With grace, feature, and high ability. Hath enormed [adorned]'. Many of these rhymed treatises offer generalized exhortations on the subject of morality and manners; others are specifically concerned with the young man who has been put in service in a household.

How the Good Wife Taught Her Daughter emphasizes industry, respectability, and obedience to the husband. Girls are advised to stay away from wrestling matches and cockfights lest they be mistaken for strumpets. The proper wife does not gad about when she goes to market to sell the cloth she and her maidens have woven; nor is the tavern the place for her to spend her time, 'For if thou be oft drunk, it will fall thee to shame'. When her husband is away, she must not allow her people to take advantage of his absence but keep them working diligently and, if necessary, work herself to set them a good example. Envy and pride are to be eschewed. If a girl marries a man who goes up in the world, she must be careful to be hospitable to her neighbours, and if her hopes of prosperity are disappointed, she must not ape the attire of wealthier folk:

> With rich robes and garlands and with rich thing,
> Counterfeit no lady as [if] thy husband were a king.

As soon as a wife gives birth to daughters, she should prudently begin gathering goods and money for the dowries; and since maidens' minds are unstable, 'Give them to spousing as soon as they be able'.

How the Wise Man Taught His Son offers advice in the same vein. The young man is warned against tavern-haunting, gambling, gossiping. The doctrine of hard work appears, rather hesitantly:

> Beware of rest and idleness,
> Which things nourish sloth,
> And ever be busy more or less—
> It is a full good sign of truth.

Choosing a wife requires prudent investigation:

> Take her not for covetise [covetousness],
> But wisely enquire of all her life,
> And take good heed, by mine advice,
> That she be meek, courteous, and wise;
> Though she be poor, take thou no heed,
> And she will do thee more good service
> Than a richer when thou hast need.

This strikes, faintly, the romantic note of virtue versus wealth which will provide so much of the stuff of the literature of the Tudor Age.

Another homely poem makes a direct appeal to ambition:

> And learn as fast as thou may and can,
> For our bishop is an old man;
> Therefore thou must learn fast,
> If thou wilt be bishop when he is past.

The more specialized manuals, whatever social degree they aim at, have one central situation in common: the young man put into a household to make his way. John Russell drew upon his experience as marshal in the hall of that cultured and erratic prince, Humphrey, Duke of Gloucester, to produce in his *Book of Nurture* a vocational guide designed to instruct the young in the duties of butler, sewer, chamberlain, marshal in a great household. Caxton's *Book of Courtesy*, the numerous variants of *Stans Puer Ad Mensam*, and other manuals assume that what any young man most needs is advice on how to behave at table. They attempt to eradicate brutishness and to force man's careless, passionate nature into a jacket of seemly modesty. The nastinesses to be avoided are almost always the same: don't slump against a post, fidget, stick your finger in your nose, put your hands in your hose to scratch your privy parts, spit over the table or too far, clean a dish by licking it with your tongue, pick your teeth, breathe stinking breath into the face of the lord, blow on your food, stuff masses of bread into your mouth, scratch your head, loosen your girdle and belch, 'burnish' bones with your teeth or probe teeth with a knife.

> Pick not your nose, nor that it be dropping with no pearls
>   clear. . . .
> And always beware of thy hinder part from guns blasting.

It is not enough to conquer mere animality, however; young men must be modest, well spoken, quick to respond to the needs and wishes of others. The page who hopes to succeed must be capable of entertaining his superiors with dance and song. He should inform his mind by reading Gower, Chaucer, Hoccleve,

and Lydgate—who, alas, have gathered all the flowers of eloquence
so that those who come after can but glean. When in doubt the
prudent young man looks to see what the cleverest are doing and
imitates them. The man not to be is 'Ruskyn Gallant', reckless
Ruskyn, 'avaunt parler in every man's tale', whose hair is so bushy
that he looks like a Breton prisoner and who is so tightly laced that
if he bows he will break somewhere. The motivation of worldly
profit is frankly exposed:

> And in especial use ye attendance
> Wherein ye shall yourself best advance.

All these instructions envisage the youth serving a master, and
they all emphasize the necessity of an alert sensitivity to differences in rank, a constant awareness of one's betters and an assid-
uous attention to pleasing them. The more elaborately a man
acknowledges a superior, the more emphatically does he assure his
own status. When Sir William Stonor was working to establish
himself in the affinity of the powerful Marquess Dorset, Stonor's
agent in the West Country, Richard Germyn of Exeter—perhaps
the son of the man Shillingford made fun of—wrote to him
admiringly, 'And ye be the greatest man with my lord, and in
his conceit. Because of your horse given [i.e., the horse you gave
him] and your attendance unto him at London, what he may do
and all his men, ye may have. His servants reporteth of you that
ye be the [most] courteous knight that ever they saw'.

The higher one's rank, the more flamboyant one's manners, for
only people of station could afford such conspicuous consumption
of leisure. The motives which enforced severe or spectacular
punishments and demanded iron assertions of authority were
likewise at work in developing accepted modes of behaviour.
The Venetian diplomat, apparently to his surprise, found the
English 'extremely polite in their language. . . . In addition to
their civil speeches, they have the incredible courtesy of remaining
with their heads uncovered, with an admirable grace, whilst they
talk to each other'. The Mayor and Mayoress of Norwich
exhibited their respect for Margaret Paston by sending their

dinners out to the manor of Hailsham where she was staying and then arriving themselves to dine with her.

Among townsmen there was developing the image of the sober, restrained man of affairs. The merchant must be thrifty, he must associate with fitting companions, he must cultivate learning and live by his intelligence:

> Man, soberly thy house begin
> And spend no more than thou mayest win,
> For a nice [over fastidious] wife, and a back door
> Maketh often times a rich man poor.
> Of all treasure cunning is the flower.
> Care not too much for anything.
> Keep thee with the wise,
> Then to riches thou shalt rise.

Yet ambition if too nakedly displayed was unseemly; self-interest must be clad in the guise of the welfare of the town or the eternal verities. Sir John Percevall, finally elected Mayor of London in 1499, had been passed over for several years because he was too pushing: 'The Bench, considering his hot appetite which he had yearly to that office, "dyspoynted hym".' The records of the Tailors Company contain an edifying contrast in manners: 'Master Heed in ungoodly wise reviled, rebuked and spake unto the said Derby with an unmeek spirit, a rude voice, unsad demeanour, and irreverent manner: "Thou liest falsely like a false harlot as thou art." Whereunto the said Derby answered soberly with a well advised mind and sad demeanour and said, "Sir, I wot and remember in what place and whose presence that I am in and if I were in another place and from hence and worshipful company I would speak as plain English unto you as ye have done unto me".' Master Derby, like Sir William Stonor, not only behaves properly but is the very image of proper behaviour. Give him the Reformation and he will be a zealous Puritan.

The film of modish conduct is, however, noticeably thin; under different circumstances Master Derby would freely exchange whoresons with Master Heed. The texture of living unshaped by polite instruction was not comely in this age. The courtesy books remind us that, beneath the middle classes struggling towards seemliness as an expression of their new status, stretches the 'low-life' world, vividly depicted in farcical morality plays and satirical ballads, where horseplay and husbands deceived by wanton clerics and wives tippling in taverns and cheerful knock-about vulgarity hold the stage. Under provocation or pressure the populace quickly turned savage. At coronations, the cloth on which royalty trod from Westminster Hall to the Abbey was regarded as the perquisite of the people. As Henry VII's Queen, Elizabeth of York, was walking in her coronation procession, the spectators suddenly pressed forward, eager to snip goodly hunks of the rich material. In a panic the guards drew weapons and before the Queen's eyes killed several of the mob.

Even in the politer reaches of society the veneer of manners sometimes slipped and social life showed rough or crude, as it would for many a decade to come. When Margaret Paston and her mother-in-law Agnes came out of the parish church on the Paston manor of Oxnead one morning, an enemy of the Paston's sent two of his men to attack their chaplain and 'called my mother and me strong whores'. Sir John Paston, who considered himself an accomplished courtier, saw no impropriety in jesting coarsely to the lovely Elizabeth Talbot, Duchess of Norfolk, and was amazed to learn that the Duchess and her followers may not have been pleased. 'My Lady Brandon and Sir William also' had told Sir John that, according to the Duchess, 'I said that my lady was worthy to have a lord's son in her belly, for she could cherish it . . . which words I meant as I said. They say too I said that my lady had sides long and large, so that I was in good hope she should bear a fair child; he was not laced nor braced to his pain, but that she left him room to play in . . . [and] it should have room enough to go out at.' Sir John adds with an injured air, 'I meant well by my troth to her, and to that she is with, as any he that oweth her best will in England'.

King Edward IV sometimes put up with conduct on the part of his lords that would have shortened them by a head at the court of his grandson Henry VIII. Just after the King's army had returned from France in 1475 without fighting a battle, the Duchess of Norfolk, who sympathized with the Paston's hopes of regaining Caister Castle, told young John how Edward had raised the issue to the Duke before they recrossed the Channel. 'She saith that the King asked my lord at his departing from Calais how he would deal with Caister, and my lord answered never a word. Sir William Brandon stood by, and the King asked him what he would do in that matter, saying that he had commanded him before time to move my lord with that matter; and Sir William Brandon gave the King to answer that he had done so. Then the King asked Sir W.B. what my lord's answer was to him, and Sir W.B. told the King that my lord's answer was that the King should as soon have his life as that place; and then the King asked my lord whether he said so or not and my lord said, Yea. And the King said not one word again, but turned his back and went his way.'

Humour was a saving grace of rough manners and a sauce of life much prized. Sometimes crude and even cruel, it could also be lively and pointed. The give-and-take in the letters between those two well educated young men, Sir John and young John Paston, resembles the witty exuberance of any age. The writer of Gregory's chronicle often shows a wry appreciation of things, as when he comments on the great debate over who won the joust between the Bastard of Burgundy and Lord Scales—'Ask of them that felt the strokes, they can tell you best.' The lower orders were always ready with a jest to deflate portentousness. Earlier in the century, when the London mob was demonstrating against Cardinal Beaufort, the enemy of their friend Humphrey Duke of Gloucester, 'low persons' shouted that they would throw the Cardinal 'into the Thames to have taught him to swim with wings'. A Paston agent neatly hit off the feeble posturing of the Duke of Suffolk, who had seized the Paston manor of Hellesdon: 'My Lord of Suffolk was there on Wednesday of Whitsun week, and there dined, and drew a stew [drained a fish pond] and took great plenty of fish; yet hath he left you a pike or two, against ye come, the which would be great comfort to all your friends, and discomfort to your enemies; for

at his being there that day there was never no man that played
Herod in Corpus Christi play better and more agreeable to his
pageant than he did. But ye shall understand that it was afternoon,
and the weather hot, and he so feeble for sickness that his legs
would not bear him, but there was two men had great pain to
keep him on his feet, and there ye were judged. Some said "slay!"
some said "put him in prison!" and forth came my lord, and he
would meet you with a spear, and have none other amends for the
trouble that ye have put him to but your heart's blood, and that
will he get with his own hands; for and ye have Hellesdon and
Drayton, ye shall have his life with it.'

Sir John Paston's friend John Pympe clearly appreciated his
own cleverness in jesting about 'the fraus' [i.e., wives] of Bruges
with their high caps 'who have given some of you great claps',
and enjoyed his slyness in thus thanking Sir John for helping him
with an *affaire du coeur*, 'And, Sir, where that sometime was a little
hole in a wall, is now a door large enough and easy passage,
whereof ye were the deviser, and have thanks for your labour of
some parties, but no thing lasteth ever'.

Young John Paston often struck a heartier, and wholesomer,
note than John Pympe. Exuberantly assuring his brother that if:
'other folks do no worse their devoir in gathering [harvesting]
of other manors than we have done in Caister, I trust to God that
ye shall not be long unpaid; for this day we had in the last comb of
barley that any man had owed in Caister town, notwithstanding
Hew Awstyn and his men hath cracked many a great word in
the time that it hath been in gathering. And twenty comb Hew
Awstyn's man had down [and] carted, ready for to have led it to
Yarmouth. and when I heard thereof, I let slip a certain of whelps
that gave the cart and the barley such a turn that it was fain to
take covert in your backhouse cistern at Caister Hall, and it
[the barley] was wet within an hour after that it came home,
and is nigh ready to make good malt all, ho! ho!'

People of the age enjoyed nonsense verses as much as did the
Victorians:

> I saw a codfish corn sow,
> And a worm a whistle blow,

And a pie treading a crow,
I will have the whetstone,[1] and I may.

I saw a stockfish drawing a harrow,
And another driving a barrow,
And a saltfish shooting an arrow.
I will have the whetstone, and I may, etc.

But there was often nothing humorous, either for parents or children, about the hunt for households of suitable—i.e., superior —rank in which to settle sons and daughters. Feelings were strictly subordinated to considerations of worldly advantage. 'As for your sister's being with my Lady,' Margaret Paston wrote to young John, 'if your father will agree thereto, I hold me right well pleased; for I would be right glad and [if] she might be preferred by marriage or by service, so that it might be to her worship and profit.' When daughters remained unplaced, motherly affection did not salve the tiresome situation. Later Margaret urged Sir John to 'purvey for your sister [a] worshipful place whereas ye think best, and I will help to her finding, for we be either of us weary of other'.

Though children were treated rigorously enough at home and though being thrust into a strange household was but the way of the world, boys and girls were often miserable. Apprentices sometimes ran away or defiantly returned to their parents or appealed to the gild against their master's ill-treatment.[2] Margaret Paston was asked to receive a girl 'for she is at Robert Lethum's, and there as she is, she is not well at her ease'. When Elizabeth Paston— she who endured so many blows at home—complained that she was being roughly used at Lady Pole's, her mother Agnes merely informed her that she 'must use herself to work readily as other gentlewomen do, and somewhat to help herself therewith'.

Dorothy Plumpton appealed eloquently and by no means spiritlessly to her father: 'I sent to you [a] message, by Wryghame of Knaresborough, of my mind, and how that he should desire you in my name to send for me to come home to you, and as yet

[1] Hung around the neck of perjurors, liars, jury-bribers, etc.
[2] Which could result in the masters being fined or even imprisoned.

I have no answer again. The which desire my lady has gotten knowledge [of]; wherefore, she is to me more better lady than ever she was before, in so much that she has promised me her good ladyship as long as ever she shall live; and if she or ye can find a thing meeter for me in this parties [parts] or any other, she will help to promote me to the uttermost of her puissance. . . . Whereof, I humbly beseech you to be so good and kind father unto me to let me know your pleasure, and write to my lady thanking her good ladyship of her so loving and tender kindness showed unto me. . . . I beseech you to send a servant of yours to my lady and to me and show now by your fatherly kindness that I am your child; for I have sent you divers messages and writings, and I had never answer again. Wherefore, it is thought in this parties, by those persons that list better to say ill than good, that ye have little favour unto me, the which error ye may now quench. . . . Also I beseech you to send me a fine hat and some good cloth to make me some coverchiefs.'

Even when the relationship between parents and children appears affectionate, social compulsions could nullify parental feelings. Under the auspices of the Queen herself, a daughter of the Stonors had been placed in a great household, probably that of the Duchess of Suffolk. The parents had apparently accepted the arrangement reluctantly and thereby incurred the Queen's displeasure. Consequently when Jane Stonor's daughter begged to come home because she found herself unwanted and knew not what to do, her mother was forced to write to her in these terms: 'Well beloved daughter, I greet you well: and I understand ye would have knowledge how ye should be demeaned. Daughter, ye wot well ye are there as it pleased the Queen to put you. . . . Also methink they should not be so weary of you that did so great labour and diligence to have you: and whereas ye think I should be unkind to you, verily that am I not, for . . . I am and will be to you as a mother should be, and if so be they be weary of you, ye shall come to me, and ye so will it; provided that my husband or I may have writing from the Queen with her own hand and else he nor I neither dare nor will take upon us to receive you, seeing the Queen's displeasure afore. . . .'

The coldness of parents toward their children was often repaid in later life by a coldness of the children, now grown, toward their parents. In wills, fathers denounced the cruelty of their offspring and hedged bequests with threats of disinheriting; suits at law and in chancery between father and sons were frequent; friends or lawyers often had to arbitrate scandalous quarrels. That tough, cold matriarch Agnes Paston, raising rows with her sons and grandsons, was by no means a unique social specimen. After the death of Thomas Stonor, Sir William and his mother carried on a series of bitter disputes over property and money, the violence of which is illustrated by a letter from an agent of Sir William's to his master: 'I have been with my mistress, your mother, and there I shall never come more by the grace of God, for I was a false varlet, thief and her traitor, and God give me grace that I never meet with her more, for I have the names of your brothers and sisters.' Even the amiable Thomas Betson could not endure the crabbedness of Lady Stonor's mother: 'I spake unto my lady your mother on St. Thomas's Day, and she would scarcely open her mouth unto me. She is displeased and I know not wherefore. . . . God send her once a merry countenance and a friendly tongue, or else shortly to the Minories [Franciscan nuns].' A little later, Thomas reported a similar experience: 'Since I came home to London, I met with my lady, your mother, and God wot she made me right sullen cheer with her countenance while I was with her. Methought it long till I was departed. . . . I had no joy to tarry with her. She is a fine merry woman, but ye shall not know it nor yet find it, nor none of yours by what I see in her.'

Margaret Paston knew that it was her duty to second her husband's managing of their children, even as she manfully seconded the managing of the estate. Yet her eldest son John, shortly to become Sir John, was not made in the same prudent, industrious mould as his father and grandfather, and when he got into trouble she could not help trying to make things easier for him. She hopefully informed her husband, 'His demeaning since ye departed hath been right good and lowly and diligent in oversight of your servants and other things, the which I hope ye would have been pleased with, and ye had been at home. He was right heavy of his

demeaning to you . . . and I beseech you heartily that ye vouchsafe to be his good father, for I hope he is chastised and will be the
worthier hereafter'.

This fall from grace occurred in 1459, when John Paston's
eldest son was already a young man of about nineteen. After he
had failed to find a place at court at the beginning of King
Edward's reign, he came home to Paston and there he remained,
not happily. This egregious breach of custom, a young man
spending his days in his father's hall, roused a clatter of malicious
tongues: 'Of one matter at reverence of God take heed', a friend
wrote urgently to John Paston, 'for in truth I hear much talking
thereof, and that is both in Norfolk, Suffolk, and Norwich, among
all men of worship, as well that love you as other, and that is of
my master, your son Sir John, cause [because] he is so at home,
and not otherwise set [provided for]. Some say that ye and he both
stand out of the King's good grace, and some that ye keep him at
home for niggard cheap [out of miserliness] and will nothing
[spend] upon him. . . . At the reverence of God, eschewing of
common language, see that he may worshipfully be set for,
either in the King's service, or in marriage. . . . I do beseech you
that this matter be kept secret'.

Two years later when he was a man grown and had been
knighted, Margaret Paston again tried to step between her son
and her husband's wrath, but Sir John flung out of the house and
went off on his own, and poor Margaret was left to bear the
brunt of her husband's displeasure because she had dared to inter-
fere. On learning of his whereabouts, she sent him a secret
message. 'Your father thought and thinketh yet that I was
assented to your departing, and that hath caused me to have great
heaviness. I hope he will be your good father hereafter, if ye
demean you well, and do as ye ought to do to him. . . . I would
ye should send me word how ye do, and how ye have shifted for
yourself since ye departed hence and that your father have no
knowledge thereof. I durst not let him know of the last letter
that ye wrote to me, because he was so sore displeased with me
at that time.'

Sir John was permitted to return to the bosom of the family, but

the interval of peace was shortlived. The following year his irate
father bodily turned him out of the house and in the late autumn
of 1465 Margaret Paston once more attempted to soften her
husband's wrath. But John Paston was not to be easily moved:
'Though in his presumptuous and indiscreet demeaning he gave
both me and you cause of displeasure, and to other of my servants
ill example, and [showed himself] weary of biding in my house;
yet that grieveth not me so evil as doth that I never could feel nor
understand him politic nor diligent in helping himself, but as a
drone amongst bees which labour for gathering honey in the
fields and the drone doth naught but taketh his part of it. . . . As
for your house and mine, I purpose not he shall come there,
neither by my will nor other, but if he can do more than look
forth and make a face and countenance.'

Torn between ingrained respect for her husband's wishes and
the prompting of her heart, Margaret tried a little later: 'I understand by John Pampyng that ye will not that your son be taken
into your house nor helped by you till such time of year as he
was put out thereof. . . . For God's sake, Sir, have pity on him;
remember ye it hath been a long season since he had aught of you
to help him with and he hath obeyed him to you and will do at
all times. At the reverence of God be ye his good father, and I hope
he shall ever know himself the better hereafter.'

But John Paston, angry to the bone, laid down to his wife what
the ambitious gentry expected of their sons: 'I let you weet I
would he did well, but I understand in him no disposition of
policy nor of governance as man of the world ought to do, but
only liveth and ever hath as man dissolute without any provision;
nor I understand nothing of what disposition he purposeth to be,
but only I can think he would dwell again in your house and mine,
and there eat and drink and sleep. Every poor man that hath
brought up his children to the age of twelve years waiteth [expects]
then to be helped and profited by his children, and every gentleman that hath discretion waiteth that his kin and servants that
liveth by him and his cost should help him forthward. As for your
son, ye know well he never stood you nor me in profit, ease or
health. . . . Wherefore give him no favour till ye feel what he is

and will be.' Sir John was at least twenty-five years of age, and his father had but a year to live.

Margaret Paston found herself going behind her husband's back to help her second son also, John Paston the younger.[1] When young John journeyed up to London, not long before his father's death, his mother lent him six marks ($£4$) for the trip, under what circumstances a hasty letter of hers shows: 'As soon as ye may without danger, purvey that I may have again the 6 marks that ye wot of, for I would not that your father wust it.' Young John was much steadier than Sir John, but apparently he too was not always a model young man, for his mother added, 'And if ye will have my good will, eschew such things as I spake to you of last in our parish church'.

From the time that Sir John succeeded to his father's estates in 1466 until his death in 1479, Margaret Paston carried on a running quarrel with him about his slipshod business dealings and his constant efforts to extract money from her. Toward the end of 1471, she was writing bitterly to young John about a hundred marks she had borrowed from 'Cousin Clere' to lend Sir John, who now in her need put off repaying her. His indifference 'is to mine heart a very spear', and in her mind simmered 'other things that I have borne these years that I speak not of'.

As Sir John continued to mortgage land and involve her in schemes for weathering his financial difficulties, she settled into a tone of harsh reproaches: 'I will not be compelled to pay your debts against my will, and [even] though I would, I may not'; there followed a threat about what might happen to him in her will.

Young John always treated his mother with respect, but he was loyal to his brother; and Margaret, as the years passed, felt shut out by both her sons. In dispatching instructions to her chaplain, Sir James Gloys, about seeing her son Walter well settled at Oxford, Margaret added, 'For I were loath to lose him, for I trust to have more joy of him than I have of them that be older'.

But there still lingered in Margaret Paston's breast a deep

---

[1] The Pastons were not the only family with two sons of the same name; Lady Stonor (Dame Elizabeth) had two brothers named John.

affection for her erring eldest son; and when in the winter of 1474-75 he wrote to her from Calais that he was ill, she replied from her lonely manor of Mauteby in a vein almost reminiscent of King Lear talking to Cordelia: 'Send me word how ye do of your sickness that ye had on your eye and your leg, and if God will not suffer you to have health, thank him thereof, and take it patiently, and come home again to me, and we shall live together, as God will give us grace to do. . . .' Several months later, perhaps feeling the wear and tear of his bachelor life, Sir John found the tenderness to write to his mother in the same vein: 'If I may do you service or ease, as ye and I have commoned heretofore, after I hear from you, as God help me, I purpose to leave all here, and come home to you, and be your husband and bailiff. . . .'

But a few months after, Sir John was negotiating mortgages again, and Margaret was once more giving vent to her indignation. On October 29, 1479, Sir John wrote to his mother from London that he had paid 5 marks to 'repledge out my gown of velvet and other gear'. He begged her to lend him 100s, for unless he could scrape up £10 'I wot not how to come home'. He never did come home; struck down a few days later by the plague then raging, he was hastily interred at the White Friars in London.

Toward the end of her life, after she had made her will, Margaret Paston felt so little confidence in her second son's affection for her that she turned to John's wife, the charming Margery, and begged her to act as an intermediary. The letter that John then wrote to his mother suggests that her action had suddenly caused him to perceive and to regret, this terrible uncertainty which was her portion in old age.

'Mother, it pleased you to have certain words to my wife at her departing, touching your remembrance of the shortness that ye think your days of, and also of the mind that ye have toward my brethren and sisters your children, and also of your servants, wherein ye willed her to be a mean to me, that I would tender and favour the same. Mother, saving your pleasure, there needeth no ambassadors nor means betwixt you and me; for there is neither wife nor other friend shall make me do that that your commandment shall make me to do, if I may have knowledge of it; and if

I have no knowledge, in good faith I am excusable, both to God and you. . . . Mother, I am right glad that my wife is anything [in] your favour or trust, but I am right sorry that my wife, or any other child or servant of yours, should be in better favour or trust with you, than myself. . . .'

Despite her naturally warm heart, Margaret Paston had shaped herself, in her dealings with her children, by her husband's precepts and the customs of the age. In her latter years she apparently sensed, without really understanding, that such conformity had cost her dear; and even when she bitterly assailed her eldest son for his spendthrift ways, she was perhaps masking with John Paston's voice the frustration that John Paston's acquisitive life had brought her to.

As the manor in the country and the gild in the town formed the matrices of society, so did the household determine, among the upper orders, the shape and colour of individual lives. Burgher or knightly, the household framed the experience of marriage and the begetting of offspring; the management of affairs; the education of children, other people's children.

It was an aggressive age, not ashamed of its quickening desires; and the household, reflecting the time in its outer fabric as in its human attitudes, was moving towards a more self-conscious decorum, an increasing enjoyment of comfort and familial privacy, and a taste for ostentation based on 'attendance' and symbolic of luxury.

Violent political alterations, the sharpening struggle for worldly success, the lure of opportunity often created challenges too severe for the head of the household to bear alone and thus required—permitted—many women to play active roles.

Though the people of the Yorkist Age thought that they looked suspiciously upon 'newfangledness' and sought to smooth the ragged edges of change in the blanket of custom, they responded to widening horizons of the future by studying, with a hard eye, the advancement of their children. Sons and daughters were baptized in the Faith Catholic, but they were reared according to a vigorous, if crude, rationalism that regarded apprenticeship (of all kinds) as the best method of fitting the young to the actual world. Though formal education was increasingly prized as the royal road to attainment, apprenticeship provided the fundamental lessons—it inserted the child firmly into the hierarchy of status, and it taught him the art of serving others as a means of furthering himself. This forcing-house of ambition, finding its form in the mediaeval past but adding urgency and calculation and widening possibilities, reveals its lineaments, a generation later, in the men pictured by Holbein, early-maturing faces shaped into the image of a wary, tough, urbane acquisitive manhood.

The subjects of Edward IV's grandson, Henry VIII, did not acknowledge this debt, or any of their debts, to the Yorkist Age. The ardent Tudor supporters who sat in Henry's Parliaments and Tudor historians had shaped the fifteenth century into a bugbear, an uncivil arena of civil strife, to remind all that the House of Tudor had rescued England from an ignominious anarchy and that the blessings of Tudor authoritarianism were, like the men who backed it, a new and wonderful phenomenon.

Subsequent ages were content, for the most part, to accept this estimate; it was not seriously challenged till the twentieth century, and then but sporadically. Yet, in the daily life of the Yorkist Age, as it has here been surveyed, the Wars of the Roses have raised but comparatively minor alarums. The time has now come, then, to examine this bugbear, to 'fight over York and Lancaster's long jars'—as Ben Jonson derisively hit off the blood-packed histories of William Shakespeare, faithful reflector of the Tudor attitude.

Epilogue

The Wars of the Roses

THE year 1450 opened gloomily: defeats in France and discontents at home sounded portents of disaster. Up from Sandwich and Dover shuffled bands of bedraggled soldiers with their women and children. Kentishmen surveyed with hard eyes these ghosts of a once-conquering army; they had had their fill of government that bungled military affairs and then subverted justice and trampled the rights of common folk so that bunglers could fill their pockets from the King's revenues. Misrule and the resentments it engendered had been growing for a long time.

The century had begun with an upheaval in the royal succession and the spilling of royal blood. By the deposition and murder of Richard II, the son of the Duke of Lancaster thrust himself on the throne as Henry IV (1399-1413). Though the usurper's reign was troubled by revolts, his mighty successor, Harry the Fifth (1413-22), the dreamer with the hands of iron, fired the dying mediaeval kingdom of England to a final blaze of French conquests. But in the reign of his feeble son, Henry VI (1422-61), the glories of Harry of Monmouth became a mockery.

Decade by decade the fabric of government, the bonds of civil harmony, unravelled in the nerveless fingers of the pious, ineffectual Henry VI. The lords who had governed the kingdom during Henry's minority quarrelled among themselves, and the court favourites who governed Henry after his coming of age (1437) plundered the treasury and the royal domain. The nobles of the realm, backed by 'affinities' of armed retainers, used intimidation or violence in competing for lands, influence, spoils of office. Demoralization at home and the progressive weakening of the

English hold on northern France interacted upon each other. The magnates, jockeying for power, could find no way to win or end the hopeless French war; and English captains brought back with them their mercenary bands to swell the 'menies' of these same magnates.

After the marriage of the beautiful, passionate Margaret of Anjou, niece of the French king, to Henry VI—a wedding of fire and milk—factional rivalries around the throne crystallized into a court party headed by the Dukes of Suffolk and Somerset and the Queen (the Lancastrians) and a group of lords excluded from power led by Richard, Duke of York (the Yorkists). The quarrel was exacerbated by the fact that York was heir to childless Henry's throne, though not so acknowledged by the House of Lancaster, and indeed could show a better title to the throne than the King.[1]

While Suffolk and Somerset arrogantly ignored a rising tide of unpopularity and mismanaged the truce with France procured by King Henry's marriage, the Duke of York was sent, in virtual exile, to govern Ireland. In the late summer of 1449 the armies of Charles VII easily overran Normandy; Somerset purchased an ignominious withdrawal to the coast towns by yielding Rouen.

So, as the ominous year 1450 began, troops which had once garrisoned Norman towns plodded up the roads of Kent 'in great misery and poverty by many companies and fellowships'. They begged, they stole; numbers of them were eventually hanged.

Early in January, Bishop Moleyns, one of the court party, rode down to Portsmouth with long-delayed wages for an unruly band of soldiers and sailors, mustered by Sir Thomas Kyriell to reinforce the Duke of Somerset. They accused Moleyns of pocketing some of their pay and cursed him as a betrayer of the English cause in France. When he haughtily rebuked them, 'they fell on him and cruelly there killed him'.

Six months later, the French crushed Kyriell's little army at Formigny. On August 19, James Gresham wrote to John Paston, 'And this same Wednesday was it told that Cherbourg is gone,

---

[1] York was descended from Lionel of Clarence, second son of Edward III; Henry VI's great-grandfather, John of Gaunt, Duke of Lancaster, was the third son.

and we have not now a foot of land in Normandy'. The loss of Guienne soon followed; of the English conquests there was left only the town of Calais.

By this time England herself heaved in the throes of violence. Within three weeks of Moleyns' murder, the Commons of Parliament, meeting at Westminster, hotly charged the Duke of Suffolk with criminal mismanagement of the realm. A strange fellow, 'Queen of the Faery', preached along the roads of Kent and Essex. Another agitator was hanged for attacking 'the rule of the lords'. Down in Canterbury, a fuller calling himself Blue Beard 'laboured to have gathered together a great fellowship'. Henry VI hastily committed Suffolk to the Tower. 'At the same time there was a great watch about the King and in the city of London every night. And the people were in doubt and fear what should befall, for the lords came to Westminster and Parliament with great powers as men of wars.'

French and Breton corsairs attacked the English coasts with impunity. On March 11, Agnes Paston wrote anxiously that a Paston acquaintance was 'taken with enemies, walking by the seaside. . . . God give grace that the sea may be better kept than it is now, or else it shall be a perilous dwelling by the sea coast'. The next day Margaret Paston sent her husband additional word that 'there be many enemies against Yarmouth and Cromer and have done much harm . . . and the said enemies be so bold that they come up to the land, and play them on Caister Sands and in other places, as homely as they were Englishmen'.

Five days later, on March 17, Queen Margaret and the court party sought to save Suffolk by commanding him to absent himself from England for five years. The next night the Duke barely escaped the rage of a London mob. On April 30 he embarked at Ipswich; off Dover, his ship was captured by a mysterious vessel which had been lying in wait for him. Two days later he was thrust into a small boat and made to kneel above a block. After a churl with a rusty sword took half a dozen strokes to smite off his head, body and head were cast upon the sands of Dover.

Rumour sped through Kentish villages that William Crowmer, sheriff of the county, and his father-in-law, Lord Say, Treasurer of England, furious at the part that Kentish men had supposedly played in the killing of Suffolk, had sworn to turn the shire into a deer park. People gathered together for the Whitsun celebrations, May 24. Suddenly they turned into armed bands. Many communities in the Weald of Kent arrayed all men of military age. The town of Lydd contributed a porpoise. From the ports, from the towns along the London-Dover road, men streamed northward. The rebels occupied Blackheath before the government or the Londoners knew what was stirring.

The leader of these thousands was a mysterious adventurer named Jack Cade, known also as Jack Amend-all, who called himself Mortimer, probably in order to suggest that he was kin to the Duke of York (York had inherited the great Mortimer estates). Jack Cade showed himself an able captain; the rebels ditched and embanked a fortified camp on Blackheath 'as it had been the land of war'.

Times had changed since Wat Tyler's day (1381), when peasants had risen against serfdom and the oppressions of the upper classes. Jack Cade's following included workers and tradesmen; sailors, fishermen from the ports; a scattering of priests; a knight who had fought at Agincourt; three men who had been sheriffs and two who had served as Knights of the Shire; some eighteen squires and seventy-four gentlemen.

Their grievances, published to the kingdom in a manifesto, were political and national. They denounced the King's evil advisers who had poisoned his mind against his true lords, like the Duke of York, and against his faithful commons. 'His false council hath lost his law, his merchandise is lost, his common people is destroyed, the sea is lost, France is lost, the King . . . oweth more than any King of England owed. . . .' The rebels demanded a programme of legal and financial reform; and they appealed to the country as moderate men respecting law.

Armed bands from Sussex and Surrey swelled the numbers on Blackheath. The commons of Essex were rising. Cade had plenty of sympathizers in London, not only among the labouring and artisan class; several wealthy merchants provided him with money and certain of the aldermen looked favourably on his cause. At first, however, the city took measures of defense. Cannon were mounted on wharves along the river; the Bridge was guarded; and barges cruised in the Thames to prevent Londoners from slipping over to Cade's camp.

News of the rising reached the King and court party at Leicester, where Parliament was meeting. Since the lords had come to the sessions with large trains of followers, the government was able to raise a sizable army in short order. Early in June, Henry VI and his nobles encamped in the open spaces of Clerkenwell and Smithfield. Other forces were marching to join them.

A delegation of royal councillors rode to Blackheath to make a pretence of considering the demands of the rebels. When Cade got word that King Henry's army was preparing to move against him, he abandoned his camp and withdrew his forces by night to the wooded region around Sevenoaks. Early the next morning the advance guard of the King's host, commanded by Sir Humphrey Stafford and his brother William, clattered across London Bridge and rode hard in pursuit of the rebels. At eleven o'clock the King, 'armed at all pieces', and an array of nobles led their forces through London and Southwark to the empty encampment on Blackheath. Later in the afternoon they received chilling news: the royal vanguard had ridden into a skilfully arranged ambush; both Staffords had been killed and their forces dispersed.

Next morning as Henry's lords attempted to muster their army on Blackheath, the troops 'made a sudden shout and noise upon the said heath saying, "Destroy we these traitors about the King!"' Men clamoured for the blood of Lord Say, Thomas Daniel, and other court favourites. Hastily the King gave order for Say, who was by his side, to be conveyed under arrest to the Tower. Henry and the men who ruled him then beat a quick retreat to Greenwich Castle; next day they fled to London by water. 'The Mayor with the commons of the city [i.e., the chief citizens] came to the King beseeching him that he would tarry in the city and they would live and die with him, and pay for his costs of household an half year.' But Queen Margaret and the court lords did not dare to face the storm; abandoning the capital to Jack Cade, they rode off with the King to Kenilworth.

Not many days later, the triumphant rebels returned to Black-heath led by the Captain of Kent, now 'arrayed like a lord' for he was wearing the handsome helmet, the brigandines 'set full with gilt nails' and the gilt spurs of Sir Humphrey Stafford. On Thursday the first of July they flooded into Southwark; Cade established his headquarters at the White Hart Inn.

With the victorious Kentishmen now at the other end of London Bridge, Cade's sympathizers in the city were able to dominate the municipal council. A rich alderman favoured by the court party, Philip Malpas, had already been deprived of his cloak of office. When Robert Horne dared to oppose admitting the Kentishmen to the city, he was promptly consigned to prison. By this time a force of rebels from Essex was gathering outside Aldgate.

In the late afternoon of Friday, July 3, Jack Cade appeared on London Bridge at the head of his host. The drawbridge was lowered. Cade swung his sword, hewed the ropes, and rode into the capital like a conqueror. Joined by a rabble of Londoners, his forces paraded the city. When the Captain of Kent reached the famous London stone on Candlewick Street, he reportedly drew his sword, struck the stone, and announced, 'Now is Mortimer lord of this city'. Stringent proclamations were cried that there was to be no robbery or violence; but a horde of Kentishmen pillaged Philip Malpas' mansion to the bare walls. In the long June twilight, Cade and most of his men rode back to their quarters in Southwark. Some remained, however, and with the aid of sympathetic Londoners spent the night terrorizing known enemies of the cause and searching for booty.

Next morning early, the hated Lord Say was surrendered by Lord Scales, Captain of the Tower, to the London magistrates. Though he claimed trial by his peers, he was promptly arraigned at Gildhall. At 11 o'clock the Captain of Kent came riding into London, clad 'in a blue gown of velvet with sable furs and a straw hat upon his head and a sword drawn in his hand', his followers marching behind him on foot. Impatient with the comedy of justice being enacted at Gildhall, the Kentishmen seized Lord Say and bore him to the Standard in Cheapside. Cade motioned an executioner to do his work. Say's corpse was stripped of clothes, the legs bound with rope and tied to a horse, and the bleeding trunk drawn through the streets of London. Say's head, thrust on a long pole, led the rebel throng as they greeted their fellows of Essex camped outside Aldgate. A prize captive of the Essex men, William Crowmer, Sheriff of Kent, was beheaded. With his head bobbing atop a pole beside Say's, the rebels marched jauntily through London, pausing now and again to make the two heads kiss. After Jack Cade had dined, he permitted his followers to rob his host; money was extorted from a number of well-to-do Londoners. Then the Captain once more retired to Southwark.

By this time the substantial citizens had had enough of Jack Cade's posturing and the pillaging of unruly bands. On Sunday morning, the Mayor and aldermen decided, with the support of Lord Scales, to rid themselves of the Kentishmen.

As darkness fell on Sunday evening, a stout body of armed Londoners and the garrison of the Tower, led by the famous captain Mathew Gough, advanced across London Bridge. The rebels rushed to meet them. In the narrow roadway, hemmed between houses and shops, a press of men hacked and thrust at each other. 'Then at night the Captain put me out into the battle at the bridge,' a captive of the rebels wrote to John Paston, 'and there I was wounded, and hurt near to death; and I was six hours in the battle, and might never come out thereof. . . .' From nine or ten that evening until eight in the morning 'there was fighting upon London Bridge, and many a man was slain or cast in Thames, harness, body and all; and among the press was slain Mathew Gough and John Sutton, Alderman'. Finally as Cade's forces began to give way, the Captain of Kent fired the drawbridge, and smoke and flame parted the combatants.

Not many hours later, a delegation of bishops arrived in Southwark bringing an offer from Lord Scales on behalf of the government. If the rebels would lay down their arms and return peacefully to their homes, they should all have 'charters of pardon' and their grievances would be considered. Jack Cade desperately, or foolishly, accepted the terms. The pardons were duly inscribed, Cade's in the name of Mortimer; the rebels dispersed to their homes; Cade withdrew with barges of booty to Rochester, made a half hearted attempt to win Queenborough Castle, and then, his followers abandoning him, fled to the weald of Sussex. A few days later he was proclaimed a traitor and a thousand marks were offered for him dead or alive, on the grounds that his pardon bore a forged name. A squire, Alexander Iden, captured and mortally wounded him. The corpse, lying naked in a cart, was identified by the hostess of the White Hart, then beheaded and quartered. The head was thrust upon London Bridge, to face Kent; pieces of the body were sent as grisly reminders to towns strongly implicated in the rising.

Two days before the Captain of Kent occupied Southwark, on June 29, Bishop Ayscough of Salisbury, the King's confessor, met a violent fate at the hands of his flock. As he was beginning to celebrate Mass at Edington, he was 'drawn from the altar and led up to an hill there . . . and they slew him horribly . . . and spoiled him unto the naked skin, and rent his bloody shirt into pieces. . . .' Throughout the summer the realm heaved in local riots and risings.

Toward the end of July more bands of soldiers who had been driven from Normandy appeared in London. When they learned that Lord Say had been worshipfully buried at the Greyfriars, they stormed into the church, pulled down Say's coats of arms affixed to pillars and replaced them upside down. On the first of August, the Duke of Somerset himself rode into the capital, 'many poor soldiers with him'. He had been hastily summoned by the court party, who were thrown into a panic at news that the Duke of York was preparing to return from Ireland. For several days thereafter, refugees from France 'in right poor array piteous to see' trudged into London dragging carts loaded with their household stuff. When St. Bartholomew's Fair opened on August 23, the city magistrates appeared with a force of three hundred men to preserve order. 'The world was so strange at that time, no man might well ride or go in no parts of this land without a strength of fellowship but that he were robbed.'

At the end of September, as the newly elected Mayor rode in procession through the city, a band of discharged soldiers, 'well armed for war with glaives and axes . . . made a countenance' at the civic dignitaries. The Mayor ordered them to disperse, was answered by a barrage of curses, and promptly 'took their weapons from them and sent various of them to prison'.

Many 'strange and wonderful bills were set in divers places, some at the King's own chamber door at Westminster. . . .' One such bill ran:

> But Suffolk, Salisbury, and Say—
> Slain were they that England betrayed.
> On the first day of May we should be afraid
> And say woe away.
> But Suffolk, Salisbury and Say
> Be done to death by May.
> England may seem well away.

The Duke of York had now returned from Ireland. Sir Thomas Tresham, Speaker of the last Parliament, was murdered as he rode to meet the Duke; but backed by a well armed fellowship, York confronted the feeble King to demand the arrest of the Duke of Somerset and reform of the government. Henry shufflingly promised to carry out his dear cousin's wishes. In a lowering atmosphere of doubts and fears Parliament was summoned to meet at Westminster. Badges of the Fetterlock, the Duke of York's cognizance, were set up at night in many places, only to be torn down and replaced by the King's arms, which were in turn removed. Daily the Mayor in full armour rode about the streets with men 'harnessed defensibly for the war'. Chains were drawn across alleys and lanes. A proclamation was cried that no Londoner 'should speak about nor meddle with any matters done in the Parliament nor the Lords'. Toward the end of November the Duke of York rode into London with some three thousand men at his back. He was supported by his brother-in-law, the Duke of Norfolk, with a great fellowship 'six clarions before him blowing', and by his powerful nephew, the Earl of Warwick (the Kingmaker).

While the armed menies of rival lords glowered at each other in the London streets, the Parliament at Westminster was shaken by angry sessions. On December 1, adherents of the Yorkist lords smashed into the Duke of Somerset's quarters at Greyfriars; they failed to lay hands on the Duke, and after a scene of wild plundering, the Mayor and his armed fellowship put down the riot.

Despite York's popularity in London and with the Commons, those who possessed the King possessed the government. The court party was soon able to get rid of Parliament. Poor King Henry, his long-jawed defenceless face with its high nose emphasizing the bewildered innocence of the dark eyes, piously hoped for the best and did as the Duke of Somerset and the Queen bade. The King of England was become no more than the inert prize of savagely contending factions. So drew to a close the turbulent unhappy year of 1450, which set the ugly pattern for the decade to follow.

In 1453 this political warfare was embittered and complicated by two events: King Henry, gripped by a 'sudden and thoughtless fright', went mad, even as his grandfather, Charles VI of France, had gone mad. Closed in an animal stupor, his lack-lustre eyes bent upon the ground, he understood nothing that was said to him. A few weeks later, Queen Margaret gave birth to an heir. All the elements of her fiery nature and haughty breeding became fused in a passionate resolve to protect the birthright of her son; frantically she worked to restore her husband to sanity and to keep power in her hands.

But with the King's incapacity, authority passed to the royal Council; towards the end of the year the Duke of Somerset was sent to the Tower, and in the spring the Duke of York became Protector of the Realm. His power lasted only until Christmas (1454), when King Henry regained his wits. The Queen and Somerset resumed the rule of the kingdom.

The Yorkists, threatened by an assembling of Lancastrian lords, gathered a small army and intercepted the royal force at St. Albans in May (1455). This so-called battle, usually taken to mark the outbreak of the Wars of the Roses, was only a skirmish. In a sudden assault, the Duke of York and the Earl of Warwick broke into the town, scattered the royal troops, and took possession of the King, who was wounded in the neck by an arrow-graze. Probably fewer than a hundred men were killed; but the Duke of Somerset, the Earl of Northumberland, and Lord Clifford lay dead in St. Peter's Street, the Duke of Buckingham's son died soon after, and Somerset's heir, Henry Beaufort, was severely wounded.

The following year (1456), the Queen managed to regain control of her husband. She abandoned London, which had grown increasingly hostile, and set about gaining adherents to her cause in Cheshire and Lancashire. The Yorkist lords retired to their strongholds, Warwick to Calais, of which he had become Captain.

While the Duke of York and the Queen manoeuvred for advantage, tensely watching each other, the realm lay virtually ungoverned. London was shaken by affrays and sudden violences. In 1456 and again in 1457 the mercers stirred riots against the Italian merchants, hated because of privileges the court party had showered upon them. Bloody fighting erupted in Fleet Street between Londoners and lawyers of the Inns of Court. Rumours coursed the streets. Ballads attacking the government were set up on church doors. 'Some said that the Duke of York had great wrong,' Gregory reports, 'but what wrong there was, no man dared say, but some "grounyd" and some lowered and had disdain of other, etc.'

The wool and cloth trade languished. The government of court lords was both too weak and too reckless to support the claims of English merchants in foreign lands or to 'keep the narrow seas'; though the Yorkist Earl of Warwick at Calais won many hearts in England by doughty exploits in the Channel. But even Warwick could not prevent the plundering of Sandwich by a French fleet in 1457. The news sent a thrill of fear and indignation throughout the realm, especially when it was whispered that Queen Margaret had secretly urged Piers de Brezé, commander of the French squadron, to attack the Yorkist stronghold. Pirates, maintained by the magnates, plundered foreign shipping, and English merchants helplessly bore the brunt of the inevitable reprisals. When the Mayor of London and a delegation of merchants complained to the Chancellor against Lord Bonvile's attacks on Burgundian vessels, they received such an empty answer that 'with one voice' they cried out furiously, ' "justice! justice! justice!" ' There was nothing the harassed Chancellor could do except hastily withdraw.

In the countryside, the great lords and their retainers ruled virtually as they pleased. The chronicler Hardyng rhymes a dismal picture:

> In every shire with jacks and sallets clean
>   Misrule doth rise and maketh neighbours war;
> The weaker goes beneath, as oft is seen;
>   The mightiest his quarrel will prefer;
> The poor man's cause is put on back full far,
>   Which, if both peace and law were well conserved,
> Might be amend, and thanks of God deserved.

The fabric of order, crumbling for a generation, had fallen to pieces. Authority had become only a name for the duel to the death between the Duke of York and Queen Margaret.

By the late summer of 1459, the Queen judged that she was strong enough to attack the Yorkists. A royal army, assembled at Coventry, began to move on the Duke of York's stronghold at Ludlow Castle. Warwick's father, the Earl of Salisbury, beat off a Lancastrian army that tried to intercept him at Blore Heath, and triumphantly brought his Yorkshiremen to Ludlow. The Earl of Warwick crossed the Channel at the head of 200 men-at-arms and 400 archers, bright in red jackets flaunting the Warwick badge of bear-and-ragged staff. Unopposed, he and his men entered London and then rode to join York.

But when the King's armies appeared before Ludlow, treachery in the Yorkist ranks forced the leaders to flee without a battle. The Duke of York and his eldest son Edmund, Earl of Rutland, took refuge in Ireland, where the Duke was received like a king, while Warwick and Salisbury and York's second son Edward, Earl of March (later Edward IV) sailed to the Earl's stronghold of Calais.

The evidence of letters and chronicles, the barrage of anti-government satires, the complaints of the trading classes indicate that, up to the end of 1459, townsmen generally and the gentry of the southern parts favoured the Yorkist cause. They had hoped that the Duke of York and his followers might restore order and revive justice in the realm. But they were wary of 'meddling betwixt lords', and they were not yet ready to take arms for the Duke against a régime that still represented their King.

Once the Yorkists were driven from England, however, they won an increasingly popular sympathy, fanned by resentment against the vengeful, reckless acts of the court party. In a Parliament packed with Lancastrians, York and his chief supporters were attainted of high treason and their lands confiscated. Three of the court lords brutally sacked the Duke's town of Newbury, hanging a number of the inhabitants. Mistrusting the hearts of the people and fearing a return of the Yorkists, the government issued streams of orders to arrest traitors and array troops and contribute money to the empty treasury. The citizens of London defied a demand for soldiers. The Master of the King's Ordinance was murdered between Dunstable and St. Albans as he was bringing a train of armaments to the capital. Placards nailed on church doors called for the return of the Yorkists; ribald songs attacked the Queen.

When the 'Calais Earls'—the Earl of Warwick and York's son Edward, Earl of March—took time by the forelock and landed at Sandwich in June of 1460—the rainiest summer in a hundred years—the sailors of the port towns and the people of Kent rose joyfully to join them. Canterbury threw open its gates; the Archbishop blessed and joined the cause. On the march toward the capital, bands of men came in from all directions to swell the host. Londoners poured across the Bridge to welcome the Yorkist chieftains.

A few days later, Warwick and the Earl of March led their forces against the King's army entrenched in the river meadows south of Northampton. The royal host was quickly routed (July 10, 1460); King Henry was taken captive in his tent and became the monarch of a Yorkist government. The Duke of York, returning from Ireland in early October, startled the realm—and, apparently, Warwick and March—by demanding, before the

Lords in Parliament, the crown of England. After some wrangling, he accepted a compromise by which he was proclaimed heir to the throne. The title of Henry VI's son, Prince Edward, was set aside—but not in the heart of his indomitable mother, Queen Margaret, who had escaped to Wales after the battle of Northampton. She and the Lancastrian magnates of the West and North began assembling an army in Yorkshire. In early December, the Duke of York set forth from London to encounter the Queen's host, leaving Warwick to guard the capital. There followed in the next three months a wild alternation of victories and defeats.

At the end of December, the Yorkists suffered at Wakefield a crushing reverse in which the Duke of York himself, his son Edmund of Rutland, Warwick's father and one of his brothers, and other captains perished. Fired by this victory, the Lancastrian host, headed by Queen Margaret and her prince and swelled by bands of Welsh and Scots and marauding borderers, swarmed southward. A trail of burning villages marked their course. Abbeys were sacked, barns and manor houses gutted, livestock killed or stolen. Refugees fled to London, spreading tales of rape and murder. The Croyland chronicler records the terror of villagers and monks as they worked frantically on their fenny island to barricade themselves against these hordes. His sigh of relief can be heard clear across the centuries as he writes exultingly after the invaders had passed Croyland Abbey—'Blessed be God who did not give us for a prey unto their teeth!'

The Earl of Warwick, hastily gathering forces, marched to St. Albans to block the Queen's advance. In a confused battle (February 17, 1461), the Lancastrians overwhelmed Warwick's elaborate defences and retook possession of King Henry, but the Earl managed to get the shreds of his army away under cover of darkness. Far from beaten, he joined forces with his protégé Edward, now the heir of York, who had overthrown a Lancastrian army at Mortimer's Cross (February 3).

The Queen hesitated, instead of striking for the capital—perhaps alarmed by the depredations of her Northerners. The Londoners, plucking up their courage, forced Mayor Lee to break off negotiations with the Lancastrians. At the end of February, Warwick and Edward of York triumphantly entered the city. Queen Margaret's army withdrew, pillaging, into Yorkshire. Young Edward, on March 4, was acclaimed King Edward IV. A few days later he and Warwick started in pursuit of their enemies.

From the southern parts, East Anglia, and the Midlands, men rushed to join the Yorkists. Their force could boast only half a dozen lords, but the ship banner of Bristol and the Elephant and Castle of Coventry and many other town flags waved above their troops. The plundering of the Northerners and rumour that Queen Margaret had promised them free pillage of all southern England created for the Yorkists the only army during the Wars of the Roses supported by popular enthusiasm.

Between Saxton and Towton, a dozen miles south of York, the pursuers found some 20,000 enemies massed on a narrow plateau bounded by a stream in flood—the full muster of King Henry's lords and their menies. Edward and Warwick brought perhaps 15,000 men to the field (Palm Sunday, March 29).

As snow began to blow in the faces of the Lancastrians, the iron ranks rushed together. Hour after hour thousands of men slashed and hacked at each other. Though savagely pressed by superior numbers, the Yorkists were bolstered by the indomitable prowess of their young King. But not till the field became cumbered with heaps of the slain and twilight was coming down did King Henry's forces crumple into flight. They were so bitterly pursued that the snowy plain all the way to York was reportedly stained with blood.

Towton was to be the longest, fiercest engagement of the Wars of the Roses, the greatest battle so far fought on English soil. Perhaps something like a quarter of the combatants perished or were mortally wounded. Europe was shaken by tidings of the casualties. A Milanese ambassador, reporting to his master that King Henry, Queen Margaret, and their prince had fled to Scotland, commented, 'Anyone who reflects at all upon the wretchedness of that Queen and the ruins of those killed, and considers the ferocity of the country and the state of mind of the victors, should indeed, it seems to me, pray to God for the dead, and not less for the living'.

The kingdom of England then experienced eight years of increasing quiet and slowly reviving trade as Edward and Warwick struggled to correct the abuses that had ruined the House of Lancaster. For a few years Queen Margaret's adherents managed to make trouble in Wales and a few other regions and to keep up an organized resistance in the far North; but the Queen herself was forced to retire to France in 1463; the victories of Hedgeley Moor and Hexham (1464) brought death to most of the remaining Lancastrian leaders; and finally, in 1465, King Henry was captured wandering helplessly in Lancashire.

Yet, though the House of York had now secured its hold on the kingdom, the Nevilles shadowed the royal government of Edward IV. George Neville, Bishop of Exeter and then Archbishop of York, was Chancellor of the realm; his brother John, Earl of Northumberland and later Marquess Montagu, ruled in the North; and the third brother, the king-making Richard, Earl of Warwick, managed military operations on land and sea and insisted on managing Edward's foreign policy as well. 'Conductor of the kingdom under King Edward', his enemy James Kennedy, Bishop of St. Andrews, called him. King Edward, however, did not intend merely to reign rather than rule, nor was he content to suffer the pretensions of overmighty subjects, which had so embroiled the realm of Henry VI. As the decade of the 1460's passed, the King and the Kingmaker moved towards a showdown to determine who was master of England.

Warwick was anything but 'The Last of the Barons'. Unlike his mediaeval predecessors, he had no desire to clip the King's powers. He worked as hard as Edward to strengthen the royal authority, but he wanted to wield it for himself. Relying on the force of the Warwick legend and carefully cultivating popularity, Warwick saw himself not as a representative of the baronage, but as a unique individual limited only by his capacity to create and exploit opportunities; he is therefore among the first of modern political adventurers.

King Edward was the mightiest warrior in Europe but he hated war; he earnestly sought to dispense justice; he had an eye for able administrators; he could not resist a brave man, especially if he was convivial, nor a pretty girl. Beneath this amiable demeanour young Edward—he was only nineteen when he became king—possessed intelligence and will, a flair for politics, an ambition to create a strong monarchy. He was grateful to the great Earl, but he meant to be the ruler of England.

A little too optimistically he soon began moving towards the accomplishment of his purpose. His secret marriage to a beautiful Lancastrian widow (Elizabeth Woodville) which thwarted Warwick's plans for a French match (1464); his dismissal of Warwick's intriguing brother George, Archbishop of York, from the chancellorship (1467), coupled with favours bestowed upon the Queen's numerous kin; and his decision to ally himself with Charles, Duke of Burgundy, rather than with Warwick's friend, Louis XI of France (1468), progressively lacerated the pride of the Kingmaker.

In the summer of 1469 the Earl of Warwick, marrying his elder daughter to Edward's shallow brother George, Duke of Clarence, inspired a rising of Northerners, who at Edgecot defeated an army under the Earls of Pembroke and Devon marching to the King's aid.

But King Edward was never better—as Louis XI said of Francesco Sforza—than when the water was up to his neck. On learning of the disaster of Edgecot, Edward chose to exchange the lion's role for the fox's. He permitted his small force to disperse. George Neville, Archbishop of York, at the head of a strong war-party, found him almost alone at Olney. Suavely the Archbishop suggested that the King entrust himself to Neville hands, and suavely King Edward agreed. On August 2 the royal captive arrived at Coventry to confront Warwick and Clarence. They seem to have prepared only the rough outline of their drama. Edward proceeded to transform it into high comedy by the impeccable style with which he played his part. He gave them fair words, he smiled, he signed whatever they put before him. About August 7 he was removed from Coventry—perhaps the citizens were becoming a little restive—and put behind the walls of Warwick Castle.

The news of the King's capture could not be disguised, and

England immediately began to show its dislike of the situation by outbreaks of disorder. London was soon hovering on the brink of mob violence. Warwick could manage the King but not the King's realm. Rapidly the country slipped out of control. Edward was suddenly conveyed by secret night marches to Middleham Castle, Warwick's stronghold in Wensleydale, Yorkshire. Doubtless the imperturbable King realized that the move signalled Warwick's weakness.

As the Archbishop of York and Clarence tried to keep up a semblance of government at Westminster, a Lancastrian rising broke out on the Scots border. The Earl of Warwick, setting about to gather men in Yorkshire, was forced to cancel the meeting of Parliament which he had summoned in order to legalize the Neville triumph. King Edward cheerfully affixed his seal to the countermanding order, and a few days later he cheerfully listened to a proposition from the Archbishop of York. Warwick, it turned out, could not raise troops to put down the Lancastrians; men refused to take arms until they knew that the King was his own master. George Neville, hastily called northward by his brother, offered King Edward a little more liberty if he would support Warwick's campaign. Amiably Edward agreed. He assured the Archbishop that he harboured no ill-will toward the House of Neville. Kept secretly in touch with affairs through Burgundian agents and his own followers, he perceived that his hour was approaching.

Edward was permitted to enter the city of York in royal state, to talk freely with those who thronged to pay him homage, and to take up official residence at Pontefract Castle. Men then flocked to Warwick's banners, and in short order he extinguished the Lancastrian rising. After riding up to York to witness the execution of the rebel leader on September 29, Edward returned to Pontefract. Appreciating to the full the alterations which the people of England had made in Warwick's drama, he now adroitly prepared his own script for the denouement. Without consulting the Nevilles, he summoned his chief lords to join him at Pontefract. They obeyed with alacrity. Lord Hastings and Edward's brother Richard, Duke of Gloucester, came riding in with several hundred armed men. Blandly the King informed the Earl of Warwick that he was returning to his capital, and there was nothing the Kingmaker could do but acquiesce. At the head of a dozen lords and a thousand horse the King of England was heartily welcomed to London by the mayor and aldermen in scarlet and 200 of the chief citizens in blue.

Edward now showed his quality as a statesman. In order to quiet the realm, he invited Warwick and Clarence to a council of peers so that all differences might be reconciled. After securing guarantees, they rode into London in December to find the King ready to forgive all and offer full pardons. But the exasperated Kingmaker, who had apparently won everything only to discover that he had gained nothing, was soon plotting with Lancastrian malcontents in Lincolnshire. Meanwhile, maintaining his affable demeanour, King Edward worked diligently to restore his position. Polydore Vergil, probably familiar with documents now lost, has high praise for the King's sagacity in this restless winter of 1469-70: 'Not to omit any carefulness, travail, nor counsel that meet was for his avail in this troublesome time, he regarded nothing more than to win again the friendship of such noble men as were now alienated from him, to confirm the good will of them who were hovering and unconstant, and to reduce the mind of the multitude, being brought by these innovations [i.e., Warwick's capture of the King] into a murmuring and doubtfulness what to do, unto their late obedience, affection, and good will towards him.'

Consequently, when Warwick secretly incited his Lincolnshire friends to take arms, the King had no difficulty crushing the rebellion. The rebel leader, Sir Robert Welles, captured after the rout of 'Lose-Coat Field' (March 12, 1470), confessed that the Earl of Warwick and the Duke of Clarence had provoked the rising in order to make Clarence king. Warwick and Clarence, who had been trying to raise troops at Coventry, sought desperately to preserve a mask of loyalty; but when Edward with a fine army at his back— 'it was said that there were never seen in England so many goodly men and so well arrayed in a field', reported a Paston correspondent—demanded that the Kingmaker and Clarence appear 'in humble wise' to explain themselves, the 'great rebels' hastily gathered up their wives, fled to Exeter, and took ship for France.

But the Earl of Warwick still had resources. Supported by Louis XI ('the universal spider'), who reconciled the Kingmaker and Henry VI's bitter Queen Margaret of Anjou,[1] Warwick and Clarence landed in the West Country in September, 1470, to win the realm for Lancaster. King Edward, who had moved into Yorkshire in order to keep watch on this Neville region, was almost captured by Warwick's brother John, Marquess Montagu, supposedly a loyal Yorkist. With a handful of lords the King managed to reach Lynn and hastily sailed for the Low Countries, ruled by his brother-in-law and ally, the Duke of Burgundy.

The kingdom fell to Warwick and the Lancastrians without a blow. Henry VI, led from his prison in the Tower, was reinstalled King of England. But only Neville adherents and diehard Lancastrians showed any enthusiasm for Warwick's shaky régime, headed by a shambling King who was no more, as Commynes phrased it, than a crowned calf, a shadow on a wall.

The fugitive Edward, meanwhile, putting all possible pressure on his reluctant brother-in-law, finally secured 50,000 crowns and a small fleet. In the middle of March, 1471, he landed at Ravenspur in Yorkshire with about 1,500 men, 1,000 English and 500 Flemings. Through a threatening countryside Edward marched his little band boldly towards York. Kingston-upon-Hull shut him out. Beverley opened its gates. The magistrates of York warned him off; but after Edward asserted that he had come only to claim his father's duchy he and his army were permitted to spend the night within the city. The Earl of Northumberland 'sat still' upon his estates, a large force of retainers gathered about him; but Edward learned that the Marquess Montagu lay in strength at Pontefract to block the road south.

Nonetheless he set forward the next morning, undismayed. Marching with great speed, he somehow slipped around the Marquess and drove onward to Sandal Castle, where a band of

---

[1] At the price of a marriage between the Earl's younger daughter Anne and Margaret's son Prince Edward.

Yorkist adherents awaited his coming. Then he continued to move rapidly southward. At Nottingham scouts brought the first sure word of the mighty forces which were gathering to crush him. Warwick had set up his standard at Coventry and was raising an army by appeals and menaces. Clarence was levying troops in the southwest counties. The Bastard of Fauconberg hovered in the Channel with a powerful fleet. Queen Margaret and her son were momently expected in England. The Duke of Exeter, the Earl of Oxford, and Viscount Beaumont had reached Newark with 'a great fellowship'. With Marquess Montagu pursuing him, Warwick to his front, and Oxford on his left flank, Edward and his force appeared to be doomed. But the King possessed important, though intangible, resources: his own peerless generalship, the loyalty of his followers, and the discontents of his brother George of Clarence.

Quickly estimating the situation, Edward made a sudden feint to the east in such ostensible force that Oxford's army fled from Newark in the night. Then hurrying his force southward to Leicester, where he was joined by some 2,500 men, he wheeled to march directly on Coventry. Warwick, deciding to await reinforcements, fell back within the city walls. On March 29, only two weeks after his landing, Edward proclaimed himself King and offered the Earl of Warwick the choice of pardon for life only or the hazard of battle. When the Earl refused to be drawn, Edward sent a small force towards Leicester to disrupt Oxford's advance once again, and marched with the rest of his men towards the on-coming army of the Duke of Clarence. Brother George, deserting his father-in-law, brought himself and his troops into the King's camp. The Yorkists turned back to Coventry, but though Marquess Montagu and Oxford had now reinforced Warwick, the Neville-Lancastrian army remained behind the city walls.

Suddenly King Edward hurled his force southward. On Sunday, April 7, he was at Daventry, on Tuesday following at Dunstable. He spent Wednesday night at St. Albans, where, in exchange for a pardon, he received the secret submission of George Neville, Archbishop of York, guarding Henry VI in London. At noon on

Maundy Thursday, April 11, the gates of that city flew open, and King Edward, without striking a blow, had regained his capital. After pausing at St. Paul's to make offering and then to pack King Henry off to the Tower, Edward hastened to Westminster in order to greet his Queen. The previous October she had taken sanctuary in the Abbey and, shortly after, given birth to her first son (later Edward V).

> The kyng comforted the quene and other ladyes eke,
> His swete babis full tendurly he did kys,
> The yonge prynce he behelde and in his armys did bere.
> Thus his bale turnyd hym to blis;
> Aftur sorow joy, the course of the worlde is.
> The sighte of his babis relesid paarte of his woo;
> Thus the wille of God in every thyng is doo.

Two days later, Easter Saturday, King Edward received the news he was hoping for: Warwick and the Lancastrians, coming in pursuit, were approaching Barnet. Ranks swelled by such stalwarts as John Howard who arrived with some 200 men, the Yorkist army marched from the city that afternoon; and after night had fallen King Edward thrust his forces so close to the enemy arrayed on the high plateau just north of Barnet, that battle could not be declined.

By dawn the next morning, Easter Sunday, a thick fog blanketed both armies. As trumpets blared and the lines of fighting men rushed together, the left wing of the Yorkists, commanded by Lord Hastings, was suddenly assailed on the flank and driven into flight by the enemy right wing under the Earl of Oxford. In the darkness of the night before, King Edward had disposed his forces so that, without his being aware, his right wing extended beyond the Lancastrian left and Hastings' left wing therefore was outflanked by Oxford. Jubilantly the Earl pursued fleeing Yorkists all the way to Barnet. Meanwhile, on the other side of the field, King Edward's right under his brother Richard, Duke of Gloucester, had no such advantage as Oxford because Gloucester's men had to scramble through a deep depression, now called Dead Man's

Bottom. Fortunately for Edward, the fog hid the disaster on the left from the main body of his troops, and though the Yorkists were outnumbered, they pressed fiercely against the centre of Warwick's army. Edward himself, as usual, set a sterling example for his men. He 'valiantly assailed [his enemies] in the midst and strongest of their battle, where he, with great violence, beat and bore down afore him all that stood in his way and then turned to range, first on that one hand and then on that other hand in length, and so beat and bore them down, so that nothing might stand in the sight of him and the well assured fellowship that attended truly upon him'.

But Oxford, having reassembled his troop in Barnet, now hastened back to take the Yorkists in the rear. Suddenly out of the mist came a hail of arrows. Then men were shouting 'Treason! Treason!' Oxford's force recoiled; the opposing ranks fell into disorder. The battle line had so twisted about that the Earl of Oxford's men had collided with their own army. As the Earl fled with a small band for the safety of Scotland, and panic ran down the Lancastrian ranks, King Edward, perceiving that his moment had come, smashed into the enemy centre. The Lancastrian-Neville army disintegrated into flight. Warwick the Kingmaker and his brother John, the Marquess of Montagu, were slain. The battle had lasted about three hours. It was but a month since Edward had come ashore at Ravenspur on what seemed to be a hopeless venture.

Queen Margaret and her son, landing this very day at Weymouth, began rallying the Lancastrians of the West Country to their banners. Three weeks later, on May 4, King Edward brought the Queen's forces to bay at Tewkesbury and quickly put them to flight. Prince Edward was slain; the chief Lancastrian captains were taken prisoner and executed. On the night that Edward IV and his victorious army entered London (May 21), Henry VI met his death in the Tower. The direct line of Lancaster thus came to an end. Queen Margaret, captured after the battle of Tewkesbury, was ransomed by Louis XI and died in France.

The wars between Lancaster and York were finished. King Edward spent the remaining dozen years of his rule in developing the strong monarchy he had aimed at since 1461. In 1474 he put an end to a costly sea-war with the Hanse towns. The following year, the Truce of Picquigny between Edward and Louis XI opened up markets in France. With the support of his able, loyal brother Richard, Duke of Gloucester, the King increased the yield of the royal domain, reorganized finances, steadily tightened his grip on the realm, and died, a much loved prince, at forty-one (April 9, 1483).

The usurpation of the throne by Richard of Gloucester (Richard III), who thrust aside his twelve-year-old nephew Edward V (reigned April 9-June 26, 1483), and Richard's crushing of the Duke of Buckingham's revolt in October of 1483 brought misery or death only to a handful of partisans. Henry Tudor's victory at Bosworth Field over Richard III (August 22, 1485) likewise had little effect upon the realm. Two years later Henry VII defeated at Stoke (June 16, 1487) the last significant Yorkist challenge to his crown in a campaign which, again, touched only a small minority of Englishmen.

The period 1455 (skirmish at St. Albans) to 1487 (Stoke Field) was not a generation of continuing campaigns and battles in which the realm of England was torn by the 'horrors of war'. Warfare came in bursts, interposed among periods of peacefulness. Even during the times of intensest strife, 1460-61 and 1470-71, most parts of the kingdom and most Englishmen were not involved in hostilities, and the brief campaigns themselves produced, except among the lords and their adherents, relatively few casualties.

Some of the chroniclers talk of hundreds of thousands of men fighting for King Edward at Towton, but such resounding figures indicate only that the Yorkists had a large force compared to the normal size of armies. On the small plateau where Towton was fought, 100,000 men could hardly be arrayed for battle.

Yorkist dispatches listed 28,000 men—20,000 Lancastrians and 8,000 Yorkists—killed in this struggle. It is doubtful if more than 35,000 were engaged on both sides, and probably not many more than 28,000 men were slain in all the battles of the Roses put together, far fewer than the number of men, women, and children who died of the plague in the same period. The methods of waging war, the size of the armies, and the battle policy of the Yorkists all helped to hold down casualties.

Knightly armour in this period reached its climax of strength and weight. In place of the old chain mail, men encased themselves in complete steel, reinforced over the shoulders by massive plates called pauldrons and bristling with protruding metal points; but only the King and the wealthiest lords could afford this cunningly articulated steel plate, the finest suits of which were made in Milan. The 'harness' worn by most men-at-arms and even many nobles consisted of a 'pair of brigandines', a leather coat covered with overlapping metal plates, often decorated with gilt nails, which was reinforced by pauldrons and steel leg-armour. Metal helmets with fearsome snouts, visored or pierced with holes, completed the equipment. These warriors wielded swords or battle-axes or spears. Sir John Paston paid £20 for a harness, but ordinary brigandines could be purchased for 16s 8d. So lapped in steel, nobles had an excellent chance of surviving the strokes of battle, but if they fought on the losing side, their cumbrous metal usually prevented them from making good their escape.

Archers wore metal helmets called sallets, covering the top of the head, and 'jacks', leather tunics reinforced with layer upon layer of deerskins and heavily padded. These offered less protection than steel armour but were remarkably effective in dulling blows and permitted their wearers far more freedom of movement than the men-at-arms enjoyed—both to handle weapons and to flee from a lost field.[1] In addition to his bow and arrows, an archer was armed with sword or long knife or bill (axe head with a spear point mounted on a pole) or even a leaden maul, and often carried a small iron shield.

Since the first feeble poppings of 'fire-vases' at Crécy, cannon had been sounding ever louder. During the fifteenth century, the King of France and the Duke of Burgundy had both developed a famous ordnance, and England under the Yorkists was not far behind. When, in 1464, the Earl of Warwick attacked Bamburgh

[1] Men wearing jacks were so infrequently killed that Louis XI decided to equip his 'francs archers' with them.

Castle, Northumberland, the great gun 'London' smashed at the walls so powerfully that chunks of masonry went flying into the sea; and 'Dijon', a shining piece of brass, sent a stone ball crashing into Sir Ralph Grey's chamber, knocking him unconscious beneath the debris. Though effective for siege-work, artillery played no part worth mentioning in any battles of the Roses, except at 'Lose-Coat Field' (March, 1470), where the first discharge of King Edward's cannon put the Lincolnshire rebels to rout. Hand-guns were slowly coming into use. The men of Lord Molynes who battered their way into the Paston manor of Gresham in 1450 carried these temperamental weapons. At the second Battle of St. Albans (February 17, 1461) Warwick's Burgundian troops used handguns which shot lead pellets or iron-tipped arrows or wildfire, but in the heat of the conflict the guns did more harm to the Burgundians than to the Lancastrians because they back-fired or burst.

The soldiers who fought each other in the Wars of the Roses enjoyed in Europe an enormous military reputation, based on the great victories in France of Crécy (1346), Poitiers (1356), Agincourt (1415). Commynes calls English troops 'the flower of the archers of the world' and declares that the mercenary bowmen in the service of the Duke of Burgundy were 'the hope of the Burgundian army'. Dominic Mancini noticed that English bows were 'thicker and longer than those used by other nations, just as their bodies are stronger than other people's. . . .'

The English captains of Edward IV's time made no change in the defensive tactics which had won the battles of the Hundred Years War. Troops, all dismounted, awaited the enemy attack arrayed in two or three 'battles' or wings. The heavily armoured men-at-arms occupied the centre of each battle, with thick salients of archers on the flanks, like this:

Drawn up to fight, an English army offered a spectacle of banners, shining armour, displays of heraldry: the archers on the wings were clad in the livery jackets of their lord or city, with town flags waving above them; and in the centre the lords and captains, coats of arms blazing over steel harness, stood beneath their pennons surrounded by their household knights and squires. When the enemy attacked, the fire of the archers not only thinned the advancing ranks but drove them into helplessly packed masses for the men-at-arms to finish off.

But in the battles of the Roses, both sides were the heirs of these tactics, and neither had any intention of enacting the role of the French at Agincourt. What usually happened, therefore, was that after one burst of arrow and cannon fire, both armies rushed together and dissolved into whirlpools of flailing swords, axes, bills. The fight was fierce and short. Except for Towton, none of the battles lasted more than three hours. As one of the lines gave way, lightly armed commons took to flight, usually successfully, while the steel-cased lords lumbered, usually in vain, toward their horse-park.

The size of the armies likewise limited casualties. The Yorkist historian who wrote an account of Edward's reconquest of his throne (spring, 1471) assigned 9,000 men to Edward's army at Barnet, and Warwick probably commanded no more than 12,000. Sir John Paston, who fought on the Lancastrian side, reported immediately after the battle that 1,000 men had been killed, an estimate that undoubtedly does not err from understatement. Since Barnet was one of the fiercest engagements, it seems safe to conclude that most of the other battles of the Roses were fought by forces of comparable size or even smaller.

For only one army during this period is the number of troops definitely known. In 1475 Edward IV invaded France with an armed force raised by indentures. Beginning with the Dukes of Gloucester and Clarence, who each brought 120 men-at-arms and 1,000 archers, lords and captains contracted with the King to furnish so many troops at so much a head. Like the Paston brothers, who spent months worrying about horses and equipment, large numbers of young Englishmen flocked to the standards: they were paid good wages; they dreamed of booty and adventure to be won in France. King Edward crossed the Channel with 11,000 archers, 1,500 men-at-arms, fifteen surgeons, and a large artillery train—'the finest army', says Commynes, 'that ever King of England led into France'.[1] Except at Towton, it appears likely that neither Yorkists nor Lancastrians were ever able to muster so large an army as this expeditionary force.

Not only were the battles of short duration and the armies small, but the ordinary soldiers were deliberately spared on the field and permitted to slide back peacefully into their daily lives. In this partisan strife, it was the chief partisans, the nobles, who were singled out for death. When the Queen's army broke into flight at Towton and the Yorkist war-steeds were hastily led forward from the horse-park, King Edward and Warwick cried to their pursuing bands, 'Spare the commons! Kill the lords!' Commynes heard an explanation of this policy from Edward himself: 'It is the custom of the English that, once they have gained a battle they do no more killing, especially killing of common people; for each side seeks to please the commons. . . . King Edward told me that in all the battles he had won, the moment he came to victory he mounted horse and shouted that the commons were to be spared and the nobles slain.' Commynes adds, 'And of the latter, few or none escaped'.

Elsewhere Commynes notes that neither the land nor the people of England suffered in the wars but 'all fell on the lords'. A rough tally of magnates killed in battle, murdered, or beheaded for treason, from the first skirmish at St. Albans (1455) to Bosworth Field (1485), gives three kings (Henry VI, Edward V, Richard III), a Prince of Wales (Queen Margaret's son), nine dukes, one marquess, thirteen earls, twenty-four barons—out of a temporal peerage that never numbered more than about thirty at any one time. Only eighteen nobles subscribed the oath taken in Henry VII's first Parliament. The line of Warwick the Kingmaker, the Beauforts of Somerset, and other noble families disappeared during this period, or, severely struck on the male side, did not last long after. Except for the Howards and the FitzAllens and the Veres and the Grey Earls of Kent and a few others, the peerage

---

[1] As a result of the Truce of Picquigny, Edward led his army home without a battle. England grumbled at this tame conclusion, but most of the soldiers probably felt like Sir John Paston: 'Blessed be God, this voyage of the King's is finished for this time. . . .'

of the sixteenth century was a creation of the Tudors. The Venetian diplomat noted during the reign of Henry VII that of the lords of the realm, 'there are very few left and those diminish daily'.

Warfare erupted to subside quickly. It did not move on a broad front but along narrow lines. The longest period of hostilities, from the Lancastrian victory at Wakefield (December 30, 1460) to the battle of Towton (March 29, 1461), occupied but three months; the campaign by which Edward regained the realm in the spring of 1471 stretched only from March 15, his landing at Ravenspur, to May 4, the final defeat of the Lancastrians at Tewkesbury. In a typical campaign two small armies, hastily raised from the adherents of the chief lords and from towns too close to the area of operations to avoid sending men, moved towards each other in mounted columns, each following a single road. Even those living along the line of march or in the neighbourhood of the fighting were not likely to suffer hurt; the realm as a whole went about its business ready to accept the arbitrament of battle.

In 1469, Warwick's northern followers moved from Yorkshire to Banbury, defeated a royal army at Edgecot, and marched home again, without disturbing any of the regions through which they passed. The taking of a horse by a soldier of the city of York, during Richard III's campaign against the Duke of Buckingham (October, 1483), was thoroughly investigated by the municipal authorities, who decided that the animal, property of one of Buckingham's followers, had been legitimately seized.

In the most troubled times, there were a few spectacular outbreaks of violence. When the kingdom was paralysed by Warwick's capture of King Edward in 1469, the Duke of Norfolk took the opportunity to besiege Caister Castle, held by the Pastons, with an army of some 3,000 men.[1] A few months later, the Berkeleys and the Talbots fought at Nibley Green. But these are isolated incidents, not the normal fare of daily living. There were disorders in England in the fourteenth century; there would be disorders in the sixteenth. To generalize about the unsettled condition

[1] Norfolk lost two men, killed by a cannon shot; young John Paston lost one man.

of the realm over the thirty-year period 1455-85 from the examples of violence to be found in complaints to the Chancellor and from the letters of people like the Pastons, who were especially embroiled in politics, would be rather like judging the present state of Great Britain by an examination of court dockets and a reading of the popular Sunday papers.[1]

During the Wars of the Roses no city withstood a siege; few cities closed their gates against an army.[2] The only towns which suffered notable damage were those that the Lancastrian host pillaged on their march southward after the victory of Wakefield (December 30, 1460). London, as might be expected, suffered the severest jars to civil life and the greatest anxieties.

The towns were chiefly affected by temporary dislocations of trade during the periods of intense warfare and by the necessity of sending contingents of troops at municipal expense when so commanded by the King. Whatever their real sympathies they generally obeyed the government in power; in periods of confused fighting, like the spring of 1461, they were sometimes forced to send bands of soldiers to both sides. These companies were usually small. Whereas Sir John Howard might raise close to a hundred men for a Yorkist campaign, the city of Norwich would send less than fifty; and it appears that towns distant from operations often sent none at all.

Cities like York and Coventry, because of their location and their affiliations, were much more deeply involved in the fortunes of York and Lancaster than other towns. A Lancastrian stronghold in 1460-61, York later did faithful service for the Earl of Warwick; then, after 1471, the city became strongly attached to Richard of Gloucester. Consequently, York provided contingents of troops, usually about 200 men each, on more than half a dozen occasions between 1460 and 1485.

---

[1] See C. L. Kingsford, *Prejudice and Promise in XVth Century England*, pp. 48-77, for a convincing refutation of the picture of widespread death and destruction drawn by certain nineteenth-century historians.

[2] London refused to admit Queen Margaret's host after the second battle of St. Albans (February 17, 1461)—see below. The town of Gloucester, heartened by tidings that King Edward was coming hard, withstood a Lancastrian army in May of 1471.

Coventry, whipsawed between Lancaster and York because of its strategic location, serves as an extreme example of town participation in the Wars. In the late 1450's, the city became, not of its own volition, the virtual seat of the Lancastrian Court. When Warwick invaded England from Calais in June of 1460, Queen Margaret lay at Coventry, and the city sent forty men to Henry VI's army defeated at Northampton by the Yorkists (July 10). As the Lancastrians rolled southward after Wakefield (January–February, 1461), the citizens received peremptory commands to provide troops and defend the city. But Coventry promptly opened its gates to young Edward of March, fresh from his victory at Mortimer's Cross (February 3, 1461), and dispatched a troop of archers with him, at the cost of £100, as he marched to join Warwick and enter London. A month later, the city sent 100 men with Edward IV and Warwick to Towton; and that summer another troop of forty men went north to aid the Earl of Warwick in his operations against the Lancastrians in Northumberland.

During the next period of troubles, 1469–71, the city of Coventry was once again pressed by both sides. Though the Earl of Warwick asked for a contingent of troops in the summer of 1469, the citizens instead sent fifty soldiers to King Edward at Nottingham, only to see that King, a few weeks later, brought to Coventry a captive by the momentarily all-powerful Earl. During these shaky days the mayor appointed captains to patrol the town, ordered guns and ammunition delivered to the gates, and established a strict watch.

In the spring of 1470 Coventry again raised troops for King Edward as he marched to meet the Lincolnshire rebels, who were allied with Warwick and Clarence. Only a few days after these soldiers departed, the Kingmaker and his son-in-law entered the city and made it their headquarters for several days. In less than a month, they were fleeing for the south coast, and Coventry promptly levied forty men to accompany the King on his pursuit. The city again supplied archers for King Edward at the end of summer (1470) as the realm uneasily awaited Warwick's return.

The moment the Kingmaker, ruling for King Henry, got word that Edward IV had landed at Ravenspur in the spring of 1471, he hastened from London to establish headquarters at Coventry. Not many days later the Yorkist army stood before the gates of the city. Warwick and his Lancastrian allies refused to issue forth to do battle; and Edward made a successful dash for London. Warwick followed in pursuit, among his forces being twenty footmen and twenty horsemen from Coventry who fought at Barnet. As soon as the news of Edward's victory reached Coventry, the citizens raised a fresh delegation of troops and sent them to Windsor, where Edward was waiting to move against Queen Margaret's forces in the West. In the hope of escaping the consequences of their enforced adherence to Warwick's cause, they made the King a gift of 400 marks, but a little later they had to pay £200 more in order to appease Edward's wrath and secure the restoration of the liberties of the city. Coventry sent a force to fight for King Richard at Bosworth Field, and cordially welcomed King Henry VII within its walls as he came from that field.

But even Coventry and York suffered no damage, and town life was not nearly so dislocated as the foregoing compressed account would suggest. Over a period of thirty years each city spent something like £600 on equipping and paying troops. The Mayor of Coventry, a city of perhaps 9,000 people, had apparently little difficulty in finding half a hundred citizens willing to leave their businesses and ride off to risk their necks in battle. The soldiers received a good wage, 6d a day; and most of them returned home, sometimes without fighting at all. Town records suggest that the sending of troops created but a ripple in the flow of municipal life. Disputes concerning common lands of the city made a far greater stir.

London, the touchstone of political fortune, saw exciting days concentrated into brief bursts of danger and fear; but on the whole the capital was less harassed during the period of the Wars themselves than in the bad decade of the fifties.

London received all armies, except two. An outburst of popular indignation forced shut the gates against Queen Margaret's

Northerners, victorious over Warwick at St. Albans (February 17, 1461). The news of the Earl's defeat produced, at first, a wave of terror in the city. Shops were closed, streets deserted; armed men patrolled the walls with the Mayor. The magistrates, who had no thought of resistance, began parleying with representatives sent by the Queen, hoping to save the capital from pillage. But once the commons discovered that the Lancastrians were moving gingerly, they took heart. Suddenly rising in arms, they plundered a supply train laden with food and money for the Queen's army, seized the keys to the gates and refused to let anyone pass out. The food disappeared into their bellies; as for the money 'I wot not how it departed', noted a chronicler who was present. 'I trow the purse stole the money.' In a few days Edward of March and Warwick were welcomed into the city.

A decade later, London even more stoutly resisted an army. About a week after King Edward had crushed the Lancastrians at Tewkesbury (May 4, 1471), the dead Kingmaker's cousin, the Bastard of Fauconberg, supported by the sailors of his fleet, rallied bands of Kentishmen to his banners. Approaching London, he sent a demand to the Mayor that the city open its gates to his forces. The Mayor replied that he was holding the capital for King Edward. Acting with Earl Rivers, in charge of the Tower, his citizens ranged cannon along the river bank and prepared to resist the Bastard's attack.

As Fauconberg sailed up the Thames with his fleet, anchoring opposite the Tower, his Kentishmen swarmed into Southwark, manhandled Flemish weavers, and burnt 'Dutchmen's Beerhouses'. The guns of the Bastard's ships opened fire on the city, but they were vigorously answered by artillery of the Tower and bombards mounted on wharves. On Sunday, May 12, Fauconberg tried to storm London Bridge, was repulsed, and set fire to some of the dwellings.

Two days later he mounted a double assault. While one force threatened the Bridge again, the main body of the rebels crossed the Thames by ship at Blackwell and attacked Aldgate. After sharp fighting, the assault was repulsed. Then the Londoners, led by their Recorder and by the Alderman of Aldgate Ward, suddenly

sallied through the gate and fell upon the enemy. At the same time
Earl Rivers issued with his garrison from a postern of the Tower
and struck the rebel flank. Fauconberg's men were put to flight;
many were killed as they took to their boats at Blackwell. By next
morning the fleet and the Kentishmen had disappeared. Not many
days later, King Edward entered the capital in triumph and
knighted a dozen prominent Londoners 'in the field'.

The countryside of England, on the whole, was no more deeply
affected than the towns. Many a squire and gentleman ignored
the summonses of Queen Margaret and King Edward and the
Earl of Warwick and Richard III and suffered not a whit for sitting
placidly upon their estates while small armies decided the fate of
England. Thomas Stonor had both Yorkist and Lancastrian connections. Yet he experienced no difficulty evading commands to
take arms, and died peacefully in 1475 without having fought in a
single engagement of the Wars of the Roses, though he was one
of the prominent landowners of Oxfordshire and adjoining
counties. John Paston, of the affinity of the Duke of Norfolk, did
not march northward to Towton with the Duke nor take part in
any of the other battles of 1459-61; yet he experienced neither
punishment nor disfavour for failing to fight for the Yorkist
cause. Throughout the Wars of the Roses, the Stanley family of
Lancashire, gentry at the beginning, played an intricate dangerous
game of shifting sides that brought Thomas the earldom of Derby
and made Sir William the richest commoner in England. They
did not always forecast the victor, but when they happened to
jump the wrong way, they were able to secure not only grace but
high office from King Edward and King Richard.

Sir Thomas Fulford, a tough and ardent Lancastrian till well
after 1471, was to be found captaining a flotilla of ships for King
Edward in the 1480's. Sir John Paston and his brother young John
fought for Warwick at Barnet; both soon procured a pardon, and
in a short time neither the Yorkist Duke of Norfolk nor King
Edward IV appeared to harbour any memory that the Pastons
had backed the wrong cause. Sir John Paston took service with the
King's favourite, Lord Hastings, by whom he was warmly
regarded; and young John continued to be numbered among the

followers of the Duke. At least three Pastons died of the plague; no member of the family was killed in battle.

If most townsmen and gentry were comparatively untouched by the Wars, partisan strife did breed a race of adventurers who risked their lives for pay in all manner of subtle or swashbuckling enterprises. In this age, however, they could not sell their memoirs after they had sold their services and most of their exploits remain hidden. The Lancastrians, Edward IV, Warwick the Kingmaker, all spent large sums of money in the underworld of spies. During the year 1468, when Warwick and his friend the King of France were doing all they could, under cover, to shake King Edward's government, Edward spent more than £2,000 for 'certain secret matters concerning the defence of the kingdom'. Some of this money probably went to John Boon of Dartmouth, whose story has fortunately been preserved in a scattering of documents, English and French. This bilingual adventurer undertook a mission that tangled his destiny with that of the greatest adventurer of the age, Louis XI.

King Edward, planning an invasion of France against Warwick's wishes, decided to sound out the Count of Armagnac, a notoriously unfaithful vassal of the French King. John Boon was chosen to deliver a packet of letters to the Count and sailed from Fowey early in 1469.

But Boon was, in reality, a secret agent of the Earl of Warwick.

When Armagnac refused to receive him or his letters, John Boon then made his way, following instructions, to the Court of King Louis at Amboise. Finding the captain of the castle at tennis, he asked to speak with the King, identifying himself as the man my lord of Warwick's herald had brought word of. That night, late—'entre chien et loup'—the captain introduced Boon into the castle of Amboise by a postern gate. He was led along a gallery and into a gloomy bedchamber lit by a single candle on a mantel over a high fireplace.

'There is the King', said the captain.

On a bench sat a man dressed in crimson velvet with a black hat pulled low over his face. Boon was ordered to seat himself on the bed and recount his mission. After he had reported his failure to see the Count and had delivered up King Edward's letters, he was dismissed with the word that further services would be required of him. The next evening he was brought into the same dark chamber at the same hour. This time the man in the room was wearing a yellow gown and a tawny hat. He took Boon genially by the hand and bade him repeat the story, explaining that he'd been slightly ill the previous evening and could not remember the details. When the Englishman finished, King Louis said, 'On your life, you will tell no one that you have already carried out your mission to the Count of Armagnac. You must do me a service'.

The next night, Boon learned what the service was to be. While a group of Louis' lords sat on the bed examining Edward's letters, the King cozily pulled Boon down beside him on the bench. Warwick's agent was to pretend that he had not yet visited Armagnac; he would absent himself from the Court for a while as if he were accomplishing the mission, and on his return he would be given papers representing the Count's answer.

Coming to the castle the following day, John Boon bluntly told the gentleman who was conducting him that he did not like King Louis' way of doing business—he had no certainty even that he had spoken to the King. When the gentleman tried to reassure him, Boon retorted that he knew the King's face and voice and the man who had hidden his features with the black hat was not the King. At this moment Louis himself appeared in the gallery. On learning the cause of the dispute, he gave Boon one of his winning smiles and congratulated him on penetrating the little game. The truth was, he had been unsure of Boon's identity and had therefore hidden in an adjoining chamber the first evening while M. du Lude (whom Louis, for good reason, called John Cleverness—'Jean des habilitez') played his part.

Heartened by the King's flattery and the jingling of the King's coins in his pocket, John Boon bought himself a horse and some French clothes and rode off on his pretended mission. On his return to the court in August (1469), John Cleverness handed him a packet of papers. 'Here are the letters in which M. d'Armagnac makes his reply to the King of England, touching what you know. Deliver them to the King [Louis] when he asks you for them.'

Boon was brought before Louis the next evening while the King was eating supper. He told his tale and extended the forged letters. Louis ordered one of his lords to undo the packet, remarking, 'You can attest that you had the letters before I ever saw them!' A few days later Louis, who liked to attend to details himself, carefully coached Boon in the official deposition he was to make. Once this document was drawn up, the King informed Warwick's emissary that if the Count of Armagnac swore he had written no letters to Edward IV, Boon would of course be required to offer to meet him in single combat. In terror, Boon protested that such a challenge went far beyond *his* daring. But Louis laughed and explained that he would only have to offer. This Boon obediently did, before the Chancellor and the royal Council.

Using Boon's accusation, Louis ordered an attack upon the Count a few years later, and Armagnac met his end on the dagger of one of the royal archers. As for Boon, he was still being actively employed by Louis, it seems, when Warwick fled to France (spring, 1470); but shortly after, he fell under the terrible displeasure of the French King and was accused of treachery. There is a hint that Boon's wife—perhaps given him by the matchmaking Louis—became one of the King's mistresses. At any rate, Boon was condemned to have his eyes put out.

But his luck did not entirely desert him. Somehow the hangman in his horrible operation missed one of Boon's pupils; and Warwick's agent, who, like Rosencrantz and Guildenstern, learned what it meant to be the tool of a King, was still able to see—'especially when the weather was clear'. He made his escape from France, only to be caught on the sea by a fellow-townsman of Dartmouth, John White. Though Boon offered 2,000 scutes for his freedom, White delivered him to the King of England. No more is known of him until Warwick, Louis, and Edward had all come to the end of their stormy rivalry. In July of 1485 he was a prisoner in the castle of Craon, between Angers and Rennes. With Louis safely in his grave, he poured out the story, in all its mazy details, of how the King of France had used him to hunt the

Count of Armagnac to death. The adventurer disappears from history on a domestic note—'married and living near Mantes'.

For the most part, those Englishmen affected by the Wars of the Roses were the ones who were drawn, or plunged, into partisan strife. Sir Thomas Cook, a wealthy merchant and former Mayor of London high in Yorkist favour, had the misfortune to run afoul of the greedy Woodvilles, the Queen's family, because he refused to sell at a loss to the Queen's mother a tapestry which had cost him £800. When a captured Lancastrian agent (1468) implicated Cook in Lancastrian plottings, the Queen's father, Earl Rivers, plundered Cook's town and country houses. Cook was found guilty only of misprision of treason, but Rivers, the Treasurer of England, exacted the enormous fine of £8,000, and River's haughty daughter mulcted Cook of a further 800 marks under the colour of an archaic privilege called 'Queen's Gold' (a total of some £300,000 in modern money). Sir Thomas, praised by a chronicler for his eloquence and intelligence, enjoyed a brief return to influential place during the Warwick-Henry VI régime of 1470-71, but on attempting to flee the realm when King Edward won back his crown, was captured at sea and suffered further hardships before he made his way back to London, to die a few years later in comparative poverty.

Sir William Stonor lived a peaceful life on his broad acres, like his father Thomas, until he became ambitious and attached himself to the retinue of the Marquess of Dorset. He was thus drawn into joining Buckingham's rebellion against Richard III, and had to flee to Henry Tudor in Brittany; but he recovered his confiscated estates when the Tudor triumphed over Richard at Bosworth Field.

One William Carnsyowe, who earned for himself the sobriquet of 'great errant Captain of Cornwall', seized on a time of violent alternations of fortune, when Queen Margaret's host of Northerners had defeated Warwick at St. Albans (February, 1461), to settle scores with a certain Henry Gyllyot, dwelling near Helston. As Carnsyowe and a band of armed men approached the house, Gyllyot slipped out a window, naked except for his shirt, and fled two miles to the Chapel of St. Sexymma. Here he remained shivering for three days until somebody brought him his breeches. Carnsyowe pillaged Gyllyot's house, maltreated his wife so that —according to Gyllyot's complaint—she 'never had a whole day after', and declared that he would hang Gyllyot at his own door. The victim went in such fear that he did not dare emerge from hiding till Midsummer. Carnsyowe, a Lancastrian partisan, asserted that Gyllyot deserved to lose life and property because he was a traitor who had fought with the Yorkists against King Henry at the battle of Northampton (July, 1460), but he may well have been using politics to mask private vengeance.

Thomas Hargrave certainly did so. After fighting for King Edward at Tewkesbury (May 4, 1471), he galloped full tilt back to Nursling in Hampshire in order to employ his credit as a good Yorkist in disposing of one Peter Marmion, suspected of Lancastrian leanings, who held the manor of Nursling to which Hargrave pretended a claim. By Saturday, May 11, a band of Hargrave's servants were threatening Marmion's life, and next day Marmion headed for the sanctuary of Beaulieu Abbey. But Hargrave intercepted him on the road, bundled him back to Nursling and tied him up with a dog collar and chain in his own hall. The Recorder of Winchester, summoned to the manor on Monday, found Hargrave lording it on the dais and Peter Marmion cringing before him in the dog collar. After Marmion had agreed, before the Recorder, to relinquish the manor to Hargrave, the party heard Mass at the parish church. As they emerged from the service, Hargrave clapped his hand to his sword and declared that if Marmion failed to keep the agreement, he would strike off his head. Trembling in terror, Marmion fell on his knees and lifting his hands to heaven, declared he would do whatever Hargrave desired. It is to be noted, however, that this story comes out in Marmion's complaint to the Chancellor and that, despite Hargrave's Yorkist service, Marmion recovered his manor of Nursling.

The times were touchy and could be anxious; eruptions of violence tested men's nerves, sometimes twisted their lives; successful merchants, become mayors, had to know how to wear harness and place cannon on city gates; the gentry joining field to field, played a tough, wary game of seeking 'good lordship' and avoiding lost causes. Despite the interruptions of the Wars, however, the subjects of King Edward IV in town and country enjoyed a time of widening prospects and displayed a hearty confidence in the way of life they bequeathed to their sons.

BIBLIOGRAPHY

The following section presents a list of the chief sources for each chapter of the volume. Since, however, a number of sources, the richest materials for social history, have been used in all or nearly all the chapters, I have grouped these separately.

PRINCIPAL SOURCES

Letters:
Letters and Papers of John Shillingford, ed. by Stuart A. Moore (Camden Soc.), 1871.
Original Letters, ed. by Henry Ellis, 3 series, vol. I of each series, 1825, 1827, 1846.
Plumpton Correspondence, ed. by Thomas Stapleton (Camden Society), 1839.
The Cely Papers, ed. by Henry Elliot Malden (Camden Soc.), 1900.
The Paston Letters, ed. by James Gairdner, several editions.
The Stonor Letters and Papers, ed. by C. L. Kingsford (Camden Soc.), 2 vols., 1919.

Household Regulations and Accounts:
Collection of Ordinances and Regulations for the Government of the Royal Household, 1790.
Household Books of John, Duke of Norfolk, and Thomas, Earl of Surrey, 1481-90, ed. by Payne Collier (Roxburghe Club), 1844.
Manners and Household Expenses of England in the Thirteenth and Fifteenth Centuries [containing household accounts of John Howard before he became Duke of Norfolk], ed. by T. H. Turner (Roxburghe Club), 1841.
The Household of Edward IV, ed. by A. R. Myers, 1959.

Wills:
Lincoln Diocese Documents, ed. by Andrew Clark (Early English Text Society), 1914.
Testamenta Eboracensia, ed. by James Raine (Surtees Society), 6 vols., 1836–1902.
The Fifty Earliest English Wills, ed. by F. J. Furnivall (E.E.T.S.), 1882.
Wills and Inventories . . . of Bury St. Edmund's, ed. by Samuel Tymms (Camden Soc.), 1850.

Foreign Travellers:

A Relation of the Island of England, ed. by C. A. Sneyd (Camden Soc.), 1847.

Calendar of State Papers and Manuscripts . . . in Milan, ed. by A. B. Hinds, vol. I, 1912.

Mancini, Dominic. *The Usurpation of Richard III*, ed. by C. A. J. Armstrong, 1936.

Robson-Scott, W. D. *German Travellers in England, 1400–1800*, 1953.

Town Records:

The Coventry Leet Book, ed. by Mary D. Harris (E.E.T.S.), Parts I–IV, 1907, 1908, 1913.

Ricart's Kalendar: Robert Ricart, The Maire of Bristowe Is Kalendar, ed. by Lucy Toulmin Smith (Camden Soc.), 1872.

York Records: Extracts from the Municipal Records of . . . York, ed. by Robert Davies, 1843.

York Civic Records, ed. by Angelo Raine, vol. I (Yorkshire Archaeological Society), 1939.

English Gilds, ed. by Toulmin Smith, 1870 (reissued 1892).

Chronicles:

An English Chronicle of the Reigns of Richard II, Henry IV, Henry V, and Henry VI, ed. by J. S. Davies (Camden Soc.), 1856.

Chronicles of London, ed. by C. L. Kingsford, 1905.

Croyland Chronicle: 'Historiae Croylandensis', *Rerum Anglicarum Scriptorum*, I, ed. by W. Fulman, 1684; English translation: *Ingulph's Chronicle of the Abbey of Croyland*, trans. and ed. by Henry T. Riley (Bohn's Antiquarian Library), 1854.

Fabyan, Robert. *The New Chronicles of England and France*, ed. by Henry Ellis, 1811.

The Great Chronicle of London, ed. by A. H. Thomas and I. D. Thornley, 1938.

Gregory's Chronicle: The Historical Collections of a Citizen of London, ed. by James Gairdner (Camden Soc.), 1876.

Six Town Chronicles of England, ed. by R. Flenley, 1911.

Three Fifteenth Century Chronicles, ed. by James Gairdner (Camden Soc.), 1880.

Warkworth, John. *A Chronicle of the First Thirteen Years of the Reign of King Edward the Fourth*, ed. by J. O. Halliwell (Camden Soc.), 1839.

Documents of State:

Calendar of the Charter Rolls, VI.

Calendar of the Close Rolls, 1454–61; 1461–68; 1468–76; 1476–85.

Calendar of the Fine Rolls, 1461–71.

Calendar of the Patent Rolls, 1452–61; 1461–67; 1467–77; 1476–85.

Foedera . . ., vol. XI, compiled by Thomas Rymer, London, 1727.

Grants of King Edward the Fifth, ed. by J. G. Nichols (Camden Soc.), 1854.

Grants of King Richard the Third: Harleian MS. 433 (British Museum).

Milanese Ambassadors: *Dispatches*. Archivio di Stato, Milan.
Rotuli Parliamentorum (Rolls of Parliament): V and VI.
Statutes of the Realm, II.

Cases in Chancery and before the Royal Council:
Early Chancery Proceedings, Public Record Office, Lists and Indexes, XII.
Select Cases before the King's Council, ed. by I. S. Leadam and J. F. Baldwin (Selden Soc.), 1919.
Select Cases in Chancery, 1364–1471, ed. by W. P. Baildon (Selden Society), 1896.

Cases also cited in:
England under the Yorkists, ed. by I. D. Thornley, 1920.
Kingsford, C. L. *Prejudice and Promise in XVth Century England*, 1925.
Scofield, Cora L. *The Life and Reign of Edward the Fourth*, 2 vols., 1923.

Useful Biographies and Collections of Biographical Sketches:
Bagley, J. J. *Margaret of Anjou*, 1948.
Blades, W. *The Life and Typography of William Caxton*, 2 vols, 1861–63.
Bennett, H. S. *Six Medieval Men and Women*, 1955.
Christie, M. E. *Henry VI*, 1922.
Holt, H. F. 'The Tames of Fairford', *Journal of the British Archaeological Association*, XXVII.
Kendall, P. M. *Richard the Third*, 1955.
———*Warwick the Kingmaker*, 1957.
MacGibbon, David. *Elizabeth Woodville*, 1938.
McClenaghan, B. *The Springs of Lavenham*, 1924.
Mitchell, R. J. *John Tiptoft*, 1938.
Power, E. *Medieval People*, 1924 (Pelican, 1937).
Scofield, Cora L. *The Life and Reign of Edward the Fourth*, 2 vols., 1923.
Vickers, Kenneth H. *Humphrey, Duke of Gloucester*, 1907.

General:
Victoria History of the Counties of England.

ADDITIONAL SOURCES FOR EACH CHAPTER
Prologue:
Armstrong, C. A. J. 'Some Examples of the Distribution and Speed of News in England at the Time of the Wars of the Roses', *Studies in Medieval History Presented to Frederick M. Powicke*, 1948.
Calendar of Letter Books . . . of London: Letter-Book L., ed. by R. R. Sharpe, 1912.
Historie of the Arrivall of Edward IV in England . . . , ed. by John Bruce (Camden Soc.), 1838.
Huizinga, J. *The Waning of the Middle Ages*, 1954.
Lincolnshire Rebellion: Chronicle of the Rebellion in Lincolnshire, 1470, ed by J. G. Nichols (Camden Soc. Misc., I), 1847.

Mankind: The Macro Plays, ed. by F. J. Furnivall and A. W. Pollard (E.E.T.S.), 1904 (reprinted 1924).

I THE MAYOR

CHAPTER ONE. THE MAYOR: AT HOME

Abram, A. *English Life and Manners in the Late Middle Ages*, 1913.

Fox, Levi. 'The Administration of Gild Property in Coventry in the 15th Century', *English Historical Review*, LV (1940).

Green, J. R. *Town Life in the Fifteenth Century*, 2 vols., 1907.

Gross, Charles. *The Gild Merchant*, 1890.

Historical Manuscripts Commission Reports, V–XII (town records).

Hudson, W. *Leet Jurisdiction in Norwich* (Selden Soc.), 1892.

Hunt, William. *Bristol*, 1887.

The Liber Custumarum of Northampton, ed. by C. A. Markham, 1895.

*London Letter Book L.***

The Macro Plays.

Miracle Plays:

    The Chester Plays, ed. b ʳ H. Deimling and G. W. Mathews (E.E.T.S., extra series), 1892, 1914.

    The Towneley Plays, ed. by George England and A. W. Pollard (E.E.T.S., extra series), 1897.

    Two Coventry Corpus Christi Plays, ed. by Hardin Craig (E.E.T.S.), 1902.

    York Plays, ed. by Lucy Toulmin Smith, 1885.

Pryce, George. *Memorials of the Canynges' Family and Their Times*, 1854.

Records of the Borough of Leicester, ed. by M. Bateson, 3 vols., 1899–1905.

Records of the City of Norwich, ed. by W. Hudson, 2 vols., 1906–10.

York Memorandum Book, ed. by Maud Sellers (Surtees Soc.), 2 vols., 1912–15.

CHAPTER TWO. THE MAYOR: ABROAD

Historical Manuscripts Commission Reports, V–XII.

Records of the City of Norwich.

Smyth, John. *The Lives of the Berkeleys*, ed. by Sir John Maclean (British and Gloucester Archaeological Society), 2 vols., vol. II, 1883.

CHAPTER THREE. REBEL AGAINST THE MAYOR

Green. *Town Life.*

Gross. *Gild Merchant.*

CHAPTER FOUR. THE MAYOR OF LONDON

Calendar of Wills Proved . . . in the Court of Husting, London, 1258–1688, ed. by R. R. Sharpe, 2 vols., 1889–90.

Hoccleve, Thomas. *Mâle Règle.*

London Letter-Book L.

* Only the title is given of works previously cited.

London Lickpenny (by John Lydgate?).

Stow, John. *A Survey of London*, ed. by C. L. Kingsford, 2 vols., 1908.

Thrupp, Sylvia L. *The Merchant Class of Medieval London*, 1300-1500, 1948.

Unwin, G. *The Guilds and Companies of London*, 1908.

II OTHER IMPORTANT PEOPLE

CHAPTER FIVE. THE KING AND THE ROYAL HOUSEHOLD

Allen, P. S. 'Bishop Shirwood of Durham and His Library', *English Historical Review*, XXV (1910).

Caxton, William. *Prefaces*. (See *The Prologues and Epilogues of William Caxton*, ed. by W. J. B. Crotch (E.E.T.S.), 1928.

Chastellain, Georges. *Oeuvres*, ed. by Kervyn de Lettenhove, vol. III, 1863-65.

Excerpta Historica (for material on Anthony Woodville), 1831.

Kingsford, C. L. *English Historical Literature in the Fifteenth Century*, 1913.

————*Prejudice and Promise in XVth Century England*, 1925.

La Marche, Olivier de. *L'État de la Maison du Duc Charles de Bourgogne dict le Hardy*, vol. III of his Mémoires, ed. by H. Beaune and J. d'Arbaumont, 3 vols, 1883-88.

Lander, J. R. 'The Yorkist Council and Administration', *English Historical Review*, LXXIII (1958).

Ministers' Accounts of the Warwickshire Estates of the Duke of Clarence, 1479-80, ed. by R. H. Hilton (Dugdale Soc.), 1952.

Mitchell, R. J. 'English Law Students at Bologna in the Fifteenth Century', *English Historical Review*, LI (1936).

More, Thomas. *The History of King Richard III*, ed. by J. R. Lumby, 1883.

Newton, A. P. 'The King's Chamber under the Early Tudors', *English Historical Review*, XXXII (1917).

————'Tudor Reforms in the Royal Household' in *Tudor Studies Presented to A. F. Pollard*, 1924.

Privy Purse Expenses of Elizabeth of York: Wardrobe Accounts of Edward IV, ed. by Sir H. Nicolas, 1830.

'Privy Purse Expenses of King Henry the Seventh' in *Excerpta Historica*.

Steel, A. *The Receipt of the Exchequer*, 1377-1485, 1954.

Tait, James. 'Letters of John Tiptoft, Earl of Worcester, and Archbishop Neville to the University of Oxford', *English Historical Review*, XXXV (1920).

Wolffe, B. P. 'The Management of English Royal Estates under the Yorkist Kings', *English Historical Review*, LXXI (1956).

CHAPTER SIX. LORDS AND GENTRY

Armstrong, C. A. J. 'Distribution and Speed of News'.

Bateson, Mary. 'The English and the Latin Versions of a Peterborough Court Leet, 1461', *English Historical Review*, XIX (1904).

Bennett, H. S. *The Pastons and Their England*, 1922.

The Boke of Noblesse, ed. by J. G. Nichols (Roxburghe Club), 1860.

Court Rolls of Tooting-Bec Manor, ed. by G. L. Gomme, 1909.

Gray, H. L. 'Incomes from Land in England in 1436', *English Historical Review*, XLIX (1934).

Haward, Winifred I. 'Economic Aspects of the Wars of the Roses in East Anglia', *English Historical Review*, XLI (1926).

'A History of the County of Wiltshire' (*The Victoria History of the Counties of England*), vol. 4, 1959.

Johnston, C. E. 'Sir William Oldhall', *English Historical Review*, XXV (1910).

Northumberland Household Book: The Regulations and Establishment of the Household of Henry Algernon Percy, 5th Earl of Northumberland, begun 1512, ed. by Percy, 1827.

Peter Idley's Instructions to His Son, ed. by Charlotte D'Evelyn, 1935.

Rowse, A. L. *Tudor Cornwall*, 1947.

Savine, Alexander 'Copyhold Cases in the Early Chancery Proceedings', *English Historical Review*, XVII (1902).

Scofield, Cora L. 'An Engagement of Service to Warwick the Kingmaker', *English Historical Review*, XXIX (1914).

———'The Early Life of John de Vere, Thirteenth Earl of Oxford', *English Historical Review*, XXIX (1914).

Smyth, John. *Lives of the Berkeleys*.

Storey, R. L. 'The Wardens of the Marches of England Towards Scotland', *English Historical Review*, LXXII (1957).

Trevelyan Papers, ed. by J. Payne Collier (Camden Soc.), 1857.

Tudor Parish Documents of the Diocese of York, ed. by J. S. Purvis, 1948.

Williams, C. H. 'A Norfolk Parliamentary Election, 1461', *English Historical Review*, XL (1925).

CHAPTER SEVEN. CHURCHMEN AND THE CHURCH

Capes, W. W. *The English Church in the Fourteenth and Fifteenth Century*, 1920.

Collectanea Anglo-Premonstratensia, ed. by Francis A. Gasquet (Camden Soc.), vols. II and III, 1906.

Firth, C. B. 'Benefit of Clergy in the Time of Edward IV', *English Historical Review*, XXXII (1917).

Jarrett, Bede. 'Bequests to the Black Friars of London during the Fifteenth Century', *English Historical Review*, XXV (1910).

Knowles, M. D. *The Religious Orders in England: The End of the Middle Ages*, vol. II, 1955.

Martin, C. T. 'Clerical Life in the Fifteenth Century', *Archaeologia*, LX (1906).

'The Pilgrim's Sea-Voyage' in *Religious and Moral Pieces* (E.E.T.S.), 1867.

Power, E. E. *Medieval English Nunneries*, 1922.

Richardson, H. G. 'John Oldcastle in Hiding, 1417', *English Historical Review*, LV (1940).

Snape, R. H. *English Monastic Finances in the Later Middle Ages*, 1926.

Visitations in the Diocese of Lincoln, 1517–31, ed. by A. H. Thompson (Lincoln Record Soc.), vol. 3, 1947.

Woodcock, Brian L. *Medieval Ecclesiastical Courts in the Diocese of Canterbury*, 1952.

CHAPTER EIGHT. MERCHANTS, PIRATES, ALIENS, AND LAWYERS

Bennett, H. S. *Chaucer and the Fifteenth Century*, 1947.

Bridbury, A. R. *England and the Salt Trade in the Later Middle Ages*, 1955.

Carus-Wilson, E. M. *Medieval Merchant Venturers*, 1954.

Chrimes, S. B. *English Constitutional Ideas in the Fifteenth Century*, 1936.

——— ' "House of Lords" and "House of Commons" in the Fifteenth Century', *English Historical Review*, XLIX (1934).

Christ Church Letters, ed. by J. B. Sheppard (Camden Soc.), 1877.

Flenley, Ralph. 'London and Foreign Merchants in the Reign of Henry VI', *English Historical Review*, XXV (1910).

Fortescue, Sir John. *The Governance of England*, ed. by C. Plummer, 1885.

Howard, Winifred I. 'Economic Aspects . . .'.

The Itineraries of William Wey (Roxburghe Club), 1857.

Kingsford, C. L. *Prejudice and Promise* . . . (for piracy).

Kirby, J. L. 'The Rise of the Under-Treasurer of the Exchequer', *English Historical Review*, LXXII (1957).

Lander, J. R. 'The Yorkist Council . . .'.

Letters and Papers Illustrative of the Reigns of Richard III and Henry VII, ed. by James Gairdner (Rolls Series), 2 vols., 1861–63.

The Libelle of Englysche Polycye, ed. by G. Warner, 1926.

Lingelbach, W. E. *The Merchant Adventurers of England*, 1902.

Lipson, E. *An Introduction to the Economic History of England*, vol. I, 1929.

McKisack, M. *The Parliamentary Representation of the English Boroughs during the Middle Ages*, 1932.

Ministers' Accounts of the Warwickshire Estates. . . .

Mitchell, R. J. *John Free: from Bristol to Rome in the 15th Century*, 1955.

Moore, Samuel. 'Patrons of Letters in Norfolk and Suffolk, *c.* 1450', *Publications of the Modern Language Association*, XXVII (1912) and XXVIII (1913).

Myers, A. R. 'Parliamentary Petitions in the Fifteenth Century', *English Historical Review*, LII (1937).

Otway-Ruthven, J. *The King's Secretary and the Signet Office in the Fifteenth Century*, 1939.

Pickthorn, Kenneth. *Early Tudor Government*, vol. I, 1934.

Pollard, A. F. 'The Growth of the Court of Requests', *English Historical Review*, LVI (1941).

The Port Books of Southampton for the Reign of Edward IV, ed. by D. B. Quinn and A. A. Ruddock, 2 vols., 1937, 1938.

Power, E. *The Paycockes of Coggeshall*, 1920.

Roskell, J. S. *The Commons in the Parliament of 1422*, 1954.

Ruddock, A. A. *Italian Merchants and Shipping in Southampton, 1270–1600*, (Southampton Record Series), 1951.

Studies in English Trade in the Fifteenth Century, ed. by Eileen Power and M. M. Postan, 1933.

Thrupp, Sylvia L. *The Merchant Class of Medieval London.*

Wedgwood, J. C. and A. D. Holt. *History of Parliament. Biographies of the Members of the Commons House, 1439–1509*, 1936.

Weiss, R. *Humanism in England during the Fifteenth Century*, 1941.

Winchester, Barbara. *Tudor Family Portrait*, 1955.

The York Mercers and Merchant Adventurers, ed. by Maud Sellers (Surtees Soc.), 1917.

III THE HOUSEHOLD

CHAPTER NINE. THE FABRIC OF LIFE

Caxton's Book of Curtesye, ed. by F. J. Furnivall (E.E.T.S.), 1868.

The Household Book of Dame Alice de Bryene, 1412–13, ed. by V. B. Redstone (Suffolk Inst. of Arch. and Nat. Hist.), 1931.

Kingsford, C. L. *Prejudice and Promise. . . .*

——'A London Merchant's House and Its Owner', *Archaeologia*, LXXIV (1925).

Leland, J. *Joannis Lelandi Antiquarii De Rebus Britannicis Collectanea*, vol. VI, 1774 (for the enthronization feast of Archbishop of York).

Lincoln Wills, ed. by C. W. Foster (Lincoln Record Soc.), 1914.

Lincolnshire Wills Proved in the Prerogative Court of Canterbury, 1471–90 (Assoc. Archit. Socs. Lincoln and Northampton, Rept. and Papers for 1933, XLI, pt. 2), 1935.

Russell, William. *The Book of Nurture* in *Manners and Meals in Olden Time* (*The Babees Book*, etc.) ed. by F. J. Furnivall (E.E.T.S.), 1868.

Salzman, L. F. *Building in England down to 1540*, 1952.

A Small Household of the XVth Century, ed. by K. L. Wood-Legh, 1956.

Somerset Medieval Wills, 1383–1558, ed. by F. W. Weaver (Somerset Record Soc.), 3 vols., 1901–05.

Thrupp, Sylvia L. *The Merchant Class. . . .*

Two Fifteenth Century Cook Books, ed. by Thomas Austin (E.E.T.S.), 1888.

Vergil, Polydore. *History*, ed. by Henry Ellis (Camden Soc.), 1844.

CHAPTER TEN. THE MARRIAGE HUNT

Child Marriages, Divorces, and Ratifications, etc., ed. by F. J. Furnivall (E.E.T.S.), 1897.

Powell, C. L. *English Domestic Relations, 1487–1563*, 1917.
Thrupp, Sylvia L. *The Merchant Class.* . . .

CHAPTER ELEVEN. WIVES

The Book of Margery Kempe, ed. by S. B. Meech (E.E.T.S.), 1940.
Caxton's Book of Curtesye.
Chastellain, Georges. *Oeuvres.*
Commynes, Philippe de. *Mémoires*, ed. by B. de Mandrot, 2 vols., 1901–03.
Hoccleve, Thomas. *Mâle Règle.*
Lettres de Louis XI, Roi de France, ed. by J. Vaesen and others, 11 vols., 1883–1909.
London Letter-Book L.
More, Thomas. *The History of King Richard III.*
Scofield, Cora L. 'Jean Malet, Seigneur de Graville, and Edward IV, 1475', *English Historical Review*, XXV (1910).
Stow, John. *A Survey of London.*
Thrupp, Sylvia L. *The Merchant Class.* . . .

CHAPTER TWELVE. CHILDREN

Caxton, William. *Dialogues in French and English* (E.E.T.S. e.s. lxxix), 1900.
Caxton's Book of Curtesye.
A Fifteenth Century Courtesy Book, ed. by R. W. Chambers (E.E.T.S.), 1914.
Fortescue, Sir John. *The Governance of England.*
Manners and Meals in Olden Time (The Babees Book, etc.).
Northumberland Household Book.
Powell, C. L. *English Domestic Relations.*
Three Prose Versions of the Secreta Secretorum, ed. by Robert Steele (E.E.T.S. e.s. lxxiv), 1898.
Thrupp, Sylvia L. *The Merchant Class.* . . .

EPILOGUE

Barnard, F. P. *Edward the Fourth's French Expedition of 1475*, 1925.
Baskerville, G. 'A London Chronicle of 1460', *English Historical Review*, XXVIII (1913).
Calmette, J., and G. Périnelle, *Louis XI et l'Angleterre*, 1930.
Chronicle of John Stone, ed. by W. G. Searle (Cambridge Antiquarian Soc.), 1902.
Chronicle of the Rebellion in Lincolnshire.
Chronicles of the White Rose of York, 1845.
Commynes, Philippe de. *Mémoires.*
Dépêches des ambassadeurs Milanais en France sous Louis XI et François Sforza, ed. by B. de Mandrot, 4 vols., 1916–19.

Excerpta Historica, 1830.

Hanserecesse, 1431–76, II, vi, ed. by G. von der Ropp, 1890.

Hardyng, John. *Chronicle*, ed. by Henry Ellis, 1812.

Historical Manuscripts Commission Reports.

Historie of the Arrivall of Edward IV in England.

Kingsford, C. L. 'An Historical Collection of the Fifteenth Century', *English Historical Review*, XXIX (1914).

———*English Historical Literature.* . . .

Political Poems and Songs relating to English History, ed. by T. Wright (Rolls Series), vol. II, 1861.

Proceedings and Ordinances of the Privy Council of England, ed. by Sir H. Nicolas, vol. VI, 1837.

Samaran, Charles. *La Maison d'Armagnac au XVe Siècle*, 1907 (for the story of John Boon; see also Scofield, *Edward IV*, I, p. 476 and p. 477 and notes).

Waurin, Jehan de. *Anchiennes Cronicques d'Engleterre*, ed. by Mlle. Dupont, vols. II and III, 1858–63.

Whethamstede, John. *Registrum Abbatiae Johannis Whethamstede*, ed. by Henry T. Riley (Rolls Series), 2 vols., 1872–73.

Worcester, William. 'Annales Rerum Anglicarum' in *Letters and Papers Illustrative of the Wars of the English in France during the Reign of Henry VI*, ed. by J. Stevenson (Rolls (Series), vol. II, 1864.

Index

INDEX

IN THE NORTON LIBRARY

Glueck, Nelson. *Rivers in the Desert: A History of the Negev.* N431

Gordon, Cyrus H. *The Ancient Near East.* N275

Grantham, Dewey W. *The Democratic South.* N299

Graves, Robert and Alan Hodge. *The Long Week-end: A Social History of Great Britain, 1918-1939.* N217

Green, Fletcher. *Constitutional Development in the South Atlantic States, 1776-1860.* N348

Gulick, Edward Vose. *Europe's Classical Balance of Power.* N413

Halperin, S. William. *Germany Tried Democracy.* N280

Hamilton, Holman. *Prologue to Conflict.* N345

Haring, C. H. *Empire in Brazil.* N386

Harrod, Roy. *The Dollar.* N191

Haskins, Charles Homer. *The Normans in European History.* N342

Herring, Pendleton. *The Politics of Democracy.* N306

Hill, Christopher. *The Century of Revolution 1603-1714.* N365

Himmelfarb, Gertrude. *Darwin and the Darwinian Revolution.* N455

Holmes, George. *The Later Middle Ages, 1272-1485.* N363

Hughes, H. Stuart. *The United States and Italy.* N396

Jolliffe, J. E. A. *The Constitutional History of Medieval England.* N417

Jones, Rufus *The Quakers in the American Colonies.* N356

Keir, David Lindsay. *The Constitutional History of Modern Britain Since 1485.* N405

Kendall, Paul Murray (editor). *Richard III: The Great Debate.* N310

Kennan, George. *Realities of American Foreign Policy.* N320

Kouwenhoven, John A. *The Arts in Modern American Civilization.* N404

Langer, William L. *Our Vichy Gamble.* N379

Leach, Douglass E. *Flintlock and Tomahawk: New England in King Philip's War.* N340

Maddison, Angus. *Economic Growth in the West.* N423

Magrath, C. Peter. *Yazoo: The Case of Fletcher v. Peck.* N418

Maitland, Frederic William. *Domesday Book and Beyond.* N338

Mason, Alpheus Thomas. *The Supreme Court from Taft to Warren.* N257

Mattingly, Harold. *The Man in the Roman Street.* N337

May, Arthur J. *The Hapsburg Monarchy: 1867-1914.* N460.

Morgenthau, Hans J. (editor). *The Crossroad Papers.* N284

Neale, J. E. *Elizabeth I and Her Parliaments,* 2 vols. N359a & N359b

Nef, John U. *War and Human Progress.* N468

Nichols, J. Alden. *Germany After Bismarck.* N463

Noggle, Burl. *Teapot Dome: Oil and Politics in the 1920's.* N297

North, Douglass C. *The Economic Growth of the United States 1790-1860.* N346

Ortega y Gasset, José. *Concord and Liberty.* N124

Ortega y Gasset, José. *History as a System.* N122

Ortega y Gasset, José. *Man and Crisis.* N121

Ortega y Gasset, José. *Man and People.* N123

Ortega y Gasset, José. *Meditations on Quixote.* N125

Ortega y Gasset, José. *Mission of the University.* N127

Ortega y Gasset, José. *The Origin of Philosophy.* N128

Ortega y Gasset, José. *What Is Philosophy?* N126

Pelling, Henry. *Modern Britain, 1885-1955.* N368

Pidal, Ramón Menéndez. *The Spaniards in Their History.* N353

Pocock, J. G. A. *The Ancient Constitution and the Feudal Law.* N387

Pollack, Norman. *The Populist Response to Industrial America.* N295

Pomper, Gerald. *Nominating the President.* N341

Robson, Eric. *The American Revolution, 1763-1783.* N382

Rostow, W. W. *The Process of Economic Growth.* N176

Roth, Cecil. *The Spanish Inquisition.* N255

Rowse, A. L. *Appeasement.* N139

Salvemini, Gaetano. *The French Revolution: 1788-1792.* N179

Silver, James W. *Confederate Morale and Church Propaganda.* N422

Spanier, John W. *The Truman-MacArthur Controversy and the Korean War.* N279

Sykes, Norman. *The Crisis of the Reformation.* N380

Thompson, J. M. *Louis Napoleon and the Second Empire.* N403

Tolles, Frederick B. *Meeting House and Counting House.* N211

Tourtellot, Arthur Bernon. *Lexington and Concord.* N194

Turner, Frederick Jackson. *The United States 1830-1850.* N308

Ward, Barbara. *India and the West.* N246

Ward, Barbara. *The Interplay of East and West.* N162

Warren, Harris Gaylord. *Herbert Hoover and the Great Depression.* N394

Wedgwood, C. V. *William the Silent.* N185

Whitaker, Arthur P. *The United States and the Independence of Latin America.* N271

Whyte, A. J. *The Evolution of Modern Italy.* N298

Wolfers, Arnold. *Britain and France between Two Wars.* N343

Wolff, Robert Lee. *The Balkans in Our Time.* N395

Woodward, C. Vann. *The Battle for Leyte Gulf.* N312

Wright, Benjamin Fletcher. *Consensus and Continuity, 1776-1787.* N402